SANT

Borrowed Words

A History of Loanwords in English

Philip Durkin

OXFORD
UNIVERSITY PRESS

OXFORD
UNIVERSITY PRESS

Great Clarendon Street, Oxford, OX2 6DP,
United Kingdom

Oxford University Press is a department of the University of Oxford.
It furthers the University's objective of excellence in research, scholarship,
and education by publishing worldwide. Oxford is a registered trade mark of
Oxford University Press in the UK and in certain other countries

Published in the United States of America by Oxford University Press
198 Madison Avenue, New York, NY 10016, United States of America

British Library Cataloguing in Publication Data
Data available

Library of Congress Cataloging in Publication Data
Data available

ISBN 978–0–19–957499–5 (Hbk.)
ISBN 978–0–19–873649–3 (Pbk.)

For Kathryn

Acknowledgements

This book has arisen primarily from my work on *The Oxford English Dictionary*, and draws heavily on the collaborative research of my many very talented colleagues on the dictionary's staff. If the *OED* did not exist, this book, like very many others, would have been entirely impossible; if I had not had the good fortune to work in such a friendly and supportive environment, writing it would have been a much less pleasant experience.

I am greatly indebted to friends and colleagues from many corners of the world who have commented on drafts of either the whole or parts of this book, especially: Rhona Alcorn, Mark Chambers, Richard Dance, Anthony Esposito, Alan Kirkness, Roger Lass, Ursula Lenker, Serge Lusignan, Seth Mehl, Inge Milfull, Sara Pons-Sanz, Herbert Schendl, John Simpson, Janne Skaffari, Katrin Thier, and Edmund Weiner. Responsibility for any errors of course remains entirely my own.

I have also benefitted hugely from comments on papers containing research for this book from audiences at the Sixteenth International Conference on English Historical Linguistics (ICEHL), Pécs, Hungary; the Fifth International Conference on Historical Lexicography and Lexicology (ICHLL), Oxford; the Seventh International Conference on Middle English (ICOME), Lviv; the LIPP Symposium on linguistic change, Ludwig-Maximilians-Universität, Munich; HELLEX 3 (New Approaches in English Historical Lexis), Helsinki; the Colloquium 'Present and future research in Anglo-Norman', organized by the Anglo-Norman Dictionary team in Aberystwyth; and seminar audiences in Cambridge, Oxford, London (Westminster), Bamberg, Poznań, and Warsaw. I am very grateful to my hosts at all of these events for providing such valuable fora for working through and debating some of the ideas in the book.

That this book looks so good in its finished form owes a great deal to many talented colleagues at OUP, including Julia Steer, Jen Moore, Vicki Hart, and Briony Ryles. I consider myself, and this book, particularly fortunate to have benefitted from the generous and expert advice of John Davey, who retired from OUP at Easter 2013; his editorial skills are legendary, as is his contribution to the world of linguistics, and it is a great privilege to have worked with him on this project and others.

Concise Contents

The companion website for the book is available at
www.oup.co.uk/companion/durkin2

Full Contents

List of Figures

List of Abbreviations

(See References for full details.)

AFW	*Altfranzösisches Wörterbuch*
ALD	*The Advanced Learner's Dictionary of Current English* (2nd edn., 1963; see also *OALD*)
AND	*The Anglo-Norman Dictionary*
BNC	*British National Corpus*
COCA	*Corpus of Contemporary American English*
DEAF	*Dictionnaire étymologique de l'ancien français*
DMF	*Dictionnaire de moyen français*
DMLBS	*Dictionary of Medieval Latin from British Sources*
DNZE	*The Dictionary of New Zealand English*
DOE	*The Dictionary of Old English*
DOST	*A Dictionary of the Older Scottish Tongue*
DSAE	*A Dictionary of South African English on Historical Principles*
ECCO	*Eighteenth-Century Collections Online*
EDD	*The English Dialect Dictionary*
EEBO	*Early English Books Online*
ESTC	*English Short Title Catalogue*
FEW	*Französisches etymologisches Wörterbuch*
GSL	*A General Service List of English Words*
HTOED	*Historical Thesaurus of the Oxford English Dictionary*
MED	*Middle English Dictionary*
OALD	*The Oxford Advanced Learner's Dictionary* (see also *ALD*)
ODEE	*The Oxford Dictionary of English Etymology*
OED	*The Oxford English Dictionary*
OLD	*Oxford Latin Dictionary*
RMLW	*Revised Medieval Latin Word-List*
SND	*The Scottish National Dictionary*
SOED	*Shorter Oxford English Dictionary*
TLF	*Trésor de la langue française*
TLL	*Thesaurus Linguae Latinae*
TOE	*Thesaurus of Old English*

Part I

Introduction

1

Introducing concepts

The topic of this book is how borrowed words have influenced the vocabulary of English over its history. A central theme is how the histories of individual words are intertwined firstly with linguistic history, that is to say with larger-scale trends and developments in the history of English; and secondly with external, non-linguistic history, that is to say with historical events and developments, such as the arrival of the Anglo-Saxons in Britain or the Norman Conquest.

In linguistics, the term 'borrowing' describes a process in which one language replicates a linguistic feature from another language, either wholly or partly. The metaphorical use of the word 'borrowing' to describe this process has some well-known flaws: nothing is taken away from what is termed the donor language, and there is no assumption that the 'borrowing' or 'loan' will ever be returned. In many ways, the idea of influence would be more appropriate. However, the term 'borrowing' has been firmly entrenched in linguistics as the usual term to describe this process since the nineteenth century, to the extent that most linguists no longer even think of it as a metaphor. This book does not attempt to change the fundamental terminology of the discipline, but keeps to the basic framework of borrowing, donors, recipients, and loans.

Words have both a form and a meaning. Either component can be borrowed. This book looks in particular at those cases where both the form and (at least some aspect of) the meaning of a word from another language have been borrowed into English. These are conventionally called loanwords. (For a more detailed account of terminology, see section 1.2.2.) The category of borrowed words is sometimes restricted to words of this type, but is often extended to include other categories, such as loan translations. For example, in modern English we have the words *omnipotent* and *almighty* in roughly the same meanings. *Omnipotent* is a loanword from Latin *omnipotēnt-, omnipotēns*; both the word form and the meaning have been replicated in English. *Almighty* is probably a (very early) loan translation of the same Latin word, based on analysis of its component parts *omni-* 'all' and *potēns* 'powerful, mighty'. This book deals primarily with loanwords, but other types such as loan translations will also be considered at various points in the historical narrative.

Chapter 1 introduces some key concepts in the study of loanwords, and will give an overall impression of the impact of loanwords on the vocabulary of modern English. Chapter 2 looks at the proportions of borrowings in the lexis as a whole (as reflected by the wordlist of the *Oxford English Diction-ary*), among the high-frequency words of contemporary English, and among those words that realize the most basic meanings. Additionally, it introduces some of the contact situations in the history of English that have led to the heaviest and most significant episodes of lexical borrowing.

1.1 A first illustration of the part played by loanwords in the vocabulary of modern English

Loanwords make up a huge proportion of the words in any large dictionary of English. They also figure largely in the language of everyday communi-cation and some are found even among the most basic vocabulary of English. Exact figures and percentages are problematic for various reasons, which are examined in the course of this chapter and in chapter 2, and which are investigated from various different points of view throughout this book. However, one easy way of illustrating the pervasive nature of loanwords in the vocabulary of modern English is simply to look at some passages from different types of contemporary writing. The following five passages are taken from (i) a book written for young children, (ii) a piece of popular fiction, (iii) a playwright's diary (as prepared for publication), (iv) a schol-arly monograph by a historian, and (v) a scientific research paper. I have underlined all loanwords (except for proper names), and all words that have been formed within English from loanwords.

'Charlie', she says, 'they look like fish fingers to me, and I would never eat a fish finger.' 'I know that, but these are not fish fingers. These are ocean nibbles from the supermar-ket under the sea—mermaids eat them all the time.'

(Lauren Child I will not ever never eat a tomato (2000).)

'Have you ever been to York Minster?' Archie broke the silence, not taking his eyes off the glossy front-door.

Kate looked at him, irritated that his thoughts could be elsewhere. 'A while ago.'

'And?' He turned to her. 'What did you think?'

She shrugged. 'I don't know. It was good. What has it got to do with us being here?'

'How good? Was it very good? Fairly good? Do you think it was better than Winchester? Did you eat in the café?'

(Claire Peate *Headhunters* (2009) 264–5.)

Switch on the radio after supper and catch most of Elgar's First Symphony, music which invariably transports me back to boyhood[1] and walking up Headingley Lane on a summer evening after a concert in Leeds Town Hall. The evocative power of music is, I suppose, greatest when heard in live performance. This is a recording but it still casts a spell because I have come on it by accident. Had I put on the recording myself the spell would have been nowhere near as powerful because self-induced. Why this should be I can't think, though doubtless Proust would know.

(Alan Bennett *Untold Stories* (2006) 253.)

To see the Host, however fleetingly, was a privilege bringing blessing. Those robbed of this privilege by misfortunes such as poor eyesight might be rescued by heavenly intervention. Conversely, the sacrilegious might be deprived of the ability to see the Host which they profaned.

(Eamon Duffy *The Stripping of the Altars* (1992) 101.)

Unique-event mutations inferred from binary marker data were used to condition the possible trees but otherwise did not contribute to the likelihood. Population splitting was modeled under strict fission with no subsequent background migration. Population growth was modeled as an exponential from an initially constant effective population size.

(*Molecular Biology and Evolution* 19 (2002) 1011=Weale et al. 2002 in main references section.)

These short extracts illustrate some key aspects of the effects of borrowing on the vocabulary of English over time. A high proportion of the words in use in everyday, non-technical conversation in modern English are not borrowed and have either been in English right back to its Germanic origins, or have been formed within English. However, it would be very difficult to conduct any sort of conversation in modern English without using some loanwords and, crucially, you would need a very good knowledge of English etymology to do so successfully. People with a good

---

[1] Some scholars consider that *boy* shows a loanword, perhaps from French, but this is one of many etymologies that are uncertain and disputed.

knowledge of French and/or Latin will probably be able to guess at a lot (but not all) of the words that have been borrowed from these languages, because their form and meaning remain relatively close to those in the donor languages; many other loanwords are much more difficult to spot, including the considerable number of borrowings from early Scandinavian found in everyday English (part IV will look in detail at the reasons for this).

As these extracts also illustrate, more formal language in modern English and/or more academic topics of discussion generally involve using a higher proportion of borrowed words than more casual everyday conversation. These are chiefly words borrowed from French and/or Latin, or words formed ultimately from elements that come from Latin or Greek. This is because more formal registers of modern English, and the specialist vocabularies of academia and technology, show many more borrowings from these sources. How this situation developed historically will be a major focus of parts V and VI. Scholars often speak about a marked stratification in the vocabulary of modern English: there is an everyday vocabulary, which itself shows many borrowings from other languages, and then there is a more learned and formal vocabulary, which shows huge influence from French and Latin in its basic constituents and in its derivational processes. This sort of binary division of the vocabulary of English is probably somewhat over-simplistic, but the concept at least provides a useful framework.

Another useful concept in this context is dissociation: as a result of borrowing, many semantic fields in English show formally unrelated words for related concepts. For example, the usual adjective corresponding to *mouth* shows the completely unrelated word form *oral*; compare the situation in modern German, in which the relationship remains clear between *Mund* 'mouth' and *mündlich* 'oral'; the vocabulary of German is often said to be relatively consociated compared with that of English.[2]

---

[2] For this famous example, see Leisi and Mair (1999) 51; the term *dissociation* originated (as German *Dissoziation*) in the first edition of this work, Leisi (1955). In the study of English in Germany it has been common to observe, as Leisi did, that English shows a much more dissociated vocabulary than modern German. It is unclear how far empirical work supports this observation (compare Sanchez (2008), Sanchez-Stockhammer (2009)), but quite aside from this question of contrasting the vocabulary of English and German, the concept of dissociation is useful in highlighting how the effects of borrowing have radically transformed the correspondence (or lack of it) between word forms and meaning relations in many semantic fields in English.

1.2 Some initial definitions of terms

1.2.1 Periods in the history of English

The history of the English language is conventionally divided into four main periods, Old English, Middle English, Early Modern English, and Later Modern English. This periodization reflects some major changes in the grammar, pronunciation, and vocabulary of English which coincide very approximately with the transition from one period to the next. However, the changes in question were not abrupt and did not occur all at the same time. Hence we can only speak of very gradual transitions between major periods in the history of the language; any precise chronological division between periods is necessarily arbitrary. Additionally, different scholars take different views on where best to place the boundary between periods.

In this book I use the same periodization that is used in the new edition of the *Oxford English Dictionary* (*OED3*): Old English denotes the period up to *c.*1150 (just under a century after the Norman Conquest); Middle English from *c.*1150 to *c.*1500 (not long after the introduction of the printing press to Britain);[3] and modern English from *c.*1500 onwards, now usually subdivided into Early Modern English, up to *c.*1750 (or sometimes *c.*1700), and Later Modern English for the period after this. Present-Day English is sometimes used to refer specifically to the language of recent decades.

The transition from Old English to Middle English is characterized by (among other things): a very gradual process of reduction in the use of distinct inflectional endings to convey grammatical relations and a greater reliance on word order; the gradual loss of grammatical gender; the beginning of a phase of borrowing from French and Latin with major consequences for the vocabulary of English; and (during the transitional period) some significant borrowing from Scandinavian languages.

Early Modern English is characterized by (among other things) a series of far-reaching changes in the pronunciation of vowels known collectively as the Great Vowel Shift and a gradual increase in the importance and influence (at first mostly in writing) of a standard form of language based largely on the English of London and the south-east of England.

---

[3] The terms 'early Middle English' (normally taken to be up to *c.*1325) and 'late Middle English' (normally taken to be roughly *c.*1400 to *c.*1500, or sometimes *c.*1375 to *c.*1500) are often used to distinguish phenomena characteristic of the opening and concluding stages of the Middle English period.

The early stages of Later Modern English are marked by greater codification of the standard variety (as in grammars and dictionaries) and, linked with this, a strongly normative tradition, i.e. the increasing importance of comment on and rules for how English should and should not be used. Additionally, the Later Modern English period shows significant shifts in the 'centres of gravity' of English use worldwide, from a language still used chiefly in the British Isles, to one used as first language in a wide variety of territories around the world, and, increasingly, as first choice as a lingua franca in international communication worldwide.

1.2.2 Types of lexical borrowing; borrowing and code switching; borrowing and imposition

Lexical borrowing occurs when the lexis of one language (commonly called the donor language or sometimes the source language) exercises an influence on the lexis of another language (commonly called the borrowing language or sometimes the receiving language), with the result that the borrowing language acquires a new word form or word meaning, or both, from the donor language.

This book concentrates on loanwords, which, as noted in the introduction to this chapter, result from the borrowing of a word form with its meaning (or a component of its meaning) from one language to another. Thus English *image* 'artificial imitation or representation of something' reflects a Middle English borrowing of French *image* in the same meaning. Similarly *friar* (Middle English *frere*) reflects a borrowing of French *frere* (modern French *frère*), but in this case only in a very particular meaning: in French this is the usual word in the meaning 'brother', but in English it denotes only a particular type of metaphorical 'brother' in a mendicant religious order.[4]

The other main types of lexical borrowing involve borrowing of meaning but not (directly) of word form, and can conveniently be referred to under the cover term *semantic borrowing*.[5] In some cases the structure of a word in the donor language is replicated by a new word in the borrowing language,

---

[4] For a detailed account of this example, see Durkin (2009) 3–7.

[5] The classic account of different types of lexical borrowing remains Haugen (1950), although the approaches and terminology adopted by different scholars vary considerably. For recent overviews, see Haspelmath (2009), Winford (2010).

e.g., as already noted, English *almighty* (Old English *ælmihtiġ*) was probably formed on the model of Latin *omnipotēns*; the components *all* and *mighty* of the English word match closely the components *omni-* 'all' and *potēns* 'mighty, powerful' of the Latin word. This is typically called a loan translation or calque. In other cases, an existing word in the borrowing language acquires a new meaning from a word in the donor language; e.g. Old English *þrōwung* 'suffering' probably acquired the additional meaning '(Christ's) passion' by a process of analogy with the meanings of Latin *passiō* 'suffering, (Christ's) passion'. This is often termed a semantic loan.

Semantic borrowing is very characteristic of the Old English period, and these examples and others are discussed in section 8.3, where the terminology that is normally used to describe semantic borrowings by scholars of Old English is presented in more detail. This is an area where terminology differs considerably. It is also an area where it is notoriously difficult to be certain that borrowing has actually occurred. Semantic borrowing does not form part of the main focus of this book, except (i) for comparison with the borrowing of loanwords, and (ii) for the special case of loanwords that show continuing borrowing of new meanings from the original donor. For instance, *to present* (borrowed from French and/or Latin *c.*1300) acquires some further meanings from French much later, e.g. 'to stage or put on (a play)' in the sixteenth century (see section 14.6).

A further, intermediate, category of loan blends is sometimes distinguished, where a borrowed word is adapted or remodelled using material from the borrowing language. For instance, Old English *fēferfuge* 'feverfew' (the name of a plant traditionally used for medicinal purposes) shows a borrowing of Latin *febrifugia*, but with substitution of Old English *fēfer* 'fever' for Latin *febris* in the same meaning. Similarly *brownetta* 'brunette' (1582) shows a borrowing of Italian *brunetta* but with substitution of English *brown* for Italian *bruno*. Cases like this, where a word from a foreign language has clearly entered English, albeit with some remodelling, are included in the scope of this book.

Loanwords in English sometimes show remodelling or suffixation of the borrowed word stem with a suffix that signals the word class that the loanword belongs to in English. For instance, in Old English borrowed verbs all need to be accommodated morphologically to one of the Old English verb classes, hence Latin *plantāre* > Old English *plantian* 'to plant', showing the infinitive ending *-ian* of verbs of the second weak class (see further section 7.5.4 on this). In later English this is seldom obligatory, although compare for instance adverbs of manner, which typically show suffixation in *-ly*. In Middle English and modern English, and especially in Early Modern English, there has been a tendency for the (borrowed) adjective-forming suffixes *-al* and *-ous* to be extended to some borrowed adjectives that do not show the equivalent ending in the donor language, hence *academical* (1549) < Latin *acadēmicus*, beside later *academic* (1579) from the same source, or *illustrious* (?1566) < Latin *illustris*. Sometimes words from other languages are directly incorporated into complex new words in English; this is particularly a feature of how words and word elements ultimately of Latin or Greek origin are drawn upon in the terminology of the modern sciences, as in *oleiferous* 'yielding or bearing oil' (1804) < Latin *oleum* 'oil' + the (ultimately borrowed) combining form *-iferous*. Chapter 14 looks in detail at some of the difficult questions of analysis and categorization posed by formations of this type.

Another important term encountered at various points in this book is code switching. This is a difficult and rather controversial topic. Most scholars consider that code switching occurs when bilingual or multilingual speakers mix elements from more than one language within a single act of communication, whether within a sentence or in successive sentences. Code switching and borrowing are distinct processes, although how distinct is a matter of some debate. One hotly contested issue is whether it is useful to call switches at the level of a single word code switches, or whether these should be regarded as borrowings, simply occurring in the language of bilingual or multilingual speakers; when single-word code switches and nonce borrowings are distinguished, criteria can vary.[6] Aside from the theoretical aspects of this question, it is important to note that when one bilingual or multilingual speaker is communicating with another, even if most of the communication is in one language, words (and larger units) from the other language(s) can readily be introduced. In some social and cultural circumstances this can be an important channel for words ultimately to enter the usage of monolingual speakers as well. This topic figures

[6] For fuller discussion and further references, see Durkin (2009) 173–7. On the question of how to treat singly occurring foreign-language words, important accounts from differing positions are offered by, on the one hand, Myers-Scotton (2002) or Thomason (2003), and, on the other, Poplack, Sankoff, and Miller (1988), Poplack and Meechan (1998), Poplack (2004), or (drawing on interesting empirical data) Poplack and Dion (2012); see also Gardner-Chloros (2010).

particularly prominently in part V of this book, when we examine English, French, and Latin in contact in the multilingual society of later medieval England.

A further theoretical distinction is sometimes drawn between borrowing and imposition, the latter term being used for the process by which speakers introduce new material into a language in the process of a shift from primary use of one language to primary use of another. This is typical in a situation of language death, where a community ceases to use one language in favour of another. This is considered in a little more detail in part IV, in the context of the Scandinavian contribution to the lexis of English.

Proper names, both place names and personal names, are excluded from the scope of this book. The methodology for studying borrowed names and name-forming elements is very different from that used in studying borrowed general lexis, and is best left to specialist studies.[7] However, in chapters 5, 9, and 10 the evidence of name studies is drawn upon to some extent for the light that it can shed on English loanwords from Celtic and Scandinavian languages.

1.3 Some different approaches to studying lexical borrowing

Because loanwords are so pervasive in English, there are numerous different ways in which they can be approached and studied. We may look at how they have entered English, which languages they have been borrowed from, and at what times and in which contact situations. Alternatively, we may look at their impact on the structure of the lexis of English, examining how they enter into word-forming patterns within English, and/or what their impact is on the meaning relations between different words. Or it is possible to approach them primarily from the point of view of their stylistic or pragmatic effects in different text types from different periods. In this book the first, fundamentally etymological and historical, approach predominates, as is more or less traditional in most loanword studies. A good deal of attention is also given to the second approach, which, like the first approach, is based fundamentally on the study of individual word histories,

---

[7] On some of the main differences in the nature of the evidence see Durkin (2009) 266–83. For an introduction to the study of the place names of England see Cameron (1996). On the available resources for English personal names and surnames see McClure (forthcoming).

drawing generalizations from these to reveal something about the lexical history and development of English. The third, essentially stylistic, approach is rather different, being fundamentally based on the analysis of texts rather than of words across time, and requiring sensitivity to speakers' perceptions about words, as well as to the facts of their history (which are often entirely opaque to speakers, and are at best reflected indirectly through aspects of word structure or phonology). This approach figures much less prominently in this book, although some perspectives of this sort are examined at various points in the historical narrative, and especially in chapters 14 and 16.[8]

Another important issue in any historical survey is whether we are interested in investigating say Middle English borrowing from the point of view of Middle English, i.e. for what it tells us about what words speakers of Middle English used and how they used them, or for what it tells us about the historical background of the English used today, essentially a teleological approach. This book tries to keep an eye on both questions, but (unlike many surveys) attempts to maintain a distinction between the two; in particular, the surveys of loanwords in the high-frequency vocabulary of modern English and in the basic vocabulary of modern English in chapter 2 will be used as a point of reference throughout this book, in order to illuminate how borrowing in the past has shaped the everyday English of today.

A recent important trend in linguistic research has been to examine lexical borrowing in the context of broader issues of language contact and to attempt to classify the different sorts of linguistic borrowing that typify different sorts of contact situations.[9] In this book lexical borrowing, and specifically loanwords, are foregrounded throughout, and there is no attempt to offer an overview of all types of linguistic borrowing (syntactic, morphological, phonological, etc.) in the history of English.[10] However,

---

[8] See Fischer (2003) for a 'typology of typologies' of lexical borrowing. He distinguishes between approaches that are predominantly morphological, those that are predominantly semantic, and those that are predominantly sociolinguistic. This book concentrates chiefly on the morphological and semantic aspects, rather than the sociolinguistic.

[9] A very influential, albeit controversial, study of this type which takes a number of its case studies from episodes in the history of English is Thomason and Kaufman (1988). See also Thomason (2001) and the various contributions in Hickey (2010). The classic seminal work on language contact in general remains Weinreich (1953).

[10] For an important attempt at such a history up to the Renaissance, see Miller (2012).

other types of linguistic borrowing are touched on with regard to certain periods when it has been suggested that there was a significant discrepancy between lexical and non-lexical borrowing; this is especially (albeit controversially) the case with regard to early contact between English and Celtic, as will be considered in chapter 5.

Many recent studies of linguistic borrowing foreground sociolinguistic perspectives. In particular, a rather broad-brush categorization of the sociolinguistic relationship between any two languages in contact is often applied. If one language has a position of lower social and cultural prestige vis-à-vis another, it is said to be a substrate and in a substratal relationship with the other language. If it has higher prestige, it is a superstrate, in a superstratal relationship. And if the levels of prestige are roughly equal, the two languages are adstrates, in an adstratal relationship. In practice, the application of these terms varies considerably, with some scholars classifying as adstratal situations where the difference in prestige is relatively small, while others would classify the same situation as showing a relationship between substrate and superstrate. In this book, these terms will be used very sparingly and mostly in relation to early contact situations in which only the broadest indications of the nature of the sociolinguistic relationships between languages can be reconstructed. Fortunately, for most of the period covered by this book, we know quite a lot about the relevant contact situations and thus a fairly fine-grained analysis is possible. This is particularly true of loanwords in the Middle English and modern English periods. See further section 2.4 for an outline of the approach taken in this study.

1.4 On evidence and hypotheses

Lists of loanwords given in handbooks and histories of English can give the appearance of being simple statements of fact. It is important to realize that they are not: they are hypotheses, sometimes supported by evidence so secure that they are not in any real doubt, but very often based on much less secure foundations.

An entirely satisfactory, secure loanword etymology might show the following characteristics:

1. The supposed borrowing is first recorded later than the supposed donor (assuming that we have a dependable documentary record for each language in the relevant period).

2. The supposed borrowing shows form(s) entirely explicable from the form(s) of the supposed donor (allowing for later known processes in the borrowing language).
3. The supposed borrowing shows meaning(s) entirely explicable from the meaning(s) of the supposed donor as starting point.
4. There is a known historical context of language contact in which the borrowing could have occurred.
5. There is no alternative explanation for the supposed borrowing, or at least none that is as convincing as the assumption of borrowing from the supposed donor.

There can be problems with all of these criteria and not all of them are amenable to rigorous objectivity. As regards (1), our documentary record is often poor, or entirely absent, for both the borrowing language and the donor in the period when the borrowing is supposed to have occurred. As regards (2), not all form developments are entirely regular or easily explained. As regards (3), it is notoriously difficult to test whether a supposed semantic development is plausible.[11] As regards (4), our historical data is often sketchy, and we may also encounter considerable uncertainties about the likely historical setting if we do not know when or where a borrowing is likely to have occurred. As regards (5), there is often a good deal of subjectivity involved in deciding whether one etymology is more convincing than another, however hard we try to base our decisions firmly on the analysis of empirical data; also, scholars differ over how much priority to give to explanations that do not involve contact with other languages over ones that do, in other words, how much priority to give to endogeny over exogeny.

This book looks in some detail at problems of evidence and its interpretation that often make us much less certain than we would like about which words have been borrowed into English, from which languages, in which places, and at which times. This involves looking at some very complicated issues, but the reader who perseveres should have a much more informed understanding of some of the assumptions, hypotheses, and uncertainties that underlie the sometimes rather bland statements made about how many words English has borrowed from other languages. Through an emphasis

---

[11] For discussion and illustration of these last two points, see Durkin (2009) chapters 7 and 8.

on how we (think we) know what we do know, I hope also to illustrate how rich a field this is for further study.

1.5 What constitutes the vocabulary of English?

Another potential pitfall is to treat 'the vocabulary (or lexis) of English' as though it were an entirely unproblematic concept. Modern standard English, as used in Britain, the USA, and other majority English-speaking communities, is the product of a number of social, cultural, and technological factors operating over a long period of time. The rise of modern standard English as a written variety was closely bound together with the development of the printing industry in early modern England, as the choices made by printers from the available pool of variation in spelling forms and in vocabulary, especially core vocabulary, gradually converged on a particular set of norms. The spread of these linguistic choices beyond the printed medium was a slow process and owed a lot to normative trends in grammatical works and dictionaries in the eighteenth and nineteenth centuries. (Chapter 14 looks more closely at these processes.)

In the modern standard variety that resulted from these processes, lexical choices are often very constrained in the core vocabulary, especially among core grammatical items. Thus, *you are* is considered the only 'correct' form of the second-person singular of the verb *be*. *Thou art* may be familiar from the works of Shakespeare and his contemporaries even to those with no specialist knowledge of the history of English, but it is considered an archaism. Where it survives in regional speech, *thou art* is considered to be non-standard, and will therefore be avoided by most speakers coming from such areas when they are speaking in more formal environments; the same applies to other forms found in other varieties of English, such as *you be*, *you is*, *you am*, or *you'm*. This differentiation between standard and non-standard is the result of the application of social norms, which can themselves change. For instance, modern spoken British English shows a good deal of variation between standard *you were* and non-standard but very widespread *you was*; typically, *you was* is perceived as uneducated or ignorant, and avoided in formal contexts; however, in contemporary Britain it can be heard regularly in the media in spoken use by people who are widely respected as high achievers in various fields (sport, business, entertainment). In the future it may become more widely accepted even in formal contexts as social attitudes shift. To take another example, some varieties of English (especially in the USA and Caribbean) have a pronoun of the type *you-all*, others do not; among those that do have it, in some varieties its use is restricted to addressing more than one person, but in others it can also be used to address just one person. A similar situation is found with *youse* (and a number of other forms) in some varieties of British and US English. Very many speakers who use *you-all* or *youse* when addressing other members of their own local communities will substitute *you* in more formal contexts, but the sociolinguistic situation is complex and fluid, and closely tied up with wider questions of regional identity and prestige.

At present, there is very little difference in core vocabulary between the major standard varieties of English worldwide. British and US English show some minor differences in grammatical vocabulary; e.g. in British English the past participle of *get* is invariably *got*, but in US English there is variation between *got* and *gotten*, depending on the semantic context. There is also some well-known variation in everyday non-grammatical vocabulary, such as *lift* versus *elevator*, *rubbish* versus *trash*. Similarly, in South African English *robot* is an everyday term for a traffic light. Today, smaller dictionaries are typically produced in editions specially tailored to different national varieties of English and reflecting these differences in lexical usage. However, this is a recent trend, linked to the growing prestige of different national varieties as markers of national identity, and the cases where usage is identical in each variety far outweigh the differences.

The differing incidence of loanwords of various origins is one of the more obvious ways in which varieties of English around the world do differ from one another. We will look at this topic more closely in chapter 15, but a first illustration can be gained by taking (very unscientifically) a passage from a contemporary South African short story and underlining all of the loan-words, in the same way as in section 1.1:

> 'Don't you <u>want</u> to see your <u>grandson</u>?'
> 'Not if that <u>moegoe</u> has to be here.'
> 'That <u>moegoe</u> is a <u>part</u> of our <u>family</u> now, whether we like it or not.' The words <u>slipped</u> out unexpectedly.
> 'Okay, I see how it is now.'
> '<u>Ag</u>, <u>suit</u> yourself then.' Pauline <u>returned</u> to her daughter.
>
> (Sean William O'Toole *The Marquis of Mooikloof and other stories* (2006) 19.)

Here, among numerous older borrowings that are common to most varieties of English, we have two distinctively South African English loanwords: *ag*, an interjection borrowed from Afrikaans; and *moegoe*, a word meaning roughly 'bumpkin', borrowed into English probably immediately from Afrikaans and Isicamtho (a mixed language of urban South Africa), but of uncertain ultimate origin. Both words are included in the full *OED*, but labelled as restricted to South African English. Some words originally found in South African English have subsequently spread to other varieties, e.g. *commando* (< Portuguese), which is found in South African English from the late eighteenth century, denoting a body of irregular troops, but is rarely found in other varieties of English until the twentieth century, having become widely familiar in Britain as a result of the Boer War of 1899–1902, and then having acquired its modern meaning as a result of specific use by Winston Churchill in 1940 during the Second World War.

However, differences of vocabulary can also be found at the micro level, between different individuals. We all have slightly different individual vocabularies, both active, i.e. the words we use ourselves, and passive, i.e. the words that we understand but are unlikely to use ourselves. These differences in individual vocabulary reflect our different experiences, educational backgrounds, professional lives, interests, friendships, and other social and cultural factors. Words can then spread from the vocabulary of one person to that of another, as a result of direct social interaction or sometimes as a result of use in published writing or broadcasting, and so on. Intra-linguistic spread of this sort is strictly a type of lexical borrowing, although the term is more usually used specifically of borrowing between languages.

One way of approaching the topic of the differing vocabularies of different individuals is to consider the vocabulary of a particular specialist field. For instance, there is a large specialist vocabulary relating to wine. There are some terms that are widely familiar and are found even in dictionaries for learners like the *Oxford Advanced Learner's Dictionary* (*OALD*), e.g. *corked*, describing wine which is spoiled because of decay in the cork; or allowing a wine to *breathe*, i.e. to begin to react with the air before it is drunk. They may be more familiar to some people than to others and some people may have a clearer idea of their meaning than others, but they are at least familiar to a large number of people. Others, like *laying down* fine wine to mature before it is drunk, or *drinking window*, denoting the period in which a mature wine is good to drink before it is past its peak, will be unfamiliar to many people, but well known to wine enthusiasts. Other people may be aware of these terms, but consciously avoid them, perceiving them to be affected 'snob' wine language. None of these terms has entered the wine vocabulary of English as loanwords, but much of the specialist vocabulary of wine has. Some of these words have been in English for a long time and have even spread outside the specialist vocabulary of wine: e.g. *vintage* entered English (late in the Middle English period) as a specific term relating to wine, but developed various metaphorical uses in other fields and can nowadays be applied also to *vintage cars,* for instance. The word is fully naturalized in English and, although it was originally a borrowing from French, it differs considerably from the modern French word form, *vendange*. There are also very many French terms that are not at all widely known, but that are known to and used by many enthusiasts for French fine wine worldwide, e.g. *barrique, cépage, cuvée, élevage, en primeur, grand cru, grand vin, négociant, premier cru,* or *vigneron*. These all show little if any naturalization in pronunciation or morphology in English, and not all of them are found even in the largest English dictionaries, such as the *OED*. But they do all occur in specialist wine publications written in English and are definitely part of the active vocabulary of some English speakers and of the passive vocabulary of others. Some speakers will know some of these words but not others. Some will be equally familiar with the specialist terminology relating to German wine, e.g. *Anbaugebiet, Auslese, Bereich, Eiswein, Kabinett, Prädikat, Qualitätswein, Spätlese, Trockenbeerenauslese,* but others may not be. The minority group of English speakers familiar with such terminology is not homogeneous: it is widely spread geographically (wherever there are people who have a strong interest in French or German fine wine) and, although its members may tend to have some other interests in common, there will be others that they do not share, and they will belong to a range of different professions. Some may be fluent speakers of French and/or German, and their use of these words may show single-word code switches to French or German, but many will not be. In the approach taken in this book such words are regarded as loanwords, even if they are rare and non-naturalized ones.[12]

---

[12] In the tradition of most German lexicography and lexicology a distinction is made between *Lehnwörter*, 'loanwords', which are taken to show full phonological and morphological integration into German (the term is often restricted partly or wholly to very early loanwords, such as *Wein* or *Strasse*, on which compare part III) and *Fremdwörter*, 'foreignisms', the latter term being used for everything from loanwords which retain some aspect of their foreign-language morphology (e.g. in the way that they form the plural) to

Thus, when we speak about the vocabulary (or lexis) of a language, it can be useful to think of a (not very precisely defined) common core of basic vocabulary, including words in everyday use and function words. This generally shows relatively little variation within narrowly defined speech communities, or within standard varieties, such as modern-day standard English as used internationally. Beyond this we can attempt to identify numerous different (overlapping) vocabularies belonging to different specialisms (e.g. activities, professions), to different functions (e.g. academic discourse), or to different stylistic registers (formal, informal, etc.).[13] In each of these, some words will be frequent and known to most if not all speakers, others will be very rare and restricted to very small numbers of speakers. Borrowed words can belong to any of these categories: some, as already seen, are in everyday use in even the simplest discourse, while others are used only very occasionally in very restricted circumstances and only ever by certain speakers.

All of these factors need to be borne in mind when we consider questions about how much borrowing from various different languages the vocabulary of modern English shows. Are we looking at the wordlist of a small dictionary, concentrating on the core plus the most frequent words from specialist vocabularies? Or are we looking at the wordlist of a very large dictionary, which will include many words not in frequent use, many of which are only known by a small minority of speakers? We explore some of the practical implications of this in chapter 2.

If we introduce a diachronic dimension, things become more complicated again. As noted above, different varieties of English today can show variation even in the area of basic vocabulary and among grammatical function words, e.g. *you-all* and *youse*. Further back in the history of English such variation becomes much more typical. Many of our surviving Old English written documents rather mask dialectal variation, because they are written in a particular form of the West Saxon dialect that was in widespread use as

completely unassimilated items like those listed in this paragraph, and often embracing any loanwords from recent centuries, whatever their degree of integration. In practice, the two categories are impossible to distinguish consistently and reliably in all instances, and the distinction is not used in this book. See further Durkin (2009 139–40), and also Polenz (1967), Eisenberg (2011), and compare sections 7.4 and 14.8.1 of this book.

[13] An early form of this model was set out by Sir James Murray in his 'General Explanations' accompanying the first completed volume of the *OED* (Murray 1888).

a written variety in the late Old English period. However, our Middle English records are far more revealing about dialectal variation and enable us to reconstruct many different local systems of phonology, morphology, and syntax. In the Middle English period vocabulary varies hugely between different local varieties, even at the level of closed-class grammatical words: in chapter 9 we look at how the borrowed third-person plural pronoun *they* (and *their* and *them*) spread gradually between different dialects, by a process of internal borrowing from dialect to dialect. In a historical context like this, where there was so much variation even in core grammatical vocabulary, the concept of a common core of basic vocabulary can probably be meaningful for a particular dialect, but it is somewhat more difficult to speak of the core vocabulary of Middle English as a whole.

It is notoriously difficult to draw a distinction between two dialects of the same language and two different languages; the old observation that a language is a dialect with an army and a navy certainly has some merit, since a lot depends on questions of politics and national identity, connected with processes of linguistic standardization. A good example is presented by Scots in the sixteenth century. It had a distinct written form, with spelling conventions very different from those in the developing London-centred standard of England. It presented significant differences from the English of England (especially southern England) in pronunciation and in some areas of grammar, and, most obviously, it had very many vocabulary items not found in other varieties of English.[14] But, on the other hand, mutual comprehension was certainly possible, and many features were shared with neighbouring dialects of northern England. Over the following centuries as political union developed, so did the influence of the standard English of England on the English used in official functions and in more formal contexts in Scotland. Thus it is a very difficult question whether Scots constituted a separate language from the rest of English in the sixteenth century; if we decide that it was a different language, and that some rural dialects remain as the descendants of this, it is still more difficult to say at which subsequent point the language used in standard functions in Scotland became something that we would want to call English rather than Scots. Whether we decide to call English and Scots in the sixteenth century two different languages or two dialects of the same language, there are

[14] On the composition of the vocabulary of Older Scots, see especially Macafee and Anderson (1997), Macafee (1997), Macafee (2002).

interesting implications for how we talk about the vocabulary of English: either there was a period in which English had a neighbour with a great deal of vocabulary in common and easy mutual comprehensibility (especially in the border regions), or there were two different emerging standard varieties of English which showed very considerable differences even in aspects of their core vocabulary.

2

Introducing the data

2.1 Assessing input from different languages in the vocabulary of modern English

Percentages are often quoted for the proportions of the vocabulary of modern English that are borrowed from French, Latin, Scandinavian languages, etc. As discussed in chapter 1, such percentages must be approached with extreme caution. Firstly, we have to bear in mind that such figures can only refer to a particular period: the proportions in contemporary English will not at all be the same as those in sixteenth- or seventeenth-century English, for example. Secondly, we must consider whose English we are talking about, as discussed in section 1.5. Thirdly, once we have decided which registers, varieties, etc. we want to take into account, we have the practical problem of arriving at a wordlist. Fourthly, once we have our wordlist, we have the problem of assessing and classifying etymologies, i.e. deciding which words are borrowed and which are not. This last problem is a major concern of this book.

Nonetheless, it can be useful to have some initial points of orientation, however much we may modify or qualify these later. The usual starting point for such discussions is the *OED*, comprising a wordlist of over 600,000 lexemes (including simplex words such as *butter*, compounds such as *butter knife*, and derivative formations such as *buttery* 'rich in butter') arranged under nearly 275,000 headword entries. Some of these words are now obsolete, but most are not. Although a total count of over 600,000 lexemes is vast, the *OED* should not be taken as a catalogue of every word or expression that ever is or has been used in English. Section 1.5 investigates how loanwords are one area (among many) in which the vocabulary of English can be hugely variable from one individual to another, and how a common core of shared vocabulary shades off into hugely varied individual repertories of lexical items depending on location, profession, interests, and individual experience. The *OED*'s selection criteria for including lexemes pay careful attention to questions of frequency of use and spread in different contexts of use, and its wordlist can be taken as a good reflection of those words that have had most impact on the lexicon of English since the mid-twelfth century (it generally includes Old English words only when they have survived into later use). No dictionary could ever list *all* English words, since the vocabulary is almost infinitely extendible by regular processes of word formation as well as by borrowing from other languages.

The *OED* has been compiled over a very long time: the first edition was published in fascicles (or instalments) between 1884 and 1928; supplements were added in 1933 and (in four volumes) between 1972 and 1986; and these were brought together with the main text in the Second Edition of 1989. A revised edition of the full text of the dictionary (*OED3*) has been in course of publication since 2000, and currently covers approximately one-third of the full text of the dictionary.

Fig. 2.1 presents the totals of loanwords from the most prolific donor languages as reflected by the two large contiguous alphabetical ranges of *OED3* that have so far been published, as of November 2012, comprising all of the letters M, N, O, P, Q, R, and A from A to ALZ. Approximately 92,500 dictionary entries fall into these alphabetical ranges, constituting the bulk of the *OED3* material so far published. For statistical purposes, I will not draw on shorter sequences of entries that have been published separately, such as *be*, *love*, or words beginning with *sub-* or *super-*, since these constitute a less representative cross-section of the English lexicon. However, for illustrative examples, I will draw freely on all of *OED3*, and also on unrevised parts of the dictionary.

The benefit of drawing statistical data from *OED3* alone is that the material has been edited over a relatively short period of time, using much the same set of resources for each word (e.g. dictionaries and databases for information about foreign languages, etc.), applying the same set of editorial principles and guidelines, and, just as importantly, employing the same style, so that data can easily be extracted computationally.[1] This portion of

---

[1] In compiling the data from *OED3* given here, as likewise in a number of other places in this book, I have made use of the sophisticated electronic tagging and search software of the computer system used by editors preparing the new edition of the *OED*. This is not

the dictionary also benefits from much more thorough treatment of recent change in the lexicon of English, including recent loanwords.[2] Additionally, any reader who wishes to compare the data presented here with data based on the whole of the *OED*, both revised and unrevised portions, can easily do so by consulting the timelines for loanwords from each donor language available at <http://www.oed.com>. For many of the languages discussed in this book, the lexicographical treatment of loanwords in *OED2* and *OED3* is very similar, and timelines based on the whole of *OED* differ very little in outline from those based only on *OED3* data. However, for some of the major donor languages, there are significant differences in treatment, reflecting issues that are discussed in detail in this book (especially in parts V and VI), and these do make a difference to the overall chronological picture. (See the discussion in sections 12.1 and 14.8 of two difficult areas that particularly affect loanwords from Latin and French, and in the latter case also loanwords from Greek and German.)

Among the 92,500 main entries that make up the alphabetical ranges M, N, O, P, Q, R, and A to ALZ in *OED3*, a little over 29,300 (approximately 32%) are identified as loanwords from other languages. Fig. 2.1 gives the twenty-five most prolific sources (twenty-four different languages, with French and/or Latin counted as a separate category).

Fig. 2.1 shows how dramatically the totals of loanwords from different languages differ. Those from the top few sources dramatically outnumber those from any other source, such that the totals cannot be made out clearly from a single chart. Fig. 2.2 therefore consists of a series of charts, each to a different scale, enabling the totals to be seen more clearly: in each successive

---

publicly available, and for this reason I have not specified the precise details of the computer searches made. However, all of the relevant data is present in the *OED* entries as published in *OED Online*, and in the companion website to this book I suggest a number of approaches for exploring *OED* data directly using *OED Online*. It should also be noted that newly revised and newly added entries are being added to *OED3* and published on *OED Online* (see chapter 17) every three months, and hence the *OED3* data presented in this book represents a snapshot of *OED*'s research at a particular point in time. See again the companion website for some ways of exploring and engaging creatively with this dynamic aspect of the *OED* today.

[2] The *OED3* text also incorporates all loanwords that have appeared in previous editions of the *OED* (including its one-volume supplement of 1933). No words added by previous editors are omitted, even if the supporting evidence appears slender; the only exception is where evidence appears to have been misinterpreted, giving rise to a 'ghost word'.

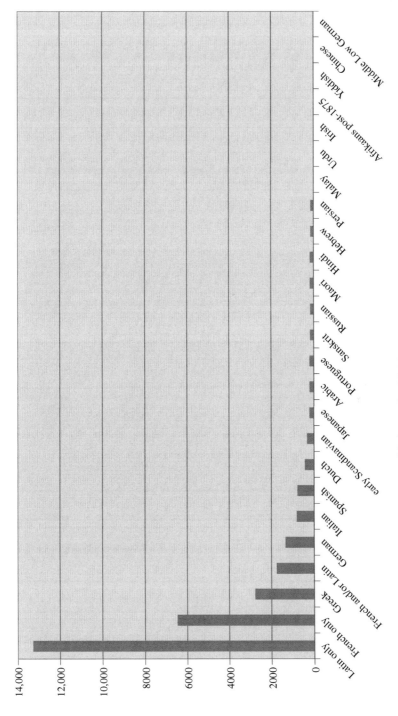

Fig. 2.1 Totals of loanwords from the 25 most prolific inputs in *OED3*.

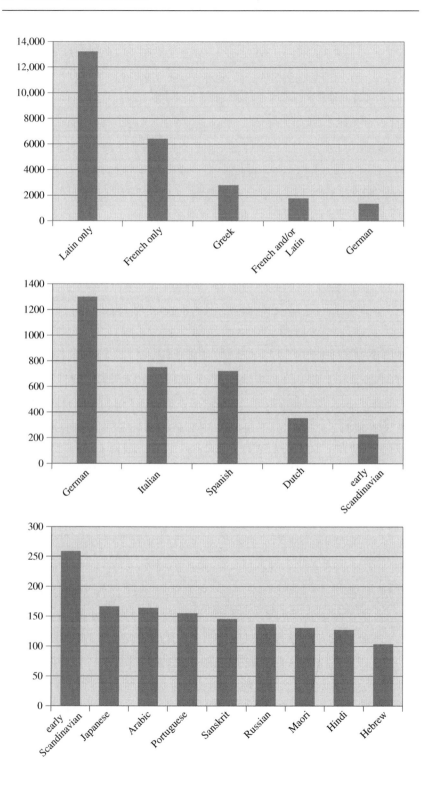

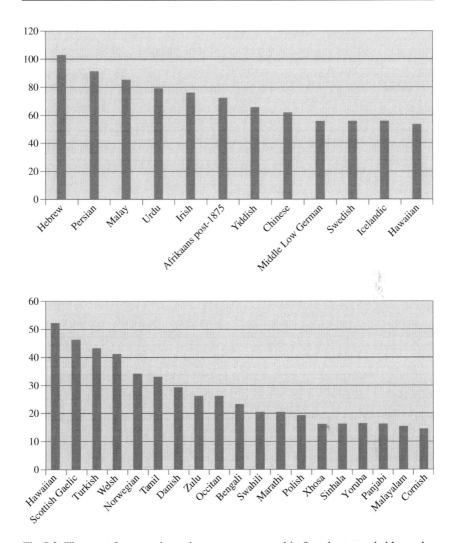

Fig. 2.2 The most frequent donor languages, arranged in five charts graded by scale.

chart, the language that was on the right-hand edge of the preceding chart appears first at the left-hand edge. These charts take the totals beyond the top twenty-five donors, so as to include Welsh and Cornish, as long-standing Celtic neighbours of English in the British Isles. (On the Celtic languages see further section 3.3.)

Some of the language names given here may be more familiar than others. See section 15.2.1 for explanation of the distinction between Low German and High German. See section 9.2 for an explanation of what is meant in this book (as in *OED3*) by the cover term 'early Scandinavian'.

It should be noted that some of the totals in these charts overlap, because many words show input from more than one language, or the language of direct origin cannot be ascertained with precision. For example, many words that may have been borrowed into Middle English or Early Modern English from Low German could alternatively have been borrowed from Dutch, or may show some input from both languages. Some more recent borrowings from Dutch show some input from Dutch as spoken in Europe, some from Dutch as spoken in South Africa, and some from Afrikaans, which developed from this variety of Dutch. (See section 15.2.1.)

By far the biggest group of words of either multiple or uncertain origin is constituted by words from French and/or Latin. In this book, I show that such words entered English in particularly large numbers at a key turning point in the history of the English lexicon, and argue that they are symptomatic of very significant historical changes. In Fig. 2.1 and Fig. 2.2, they are therefore presented as a separate category.

Loanwords from all of the twenty-five most prolific inputs listed in Fig. 2.1 are looked at in the course of this book. However, it should be noted that these raw numbers (in Fig. 2.1 and Fig. 2.2) do not reflect qualitative differences in impact on the vocabulary of modern English. We will look at this topic more closely in sections 2.2 and 2.3. It will be noted that, for example, in these charts the total of loanwords from Japanese comes next after the total from early Scandinavian. However, Japanese has (so far at least) contributed no words to English which form part of the basic vocabulary of modern English, whereas early Scandinavian contributed several, including even the third-person plural personal pronoun *they*. Such qualitative differences are a major determining factor in the amount of discussion devoted to loanwords from various source languages in the course of this book. Additionally, it should be noted that not all loanwords from a particular source language are of similar importance in the vocabulary of English. For instance, the majority of the words that figure in the huge total of English loanwords from Latin are of relatively rare occurrence, but some occur very frequently, and have an important role in the language of everyday discourse. Such words are looked at particularly closely in this book.

In fact, the ultimate contribution of loanwords to the vocabulary of English is much higher than even these numerical totals suggest, if we also take into consideration all of the words formed within English from borrowed words. The inherited portion of the vocabulary of English that

(i) *OED* headword entries only   (ii) All lexical items in *OED*

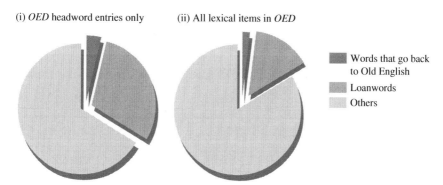

Words that go back
to Old English

Loanwords

Others

Fig. 2.3 All items in *OED* classified by origin. (i) *OED* headword entries only. (ii) All lexical items in *OED*.

goes back to Old English is relatively small: the *OED* lists among its 275,000 headword entries approximately 9,600 words (around 3.5%) surviving beyond 1150 that were first attested before 1150. (Even this total includes several hundred pre-1150 loanwords from Latin and smaller numbers of loanwords from Scandinavian and Celtic languages, but these are very approximately counterbalanced by words not recorded until after 1150 that are nonetheless generally considered to be of native origin and to have existed already in Old English.)

Thus, if we put together all of the words found before 1150 and all of the words known to have been borrowed subsequently from other languages, we have only about one-third of the *OED* headword list. Some of the remaining words are of unknown origin, and may be borrowings, while others can be identified pretty confidently as imitative formations reflecting non-linguistic sounds in the external world (e.g. bangs or crashes, animal cries, or natural utterances such as groans), and others are derived from proper names. However, the vast majority are formed from those words that are either inherited or borrowed, chiefly by processes of compounding, derivation, or conversion, e.g. from *fork*, we find *fork handle*, *forked*, and *to fork*. In some cases the relationship with the parent word(s) remains transparent; in others it has become opaque, e.g. in *lord* or *lady*, both of which originally showed compounds of *loaf*.

Fig. 2.3 shows the proportions of words of each type in modern English, as reflected by the *OED*. Here, (i) shows the relative proportions among *OED* headword entries only, while (ii) shows what we find if we take into account all lexical items in *OED*, including the huge numbers of compound

Table 2.1 Proportions of words of different origins in modern English.

	SOED (%)	ALD (%)	GSL (%)
Inherited[3]	22.2	27.43	47.08
French	28.37	35.89	38.2
Other Romance languages	1.86	1.6	0.2
Latin	28.29	22.05	9.59
Greek	5.32	1.59	0.25
Scandinavian element	2.16	2.51	3.11
Dutch, Low German, Frisian	1.42	1.61	0.7
High German (incl. Yiddish)	0.5	0.28	0
Celtic	0.43	0.32	0.025
Other European languages	0.13	0.11	0
Non-European languages	2	1.12	0.05
Unknown etymology	4.03	3.84	0.98
Proper names	3.29	1.96	0

Source: Scheler (1977) 72

and derivative words that are listed under a parent word as subordinate entries, rather than as separate entries.

Thus, in both of these charts the category 'others' is by far the largest. The vast majority of the words in this category are formed by compounding, conversion, or derivation, either from words that go back to the earliest stage of the English language, or from words that have been borrowed from other languages. Attempting to estimate what proportion of the vocabulary of English is formed ultimately from inherited words, and what proportion from words of Latin origin, French origin, etc., is fraught with difficulties. Any figures arrived at can only be very approximate, depending on how one deals with a great many variables. However, if they are approached with due caution, such figures can be illuminating. Scheler (1977 72) presents the figures reproduced in Table 2.1, drawn from Finkenstaedt et al. (1973). The first column shows data taken ultimately from the *Shorter Oxford English Dictionary* (*SOED*), the second from the *Advanced Learner's Dictionary of Current English* (*ALD*, 1963 edition), and the third from a basic vocabulary list, the *General Service List of English Words* (*GSL*). Broadly the same data from Finkenstaedt et al. (1973) is drawn upon in many of the accounts found in current handbooks of English (often via the analysis in Wermser (1976)).

---

[3] Including some words of unknown etymology recorded for the first time in Old English or Middle English.

Some important caveats need to be noted about these figures. The *SOED* figures are derived from the first edition of that dictionary, which was based on the first edition of the *OED*. The *SOED* omitted some rarer words, especially obsolete ones, and summarized and in some cases simplified etymologies. This data was then classified under various summary types in Finkenstaedt (1973), including some rather arbitrary decisions about how to classify words compounded from elements of different origins.[4] The *ALD* figures use *SOED*'s etymologies, and only include those words from the wordlist of the 1963 edition of *ALD* that were also found in *SOED*. The *GSL* figures include only its headwords (which are all high-frequency items), rather than subordinate entries, with etymologies being taken from the *Oxford Dictionary of English Etymology* (*ODEE*).

One important point to note is that the figure for words from Latin reflects some assumptions on which thinking has changed considerably since the first edition of the *OED* (and since *ODEE*, which mirrored its approach closely): in *OED3*, many of these words are given as potentially being borrowed immediately from French, either partly or wholly (see further section 11.3); additionally, a great deal of scientific vocabulary is classified as directly from Latin (or Greek) in the first edition of *OED*, which in *OED3* is presented as formed within English or in other modern languages from elements ultimately of Latin or Greek origin (see further section 14.8.1).

The figures therefore do need to be approached with caution, from various points of view. However, they are valuable for the perspective they give on the composition of the vocabulary of modern English. It is evident at a glance that the proportion of words ultimately reflecting borrowing from most languages (or language groups) declines steadily as one moves from the fuller wordlist of *SOED* to the high-frequency wordlist of the *GSL*. The exceptions to this are French and Scandinavian, the proportions of which actually increase from left to right of Table 2.1. This reflects some important characteristics of borrowing from these two languages, which are explored in detail in this book.

In the following two sections, I turn aside from the wordlists of dictionaries, to see what light can be shed by corpus data (see section 2.2) and basic meaning lists (see section 2.3) on the contribution of borrowing from

---

[4] See further Durkin (2002a) on what is lost through this approach.

different languages to the core vocabulary of English. However, before doing so, it is worth illustrating how using *OED* data also enables us to explore the diachronic (i.e. historical) dimension. As already seen, Latin and French are by far the biggest contributors of loanwords in English. If we look at the dates of first attestation of the 21,393 loanwords from Latin, French, and Latin and/or French in *OED3*, we get the pattern shown in Fig. 2.4. (The chart begins from 1150, because the *OED* does not provide a complete record for the lexis of Old English. There are in fact 238 words in parts of *OED3* so far completed borrowed from French or (mostly) Latin before 1150: see section 12.1.2.)

We can thus see at a glance that the number of words borrowed from Latin has shown some dramatic peaks and troughs in different fifty-year periods, while the number of loanwords from French has remained much steadier. The totals of words assigned to French and/or Latin are much higher in the period 1350–1450 than in any other. We will look at the historical factors determining these patterns in detail in chapters 11 and 14. For the present, it is important to note that raw figures like these do not necessarily give the full picture. It is rather revealing if we compare Fig. 2.4 with a chart showing the totals of new words of all origins per half century, or in other words the lexical growth of English as reflected by the *OED*, as shown by Fig. 2.5.

One thing that is immediately apparent is that the chart for loanwords purely from Latin is quite similar in shape to the chart for quantities of new words of all origins first recorded in each half century (even though the totals are obviously much lower), especially for the period up to around 1800. By contrast, the charts for words purely from French and from French and/or Latin are rather different. This is brought out even more clearly if we look in Fig. 2.6 at loanwords from each source language as a proportion of all new words recorded in each half century.

These charts point to some important themes that are explored in detail in chapters 11 and 14: in the Middle English period, loanwords from French make up a huge proportion of all new words recorded in English, falling away rather sharply after 1500. Loanwords from Latin, by contrast, make up a much less significant proportion of the total until the second half of the fourteenth century, but make up around one-fifth of the total of new words in the sixteenth and seventeenth centuries, before falling away somewhat in the eighteenth and nineteenth centuries, and then declining much more dramatically in the twentieth century. In the following section we see how the *OED*'s diachronic data can shed further light on loanwords in the history

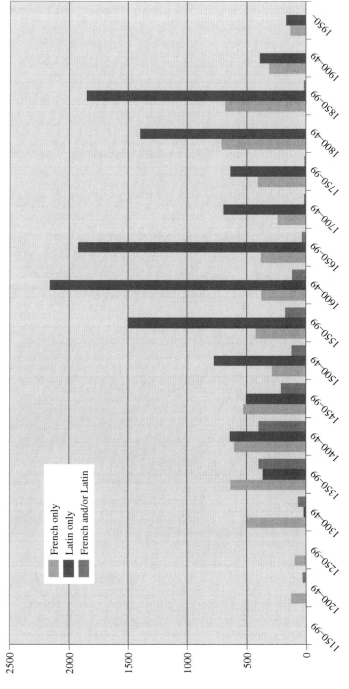

Fig. 2.4 Loanwords from French, Latin, and French and/or Latin in parts of *OED3* so far completed, arranged chronologically.

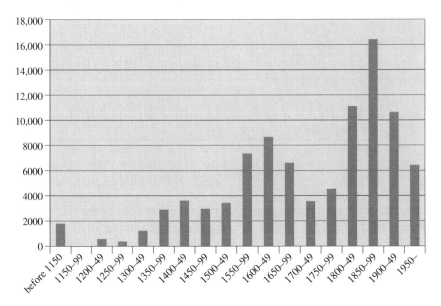

Fig. 2.5 New words of all origins as reflected by parts of *OED3* so far completed, arranged chronologically.

of English if we narrow our focus to just the high-frequency words of modern English.

2.2 Examining loanwords in the high-frequency vocabulary of modern English

Examining the incidence of loanwords among the high-frequency words of modern English can give a valuable insight into the composition of the core vocabulary. This section looks at the 1,000 most frequent words in the *British National Corpus* (*BNC*). I have chosen this corpus because a carefully produced frequency list is readily available both online (<http://ucrel. lancs.ac.uk/bncfreq/>) and in a published book (Leech et al. (2001)). Using *BNC* data is open to the objections that the corpus is now a little dated (it was compiled in the early 1990s), represents only British English, and mostly reflects written language, although these factors become less important when we are taking a long panoramic view, as here. Very similar results will be found if the same procedure is repeated on other contemporary corpora, as I will show.

It should be noted that the frequency list I use here, like other corpus frequency lists, distinguishes 'words' syntactically, thus *to rest* is distinguished

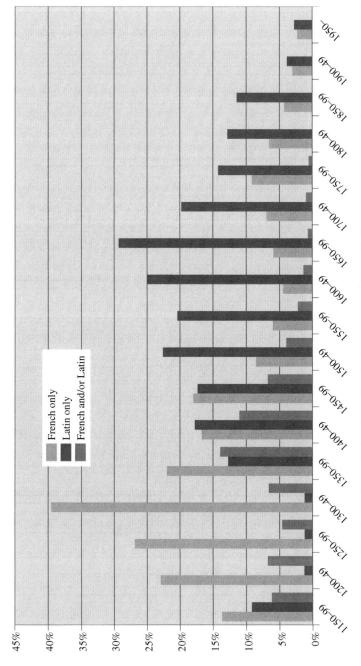

Fig. 2.6 Loanwords from French, Latin, and French and/or Latin as a proportion of all new words, as reflected by parts of *OED3* so far completed.

from *a rest*, but it does not distinguish between identical word forms that show distinct meanings and distinct histories, thus *rest* in *to take a rest* is not distinguished as a separate word from *rest* in *the rest of.* This phenomenon, known as 'homonymy', is very difficult to define and identify if language is looked at purely from a synchronic, non-historical viewpoint (although there is a good deal of work establishing it as a psychological reality for speakers). In a diachronic, historical study such as this one, the etymological criterion is the essential one: *rest* in *to take a rest* is a word of native Germanic origin, but *rest* in *the rest of* is a loanword of French origin. Fortunately, homonymy is fairly limited among the thousand most frequent words in contemporary English and, in the cases that do arise, pragmatic decisions can be made without too much difficulty: for instance, the loanword *rest* is of more frequent occurrence in the corpus than the non-loanword *rest*, and belongs among the 1,000 most frequent words on its own account. Similarly, *bank* 'financial institution' (from French, perhaps with some input directly from Italian: see section 15.2.4) is much more common than *bank* (of earth) (probably from early Scandinavian). When we come to look at historical corpora, in chapter 14, the much greater degree of spelling variation found in earlier stages of English poses much greater challenges for this sort of work, and makes comparison of data between different periods extremely problematic.

Taking the 1,000 most frequent words in a corpus is to a certain extent arbitrary, but not entirely so, since above this number, long runs of words are found with very similar frequency numbers. Among the very most frequent words (e.g. in the top 100 or 200 words) the incidence of loanwords is much lower. (See the end of this section for the situation among the 100 most frequent words in the *BNC*.)

My procedure has been to take the 1,000 most frequent items in the *BNC* frequency list, after making some subtractions of problematic items such as numerals, symbols, and proper names.[5] I have followed the decisions of the

---

[5] I have eliminated from this frequency list: numerals and symbols; proper names; adjectives referring to particular nationalities: *English, British, American, European*, and (showing the age of the *BNC*) *Soviet*; also *St.*, since, whether representing *Saint* or *Street*, the overwhelming majority of instances are in names. I have included the titles *Mr* and *Mrs* (particularly since they have their own pronunciations distinct from their etymons *master* and *mistress*), and also (although it is very much a borderline case) *hon.* for *honourable* (in the titles of MPs, etc.). Both *Dr* and the full form *doctor* occur as separate items in the frequency list, but I have counted them only once.

Table 2.2 Loanwords and words formed from loanwords, among the 1,000 most frequent words in the *BNC*.

Number of words (percentage of total)	Language borrowed from	Notes
487 (92%)	French, Latin or French and/or Latin	Comprising (tentatively): • 220 probably just from French • 58 probably just from Latin • 209 from French and/or Latin
32 (6%)	Scandinavian	
4 (1%)	Italian	Although three of these, *manage*, *management*, and *manager*, all reflect the same one borrowing, and also probably show some influence from French
1 from each language noted (collectively 1%)	Welsh; Middle Low German; Spanish and/or Italian; French or Italian; French or Latin with maybe some direct Greek input; 1 hybrid formation from 1 (ultimately) Scandinavian element and 1 Latin and/or French element	

list compilers on questions of grammatical and syntactic analysis, although this gives some oddities for present purposes, such as counting *used to* separately from other instances of the verb *use*. I have made my own assessment of etymologies, based on the *OED*, and I have taken dates of first attestation for words from the *OED*.

Some 529 (53%) of these 1,000 words are either loanwords, or (in about 58 cases in total) are formed from loanwords, either by conversion or derivation, or (in a very few cases) showing compounds or lexicalized phrases with a borrowed word as one of their elements. I treat all of these cases together, since for present purposes the most important point is that all of these high-frequency lexemes have loanwords as their basis, either directly or indirectly.

The breakdown of donor languages is shown in Table 2.2.

Chapter 11 investigates in detail the question of loanwords from French and/or Latin; these have a distinctive and important role in the lexical history of English. The division I have made in Table 2.2 into loanwords from French, Latin, and French and/or Latin among the *BNC* high-frequency

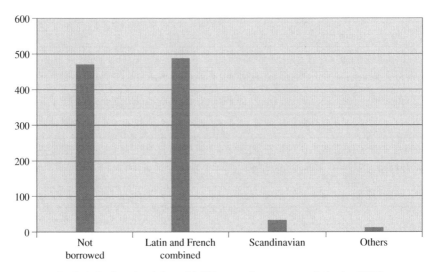

Fig. 2.7 (Indirect) origins of 1,000 most frequent words in the *BNC.*

words is very tentative. This is because the etymologies of many of these words have not been reviewed in detail for a long time. They need to be reviewed very carefully in view of the documentation currently available for each language using a consistent interpretative framework, as is currently being done for all words in *OED3* (see section 11.3). Provisionally, for all words not yet researched in detail for *OED3*, I have allocated each word to one of these three groups on the basis of the evidence currently available in English dictionaries compared briefly with that for Latin and French.

The overall totals of words of different origin, regardless of date of borrowing, are as represented in Fig. 2.7.

Fig. 2.8 gives a chronological breakdown of the loanwords from each of the major sources. It is evident that loanwords first attested in the Middle English period, and especially in the later Middle English period, are very numerous in the high-frequency vocabulary of modern English. This is one of the reasons why examining loanwords from the Middle English period is a central focus of attention in the remainder of this book. In particular, at many points in parts V and VI, I take as my examples words from French and Latin in this list, since the enormous volume of such borrowings can otherwise make the selection seem somewhat arbitrary.

As noted, very similar results are found if a similar study is conducted on other corpora of contemporary standard English. The *Corpus of Contemporary American English* (*COCA*) is a large body of contemporary US spoken and

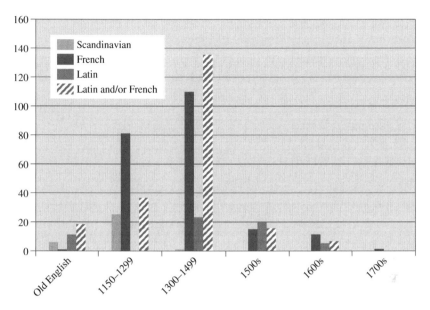

Fig. 2.8 Totals of loanwords from Scandinavian, French, Latin, and French and/or Latin in the 1,000 most frequent words in the *BNC*, arranged chronologically.

written English compiled by Mark Davies at Brigham Young University (see <http://corpus.byu.edu/coca/>). Frequency lists are available for this corpus, both online and (based on an earlier version of the same corpus) in print form (Davies and Gardner (2010)). If we look at the top 1,000 items in this and the *BNC* list, over 80% of items are shared (and many of the differences that are found result from differences in lemmatization of phrasal or grammatical constructions, rather than directly from differences in the content of the two corpora). Even more striking for the purposes of this study is that where the two lists do differ in the actual words that they contain, the proportions of words of French, Latin, and native origin remain extremely similar (to within a couple of percentage points), as does the chronological profile of the borrowing.[6] Similar results are found with very large corpora of global English, such as the *Oxford English Corpus*.

---

[6] See Berndt (1989 69) for the very different results of a similar survey of a high-frequency list compiled before the age of digital corpora, which finds inherited material making up 83% of the 1,000 most frequent words, but only 35% of the next 1,000, down to 28.5% of the 9,000th to 10,000th most frequent items.

If we narrow the focus still further, to look just at the 100 most frequent items in the *BNC*, then the picture becomes rather different. The proportion of borrowings is much lower than in the top 1,000 words (just 11%), and the Scandinavian contribution significantly exceeds that from French and Latin combined:

Scandinavian: *they, their, to get, to take, to give, like, to want*
French: *people, very*
French and/or Latin: *just, to use*

Whether we are looking at the 1,000 most frequent words in the *BNC*, or the 100 most frequent, one important consideration should be borne in mind. We can establish pretty confidently that these are high-frequency words in the English of the late twentieth century (although the precise results we get may vary depending on the corpus we use and how we process the data). We can also check what the date of first attestation is in the dictionary record (although we may sometimes suspect that there was in fact earlier use, and the dates for early periods are generally rather problematic). However, it would be wrong to assume that these words have shown the same high frequency throughout their history in English. Firstly, the discourse of different eras shows different biases in the topics and concepts discussed. For instance, the practices and terminology of agriculture are more remote for most individuals in modern western societies than they were in earlier times, while many new technologies have become ubiquitous. Religious discourse is less important than it was in the lives of many individuals, whereas some scientific concepts have become a touchstone for modern culture. Secondly, many of these borrowed words have replaced earlier words as the (more or less) usual word used to realize a particular meaning: for instance, the borrowed verb *to carry* has taken on meanings that were earlier typically realized by *to bear*, while borrowed *to take* has completely ousted the native word *nim* (Old English *niman*). This process is extremely difficult to assess diachronically. The topic is examined in some detail in chapter 16. For the time being, it is important to note that many of these words have only very gradually come to be high-frequency words in English, often following centuries of competition with earlier synonyms or near-synonyms. However, looked at from a very long historical perspective, it is clear that borrowing in the Middle English period has made by far the largest contribution to the high-frequency vocabulary of modern English.

2.3 Assessing the impact of borrowing on the 'basic' vocabulary of English

Word frequency is not the only perspective from which the impact of borrowing on everyday English can be considered. Another approach is to consider to what extent borrowed words are found as the usual, everyday realization of basic meanings, which are necessary for communication in the simplest and most universal social situations. This sort of definition of 'basic' vocabulary is fraught with difficulties: meanings that seem essential in one cultural setting may not be relevant at all in another. However, the concept of basic vocabulary can be very useful in trying to compare the use of borrowed words in different languages and in different periods of a language's history. The high-frequency words from the *BNC* are very much a reflection of the typical discourse of everyday life in late twentieth-century Britain (especially in print media), but many of them realize meanings that would have little or no relevance in some other cultures or societies (e.g. *committee, director, research, secretary*). In order to make wide-ranging comparisons between languages, linguists sometimes look instead at the words realizing meanings that are 'basic' to social situations that are (so far as possible) universal across all human societies. A recent important collaborative project along these lines is the World Loanwords Database project (WOLD), the results of which are reflected in Haspelmath and Tadmor (2009) and in a number of associated research articles. In this project an extended version of the Intercontinental Dictionary Series meaning list has been used as the basis of a wide-ranging cross-linguistic survey of lexical borrowing. This gives a large list of 1,460 meanings across a range of core vocabulary areas, designed to be relatively neutral as to geographical location. Nonetheless, some items such as 'elephant', 'camel', 'lion', 'panther', or 'kangaroo' are clearly more relevant to some geographical locations than to others, and the list includes a very few meanings such as 'bank', 'film/movie', or 'driver's license' which in most societies in the world will reflect relatively recent cultural importations from elsewhere (but may not necessarily be realized by a loanword).

As part of this project, Anthony Grant looked at contemporary British English and found that 41% of the meanings in this full meaning list were normally realized by words which can (in some cases rather tentatively) be identified as loanwords (see Grant (2009)).[7] One of the major outputs from

---

[7] Meanings that map to more than one usual modern English word, e.g. 'maize/corn', mean that there were in fact 1,516 words in Grant's sample, as reproduced at <http://wold.clld.org/vocabulary/13>.

this project was a collated list of the 100 meanings that seemed on average most resistant to borrowing across all of the languages surveyed; this list is called the Leipzig-Jakarta List of Basic Vocabulary, after the two main centres where the research was carried out.[8] In this list, twelve meanings (i.e. 12% of the total) are normally realized by a borrowed word in modern British English:

> Scandinavian (or Scandinavian-influenced): *root*,[9] *wing, to hit, leg, egg, to give, skin, to take*
> French: *to carry, soil, to cry,* (probably) *to crush*

It is notable that the proportion of the Scandinavian element to the French element is roughly the same as in the most frequent 100 words in the *BNC* discussed in section 2.2.

In the full WOLD meaning list on which this research was based, the totals of borrowings are roughly as follows:[10]

French: 398
Latin: 135
Scandinavian: 62
Dutch: 21
Spanish: 19

---

[8] The full 100 meaning list is as follows, divided into semantic categories: 'natural phenomena': water, fire, night, wind, rain, smoke, stone/rock, salt, sand, soil, ash, shade/shadow, star; 'human body parts': nose, mouth, tongue, eye, tooth, hair, ear, arm/hand, neck, breast, navel, liver, back, leg/foot, thigh, knee, skin/hide, flesh/meat, bone, blood; 'animal and plant parts': wing, horn, tail, egg, root, leaf, wood; 'humans and animals': child (descendant), fish, bird, dog, ant, fly, head louse; 'cultural items': house, name, rope; 'properties': old, new, big, small, long, wide, far, thick, good, red, black, heavy, sweet, bitter, hard; 'actions': go, come, run, fall, carry, take, eat, drink, cry/weep, tie, laugh, suck, hide, stand, bite, hit/beat, do/make, burn (intr.), blow, know, see, hear, give, say, crush/grind; 'deictic/grammatical': 1SG pronoun, 2SG pronoun, 3SG pronoun, who?, what?, this, one, not, yesterday, in.

[9] This is placed by Grant (2009) in the category 'no evidence for borrowing', which is surprising, since the Scandinavian etymology has been well established for a long time.

[10] I give here the totals as given in Grant (2009) 381–3; they do not agree precisely with the data presented at <http://wold.clld.org/vocabulary/13>. I have here followed Grant's analysis of etymologies, which would not in every instance agree with my own. A very few of the etymologies are manifestly erroneous, rather than just showing differences of opinion or methodology; I have included them in the totals here, but removed clearly wrong cases from the data in Fig. 2.9: see further n. 11.

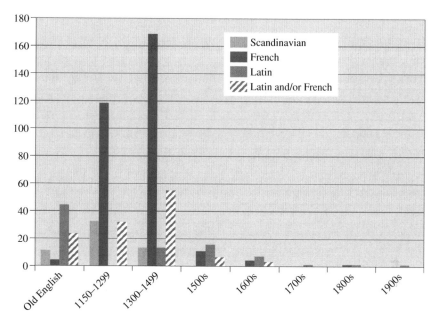

Fig. 2.9 Loanwords from Scandinavian, French, Latin, and French and/or Latin in the full WOLD meaning list, arranged chronologically.

Middle Low German: 4

Portuguese: 4

Greek: 3

Italian, Welsh, Scottish Gaelic: 2 from each

British Celtic, Malay, Tahitian, Tongan, Guugu Yimidhirr, Dharuk, Virginia Algonquian, Eastern Abenaki, Massachusett, Mikmaq, Tupi: 1 from each

Of unknown origin: 41

Fig. 2.9 gives the chronological pattern for loanwords from the four major sources using the same framework as in section 2.2, with borrowings from French and/or Latin separated out (very tentatively) from those solely from French and those solely from Latin, and using the *OED*'s dates of first attestation.[11] (In some cases, the basic meaning in the WOLD list is not the

---

[11] In the data for this figure I have generally followed Grant's estimates of etymologies, rather than reassess the whole meaning list, but I have rejected a number of clearly wrong or extremely doubtful etymologies, twelve from his lists of loanwords from Latin and French, and two from his list of borrowings from Scandinavian. I have also moved some words from the French list to the Latin list, and vice versa, as well as separating out the words potentially borrowed from either language (or both: compare section 11.3).

original meaning of the word in question at the time of its borrowing into English, but this is not sufficiently often the case to affect the overall chronological picture significantly.)

In broad outline this is rather similar to Fig. 2.8, illustrating the high-frequency words from the *BNC*. There are some interesting differences: the contribution of words borrowed solely from French is markedly stronger and very much concentrated in the period before 1500. There are relatively few words of any origin from later than 1500 and these include a number of names of recent innovations (e.g. *bicycle*, *cigarette*) or of things new to English-speaking communities (such as most of the loans from more exotic languages already summarized). It is interesting that the biggest total of loanwords solely from Latin in this basic meaning list is of words first attested in the Old English period, e.g. *cup*, *dish*, *fever*, *fork*, *kettle*, *pan*, *wall*, although not all of these words are of common occurrence in Old English (see further section 7.5.2). We look in detail in chapter 16 at some of the potential, as well as some of the drawbacks, of considering the impact of loanwords on the basic vocabulary of English over a long time span.

An interesting outcome of this research project is that it enables comparisons to be made, however imprecisely, between different languages in terms of how many loanwords they show in their basic vocabulary. English ranked fifth out of forty-one languages in this survey (Tadmor (2009) 56–7). In a subsequent article (Tadmor et al. 2010), the leaders of this research project concluded that their survey had probably rather over-represented languages with high levels of borrowing; hence the status of English as a language with an unusually high level of borrowing starts to become very evident, although it is by no means unique in this respect. The languages that ranked higher than English in this survey were, by a considerable margin, Selice Romani and Tarifiyt Berber, and, by much smaller margins, Gurindji and Romanian. Among other languages from highly developed industrialized societies included in this survey, Japanese was not very far behind English (showing major waves of borrowing from Chinese and, much more recently, from English), while Dutch showed a much lower total of 19.1% of borrowed words in its basic vocabulary (Tadmor (2009) 56–7).

A further important output of this project was some empirical support for the observation that, cross-linguistically, nouns are typically borrowed much more often than verbs,[12] supplemented by some important observations about other parts of speech, and about function words:

---

[12] Compare also Wohlgemuth (2009) on this topic.

Adjectives (and adverbs) are almost as hard to borrow as verbs—this is a much less well-known fact which has hardly received any attention so far…Words with grammatical meanings ('function words') are even harder to borrow than verbs…Only about 12% of all function words are borrowed.

(Tadmor et al. (2010) 231.)

2.4 Some implications of this data for the shape of this book

The figures in section 2.1 show that the largest contributions of loanwords to the vocabulary of modern English come from Latin and French. Greek and German are also important, although, as already noted, in both cases this owes a great deal to the modern language of science, and the picture would look very different if the figures were restricted to non-technical vocabulary (compare the data from Scheler (1977) considered in section 2.1). The next most numerous contributors are Italian, Spanish, Dutch, and (perhaps rather surprisingly) Japanese, followed by early Scandinavian, with a number of other languages following rather closely behind.

If we look, as in section 2.2, at the 1,000 most frequent words in the *BNC*, Latin and French emerge very clearly as the most prolific donor languages in the high-frequency vocabulary of modern English. The chronology of these borrowings shows that by far the majority were borrowed in the Middle English period. Early Scandinavian emerges clearly as the third most important contributor to the 1,000 most frequent words. All of the early Scandinavian loanwords in this list are first attested in English before 1500, most of them considerably earlier than this.

When the focus is narrowed to the 100 highest-frequency items in the *BNC* (or in other corpora), the proportion of loanwords overall becomes much lower and early Scandinavian is the major contributor, followed by French. Looking at basic meanings in section 2.3 gives a similar picture for the core list of 100 meanings least susceptible to borrowing, while the larger list of 1,460 meanings puts Latin and French jointly well ahead of early Scandinavian, rather like the data from the 1,000 most frequent words in the *BNC*.

These various observations shape much of the rest of this book. By far the largest amount of space is devoted to examining how loanwords from Latin and French have transformed the vocabulary of English at all levels. Aside from a sizeable contribution (particularly from French) to the vocabulary of everyday life, loanwords from Latin and French have provided the core vocabulary of many intellectual, cultural, and technical fields. Just as importantly, they have provided scope for lexical variation, i.e. for the selection of alternative words with the same or similar meaning, that has been exploited in the highly developed stylistic registers of modern English.

Another major topic for investigation is how the numerically much smaller number of borrowings from Scandinavian languages have penetrated even more deeply into the most basic levels of the vocabulary. Chapter 6 looks in detail at the particular social and cultural circumstances that led to this.

As shown already by the chronological data looked at in this chapter, developments in the (late) Old English period and, especially, in the Middle English period are crucial to both of these narratives, and therefore a good deal of the focus of this book is on borrowings that occurred in the period before 1500, although viewed from the perspective of their impact on the later development of the vocabulary of English, in addition to their impact on the vocabulary of Old English and Middle English.

The shape of the rest of this book is therefore as follows.

Part II consists of three chapters investigating aspects of the early linguistic and non-linguistic history of English. Chapter 3 gives a brief introduction to the most relevant aspects of external, non-linguistic history up to roughly 1150, on the grounds that many readers may find it useful to have some historical points of reference for this early period. Chapter 4 looks at some very early borrowings into Germanic, the ancestor language of Old English, and also introduces some key concepts in the study of early linguistic history. Chapter 5 examines in some detail the contact between Old English and the Celtic languages spoken by the conquered peoples of post-Roman Britain, even though this resulted in few loanwords. This may seem a little perverse, since there are so many episodes in the history of English in which many words have been borrowed, but this chapter will try to show that extensive borrowing of lexis is not a necessary outcome of language contact and, in a situation where one population has low prestige in the eyes of another population, there may be very little lexical borrowing indeed.

The three chapters making up part III investigate in greater depth borrowing from Latin in Old English, and also in the period before the Anglo-Saxons came to Britain, which we might term 'proto-Old English'. Contact between the Germanic peoples and the materially advanced culture of ancient Rome led to borrowing of some important lexis into Germanic, as did the process of conversion to Christianity. Most of this happened before the period of our surviving Old English texts and this poses some interesting (and in many cases insoluble) challenges for attempts to ascertain in precisely which time and context particular loanwords were borrowed. Within the period of our surviving texts, borrowing seems mostly to have been confined to relatively learned vocabulary, although our sources often do not give us as much certainty about this as we would ideally like.

Part IV consists of two chapters that look at borrowing from the Scandinavian languages spoken by the raiders, conquerors, and settlers who came to Britain from the late eighth century onwards. In this instance, borrowing took place from a closely related language in a situation where Scandinavian speakers and English speakers lived in close proximity; this is reflected by a significant amount of borrowing of basic vocabulary, but also by the fact that a significant proportion of borrowings remain restricted to those geographical areas where contact between the different populations was most intense. Because of the similarity of the languages, there are many cases where we cannot be certain that borrowing in fact occurred and many etymologies depend on the balance of probabilities rather than on definite facts. Some of the loanwords probably reflect borrowing by English speakers as they came in contact with Scandinavian customs and culture; other words probably reflect importations as originally bilingual (or even monolingual Scandinavian-speaking) communities gradually switched to using English only. The fact that many of these words subsequently became firmly entrenched in the basic vocabulary of modern standard English reflects some important processes of internal borrowing between varieties of Middle English.

Part V begins with two chapters that examine contact between English, French, and Latin in the Middle English period, investigating developments that had far-reaching consequences for the future shape of the vocabulary of English. It is argued that the most significant fact is not that England was conquered per se, nor that the Normans were particularly advanced culturally in comparison with Anglo-Saxons (in fact in most respects except military expertise the Normans were, if anything, rather less advanced), but that they spoke a form of French. This was of crucial importance for several reasons:

- French was a descendant of Latin, the prestige language of learning, religion, and officialdom in western Europe, and some French words showed their Latin descent in clear and obvious ways.

- French was soon to enter a remarkable period as the leading vernacular language of learning and culture in north-western Europe, with much of the early flowering in fact taking place in England in the medium of Anglo-French. It also became an important language of international commerce. In fact, for most of the period up to *c.*1800 or beyond, French had a reasonable claim to be regarded as the leading and most important vernacular of western Europe (albeit following largely in the cultural wake of Italian in the early stages of the Renaissance).
- (Related to both of the preceding points.) At the time of the Conquest and for centuries afterwards, classicizing influence on French was enormous and many Latin words became re-borrowed into French, while many French words became remodelled after their ultimate Latin etymons (i.e. the Latin forms that had been the original starting-point for their development in French).

Consequently, English entered a period of evolving and changing but nonetheless unbroken contact with French, and with Latin both via French and directly, which was to last well into the Early Modern period. The section ends with a chapter that looks at the impact of loanwords from Latin and French as well as from early Scandinavian, as reflected by a series of passages from Middle English texts of different dates and from varying geographical locations and cultural milieux. It also looks at some of the ways in which interaction between different languages in the multilingual society of later medieval England can be traced in the surviving linguistic records.

Chapter 14 looks at the complex histories of borrowing from French and Latin in the Early Modern and Later Modern periods, in which borrowing from the two languages proceeds along increasingly divergent pathways. More and more words come to be borrowed directly from Latin without being mediated by French, and many others show increasing Latin influence in their form in English. In Early Modern English loanwords from both languages are exploited in order to develop new stylistic and technical registers in the vocabulary of English. Over time, Latin words and word-elements come to be especially associated with the vocabulary of science, in which elements ultimately of Latin (or sometimes Greek) origin are deployed across the vernacular languages of scientific scholarship to form new words denoting new things and concepts unknown to the ancient world. Borrowing from French, on the other hand, begins to show a pattern much more like that shown by borrowing from other modern European languages, reflecting areas of particular French social and cultural prestige, as well as reflecting the role of French as one of the major international languages of scholarship.

Chapter 15 looks at some other languages that have contributed considerable numbers of loanwords, although with less dramatic consequences for the vocabulary of modern English, including: Dutch and Low German, which have contributed many loanwords as a result of geographical proximity and close cultural and trading links, although the similarity of the languages to English often makes it difficult to be certain that borrowing has occurred; (High) German, which has contributed many loanwords in more recent centuries, although many of these belong to technical registers, and many will not be recognized as German loanwords by most speakers because they are formed from elements ultimately of Latin or Greek origin; and Spanish, Portuguese, and Italian, which from the Renaissance onwards have shown particular patterns of cultural influence on the vocabulary of English. It looks at how Dutch, Spanish, and Portuguese in particular have often acted as conduits for borrowing of words ultimately from languages from outside Europe, as a result of trade and colonialism. It also examines how the international spread of English has had implications for patterns of lexical borrowing. Words have been borrowed from other European languages in places and contexts far outside Europe, e.g. from Dutch and its descendant Afrikaans in South Africa, and then in some cases they have spread by internal borrowing from one variety of English to another. Additionally, very many words have been borrowed from languages originating outside Europe, sometimes into particular local varieties of English (perhaps with subsequent spread), sometimes into numerous varieties of English more or less simultaneously. This huge topic will be looked at here through those languages that figure among the twenty-five most prolific donor sources listed in section 2.1.

Prestige borrowing from other languages has greatly declined in contemporary English for one simple reason: right now, English is the prestige language of learning and of many aspects of contemporary cultural life, both within Anglophone societies and beyond, and the predominant pattern is for other languages to borrow from English, and not vice versa. Recent borrowings are, however, generally very salient: most speakers will be aware that *sushi* or *wasabi* are not native English words. Loanwords typically become much less salient to speakers over time, particularly if they become part of everyday discourse and especially when, as in the case of Scandi-navian borrowings such as *they* or *call*, there is no obvious indication of loanword status for the non-specialist. Chapter 16 looks in a little more detail at how thoroughly integrated various different layers of loanwords have become in the vocabulary of modern English, and in particular at how words that have been borrowed in different chronological periods and in different borrowing contexts have had different characteristic impacts on the development of the English lexicon.

Part II

Early Contacts in Continental Europe and Britain

3

Historical and cultural background to c.1150

Before we consider the linguistic evidence for contact between Old English (and proto-Old English) and other languages, it may be useful to sketch the historical circumstances in which some of the most significant contact situations arose. This is not intended as a potted history of early medieval Britain: it aims only to highlight those historical factors which are most significant for linguistic borrowing in the early history of English.

3.1 The Germani at the dawn of their recorded history

English is one of the Germanic languages. These developed from an unrecorded language known as proto-Germanic, which was spoken by people often referred to under the collective cover term of the 'Germani'. (On reconstructed languages such as proto-Germanic and on language families, see section 4.1.) At roughly the time when ancient Greece was at its cultural peak and when Rome was becoming an important power in Italy, the Germani were probably living mainly in southern Scandinavia and in parts of northern Germany. For centuries the Celts were among their most important neighbours in north-west Europe. This situation probably gave rise to some very early loanwords (e.g. one reflected by modern English *rich* and modern German *Reich* 'kingdom': see section 4.2). Some other early loanwords suggest that the Germani also lived near to speakers of Finnish and other Uralic languages (see section 4.1) and to speakers of Baltic and Slavonic languages. This accords well with what we would expect from the later geographical location of the speakers of these various languages.

By the time of the earliest Roman emperors a process was well underway that saw some of the Germanic peoples spread initially to the south and east (giving rise to Gothic and other, mostly unattested, East Germanic varieties), while others went west and south (leading ultimately to the development of the West Germanic languages: see section 4.1). The resulting geographical proximity meant that Romans and Germani were often in conflict, but also had extensive cultural exchange. In the first century AD the Roman historian Tacitus wrote an important treatise about them. Although he had no direct contact with them, at least some of what he said about them is generally held to have been based on reliable sources. However, his main concern was to describe something that bears many similarities to later European conceptions of the 'noble savage', probably intended more to contrast with contemporary Roman society than to record entirely truthful information about the Germani.

For this period we have no direct linguistic evidence, only what we can infer from the evidence of later centuries. (Even the earliest Runic inscriptions probably date from a little later than this, although some information is inferable from names or words cited by Latin or Greek writers.) We also have little historical evidence, only what can be gleaned from references by Greek and Roman historians. There is more archaeological evidence, but marrying up archaeological, ethnic, and linguistic history is a problematic enterprise.

3.2 The Germani on the continent in later Roman times

The ethnographic, linguistic, and cultural situation along the western European boundaries of the Roman Empire changed a great deal in the centuries between Julius Caesar's conquests in Gaul and the fall of the Western Empire. The imperial boundary for a long period followed roughly the course of the rivers Rhine and Danube, joined by a line enclosing territory roughly from modern Koblenz to modern Regensburg. It was an important defensive frontier, but it is wrong to think of a crude ethnic division between Germani outside the Empire, and Roman imperial rulers and their Celtic subjects within it. There was a steady influx of Germani on account of the Roman habit of recruiting from outside the Empire into parts of their military (with different circumstances at different times and in different places). Additionally, although the precise details of which languages were spoken where and by whom are often uncertain, it is not in doubt that some of the peoples who fell inside the late imperial boundaries were Germani. Perhaps most importantly, linguistic, historical, and archaeological evidence all point to considerable interchange of traded goods across the imperial boundary. Some borrowings from Latin can be dated to this period on linguistic grounds with reasonable certainty; for many others a good circumstantial case can be made. Some probable examples include such familiar modern English words as *pound, kettle, cheap* (which could all be extremely early: see section 4.3), and *street, wine, pit, copper, pin, tile, post* ('wooden shaft'), *cup*.

Subsequently, as the Roman Empire declined, very many more people speaking Germanic languages came into the western parts of the Empire, whether as invited guests to provide protection against other invaders, or as conquerors (or in some cases as a complex blend of the two). This had an enormous effect on the future history of western Europe, not least linguistically, and not least in Britain.

3.3 Britain before the Romans

At the beginning of the first century AD Britain was one of the many areas of Europe inhabited either entirely or predominantly by Celtic peoples, speaking languages belonging to the Celtic branch of Indo-European.[1]

Celtic as spoken in recent centuries divides into two groups of languages: Goidelic, consisting of Irish and its later offshoots Scottish Gaelic and Manx (which result from the settlement of Irish invaders in Scotland and the Isle of Man in large numbers); and Brittonic (or Brythonic), reflected today by Welsh, Cornish, and (as a result of migration from Britain) Breton. In the first century AD some form of Celtic language was also spoken in all of what historians of this period sometimes refer to as Lowland Britain, i.e. roughly modern England. Across the other side of the Channel another Celtic language, Gaulish, continued to be spoken in Roman Gaul. Unfortunately, there are very few records for Gaulish or for any of the other ancient continental Celtic varieties: the corpus is restricted largely to inscriptions and what can be gleaned from names, plus the evidence of Celtic words borrowed into other languages. There is also extremely little direct evidence for any of the Celtic languages in the British Isles until considerably later in

---

[1] What was spoken by the Picts, who are thought to have occupied much of modern Scotland at this time, has been the subject of a great deal of uncertainty and debate. Most scholars today take the view that in this period probably the only language spoken by the Picts was a form of the same Celtic language that was spoken in the southern part of mainland Britain, i.e. the ancestor of Welsh, Cornish, and Breton: see e.g. Forsyth (1997).

the medieval period.[2] It is normally assumed that the Celtic language spoken in Lowland Britain at this time was essentially identical to the ancestor of the modern Welsh and Cornish languages, and this is often termed proto-Brittonic. However, even this assumption has recently been challenged by Schrijver (2009), who contends that Old Irish may have been an offshoot from Lowland British Celtic, resulting from migration, probably from northern England to Ireland, perhaps in the wake of the Roman Conquest of the first century AD. This remains a minority view and fortunately has only very limited implications for the history of lexical borrowing into English (to which we return in section 5.1), but it is a reminder of how little is certain about the linguistic situation in Britain at this time.

3.4 Roman Britain and its linguistic situation

A great deal changed in the British Isles during the course of the first century AD, as a consequence of the successful Roman invasion during the reign of Emperor Claudius in AD 43 (following Julius Caesar's temporary incursions in 55 and 54 BC). The Roman conquest of southern Britain proceeded rapidly and from the first century until at least the late fourth century most of mainland Britain (excluding most of Scotland) was part of the Roman Empire. There was frequent conflict, but, after the suppression of the revolt led by Boudicca in the first century AD, subsequent conflict largely took the form not of liberation struggles between occupied and occupier, but of struggles for control of a Romanized society. These were part of the wider picture of conflicts and power struggles within the Empire, punctuated by periodic incursions by 'barbarian' peoples from beyond the imperial frontiers.[3]

Documentary records concerning Roman Britain are at best patchy and much of what is known about Britain in these centuries comes from the archaeological record. Administration and much economic life was centred on Roman military installations, cities, and towns; agricultural production appears largely to have fallen under the control of these units, and/or of

---

[2] On the Celtic languages and the relationships between them, see especially the various survey essays in Ball and Müller (2009).

[3] On the general history of Roman Britain, see Salway (2001), Frere (1999); a short account focusing on the implications of this period for the later history of Anglo-Saxon England is provided by Campbell (1982a).

Romano-British villas, or of villages or other small settlements which appear to have differed from the towns largely in their administration and (generally) in their size. There were clearly periods of relative political and economic stability during these centuries and also periods of great instability. The archaeological record suggests the second half of the fourth century was a period of considerable prosperity. However, both the archaeological and documentary records indicate very troubled times indeed in the early fifth century. The Roman legions departed in the very early years of the fifth century, never to return, being drawn into the continuing power struggles on the continental mainland, and the struggle to defend receding imperial frontiers. There appears to have been a complete economic collapse probably around AD 420, after which pre-Anglo-Saxon Britain never saw the full restoration of an economy based on the circulation of currency.

Our knowledge of what was happening in Britain in this period is uncertain, and attempts to understand it also highlight some considerable uncertainties about the preceding centuries. Almost certainly, the situation differed greatly from place to place. However, the imperial system of administration based on urban centres seems to have lasted only a short time, as did any extensive economic activity. Many cities, towns, and Roman forts may well have continued to be focal strongpoints for defensive purposes (or indeed bases for offensive operations), but this is not at all the same thing as the survival of Romanized urban life. It is possible that society was refocused around strong men and their followers, who offered some security against incursions by Irish, Pictish, and Germanic raiders. Probably Christianity was the religion of the majority, although it is uncertain how far paganism may have survived in more rural areas.

Unfortunately for our purposes, the linguistic situation is one of the things about which we know the least. During the period of Roman imperial domination, Latin was certainly the language of administration and of much of the elite; what is much less certain, and rather hotly disputed, is whether it was also the language of the 'man in the street', and if it was, whether it remained so in more troubled times before the arrival of the Anglo-Saxons. The assumption made by most scholars is that Latin had relatively little currency outside the urban areas; that (some form of) Celtic was the language of the majority, except in the Roman military, where Latin was the crucial lingua franca; while auxiliaries recruited from many locations both inside and outside the Roman Empire probably spoke their own native languages. There were certainly Germani among such auxiliaries. There were probably also slaves of Germanic origin in Britain and in the later stages of Roman Britain there were also certainly at least some mercenaries and other irregular forces of Germanic origin, and some settlements associated with such people. They may have been quite numerous, but it is unlikely that they had any significant impact on the subsequent linguistic history of Britain.

One tantalizing comparison is with Roman Gaul. It is generally thought that under the Empire the linguistic situation was broadly similar in Gaul, with Latin the language of an urbanized elite and Gaulish remaining the language in general use in the population at large. Like Britain, Gaul was subject to Germanic invasions, and northern Gaul eventually took on a new name from its Frankish conquerors. However, France emerged as a Romance-speaking country, with a language that is Latin-derived in grammar and overwhelmingly also in lexis. One possible explanation for the very different outcomes in the two former provinces is that urban life may have remained in much better shape in Gaul than in Britain; Gaul had been Roman for longer than Britain, and urban life was probably much more developed and on a larger scale, and may have proved more resilient when facing economic and political vicissitudes. In Gaul the Franks probably took over at least some functioning urban centres where an existing Latin-speaking elite formed the basis for the future administration of the territory; this, combined with the importance and prestige of Latin as the language of the western Church, probably led ultimately to the emergence of a Romance-speaking nation. In Britain the existing population, whether speaking Latin or Celtic, probably held very little prestige in the eyes of the Anglo-Saxon incomers, and this may have been a key factor in determining that England became a Germanic-speaking territory: the Anglo-Saxons may simply not have had enough incentive to adopt the language(s) of these people.[4]

---

[4] For accounts of the historical situation from differing perspectives, see: Hills (1979), the various chapters in Campbell (1982b), Evans (1990), Hines (1990), Ward-Perkins (2000), Bassett (2000), Higham (2002), and the various contributions in Higham (2007). On the linguistic situation, see especially Evans (1983), Polomé (1983), Schrijver (2002), Adams (2003), Adams (2007), Schrijver (2007), Schrijver (2009); see also Wollmann (1993) for an interesting comparison with the situation in the Balkans in broadly the same period.

3.5 From the Anglo-Saxon 'Settlement' to the first Christian centuries

Almost all aspects of the process by which Germanic peoples came to Britain and came to dominate its lowland areas are the subject of intense scholarly debate, including such basic questions as when they came and how many of them came either at any one particular time or over the settlement period as a whole. Interpretations vary between, on the one hand, a take-over by an elite and its followers, with little change in the population at large; and, on the other hand, a wholesale resettlement of peoples across the sea. Opinions also differ very greatly on what was the typical fate of the existing Romano-British population: assimilation, extermination, enslavement, and being driven out to other parts of Britain probably all played some part, but to what extent is much harder to tell. The fifth and sixth centuries in Britain are truly dark for both historians and historical linguists, because there is so little evidence available; the information is also rather sparse for archaeologists, and historical population studies in fields such as genetics or the study of blood groups have so far produced rather contradictory results.[5]

It is certain that in the course of the sixth century Anglo-Saxon domination spread from a series of relatively shallow pockets along the eastern and south-eastern coasts of England, to include by around AD 600: all of southern England to a line somewhere west of Bath; nearly all of the English midlands except a strip down the Welsh marches; and large parts of the north-east of England. By about fifty years later, most of modern England was in Anglo-Saxon hands, with the exception of an area in the west country roughly corresponding to modern Devon and Cornwall, and a largish pocket in the north-west including, but rather larger than, the modern Lake District; parts of modern Scotland, including Edinburgh, were also by now under Anglo-Saxon control.[6] The picture that historical sources give us of the seventh century and later is of a series of gradually more stable Anglo-Saxon kingdoms in southern and eastern parts of Britain (by now all of them converted to Christianity), bordered by Celtic kingdoms in the west.

---

[5] In addition to the references in footnote 4, for some of the conflicting evidence from population studies see e.g. Weale et al. (2002), Capelli et al. (2003), Thomas et al. (2006), Sykes (2006), Pattison (2008), Thomas et al. (2008), Pattison (2011).

[6] See the map in Jackson (1953) 208–9, also much reproduced elsewhere.

It is quite possible that the emergent Anglo-Saxon kingdoms absorbed many Britons, who decided that an Anglo-Saxon identity spelled future success and who consequently adopted English, the language of the conquerors. On the other hand, many Britons may have found their options much more constrained: slavery was a common part of life in Anglo-Saxon England, as it had been in the Roman Empire, and as it remained in much of contemporary Europe. Lower status prisoners from battles were typically enslaved while higher status ones were typically executed or sometimes held hostage; this appears to have applied to conflicts between Anglo-Saxon tribes or kingdoms, as well as to those between Anglo-Saxons and Britons. Slaves were frequently sold overseas and such people would have had no impact on the future linguistic development of society. Those who remained in Britain would seem, at least in later centuries, to have had a highly disadvantageous status, but one which carried with it at least some rights, and which was likely to have involved a good deal of interaction with both their owners and with others in rural communities.[7]

Lexical evidence is significant here: one of the Old English words for a slave (or sometimes specifically a British slave), *wealh*, shows a semantic specialization of a word for a Briton or (originally) any foreigner; it is also used attributively with the meaning 'foreign' in e.g. *wealh-hnutu* 'walnut'. However, this evidence needs to be handled carefully. Pelteret (1995 261–330) looks at the whole of this semantic field in detail and concludes that the meaning 'slave' for *wealh* is predominantly a southern phenomenon and probably arose relatively late, in the context of West-Saxon conquests over the Britons in the south-west. Clark (1992 463–4) argues that early place-name evidence also points to *wealh* probably not having strongly negative connotations in early use (but this is a very difficult area). As Lutz (2009) argues, however, the situation may be rather different with the derivative formation *wīln*, which always means 'female slave' in the surviving texts, and which shows a relatively early Old English sound change called *i*-mutation (see section 8.1), thus indicating a relatively early origin for this word form. She argues that this word may just illustrate a scenario in early Anglo-Saxon England in which British women were often slaves and female slaves were typically British.

---

[7] See Pelteret (1980), Pelteret (1995).

The West-Saxon king Ine's law code, dating from the late seventh century, accords a disadvantageous status to Britons compared with Anglo-Saxons, although some have argued in recent decades that this may have been intended to encourage the adoption of an Anglo-Saxon (or in fact specifically English) identity, especially in dangerous border areas, where it would have been very advantageous to assimilate conquered populations rapidly.[8] Whether or not this was an intended consequence, it is highly likely that, given the opportunity, Britons would have adopted advantageous Anglo-Saxon identities when they perceived themselves as irreversibly a part of Anglo-Saxon communities. If the main shift required was to begin speaking English rather than Brittonic Celtic, then it is likely that many would have done so if they could, still more so in the case of subsequent generations born under Anglo-Saxon rule. However, it remains far from certain that these were the prevailing conditions, and the uncertainty only becomes greater the further back in time we attempt to look.

The question of how much English may have borrowed from either Celtic or Latin during the process of Anglo-Saxon territorial expansion is controversial. We may anticipate slightly the findings of the next chapter, and state immediately that one of the few things we do know with some confidence is that lexical borrowing from Celtic into Old English was relatively slight, although estimates of the precise number of words vary greatly; it has remained relatively slight throughout the many centuries of contact between speakers of English and Celtic languages in the British Isles, at least so far as influence on the general vocabulary of English is concerned. However, some scholars consider that English may have shown a good deal of grammatical and structural influence from Celtic, either during the settlement period or in subsequent centuries. Chapter 4 looks a little more closely at all of these questions.

By contrast, Old English borrowed a great many words from Latin. The problem is to determine when. A number of earlier scholars considered that a great deal of lexis was probably or even certainly borrowed from Latin in Britain in the period of the Anglo-Saxon settlement. However, recent reassessments have cast considerable doubt on the criteria employed and the majority view today is that there are few if any words that could not be explained either by earlier borrowing (i.e. on the continent before

---

[8] See Ward-Perkins (2000).

Anglo-Saxons came to Britain) or by continuing contacts with the contin-ent. This does not, however, rule out the possibility that early borrowing may also have occurred in Britain. We look at this more closely in part III.

3.6 The influence of Latin after the conversion

The conversion to Christianity was taking place concurrently with the later stages of the expansion of Anglo-Saxon control over most of what would come to be known as England.

The Anglo-Saxon kingdom of Kent was converted to (Roman) Christian-ity at the very end of the sixth century. Anglo-Saxons had certainly encoun-tered ethnically Celtic Christians much earlier than this, and Celtic (especially Irish) Christianity played an important part in missionary activ-ity among the Anglo-Saxons, especially in the north. By the end of the seventh century all of the Anglo-Saxon kingdoms had been converted to Christianity, and looked ultimately towards Rome as the source of Chris-tian authority.

Our knowledge about England in the seventh, eighth, and early ninth centuries is sadly rather limited. Thanks especially to Bede, we know a fair amount about the thriving Christian cultural life in Monkwearmouth and Jarrow (near Newcastle-upon-Tyne) in the 730s, and his *Ecclesiastical History of the English People* tells us much of what we know about the religious and secular history of the seventh century as well. We also know a fair amount about the political ascendancy of Offa of Mercia in the second half of the eighth century, but not nearly enough. We only begin to know much more about Anglo-Saxon history in general when we reach the age of Alfred the Great in the late ninth century, by which time the Viking onslaught had already progressed a long way and the events of the Anglo-Saxon settlement were some 400 years in the past.

If we consider what documentary evidence we have specifically for the English language in this period, things are darker yet. We have almost nothing from before the eighth century (mostly just what we can tell from the forms of Germanic personal and place names recorded in Latin docu-ments), and there is little even from that century: what survives from the Age of Bede is almost entirely in Latin, with the exception of the short poetical fragments of Cædmon, Bede's Death Song, and the Leiden Riddle; there are some important early inscriptions, although precise dating is difficult; manuscript evidence for the eighth and most of the ninth centuries is largely confined to interlinear glosses and Latin–English glossaries, which yield crucial early linguistic evidence. We have to wait until the time of Alfred the Great in the late ninth century before we begin to have large amounts of connected writing in Old English. The majority of the surviving material comes from the late tenth century or later. (Some of the verse that survives may show later recensions of material that existed earlier, but this gives us only extremely limited linguistic evidence for earlier periods.)

It is also worth noting at this point that all of our surviving Old English material, right up to the middle of the twelfth century, only amounts to a collection roughly five times the size of the complete works of Shakespeare (although this is large in comparison with what survives for many other European languages in the same historical period). The vast majority of it is in the West-Saxon dialect, which was widely used as a written standard in later Anglo-Saxon times, and it was nearly all mediated through the Church, which was the home of learning and of manuscript production.

This is no more than a crude sketch of the surviving Old English material, but it is sufficient to highlight one key fact: the conversion to Christianity lies far back in the pre-literary period, and the bulk of our texts come from several hundred years later. The impact of Christianization, just like the traces of early contact between Latin and Celtic speakers on the continent or in Britain, must thus be traced through the techniques of linguistic reconstruction. The impact of Latin, through the Church, on Old English was considerable. There is good evidence for borrowing of lexis either connected with or borrowed via the Church from the period of the conversion (or even a little before) right through to the end of the Old English period. Particularly in the later centuries, many of the borrowings are markedly learned in character, but, because of our restricted range of surviving texts, judgements can be hard to make. Additionally, it is often difficult to draw the line between borrowed words and references to Latin words in an English context. As well as borrowing words from Latin, Old English shows considerable semantic influence from Latin, both in the meaning development of existing words and in the formation of loan translations: most indications are that semantic borrowing, rather than borrowing of loanwords, was the characteristic means of accommodating new concepts in the vocabulary of Old English. All of these topics are investigated in detail in part III.

3.7 Anglo-Saxons and Scandinavians

Scandinavian (or Viking) raids on points in eastern and southern England began in the late eighth century. Substantial armies arrived in AD 865 and 871, engaging in invasion and conquest rather than just raiding. The famous struggles between the Scandinavians and Alfred the Great ensued, leading to a treaty in the 880s establishing Scandinavian control over a huge area generally referred to as the Danelaw extending very roughly east and north of the line of Watling Street, which ran from London to Chester. The name 'Danelaw' refers collectively to areas where Scandinavian law, rather than West-Saxon or Mercian law, applied. The name arises from the fact that the invaders in the east and north-east were largely Danish. (See further section 9.1 on the rather difficult topic of how Scandinavianized the Danelaw areas were.)

Alfred was engaged in further military conflict with the Scandinavians only a few years later, and subsequent military and political conflicts and relationships between the Anglo-Saxons and the Scandinavians were complex: Alfred's son, Edward, conquered the Danelaw in the early tenth century, incorporating it into an English kingdom; in the late tenth and early eleventh centuries there were renewed invasions from Scandinavia, and ultimately in 1016 the Danish king Cnut became king of England; in 1042 there was once again an English rather than a Scandinavian king, but as a result of complex dynastic succession (Cnut having married the widow of his English predecessor) rather than a liberation struggle; in 1066 Harold defeated a Norwegian invading army at Stamford Bridge only weeks before his own defeat by the Normans at Hastings.

From the point of view of linguistic history these complex political relations are in themselves of less importance than the fact that much of eastern and northern England experienced a replacement of its Anglo-Saxon nobility by Scandinavians (chiefly Danes), and that there was at least some settlement of Scandinavian populations in parts of the Danelaw; there were also predominantly Norwegian invasions and settlements in parts of the north-west. Much of the evidence for this settlement is in fact linguistic, from place names, personal names, and the evidence of different varieties of Middle English (and even of modern English). It is pretty certain that some Scandinavian was in use in some communities in Britain in the eleventh century, and possibly in places even in the twelfth century.[9] When the bulk of the lexis was borrowed into English (and particularly the important basic vocabulary items) is an intriguing question and we examine some different approaches to this in part IV.

3.8 The Norman Conquest

The story of the events leading up to William of Normandy's invasion of England in 1066 is thrilling, but is told too well in too many other places to justify its being told again here.[10] For our purposes, the most important thing is that in the decades after 1066 the Anglo-Saxon political and religious elite was largely replaced by an imported one consisting of Normans and other French-speaking allies of William. Now there were French speakers in influential positions on English soil and, for centuries to come, French (of one sort or another) was to have a major influence on the development of English lexis. In the immediate post-Conquest period, there were native speakers of French as well as of English, Scandinavian languages, and Celtic languages forming part of the population of Britain. Long after the period in which it was anyone's first language in Britain, French remained important, like Latin, as a language used in various technical functions as part of many people's everyday lives. Arguably it was in this latter period that French had its most far-reaching impact on the development of English lexis. We look at this topic in detail in part V.

[9] Compare Parsons (2001), Townend (2002), Townend (2006).
[10] For a good brief account, see John (1982).

4

Very early borrowings into Germanic

Some borrowings into Germanic can be identified with reasonable confidence as having occurred very early, probably before the separation of the various branches of Germanic. Since this period is long before our earliest written evidence for any of the Germanic languages, the arguments are heavily dependent on the method known as comparative reconstruction. We look briefly here at some of the key concepts involved.[1]

4.1 Language families and comparative reconstruction

English is a Germanic language. That is to say, it shares a common ancestry with Dutch, German, and Frisian (which are, like English, West Germanic languages), and rather more remotely with Icelandic, Norwegian, Swedish, and Danish (which are North Germanic languages), and with the extinct language Gothic (an East Germanic language). These languages (and others not listed here) are developments from branches (West, North, and East Germanic) of an unattested language that scholars call proto-Germanic.[2] This is traditionally represented with a tree diagram, as in Fig. 4.1.

In the case of some other language families we are fortunate enough to have documentation for both the parent language and its daughters.

---

[1] For an introduction to some of the basic concepts involved in comparative reconstruction and, in particular, for an introduction to the concept of sound change, see Durkin (2009).

[2] This summary in fact simplifies what was probably a rather more complex picture. For more detail and further references see Durkin (2009) 8–9.

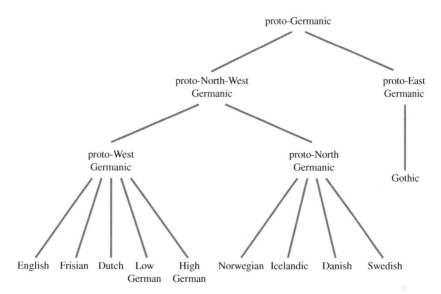

Fig. 4.1 The major Germanic languages.

French, Spanish, Italian, and the other Romance languages developed from Latin, which is of course preserved in documents from antiquity, although reconstruction from the Romance languages sometimes indicates differences from the literary Latin of most of our records. (Of course, Latin then continued in use for many centuries as a learned language, alongside its Romance daughter languages.) Proto-Germanic, on the other hand, can only be reconstructed on the basis of comparison of its surviving daughter languages, using what is called the comparative method. This same method enabled scholars to identify that Latin (and its smaller sisters among the Italic languages) and proto-Germanic are also ultimately related to one another. They both developed from an unattested language that is given the name proto-Indo-European, on account of the spread of its daughter languages at the dawn of the historical period across Europe, parts of the Near East, and South Asia (that is, before the global spread of some Indo-European languages, like English, French, and Spanish, to many other corners of the world in historical times). From the perspective of proto-Indo-European, the Germanic and Romance languages are thus more properly identified as no more than branches of a larger family: the Indo-European language family. Beside Germanic and Italic, some other major branches of Indo-European are Celtic (see section 3.3), Hellenic (i.e. Greek),

Slavonic, Baltic, Indo-Iranian, and Anatolian (including the important very early documents for Hittite). In fact, comparison with other branches of Indo-European often tells us things about proto-Germanic that we would not know simply from comparing the Germanic languages with one another, and this is the same for the other branches of Indo-European as well.

By the method of comparative reconstruction we can establish links between words that have developed from a common ancestor and often establish, at least approximately, what that common ancestor sounded like. Some instances of lexical borrowing between languages can even be established at this level of comparative reconstruction. A relatively simple example of the methodology involved can be taken from a case of borrowing from proto-Germanic into Finnish. English *ring* (Old English *hring*) has numerous cognates in other Germanic languages, including Old High German *ring* and Old Icelandic *hringr*; that is to say, all of these forms are assumed to be descended from a shared ancestor, which can be reconstructed with some confidence as proto-Germanic **hring-a-*. (The hyphens indicate that the *a* is a stem-forming suffix, to which inflectional endings were added. The asterisk indicates a reconstructed form, as opposed to one evidenced in surviving documents.) Investigation of the likely further etymology of this word suggests that its earlier form was probably **hreng-a-*, not **hring-a-*, and that the change in the vowel resulted from a regular proto-Germanic sound change *e* > *i* before *n* (also shown by, e.g. the ancestor of modern English *wind*, which is cognate with Latin *ventus*); the word is probably related etymologically to the proto-Germanic verb that is the ancestor of modern English *shrink* (which probably shows the same sound change). Thus we have a prehistory for this word along the following lines:

> proto-Germanic **hreng-a-*
> > (with raising of *e* > *i* before *n*) **hring-a-*
> > Old English *hring*, Old High German *ring*, Old Icelandic *hringr*, etc.

This hypothesis is supported by the Finnish form *rengas*. Finnish is a non-Indo-European language, and *rengas* appears to show an early borrowing from proto-Germanic **hreng-a-*, before this sound change occurred.[3]

Unfortunately, most hypotheses of borrowing at this time depth are much more complex, and many involve much greater uncertainty, and this applies

---

[3] For a survey of contact between Germanic and Finnish, see Koivulehto (2002).

to most of the likely cases of early borrowing into Germanic from Celtic and Latin.[4]

4.2 Very early borrowings from Celtic

Some probable early borrowings from Celtic into Germanic are reflected by the English words *rich* (and German *Reich* 'kingdom'), *iron*, and *leech* 'physician'. Some others are reflected by Old English words that did not survive into modern English: *ambiht* 'servant' (although this could perhaps have come to Germanic via Latin *ambactus*), *byrne* (later also *bryniġe*, < early Scandinavian) 'coat of mail', *ġīsl* 'hostage', and *wealh* 'foreigner, (later) slave' (on which see further section 3.5).[5] Some of the things denoted by these words suggest that at least some of the Celts and their culture may at this point have had considerable prestige for at least some of the Germani.

When one is operating at this sort of time depth, considerably before the earliest surviving records, the arguments supporting the hypothesis that a word is borrowed can be rather intricate and complex. To show the sorts of argument that are typically involved, we can work through one example in detail.

English *rich* shows the reflex (or descendant) of Old English *rīċe* 'powerful, wealthy'. This has a clear set of cognates in the other major Germanic languages, including (from the oldest recorded stages of each language):

> Old Frisian *rīke*, Old Dutch *rīki*, Old Saxon *rīki*, Old High German *rīhhi*, Old Icelandic *ríkr*, Old Swedish *rīker*, Old Danish *rikær*, Gothic *reiks*

Their common ancestor can be reconstructed fairly certainly as a proto-Germanic adjective **rīk-ja-*, showing a root **rīk-* and a suffix **-ja-* which forms adjectives. The same suffix could also form nouns, and a noun formation **rīk-ja-* is reflected by Old English *rīċe* 'kingdom' and by a

---

[4] Outside the scope of this book is the difficult and vexed question of whether Germanic shows an unusually large proportion of words of unknown etymology in comparison with other branches of Indo-European, and whether, if it does, this indicates large-scale borrowing from one or more other languages. For some overview of the large literature on this topic, see Roberge (2010).

[5] This short list follows Ringe (2006) 296. For more extensive surveys and discussion of less certain examples, see Birkhan (1970), Green (1998); for further literature on this topic, see references in Roberge (2010).

similar range of cognates, including Old High German *rīhhi* (> modern German *Reich*). There is also evidence for a root noun from the same base, in which the inflectional endings were added directly to the root **rīk-*. This is reflected by Gothic *reiks* 'ruler' (an *-ei-* spelling in Gothic regularly reflects Germanic **ī* /iː/).

It is tempting to try to connect this proto-Germanic root **rīk-* with a series of words of similar form and meaning in other branches of Indo-European, such as Latin *rēx* 'king', Gaulish *rix*, *rig-*, probably 'king', and Sanskrit *rājā* 'king, prince, sovereign' and *rāj-* 'to rule'. These all reflect a proto-Indo-European root **rēg-*. The problem is that proto-Germanic **rīk-* cannot easily be explained as the development of proto-Indo-European **rēg-*. It clearly has the same initial consonant and we would indeed expect proto-Indo-European **r* to be reflected by **r* in proto-Germanic. Proto-Germanic **k* for proto-Indo-European **g* may at first appear more surprising, but this is in fact perfectly regular. It is explained by a famous sound change called Grimm's Law, which is one of the most important distinguishing features of the Germanic languages: in most positions in a word, where we find **g* in a proto-Indo-European form we expect to find **k* in its proto-Germanic reflex. (Compare Latin *ager* with Gothic *akrs*, English *acre*.)[6] However, the vowel **ī* in proto-Germanic **rīk-* is more difficult to explain. What we know of comparative Germanic philology indicates that the various attested forms definitely reflect proto-Germanic **rīk-*, not **rēk-*, but what we know of comparative Indo-European philology tells us that proto-Indo-European **rēg-* should give proto-Germanic **rēk-*, not **rīk-*. Thus:

proto-Indo-European **rēg-* > proto-Germanic **rēk-*

but

proto-Germanic **rīk-* + **-ja-* > **rīk-ja-* 'powerful, wealthy' > Old English *rīċe*, Old Frisian *rīke*, etc.

It is rather improbable that the close resemblance in meaning between the Germanic words and the words in other Indo-European languages is entirely the result of chance, and that they are not related at all. On the other hand, comparative linguists will normally try to avoid at all costs positing a one-off exception to an otherwise regular sound correspondence, since this greatly reduces the robustness of our results, and could lead us to

---

[6] See further Durkin (2009) 17–19, 180–2.

accept all manner of incorrect etymologies, and damage the foundation for further research work.

An elegant solution is provided by the hypothesis that the word was borrowed from Celtic into Germanic. In proto-Celtic, Indo-European *$\bar{e}$ regularly develops to *$\bar{\imath}$, and thus Gaulish *rix, rig-* is a quite regular reflex of proto-Indo-European *$r\bar{e}g$-*.[7] We therefore have a viable word history that can explain the vowel in the Germanic forms as well:

> proto-Indo-European *$r\bar{e}g$-* > proto-Celtic *$r\bar{\imath}g$-* which is borrowed as proto-Germanic *$r\bar{\imath}g$-*

This leaves unaddressed the question of the final consonant *k in Germanic, but this is explained if we assume that the borrowing from Celtic was very early, before the operation of Grimm's Law. This then gives our final step to arrive at the form that lies behind the attested forms in the various Germanic languages:

> proto-Germanic *$r\bar{\imath}g$-* develops (by the operation of Grimm's Law) to *$r\bar{\imath}k$-*

So we now have a complete narrative from proto-Indo-European to the attested forms in the Germanic languages, involving borrowing from Celtic to Germanic:

> proto-Indo-European *$r\bar{e}g$-* > proto-Celtic *$r\bar{\imath}g$-* > proto-Germanic *$r\bar{\imath}g$-* > (by Grimm's Law) *$r\bar{\imath}k$-*
>
> proto-Germanic *$r\bar{\imath}k$-* + *-ja-* > *$r\bar{\imath}k$-ja-* 'powerful, wealthy' > Old English *rīċe*, Old Frisian *rīke*, etc.

As is typical with arguments of this sort of complexity at this sort of time depth, different hypotheses have been offered to explain the proto-Germanic word form, but the explanation I have sketched here is accepted by most scholars who have looked at this question.

If we accept this etymology, it casts an interesting light on relations between at least some Germanic speakers and some Celtic speakers in a period before our earliest substantial records for languages from either group. A borrowing would appear to have occurred involving a major term to do with the highest levels of a social hierarchy, and the direction appears to have been from Celtic to Germanic. As we have seen, some of the

---

[7] See Szemerényi (1996) §4.1.4, Matasović (2009) 8, 311.

other probable early borrowings also point towards borrowing for reasons of prestige. Others, especially *iron*, a term of central importance in the Iron Age, suggest transfer of technology from Celts to Germani as well.

A number of scholars, especially in earlier times, have attempted to sketch more specific possible scenarios for this exchange, but it is probably best to exercise a good deal of caution at this point.

Another word sometimes mentioned in this connection is *wire*. In this instance, the cognates do not all show the same stem vowel: Old English *wīr*, Middle Low German *wīre*, and Old Icelandic *vírr* all suggest proto-Germanic *$\bar{i}$, but Old High German *wiara*, *wiera* suggests proto-Germanic *$\bar{e}$. Because of this, it has been proposed that the word may show a borrowing from Celtic, in which proto-Indo-European *ei* developed variably to $\bar{e}$ or $\bar{i}$. In the early Germanic languages, *wire* and its cognates often denote high-status, finely crafted metalwork and so perhaps we have another borrowing to place in a milieu similar to *rich*. However, in this instance another, much more economical, explanation is possible: the unusual forms in Old High German may simply reflect a lowering of $\bar{i}$ to $\bar{e}$ before *r*, for which parallels can be found. An apparently rather exciting example of early Celtic borrowing/influence in Germanic thus appears to fall away in the face of a rather more prosaic explanation.[8] Such reassessments are not uncommon in the world of comparative linguistics and show why caution is needed in constructing elaborate hypotheses about early contact situations on the basis of a small number of examples.

4.3 Very early borrowings from Latin

Unlike (probably) English *rich*, etc. from Celtic, there appear to be no borrowings from Latin into proto-Germanic that are sufficiently early to show Grimm's Law. However, there are several words that were probably borrowed before the separation of the various Germanic varieties. These include (giving in each case the likely proto-Germanic forms):

---

[8] For advocacy of borrowing from Celtic in this case, see Green (1998) 155 and further references given there. On the possible Germanic sound change, see Ringe (1984). I am very grateful to Patrick Stiles for advice given during work on the etymology of this word for the new edition of the *OED*.

*Rūmōnīz 'Romans' (< Latin Rōmānī), *punda 'pound' (< Latin pondō 'by weight'), *katilaz 'kettle' (probably < either Latin catīnus 'food vessel' or its diminutive catillus), and various words to do with trade from a root *kaup (< Latin caupō 'merchant').[9]

*Rūmōnīz has no direct reflex in Old English, and so it will not concern us further here. (The various Old English names for the Romans are later independent borrowings.) We now look at the arguments for and against early borrowing for each of the other words.

Old English pund probably reflects early borrowing in Germanic. There are related forms in all three branches of Germanic: e.g. Old Frisian pund, Old High German phunt, Old Icelandic pund, Old Swedish pund, Gothic pund. However, the mere existence of forms in each language proves little, since most of the Germanic languages continued to have contact with Latin long after the proto-Germanic period and, therefore, separate instances of borrowing in each language are a real possibility. The shared raising of Latin o > u before a nasal is not very much stronger evidence for shared descent, since although this change is common in early borrowings it is certainly not confined to the proto-Germanic period (compare the discussion of Old English mynster and mynet in section 8.1.3). The strongest evidence for shared early borrowing in this case comes from the fact that all of these words show the same semantic innovation: Latin pondō is the ablative case of a word pondus (not attested in the nominative case) which occurred in uses with a numeral, in which it was short for lībra pondō 'a pound by weight, a pound weight', so e.g. trēs (lībrae) pondō 'three pounds in weight'; the Latin word was reinterpreted by Germanic speakers as itself denoting a pound weight, and it is this reinterpretation that is reflected by the attested word in the various Germanic languages. From the point of view of cultural history, we can see how such a borrowing could have occurred very early in trading situations in which accurate measurement of weight is essential.

Modern English kettle probably goes back to a common Germanic borrowing *katilaz, as do the Old English forms ċietel /tʃɪətel/[10] and ċetel /tʃetel/. Again, there are parallels or cognates in all three branches of

---

[9] For this list, see Ringe (2006) 296, although he does not discuss the reasons for regarding each word as an early borrowing.

[10] Some scholars would instead interpret this spelling as reflecting /tʃetel/: see section 8.1. See section 6.3 on ċ in Old English spellings; this is a convention introduced by modern scholars in order to distinguish (what is assumed to be) /tʃ/ from /k/.

Germanic, e.g. Old Saxon *ketel*, Old High German *kezzil*, Old Icelandic *ketill*, Gothic *katils*. The forms found in Old English suggest that this is not a late borrowing, because it appears to show some early sound changes (fronting, palatalization, and *i*-mutation: see section 8.1),[11] although it could certainly have been borrowed much later than the common Germanic period and still show all of these sound changes. Shared semantic innovation strengthens the hypothesis of early borrowing in proto-Germanic, although the innovation 'food vessel' > 'kettle' is perhaps rather more predictable than that shown by *pound* and hence slightly more likely to be coincidental. From the point of view of cultural history and archaeology, it is known that such vessels have been traded from south to north since very early times,[12] and so very early borrowing is historically plausible. Thus, we can say that there is a reasonable amount of evidence in favour of shared early borrowing and nothing against, although this amounts to much less than a certainty. (One later uncertainty is the relationship between modern English *kettle* and the Old English word; it probably shows at least formal influence from Scandinavian and may be a new Scandinavian borrowing, replacing the earlier word. Compare section 10.2.2.)

A rather less secure example of borrowing at the common Germanic stage is shown by the group of words related to modern English *cheap*. This large word group includes:

- The noun Old English *ċēap* /tʃæːɑp/ 'purchase or sale, bargain, business transaction, market, possessions, livestock'; the modern adjective *cheap* originates from a shortening of the phrase *good cheap* 'good bargain'. Cognates include Old Frisian *kāp*, Middle Dutch *coop*, Old Saxon *kōp*, Old High German *chouf*, Old Icelandic *kaup*.
- The Class II weak verb Old English *ċēapian* 'to buy and sell, to make a bargain, to trade' (< **kaupōjan*), which has cognates or parallels in all three branches of Germanic, including significantly Gothic *kaupōn* 'to trade, to buy and sell' (compare also Old High German *koufōn*, also *koufen* > modern German *kaufen*).
- The Class I weak verb Old English *ċȳpan* 'to sell' (< **kaupjan*) with cognates or parallels in other West Germanic languages.

---

[11] The stages in the pronunciation of the word would thus be /katil-a/ > /kætil-a/ > /kætil-/ > /tʃætil/ > /tʃetil/ > /tʃetel/.

[12] Compare Lehmann (1986) under **katils*.

- Old English *čȳpa*, *čēapa* 'merchant, trader', and numerous other derivative formations from the same base, such as *čēapung*, *čȳping* 'trade, buying and selling, market, market place' (from which come place names such as *Chipping Campden*) and *čēapman*, *čȳpeman* 'merchant, trader' (hence, albeit with a complicated sound history, modern English *chapman*).

It is not in doubt that this word group ultimately reflects borrowing from Latin, either from *caupō* 'petty trader' or its derivative *caupōnārī* 'to traffic, to trade'. The existence of Gothic *kaupōn* is often taken as showing that this borrowing took place before the split of Gothic from the other Germanic languages. However, it has also been argued with reasonable plausibility that the borrowing could have been into West Germanic (in the context of language contact in the middle or lower Rhine area, with Latin *caupō* as the starting point), and that the words found in North Germanic and Gothic reflect spread from West Germanic.[13]

Section 8.2.1 considers some words that many earlier scholars thought likely to be early borrowings into Germanic from Greek, but that are now generally seen in a different light.

An interesting fact about proto-Germanic is that its reconstructed vocabulary shows an unusually high proportion of words with no known connections elsewhere in Indo-European; one explanation for this is some sort of language contact, and perhaps at least one language shift situation, where words have entered Germanic from a substrate as large numbers of speakers have switched to Germanic from another language, but it is unlikely that certainty will ever be reached on this point.[14]

---

[13] See Brüch (1951).

[14] For an introduction to some very controversial ideas on this topic, see Vennemann (2010).

5

Old English in contact with Celtic

This chapter looks in some detail at a contact situation that resulted in little lexical borrowing in English. Given that English shows so many loanwords from other languages resulting from other contact situations, this may seem a little perverse. However, this major incident of non-borrowing comes at the beginning of the story of the use of English in the British Isles, and it gives a useful basis for comparison with different contact situations where extensive borrowing did occur.

The number of generally accepted early Celtic borrowings in English is very small. This much is agreed by nearly all scholars, but almost every other aspect of Celtic influence on early English is bedevilled with controversy. A thorough reappraisal of all possible cases of Celtic borrowing in Old English, conducted by someone equally learned in Celtic languages and in Old English, is long overdue. This chapter makes no pretence to be such a reappraisal. Instead I attempt to provide a brief summary of some of the words most frequently thought to show Celtic borrowing in Old English and some reflections on what they seem to indicate about the nature of early contact between English and Celtic languages. I then look very briefly at some of the (very controversial) ideas about possible influence from Celtic languages on English in areas other than lexis that have come to prominence in the scholarly literature in recent years. Finally, I look at some later borrowings into English from Celtic languages.

5.1 Lexical borrowings from Celtic into Old English

The normal assumption is that contact between Anglo-Saxon settlers and the existing population of Britain involved Brittonic rather than other varieties of Celtic (compare section 3.3), and therefore I begin with those words for which borrowing from Brittonic is likely or at least possible. It should be noted, though, that most of these words need not have been very early borrowings: they could have occurred in the early part of the Anglo-Saxon settlement, but they could have occurred later, as a result of cultural contacts with Celtic neighbours, or in the context of conquest of further Celtic territory.[1]

Brock 'badger' (Old English *brocc*) is a clear borrowing from Celtic, although there is no clear linguistic evidence as to which variety of Celtic it was borrowed from.[2] There are no other words for the badger recorded from the Old English period, so the assumption must be that *brock* was the usual word for this animal, which it remained until the appearance of *badger* in the early modern period. *Bin* (Old English *binn*), which in early use denoted various kinds of receptacle, especially a manger, is probably another early Celtic borrowing, but was probably borrowed via Latin (compare section 7.1), perhaps on the continent.

Coomb 'valley' (Old English *cumb*) is a fairly certain Celtic borrowing, but it has only a tenuous existence in Old English outside place names, and its modern currency (such as it is) mainly reflects recent (re-)borrowing from Welsh and uses in place names. Other items found in place names and with occasional independent uses in Old English include *luh* 'lake', *torr* 'rock, hill', and (ultimately of Latin origin) *funta* 'fountain'.[3] The occurrence of

[1] For summaries of this topic, see Campbell (1959) 219–20, Kastovsky (1992) 318, Breeze (2002), Coates (2007), Filppula et al. (2008) 126–31. For a very influential early account, see Förster (1921).

[2] Because of the many difficulties involved in reconstructing early Celtic donor forms, and because they are unlikely to be illuminating for most readers, such reconstructions are not given in this chapter. However, see section 5.5. for some more fully worked through examples involving somewhat later loanwords from Celtic languages.

[3] On *funta* in particular, see Gelling (1977), who argues that the distribution of place names containing this element argues strongly for an association with Roman remains and speculates that borrowing directly from Latin is a possibility, although not the only one. For some further examples of words found only or chiefly in place names, see Coates (2007), and see also discussion in Parsons (2011).

such topographic terms, whether in place names or in occasional independent use, is to be expected in the context of the settlement of a new territory. *Pen* 'hill, promontory' has slightly more currency in Old English, but is largely confined to place names later.

Another geographical word, *dūn* 'hill', is often attributed to Celtic borrowing. As well as being the basis of modern English place names such as *The Downs*, *dūn* 'hill' is the origin of the modern adverb and preposition *down*, which was derived, entirely within English, < *adūne* < *of dūne* 'off the hill or height'. If this word is a Celtic borrowing, it has thus contributed a basic spatial term to the vocabulary of modern English, albeit indirectly. However, this borrowing is unlikely to have taken place in Britain, since the relevant Celtic word in Britain seems only to have meant 'hillfort', while it may also have meant 'hill' on the continent; the English word, even in the earliest place names, gives no hint of denoting any sort of fortified place, only a hill. Also, Old English *dūn* has either parallels or cognates in other West Germanic languages (including the Dutch word from which English *dune* 'sand dune' was ultimately borrowed, via French). If English *down* reflects borrowing from Celtic, then the borrowing seems likely to have taken place on the continent. Some scholars have doubted that it is borrowed at all, regarding the formal and semantic similarity as mere accident.[4]

Crag, which is first recorded in Middle English, may reflect earlier borrowing from Celtic (although the vowel presents problems), as may *coble* 'type of flat-bottomed rowing boat' (which is probably related to *cuopel* found in the Northumbrian dialect of Old English).

Some suggested, but variously debated and disputed, further possible loanwords are (giving the Old English forms in each case): *bannuc* 'bit' (compare the later borrowing *bannock* from Scottish Gaelic), *becca* 'fork', *bratt* 'cloak', *carr* 'rock', *dunn* 'dun, dull or dingy brown', *gafeluc* 'spear', *mattuc* 'mattock' (also suggested as a Latin loan: see section 6.3.1), *toroc* 'bung', and (ultimately from Latin: see section 6.3) *assen* and *assa* 'ass' and perhaps also *stær* (or *stær*) 'history', *stōr* 'incense', and *cæfester* 'halter'. Very

---

[4] For summaries of views, see Gelling (1984) 140–1, Gelling and Cole (2000) 32–3, Watts (2004) xliii, Philippa (2003–9) I 643. It is also uncertain whether the Celtic word is ultimately related to the Germanic base of English *town*, at a period before the Grimm's Law change *$*d$ > *$*t$ in Germanic. If so, *town* could reflect a very early Celtic borrowing in Germanic, like those considered in chapter 4, although the relationship could be the other way around, or both words could reflect a common ancestor, or perhaps there could be no relationship between them at all.

few of these are common words in Old English (or later), some of them are very doubtfully of Celtic origin, and others could be from Old Irish rather than from Brittonic. For instance, Breeze (1993) argues convincingly on grounds based on word form as well as the documentary record for each language that *gafeluc* came to English from Irish (probably via Scandinavian), rather than from Brittonic or later Welsh.

Hog (Old English *hogg*) could be a borrowing from Celtic (compare Old Welsh *huch*, Old Cornish *hoch*), but this hypothesis is probably only viable if we assume that its form was altered as a result of association with *dog*, *frog*, *pig*, *stag* or other animal names of similar shape (most of which are complete etymological puzzles, and first appear in late Old English).[5]

Borrowing specifically from Old Irish is probably shown by *drȳ* 'magician'. It is perhaps also shown by *bratt* 'cloak' and *ancra*, *ancor* 'anchorite' (ultimately < Latin *anachōrēta*),[6] and just possibly by *cursung* 'cursing' and related words (perhaps ultimately < Latin *curas agere*). One or two further very rare Old English words that may be borrowed from Irish are *clugge* 'bell', *æstel* 'bookmark', *ċine* (or *ċīne*) 'sheet of parchment folded in four', and *mind*, a type of head ornament. Most of these words could (as often assumed) reflect activity among the pagan Anglo-Saxons by Irish missionaries, although other contact situations are also possible. Another word perhaps belonging to this group is *cros* 'cross', although this is attested in Old English only in descriptive place names and only in twelfth-century texts, and may well be via Scandinavian (the usual word for 'cross' in Old English is *rōd*).[7]

A number of additions to the list of Old English borrowings from Celtic have recently been suggested by Andrew Breeze.[8] Many of the words concerned are rare both in Old English and later, but some are much commoner, most notably *wan* 'pale' (Old English *wann* 'dark, gloomy, black'). Other fairly prominent Old English words for which he suggests

---

[5] Compare Hogg (1982), Coates (1982) 203.

[6] For an overview of opinions on this example, see Durkin (2011).

[7] The history of Old English *cros* and of Middle English *cros* (> modern English *cross*) has been much discussed. For recent views, see on the one hand Diensberg (1997), who assumes that Old English *cros* is from Old Irish, and suggests that Middle English *cros* could, like the form *crois*, show a new borrowing from French; on the other hand, Dance (2003) 417–18, who argues (in my view convincingly) that both Old English *cros* and Middle English *cros* very likely came into English via Scandinavian.

[8] See especially Breeze (2002) and <http://www.unav.es/linguis/AndrewBreeze/> for references to his many publications on this topic.

Celtic etymologies are *trum* 'strong', *dēor* 'fierce, bold', and *syrce, syrc, serce* 'coat of mail'; these, together with one or two other less frequent terms, may suggest that British military tactics and armour may in particular have prompted lexical borrowing by the Anglo-Saxons (see Breeze (2002) 176). Among contributions from other scholars, see e.g. Ahlquist (1988) for suggested Celtic etymologies for *jilt* and *twig*. It remains to be seen how many of these suggestions will stand the test of time; even if all are ultimately accepted by the scholarly community at large, the total of Celtic borrowings in Old English will remain tiny in comparison with the number of Latin borrowings.

It is possible, although impossible to prove, that large numbers of borrowings from Latin could have passed into English via Celtic in the very early stages of the Anglo-Saxon settlement without any change in form that would make this route of transmission clear. However, the balance of recent scholarship has been that there are no 'smoking gun' examples that definitely show transmission via Celtic in Britain in the settlement period.[9]

Another possibility is that some of the Celtic borrowings found later in the history of English (in some cases only in regional varieties) could in fact have been borrowed much earlier and simply do not show up in the documentary record in the Old English period (or in many cases in the Middle English period also). This case is argued briefly in a recent survey volume on possible Celtic influence on English (Filppula et al. (2008) 126–32). What has not been undertaken to date is a thorough study of the plausibility of this hypothesis for individual word histories, to identify which could plausibly have been in English far longer than the documentary record would indicate, and which cases are ruled out on the grounds of intervening sound changes in the history of either English or the Celtic languages. Given the extensive sound changes that occurred in this period, one would expect to find at least some examples that are only fully explicable if borrowed much earlier, if it is really the case that large numbers of words were borrowed much earlier than the historical record would suggest. Such work is essential if this hypothesis is to be pursued further.

A major desideratum for this subject is a comprehensive survey of all (attested or reconstructed) Old English words that may show borrowing from a Celtic language, giving full reconstructions of the suggested Celtic

---

[9] See especially Wollmann (1993) 19–24.

donor forms, and thorough argumentation for the linguistic or historical reasons for the suggested route of transmission in each case.

In the present state of knowledge, the likely Celtic loanwords in English are a fairly disparate group and seem to reflect several different contact situations. There are toponymic terms, presumably linked with the Anglo-Saxon conquest of various parts of England. Rural *brock* and agricultural *bin* may (but need not) belong with these. The military terms suggested by Andrew Breeze point to borrowing in the context of the many armed conflicts between Anglo-Saxons and Britons. Most of the other words that suggest any sort of specific milieu seem instead to belong to the world of the Church and learned culture. Probably they reflect contact with the Celtic churches during the period of conversion of the Anglo-Saxons or later, rather than contacts during the period of Anglo-Saxon paganism. Most of the remaining non-religious words could also easily belong to this later period, since conflicts with Britons in the west and conquest of new territory continued well into the period of Anglo-Saxon Christianity (compare section 3.5).

5.2 The evidence of personal names and place names

Celtic personal names occurring in Anglo-Saxon England as the names of people not explicitly identified as Celts are few but in some cases rather significant. The ox-herd poet *Cædmon*, whose existence and verse is recorded by Bede, has a name of Celtic origin. Several Celtic names occur among the earlier parts of the genealogies of the West Saxon kings (*Ċerdiċ, Ċeawlin, Ċeadda, Ċeadwalla*), although historians are divided on the precise significance of these. There are two bishops (in fact brothers) recorded in the seventh century with the names *Ċedd* and *Ċeadda*, and the name *Cumbra* is found among the West-Saxon nobility.[10]

The place-name evidence is complex, but on the whole more plentiful than the evidence of personal names or general lexis. It is also, obviously, much more closely associated with particular geographical localities, and this brings with it certain implications: although there are often uncertainties, we can be pretty sure that a place name in the east of England reflects

[10] See further Clark (1992) 463, Filppula et al. (2008) 125–6.

contact either before or at the time of extensive Anglo-Saxon settlement in that area, rather than, say, later contact with Irish or Welsh. We have already noted some elements in Old English place names that are ultimately of Celtic origin. However, the general picture is that survival of Celtic place names was rather limited, except in those areas in the north and west that came under Anglo-Saxon domination later. Rivers and other major geographical features are the most likely to preserve their Celtic or pre-Celtic names (e.g. *Thames*, *Severn*, *Trent*), but again this is much more common the further west one goes in England. Other types of place names are only very sparsely preserved outside those areas known to have been settled late. For instance, the far south-eastern county of *Kent* preserves its Celtic name; given its geographical location and its continental connections, this name was very probably known to the Anglo-Saxons before they came to Britain. Within this county we find additionally that the Celtic names of *Dover*, *Reculver*, and *Sarre* are retained, and additionally (of pre-Celtic origin) *Thanet* (sometimes also identified by its Celtic name *Ruoihm*). Elements of Celtic names (in combination with Old English place-name elements) are preserved in *Chevening*, *Chattenden*, *Chatham*, and perhaps also *Rochester*. A pre-Celtic element is preserved in the name of *Richborough*.[11] This is a small showing for a large and populous county, in which it is often thought that Romano-British culture may have suffered less total disruption than in most other parts of Britain. In some parts of the east of England the place-name evidence is much thinner than this (although for some areas this may partly reflect the variable degree of detail of the existing place-name scholarship). Modern scholarship is identifying more Celtic place names than are being eliminated as previous wrong guesses and the general picture is of greater preservation of Celtic names than was previously thought (see especially Coates and Breeze 2000). Nonetheless, Celtic place names are still generally few and far between in the core areas of early Anglo-Saxon domination, although they are rather better preserved in some western parts of England.[12]

[11] For all of this Kentish data, see Coates and Breeze (2000) 315–16, 381, also Coates (2002).

[12] See Coates and Breeze (2000), Gelling (1992), Coates (2000). For an interesting comparison with Latin elements in English place names, see Parsons (2011).

5.3 A comparison: borrowing from Celtic into French

It is useful to compare the situation in English with that found in French. As we have already noted (see section 3.4), in the Roman province of Gaul the use of Gaulish appears to have persisted, particularly in the countryside, for hundreds of years after the Romans arrived, even though Latin (and the proto-Romance developing from it) gained an increasing purchase in urban areas. In the post-Roman (or sub-Roman) period this situation was complicated still further by the arrival of new Germanic overlords, but Latin/ proto-Romance remained the dominant language in urban areas.

Lambert (1995) notes that estimates of the number of borrowings ultimately from Gaulish in French vary between around 50 and 500; most put the number at least over 100. He supplies a (not entirely exhaustive) list of 133 reasonably plausible borrowings, although it should be noted that this list includes some words ultimately of Celtic origin that only reached French by a rather indirect route, and hence cannot be counted as showing direct Gaulish influence on French. For example, he includes *ambassade*, which was probably borrowed into French < Italian < Occitan < Old High German, and ultimately shows the same very early borrowing from Celtic as Old English *ambiht* noted in section 4.2. Similarly, he includes *brigand*, a borrowing into French from Italian *brigante*, but it is only the Italian word that shows the result of direct Celtic influence. Even when such examples are eliminated, and also after allowing for some very uncertain etymologies, it remains clear that French owes a good number of words to Gaulish.[13]

The documentary record shows that some of these words had been borrowed into Latin before (in a few cases long before) Caesar's conquests in Gaul, hence potentially in contact situations other than that between dominant superstrate and governed substrate; others can be shown clearly to belong to later centuries; but for many it is simply not possible to say with certainty when the borrowing occurred.

Interestingly, various semantic groupings can be identified among these borrowings:

---

[13] For some very useful analysis of the numbers of Celtic etymologies suggested by various different etymological dictionaries of French, and of differences of opinion among the dictionaries, see Felixberger (2002), Felixberger (2003). For an older but still very readable account, see Wartburg (1969) 21–31. For more detailed analysis of most of these words, see also Delamarre (2001).

- Names of animals (interpreted broadly, but omitting some words from Lambert's lists that are now obsolete or regional, or else are extremely doubtfully of Gaulish origin): *bièvre* 'beaver', *blaireau* 'badger', *bouc* 'billy goat', *mouton* 'sheep', *vautre* 'type of hunting dog', and the hybrid formation *palefroi* 'palfrey', with a second element of Gaulish origin; more doubtfully also *chamois* 'chamois' and *truie* 'sow'.
- Names of birds: *alouette* 'lark' and (with substantial alteration in form resulting from folk etymology) *chat-huant* 'tawny owl'.
- Names of fishes: *alose* 'shad', *loche* 'loach', *lotte* 'burbot', *tanche* 'tench', *vandoise* 'dace', and perhaps ultimately *brochet* 'pike'; *limande* 'dab' probably shows a suffix of Gaulish origin.

Some of these words are even familiar in English, as a result of borrowing from French: *mutton, palfrey, loach, tench, chamois*. (English *buck* is of Germanic origin, and is probably related to the Celtic and French words only at the Indo-European level; likewise French *bièvre* 'beaver' (now only an archaism) is only extremely distantly related to English *beaver*, if at all.)

From the world of brewing beer, we find *brasser* 'to brew (beer)' (and hence *brasserie* > English *brasserie*), ultimately reflecting borrowing of a Gaulish noun. We also find *cervoise* 'beer', reflecting Latin *cervesia*, a borrowing from Celtic first recorded in the first century AD in Pliny the Elder, although this word was later ousted in French by the Germanic borrowing *bière*. (It remains in the Romance languages of the Iberian Peninsula: Spanish *cerveza*, Portuguese *cerveja*, Catalan *cervesa*.)

Some other reasonably common modern French words generally held to be (probably or possibly, wholly or partly) of Celtic origin are:

arpent 'measure of land', *bec* 'beak', *béret* 'beret', *borne* 'boundary (marker)', *boue* 'mud', *bouge* 'hovel, dive' (earlier 'bag'), *bruyère* 'heather, briar-root', *changer* 'to change', *char* 'chariot' (reflecting a borrowing which had occurred already in classical Latin, whence also *charrue* 'plough'), *charpente* 'framework' (originally the name of a type of chariot), *chemin* 'road, way', *chêne* 'oak', (partly) *craindre* 'to fear', *crème* 'cream', *drap* 'sheet, cloth', *javelot* 'javelin', *lieue* 'league (measure of distance)', *marne* 'marl' (earlier *marle*, hence English *marl*), *pièce* 'piece', *ruche* 'beehive', *sillon* 'furrow', *soc* 'ploughshare', *suie* 'soot', *vassal* 'vassal'; perhaps also *barre* 'bar', *jaillir* 'to gush, spring, shoot out', *quai* 'quay'. (Compare also section 13.1.3 for obsolete *druerie* 'love', a derivative of *dru* 'thick, dense, rich', also 'lively, beloved'.)

This is if we omit items such as *mine* 'facial expression', *petit* 'small', *roche* 'rock', or *tonne* 'tonne, originally barrel', where the supposition of a Celtic origin rests chiefly or solely on geographical spread, rather than on any plausible reconstructible etymon.

Lambert also lists a number of words (in addition to the 133 already mentioned) of possible Celtic origin that are found in Latin (often only rarely and/or in late sources) but that are not reflected in French, although it should be noted that this list contains some words of very uncertain origin.

It would be easy to overemphasize the impact of Gaulish words on the vocabulary of modern French. A page drawn at random from a book in French may well contain no words at all of Gaulish origin. However, *changer* is quite a high-frequency word, as are *pièce* and *chemin* (and its derivatives). If admitted to the list, *petit* belongs to a very basic level of the vocabulary. The meanings 'beaver', 'beer', 'boundary', 'change', 'fear' (albeit as noun), 'to flow', 'he-goat', 'oak', 'piece', 'plough' (albeit as verb), 'road', 'rock', 'sheep', 'small', and 'sow' all figure in the list of 1,460 basic meanings used in Haspelmath et al. (2009) (see further section 2.3 on this). Ultimately, through borrowing from French, the impact is also visible in a number of high-frequency words in the vocabulary of modern English, e.g. (in addition to the animal names already mentioned above) *beak*, *carpentry*, *change*, *cream*, *drape*, *piece*, *quay*, *vassal*, and (ultimately reflecting the same borrowing as French *char* 'chariot') *carry* and *car*.

If we compare the situation in French with the direct borrowing from Celtic found in Old English, the contrast is striking. There could be various explanations for this. In the case of French, we are looking at a Romance language that developed from the Latin used in Gaul right from the beginning of the Roman occupation and shows some Celtic words that were probably borrowed even earlier, when the Gauls were northern neighbours of the Romans. A Gaulish-speaking rural peasantry appears to have had many centuries of relatively stable interaction with the increasingly Latin/Romance-speaking towns and cities; the major change over the centuries was that Latin/Romance appears to have spread more and more at the expense of Gaulish, until Gaulish ceased to be used at all (except in Brittany, where it was probably reinforced by and blended with Brittonic Celtic brought by Celts fleeing post-Roman Britain). For people in the countryside there was thus probably a very long period in which a situation of diglossia existed, with Latin being used in dealings (of an economic or administrative variety) with townfolk, but Gaulish remaining the language of everyday interaction with other rural folk. A similar situation, with broadly similar social conditions, surely existed in Britain until at least the end of the fourth century. But whereas in Gaul the Germanic conquerors arrived with relatively little disruption to the existing linguistic situation, in Britain we find a complete disruption, with English becoming the language in general use in (it seems) all contexts. Thus Gaul shows a very gradual switch from Gaulish to Latin/Romance, with some subsequent Germanic input, while Britain seems to show a much more rapid switch to English from Celtic and (maybe) Latin (that is, if Latin retained any vitality in Britain at the time of the Anglo-Saxon settlement).

It is thus not surprising that Old French contained many more words of Celtic origin than Old English did, including a number of words with quite basic meanings. Just as interesting is how small a mark Gaulish left on the vocabulary of Old French, given that Gaulish and Latin/ Romance speakers were living in close proximity for such a long time, and given that the Gaulish speakers ultimately switched to Latin/ Romance/French. This may point us to an important parallel with the situation in Britain. French appears to have borrowed fairly sparingly from Celtic, probably because throughout the contact period Gaulish was a low-status language relative to Latin/Romance, the language of urban life and administration.

Turning aside for a moment from lexis, only very limited structural influence on French is usually attributed to Gaulish. Among phonological developments frequently (but very controversially) attributed to Gaulish influence on French (or to Celtic influence on Romance more generally) are:[14]

- The development of Latin /pt/ to /xt/ (thus merging with the reflex of /kt/) and of /ps/ to /xs/ (thus merging with the reflex of /ks/) at an early stage in the development of French, hence *capsa* > **kaxsa* (ultimately > *caisse*), *captīvus* > **kaxtivus* (ultimately > *chétif*). The development shown by /kt/ in most of western Romance is itself also frequently attributed to Celtic influence, e.g. *factum* > **faxtum* (ultimately > *fait*).
- The rounding of /u/ to /y/.
- The weakening of /pt/, /t/, /k/ in intervocalic position.

---

[14] See Lambert (1995) 46–7. For general surveys of the question and extensive further literature, see Felixberger (2003), Stefenelli (1996).

In syntax, it is sometimes speculated that cleft constructions in French may have arisen as a result of influence from a Gaulish substrate.[15] It has also been suggested that there may be a connection between the mixed system of decimal and vigesimal counting found in modern French and the similar systems found in some of the modern Celtic languages; compare French *quatre-vingt-dix* 'ninety', literally 'four-twenty-ten' (which gradually replaced *nonante* 'ninety') with Breton *pevar-ugent* 'eighty', literally 'four-twenty'; but there are problems with the hypothesis of Celtic substratal influence and rival explanations exist.[16]

5.4 The hypothesis of structural borrowing from Celtic in English ('the Celtic hypothesis')

By contrast with the situation as regards French, a great many claims have been made for non-lexical, contact-induced influence of Celtic on English. This has been a particular focus of scholarly attention in the past two decades, although all of these claims remain controversial. To catalogue all of the claims of Celtic influence would take far more space than is available in this book and would take us a long way from our central theme of lexical borrowing. Fortunately, good general surveys of this topic are now available and it will be sufficient here to give some pointers to some of the main topics.[17]

One perennial suggestion of Celtic influence concerns the verb *to be*. In English, this verb shows a mixed (or suppletive) paradigm, showing forms that originated as forms of three (or perhaps four) different, unrelated verbs; thus (i) *be*, (ii) *am, is,* and (iii) *was, were* all ultimately reflect different verbs (and *are* and *art* could just show another origin again, although they may belong with (ii)). In this respect, English is not very different from the other West Germanic languages. However, it does show interesting differences in how it uses these forms. In Old High German and Old Saxon, forms of types (i) and (ii) simply form part of a mixed paradigm of present tense forms; compare modern German *ich bin* 'I am' but *er ist* 'he is'. However, in Old

---

[15] Compare Lambert (1995) 68 and compare section 4.4 for similar suggestions with regard to English.

[16] See Felixberger (2003) 598.

[17] For recent overviews and references to some of the key literature, see Filppula et al. (2008), Filppula (2010).

English, fairly full sets of inflections exist for both types (i) and (ii), and some distinctive patterns can be detected in the ways that the different forms are used. For instance, the *be*-forms (type (i)) are often used for future time reference, and sometimes for iterative or durative present tense, while they are much less likely than the *am/is*-forms (type (ii)) to be found with adverbs such as *nū* 'now' or *ġȳt* 'yet'. Many scholars have drawn attention to the parallel with the way that two sets of forms (ultimately of the same origin as the Old English types (i) and (ii)) are used in Celtic languages, as for instance Welsh *byddaf,* which can realize consuetudinal present meaning ('I am wont to be') and also future ('I shall be'). Consequently, some scholars have seen the pattern in Old English as resulting from the influence of a substrate of Celtic speakers who had switched to English but had imported some Celtic habits of speech in their use of the forms already available in English; others have seen this as a pattern already in development in some varieties of West Germanic, which was reinforced by contact with Celtic languages; and others still have denied the possibility of Celtic influence entirely. Additionally, some have seen the mixed paradigm in other West Germanic languages as itself resulting ultimately from an earlier (probably adstratal or superstratal) period of Celtic contact, while many others have not.[18]

It has also been suggested that Celtic contact may have influenced the development of the English intensifier and reflexive forms in -*self* (e.g. *myself, yourself,* etc.),[19] or the development of the progressive construction using *be* plus the -*ing* form of the verb.[20]

The special numerals *yan, tan, tethera,* etc. (also found in many variants) that are used for sheep-counting, children's games, and other purposes in some northern varieties of English, owe at least something to one or more Celtic languages, although the nature and date of the input is uncertain; it could be substratal, or it could result from later, perhaps very much later, importation.[21]

One of the best-explored suggestions is that periphrastic constructions with the verb *do* result from Celtic contact. In English, a periphrastic construction with *do* is found in declarative sentences (e.g. *I do think this*)

---

[18] For discussion and references to the main contributions, see Filppula et al. (2008) 40–2, Lutz (2009) 227–49.

[19] See Poppe (2009), Filppula et al. (2008) 95–7.

[20] See Filppula et al. (2008) 59–72, 176–81.

[21] See especially Jackson (1955) 88, Barry (1969), Filppula et al. (2008) 102–5.

from the thirteenth century onwards (earliest in rhyming verse), and a little later in negative sentences and questions (e.g. *I do not think this, Do I think this?*). This appears to be at first a south-western feature, which spread to the standard variety, and thence to many other varieties; in modern use, it has shrunk back again to the south-west in declarative sentences, but remains usual in negative sentences and questions. Celtic has similar sentence types with its verb meaning 'do' plus a verbal noun (the Celtic languages have no infinitive), and it has been suggested that the English construction results from Celtic influence, probably from a substrate of speakers who imported this construction type when they switched from Celtic to English. The explanation normally given for this feature appearing so late in English is that it was in sociolinguistic terms a change from below, affecting first the speech of those people of low social status whose speech was least likely to be reflected in literary usage, and only spreading slowly into the sorts of high-prestige varieties reflected in written sources; the conservatism of the written language in the Old English period is often also cited as a factor. (It should be noted that there are at least two viable alternative explanations of periphrastic *do* that do not involve Celtic contact, and there are also similar phenomena in some continental Germanic varieties, which complicate explanations, if they are not taken to be coincidental independent developments.)[22]

Moving further away from lexis, other suggested areas of syntactic influence are: the shift from the external possessor to the internal possessor type of construction (e.g. *he has a pimple on his nose* rather than **he has a pimple on the nose*); the system of verbal agreement found in some northern varieties of Middle English known as the Northern Subject Rule;[23] the frequency of zero-relative or contact clauses in English, e.g. *a man I know* as opposed to *a man who I know*;[24] or the frequency of *it*-clefting, as in e.g. 'It was a bike that he bought (not a car)' or 'It was last year that he decided to buy a new bike',[25]

---

[22] For useful summaries of the now large literature in favour of Celtic influence on this feature, see van der Auwera and Genee (2002), Klemola (2002), Filppula et al. (2008) 49–59; for discussion of important alternative explanations, see Denison (1985), Denison (1993), and Garrett (1998, especially on the intertwined history of specifically habitual *do*).

[23] See Benskin (2011) for a recent assessment.

[24] See Filppula et al. (2008) 30–40 and 84–94 respectively.

[25] For these examples and further discussion, see Filppula (2009); see also Filppula et al. (2008) 72–84.

it being suggested that the very slow spread of such constructions in English results from underlying Celtic substratal influence.

The influence of a Celtic substrate is also sometimes suggested in various areas of phonology. For instance, Laker (2009) argues that the development of a phonemic contrast between /f/ and /v/ and /θ/ and /ð/ (and indirectly also between /s/ and /z/) in English is attributable to Celtic learners of English interpreting the allophonic distinction in English as a phonemic one (i.e. a distinction that can convey differences of meaning), since such phoneme pairs existed already in their own native language. It has also sometimes been suggested that the retention in English (unlike in other Germanic languages) of voiced and voiceless /θ/ and /ð/, and also of /w/, may owe something to Celtic influence.[26]

Although they are often presented collectively as the Celtic hypothesis, these suggestions are nearly all independent of one another, having in common simply the idea that there may have been Celtic substratal influence on English. For our purposes, the interesting question is how this would be likely to correlate with lexical borrowing. According to the current prevailing model in contact linguistics, perhaps rather surprisingly, extensive structural borrowing and minimal lexical borrowing are actually very compatible in situations where speakers have switched from a low-prestige to a high-prestige language:[27] speakers switching from Celtic to English may have had little motivation to bring words from the abandoned low-prestige language into the newly adopted high-prestige language, but various aspects of their linguistic behaviour (including perhaps aspects of their use of basic function words such as *be* or *do*) may have been shaped by their background as speakers of Celtic languages learning English. Thus, even if all of the suggestions listed do correctly identify Celtic influence on English (which many scholars would consider very unlikely), this still does not necessarily conflict with the observation that English shows little lexical borrowing from Celtic languages.

[26] This is one of a number of suggestions made in an early contribution to this debate by Tolkien: Tolkien (1963). For two important contributions suggesting either direct or indirect Celtic influence in other areas of phonology, see Schrijver (1999), Schrijver (2009).

[27] See especially Thomason and Kaufman (1988), Thomason (2001), Thomason (2003).

5.5 Epilogue: later lexical borrowing from Celtic languages

The varieties of english spoken in Wales, Cornwall, Scotland, the Isle of Man, and Ireland all show considerable lexical borrowing from the various Celtic languages spoken in those areas, although both the number of words borrowed and the sorts of loanwords that are found differ greatly in different times and places. This results from a number of complex factors, such as the relative prestige of the Celtic languages in each place and the manner in which English has been acquired and taught. Cultural loans predominate, especially words relating to the particular social and cultural practices of specific communities, and words relating to agriculture and topography. The (limited) extent to which any of these words have entered the general English vocabulary is a reflection of the (generally low) levels of prestige and interest that have been felt towards the different Celtic nationalities at different times.

Several words of Celtic origin that do not appear in Old English have since become part of the core vocabulary of English. Apart from *rich* and *down* (on the Old English and earlier histories of which see sections 4.2, 5.1), four other words of possible Celtic origin occur in Grant's survey of the 1,460 basic meanings in the Leipzig-Jakarta list as part of the cross-linguistic survey in Haspelmath and Tadmor (2009) (see further section 2.3): *baby*, *gull*, *trousers*, and *clan*. *Baby* also figured in the 1,000 most frequent words from the *BNC* considered in section 2.2.

There is a reasonable case to be made for *baby* ultimately showing a Celtic origin. Its antecedent could even have been borrowed as early as the Old English period; it would seem a natural borrowing in a situation where an English-speaking child had either a Celtic-speaking mother or a Celtic-speaking nurse. However, it is also quite possible that it shows no connection with Celtic whatever. The word *baby* is first attested in the late fourteenth century in Langland's *Piers Plowman*. It is a derivative formation from *babe*, with which it overlaps very considerably in meaning, plus a suffix *-y* which forms diminutive and hypocoristic formations (i.e. the addition of this suffix to a word conveys connotations of smallness and/or affection). *Babe* is also first attested in the late fourteenth century, also in a literary text, Gower's *Confessio Amantis*. *Babe* may have originated as a clipped form of *baban* 'baby, infant', a very rare word that is first attested in the first half of the thirteenth century in one of the manuscripts of the *Ancrene Wisse*, a devotional guide for anchoresses (see further sections 12.1.3, 13.1.3 on this text). This word may well be a borrowing from Welsh *baban*, which (although not itself recorded until the fourteenth century) may be a variant of *maban* 'little boy, infant' (first recorded in the thirteenth century, but there are good reasons for thinking it may be much earlier), itself a diminutive formation < *mab* 'son'. Welsh *maban* has the inflected form *faban*, which could also theoretically be the inflected form of a word *baban*. (This situation results from a sound change very early in the history of Welsh called lenition, and the resulting alternation of sounds is called soft mutation.) Hence *faban* may have been reanalysed as the inflected form of *baban*, and *baban* may thus have arisen as a variant of *maban*. So:

Welsh *mab* + *-an* > *maban*
maban, inflected *faban* > (by reanalysis) *baban*, inflected *faban*
Welsh *baban* > English *baban*
(English) *baban* > *babe*
babe + *-y* > *baby*

However, different explanations are possible at every turn in this story. The syllable /ba/ is (cross-linguistically) very common in familiar words for relationships within the close family group, because it is characteristic of early infantile vocalization, especially when reduplicated, i.e. it recalls the /ba/, /ba/ sounds made by very small children; compare /da/, /ma/ and e.g. *dada*, *mama*, etc. For this reason words of this shape are notoriously problematic for etymologists, because there is always the possibility that they have been created anew from the same, universal, source material. Thus *baby* could be a formation from reduplicated /ba/ with the ending remodelled after diminutive/hypocoristic *-y* (compare *daddy*, etc.); *babe* could be a clipping of **baba* < /ba/ /ba/. English *baban* could just about show a similar origin, although the *-n* would be a little difficult to explain; Welsh *baban* could itself be from /ba/ /ba/ with the Welsh diminutive suffix *-an*, rather than a variant of *maban*. It thus seems very likely that early Middle English *baban* is a borrowing from Welsh *baban*, because this gives us a better explanation for its form than any alternative explanation, but every other step in the chain of possible links between English *baby* and Celtic is very uncertain.

The bird name *gull* certainly shows a Celtic borrowing. It is first recorded in English in the middle of the fifteenth century in a Scottish text. Lockwood (1993 76–7) makes a good case for this being reasonably close to the date when it entered English, although it probably did so at the other end of the British Isles: the likeliest immediate donor form is late medieval

Cornish *gullen* < earlier *gullan* < *guilan*, cognate with Welsh *gwylan*, both from earlier *uilan*. The ending of *gullen* was probably perceived as a plural ending in Middle English (especially in south-western varieties), hence English *gull*.

Trouse, the antecedent of *trousers*, is a borrowing from Irish and Scottish Gaelic *triubhas*, as is *trews*. The borrowing is first recorded (as *trewis*) in Older Scots (compare section 1.5) at the beginning of the sixteenth century, denoting a distinctive (Highland) Scottish garment. It is also found in English sources from the second half of the sixteenth century, denoting a distinctive Irish garment, probably showing a separate borrowing from Irish, probably in the context of the Tudor reconquest of Ireland. It is only later found in extended use denoting similar garments coming to be worn elsewhere in Britain. The form *trouse* reflects a form that participated in the English Great Vowel Shift change /u:/ > /au/. Although the word is singular in Irish and Scottish Gaelic (and also sometimes in early use in English) the *-s* ending was perceived as plural in English, and *trouse* and *trews* came to be used with plural concord, and often also with a plural ending, hence *trouses*. Subsequently, this was remodelled after words such as *drawers*, giving the usual modern form *trousers*.

Clan is found from the fifteenth century, again at first only in Older Scots, and only with reference to a (chiefly Highland) Scottish cultural phenomenon, later spreading to other varieties of English, and also (at first in Scottish sources) coming to be applied to similar cultural phenomena outside Scotland. (The Scottish Gaelic and Irish word from which it is borrowed probably ultimately shows a borrowing from Latin *planta* 'young plant' in a specialized metaphorical use, 'children collectively'.)

The borrowing and subsequent spread of both *trouse/trews* and *clan* probably reflect the general perception among English speakers in these centuries of Highland Scotland and Ireland as archetypal representatives of the 'wild' and 'primitive', somewhat exotic places where different words are appropriate to refer to different social and cultural practices. The subsequent history of these words shows their extension in meaning to apply to similar garments or cultural phenomena from elsewhere.

The impact of such loanwords on the general vocabulary of English is tiny. As shown by Fig. 2.1 in section 2.1, among the Celtic languages, only Irish ranks among the twenty-five most prolific inputs in parts of *OED3* so far completed. If, as in Fig. 5.1, the first dates of Irish loanwords in *OED3* are mapped chronologically, it will be seen that they are spread fairly

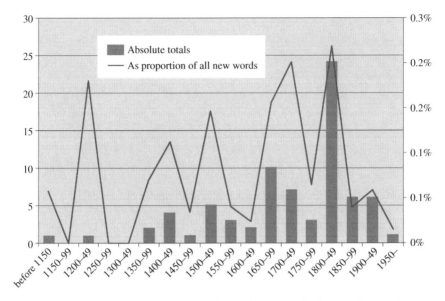

Fig. 5.1 Loanwords from Irish, as reflected by *OED3* (A–ALZ and M–RZ).

evenly across the history of English. The absolute totals of loanwords (the bars in the chart) show a peak in the early nineteenth century, but when the total is expressed as a proportion of all new words recorded by *OED3* in each period (the line in the chart), the variation appears much less significant. Most notably, the totals are very small in all periods (even if one takes into account that they reflect a little under one-third of the whole *OED*), and the percentage of all new words that come from Irish never reaches above 0.25% in any sub-period. The historical fluctuations appear erratic, although the sharp falling away after the mid nineteenth century is interesting. (Compare the much more revealing patterns shown by loanwords from many of the other languages among the top twenty-five donors, as examined in chapter 15.)

5.6 Conclusions

As stated at the beginning of this chapter, the amount of lexical borrowing from Celtic languages in early English is very small. The number of words of Celtic origin in the general vocabulary of modern English remains small, in spite of considerable later borrowing into the varieties of English spoken in Wales, Cornwall, Scotland, the Isle of Man, and Ireland.

A comparison with French showed that there is a much greater Celtic element in the lexis of modern French than in that of modern English, and that this penetrates more deeply into basic levels of the vocabulary. Indeed, the general vocabulary of modern English shows more words ultimately of Celtic origin as a result of later borrowing from French than it does from direct borrowing from Celtic languages. However, as we have seen, the Celtic contribution to the vocabulary of French is not in itself huge: it is relatively insignificant in comparison with what English has taken from French or Scandinavian, for instance. Yet Gaul would have seen hundreds of years in which Latin and Gaulish were in intimate contact as Latin gradually became dominant in the countryside as well as in the towns. The paucity of the borrowing probably comes down to social factors: Roman culture was the prestige culture and there was relatively little that the Romans wanted to learn from the Gauls, or even that the Gauls themselves needed to import Gaulish words to describe when they began to speak Latin. The borrowings that are found can mostly be ascribed to various fairly predictable areas: agricultural life, and one or two areas in which Gaulish technology was distinctive, such as brewing beer or the construction of various types of carts and chariots.

A similar explanation may lie behind why we find so little Celtic borrowing in Old English: by the time the Anglo-Saxons came, Roman Britain, whatever its former glories, had been long enough collapsed that there was little of interest to pass on to the Anglo-Saxons that they did not already know about from the continent. The Anglo-Saxons may have been barely at all more advanced in material culture, but they were in charge and held prestige as the new masters of Lowland Britain. Even if we take the view that the majority of the population remained of Celtic origin (the most difficult of the competing scenarios to accommodate from the point of view of the lexical evidence, if not from other perspectives), then it seems plausible that the switch to English may have taken place with so little lexical borrowing precisely because of the lower status of Celtic speakers and the absence of obvious technological or cultural novelties entering the new society from a Celtic source.

By contrast, the Anglo-Saxons did borrow a great deal of lexis from Latin even before the conversion to Christianity. However, as we will see in chapter 6, it is quite possible that this mostly took place either before the settlement in Britain or as a result of continuing contact with the continent after the settlement.

Part III

Old English and Proto-Old English in Contact with Latin

Introduction to part III

The three chapters in part III examine borrowing that took place across a very long historical period, from the relationships of Germani with Romans on the continent in imperial times, through to the aftermath of the Norman Conquest of 1066. One of the most interesting facts about many of the word histories looked at here is the difficulty of pinning down precisely when borrowing occurred, and in which social and cultural conditions. The overall number of borrowings is large (well over 500 loanwords, plus many semantic borrowings, plus many derivatives and compounds formed on the loanwords), but not so large that it is not feasible to take some account of all of the major borrowings in this period and of a large sample of the rarer ones as well. This period thus provides a useful way of examining in miniature many of the themes and issues that recur in the remainder of this book.

6

An overview of Latin loanwords in Old English

6.1 Estimating the scale of the contribution

It is no easy matter to identify how many distinct words there are in our total surviving Old English records, for both theoretical and practical reasons. The *Thesaurus of Old English* (*TOE*) lists approximately 34,000 distinct word forms. This is much higher than the *c.*18,000 contained in the concise dictionary Clark Hall (1960), or the estimate in the region of 23,000 or 24,000 in Scheler (1977 14, 74).[1] Completion of the *Dictionary of Old English* (*DOE*), which is being prepared in Toronto on the basis of a near-complete corpus of the surviving texts, will give a much clearer picture of the size of the Old English lexicon, although many rather grey areas will remain, especially concerning how we regard words that appear with their Latin inflections in Old English sentences.

There has been no recent complete appraisal of all of the Old English words that may be of Latin origin. It would be a very large task and it is unlikely to be attempted before the completion of the *DOE*, which would certainly make the task somewhat easier. Earlier scholarship was rather more adventurous in attempting comprehensive listings. An influential and still very useful list which drew on most of the available earlier scholarship is found in Serjeantson (1935).[2] Her Appendix A lists just over 520 loanwords

---

[1] Scheler's figures are drawn on also in the discussion in Kastovsky (1992), one of the most detailed recent surveys of the lexis of Old English.

[2] Compare the assessment in Wollmann (1990a) 63.

immediately from Latin. There are some inclusions that are very dubious, but many more omissions (including some doubtless accidental omissions of words that are actually mentioned in her main text but omitted from the appendix). Words which there are strong grounds for regarding as post-Conquest borrowings into Old English from Latin and/or French (i.e. words borrowed between 1066 and 1150) are largely omitted from her list, although there are varying opinions on some cases, and certainly some of the words she does include are first attested in manuscripts dating from after the Conquest. Scheler (1977 38) estimates a further 50 borrowings between 1066 and 1150, but the precise basis for this estimate is not clear. (We look at a few such cases in part V.)

Probably the number of fairly securely identified pre-Conquest Latin loanwords can be put at at least 600.[3] I give in section 6.3 what is intended as a comprehensive list of words that have a reasonable likelihood of being early borrowings (although some are only doubtfully of Latin origin, and a few are not entirely securely attested as English words): these come to 261 in total. I then list a further 36 words for which early borrowing has often been suggested but is less certain. Finally, I give a very selective list of 137 examples of later loanwords. This third list could easily be extended very considerably with further secure examples of later borrowing, although, as we will investigate, it is extremely difficult to establish a definitive list of later borrowings.

If we take an estimate of at least 600 words borrowed (immediately) from Latin, and a total of around 34,000 words in Old English, then, conservatively, around 1.75% of the total are borrowed from Latin. If we include all compounds and derivatives formed on Latin loanwords in Old English, then the total of Latin-derived vocabulary probably comes closer to 4.5% (see further section 7.2 on this), although this figure may be a little too high, since estimates of the total size of the Old English vocabulary (native and borrowed) probably rather underestimate the numbers of compounds and derivatives.

This total includes some relatively common words and there is some penetration even among quite basic levels of the vocabulary. A good number of these borrowings survive into modern English, especially from among the earliest borrowings. It is also worth bearing in mind that the lexis of Old English overall showed an extremely large degree of transparency, having a great many large word families consisting of a root word plus very

---

[3] Compare Wollmann (1993) 1.

many analysable compounds and derivatives formed from this root word;[4] even allowing for the fact that many Latin loanwords in Old English also have compound and derivative formations, it is still probably the case that the Latin contribution to the stock of root words in Old English is rather higher than 1.75%.

On the other hand, it is clear that many of the Latin-derived words, particularly the later ones, belonged only to specialist learned discourse, although our surviving records seldom tell us quite as much as we would like to know about the register or degree of currency of particular words.

As already mentioned, quite aside from the loanwords there are large numbers of loan translations and other instances of semantic borrowing, although this is an area where certainty is often elusive. See further section 8.3 on this.

6.2 Earlier and later borrowings

6.2.1 Identifying earlier and later borrowings

We can divide the Latin borrowings fairly confidently into two broad groups, earlier borrowings and later borrowings, although there are many doubtful individual cases. Probably the dividing line between the two falls around the middle of the seventh century, but this can only be regarded as a very rough estimate, since it is before the period for which we have any substantial Old English written records.

Unlike the situation in most later periods of the history of English, when we are looking at Old English evidence the date of the first document in which a word is recorded is seldom a very sound guide to the date at which it was borrowed. If we encounter words first in texts from the second half of the eleventh or the twelfth century (i.e. from the time of the Norman Conquest or after), then we may attach some weight to this fact, and consider them late introductions to Old English, since we have a large body of earlier records against which to compare. However, even in this late Old English period there are anomalous cases of words first recorded in

---

[4] For useful illustration of this, see Kastovsky (1992) 294–8; see also the introductory presentation of high-frequency words arranged by word group in Barney (1985), although this includes only a small selection of illustrative compound and derivative formations for most word families.

very late sources that must have existed much earlier. For example, *pīn* 'pain, torture, anguish, punishment' is attested in only one reasonably secure pre-Conquest example (from a severely damaged manuscript), but it was probably a relatively early borrowing, and derivative formations formed from it are much better attested in Old English sources.

As noted in section 3.6, our written records are very patchy until we reach the large body of English texts of the late tenth and early eleventh century which, directly or indirectly, reflect the great impetus in vernacular writing and learning arising from the Benedictine reforms of the late tenth century. With the exception of words with basic core meanings, omission from the literary record before the late tenth century gives no good indication that a word did not exist earlier. It should also be borne in mind that our knowledge of all dialects of Old English other than West Saxon is extremely limited, for all periods.

The evidence on which Latin borrowings can be divided into an early and a late group comes instead from internal, linguistic evidence, and especially from whether words show the effects of the major sound changes that took place (largely or entirely) before the date of our earliest surviving texts. If a borrowed word shows a phonetic environment in which a particular change would normally have occurred but fails to show this change, the normal assumption is that it was borrowed later than the period in which this change operated. If the word does show this change, then it is normally assumed that it was in the language by the time this change occurred. (There are complicating factors, especially as regards the latter assumption: see examples in section 8.1.) Sound changes that affected words in Vulgar Latin before they were borrowed into English are also of importance. In the past, the assumption has often been made that a more or less definite date can be assigned to a sound change and this can therefore be used as a firm dating criterion for word histories. However, more recent work on sound change stresses the extent to which most changes are very gradual, spreading slowly from word to word, and from community to community. In this perspective, drawing dating information from the presence or absence of various sound changes becomes a rather more tentative, at times even precarious, affair.

Another important criterion in assessing the date of borrowing is whether there are parallel borrowed forms in other Germanic languages. If all of the forms in other Germanic languages show the same linguistic features pointing to early borrowing, this can be a strong piece of corroborating evidence for early borrowing.

Semantic criteria are also often applied. Words to do with the detail of the life of the Church are unlikely to have been borrowed before the early seventh century at the earliest, although some basic words to do with Christianity (and especially its buildings and material culture, as well as the basics of belief) may have been known even to pagans. More elaborate claims are sometimes based on semantic criteria, for instance that plant names are likely to have been introduced in the context of monastic gardens: however, such approaches run the risk of oversimplification and of overestimating how much we know about precise cultural contexts, especially in the early period.

6.2.2 Characteristics of earlier and later borrowings

The context for most of the later borrowings is certain: they are nearly all words connected with the religious world or with learning, which were largely overlapping categories in the Anglo-Saxon world.[5] Many of them are only very lightly assimilated into Old English, if at all. In fact it is debatable whether some of them should even be regarded as borrowed words, or instead as single-word switches to Latin in an Old English document, since it is not uncommon for words only ever to occur with their Latin case endings.

The earlier borrowings include many more words that are of reasonably common occurrence in Old English and later, for instance names of some common plants and foodstuffs, as well as some very basic words to do with the religious life. If we could pin down the time and place when these words were borrowed, this would cast real light on the darkest periods of Anglo-Saxon history. As we will see, though, internal linguistic evidence can in most cases give us only very limited insights. We can often establish with reasonable certainty that one word is an earlier borrowing than another. It is much more difficult to progress from this relative dating to an absolute dating, or in other words to establish clear points of connection between linguistic and non-linguistic history. It is generally even more difficult to establish the place and cultural context of a particular borrowing with any certainty: all too often there are multiple possibilities and it can be rash (and sometimes a real distortion of the evidence) to pick out one possible context to the exclusion of others.

---

[5] For a very useful short assessment of the language contact situation, see Timofeeva (2010).

One particularly difficult problem is determining whether words were borrowed after the Anglo-Saxon settlement of Lowland Britain, or before this, on the continent. In fact, it is probably wrong to think of a very sharply defined 'before' and 'after', since the process of settlement was a gradual one, and there were also continuing close contacts with the continent after this period. The linguistic evidence often leaves very considerable doubt as to whether a borrowing occurred on the continent as far back as late imperial times, or in England, perhaps as late as the introduction of Christianity or even later.[6]

6.2.3 Attempts to distinguish chronological and geographical layers of borrowing among the early loanwords

A major focus of earlier scholarship, most notably Pogatscher (1888), was to attempt to distinguish between words borrowed while the Anglo-Saxons were still on the continent, and words borrowed after they came to Britain, largely on the basis of sound changes in Old English and in Latin. Serjeantson (1935) drew on this scholarship to divide her list of Latin loanwords into three chronological groupings, described as:

(A) Words from the Continental period, up to about 400, showing early borrowing by corresponding forms in other Germanic dialects, or by their phonological form (i.e. absence of early Romance changes, or presence of sound-changes which took place before or very shortly after the settlement of the English in this country).

(B) Words probably borrowed in Britain, 450–650. These are still loans from the spoken language.

(C) After 650. Late loan-words, including those of learned origin introduced through the written language (marked L).

(Serjeantson (1935) 271, 277, 281.)

There are echoes of this approach in most of the current handbooks on the history of English (albeit often unacknowledged), but the division between Serjeantson's periods A and B is very problematic. Certainly, there are some words that are almost certainly very early borrowings, and there are some that can be confidently regarded as much later borrowings, probably

---

[6] Several key references in the voluminous literature on this subject are Pogatscher (1888), Jackson (1953, especially 246–56), Wollmann (1990a), Wollmann (1990b), Wollmann (1993), Gneuss (1993); the latter two pieces are particularly suitable starting places for further reading.

attributable to very roughly the first half of the seventh century. However, recent scholarly surveys, especially Wollmann (1990a), have suggested strongly that there are too many very doubtful cases to divide the material into periods A and B as Serjeantson does. Indeed, as already noted, the settlement itself seems to many modern scholars a rather more fuzzy division than it seemed to most earlier scholars: even once the main period of settlement was over, continuing contacts with the continent may well have remained a significant factor, right up until the Conversion and beyond. The material awaits a thorough reappraisal: Wollmann's survey looks at only a small number of words in depth, and aspects of his methodology have been criticized;[7] Feulner (2000) provides a detailed account of the not insignificant number of words that are ultimately of Greek origin (see further section 8.2.1), establishing a very sound methodology for their investigation, but is often rather agnostic on some of the more disputed questions of dating. However, from the current state of the subject, it seems very unlikely that a confident assignment of all of the material to pre- and post-settlement phases of borrowing could again be attempted.

In the listing given here, I attempt only a broad division into (probable) earlier and later borrowings, roughly either side of AD 650,[8] although in chapter 8 I return to some of the criteria by which at least some of the pre-AD 650 borrowings can be tied to a narrower dating with at least a reasonable degree of confidence.

6.3 The loanwords

This section offers what is intended to be a comprehensive list of early borrowings (before c.650), followed by a selection of the later borrowings.

For the later period, I have included words that are attested more frequently, or that show signs of greater phonological or morphological integration into Old English, as well as a sample of rarer, less thoroughly integrated words. I have listed all words that could potentially show any continuity with later English words (see further section 7.5.1 on these). Very

---

[7] See Dietz (1992), but see also Dietz (2011) for an account critical of attempts that have been made to use place-name evidence to support the supposition of very early insular borrowing of certain words.

[8] Compare the broad framework adopted for the detailed discussion of individual cases in Campbell (1959).

many of the later borrowings appear to have been confined to learned contexts in Old English. For several (partly overlapping) reasons it is very difficult to count the number of such words in Old English accurately. The completion of the *DOE* will give a much clearer picture, as individual contexts and uses are re-examined carefully; it will doubtless also bring to light further loanwords omitted from earlier dictionaries and surveys. However, there are also difficult theoretical issues: many of these words appear sometimes with English inflections and sometimes with Latin inflections but embedded in English sentences, and there are some interesting and not yet completely resolved questions concerning what constitutes an Old English word in such contexts (see section 7.4).

Some general notes on these listings:

Some of the Old English words are marked with an asterisk. These fall into two groups. Firstly, words that are not directly attested in Old English, but whose existence is implied either by words that seem to be derivatives from them, or by later English words (or by both). In all such cases the asterisked form is followed by a comment in parentheses explaining what the evidence implying its existence is. See e.g. *cōfrian, *mūtian, *platian. Secondly, there are words whose existence depends on the interpretation of doubtful or disputed attestations. See e.g. *ċiċeling, *delfīn, *sīric.

Many borrowings occur in Old English in a variety of different word forms. These can reflect any of several different factors: (a) different chronological layers of borrowing from Latin; (b) remodelling of an existing borrowing after its Latin etymon, giving the appearance of the reversal of earlier sound changes; or (c) more or less contemporary borrowing of the same Latin word in forms that show different degrees of assimilation to the Old English sound system. In some, especially older, listings of loanwords there is a strong bias towards assuming that most such cases show different chronological layers of borrowing from Latin, and such variants are hence ascribed to different historical sub-periods; this is the approach frequently (although by no means consistently) taken in Serjeantson (1935). My approach here is different and more in line with that generally taken in the *DOE*: in most cases I list such forms side by side, without explicit comment, but normally with the earlier form(s) listed before later ones. For comment on some examples, see section 8.1. In a very few cases, where the later form differs from the earlier one in ways that could not be explained by substitution of one or two sounds from the Latin word, I have marked the later forms explicitly with 'also (later)' (see e.g. later *antifon, antyfon* beside earlier *antefn*, or later *lātīn* beside earlier *læden*). I have only listed borrowings entirely separately from one another when there is a very significant difference in meaning as well as word form, e.g. *ynċe* 'inch' and *yntse* 'ounce' (both < Latin *uncia*).[9]

To make the forms more transparent for readers less familiar with Old English, I have added macrons to indicate long vowels, and I have used dotted *ċ* and *sċ* to represent /tʃ/ and /ʃ/ respectively and *ġ* to represent /j/ (on the origins of these sounds, see section 8.1.1). However, it should be noted that these diacritics are 'editorial' interventions in the forms, often based on suppositions about the likely pronunciation of a word form, rather than on hard evidence. I have generally passed over questionable or doubtful cases silently.

The Latin forms given as etymons are mostly attested forms (rather than reconstructed ones), and I have selected the attested forms that are most similar to the form or forms that were probably borrowed into Old English. I have given asterisked (i.e. unattested, reconstructed) forms only sparingly, normally only in cases where the form that is usually assumed as the direct etymon of an Old English form differs very significantly from the attested forms. I have not indicated vowel length in any of the Latin forms, since to record only the classical Latin quantities could be misleading without detailed notes on the changes in quantity that are taken to underlie many of the borrowings into Old English. For similar reasons I have not periodized any of the Latin forms. I have not distinguished here those words that had come into Latin from other languages: see especially section 8.2.1 on words ultimately of Greek origin.

I have omitted borrowed names of peoples (and places), and transparent derivatives from these, e.g. *rōmānisċ* 'Roman' < *Rōmāne* 'the Romans'.

6.3.1 Early borrowings (to *c.* AD 650)

I have grouped nouns into a series of semantic categories, although in some cases the assignment to a particular category is less secure than in others. I have given footnotes on some of the most difficult cases. Verbs and adjectives are listed separately.

---

[9] Compare similarly: *tæfl* and *tabele, tabul, tabule*; *clūstor* and *clauster*; *lopust* and *loppestre, lopystre*.

Religion and the Church   Abbod, *abbot* 'abbot' [L *abbat-, abbas*]; *abbodesse* 'abbess' [L *abbatissa*]; *antefn*, also (later) *antifon, antyfon* 'antiphon (type of liturgical chant)' [L *antifona, antefona*];[10] *ælmesse, ælmes* 'alms, charity' [L **alimosina*, variant of *elemosina*]; *bisċeop* 'bishop' [probably L *episcopus*];[11] *cristen* 'Christian' [L *christianus*]; *dēofol, dīofol* 'devil' [perhaps Latin *diabulus*]; *draca* 'dragon, monstrous beast; the devil' [L *draco*]; *engel, angel* 'angel' [probably L *angelus*]; *mæsse, messe* 'mass' (the religious ceremony) [L *missa*]; *munuc* 'monk' [L *monachus*]; *mynster* 'monastery; important church' [L *monasterium*]; *nunne* 'nun' [L *nonna*]; *prēost* 'priest' [probably L **prebester, presbyter*]; *senoð, seonoð, sinoð, sionoð* 'council, synod, assembly' [L *synodus*].

Learning and scholarship   Læden 'Latin; any foreign language', also (later) *lātīn* 'Latin' [L *Latina*]; *sċolu*, also (later) *scōl* 'troop, band; school' [L *schola*].[12]

Plants, fruit, and products of plants   Bēte 'beet, beetroot' [L *beta*]; *billere* denoting several water plants [L *berula*]; *box* 'box tree', later also 'box, receptacle' [L *buxus*];[13] *celendre, cellendre* 'coriander' [L *coliandrum*]; *ċerfille, ċerfelle* 'chervil' [L *caerefolium*]; **ċiċeling* 'chickpea' [L *cicer*]; *ċīpe* 'onion' [L *cepe*]; *ċiris-*(bēam) 'cherry tree' [L **ceresia, cerasium*]; *ċisten-, ċistel-, ċist-*(bēam) 'chestnut tree' [L *castinea* or *castanea*]; *coccel* 'corn cockle, or other grain-field weed' [L **cocculus < coccum*]; *codd-*(æppel) 'quince' [L *cydonium, cotoneum*, or *cotonium*]; *consolde* '(perhaps) daisy or comfrey' [L *consolida*]; *corn-*(trēo) 'cornel tree' [L *cornus*]; *cost* 'costmary'

[10] The form *antefn* probably shows a borrowing very early in the Christian period. See Feulner (2000) 79–81.

[11] On the possibility of borrowing from Greek via Gothic in the case of this word and in those of *dēofol*, *engel*, and *prēost*, see section 8.2.1.

[12] Since the written forms of *sċolu* and *scōl* in Old English manuscripts differ only in the nominative singular (*scolu* and *scol*), most of the surviving examples could theoretically reflect either word form. It is certain that the early form *sċolu* occurs in the meanings 'band, troop' as well as 'school'. It is very likely that the later form *scōl* does as well, but this cannot be proven completely satisfactorily. On the origin of both form types, see section 8.1.4.

[13] On the complicated question of whether the meaning 'box, receptacle' shows a re-borrowing or subsequent semantic influence (or even a coincidental semantic development within English), see Wollmann (1990a) 324–39.

[L *costum*]; *cymen* 'cumin' [L *cuminum*]; *cyrfet* 'gourd' [L *cucurbita*]; *earfe* plant name, probably vetch [L *ervum*]; *elehtre* '(probably) lupin' [L *electrum*]; *eofole* 'dwarf elder, danewort' [L *ebulus*]; *eolone, elene* 'elecampane' (a plant) [L *inula, helenium*]; *finol, finule, finugle* 'fennel' [L *fenuculum*]; *glædene* a plant name (usually for a type of iris) [L *gladiola*]; *humele* 'hop plant' [L *humulus*]; *lāser* 'weed, tare' [L *laser*]; *leahtric, leahtroc*, also (later) *lactuce* 'lettuce' [L *lactuca*]; **lent* 'lentil' [L *lent-, lens*]; *lufestiče* 'lovage' [L *luvesticum*]; *mealwe* 'mallow' [L *malva*]; **mīl* 'millet' [L *milium*]; *minte, minta* 'mint' [L *mentha*]; *nǣp* 'turnip' [L *napus*]; *nefte* 'catmint' [L *nepeta*]; *oser* or *ōser* 'osier' [L *osaria*]; *persic* 'peach' [L *persicum*]; *peru* 'pear' [L *pirum, pera*]; *pič* 'pitch' (the resinous substance) [L *pic-, pix*]; *pīn* 'pine' [L *pinus*]; *pipeneale* 'pimpernel' [L *pipinella*]; *pipor* 'pepper' [L *piper*]; *pirie* 'pear tree' [L **pirea*]; *pise, *peose* 'pea' [L *pisum*]; *plūme* 'plum; plum tree' and *plȳme* 'plum; plum tree' [both perhaps L *pruna*];[14] *pollegie* 'pennyroyal' [L *pulegium*]; *popiġ, papiġ* 'poppy' [L *papaver*]; *porr* 'leek' [L *porrum*]; *rǣdič* 'radish' [L *radic-, radix*]; *rūde* 'rue' [L *ruta*]; *syrfe* 'service tree' [L **sorbea, sorbus*]; *ynne-* (in *ynnelēac*) 'onion' [L *unio*].

Animals   *Assa* 'ass' [L *asinus*, perhaps via Celtic];[15] *capun* 'capon' [probably L *capon-, capo*]; *cat, catte* 'cat' [L *cattus*]; *cocc* 'cock, rooster' [L *coccus*]; **cocc* (in *sǣcocc*) 'cockle' [perhaps L **coccum*]; *culfre* 'dove' [perhaps L **columbra, columbula*]; *cypera* 'salmon at the time of spawning' [L *cyprinus*]; *elpend, ylpend* 'elephant', also shortened to *ylp* [L *elephant-, elephans*]; *eosol, esol* 'ass' [L *asellus*]; *lempedu*, also (later) *lamprede* 'lamprey' [L *lampreda*]; *mūl* 'mule' [L *mulus*]; *muscelle* 'mussel' [L *musculus*]; *olfend* 'camel' [probably L *elephant-, elephans*, with the change in meaning arising from semantic confusion]; *ostre* 'oyster' [L *ostrea*]; *pēa* 'peafowl' [L *pavon-, pavo*]; **pine-* (in **pinewincle*, as suggested emendation of *winewincle*) 'winkle' [perhaps L *pina*]; *rēnġe* 'spider' [L *aranea*]; *strȳta* 'ostrich' [L *struthio*]; *trūht* 'trout' [L *tructa*]; *turtle, turtur* 'turtle dove' [L *turtur*].

Food and drink (see also plants and animals)   *Cȳse, čēse* 'cheese' [L *caseus*]; *foca* 'cake baked on the ashes of the hearth' (only attested with reference to Biblical contexts or antiquity) [L *focus*]; *must* 'wine must, new wine'

---

[14] For summary of the controversy surrounding these two words, see Feulner (2000) 408–11.

[15] Compare section 5.1.

[L *mustum*]; *seim* 'lard, fat' (only attested in figurative use) [L **sagimen, sagina*]; *senap, senep* 'mustard' [L *sinapis*]; *wīn* 'wine' [L *vinum*].

Medicine   Butere 'butter' [L *butyrum, buturum*];[16] *ċeren* 'wine reduced by boiling for extra sweetness' [L *carenum*]; *eċed* 'vinegar' [L *acetum*]; *ele* 'oil' [L *oleum*];[17] *fēfer* or *fefer* 'fever' [L *febris*]; *flȳtme* 'lancet' [L *fletoma*].[18]

Transport; riding and horse gear   Ancor, ancra 'anchor (also in figurative use)' [L *ancora*]; *cæfester* 'muzzle, halter, bit' [L *capistrum*, perhaps via Celtic];[19] *ċæfl* 'muzzle, halter, bit' [L *capulus*]; *ċearriċge* (meaning very uncertain, perhaps 'carriage') [perhaps L *carruca*];[20] *punt* 'punt' [L *ponton-, ponto*]; *sēam* 'burden; harness; service which consisted in supplying beasts of burden' [L *sauma, sagma*]; *strǣt* 'road; paved road, street' [L *strata*].

Warfare and weapons   Camp 'battle; war; field' [L *campus*];[21] *cocer* 'quiver' [perhaps L *cucurum*].[22]

Tools and implements   Cucler 'spoon' [L *coclear*]; *culter* 'coulter; (once) dagger' [L *culter*]; *fæċele* 'torch' [L *facula*]; *fann* 'winnowing fan' [L *vannus*]; *forc, forca* 'fork' [L *furca*]; **fossere* or *fostere* 'spade' [L *fossorium*]; *inseġel, insiġle* 'seal; signet' [L *sigillum*]; *līne* 'cable, rope, line, cord; series, row, rule, direction' [probably L *linea*]; *mattuc, meottuc, mettoc* 'mattock'

---

[16]   For a summary of sharply diverging opinions on the dating of this word, see Feulner (2000) 108–10. As regards the semantic category to which this word belongs, I have placed it here rather than under Food because, as noted in the *DOE*, although there are references to use as food in Old English texts, the majority of the *c.*200 recorded instances in Old English texts are in medical recipes. See further section 7.5.2.

[17]   Placed in this category because of its frequent occurrence in medical recipes, but the word could also be placed under Food (because of occurrences referring to use in baking) or under Religion and the Church (because of occurrences with reference to use of oil in anointing people).

[18]   See Feulner (2000) 232–4 on various views concerning the date and circumstances of borrowing of this very rare word.

[19]   See especially Wollmann (1990a) 613–24, (1993) 20–1.

[20]   This word occurs only in glosses, as a gloss of a Latin (or perhaps Greek) word that is similarly obscure: see the *DOE*.

[21]   On this word, see further Dietz (2011) 274–9.

[22]   This is only very doubtfully a Latin loanword and should perhaps be omitted from any listing: see Wollmann (1990a) 187.

[perhaps L *matteuca]; mortere 'mortar' [L mortarium]; panne 'pan' [perhaps L panna]; pægel 'wine vessel; liquid measure' [L pagella]; pihten part of a loom [L pecten]; pīl 'pointed object; dart, shaft, arrow; spike, nail; stake' [L pilum]; pīle 'mortar' [L pila]; pinn 'pin, peg, pointer; pen' [probably L penna]; pīpe 'tube, pipe; pipe (= wind instrument); small stream' [L pipa]; pundur 'counterpoise; plumb line' [L ponder-, pondus]; seġne 'fishing net' [L sagena]; sicol 'sickle' [L *sicula, secula < secare 'to cut']; spynġe, also (later) sponge 'sponge' [L spongia, spongea]; timple instrument used in weaving [L templa]; turl 'ladle' [L trulla].

Buildings and parts of buildings; construction; towns and settlements
Ċeafor-(tūn), cafer-(tūn) 'hall, court' [L capreus]; ċealc, calc 'chalk, plaster' [L calc-, calx]; ċeaster, ċæster 'fortification; city, town (especially one with a wall)' [L castra]; ċipp 'rod, stick, beam (especially in various specific contexts)' [probably L cippus]; clifa, cleofa, cliofa 'chamber, cell, den, lair' [perhaps L clibanus 'oven']; clūse, clause 'lock; confine, enclosure; fortified pass' [L clausa]; clūstor 'lock, bolt, bar, prison' [L claustrum]; cruft 'crypt, cave' [L crupta]; cyċene 'kitchen' [L coquina]; cylen 'kiln, oven' [L culina]; *cylene 'town' (only as place-name element) [L colonia]; mūr 'wall' [L murus]; mylen 'mill' [L molina]; pearroc 'enclosure; fence that forms an enclosure' [perhaps L parricus]; pīsle or pisle 'warm room' [L pensilis]; plætse, plæce, plæse 'open place in a town, square, street' [L platea]; port 'town with a harbour; harbour, port; town (especially one with a wall or a market)' [L portus]; post 'post; doorpost' [L postis]; pytt 'hole in the ground; well; excavated hole; pit; grave; hell' [perhaps L puteus]; sċindel 'roof shingle' [L scindula]; solor 'upper room; hall, dwelling; raised platform' [L solarium]; tīġle, tīgele, tigele 'earthen vessel; potsherd; tile, brick' [L tegula]; torr 'tower' [L turris]; weall 'wall, rampart, earthwork' [L vallum]; wīċ 'dwelling; village; camp, fortress' [L vicus].

Containers, vessels, and receptacles   Amber 'vessel, dry or liquid measure' [L amphora, ampora];[23] binn, binne 'basket, bin; manger' [L benna]; (for box 'box, receptacle' see under Plants); buteruc 'bottle' [perhaps from a derivative of L buttis]; byden 'vessel, container; cask, tub; tub-shaped geographical

---

[23] The second element of this word was probably remodelled as a result of association with beran 'to bear' or its Germanic base.

feature' [probably L *butina]; bytt 'bottle, flask, cask, wine skin' [L *buttia]; ċelċ, cælic, calic 'drinking vessel, cup' [L calic-, calix]; ċist, ċest 'chest, box, coffer; reliquary; coffin' [L cista]; cuppe 'cup', also copp 'cup, beaker; gloss for Latin spongia sponge' [L cuppa]; cȳf 'large jar, vessel, or tub' [L *cupia < cupa]; cȳfl 'tub, bucket' [L cupellus]; cyll, cylle 'leather bottle, leather bag; ladle; oil lamp' [L culleus]; ċytel, ċetel 'cooking-vessel (usually of metal), kettle, cauldron' [L catillus]; disċ 'dish, bowl, plate' [L discus]; earc, earce, earca, also arc, arce, arca 'ark (especially Noah's ark or the ark of the covenant), chest, coffer' [L arca]; gabote, gafote kind of dish or platter [L gabata]; ġellet 'jug, bowl, or basin' [L galleta]; læfel, lebil 'spoon, cup, bowl, vessel' [L labellum]; orc 'pitcher, crock, cup' [L orca]; pott 'pot' [perhaps L pottus]; sacc, also sæcc 'sack, bag' [L saccus]; sester 'jar, vessel; a measure' [L sextarius]; spyrte 'basket' [probably L sporta, *sportea].

Coins, money; weights and measures, units of measurement Dīner, dīnor type of coin, denarius [L denarius]; mīl 'mile' [L milia]; mydd 'a measure' [L modius]; mynet 'a coin; coinage, money' [L moneta]; oma 'a liquid measure' [L ama]; pund 'pound (in weight or money); pint' [L pondo]; trimes 'unit of weight, a drachm; name of a coin' [L tremissis]; ynċe 'inch' [L uncia]; yntse 'ounce' [L uncia].

Transactions and payments Ċēap 'purchase, sale, transaction, market, possessions, price' [L caupō or caupōnārī: see section 4.3]; toll, also toln, tolne 'toll, tribute, rent, duty' [L toloneum]; trifet 'tribute' [L tributum].

Clothing; fabric Belt 'belt, girdle' [L balteus]; bīsæċċ 'pocket' [L bisaccium]; cælis 'foot-covering', also (later) calc 'sandal' [L calceus]; ċemes 'shirt, undergarment' [L camisia]; ġecorded 'having cords, corded (or perhaps fringed)' [L corda]; cugele '(monk's) cowl' [L cuculla]; fīfele 'broach, clasp' [L fibula]; mentel 'cloak' [L mantellum]; pæll, pell 'fine or rich cloth; purple cloth; altar cloth; rich robe' [L pallium]; pyleċe 'fur robe' [L pellicia]; seolc 'silk' [perhaps L sericum]; sīde 'silk' [L seta]; *sīric 'silk' [perhaps L sericum]; socc 'light shoe' [L soccus]; swiftlēre 'slipper' [L subtalaris].

Furniture and furnishing Meatte, matte 'mat; underlay for a bed' [L matta]; mēse, mīse 'table' [L mensa]; pyle, pylu 'pillow, cushion' [L pulvinus]; sċamol, sċemol, sċeomol, sċeamol 'stool, footstool, bench' [L *scamellum]; stræl, strēaġl 'curtain; quilt, matting, bed' [L stragula]; stræt 'bed' [L stratum].

Precious stones   Ġimm 'gem, precious stone, jewel; also in figurative use' [L *gemma*]; *meregrot* 'pearl' [L *margarita*, but showing folk-etymological alteration after an English word for 'sea' and (probably) an English word for 'fragment, particle']; *pærl* '(very doubtfully) pearl' [perhaps L *perla*].

Roles, ranks, and occupations (non-religious or not specifically religious) Cāsere 'emperor; ruler' [L *caesar*]; *fullere* 'fuller' [L *fullo*]; *mangere* 'merchant, trader' [L *mango*]; *mæġester*, also (later) *māġister* or *magister* 'leader, master, teacher' [L *magister*]; *myltestre* 'prostitute' [L *meretrix*, with remodelling of the ending after the Old English feminine agent noun suffix -*estre*]; *prafost*, also *profost* 'head, chief, officer' [L *praepositus, propositus*]; *sūtere* 'shoemaker' [L *sutor*].

Punishment, judgement, codes of behaviour   Pīn 'pain, torture, anguish, punishment' [L *poena*];[24] *regol, reogol* 'rule; principle; code of rules; wooden ruler' [L *regula*]; *scrift* 'something decreed as a penalty; penance; absolution; confessor; judge' [L *scriptum*].

Verbs   *Cōfrian 'to recover' (implied by *acōfrian* in the same meaning) [L *recuperare*]; *cyrtan 'to shorten' (implied by *cyrtel* 'garment, tunic, cloak, gown' and (probably) *ġecyrted* 'cut off, shortened') [L *curtus*, adjective]; *dīligian* 'to erase, rub out; to destroy, obliterate' [L *delere*]; *impian* 'to graft; to busy oneself with' [L *imputare*]; *mūtian (implied by *bemūtian* 'to exchange' and *mūtung* 'exchange') [L *mutare*];[25] *nēomian 'to sound sweetly' or *nēome 'sound' [L *neuma*, noun];[26] *pinsian* 'to weigh, consider, reflect' [L *pensare*]; *pīpian* 'to play on a pipe' [L *pipare*]; *pluccian* 'to pluck' [perhaps L *piluccare*]; *pundrian (implied by *apyndrian, apundrian* 'to weigh, to adjudge') [L *ponderare*, if not a derivative of OE *pundur*]; *pynġan* 'to prick' [L *pungere*]; *scrīfan* 'to allot, prescribe, impose; to hear confession; to receive absolution; to have regard to' [L *scribere*]; *seġlian* 'to seal' [L *sigillare*]; *seġnian* 'to make the sign of the cross; to consecrate, bless'

[24] See section 6.2.1 on the complications with this example.

[25] Opinions are divided on the date of borrowing, although most scholars favour the hypothesis of early borrowing: see Wollmann (1990a) 167.

[26] The single example, from the poem 'The Fortunes of Men', reads in the manuscript *neome cende*; for a long time this has been emended to *neomegende*, taken to be the present participle of a verb *nēomian 'to sound sweetly'; see Stanley (2003) for an interpretation as a noun *nēome (ultimately of the same origin), reading the half-line of the poem tentatively as *næġl neoma[n] cende* 'the plectrum brought forth the melody'.

[L *signare*, if not < OE *seġn*]; *-stoppian* (implied by *forstoppian*) 'to obstruct, stop up' [perhaps L *stuppare*]; *trifulian* 'to break, bruise, stamp' [L *tribulare*]; *tyrnan*, *turnian* 'to turn, revolve' [L *turnare*].[27]

Adjectives Cirps, crisp 'curly, curly haired' [L *crispus*]; *cyrten* 'beautiful' [perhaps L *cortinus*]; *pīs* 'heavy' [L *pensus*]; *sicor* 'sure, certain; secure' [L *securus*]; *sȳfre* 'clean, pure, sober' [L *sobrius*]; *byxen* 'of box wood' [probably L *buxeus*].

Miscellaneous Candel, condel 'candle, taper', (in figurative contexts) 'source of light' [L *candela*]; *ċēas*, *ċēast* 'quarrel, strife; reproof' [L *causa*]; *ċeosol*, *ċesol* 'hut; gullet; belly' [L *casula*, *casella*]; *copor* 'copper' [L *cuprum*]; *derodine* 'scarlet' [probably L *dirodinum*]; *munt* 'mountain, hill' [L *mont-*, *mons*]; *plūm-*, in *plūmfeðer* '(in plural) down, feathers' [L *pluma*]; *sælmeriġe* 'brine' [L **salmuria*]; *sætern-* (in *sæterndæġ* 'Saturday') [L *Saturnus*]; *seġn* 'mark, sign, banner' [L *signum*]; *tasul*, *teosol* 'dice; small square of stone' [L *tessella*, **tassellus*]; *tæfl* 'piece used in a board game, dice; type of game played on a board, game of dice; board on which this is played' [L *tabula*].

Also, possibly, two important suffixes: *-ere*, forming agent nouns [probably L *-arius*; if so, borrowed very early]; *-estre*, forming feminine agent nouns [perhaps L *-istria*].

6.3.2 Some cases where an early date has often been suggested but is less certain

Religion and the Church Ancra, ancor 'anchorite' [L *anachoreta*, perhaps via Old Irish *anchara*];[28] *ærċe-*, *erċe-*, *arce-* 'arch-' (in titles) [L *archi-*]; *relic-* (in *relicgang* (probably) 'bearing of relics in a procession') [clipping of L *reliquiae* or OE *reliquias*]; *reliquias* 'relics' [L *reliquiae*].

Learning and scholarship Græf 'stylus' [L *graphium*]; *stǣr* (or *stær*) 'history' [probably ultimately L *historia*, perhaps via Celtic];[29] *traht* 'text, passage, commentary' [L *tractus*]; *trahtað* 'commentary' [L *tractatus*].

---

[27] For summary of scholarly opinions on this case see Feulner (2000) 383–4.

[28] See section 5.1.

[29] For summary of some of the arguments for and against borrowing via Irish or other Celtic languages see Feulner (2000) 248–51.

Plants and products of plants   *Æbs* 'fir tree' [L *abies*]; *croh*, *crog* 'saffron; type of dye; saffron colour' [L *crocus*];[30] *fīċ* 'fig tree, fig' [L *ficus*]; *plante* 'young plant' [L *planta*]; *sæðerie*, *satureġe* 'savory (plant name)' [L *satureia*]; *sæppe* 'spruce fir' [L *sappinus*]; *sōlsēċe* 'heliotrope' [L *solsequium*, with substitution of a derivative of OE *sēċan* 'to seek' for the second element].

Tools and implements   *Stropp* 'strap' [L *stroppus* or *struppus*]; *trefet* 'trivet, tripod' [L *tripes*].[31]

Buildings and parts of buildings   *Port* 'gate, gateway' [L *porta*];[32] *portiċ* 'porch, portico, vestibule, chapel' [L *porticus*].

Containers, vessels, and receptacles   *Cæpse* 'box' [L *capsa*]; *sċrīn* 'chest; shrine' [L *scrinium*]; *sċutel* 'dish, platter' [L *scutella*]; *tunne* 'cask, tun, barrel' [L *tunna*].[33]

Clothing and fabric; furnishing   *Orel*, *orl* 'robe, garment, veil, mantle' [L *orale*, *orarium*]; *purpure*, *purpur* 'deep crimson garment; deep crimson colour (imperial purple)' [L *purpura*];[34] *saban* 'sheet' [L *sabanum*];[35] *tæpped*, *teped* 'cloth wall or floor covering' [L *tapetum*, *tappetum*].

Verbs   *Cystan* 'to get the value of, exchange for the worth of' [L *constare*]; *dihtan*, *dihtian* 'to direct, command, arrange, set forth' [L *dictare*]; *glēsan* 'to gloss, explain' [L *glossare* (verb) or *glossa* (noun)]; *lafian* 'to pour water on, to bathe, wash' [L *lavare*]; **pilian* 'to peel, strip, pluck' (see section 8.1.2) [L *pilare*]; *plantian* 'to plant' [L *plantare*, or < OE *plante*]; **pyltan* 'to pelt' (implied by later *pilt*, *pelt*) [perhaps L **pultiare*, alteration of *pultare*]; *sealtian* 'to dance' [L *saltare*]; *trahtian* 'to comment on, expound; to interpret' [L *tractare*, if not < OE *traht*].

---

[30] For a recent discussion of this difficult case, see Dietz (2011) 280–3.

[31] This could be a much later borrowing. Compare Wollmann (1990a) 659–65.

[32] For a recent sceptical account, see Dietz (2011) 285–6.

[33] On doubts about the date of this borrowing, see Wollmann (1990a) 165.

[34] On this example, see further Feulner (2000) 314–16.

[35] Although opinions differ, this word, preserved in only a single attestation, seems more likely to be a later borrowing: compare Feulner (2000) 319–20.

Adjectives   *Cūsc* 'virtuous, chaste' [L *conscius*, perhaps via Old Saxon *kusko*].

Miscellaneous   *Coron-*(bēag) 'crown' [L *corona*]; *diht* 'act of directing or arranging; direction, arrangement, command' [L *dictum*]; **pill* (perhaps shown by *pillsāpe* soap for removing hair, depilatory) [perhaps L *pilus* 'hair'].

6.3.3 Some later loanwords (probably after AD 650)

I have given only a selection of words here and the numbers of words in each semantic category should not be taken as being representative.

Religion and the Church   *Acolitus* 'acolyte' [L *acoluthus, acolitus*]; *altare, alter* 'altar' [L *altare*]; *apostata* 'apostate' [L *apostata*]; *apostol* 'apostle' [L *apostolus*]; *canon* 'canon, rule of the Church; canon, cleric living under a canonical rule' [L *canon*]; *capitol* 'chapter, section; chapter, assembly' [L *capitulum*]; *clauster* 'monastic cell, cloister, monastery' [L *claustrum*]; *cleric*, also (earlier) *clīroc* 'clerk, clergyman' [L *clericus*]; *crēda, crēdo* 'creed' [L *credo*]; *crisma* 'holy oil, chrism; white cloth or garment of the newly baptized; chrismatory or pyx' [L *chrisma*]; *crismal* 'chrism cloth' [L *chrismalis*]; *crūc* 'cross' [L *cruc-, crux*]; *culpa* 'fault, sin' [L *culpa*]; *decan* 'person who supervises a group of (originally) ten monks or nuns, a dean' [L *decanus*]; *dēmōn* 'devil, demon' [L *daemon*]; *dīacon* 'deacon' [L *diaconus*]; *discipul* 'disciple; follower; pupil' [L *discipulus*]; *eretic* 'heretic' [L *haereticus*]; *grapul* 'gradual (antiphon sung between the Epistle and the Gospel at Mass)' [L *graduale*]; *īdol* 'idol' [L *idolum*]; *lētanīa* 'litany' [L *letania*]; *martir, martyr* 'martyr' [L *martyr*]; *noctern* 'nocturn, night office' [L *nocturna*]; *nōn* 'ninth hour (approximately 3 p.m.); office said at this time' [L *nona (hora)*]; *organ* 'canticle, song, melody; musical instrument, especially a wind instrument', also *orgel-* (in *orgeldrēam* 'instrumental music') [L *organum*]; *pāpa* 'pope' [L *papa*]; *paradīs* 'paradise, Garden of Eden, heaven' [L *paradisus*]; *passion* 'story of the Passion of Christ' [L *passion-, passio*]; *prīm* 'early morning office of the Church' [L *prima*]; *prior* 'superior officer of a religious house or order, prior' [L *prior*]; *sabat* 'sabbath' [L *sabbata*]; *sācerd* 'priest; priestess' [L *sacerdos*]; *salm, psalm, sealm* 'psalm, sacred song' [L *psalma*];[36] *saltere, sealtere* 'psalter, also type of stringed instrument' [L *psalterium*], *sanct* 'holy person, saint' [L *sanctus*]; *stōl, stōle* 'long outer garment; ecclesiastical vestment' [L *stola*]; *tempel* 'temple' [L *templum*].

---

[36] See section 8.1.2 on the questions raised by the form *sealm*.

Learning and scholarship   *Accent* 'diacritic mark' [L *accentus*]; *bærbære* 'barbarous, foreign' [L *barbarus*]; *bibliopēce, biblipēca* 'library' [L *bibliotheca*]; *cālend* 'first day of the month; (in poetry) month' [L *calendae*]; *cærte, carte* '(leaf or sheet of) vellum; piece of writing, document, charter' [L *charta, carta*]; *centaur* 'centaur' [L *centaurus*]; *circul* 'circle, cycle' [L *circulus*]; *comēta* 'comet' [L *cometa*]; *coorte, coorta* 'cohort' [L *cohort-, cohors*]; *cranic* 'chronicle' [L *chronicon* or *chronica*]; *cristalla, cristallum* 'crystal; ice' [L *crystallum*]; *epistol, epistola, pistol* 'letter' [L *epistola, epistula*]; *fers, uers* 'verse, line of poetry, passage, versicle' [L *versus*]; *gīgant* 'giant' [L *gigant-, gigas*]; *grād* 'step; degree' [L *gradus*]; *grammatic*-*cræft* 'grammar' [L *grammatica*]; *legie* 'legion' [L *legio*]; *meter* 'metre' [L *metrum*]; *nōt* 'note, mark' [L *nota*]; *nōtere* 'scribe, writer' [L *notarius*]; *part* 'part (of speech)' [L *part-, pars*]; *philosoph* 'philosopher' [L *philosophus*]; *punct* 'quarter of an hour' [L *punctum*]; *tītul* 'title, superscription' [L *titulus*]; *þēater* 'theatre' [L *theatrum*].

Plants, fruit, and products of plants   *Alwe* 'aloe' [L *aloe*]; *balsam, balzam* 'balsam, balm' [L *balsamum*]; *berbēne* 'vervain, verbena' [L *verbena*]; *cāl, cāul, cāwel* (or *cawel*) 'cabbage' [L *caulis*]; *calcatrippe* 'caltrops, or another thorny or spiky plant' [L *calcatrippa*]; *ceder* 'cedar' [L *cedrus*]; *coliandre, coriandre* 'coriander' [L *coliandrum, coriandrum*]; *cucumer* 'cucumber' [L *cucumer-, cucumis*]; *cypressus* 'cypress' [L *cypressus*]; *fēferfuge* (or *feferfuge*), *fēferfugie* (or *feferfugie*) 'feverfew' [L *febrifugia*, with substitution of Old English *fēfer* or *fefer* for the first element]; *laur, lāwer* 'laurel, bay, laver' [L *laurus*]; *lilie* 'lily' [L *lilium*]; *mōr-* (in *mōrberie, mōrbēam*) 'mulberry' [L *morus*]; *murre* 'myrrh' [L *murra, murrha, myrrha*]; *nard* 'spikenard (name of a plant and of ointment made from it)' [L *nardus*]; *palm, palma, pælm* 'palm (tree)' [L *palma*]; *peonie* 'peony' [L *paeonia*]; *peruince, perfince* 'periwinkle' [L *pervinca*]; *petersilie* 'parsley' [L *petrosilenum, petrosilium, petresilium*]; *polente* (or perhaps *polenta*) 'parched corn' [L *polenta*]; *pyretre* 'pellitory' (a plant) [L *pyrethrum*]; *rōse* (or *rose*) 'rose' [L *rosa*]; *rōsmarīm, rōsmarīnum* 'rosemary' [L *rosmarinum*]; *safine* 'savine (type of plant)' [L *sabina*]; *salfie, sealfie* 'sage' [L *salvia*]; *spīce, spīca* 'aromatic herb, spice, spikenard' [L *spica*]; *stōr* 'incense, frankincense' [probably L *storax*];[37] *sycomer* 'sycamore' [L *sycomorus*]; *ysope* 'hyssop' [L *hyssopus*].

---

[37] Perhaps via Celtic; for a summary of scholarship on this difficult word, see Feulner (2000) 353–5.

Animals   *Aspide* 'asp, viper' [L *aspid-, aspis*]; *basilisca* 'basilisk' [L *basiliscus*]; *camel, camell* 'camel' [L *camelus*]; **delfīn* 'dolphin' [L *delfīn*]; *fenix* 'phoenix; (in one example) kind of tree' [L *phoenix*]; *lēo* 'lion' [L *leo*]; *lopust* 'locust' [L *locusta*]; *loppestre, lopystre* 'lobster' [probably L *locusta*]; *pandher* 'panther' [L *panther*]; *pard* 'panther, leopard' [L *pardus*]; *pellican* 'name of a bird of the wilderness'[38] [L *pellicanus*]; *tiger* 'tiger' [L *tigris*]; *ultur* 'vulture' [L *vultur*].

Medicine   *Ātrum, atrum, attrum* 'black vitriol; atrament; blackness' [L *atramentum*]; *cancer* 'ulcerous sore' [L *cancer*]; *flanc* 'flank' [L **flancum*]; *mamme* 'teat' [L *mamma*]; *pigment* 'drug' [L *pigmentum*]; *plaster* 'plaster (medical dressing), plaster (building material)' [L *plastrum, emplastrum*]; *scrofell* 'scrofula' [L *scrofula*]; *tyriaca* 'antidote to poison' [L *tiriaca, theriaca*].

Tools and implements   *Pāl* 'stake, stave, post, pole; spade' [L *palus*]; (perhaps) *paper* '(probably) wick' [L *papirus, papyrus*]; *pīc* 'spike, pick, pike' [perhaps L **pic-*]; *press* 'press (specifically clothes-press)' [L *pressa* or French *presse*: see section 7.1].

Building and construction; settlements   *Castel, cæstel* 'village, small town; (in late manuscripts) castle'[39] [L *castellum*]; *foss* 'ditch' [L *fossa*]; *marman-, marmel-* (in *marmanstān, marmelstān*) 'marble' [L *marmor*].

Receptacles   *Purs, burse* 'purse' [L *bursa*].

Money; units of measurement   *Cubit* 'cubit, measure of length' [L *cubitum*]; *mancus* 'a money of account equivalent to thirty pence, a weight equivalent to thirty pence' [L *mancus*]; *talente* 'talent (as unit of weight or of money)' [L *talentum*].

[38] For a discussion of the interesting questions raised by the various Old English renditions of this biblical bird name, see Lass (1997) 84–8.

[39] The sense 'castle' may well reflect a later separate borrowing, from French and Latin: see sections 7.5.2, 12.2.1, 13.1.1.

Clothing *Cæppe*, also (in cantel-*cāp* 'cloak worn by a cantor') *cāp* 'cloak, hood, cap' (with uncertain relationship to *cōp* in the same meaning) [L *cappa*]; *tuniče*, *tuneče* 'undergarment, tunic, coat, toga' [L *tunica*].

Roles, ranks, and occupations (non-religious or not specifically religious)
Centur, *centurio*, *centurius* 'centurion' [L *centurion-*, *centurio*]; *cōc* 'cook' [L **cocus*, *coquus*]; *consul* 'consul' [L *consul*]; *fiþela* 'fiddler' (also *fiþelere* 'fiddler', *fiþelestre* '(female) fiddler') [probably L *vitula*].

Warfare *Mīlite* 'soldiers' [L *milites*, plural of *miles*].

Verbs *Acordan* 'to reconcile' [perhaps L *accordare*, although more likely a post-Conquest borrowing from French]; *acūsan* 'to accuse (someone)' [L *accusare*]; *ġebrēfan* 'to set down briefly in writing' [L *breviare*]; *dēclīnian* 'to decline or inflect' [L *declinare*]; *offrian* 'to offer, sacrifice' [L *offerre*]; **platian* 'to make or beat into thin plates' (implied by *platung* 'metal plate' and *ġeplatod* and *aplatod* 'beaten into thin plates') [L *plata*, noun]; *predician* 'to preach' [L *predicare*, *praedicare*]; *prōfian* 'to assume to be, to take for' [L *probare*]; *rabbian* 'to rage' [L *rabiare*]; *salletan* 'to sing psalms, to play on the harp' [L *psallere*];[40] *sċrūtnian*, *sċrūdnian* 'to examine' [L *scrutinare*]; **spendan* 'to spend' (recorded in Old English only in the derivatives *spendung*, *aspendan*, *forspendan*) [L *expendere*]; *studdian* 'to look after, be careful for' [L *studere*]; *temprian* 'to modify; to cure, heal; to control' [L *temperare*]; *tonian* 'to thunder' [L *tonare*].

Adjectives *Fals* 'false' [L *falsus*]; *mechanisċ* 'mechanical' [L *mechanicus*].

Miscellaneous *Fals* 'fraud, trickery' [L *falsum*]; *rocc* (only in *stānrocc*) 'cliff or crag' [L *rocca*]; *sott* 'fool', also adjective 'foolish' [L *sottus*]; *tabele*, *tabul*, *tabule* 'tablet, board; writing tablet; gaming table' [L *tabula*].

---

[40] See section 7.5.4.

7

Interrogating the data from chapter 6

This chapter looks in detail at the data presented in section 6.3, as a way of investigating some of the key issues concerning loanwords in Old English. It examines some cases of uncertainty about whether a particular word shows a Latin borrowing at all, from several different perspectives, and also looks at questions concerning the degree of integration of Latin loanwords into the lexicon of Old English. It complements this by also examining the data from a long historical perspective, to see to what extent Latin loanwords found in Old English survived into Middle English and beyond, and hence ultimately what the contribution of borrowing from Latin in this period was to the future shape of the English lexicon.

7.1 Concerns about etymologies

Some of the words listed in section 6.3 are not certain borrowings from Latin. In such cases I have qualified the Latin etymon with either 'probably' or 'perhaps'. Most of those qualified with 'perhaps' are only very doubtfully Latin borrowings and their inclusion reflects the fact that there is insufficient evidence to reject Latin borrowing outright. I have omitted entirely some untenable suggestions from the older literature; some retained here, e.g. *pīc*, are nonetheless very unlikely.

A very few words are ultimately from Celtic and could have come directly from Celtic, e.g. *binn* or *stōr* (compare section 5.1). Likewise, *cūsc* 'virtuous, chaste' (ultimately < Latin *cōnscius*) may have been borrowed via Old Saxon.

In a very few cases post-Conquest borrowing from Latin or even from French may explain all of our evidence: for instance, *press* 'press (specifically clothes-press)' is recorded only in a post-Conquest manuscript and could show a French borrowing; *acordan* 'to reconcile' and *bærbære* 'barbarous, foreign' are recorded only in manuscripts of the twelfth century and later, and could be post-Conquest borrowings from Latin.

A very few words seem safe to assume as borrowings but nonetheless present unexplained formal anomalies. Perhaps the clearest example of this is *purs* 'purse', which appears to be a borrowing of Latin *bursa* in the same meaning, but shows completely unexplained initial /p/ (see Durkin (2009) 212–13); the form we should expect, *burse*, is found a couple of times in late Old English, but then not in Middle English (until *burse*, *bourse* is found as a re-borrowing in the fifteenth century); the inexplicable *purs* is found once only in late Old English, but is the dominant form in Middle English and later.

7.2 Derivatives and compounds of loanwords

Many of the loanwords give rise to new derivatives and compounds in Old English. This provides important evidence for their degree of integration into the lexis. Some of the more notable examples include the following:

> *assen* 'female ass' < *assa*;
> *campian* 'to fight' < *camp*;
> *cāsering* any of various coins from the Roman Empire < *cāsere*;
> *ċēapian* 'to buy and sell, to buy, to trade' < *ċēap*;
> *cirpsian* 'to make curly' < *cirps, crisp*;
> *clȳsing* 'enclosed place', *beclȳsan, forclȳsan*, both 'to close', *mynsterclūse* 'monastic enclosure, cell', *muntclȳse* 'mountain prison', all < *clūse*;
> *cōcor-panne* 'cooking pan', *ġecōcnod* 'seasoned', *ġecōcsod* 'cooked', *cōcnung* and *cōcor-mete* both 'cooked food' (in different precise senses) < *cōc*;
> *culpian* '(perhaps) to make humble obeisance to, or to beg' < *culpa*;
> *cyperen* 'made of copper' < *copor* (although see further section 8.1.3);
> *dihtend* 'director', *dihtere* 'deviser, interpreter, authority', *dihtung* 'arrangement', *ġediht* 'dictated, written, appointed, arranged, etc.', all ultimately < *diht*; similarly *ġedihtan* 'to dictate, compose, command, arrange, etc.' < *dihtan*;
> *fersian* 'to versify' < *fers*;
> *gimmian* 'to put forth gem-like buds', *ġeġimmod* 'bejewelled', *ġimmisċ* 'jewelled' (and also many compounds) < *ġimm*;
> *mangian* 'to trade, to gain by trading' < *mangere*;
> *myneċen, myneċenu* 'nun' < *munuc*;

organystre 'person who plays an instrument', *orgnian, organian* 'to sing to an instrumental accompaniment' < *organ;*

pællen 'made of fine or rich cloth' < *pæll;*

pīlere 'person who pounds in a mortar', *pīlian* 'to pound in a mortar' < *pīle;*

pīnere 'tormenter, torturer', *pīnian* 'to torture, torment', *pīnung* 'torment, torture' < *pīn;*

pīpere 'piper' < *pīpian* or *pīpe;*

pundere 'scholar (i.e. person who weighs or evaluates)' < **pundrian;*

sealticge 'dancer' < *sealtian;*

tynċen 'small barrel' < *tunne;*

tæppel- in *tæppelbred* 'footstool' < *tæpped*

Beside the noun *læden* 'Latin' there is an adjective, with the same spelling in the nominative singular. Beside borrowed *traht* 'text, passage, commentary', *trahtað* 'commentary', and *trahtian* 'to comment on, expound; to interpret' (probably formed on the Latin verb stem rather than the Old English noun) there are the derivatives *trahtere* 'expounder, commentator' and *trahtnung* 'explanation, exposition, commentary'. *Platung* 'metal plate' is paralleled by *ġeplatod* and *aplatod* 'beaten into thin plates', which probably collectively point to an otherwise unrecorded Old English verb **platian* formed on the Latin noun *plata*. Beside the compound *grammatic-cræft* there is a simplex *grammatica, grammatice* 'grammar', as well as an agent noun *grammaticere* 'grammarian' and an adjective *grammatisċ* 'grammatical'. However, some of these words, particularly some of the verbs, could alternatively be explained as being further Latin loanwords: compare sections 7.3, 7.5.4.

For those letters of the alphabet that it covers (currently up to the end of G), the *DOE* provides very full listings of compounds and derived words. These show that many of the earlier borrowings gave rise to multiple compounds and derivatives in Old English. More than ten compounds or derivatives are shown by each of the following borrowed words: *camp* 'battlefield, etc.'; *candel* 'candle, etc.'; *ċēap* 'purchase, etc.'; *ċeaster* 'fortification, etc.'; *ele* 'oil'; *ġimm* 'gem, etc.'. For the approximately 120 words beginning with the letters A to G listed in sections 6.3.1 and 6.3.2 that gave rise to derivatives and compounds in Old English, approximately 300 compounds and derivatives are listed in the *DOE* (only an approximate total is possible without detailed comment on difficult cases). If this ratio held true for all words listed in sections 6.3.1 and 6.3.2, it would be a very substantial addition to the overall number of Latin-derived words in Old English. The later borrowings listed in section 6.3.3 generally give rise to fewer compounds and derivatives, although there are some. Thus, if the question of interest to us is 'What proportion of the surviving Old English lexis can be traced back to Latin borrowing, either directly or indirectly?', the total has increased significantly; even if our focus is instead on direct borrowing, these figures are important, because they show the productivity of very many of the early borrowings within English, hence providing an important insight on their degree of integration into the language.

7.3 Uncertain cases of derivation or independent borrowing

Since many of the borrowings show assimilation to derivational patterns that were productive in Old English, a number of the words given in the lists in section 6.3 could likewise alternatively be explained as derivative formations from other borrowed words. In some cases probability seems to point much more strongly to independent borrowing, but this cannot be taken to be a certainty. For example, while *nōt* 'note, mark' < Latin *nota* and *nōtere* 'scribe, writer' (< Latin *notārius*) very probably show independent borrowing of (related) Latin words, another word in the same family, the very rare verb *nōtian*, could likewise show borrowing directly < Latin *notāre*, but could equally be derived from the noun *nōt* within English. Compare the comments on **pundrian*, *seġnian*, and *trahtian* in the listings in section 6.3.

Similarly, alongside the noun *apostol* there is a (relatively frequently attested) adjective *apostolič*, *apostollič*, which may be a loanword from Latin *apostolicus* (probably with assimilation to adjectives in *-ič*), or may be a derivative from *apostol* within Old English.[1] Likewise *sēamere* 'beast of burden' may be a loanword from post-classical Latin *saumarius*, variant of *sagmarius*, or may be a derivative of *sēam*. *Cempa* 'warrior, combatant, soldier' may be a (fairly early) derivative < *camp* in Old English, but could be a loanword from the Latin derivative *campio*.[2]

7.4 Problems concerning learned borrowings

The morphology of Old English has a number of distinct inflections, which realize distinctions of tense, person, number, and mood in the verb, and of case, number, and gender in nouns and adjectives. Words belong to a

---

[1] See Feulner (2000) 85–6 for more on this example.
[2] See Green (1998) 234.

variety of different verbal, nominal, or adjectival paradigms, mostly based on inherited patterns, which determine the particular inflections that each word will show. With the exception of the special type discussed in the next paragraph, loanwords in Old English are assimilated to one or other of these paradigms and hence show similar inflections to inherited words. Some patterns are discernible in assignment of words from particular Latin paradigms to particular Old English paradigms, e.g. many Latin second- and fourth-declension nouns (with nominative singular in *-us*) are assimilated to the Old English strong masculine *a*-declension (so called because of the thematic vowel that characterized this declension at an earlier stage in its history); thus Latin *angelus* > Old English (or proto-Old English) *engel*, Latin *grādus* > Old English *grād*. Many Latin feminine nouns of the first declension are assimilated to the Old English weak feminine declension (which in traditional grammars are called *-ōn-* stems, for reasons of the pre-history of the forms); thus Latin *sabīna* > Old English *safine*, Latin *murra, murrha, myrrha* 'myrrh' > Old English *murre*. See section 8.1.3 for an assumption of a similar development in the etymology of *mass*. For some useful discussion and further references see especially Gneuss (1996a). On verbs see further section 7.5.4.

However, there is also a widespread phenomenon in Old English texts of using Latin words with their Latin inflections, embedded in what are otherwise Old English sentences. Our surviving texts indicate that this was predominantly a feature of learned discourse in Old English. If a Latin word, with its usual Latin inflections, occurs in an Old English sentence, we could perhaps analyse this as a single-word code switch, or we could assume that the Latin word has been borrowed into Old English with its full paradigm of Latin endings (this is the approach that grammars of classical Latin typically take with similar borrowings of Greek words). The situation is greatly complicated by the fact that many words occur sometimes with Old English inflections, sometimes with Latin ones (and in some cases the inflection in both languages is identical, hence the analysis is ambiguous). It may be best to look at some examples before looking at the various analyses that scholars have attempted.

Acolitus 'acolyte' is included in the *DOE*. It only ever appears with its Latin inflections, five times in the nominative, *acolitus* (or three times, if very similar examples in Ælfric's *First Old English Letter for Wulfstan* and *Letter to Wulfsige* are counted once only), and once in the accusative, *acolitum*, in positions where the Old English sentence requires these cases. In all of the examples of its occurrence the word is explained and there is some degree of meta-textual citation in its use:

> *Acolitus is seþe tapor byrð æt Godes þenungum.*
>
> 'An acolyte is one who bears a light at God's services.'
>
> (Ælfric, *First Old English Letter for Wulfstan*; my translation; a similar passage occurs in Ælfric's *Letter to Wulfsige*.)
>
> *Seofon hadas syndon gesette on cyrcan: an is hostiarius, oðer is lector, þridda is exorcista, feorða acolitus, fifta subdiaconus, sixta diaconus, seofoða presbiter.*
>
> 'There are seven ranks established in the church: the first is hostiarius, the second lector, the third exorcist, the fourth acolyte, the fifth subdeacon, the sixth deacon, the seventh priest.'
>
> (Ælfric, *Letter to Wulfsige*; my translation; a similar passage occurs in Ælfric's *First Old English Letter for Wulfstan*.)
>
> *Sanctus Siluester cwæð: ne sceal nan acolitus, þæt is huslþen, forsecgan nanne subdiacon; ne nan exorcista, þæt is halsere, forsecgan nanne acolitum...*
>
> 'St. Silvester says, "No acolyte, that is to say assistant at the administration of the sacrament, shall accuse a subdeacon; nor any exorcist, that is to say expeller of evil spirits, accuse any acolyte..."'
>
> (Old English version of Chrodegang of Metz, *Regula Canonicorum*; my translation.)

In some analyses, including that adopted by the *DOE*, the uses from the Old English version of Chrodegang of Metz's *Regula Canonicorum* are regarded as not Old English, on the grounds that the word is explained explicitly on its first appearance in the passage, '*acolitus, þæt is huslþen*'.[3]

There are three examples of *absinthium* 'wormwood' embedded in Old English sentences, all from the same text (a translation of the *Herbarium Apulei*), and all in the same chapter. In one of the manuscripts of this text *absynthius* also occurs in the heading of this chapter (and *herba absinthius þæt is wermod* 'the plant absinthius, that is, wormwood' also occurs in the introductory list of chapters):

> *CII. Wermod absynthius*
>   *Ðeos wyrt þe man absinthium & oþrum naman wermod nemneð byþ cenned on beganum stowum & on dunum & on stænihtum stowum.*

---

[3] Compare also Feulner (2000) 59–60. The count of four occurrences from the *DOE* given in section 7.5.2 thus reflects only the matches from Ælfric's letters.

> *Wið þæt man læla & oðre sar of lichaman gedo genim þas wyrte absinthium,*
> *seoð on wætere, do þonne on anne clað, lege to þam sare, gyf þonne se lichoma*
> *mearu sy, seoð on hunige, lege to þam sare.*
>
> *Wið þæt rengwyrmas ymbe þone nafolan derigen genim þas ylcan wyrte*
> *absinthium & harehunan & elechtran, ealra gelice mycel, seoð on geswettum*
> *wætere oþþe on wine, lege tuwa oððe þriwa to þam nafolan, hyt cwelþ þa wyrmas.*

'102. Wormwood, absinthius.

This plant that one calls absinthius and by another name wormwood is known in cultivated places and on hills and in stony places.

In order that one may remove weals and other sores from the body, take this same plant absinthius, boil it in water, put it on a cloth, and put it on the sore; if the body is tender, boil [this plant] in honey, and put it on the sore.

If ringworms are causing harm around the navel, take this same plant absinthius and horehound and lupin, the same amount of each, boil in sweetened water or in wine, put it on the navel two or three times, and it will kill the worms.'

(Old English translation of *Herbarium Apulei*; text from De Vriend (1984) 148; my translation.)

If we leave the chapter heading out of account for a moment, the Old English sentences show the form *absinthium* three times, in each case in a position where the syntax of the Old English sentence requires a form in the accusative. *Absinthium* is indeed the Latin accusative form, both of the usual classical Latin neuter noun *absinthium* (which is what occurs in at least one manuscript of the Latin text being translated here), and also of its masculine variant *absinthius* (which is reflected by the heading 'Wermod absynthius' in one manuscript of the Old English text). Interpreting the implications of this short passage for the lexis of Old English is a difficult task and also non-trivial when we consider that there are many word forms occurring equally rarely in equally complicated circumstances. The word is not explicitly flagged as not being English, although the use of the native synonym *wermōd* perhaps implies that it is anticipated that it may be unfamiliar to some of the audience. The formula in the following sentence, *genim þas ylcan wyrte absinthium* 'take this same plant absinthium', is very typical of this text and probably does not signal anything about the status of the word. Note that the learned borrowing *elehtre* '(probably) lupin' also occurs in this passage, as does the early borrowing *wīn* 'wine'. *Absinthium* is not included in the *DOE*, presumably being regarded as a Latin word occurring in an Old English context.[4]

---

[4] It is explicitly excluded from the specialist studies by Feulner (2000) 459 and Bierbaumer (1975–9) II, 140.

It is included in *OED3*, but the next examples date from the late fourteenth century, and examples where it could not reasonably be argued that a Latin word is shown are later still. There is therefore extremely little likelihood of any continuity between the examples in Old English texts and later use, although this cannot be ruled out completely. However, whether or not we say that Old English had a word *absinthium* will depend on some theoretical assumptions and on how we apply these when we consider the precise contexts of our surviving examples in Old English texts.

In a similar example, Latin *absolutio* 'absolution' occurs five times in Old English sentences, always in the accusative form *absolutionem*, in positions where the (Old English) syntax requires an accusative form. Two of the examples are these:

> On ðone þurnesdæg ær Eastron... him þonne se biscop ofer singeð and absolutionem deð.

> 'On the Thursday before Easter... the bishop then sings over him and grants absolution.'

> (*Handbook for Use of Confessor* in *Anglia* (1965) 83 20; my translation.)

> Ðonne absolutionem bisceopas ofer hy rædað.

> 'Then bishops read absolution over them.'

> (Wulfstan *Homily on First Sunday in Lent*; my translation.)

This word is excluded by the *DOE*. It is included in an important early study of learned words by Funke (1904 108) as a 'foreignism' (see later in this section on the categories he distinguishes).

The picture is complicated still further by the fact that some words occur sometimes with Old English endings and sometimes with Latin endings. Thus, the rather commoner word *comēta* 'comet' mostly shows Old English case endings, *comēta* in the nominative singular (although this is identical to the Latin nominative singular, and hence ambiguous), *comētan* in all other cases in the singular and in the nominative and accusative plural (the genitive and dative plural do not occur). However, instances are also found in Old English sentences of the Latin ablative singular form *comētā* and the nominative plural *comētē* (a common post-classical Latin form corresponding to classical Latin *comētae*), in places where these cases are appropriate to the syntax of the Old English sentence.

The *DOE* lists five occurrences of *centaur* 'centaur', but only two of these show Old English morphological endings (both showing the genitive singular *centaures*). The other three show Latin case endings, in one instance showing agreement with a Latin proper name also showing its Latin dative ending, *& lǣcedom Chironi centauro syllan* 'and gave this medicine to Chiron the centaur'.

The *DOE* often provides useful comments on words that show Latin inflections in Old English sentences. Among the words I have listed in section 6.3, in addition to those already discussed, the *DOE* shows that: *cypressus* 'cypress' is found mostly with Latin inflections; *discipul* 'disciple, etc.', sometimes shows Latin inflections and sometimes Old English inflections; *dīacon* 'deacon' and *fers, uers* 'verse, line of poetry, passage, versicle' are found occasionally with Latin inflections. At *epistol, epistola* 'letter' the *DOE* notes 'Only those examples which show evidence of naturalization of the Latin word in English have been treated in this entry'; at *crūc* 'cross' examples of the Latin accusative form *crūcem* are listed separately, with the comment 'Cf. Latin forms in Old English context', and these are excluded from the *DOE*'s count of four instances of *crūc* in Old English.

Scholarly responses to this material have varied greatly. Funke (1904 44) distinguishes several distinct types of borrowings on morphological grounds: (1) loanwords (*Lehnwörter*), showing full integration to the declensional classes of Old English; (2) foreignisms (*Fremdwörter*), which retain their Latin case endings; (3) words occupying a middle stage between these two, which show the Latin ending in the nominative singular, but otherwise show the Old English case endings. In addition to the mixed evidence that can result if a word is becoming more fully integrated into the Old English morphological system over time, he suggests that some words also appear to present mixed paradigms as a result of the coexistence of an early, more fully integrated borrowing and a later, learned re-borrowing, which is less fully integrated. Campbell (1959 §563) comments much more curtly 'Very often ... late loan-words retain their Lat[in] declensional endings whole or in part' and proceeds to give some examples. In this context, it can be useful to compare the variation between e.g. *indexes* and *indices* as the plural of *index* in modern English. Additionally, as we have seen, many scholars, including the *DOE* editors, take into account the degree of glossing or explanation that is found when assessing whether a particular example of a word form with a Latin ending shows an Old English borrowing; some scholars also try to take into account the specific characteristics of the texts in which such words occur and whether there is a high incidence of other words with Latin endings embedded in Old English sentences. Words that retain their Latin endings in Old English contexts rarely show any signs of phonological adaptation to the Old English sound system, nor are they productive in forming compounds or derivatives, but this does no more than indicate that they were at best somewhat marginal items in the lexis of Old English. Later currency is generally not very helpful, because in nearly all cases later re-borrowing cannot be ruled out (see section 7.5.1). A particularly full summary of these and other criteria employed by some scholars is provided by Feulner (2000 35–44), in the context of a consideration specifically of those words that are ultimately of Greek origin. See also Milfull (2009) for a discussion of the issues raised by such words for lexicographers.

A reappraisal of this topic is overdue, taking into account modern perspectives on code switching and mixed-language texts. It is unlikely that anyone will undertake this before the *DOE* is completed and, even then, the task of combing the *DOE* Corpus or a successor for cases omitted by the *DOE* (like *absinthium* and *absolutionem*) will remain a very large one. Pending such research, we can at least note that present estimates of the precise number of morphologically integrated or semi-integrated Latin words occurring in our surviving Old English texts are likely to be unreliable.

7.5 Assessing the influence of Latin loanwords in Old English

7.5.1 Survival in modern English

A large number of the loanwords found in Old English have reflexes in modern English, although it is normally much easier to be certain about this in the case of earlier borrowings than with later borrowings. The reason for uncertainty is that English continued to be in contact with Latin (and subsequently also with French) for many centuries and it is often difficult to be certain that the modern word does not result from later re-borrowing from Latin (and/or from French).

Sometimes semantic considerations point strongly to a word's continuous existence in English, because it shows a meaning distinct from that in the donor language: some examples of this type are discussed in section 4.3.

Much more typically, the arguments are based on word form. This is why there is much more often certainty of continuity in the case of early borrowings, because they frequently reflect the results of Old English sound changes, or otherwise show greater evidence of integration into the Old English sound system; indeed, this is normally the main criterion on which they are identified as early borrowings. Thus, we can be certain that modern English *kitchen* is the direct reflex of Old English *cyċene* rather than the result of later re-borrowing from Latin *coquina* because a later re-borrowing would not show the same development of the vowel in the first syllable nor of the following consonant (which respectively show the sound changes *i*-mutation and palatalization followed by assibilation: see section 8.1.1).

Additionally, some sound changes that occurred in late Old English or early Middle English can give further clues to help identify modern English words whose form clearly goes back to borrowings that occurred in Old English. Thus, the vowel in modern English *noon* points strongly to continuity with Old English *nōn* rather than later re-borrowing from Latin *nōna* or (Anglo-)French *none*, because, in early Middle English, *ō* in words inherited from Old English was a distinct (higher) vowel sound than *ō* in words newly borrowed from French or Latin, and the subsequent development of the two sounds remained distinct (giving in modern British English /uː/ and /əʊ/ respectively). This does not mean that there was definitely no subsequent influence from the Latin and/or (Anglo-)French word: in fact, in this particular instance it is very likely that the meaning 'midday' (rather than 'ninth hour of the liturgical day', originally about 3 p.m.) resulted from later influence from either Latin or Anglo-French or both. However, the word form *noon*, with /uː/, points strongly to continuity with the Old English word, rather than a completely new borrowing. Conversely, the vowel in modern English *note* points strongly to re-borrowing in Middle English, since otherwise we would expect the modern pronunciation /nuːt/ (assuming that the vowel was long in Old English: compare section 8.1.4).

In some cases, it is impossible to prove that there was no continuity, but at least some subsequent borrowing from Latin or French is proved on formal grounds, e.g. *feverfew*, where the final syllable of the modern word form reflects the French form rather than the Old English one. Similarly, the diphthong shown by modern English *mount* results from Middle English borrowing of Anglo-French *mount*, rather than from continuity with the early Old English borrowing *munt*, with a short vowel.[5] The diphthong in modern English *oil* clearly reflects Middle English borrowing from

---

[5] On the phonology of the later word, see Short (2007) §6.7, Jordan (1934) §229, Bliss (1952–3).

Anglo-French, rather than the early Old English borrowing *ele*. (See further section 11.4 on this example.)

In many other cases certainty is unattainable: continuity is feasible, but the subsequent history could just as easily be explained by the scenario that the (possibly very rare) Old English form did not survive and the word was re-borrowed in Middle English. For more detailed discussion of those words of this type that fall in the most frequent 1,000 items in the *BNC*, see section 11.4.[6]

7.5.1.1 *Survivals from probable earlier borrowings*   (a) Words where continuity is (in most cases) certain or (in a few cases) highly likely (including some derivatives of borrowed words):

Abbot; alms; anthem; ass; belt; bin; bishop; box; butter; candle; chalk; cheap; cheese; chervil; chest; cock; cockle (plant name); *copper; coulter; cowl; cup; devil; dight; dish; fennel; fever; fork; fuller; inch; kiln; kipper; kirtle; kitchen; line; mallow; mass* (= Eucharist); *mat;* (perhaps) *mattock; mile; mill; minster; mint* (for coinage); *mint* (plant name); *-monger; monk; mortar; neep* (and hence tur*nip*); *nun; pail; pall* (noun); *pan* (if borrowed); *pear;* (probably) *peel; pepper; pilch* (noun); *pile* (= stake); *pillow; pin; to pine; pipe; pit; pitch* (dark substance); (perhaps) *to pluck;* (perhaps) *plum;* (perhaps) *plume; poppy; post;* (perhaps) *pot; pound; priest; punt; purple; radish; relic; sack; Satur*day; *seine; shambles; shrine; shrive* (and *shrift, Shrove Tuesday*); *sickle;* (perhaps) *silk; sock; sponge;* (perhaps) *stop; street; strop* (and hence *strap*); *tile; toll; trivet; trout; tun; to turn; turtle*-dove; *wall; wine.*

(b) Words where it is uncertain how great a role was played by later borrowing from Latin and/or French:

Anchor; angel;[7] *antiphon; arch-; ark; beet* and *beet*root; *capon; cat; crisp; drake* (= dragon, not duck); *fan; Latin; lave; master; mussel;* (wine-)*must; pea; pine* (the tree); *plant; to plant; port; provost; psalm; scuttle; table;* also (where the re-borrowing would be from early Scandinavian) *kettle.*

7.5.1.2 *Survivals from later borrowings*   Among the later words, because of the less extensive integration they show to the Old English sound system and the lack of distinctive semantic developments within English, there are very

---

[6] For discussion of related issues, see also Durkin (2009) 70–1.

[7] In this instance the later form, with /dʒ/ rather than /g/, is clearly due to French influence.

few cases where we can say with confidence that there was direct continuity from Old English through to modern English:

> *Aloe*; *cook*; *cope* (= garment); *noon*; *pole*; *pope*; *school*;[8] (if borrowed) *fiddle*; (in some of these cases re-borrowing in very early Middle English could also be possible).

Some cases from among the later borrowings where at least some degree of continuity seems reasonably likely include:

> *Altar*; *canker*; *cap*; *clerk*; *comet*; *creed*; *deacon*; *false*; *flank*; *hyssop*; *lily*; *martyr*; *myrrh*; *to offer*; *palm* (tree); *paradise*; *passion*; *peony*; *pigment*; *prior*; *purse*; *rose*; *sabbath*; *savine*; *sot*; *to spend*; *stole*; *verse*; also (where the re-borrowing would be from early Scandinavian) *cole*.

7.5.2 Word frequencies and textual distribution

The *DOE* gives extremely useful frequency numbers for the parts of the alphabet that it covers, currently a, æ, b, c, d, e, f, g, drawing on the near-comprehensive corpus of surviving Old English texts on the basis of which the *DOE* is compiled. The numbers given below are the frequency numbers for the words beginning with a–g from the listings in section 6.3. They reflect the frequency of the simplex word, rather than for the simplex word and its compounds and derivatives; in some particularly notable instances, especially when a compound or derivative is more frequent than the simplex, I have given its frequency also, in brackets after the simplex. (Totals greater than 30 have been rounded up or down for economy of presentation, in this list and in the following discussion.)

3,700: *bisċeop* 'bishop'
2,500: *dēofol, dīofol* 'devil'
2,250: *engel, angel* 'angel'[9]
1,400: *apostol* 'apostle'
1,100: *abbod, abbot* 'abbot'; *cristen* 'Christian'
950: *ċeaster, ċæster* 'fortification, etc.'
900: *cāsere* 'emperor; ruler'
500: *ele* 'oil'
475: *ælmesse, ælmes* 'alms, charity'

---

[8] It is clearly the later form *scōl* that survived. Modern English *shoal* is sometimes thought to show continuity with the form *sċolu* in a specialized meaning, but later borrowing of the cognate word from Dutch is more likely: compare section 15.2.

[9] *Engel* is much the commoner form. On the origin of the two forms, see section 8.2.1.

300: *dīacon* 'deacon'

250: *eċed* 'vinegar'

225: *abbodesse* 'abbess'; *consul* 'consul'; *draca* 'dragon, etc.'

200: *butere* 'butter'; *culfre* 'dove'

175: *ċeafor*-(tūn), *cafer*-(tūn) 'hall, court'; *ċēap* 'purchase, etc.'; *ċelċ, cælic, calic* 'drinking vessel, cup'

150: *fers, uers* 'verse, etc.'

140: *castel, cæstel* 'village, etc.'; *earc, earce, earca, arc, arce, arca* 'ark, etc.'

120: *assa* 'ass'

110: *antefn, antifon, antyfon* 'antiphon'; *discipul* 'disciple, etc.'; *fēfer* or *fefer* 'fever'; *ġimm* 'gem, etc.'

100: *diht* 'act of directing, etc.'

90: *finol, finule, finugle* 'fennel'

80: *disċ* 'dish, bowl, plate'; *eolone, elene* 'elecampane'

75: *circul* 'circle, cycle'

70: *capitol* 'chapter'; *cleric, clīroc* 'clerk, clergyman'; *dihtan, dihtian* 'to direct, etc.'

60: *bytt* 'bottle, etc.'; *ċist, ċest* 'chest, etc.'; *elehtre* '(probably) lupin'

50: *amber* 'vessel, etc.'; *ancra, ancor* 'anchorite'; *binn, binne* 'basket, bin; manger'; *crēda, crēdo* 'creed'; *ċȳse, ċēse* 'cheese'

45: *candel, condel* 'candle, etc.'; *cymen* 'cumin'

40: *canon* 'canon'; *ċēas, ċēast* 'quarrel, etc.'; *cyċene* 'kitchen'; *ċytel, ċetel* 'cooking-vessel, etc.'; *cyll, cylle* 'leather bottle, etc.'; *fenix* 'phoenix, etc.'

35: *altare, alter* 'altar'; *byden* 'vessel, etc.'; *camp* 'battlefield, etc.' (> *campian* 'to fight' *c*.70, *cempa* 'warrior, combatant, soldier' *c*.400); *cærte, carte* 'vellum, etc.'; *cuppe* 'cup'; *cyrtel* 'garment, etc.' (< **cyrtan*); *glædene* plant name

30: *clauster* 'monastic cell, cloister, monastery'

29: *comēta* 'comet'; *elpend, ylpend* 'elephant'

27: *cost* 'costmary'; *cucler* 'spoon'

26: *ancor, ancra* 'anchor'; *bēte* 'beet, beetroot'; *cancer* 'ulcerous sore'; *celendre, cellendre* 'coriander'; *clūse* 'lock, etc.'

25: *alwe* 'aloe'; *crisma* 'chrism, etc.'; *fēferfuge* or *feferfuge, fēferfugie* or *feferfugie* 'feverfew'; *gīgant* 'giant'

24: *cæppe* 'cloak, hood, cap'; *ċerfille, ċerfelle* 'chervil'; *cugele* '(monk's) cowl'; *cocer* 'quiver'

23: *bibliopēce, biblipēca* 'library'; *clifa, cleofa, cliofa* 'chamber, etc.'

22: *cocc* 'cock, rooster'; *decan* 'dean'

21: *cāl, cāul, cāwel* (or *cawel*) 'cabbage'

20: *eosol, esol* 'ass'

19: *fīċ* 'fig tree, fig'

18: *dīligian* 'to erase, etc.'

17: *ċeren* 'wine reduced by boiling'; *cōc* 'cook'; *coccel* 'corn cockle, etc.'

16: *balsam, balzam* 'balsam, balm'; *fals* 'fraud, trickery'

15: *box* 'box tree; box, receptacle' (8 box tree, 7 receptacle)

14: *cristalla, cristallum* 'crystal; ice'

13: *ċīpe* 'onion'; *cȳf* 'large jar, vessel, or tub'

11: *ċisten-, ċistel-, ċist-*(bēam) 'chestnut tree'; *cyrfet* 'gourd'; *græf* 'stylus'

10: *ceder* 'cedar'

9: *camel, camell* 'camel'; *centur, centurio, centurius* 'centurion'; *dīner, dīnor* type of coin, denarius; *epistol, epistola* 'letter'; *fann* 'winnowing fan'

8: *ātrum, atrum, attrum* 'blackness, etc.'; *cat, catte* 'cat'; *ċealc, calc* 'chalk, plaster'; *ċipp* 'rod, etc.'; *ċiris-*(bēam) 'cherry tree'; *cruft* 'crypt, cave'; *grād* 'step; degree'

7: *acordan* 'to reconcile'; *berbēne* 'vervain, verbena'; *billere* denoting several water plants; *buteruc* 'bottle'; *ċeosol, ċesol* 'hut; gullet; belly'; *croh, crog* 'saffron, etc.'; *culter* 'coulter; (once) dagger'; *fals* 'false'

6: *coliandre, coriandre* 'coriander'; *cylen* 'kiln, oven'; *cyrten* 'beautiful'

5: *æbs* 'fir tree'; *belt* 'belt, girdle'; *cālend* 'first day of the month; (in poetry) month'; *centaur* 'centaur'; *clūstor* 'lock, etc.'; *copp* 'cup, etc.'; *corn-*(trēo) 'cornel tree'; *cypressus* 'cypress'; *fæċele* 'torch'

4: *accent* 'accent'; *acolitus* 'acolyte'; *aspide* 'asp, viper'; *cranic* 'chronicle'; *crūc* 'cross'; *forc, forca* 'fork'; *fullere* 'fuller'; *gabote, gafote* kind of dish or platter

3: *apostata* 'apostate'; *capun* 'capon'; *cæfester* 'muzzle, halter, bit'; *ċearricge* (uncertain meaning); *ċemes* 'shirt, undergarment'; *cirps, crisp* 'curly, curly haired' (> *cirpsian* 'to make curly' 5); *copor* 'copper' (probably > *cyperen* 'made of copper' 21); *dēclīnian* 'to decline or inflect'; *derodine* 'scarlet'; *earfe* plant name, probably vetch; *fifele* 'broach, clasp'; *foca* 'cake baked on the ashes of the hearth'; *glēsan* 'to gloss, explain'; *ġebrēfan* 'to set down briefly in writing'

2: *basilisca* 'basilisk'; *byxen* 'of box wood'; *ċæfl* 'muzzle, halter, bit'; *calcatrippe* 'caltrops'; *acōfrian* 'to recover' (< **cōfrian*); *coorte, coorta* 'cohort'; *cucumer* 'cucumber'; *cȳfl* 'tub, bucket'; *cypera* 'salmon at the time of spawning'; *cystan* 'to get the value of, etc.'; *dēmōn* 'devil, demon'; *eretic* 'heretic'; *fiþelere* 'fiddler'; *flȳtme* 'lancet'; *foss* 'ditch';[10] *grammatic-*cræft 'grammar'

1: *acūsan* 'to accuse (someone)'; *bærbære* 'barbarous, foreign'; *bīsæċċ* 'pocket'; *calc* 'sandal'; cantel-*cāp* 'cloak worn by a cantor'; *cælis* 'foot-covering'; *cæpse* 'box'; *consolde* '(perhaps) daisy or comfrey'; *codd-*(æppel) 'quince';[11] *coron-*(bēag) 'crown'; *crismal* 'chrism cloth'; *cubit* 'cubit, measure of length'; *culpa* 'fault, sin'; *cūsc* 'virtuous, chaste'; *cyrtan* 'to shorten' (debatably); *eofole* 'dwarf elder, danewort'; *fiþela* 'fiddler'; *fiþelestre* 'fiddler'; *flanc* 'flank'; *fostere* 'spade'; *ġecorded* 'having cords, etc.'; *ġellet* 'jug, bowl, or basin'; *graþul* 'gradual';

(0: *ċiċeling* 'chickpea'; *cocc* 'cockle'; *delfīn* 'dolphin')

The two most frequently attested formations showing *arce-, ærċe-* 'arch-' in titles are *arce-bisċeop* (*c.*800 examples) and *arce-dīacon* (*c.*35 examples).

There are thus huge disparities in the frequency of the surviving attestations of these words. A few, like *bisċeop, dēofol,* or *engel,* form part of the

---

[10] Although both examples may instead show a proper noun, the name of the Fosse Way.

[11] Additionally, the two instances of *gōdæppel* may show a folk-etymological alteration of this word; compare Bierbaumer (1975–9) III 115, Feulner (2000) 150–2.

core vocabulary of religion or the Church, and are amply attested in our surviving sources. However, these figures need to be handled carefully. The surviving corpus of Old English writings is relatively small (see section 3.6). Many of our surviving texts incline strongly towards various technical registers and almost all texts have been mediated through clerics. The surviving material is also mostly from the late tenth century and later, and is mostly written in the West Saxon dialect, and in particular in that variety of West Saxon that came in later Old English to serve as a written variety in learned communities throughout England. The (very small) body of surviving verse is written in a highly stylized and archaic language, which is dialectally mixed and contains some special vocabulary that may be very old.

Some words appear to be very frequent from the raw frequency numbers, but most of the examples are found in only one or two particular texts. For instance, *consul* is found 225 times, but all but five of these examples are from the same text, the translation of *Orosius* from the circle of Alfred the Great. *Castel* 'village, small town; (in late manuscripts) castle' is found 140 times, but mainly in the *Anglo-Saxon Chronicle* (in late uses in the meaning 'castle' perhaps as a separate borrowing from Anglo-French: see sections 12.2.1, 13.1.1). Another word found chiefly in the *Anglo-Saxon Chronicle* is *comēta* 'comet', which is recorded 29 times in total. *Antefn, antifon, antyfon* 'antiphon (type of liturgical chant)', recorded 110 times, is found mainly in the *Benedictine Rule* and *Regularis Concordia*. *Circul* 'circle, cycle', recorded 75 times, is found mainly in Byrhtferth's *Manual*.

Butere 'butter' has no exact synonyms in Old English (although *smeoru* 'fat, grease, lard' comes close), but its high frequency rate (around 200 examples, plus uses in compounds) is largely due to its frequent occurrence in surviving medical recipes; without the survival of these, the word would have left a very much smaller trace in our documentary record (although there are references to production of butter for culinary use, notably in the Old English translation of Ælfric's *Colloquy*). Other words that the *DOE* notes are recorded only or mostly in medical recipes are: *fēfer, fefer* 'fever'; *finol, finule, finugle* 'fennel'; *cucler* 'spoon'; *eċed* 'vinegar'; *eolone, elene* 'elecampane'; *elehtre* '(probably) lupin'; *ċerfille, ċerfelle* 'chervil'; *alwe* 'aloe'; *fēferfuge* (or *feferfuge*), *fēferfugie* (or *feferfugie*) 'feverfew'; *cāwel, cawel* 'cabbage'. Others are found mostly in medical recipes and in glossaries, e.g. *cyrfet* 'gourd'; *glædene* a plant name; *cost* 'costmary'; *croh, crog* 'saffron'; *bēte* 'beet, beetroot'; *ātrum, atrum, attrum* 'black vitriol; atrament; blackness'; *berbēne* 'vervain, verbena'.

As already noted, the language of Old English verse is highly stylized and traditional; it is notable that many of the borrowings, especially the later ones, figure little if at all in the surviving verse texts. For instance, the *DOE* notes that just four of the 1,400 examples of *apostol* 'apostle' are in verse. All of the five examples of *clūstor* 'lock, etc.' are in verse, but this is not true of the later doublet *clauster* 'monastic cell, etc.'.[12]

Sometimes the evidence of proper names can be a very helpful supplement to the literary record: for instance, *ċealc* 'chalk' is rare in the literary record but common in place names, and so it must have been a common word at least at one time; *byxen* 'of box wood' has only two attestations, but also occurs in a place name.

Old English lexis shows a high degree of full or partial synonymy, with more than one word realizing (so far as we can determine) the same meaning; the *Thesaurus of Old English* (Roberts and Kay (1995), henceforth *TOE*) and the *Historical Thesaurus of the Oxford English Dictionary* (*HTOED*) now give us wonderful tools for exploring such situations. Thus *bīsæċċ* 'pocket', *ċeosol* in the sense 'belly', and *ċipp* 'beam' can all quite easily be seen to be fairly rare synonyms of other words in these basic meanings. *Altare* and *alter* 'altar' are recorded 35 times altogether; but *wēofod*, the first element of which reflects a heathen word for an idol, is much commoner in Old English in this meaning. However, the surviving written records sometimes leave rather more uncertainty about which was actually the more commonly used term in a pair or group of synonyms. *Belt* shows a basic meaning 'belt' and is the usual word in this meaning in modern English, but the *TOE* and *HTOED* show that *gyrdel* exists as a synonym, and the *DOE* shows that it is more common in our surviving texts (35 examples for *gyrdel*, as opposed to five, mainly glossarial, examples for *belt*); our records are not sufficient to tell us whether there may have been some difference of register between these two words.

Copor 'copper' is recorded only three times, but there are no synonyms recorded for this word in Old English, and the related adjective *cyperen* 'made of copper' is rather commoner in the surviving texts. *Cirps, crisp* 'curly, curly haired' is also only recorded a handful of times, but also has no recorded synonyms. The derivative *cirpsian* is recorded very slightly more often. The surviving text types may well play a part in its being recorded

---

[12] For a good deal of useful comment on the occurrences of the borrowings in verse texts, see Serjeantson (1935) 18–22, 43–4.

so rarely. The same probably applies to *culter* 'coulter', recorded only six times in this sense. *Culfre* 'dove' is recorded 200 times; interestingly, there are no secure examples of **dufe*, the ancestor of modern *dove*, although the evidence of other Germanic languages suggests that the word probably existed in Old English.

By contrast, *elpend, ylpend* 'elephant' is recorded 29 times in the surviving literature (excluding the shortened form *ylp*), but elephants were hardly central to Anglo-Saxon society; ivory was much prized, but much of it came from walrus tusks. *Olfend* 'camel' is even more common in the surviving texts, reflecting their frequent focus on the Bible and the Holy Land. The relatively high frequency of *fenix* 'phoenix' also reflects the predominance of texts with a religious focus. *Cāsere* 'emperor, ruler' is very common in our literary records, but occurs largely denoting either ancient Roman emperors or modern continental (Holy Roman) emperors, or sometimes in extended application to various other rulers or in certain collocations in rather elevated language. In spite of its high frequency, it seems unlikely that it was an everyday word in the vocabulary of Old English and it is notable that no regularly developed reflex **coser* survives in later English.

An interesting perspective is given by *discipul*, recorded 110 times, and hence one of the higher-frequency items in these lists. However, the meanings of Latin *discipulus* are also rendered in Old English by the loan translation *leorningcniht*, for which the *DOE Corpus* gives 445 examples, as well as by a number of other terms (for which see the *TOE* and especially MacGillivray (1902) 43–51); completion of the *DOE* will make a thorough re-investigation of this complex word group much more feasible.

7.5.3 Loanwords showing basic meanings

Comparison with a list of basic word meanings gives one useful measure of how borrowing from Latin affected some fairly basic areas of vocabulary. If we return to the tools examined in section 2.3, none of the Old English borrowings from Latin are the usual realization in Old English of a meaning from the 100-meaning Leipzig-Jakarta List of Basic Vocabulary. However, the 1,460-meaning list that was used as the basis for the WOLD survey contains a number of the meanings found among the Latin borrowings in Old English. As already noted in section 2.3, this list contains some items (e.g. 'bank', 'film/movie', or 'driver's licence') that are self-evidently entirely anachronistic if we are looking at Old English, and others such as 'elephant', 'camel', 'lion', or 'panther' that are very marginal from the standpoint of Anglo-Saxon society; all four of these 'exotic' meanings are realized by Latin loanwords in Old English, but they can hardly be regarded as core vocabulary items from the perspective of Old English. However, these disadvantages are at least partly offset by the benefits of using a list that has proved workable in Haspelmath and Tadmor (2009) in examining the vocabularies of a wide range of contemporary languages from widely varying cultures, as well as a few older languages (such as Old High German).

By my calculation, 137 of the 1,460 meanings in this list, a little under 10%, are sometimes realized by one or more words borrowed from Latin in Old English; this includes meanings from 21 of the 24 categories, only Kinship, Quantity, and Miscellaneous function words not being represented at all. (Although the representation of some categories, such as Animals, would be considerably reduced if we pruned out some words of very limited relevance to everyday life in Anglo-Saxon England.) I have omitted from this total words that only come to realize basic meanings from the list later than the Old English period, such as *ċist, ċest*, which only comes to denote 'chest' as part of the body very much later, or similarly *nōn,* which only acquires the meaning 'noon' in early Middle English, or *forc, forca,* which does not denote a fork as an item of cutlery in Old English (this meaning, indeed, being a poor candidate for a basic meaning in the early Middle Ages, forks having been very rare in the West until the early modern period or even later).

Section 7.5.2 looks at how using frequency information in conjunction with the *TOE* and *HTOED* can give some important insights into the impact of words borrowed from Latin on the vocabulary of Old English. Using this list of 1,460 basic meanings in conjunction with the same tools can help narrow the focus on the impact of Latin borrowing on basic levels of the vocabulary.

Some of the meanings in this list seem, from our surviving records, always to be realized by a borrowed word, i.e. the borrowed words have no (exact) synonyms in the relevant meanings: *butere* 'butter' (and its compounds: although compare section 7.5.2); *ele* 'oil'; *cyċene* 'kitchen'; *ċȳse, ċēse* 'cheese'; *wīn* 'wine' (and its compounds); *sæterndæġ* 'Saturday'; *mūl* 'mule'; *ancor* 'anchor'; *līne* in the meaning 'line, continuous length'; *mylen* (and its compounds) in the general meaning 'mill'; *scōl* and *sċolu* (and the compound *leornungscōl*) in the meaning 'school' (although there are other words recorded in the meanings 'school-house' and 'monastic school-house').

Thus, if we can be confident that these concepts were important ones in Anglo-Saxon society (which in some cases would require the input of a cultural historian rather than a linguist to confirm), then we can also be confident that these loanwords were the words used to realize them. (*Pipor* 'pepper' also has no synonyms, but this probably falls among the meanings from the WOLD meaning list that, for cultural and historical reasons, fell outside the core vocabulary of Old English, like *olfend* 'camel', *lēo* 'lion', etc.)

In other cases a borrowed word is the usual, but not the only, word in a particular meaning from the list: *weall* for 'wall'; *pīpe* for 'pipe, tube'; *pīle* for 'mortar' (i.e. vessel in which something is ground); *disċ* for 'plate/platter/bowl/dish'; *candel* for 'lamp, lantern, candle' (but with some complex overlap with other words in the same semantic field); *torr* for 'tower'; *prēost* and *sācerd* (both borrowed) for 'priest'.

In some other cases probably the most that we can say is that a borrowed word is more frequent than its synonyms in a particular basic meaning. *Port* is probably rather more common than *hæfen* or *hȳþ* in the meaning 'harbour'. *Munt* appears to be more frequent than *beorg, hylle, dūn*, or *cnoll* for 'mountain or hill' (although it should be noted that it occurs chiefly in Biblical contexts). Contrast section 7.5.2 on *belt* beside *gyrdel*. In a more complex case, *ċelċ, cælic, calic* is (if, like the *DOE*, we take these forms together) the most frequent of the 'drinking vessel' words in the surviving texts (not, in spite of its later dominance, borrowed *cuppe* or *copp*, nor non-borrowed *sċenċ* or *drenċfæt*); however, the *DOE*'s figures do not distinguish between the general meaning 'cup, drinking vessel' and specific meanings such as 'the cup or chalice in which the wine of the Eucharist is administered' (both of these meanings are well represented by quotations in the *DOE*).

7.5.4 A closer examination of borrowed verbs

One immediate point of interest is the verbs in this list. They are relatively few, but this is normal in borrowing situations. Section 7.4 looked at how words are normally accommodated to the morphological paradigms of Old English. The verb conjugations in Old English are divided into two main groups: weak and strong. The weak verbs form their past tense by means of a dental suffix (modern English -*ed*), while the strong verbs show alternation in the vowel of the root syllable. The type of vowel alternation involved goes back to proto-Indo-European and is referred to by philologists as ablaut. It plays a major role in the morphological paradigms and word-formation processes of reconstructed Indo-European. In proto-Germanic, ablaut relationships were exploited in a systematic way in realizing distinctions of time and number in the verb system. Such strong verbs often convey basic or primary meanings, and tend to stand at the heart of groups of related words. Weak verbs tend to convey less primary meanings and are often fairly transparent derivatives from nouns or adjectives or from strong verbs. For instance, we find numerous pairings where the strong verb has primary meaning and the related weak verb has causative meaning or inchoative meaning, e.g. *settan* 'to set' is a weak derivative from the past stem of *sittan* 'to sit'.[13] Few if any new strong verbs were formed within the documentary period, although we do find very occasional examples of weak verbs shifting to one of the strong classes (a late example is *ring*); a number of strong verbs were borrowed from early Scandinavian and accommodated to the English strong verb classes; *strive* shows a very rare example of a French borrowing giving rise to a verb that is normally strong in English.

Borrowed verbs in Old English are normally weak. Some belong to the Old English first weak class, with infinitive in -*an*, but more belong to the second weak class, with infinitive in -*ian*; some vary in conjugation. In the first weak class the inflectional endings were originally preceded by a formative element *-*i*- or *-*j*- which was lost before the period of our documentary evidence, but had an effect on certain vowels in the preceding syllable, as e.g. in *pynġan* < Latin *pungere*. On the sound change involved here, see section 8.1.1.

For all of the Old English verbs that show likely direct borrowings from Latin, see the listings in sections 6.3.1, 6.3.2, and 6.3.3, but see also sections 7.2 and 7.3 for the possibility that some of these words may be derivatives from other borrowed words. A few Old English verbs are probably formed on Latin words from other word classes, e.g. **cyrtan* 'to shorten' (< *curtus*, adjective) or **platian* 'to make or beat into thin plates' (< *plata*, noun) (although it should be noted that in both of these cases the Old English

---

[13] For further explanation and further examples, see Lass (1994) 166–9.

verb is not directly attested and its existence is simply assumed from the existence of apparent derivatives). In two cases verbs have probably been remodelled with native suffixes: *salletan* (< Latin *psallere* and preserved in only a single attestation) probably shows remodelling with the Old English frequentative suffix *-ettan*, probably prompted by the Latin imperative form *psallite*, which it glosses; *scrūtnian*, *scrūdnian* 'to examine' (< Latin *scrūtināre*) probably shows remodelling with the native verbal suffix *-nian*.

In addition, there are numerous weak verbs that were (definitely or probably) formed on other words borrowed from Latin, such as *campian* 'to fight'; *ceapian* 'to buy and sell, etc.'; *mangian* 'to trade, etc.'; *orgnian*, *organian* 'to sing to an instrumental accompaniment'; *pīlian* 'to pound in a mortar'; *pīnian* 'to torture, etc.': see section 7.2 for further examples.

The loanword *scrīfan* (< Latin *scrībere*; modern English *shrive*) is especially interesting because it is a strong verb. It belongs to the Class I conjugation of strong verbs, showing infinitive *scrīfan*, past tense singular *scrāf*, past plural *scrifon*, past participle *scrifen*; the pattern is preserved to some extent in modern English in the participle *shriven* and probably also in the related *Shrove Tuesday*. This verb therefore belongs to the same class as *rīdan* 'to ride', *glīdan* 'to glide', *wrītan* 'to write', and a large number of others. Nothing else about the form of *scrīfan* points to particularly early borrowing: occurrence of medial *f* in a word with Latin *b* is normal in all but late learned borrowings (e.g. *cubit*); the change /sk/ to /ʃ/ presents a number of notoriously thorny problems for Old English philologists, but does not point to a particularly early borrowing (and our first secure evidence that this change actually happened in this word comes from much later spellings). However, we do find (apparent) cognates in other West Germanic languages, including: Old Frisian *scrīva*, Old Dutch *skrīvan*, Old Saxon *skrīban*, Old High German *scrīban*; we also find Old Swedish *skrīva*, and (with a short stem vowel) Old Icelandic *skrifa*. These infinitive forms are all fairly predictable phonological shapes for borrowings of Latin *scrībere* and so we might want to exercise caution in ruling out parallel borrowing from Latin in each case. However, with the exception of Old Icelandic *skrifa* and some other rare instances in Scandinavian languages, they are all conjugated strong, e.g. Old Frisian *scrīva*, *skref*, *skreven*, etc. As already discussed, this verb is exceptional in being a borrowed verb accommodated to the strong conjugation (although there is the occasional later parallel, such as *strive*, as already noted a fairly certain early Middle English borrowing from French); it would be stretching coincidence too far to suggest that this had happened independently in each of these languages, although we cannot entirely rule out some very early borrowing between various Germanic varieties, with substitution of the vowel alternations found in Class I verbs in each language. The balance of probability certainly points to *scrīfan* reflecting a fairly early borrowing from Latin into continental Germanic.

We may also perhaps speculate a little about a possible cause for this verb becoming a strong Class I verb. As already noted, such verbs are fairly numerous and so they probably exercised a strong analogical attraction for a borrowed verb with stem vowel *ī*. It is tempting to speculate that there could have been some particular analogical influence from the ancestor of *wrītan* 'to write' and its cognates; it is normally assumed that the ancestor of *wrītan* showed in proto-Germanic the senses 'to tear' and 'to scratch', and hence the meaning 'to write' developed in the context of runic inscriptions. In Old English *scrīfan* does not show the meaning 'to write', instead only showing various metaphorical meanings that had developed from it already in Latin, but it does mean 'to write' from an early date in Old High German (and became the usual verb in this meaning in German: modern German *schreiben*); thus this may reflect the earliest meaning of an early Germanic borrowing. However, as so often, radically different explanations have been offered by some scholars, who would see the strong conjugation of *scrīfan* and its Germanic relatives as evidence that they are not borrowings from Latin at all, but instead show Latin semantic (and perhaps also formal) influence on an otherwise unevidenced inherited Germanic strong verb. Alternatively, some assume that the sense 'to write' in continental Germanic languages results from secondary borrowing. (For useful discussions, see Seebold (1970) 419–20, Pfeifer (2000) 1242, Kluge (2002) 825.) For a different account again, which actually assumes separate borrowing of the Latin word into Old English and Old High German and then overlapping influence of each on other Germanic languages, see Green (1998) 263–4; however, this account offers no explanation for the enormous coincidence of the verb being strong in each case. An additional reason for suspecting that there is at least some connection between all of the Germanic verbs is the existence of formal parallels of the derivative noun *shrift* in a number of languages (although the meanings of these nouns differ widely).

8

Methodologies: sound change; word geography; loanwords versus semantic borrowing

8.1 Evidence based on English and Latin sound change

Chapter 4 looked in general terms at the methodology by which regular sound changes can be used to help determine the likely relative dates of borrowing of different words. The present section looks at some practical examples where sound change plays a key role in suggesting when a borrowing occurred, at least relative to other word histories. Assigning an exact historical date to a sound change is a much more difficult matter for a number of reasons, especially in this period when both our linguistic and our historical knowledge is so limited.[1]

It will make sense to look first at a very broad outline of some of the most important Old English and proto-Old English sound changes. Some of these changes occur only in one or more of the four Old English dialects that have been identified on the basis of the surviving evidence: West Saxon (centred on the south and south-west, but also the basis for a late Old English literary

---

[1] In addition to the studies listed in n. 6, chapter 6, Luick (1914–21) and Campbell (1959) are invaluable for their detailed accounts of sound changes and other formal developments affecting earlier and later loanwords. In addition to these two grammars, Hogg (1992a), Hogg (1992b), and Lass (1994) all give excellent accounts of the sound changes; Hamer (1967) and Brook (1947) are both very useful for the beginner, as is Appendix 1 in Smith (2007).

variety very widely used in writing), Kentish (centred on Kent), Northumbrian (centred on the north), and Mercian (centred on the midlands). Features shared by Northumbrian and Mercian are referred to collectively as Anglian.

8.1.1 A selective list of changes

What follow are short summaries of some of the main changes that are shown by words discussed below, arranged in what is generally taken to be very roughly their chronological sequence. For ease of reference, I have assigned an identifier to each, as 'Change A', 'Change B', etc.

In the presentation of the changes here, the output forms are the orthographic forms found in most of the surviving Old English texts, although with added macrons to distinguish vowel length; the input forms are the reconstructed sounds of an earlier stage of the language, rendered using the same alphabetical characters with the same orthographic values; I have only given transcriptions in the International Phonetic Alphabet where the orthographic forms are likely to be found confusing.

In proto-Germanic:
e > *i* before a nasal plus another consonant   (Change A)

In proto-Old English:
Fronting:[2]   (Change B)

    when not immediately followed by a nasal consonant
      (i) (generally called First Fronting)
         a > *æ*
         (which, at different dates, > *e* in south Mercian and in Kentish)
      (ii) (in a similar but distinct change)
         ā (earlier *ǣ*) > *ǣ* (in West Saxon), *ē* (in Anglian and in Kentish)

---

[2] Very similar changes occur in Old Frisian, although the supposition that they therefore indicate a shared 'Anglo-Frisian' stage of common development is now considered unlikely: for a recent short overview of the various complications and alternative hypotheses, see Bremmer (2009) 125–8. Certainly, these early changes must reflect what were at least tendencies in proto-Old English at the time of the Settlement. Old Frisian also presents some intriguing but not entirely precise parallels to the next change outlined below, breaking. It should be noted that many of the West Germanic languages show very similar developments to English long after English had come to Britain, most notably *i*-mutation and the lengthening in open syllables which occurred in early Middle English.

Monophthongization of *ai > ā*   (Change C)

Breaking: (Change D)

> *i > io* before *h, hC, rC* (where C = any consonant)
>
> *e > eo* before *h, hC, rC, lh*, sometimes *lC*
>
> *æ > ea* before *h, hC, rC*, and (in West Saxon and Kentish) *lC*
>
> *ī > īo* before *h, hC*
>
> *ǣ > ēa* before *h, hC*
>
> *ē > ēo* before *h* (in the Anglian dialects only)

Restoration: (Change E)

> Fronted *æ > a* before a following back vowel, thus nominative and accusative plural *dagas* 'days' beside nominative and accusative singular *dæg*

Palatalization of velar consonants: (Change F)

> Velar *g* and *c* (and *sc*) become palatalized (or fronted) before front vowels; eventually, these became /j/ and /tʃ/ (the latter change is normally called assibilation)
>
> *sc* became (eventually) /ʃ/ before front vowels and usually also before back vowels and consonants as well[3]

In the orthographic forms typically given in grammars and dictionaries, and in this book, these sounds are represented by *ġ, ċ, sċ* respectively.

Palatal diphthongization: (Change G)

> (Somewhat controversially and chiefly in West Saxon) after palatalized *ġ, ċ*, and *sċ*
>
> *e > ie*
>
> *ē > īe*
>
> *æ > ea*
>
> *ǣ > ēa*

i-mutation: (Change H)

> Before *i* or *j* in the next syllable, back vowels were fronted:
>
> *a > æ*
>
> *ā > ǣ*
>
> *o > oe* /ø/ (later > *e*)

---

[3] See further section 10.2.1 on the detail of this sound change, which is important in the identification of Scandinavian influence.

$\bar{o} > \bar{o}\bar{e}$ /ø:/ (later $> \bar{e}$)
$u > y$ /y/
$\bar{u} > \bar{y}$ /y:/

Also, in the low front vowels, $æ > e$, and (if not regarded as the result of an earlier parallel change) $e > i$

Note: The i or j causing the mutation was typically lost (or lowered to e) before the period of our Old English documents, so the trigger for the change is normally invisible in our surviving forms. (However, some of the earliest documents may preserve some unmutated forms: see Lass (1994 62–3).)

Back mutation: (Change I)
   In certain conditions, $æ$, e, i were diphthongized to ea, eo, io before a back vowel in the following syllable.

Later changes, in the period of our documentary evidence:
In late West Saxon:[4]   (Change J)

$ie > y$
$\bar{\imath}e > \bar{y}$

In Kentish: (Change K)

$æ > e$
$\bar{æ} > \bar{e}$
$y > e$
$\bar{y} > \bar{e}$

8.1.2 Examples of Latin borrowings involving these changes

The proto-Germanic change $e > i$ before a nasal consonant followed by another consonant (Change A) is apparently shown by, for example, *minte* 'mint (the plant)' (< Latin *mentha*) and *ġimm* 'gem' (< Latin *gemma*; this word also shows palatalization of the initial consonant; modern English *gem* shows a Middle English borrowing from French; compare also the later Old English borrowing *ġemme*). However, it is not entirely a foregone conclusion that

---

[4] See Hogg (1992b) 117 on the complexity of the underlying process.

these words were therefore borrowed extremely early into proto-Germanic, before this raising occurred. They could instead show substitution of *i* for *e* in a phonetic environment where *e* did not occur in Old English words. This could have applied at any period up to that of *i*-mutation, when *e* again appeared before nasals in some Old English words. In the case of *minte*, the existence of Middle Dutch *minte*, Old Saxon *minta*, and Old High German *minza* probably confirms the hypothesis of shared early borrowing, although these could show parallel, independent borrowing (and there is the complicating factor that we also find Middle Dutch *munte*, *muynte*, *muente* and Old High German *munza* with unexplained variation in the stem vowel: compare Durkin (2009 202)). *Ġimm* has a cognate or parallel in Old High German *gimma* (although this word differs in gender and morphological class; on the distinction between cognates and parallels, see further section 8.2). Certainly these words can be contrasted with later borrowings that preserve Latin *e* before a nasal plus another consonant, such as *tempel* 'temple' (< Latin *templum*) or *-spendan* 'to spend' (< Latin *expendere*).

Strǣt 'road, paved road, street' (< Latin *strāta*) is almost certainly a very early Old English borrowing, because it shows fronting of *ā* > *ǣ* (Change B). It need not have preceded this particular change, since the sound *ā* did not exist in Old English after the fronting of *ā* > *ǣ* until a subsequent change *ai* > *ā* (Change C) restored this sound to the sound system of Old English (albeit with a very different distribution); thus, *strǣt* could have been borrowed during the interval between these two changes. However, since the change *ai* > *ā* was also extremely early (before breaking: Change D), we can still be confident that this was a very early borrowing. Exactly the same considerations apply to *nǣp* 'turnip' (< Latin *nāpus*) and *rǣdiċ* 'radish' (< Latin *rādīc-*, *rādīx*). The hypothesis that *strǣt* was borrowed very early is reinforced by the existence of cognates or parallels in other West Germanic languages: Old Frisian *strēte*, Old Dutch *strāta*, Old Saxon *strāta*, and Old High German *strāza*. All of these accord well with the idea that the word was borrowed early into proto-West Germanic, before the fronting of *ā* > *ǣ* in Old English and Old Frisian; they do not provide absolute proof, but enough to satisfy most scholars and dictionaries that this can in all likelihood be taken to be a common proto-West Germanic borrowing. By contrast, *nǣp* does not have cognates or parallels in other early Germanic languages (forms found in North Germanic languages are probably borrowed from English), and in the case of *rǣdiċ* the early borrowings from Latin *rādīc-*, *rādīx* found in other West Germanic languages show (apparently unexplained) shortening of the stem vowel: Middle Dutch *radic*, Old Saxon *redik*, and Old High German *ratih*.

Another word with *ǣ* for Latin *ā* is the ancestor of modern English *cheese*. Latin *cāseus* was borrowed very early into proto-Old English as **kāsi* /kɑːsi/. It then showed fronting of *ā > ǣ*, **kǣsi* /kæːsi/ (Change B). The velar was then palatalized, giving **ćǣsi* /tʃæːsi/ (Change F). Palatal diphthongization then followed, giving (if we simplify the details very slightly) **ćēasi* /tʃæasi/ (Change G), and *i*-mutation then gave **cīesi* /tʃiːysi/ (Change H). Lowering of final *i* gave **ćīese* /tʃiːyse/, which is what we should expect to find in early West Saxon, except that the word is not recorded in any of our surviving early West Saxon texts. With the late West Saxon change *īe > ȳ* (Change J) we finally reach the recorded form, late West Saxon *ćȳse* /tʃyːse/. To summarize:

*kāsi /kɑːsi/ > **kǣsi* /kæːsi/ > **ćǣsi* /tʃæːsi/ > **ćēasi* /tʃæasi/ > **cīesi* /tʃiːysi/ > **ćīese* /tʃiːyse/ > *ćȳse* /tʃyːse/

In fact, modern English *cheese* is not derived from late West Saxon *ćȳse* but from the Anglian form *ćēse*, which shows a much simpler history:

*kāsi /kɑːsi/ > (with fronting, Change B) **kēsi* /keːsi/ > (with palatalization of the velar, Change F, and lowering of final *-i*) *ćēse* /tʃeːse/

This word history has considerable importance, even notoriety, in Old English studies. Since the middle of the twentieth century a dispute has been raging among Old English scholars about whether the change called palatal diphthongization ever actually occurred, or whether what appear to be diphthongs are in fact simply digraph spellings intended to signal the palatal quality of the preceding consonant, since the graphs <c> and <g> were used for both the palatal and velar sounds. Late West Saxon *ćȳse* has assumed crucial importance in this debate because it is the only Old English form that probably cannot be explained except by palatal diphthongization. However, some scholars have countered that sound changes are not normally constructed on the basis of single word forms, on the principle that a single word history may simply be anomalous.[5] Fortunately, the much less problematic history of the non-West Saxon form *ćēse* also supports the hypothesis that the borrowing was very early, before the fronting of *ā > ǣ/ē*.

---

[5] For summaries and further references, see Hogg (1992a) 119–21, Hogg (1992b) 112, Lass (1994) 81–2.

Earc and *arc* 'ark, chest, coffer' (Latin < *arca*) apparently show parallel earlier and later borrowings, the first with fronting of *a* > *æ* (Change B) and breaking of *æ* > *ea* (Change D), and the second without these changes. A similar pairing is shown by *ċealc* (which additionally shows palatalization, Change F) and *calc* 'chalk, plaster' (< Latin *calc-*, *calx*), and perhaps also by *sealm* and *salm* 'psalm' (< Latin *psalma*), unless the occurrence of *salm* in West Saxon texts simply reflects the adoption of an Anglian form, or, alternatively, the word in all of its forms was a late borrowing and *sealm* arose by analogy with other words of this shape. Theoretically these alternative scenarios could apply to *arc* as well. Compare similarly *salter*, *sealtere* 'psalter, also type of stringed instrument', which is surely a learned borrowing after the period of conversion to Christianity, but which nonetheless shows similar variation.

*Pilian 'to peel, strip, pluck' (< Latin *pilāre*) is not attested at all in Old English. However, its later form history suggests that not only did it exist in Old English, but it was probably a (reasonably) early borrowing, since it seems likely that it showed variants **piolian*, **peolian*, resulting from back mutation (Change I) in parts of the paradigm where a back vowel immediately followed the *l*.

8.1.3 Examples involving changes in Latin as well as English

Some loanword etymologies involve unattested form developments in Latin. For instance, *mynster* 'minster' shows a borrowing ultimately from Latin *monastērium* (which is in turn of Greek origin), but its phonology involves several reconstructed steps. The *y* in the Old English form apparently results from *i*-mutation of earlier **u* (Change H). Old English *u* is regularly found for Latin *o* before a nasal and/or *i*/*j* in the next syllable, hence we have an explanation for **u* in this word. However, the *i*-mutation of **u* > *y* still needs an explanation. One explanation, accepted by many scholars, is that the donor form may in fact have been an unrecorded Latin variant **monistērium*, with raising of the unstressed vowel in the second syllable. This hypothesis is supported by Old High German *munistri* (and by modern German *Münster*, showing the results of *i*-mutation). Among other forms in West Germanic languages are Middle Dutch *monster*, *munster*, Middle Low German *münster*, *mönster*, Old High German *munster*, *monster*; the relationships among them are very uncertain and it is not unlikely that various borrowings between Germanic languages occurred during the process of Christianization. In fact, an alternative explanation was advanced for the Old English form by the distinguished grammarian Alistair Campbell, who assumed loss of the second syllable of the Latin word when it was borrowed into English and development of borrowed $\bar{e} > i$ in an unaccented syllable, hence *munstir-*, with resultant *i*-mutation. This same explanation would also work plausibly for Old High German *munistri* (and modern German *Münster*). It also works well for another word, Old English *mynet* 'coin, etc.' This is ultimately from Latin *monēta*, and probably again shows development of borrowed $\bar{e} > i$ in an unaccented syllable and development of $o > u$ before a nasal and/or *i/j* in the next syllable. The same explanation also works for the corresponding forms found in other West Germanic languages in the same meaning: Old Frisian *menote, mente, munte*, Middle Dutch *munte, muynte, monte, moente*, Old Saxon *munita*, Old High German *munizza* (modern German *Münze*).

Both of these explanations involve hypothesizing stages of development in either Latin or Old English which would not be surprising in each language, but which reflect tendencies rather than regular sound changes. Many other word histories involve sound changes that are regular in Vulgar Latin, just as fronting or *i*-mutation are in Old English. Vulgar Latin is the term usually used to denote the regular descendant of spoken Latin of the imperial era, from which the Romance languages ultimately developed. Many of its most important characteristics can only be traced through the later evidence of the Romance languages and through loans into other languages, since written Latin remained very conservative and yields only limited clues about changes that were happening in the spoken language. Later (although precisely when is the subject of considerable controversy) a more conservative 'Church Latin' spoken variety developed on the basis of the written forms (although it showed many differences of quantity and accentuation from classical Latin) and this slowly came to be distinguished, as 'Latin', from the vernacular Romance languages that developed from spoken Vulgar Latin.[6] (Although nomenclature varies, 'post-classical Latin' is often used as a cover term when it is not necessary to distinguish Vulgar Latin from the learned variety. This is the usual practice for instance in *OED3*.)

---

[6] Some important, although controversial, perspectives on this topic are found in the work of Roger Wright: see especially Wright (1982), Wright (2002), and the edited collection Wright (1996).

Some of the most important of Vulgar Latin changes are (in very crude summary):

Vowel lowering: (Change α)

   i > e
   u > o

Occlusivization (or hardening):   (Change β)

   v /w/ > /v/

Voicing of stops intervocalically: (Change γ)

   p > b, t > d, k > g

We can see the implications for the dating of loanwords into Old English from examples such as *disċ* 'dish, bowl, plate' (< Latin *discus*) and *piċ* 'pitch' (< Latin *pic-, pix*), which do not show Vulgar Latin lowering of *i > e* (Change α), beside *peru* 'pear' (< Latin *pirum*, later *pera, pira, *perum*) and *seġn* 'mark, sign, banner' (< Latin *signum*, Vulgar Latin **segnum*) which do, and are therefore probably later borrowings than *disċ* and *piċ*. Similarly *culter* 'coulter' (< Latin *culter*) and *must* 'wine must, new wine' (< Latin *mustum*) do not show lowering of *u > o* (Change α), but *copor* 'copper' (< Latin *cuprum*, earlier *cyprum*, Vulgar Latin **coprum*) does. *Cyperen* 'made of copper', however, apparently shows *i*-mutation of *u*, not *o* (Change H); it may therefore show separate borrowing of Latin *cuprīnus*, with substitution of a native suffix for the ending of the Latin word. A similar situation is probably shown by *byxen* 'of box wood' beside *box* 'box tree' (although see further Pogatscher (1888) §§224–6, Wollmann (1990a) 330–1). The case of *cypera* 'salmon at the time of spawning' is very uncertain.

It can be useful to combine this approach with an examination of comparative evidence from other Germanic languages. For example, *piċ* has cognates or parallels in other West Germanic languages, albeit with variable vocalism: Middle Dutch *pec, pic*, Old Saxon *pik*, Old High German *beh, peh*. There is a straightforward cognate or parallel for *disċ* in Old High German *tisc* 'plate'; Old Saxon *disk* 'table' shows a sense development either parallel to or linked with the sense development in Latin and the Romance languages which ultimately gives rise also to modern English *desk* (a Middle English borrowing, probably from medieval Latin).

Turning to Change β, we can tell that Old English *wīn* 'wine' (< Latin *vīnum*) and *wīċ* 'dwelling, etc.' (< Latin *vīcus*) were borrowed before the Vulgar Latin change /w/ > /v/ (Change β), as was *weall* 'wall, rampart' (< Latin *vallum*), which we can see entered Old English early because it shows the Old English changes fronting of *a* > *æ* (Change B) followed by breaking of *æ* > *ea* (Change D). A similar situation is shown by *mealwe* 'mallow' (< Latin *malva*). Borrowings after the Vulgar Latin change /w/ > /v/ normally show spellings in *f* in Old English, because [f] and [v] were positional allophones of a single phoneme in Old English, [v] being found intervocalically and [f] in all other positions, and *f* was the symbol normally used to represent this phoneme. Hence we find e.g. *fann* 'winnowing-fan' (< Latin *vannus*), *fers* 'verse' (< Latin *versus*), *salfie, sealfie* 'sage' (< Latin *salvia*).

If we return to the example of *strēt* 'street' and the parallels in other West Germanic languages already discussed, we see that it also preserves the voiceless intervocalic stop of Latin *strāta*, which is another piece of evidence arguing for early borrowing (compare Change γ). The same applies to *mynet* 'coin, etc.' < *monēta*.

A very interesting word history involving aspects of both Vulgar Latin and Old English sound history is shown by *mæsse, messe* 'mass' (the religious ceremony). The Old English form found in the early West Saxon translation of Bede's *Ecclesiastical History* and in many other documents is *mæsse*, hence with a low front vowel in the first syllable. Other recorded forms are *mæssa, messe, masse*, and (in Northumbrian texts) *mesa, measse*. The word is clearly ultimately a borrowing of Latin *missa*, and Vulgar Latin lowering of *i* > *e* (Change α) would give *messa (as reflected by forms in modern Romance languages such as French *messe*). We do not find *messa as a borrowed form in Old English, but we do find *mesa* (in which the single *s* spelling perhaps reflects sporadic simplification of double consonants) and *messe*, in which the final vowel could show a common development of *a* > *e* in an unstressed syllable, but more likely has a morphological explanation: in Latin, *missa* is a feminine noun of the first declension and in Old English it has been taken into the numerous class of weak feminine nouns (compare section 7.4), hence Vulgar Latin *messa > Old English *messe*.

Thus far we have a story that can be paralleled by numerous other cases; it is also one for which it is difficult to give any very precise historical context. However, the form *mæsse*, which is by far the most frequently found in our Old English documents, is much more difficult to explain, as are other forms reflecting a low front or back vowel (*mæssa, masse*).

The usual explanation is as follows. One of the major dialect distinctions in Old English is that where we find *æ* in the other dialects of Old English we normally find *e* in Kentish (this is because of the Kentish change *æ* > *e*, Change K). Vulgar Latin *messa may have been borrowed into the Kentish dialect of Old English and then speakers of other dialects may have introduced *æ* by analogy with all of the other words in which an *e* in Kentish corresponded to *æ* in their own dialect, therefore we find in West Saxon or Mercian *mæsse*. Thus:[7]

> Kentish *fet* 'vessel', *glednes* 'joy', etc. : *messe* 'mass'
> = West Saxon and Anglian *fæt*, *glædnes*, etc. : *mæsse*

If this hypothesis is correct, it carries with it a very plausible and tempting historical scenario: this crucial word in Christian life would appear to have been borrowed first in Kentish, which fits nicely with the earliest arrival of Augustine's mission in Canterbury and the spread of (Roman as opposed to Irish) Christianity from this Kentish base.[8]

However, other explanations are possible. Wollmann (1990b) argues instead for much earlier borrowing of a Vulgar Latin form in which the *e* had a more open quality, and hence the variation between *æ* and *e* in this word might very well go back to continental times: he thus attaches *mæsse* to a group of words connected with Christianity assumed to have belonged to Old English in pagan times, reflecting familiarity with some very basic aspects of Christianity even among the pagan Anglo-Saxons. He adduces the parallel of the Old High German form *mësse* beside *misse* in support of this, although he acknowledges that the form *mësse* could also be explained by a sound change within Old High German. This alternative explanation has not won widespread support and seems to me less plausible than borrowing of the word in the context of the Christian conversion; certainly the fact that both *mæsse* and *messe* are found in non-Kentish records seems not to argue against the assumption that *mæsse* reflects analogical substitution, since the two forms could have spread in parallel, and currency of *messe* would have been reinforced by the Vulgar Latin pronunciation *messa, so long as this pronunciation retained currency in the Church. However, the fact that a workable alternative explanation can be constructed shows how very tentative any attempts to establish links between

---

[7] On proportional analogy of this type, see Durkin (2009) 198–9.
[8] See Campbell (1959) §208 for an explanation of the form *measse*.

philological arguments and historical arguments must be in this very poorly documented period.

8.1.4 Changes of quantity reflected by late borrowings

Changes of quantity in the 'Church Latin' pronunciations of words appear to be reflected by some late loanwords: Old English *lilie* 'lily' and *cleric* 'clerk, clergyman' both reflect Church Latin pronunciations with shortening of a stressed vowel before two unstressed syllables (compare classical Latin *līlium* and *clēricus*); Latin lengthening in a stressed open syllable when one unstressed syllable followed is probably shown by e.g. Old English *grād* 'step; degree' (compare classical Latin *gradus*) and *scōl* 'school' (beside probably much earlier *scolu*; compare classical Latin *schola*), and probably also in *nōt* 'note' and related words.[9] However, questions of vowel quantity raise difficult issues of both evidence and interpretation that cannot be entered into in detail here.[10]

8.1.5 How analogy can produce misleading forms: *proud* and *pride*

As already noted, sound change is not always a completely trustworthy guide to chronology, for a variety of reasons. A clear example of this is provided by Old English *prūd* 'proud' and *prȳdo* 'pride'. Both phonology and semantics point to *prūd* being a borrowing from very early Old French (i.e. from the descendant of Latin spoken in Gaul), reflecting a sound change that was probably not earlier than the ninth century. However, the Old English derivative *prȳdo* 'pride' appears to show *i*-mutation (Change H), even though the period of *i*-mutation was earlier than this. Probably analogy with existing word pairs such as *full* 'full' and *fyllu* 'fullness' has given rise to the same vowel alternation in *prūd* and *prȳdo*, giving the false appearance that *i*-mutation has taken place here.[11]

---

[9] The single piece of evidence from Old English for the vowel quantity of *nōt* 'note' and related words appears to come from an instance of the compound *wællnōt* (probably 'deadly mark') in verse.

[10] On the difficult question of dating open syllable lengthening in Vulgar Latin or proto-Romance, see especially the overview in Loporcaro (2011).

[11] See further Durkin (2009) 149, 190–1.

8.2 The problem of parallels/cognates in other Germanic languages

Many of the Latin borrowings found in Old English are also found in some or all of the other West Germanic languages, and in many cases also in North Germanic and in a very few cases also in Gothic. A number of such cases have already been encountered in this chapter and also in chapter 4. This section looks in more detail at some of the issues raised.

In many cases there is clear evidence that two (or more) separate borrowings have taken place, and that we do not have the reflex of a shared earlier borrowing. For instance, Old English *cōc* 'cook' is probably from a Church Latin form **cōcus* < earlier **cocus* < classical Latin *coquus*, thus reflecting the same lengthening in an open syllable that we saw in the case of *grād* and *scōl* in section 8.1.4. By contrast, forms in other West Germanic languages show a short vowel (Old Saxon *kok*, Old High German *koh*) and probably reflect a distinct borrowing < Latin **cocus*.

If there is no such evidence arguing against shared borrowing, it is sometimes rather readily assumed that related forms show the reflexes of a shared borrowing at a date before the various languages definitively split from one another. However, it is possible to apply much more stringent criteria and say that parallel borrowing into different languages, probably in very similar social and cultural circumstances, cannot be ruled out except where there is positive evidence in favour of shared borrowing. Such criteria were applied in chapter 4 when looking at possible borrowings into proto-Germanic, where shared innovation in form or meaning was used as the criterion for identifying probable shared early borrowings.

Even when we make our criteria very strict indeed, it is often difficult to rule out the possibility that borrowing between different Germanic varieties has occurred, giving a false appearance of either shared or parallel early borrowing. Occasionally either phonology or morphology reveals that such borrowing between Germanic varieties has indeed occurred. For instance, Old Frisian *kiste* 'chest' might be assumed to be an early borrowing from Latin, like Old English *ċist*, *ċest* 'chest' and probably also Middle Dutch *kiste*, Middle Low German *kiste*, and Old High German *kista*. However, the absence of palatalization and assibilation of the initial consonant in Old Frisian points to this word being a later borrowing, probably from either Middle Dutch or Middle Low German, which are contemporary with the earliest substantial records for Frisian.[12] Generally, the earlier we go the more difficult it becomes to detect such borrowing between Germanic varieties, although that does not necessarily mean that it was not happening.

Most etymological dictionaries make little or no attempt to reflect these multiple possibilities, and clarity is not aided by the often rather loose use of the term 'cognate' in the historical linguistics literature: sometimes 'cognate' is used in a narrow sense 'definitely showing a single shared word history' (its usual meaning in this book), but sometimes it is used in a much wider sense to mean something like 'showing ultimately the same origin and not clearly identifiable as showing a divergent or distinct strand of development', and more often it is used rather indiscriminately to describe either situation, with little thought as to which is the more likely in a given instance.

This looseness in the application of terminology is not (purely) the result of lazy thinking or lack of scholarly insight: the relationships between the various attested early West Germanic varieties in particular are extremely complex and do not give us any reliable set of linguistic criteria for establishing the precise word histories of very early borrowings. The nature of our evidence condemns us to some degree of uncertainty.

Some readers may consider that the hypothesis of parallel borrowing sounds rather far-fetched and artificial, and that either shared borrowing or spread between different Germanic languages seem more natural and obvious hypotheses. If so, it is perhaps worth pausing to consider a comparable situation from a historical period for which we have much better evidence. Very many of the borrowings from French found in Middle English are also found in Middle Dutch. Particularly in the later medieval period, the borrowings often show no formal or semantic distinction in either language that would rule out the hypothesis that Dutch received the word via English rather than directly from French, or vice versa. However, this hypothesis is not normally considered unless there are very strong formal or semantic factors arguing for it, since we know that, although Middle English and Middle Dutch showed considerable contact with one another, both showed rather more contact with French.

When we come to the prehistory of the various West Germanic languages, we simply do not have this level of historical knowledge, although we can be fairly certain that all of the West Germanic varieties had at least

---

[12] See Bremmer (2009) 95.

some direct early contact with Latin and that they continued to do so throughout the period that concerns us here.

An approach that offers at least some way forward in this situation is word geography, i.e. looking at the geographical spread of Latin borrowings among the West Germanic languages and beyond. The most significant body of work in this area was undertaken by Theodor Frings in the early to mid twentieth century and published under the collective title *Germania Romana* (the second edition of which comprises two volumes: Frings (1966) and Frings and Müller (1968); there is also a useful summary of the main ideas in Frings (1957)). Frings's arguments are complex and should be pursued at first hand by anyone who has a strong interest in this subject (and a reading knowledge of German); it should also be noted as an initial caveat that the Old English data is in many cases rather marginal to his main focus on discerning the intricacies of word histories in the Rhine area. To summarize some of his key findings very simply: some Latin words with non-religious meanings found in Old English have parallels in the Netherlands and (in some cases) in Frisian-speaking areas and (in some cases) in parts of Germany centred on Cologne and Trier (which were Roman provincial cities and, later, seats of church provinces), but (crucially) not further south. Frings expresses the notion in terms of a series of areas; thus there is an England-Netherlands area, an England-Cologne area (i.e. with England at one geographical extreme and Cologne at the other), and an England-Trier area, each defined by the geographical distribution of various Latin loanwords; similarly, there are numerous areas excluding England, such as a Netherlands-Trier area and a Cologne-Trier area. Two Old English words that fall in the largest area, England-Trier, are *culter* 'coulter' and (if borrowed) *pytt* 'hole in the ground, etc.', that is to say, these words have parallels throughout this geographical area. It is tempting to see many of these patterns as reflections of early borrowing along Roman trading routes. However, an argument that Frings was at pains to make (to the frustration of some later scholars) was that these patterns do not necessarily reflect shared borrowing, but may instead show parallel borrowing in shared social and cultural circumstances. Some of the words we have considered elsewhere in this chapter fall into Frings's various areas as follows:

- England-Trier: (in addition to *pytt* and *culter*) *bytt* 'bottle, etc.', *ċemes* 'shirt, undergarment', *copor* 'copper', *fullere* 'fuller', *forc, forca* 'fork', *impian* 'to graft, etc.', (perhaps) *munt* 'mountain, hill', *nefte* 'catmint', *peru* 'pear', *pinn* 'pin, etc.', *punt* 'punt', *stropp* 'strap', *tīgle*, *tīgele*, *tigele* 'tile, etc.', *wīċ* 'dwelling, etc.', *ynne-* (in *ynnelēac*) 'onion'; also (almost certainly late in Old English) *peruince*, *perfince* 'periwinkle' and *salfie*, *sealfie* 'sage'.

- England-Cologne: *ċeaster*, *ċæster* 'town', *eċed* 'vinegar', *cyll*, *cylle* 'leather bottle, etc.', *cuppe* 'cup', (perhaps) *-estre*, suffix forming feminine agent nouns, *mangere* 'merchant, trader', *pæġel* 'wine vessel; liquid measure', *pīn* 'pine (= type of tree)', *post* 'post', *regol*, *reogol* 'rule, etc.', *sæterndæġ* 'Saturday', *spynġe* 'sponge'.
- England-Netherlands: *torr* 'tower'.

Frings's lists for each of these areas include further examples, but I have listed only those that are reasonably secure. Some of Frings's suggestions have yet to be considered in detail in the literature specifically on Old English. This would be a significant desideratum for any new etymological dictionary of Old English.

A similar argument can be made for some words reflecting specifically Christian borrowing in a similar geographical area, reflecting the influence of the Gaulish church, a key example here being *offrian* 'to offer'. In this case the assumption of parallel borrowing may appear more tempting, with parallel borrowing by Anglo-Saxons in England after the Conversion, although various other scenarios are at least imaginable.

Frings's findings from word geography thus place a number of the Old English loanwords from Latin in a particular context, showing at the very least parallels with items in other West Germanic varieties near to northern Gaul. However, Frings also draws attention to the large number of apparently early loanwords in Old English that do not have such parallels: the list of such words in Frings and Müller (1968 518–19) comes to forty-six words in total, bigger than any of the lists of shared items, and this list could be increased greatly. Some of these words are undoubtedly early in Old English, but what they imply about where and in what circumstances borrowing took place remains an open question.

8.2.1 Greek words, the hypothesis of the 'Danube mission', and some word histories that have shown frequent reappraisals

Very many words ultimately of Greek origin came into Old English through Latin. Feulner (2000) provides an excellent account of these. Her count of loanwords ultimately of Greek origin in Old English comes to over 250 words attested before 1100 (although some are very rare and some only ever appear in the Latin nominative form), plus some extensive appendices of uncertain or rejected items (including some items of the type looked at in section 7.4). There are early borrowings and many later learned ones. A few representative examples are *byden* 'vessel, etc.', *copor* 'copper', *ele* 'oil', *pæll* 'fine or rich cloth, etc.', *pīn* 'pain, etc.', or (among the more learned words) *apostata* 'apostate', *balsam*, *balzam* 'balsam, balm', *circul* 'circle, cycle', *paradīs* 'paradise, etc.', *philosoph* 'philosopher'. What knowledge even the most learned Anglo-Saxon scholars had of the ultimate Greek origin of some of these words is uncertain.

It has long been hypothesized that a number of Old English (and modern English) words ultimately of Greek origin did not come into English via Latin, but instead were early loanwords directly from Greek into Gothic and spread from Gothic to other Germanic languages. It is not at all controversial that Gothic had very extensive contact with Greek; what is much more controversial is what implications this had for other Germanic languages. A classic argument, which now has few adherents, is that words of Greek origin spread from Gothic to other Germanic languages as a result of a Danube mission by Gothic missionaries. This idea was put forward in its most influential form by the great etymologist Friedrich Kluge in the early years of the twentieth century (Kluge 1909), although the precise list of words involved has varied in later formulations of broadly the same idea.

In most more recent scholarship, there is only one Old English word for which the hypothesis of borrowing from Greek unmediated by Latin meets with widespread support, and even in this case the context of borrowing was probably very different from a Gothic Danube mission. The word in question is *church*, Old English *ċiriċe* (in late West Saxon more normally *ċyriċe*). This has parallels in other early West Germanic languages: Old Frisian *kerke*, *zerke*, Old Saxon *kirika*, *kerika*, and Old High German *kirihha*, *kilihha*. Crucially, there are no plausible donor forms in post-classical Latin nor in any variety of Romance from Gaul or Italy. The ulterior etymology of the Germanic word was long the subject of dispute, but it is now generally agreed that it is from a derivative of the (New Testament) Greek adjective κυριακός (*kyriakós*) 'holy'. The *i* /i/ in the Germanic words was a natural substitution for Greek *υ* regardless of whether that had the (earlier) value [y] or the (later) value [i], since proto-Germanic had no [y]. In Old English both velars were palatalized as we would expect (see section

8.1.1) and the late West Saxon form with *y* shows a frequent development before *r*; the forms with *e* in the first syllable in other West Germanic languages likewise have satisfactory explanations as developments in this phonetic environment. The hypothesis that the word was taken directly from Greek into at least one early Germanic language thus seems highly probable, but modern scholarship has moved the focus a long way from a hypothetical Danube mission by the Goths, who seem to have had no corresponding noun in this sense. Instead, it is now generally thought much more likely that the word reached the Germanic languages through the western church, the likely point of contact again being the colonial cities of what Frings termed 'Germania Romana' (compare section 8.2); Greek was very commonly used as the main ecclesiastical language throughout the west in late antiquity (and remained in widespread use as a liturgical language into the fourth century),[13] and it is now thought most probable that a Greek derivative noun with the meaning 'church' (or literally 'God's (house)') was borrowed into a West Germanic variety, most probably proto-Frankish, and then spread to the other early West Germanic varieties.

All of the other English words for which early borrowing directly from Greek was formerly posited are now thought by most scholars to have been borrowed via Latin, in some cases perhaps very much later than the proto-West Germanic stage. Some of the words frequently mentioned in this connection are *dēofol, dīofol* 'devil', *engel* 'angel', *prēost* 'priest', *Crēcas* 'the Greeks', and *bisċeop* 'bishop'. There are a bewildering number of attempts at explaining Old English *dēofol, dīofol* 'devil', starting out from either Greek διάβολος (*diábolos*) or (ultimately Greek-derived) Latin *diabulus*, but there is no entirely satisfactory explanation for it, nor for how the word may have spread between various Germanic languages, although it is not in doubt that it shows a very early borrowing. A good summary of the various debates is provided by Feulner (2000 192–5).

Kluge appears to have grouped *engel* 'angel' (ultimately < Greek ἄγγελος *ággelos*) together with *dēofol* as a borrowing via Gothic essentially on semantic grounds, although a reasonable case can be made on formal grounds. The word must be a fairly early borrowing in Old English because it shows *i*-mutation (see section 8.1.1) resulting from an earlier form **angil-*, unlike later Old English *angel*, which either shows re-borrowing from Latin

[13] Compare Polomé (1983) 510–11.

angelus or remodelling after the Latin word. Cognates or parallels in other West Germanic languages suggest a similar developmental pathway, but the form **angil-* is not very easily explained, since it is only in Gothic that such raising of the vowel in the second syllable would be normal, as reflected by the Gothic *aggilus*. However, most recent scholars have (explicitly or tacitly) preferred to explain the West Germanic forms as resulting from remodelling of the second syllable after words showing the native diminutive suffix **-ila-*, rather than assuming a borrowing from Gothic.

Prēost 'priest' is ultimately < Greek πρεσβύτερος (*presbúteros*); its phonology presents many points of difficulty (for a good summary, see again Feulner (2000 311–13)), but most scholars now consider it to have been a loan via Latin *presbyter* (perhaps via an unattested Latin form **prebester*); similar considerations apply to *Crēcas* 'the Greeks' (ultimately < Greek Γραικοί (*Graikoi*), the usual name for the Greeks among the Romans). The phonology of *bisċeop* 'bishop' has prompted still more discussion and leaves many questions unanswered,[14] but the balance of current scholarly opinion points to borrowing via Latin (although the precise form involved is much disputed) rather than directly from Greek ἐπίσκοπος (*epískopos*), and to a borrowing somewhere in the west rather than via Gothic or in some other eastern contact situation.

8.3 Semantic borrowing

So far we have looked only at loanwords, i.e. words that show borrowing of a word form and at least one of its associated meanings. However, various types of semantic borrowing were very typical of Old English, as they have remained typical of some of its close relatives, such as modern German, where the tendency towards semantic borrowing has been reinforced by puristic linguistic movements in recent centuries. In this chapter an exception is therefore made to the general rule elsewhere in this book, and semantic borrowing is looked at in a little detail, especially for how it compares with borrowing of loanwords in the same period. (For an introduction to the concepts involved, see section 1.2.2.)

---

[14] For some important recent discussions, see Rotsaert (1977), Wollmann (1993) 22–3, Feulner (2000), Grzega (2003).

It is usually accepted by scholars that semantic borrowing from Latin was a much more common process in Old English than borrowing of loanwords and there seems no good reason to doubt this, although it is very difficult to quantify reliably, because so much uncertainty surrounds the identification of cases of semantic borrowing. Very often non-linguistic criteria are involved in such assessments: for instance, it is normally felt that the identification of semantic borrowings is most secure in the area of religious vocabulary, since we know that the Anglo-Saxons adopted a new religion, Christianity, and had to find ways of rendering its key terms.

The most authoritative and thorough account of semantic borrowing in Old English is given by Gneuss (1955); a very useful overview and summary (in English) is given by Kastovsky (1992). My discussion here largely follows this framework, although not in all details.

Semantic borrowing can be divided into two main types, namely cases in which an existing word acquires a new meaning, and cases in which a new word is created from elements that already form part of the borrowing language in order to realize a meaning found in the donor language. Various subtypes are typically identified, especially to distinguish how much (if at all) newly created words are modelled morphologically on the word whose meaning they render.

8.3.1 Cases where existing words acquire a new meaning

In some cases, semantic borrowing involves a type of proportional analogy: a word in the donor language and a word in the borrowing language both share one meaning (A); the word in the donor language also shows a meaning (B); by semantic borrowing, the word in the borrowing language also acquires meaning B. For example:

> Latin *passiō* 'suffering' : '(Christ's) passion' = Old English *þrōwung* 'suffering' : '(Christ's) passion'
> Latin *lingua* 'tongue' : 'language' = Old English *tunge* 'tongue' : 'language'

We are almost always dealing with probabilities rather than certainties in such cases. For instance, 'language' may anyway seem a natural development from 'tongue', with or without Latin influence. The meanings 'faculty of speech', 'language' (in the abstract) are found in Old English, as well as 'a (particular) language', and the bridge seems an easy one; the *OED* (first edition) in fact comments, 'in many contexts it is impossible to separate the sense of the organ from that of its work or use'. A similar range of meanings is found in some of the other early Germanic languages, e.g. Old High German, although this may again result from Latin influence. In the case of *þrōwung* it would perhaps be arguable that use with reference to Christ's passion is simply a contextual use of 'suffering', with the particular details determined by the particular circumstances of Christ's scourging and crucifixion, rather than a truly distinct meaning, although this argument is less easy to maintain when the specific meaning 'suffering unto death' is applied also to Christian martyrs.

Another example offered by Kastovsky interestingly shows a single Old English verb probably acquiring meanings from two different Latin verbs as a result of similar processes:

> Latin *aedificāre* 'to build' : 'to edify' and Latin *instruere* 'to build' : 'to instruct' = Old English *ġetimbran* 'to build, construct, erect' : 'to edify', 'to instruct'

In some cases a word appears to acquire a meaning by association with a Latin word with which it does not show an exact semantic correspondence. For instance, *cniht* 'child, servant, retainer' acquired the additional meaning 'disciple, follower of Christ' from Latin *discipulus*, originally 'learner, pupil' (see sections 7.5.2 and also 8.3.2 on the compound *leorning-cniht*). The assumption is that the Old English word was used as a translation equivalent of the Latin word and hence came to acquire this meaning as one of its range of meanings; the initial suitability of the translation equivalent depends on at least a loose semantic correspondence between the two words. A similar process is often found in rendering specific terms relating to antiquity, e.g. Latin *cēnsor* as the title of a particular official is often rendered by *ġerēfa* 'reeve' and arguably gives rise to a new, context-specific meaning of this word; similarly, *gladiātor* 'gladiator' is rendered by the more general *cempa* 'fighter' (itself a derivative formation from a word borrowed from Latin), *rēspublica* 'republic' by *cynedōm* 'kingdom', etc. This list could be multiplied very greatly. It is perhaps questionable how far such context-specific uses of words can be said to show semantic borrowing if these meanings are entirely determined by their context, i.e. the description of events in the ancient world in texts such as the Old English translations of Orosius or of Boethius, and could not be used in other contexts without some explicit cues to the meaning. However, they do illustrate very well the strong tendency in Old English to use an existing word in a way that diverges strongly from its usual meaning, rather than resort to a loanword, as would be more typical of modern English.

8.3.2 Cases where a new word is created

The most characteristic examples of creation of a new word in a borrowing situation are loan translations, in which the newly created word to some degree 'translates' the compositional elements of the foreign-language word. In some cases this is quite exact, as in Old English *ælmihtiġ* 'almighty' which was probably formed as a loan translation of Latin *omnipotēns* (there are parallels in other West Germanic languages, such as Old High German *alamahtic*, but all of them are probably modelled ultimately on the Latin word), or similarly *godspel* 'gospel', literally 'good message', a loan translation of the (Greek) meanings of the elements of Latin *evangelium* (itself a borrowing from Greek).[15] Such formations often occur in smaller or larger groups, such as *eorþtilia*, literally 'earth-tiller', rendering the elements of Latin *agricola* 'farmer', beside *eorþtilþ*, literally 'earth-tilth', and *eorþtilung*, literally 'earth-tilling', both rendering Latin *agricultūra* 'agriculture'.

In some cases copying the morphological structure of the Latin word results in apparently redundant prefixation in an Old English word, such as *ontimbran* (beside *ġetimbran* already mentioned) in the meaning 'instruct' after Latin *instruere*. However, the large number of loan translations in Old English seems to have resulted in very few, if any, new word-formational patterns in Old English. One instance may be the type of exocentric (or bahuvrihi) compound formed from a numeral plus a noun which is shown by a very small number of plant names including *fīf-lēafe*, *fīf-lēaf* 'cinquefoil', literally 'five-leaf (plant)', modelled on Latin *quinquefolium*; however, even this pattern did not become productive in Old English.[16]

In other cases the morphological match is less exact; these are often referred to as loan renditions rather than loan translations. Very often a Latin noun phrase gives rise to a compound in English, e.g. Old English *handbōc* for Latin *liber manuālis* 'handbook', or Old English *ċildamæssedæġ* for Latin *innocentium festivitas* 'Childermas, the feast of the Holy Innocents'. This reflects general tendencies in the word-formation patterns of each language, compounds being much rarer in Latin than they are in Old English. Sometimes it may be unclear precisely which Latin word provided

---

[15] The short vowel in *godspel* probably reflects early shortening of original **gōdspel* (see Hogg (1992a) §5.199, Luick (1914–40) §204 note 1); on the evidence for later reinterpretation as 'God's message' shown by formations modelled on the English word in other Germanic languages, see Green (1998) 346–7.

[16] See further Sauer (2003) 165–6, 171.

the model: for instance, Old English *handbōc* could instead be modelled on Latin *manuāle* rather than *liber manuālis*. Often such uncertainty about the precise model can cut across distinctions between loan translations and loan renditions, and such considerations make these categories somewhat fluid.

The often-cited example *leorning-cniht*, a compound of *leorning* 'learning' and *cniht* 'child, servant, retainer', is a less clear case of loan translation than is sometimes suggested. It clearly renders Latin *discipulus* 'disciple', almost certainly reflecting the (very possibly incorrect) assumption usually made in antiquity that its first element was the verb *discere* 'to learn'; the identity of the *-pulus* element was and remains unexplained. The Old English word is thus a partial translation on the basis of a quite possibly mistaken etymological assumption about the Latin word.

It can also be important to pay attention to the contexts in which loan translations and renditions occur, in order to assess their role and function, and to try to gain some impression of what part (if any) a particular formation may have played in the broader Old English vocabulary. For instance, a loan formation that is much discussed is Old English *dǣlnimend* (< *dǣl* 'part' and *nimend* 'taking') meaning '(grammatical) participle', on the model of Latin *participium* (ultimately < *part-*, *pars* 'part' and *capere* 'to take'). The Old English word in fact occurs rather more widely in the meaning 'participant', frequently rendering other Latin word forms from the same word family as *participium*. The grammatical meaning occurs only in Ælfric's *Grammar*, but, as Kornexl (2001) notes, it is often overlooked that the word as it occurs in this context serves a very specific purpose, making Latin grammatical terminology more transparent to learners, and it may be rash to assume that the word would have occurred so readily in other contexts. As Kornexl comments:

Ælfric's famous grammatical terminology...which largely consists of loan-formations of Latin terms that are usually placed side by side with their foreign models, or are clearly embedded in an explanatory context that refers to these models, has been credited with a degree of lexical and semantic autonomy by historical linguists and lexicographers that may neither do justice to the author's intentions nor to actual usage.

(Kornexl (2001) 204–5.)[17]

---

[17] On the grammatical terminology in Ælfric's *Grammar*, compare also Kastovsky (2010).

A third category, loan creations, is often (although somewhat controversially) identified in the scholarly literature, namely words that appear to have been created purely to provide an equivalent of a particular Latin word, but without reflecting its morphology at all, e.g. *ċeasterwaran*, literally 'city-inhabitants', as an equivalent of Latin *civēs* (plural) 'citizens'; or *fulwian* and *fulwiht*, literally 'consecrate fully' and 'full consecration', as equivalents of late Latin *baptizāre* 'baptize' and *baptismum* 'baptism'. These are normally the most difficult type to identify with any certainty.[18]

8.4 Word-geography, borrowing, and loan rendition reflected by the names of the days of the week in Old English and other Germanic languages

The modern English names of six of the days of the week reflect Old English or (probably) earlier loan renditions of classical or post-classical Latin names; the seventh, *Saturday*, shows a borrowed first element. In the cases of *Tuesday*, *Wednesday*, *Thursday*, *Friday* there is substitution of the names of roughly equivalent pagan Germanic deities for the Roman ones, with the names of Tiw, Woden, Thunder or Thor, and Frig substituted for Mars, Mercury, Jupiter, and Venus respectively; in the cases of *Monday* and *Sunday* the vernacular names of the celestial bodies 'Moon' and 'Sun' are substituted for the Latin ones. The first element of *Saturday* (found in Old English in the form types *Sæternesdæġ*, *Sæterndæġ*, *Sætresdæġ*, and *Sæter-dæġ*) uniquely shows borrowing of the Latin name of the Roman deity, in this case *Saturn*. Most of the names are common to all of the West Germanic languages (although in the case of 'Tuesday' modern Dutch and German show distinct formations perhaps showing the name of a different Germanic deity as first element), but there are some interesting differences in the cases of the words for 'Saturday' and 'Wednesday':

- The type reflected by modern English *Wednesday* is usual in England, the Netherlands, Frisia, and traditionally in the Church province of Cologne.
- The type reflected by modern German *Mittwoch*, which is the usual word in regional use in most parts of Germany, perhaps shows a loan rendition of a post-classical Latin name in Christian use, *media hebdomas*.

---

[18] For an argument that loan creations should not be considered as a type of borrowing at all, see Höfler (1981).

(See Frings and Müller (1968) 318–20.)

The case of the words for 'Saturday' is more complicated:

- The type reflected by modern English *Saturday* is again usual in England, the Netherlands, Frisia, and traditionally in the Church province of Cologne; its first element shows borrowing of the name of the pagan god Saturn, as found in the classical Latin name of the day *Sāturnī diēs*, and perhaps came to Germanic languages via Gaul, although it was later replaced there by a formation based on *sambata* which is reflected by modern French *samedi*.

- The type reflected by modern German *Samstag*, the first element of which ultimately shows borrowing of a variant *sambata* of Latin *sabbata*, ultimately of Hebrew origin, is traditionally southern German (found as far north as the Church province of Trier).

- The type reflected by modern German regional (central and northern) *Sonnabend* is paralleled by Old English *sunnanǣfen* and is found also in Frisian, and ultimately shows a partial calque on Latin *vigilia*. The route of transmission of this form is disputed, but one possibility is that it reflects the activity of Anglo-Saxon missionaries on the continent.

(See Frings and Müller (1968) 444–7.)

This variation in the name forms is interesting from at least two points of view. Firstly, it reminds us that little is inevitable in borrowing and there can be very different outcomes from very similar contact situations. Secondly, the distribution of the forms points again to the importance of either shared or parallel borrowing reflected by the Germanic varieties spoken in England, the Netherlands, and in the area of the old Roman colony of Cologne (compare section 8.2).

Conclusions to part III

The following remarks draw together some of the main threads from the three preceding chapters.

In section 6.3 the loanwords are divided into two chronological groups, early and late, the dividing line between them falling somewhere around AD 650, thus in the middle of the period of conversion to Christianity and considerably after what is assumed to have been the main period of settlement in Britain. In some cases, like *strǣt* 'road, paved road, street', linguistic evidence from Latin and English, and comparative evidence from other Germanic languages, all points towards very early borrowing. But in very many cases such evidence is lacking, or what evidence we have seems to point in different directions. Furthermore, events in linguistic history (such as sound changes) and events in non-linguistic history (such as the Settlement or the Conversion) cannot be aligned with one another with any great precision. For these reasons I have generally refrained from attempting to assign particular words to either 'continental' or 'insular' borrowing.

The earliest Old English (or proto-Old English or West Germanic or even North-West Germanic) borrowings from Latin include a number of words that are of relatively high frequency in modern English and that have fairly basic meanings, such as *cheese*, *wine*, *belt*, although the case of *belt* shows that although we can know that a word existed in Old English and had (within some margin of error) a particular meaning, we have to be careful about making assumptions that it was the usual word in that meaning. When considering basic meanings we must also remember that what is 'basic' is to a certain extent culturally and historically relative: for instance, the Anglo-Saxons were not great drinkers of wine, and hence the fact that a loanword is the only word in Old English recorded in the meaning 'wine' is hardly of the same significance as it would be if we were considering the vocabulary of a southern European wine-drinking culture.

Viewed from the perspective of the later history of English, another important characteristic of many of the early borrowings is that they show word forms that it would be either impossible or at least extremely unlikely for us to find as a result of later, post-Old English, (re-)borrowing of the same Latin word or of one of its Romance reflexes. Only a small proportion of the later borrowings show word forms that enable us to rule out this hypothesis.

It is also from the earlier loanwords that we find the largest numbers of Old English derivatives and compound formations. Few of the loanwords of any date show significant divergence in meaning from their Latin etymons during the Old English period.

The impact of these loanwords on the wider linguistic system of Old English seems to have been very limited. Apart from early borrowing of (probably) the masculine agent-noun suffix -ere and (perhaps) the feminine agent-noun suffix -estre, the only (marginally) productive borrowed affix is ærče-, erče-, arce- 'arch-' (in titles). There is no clear impact on the phonology of Old English from these loanwords, although certainly the frequency of word-initial /p/ increased considerably as a result. (For a reason that is not properly understood, initial /b/ was very rare in proto-Indo-European and hence, as a result of the operation of Grimm's Law, word-initial /p/ was rare in proto-Germanic.)

In many ways it is the later borrowings, belonging to the period of Anglo-Saxon literacy, that are the most tantalizing in terms of the later history of English, although they generally show much less dramatic developments in terms of sound change or morphological adaptation. We see borrowing in the period between *c.*650 and the Norman Conquest, and especially the latter part of this period, largely through the lens of scholars' written language, and we know much less than we would like about how well established many of these words may or may not have been outside the written language of scholars. We can see that semantic borrowing was common, as an alternative to the introduction of new loanwords. In cases where loanwords and semantic borrowings both existed for the same meaning, we can see that the semantic borrowings often occur with much higher frequency in our surviving texts. (Compare section 12.1.2.1 on the very different situation in Middle English.) When it comes to assessing whether or not an Old English borrowing may show continuity with a later English word, we can generally have very little certainty unless there are clues from word form or meaning change. This is all the more frustrating because it robs us of some valuable context for understanding the changes that took place after the Norman Conquest. However, from the perspective of the later history of English, perhaps what is most striking is how little even the language of Christianity was affected by loanwords in this period: there is no doubt that English before the Conquest was much less receptive of loanwords from Latin (and very early French) than it was in the centuries after, and to find the explanation for this, and for much of the subsequent history of the lexis of English, we must look ahead to the developments discussed in part V. Before that, however, it is necessary to turn in the next part of this book to a very different contact situation with another Germanic language that had important effects on English lexis in the late Old English and early Middle English periods.

Part IV

Scandinavian Influence

Introduction to part IV

Scandinavian influence on the lexis of English is unusual for a variety of reasons. There is some influence even at the most basic level of the vocabulary of modern English (most notably the pronoun *they*), but the overall number of Scandinavian loanwords is not nearly as big as that from Latin and French. There is also considerable variation between different varieties of English in the incidence of Scandinavian-derived or Scandinavian-influenced words: in particular, there is still some correlation between the geographical distribution of Scandinavian words in Britain and the patterns of Scandinavian settlement.

Several factors make it difficult to determine whether many English words are in fact borrowings from Scandinavian. Firstly, if we leave aside some important early inscriptions, our earliest substantial records for any of the Scandinavian languages date from later than the period of contact with English. Secondly, we have very little contemporary evidence for the varieties of English into which most of the initial borrowing occurred. Finally, and most importantly, the close family relationship of English and Scandinavian means that intricate philological work is often required to determine whether a loan has occurred in particular instance, or alternatively another type of influence, or even no influence at all. An investigation of such methodology therefore occupies a central place in this part of the book, at the beginning of chapter 10.

Because the overall number of (possible) loanwords is large and varies from dialect to dialect, and because of the complications involved in deciding whether or not a particular word is borrowed, examples are drawn principally from among those words that are familiar as part of the general vocabulary of modern English, and especially those that form part of its core and high-frequency vocabularies (as explored in sections 2.2 and 2.3).

9

Introduction to Scandinavian loanwords in English

9.1 Areas of Scandinavian settlement in England

The historical background is sketched very briefly in section 3.7. From the late ninth century until at least the end of the Anglo-Saxon period, there was an important divide between the Danelaw, under Scandinavian law, and the rest of England, under Anglo-Saxon law. The boundary probably ran very approximately from London to Chester, thus diagonally across the English midlands.[1] North and east of this was the Danelaw. Scandinavian influence was generally heaviest in the Danelaw areas and it is generally assumed that any heavy settlement of Scandinavian populations in England was confined to the Danelaw. However, the nature and extent of Scandinavian settlement in Britain is the topic of much controversy. There is very little evidence in the documentary record. Much of the most important evidence comes from two types of linguistic data: firstly, the evidence of place names (and to a certain extent of surnames), and secondly, the evidence of Scandinavian influence in different regional varieties of English, both medieval and modern. The place-name evidence is of various types: (i) Scandinavian names for new settlements, (ii) new Scandinavian names for existing settlements (or natural features, etc.), and (iii) the 'Scandinavianization' of existing place names. The last of these processes consists either of substituting early Scandinavian words

---

[1] On the many difficulties surrounding our knowledge about the Danelaw, see Holman (2001).

for similar-sounding (and normally directly cognate) English ones, or of substituting early Scandinavian sounds for English ones, on the patterns established by cognate word pairs.

It is generally held (particularly from the place-name evidence) that Scandinavian influence and probably also settlement was most intense in a band from the east midlands (beginning round about Northampton and Leicester) up to around the river Tees (i.e. roughly the northern boundary of later Yorkshire), and also in eastern areas of East Anglia, and in parts of the north-west.[2] The evidence of later English dialects and, to a certain extent, of Middle English materials, points to the importance of what has been described as a 'Great Scandinavian Belt' stretching across northern England 'from Cumberland and Westmorland in the west to the North and East Ridings of Yorkshire in the east, often including part of Lincolnshire but excluding the old kingdom of Bernicia in Durham and Northumberland' (Samuels (1985) 269). Why the (non-onomastic) linguistic evidence is less dense in more southerly areas for which other evidence (especially from place names) suggests heavy settlement has not as yet been fully resolved.

The situation further north, and especially in Scotland, presents many difficulties and some fundamental areas of uncertainty. It is not in doubt that there was considerable Scandinavian (chiefly Norwegian) settlement in large parts of (especially northern and western) Scotland. What is more uncertain is how much contact with Scandinavian varieties within Scotland influenced the vocabulary of Scots, since it is thought there was also a great deal of immigration to Scotland by English speakers from further south in the area of the Great Scandinavian Belt in England, bringing with them many linguistic features including numerous Scandinavian borrowings. Recent vocabulary studies suggest it may be possible to distinguish some distinctive rural vocabulary in Scots as resulting from Scandinavian contact within Scotland, but that most Scandinavian vocabulary in Scots may well result from immigration from England.[3]

---

[2] For useful maps, see Lapidge et al. (1999) 370, 519 and also Macafee (2002) §2. For an introductory summary of the evidence of place names and further references, see Cameron (1996). See also the useful summary of scholarship by historians and place-name scholars in footnotes to Dance (2003) 20–2.

[3] See Macafee (2002) §2.3.3 and further references given there, and also Kries (2003).

9.2 What is meant by 'early Scandinavian'

One important, albeit slightly arcane, initial question concerns terminology. Traditionally, the term 'Old Norse' has been used to denote two different things: (i) the language of the earliest substantial documents in any Scandinavian language, namely the rich literature largely preserved in Icelandic manuscripts dating from the twelfth century and (mostly) later; and (ii) the language that was in contact with English in the British Isles. In fact this is somewhat misleading, since English was in contact with the ancestor varieties of both West Norse (Norwegian and Icelandic) and East Norse (Danish and Swedish), but at a time earlier than our earliest substantial surviving documents for any of the Scandinavian languages, and at a time when the differences between West and East Norse were still very slight. Thus it is only rarely that English words can be attributed to either West or East Norse influence with any confidence.[4] In this book I follow the terminology used in the new edition of the *OED*, using 'early Scandinavian' as a catch-all for the early West Norse and East Norse varieties which were in contact with English, and distinguishing this from 'Old Icelandic' denoting the language of the early Icelandic texts, and from 'Old Norwegian', 'Old Danish', 'Old Swedish' denoting the oldest literary records of each of these languages.

9.3 An illustrative example of some of the main issues: *they*

Some of the most distinctive aspects of Scandinavian influence on English lexis can usefully be approached through an extended example. I will therefore begin with a consideration of one of the most important and surprising Scandinavian borrowings to have entered the general vocabulary of modern English: the third-person plural personal pronoun *they*.

In this instance it is probably easiest to work backwards, from Early Modern English to the period of direct contact with early Scandinavian. If we take any text written in London and its surrounding area in the emerging standard variety of the sixteenth century, we find that the usual third-person plural personal pronoun forms are *they* (subject form), *them*

---

[4] For a useful discussion of this topic, see Coates (2006). For a classic summary of the few items that can be with any confidence ascribed to distinctively West or East Norse input, see Björkman (1900–2) 281–8. See also Thorson (1936) 16–19 on the evidence of modern English regional forms.

(object form), and *their* (possessive form), just as in modern English; we may also sometimes find *hem* or *em* as unstressed object forms. All three of the forms *they*, *them*, and *their* are of Scandinavian origin. This is a first point of great significance: personal pronoun forms are among the 'closed-class' grammatical items least likely to be borrowed from another language (although third-person forms are perhaps less resistant to borrowing than first- and second-person ones). This borrowing attests to very intimate contact between Scandinavian and English, and also owes a lot to the similarity between early Scandinavian and medieval English.

If we go back further to the most important early manuscripts of Chaucer's *Canterbury Tales*, from the early fifteenth century, we typically find *they* as subject form, but the native (i.e. non-borrowed) *hem* and *her* as object and possessive forms. If we then go back a little further still, to London English of the early fourteenth century, we typically find the native forms *he* or *hi* for the subject form of the third-person plural pronoun. However, this does not mean that *they* was borrowed from Scandinavian at some point in the course of the fourteenth century and *them* and *their* a little later. The borrowing certainly happened much earlier, probably in the late Old English or very early Middle English period, in areas where early Scandinavian was extensively spoken and was in extended contact with English; the pronouns may (but need not) have been imported into English by speakers switching language from Scandinavian to English.[5]

Even in texts showing much earlier evidence of extensive Scandinavian influence, *they* typically appears rather earlier than *their* or *them*. The *Ormulum* is an east midland text from (probably) the second half of the twelfth century (see further section 9.4.2). It always has Scandinavian *þeʒʒ* for the subject form, usually Scandinavian *þeʒʒr* but also native *heore*, *here* for the possessive form, while for the object form it usually has native *hemm* but also (chiefly after a vowel) Scandinavian *þeʒʒm*.

The early appearance of *they* relative to *their* and *them* is possibly explained by some peculiarities of the pronoun system that survived from Old English: as a result of various phonological developments, in some varieties of early Middle English the pronoun forms for third-person singular masculine, third-person singular feminine, and third-person plural could

---

[5] There is almost certainly no direct connection with the rare Old English demonstrative pronoun form *þæge*, for a recent discussion of which and references to earlier scholarship see Dance (2003) 456–7.

all appear as *hē,* as a result of regular development from the distinct Old English forms *hē, hēo,* and *hīe.* It is therefore possible that the widespread adoption of the Scandinavian-derived form *they* had what is sometimes called a therapeutic motivation, restoring a clear formal contrast in grammatical number that was lacking in the inherited pronoun system; the new form *she* (on which see further below) probably served a similar function in giving a clear distinction between masculine and feminine singular forms.[6]

There are several factors that probably eased the adoption of the Scandinavian third-person plural pronoun forms. Firstly, Old English sometimes used the demonstrative form *þā* in functions overlapping with the third-person plural pronoun; the early Middle English reflexes of this are (early) *þā,* (later, after *c.*1200, southern) *þō,* (later still, northern) *þae.* Existing use of a form with initial /θ/ in the functions of the third-person plural pronoun may thus have eased the way for adoption of *they* (voicing of the initial consonant to /ð/ was a later development). Additionally, it is important to note the clear similarity of the Scandinavian-derived object and possessive forms *them* and *their* to the inherited ones *hem* and *hēr* (both of which show a good deal of variation as regards the stem vowel), as well as to the demonstrative forms *þǣm* or *þām* and *þǣra* or *þāra* in similar use. (Indeed, it is just possible to construct an etymology for the form *them* that does not involve Scandinavian contact at all, although *theim,* with which it varies in Middle English, certainly must.) Thus, there were very possibly a number of factors at play making adoption of the Scandinavian forms and their subsequent spread between varieties of English a rather less dramatic shift than it might otherwise appear.[7]

The later appearance of the Scandinavian-derived pronouns in southern (and western) varieties reflects a process of internal spread within English. In the case of London English, this can be observed to be part of a general process in which features typical of midland or eastern varieties come to be more frequent in the language of London and its immediate surroundings, correlating with the prestige of incomers to the city from further north, particularly from the midland areas and East Anglia. The fact that *they* generally appears to have travelled rather faster than *them* and *their* may again be attributable to a therapeutic role in restoring a clear distinction between singular and plural in the third-person pronouns.

---

[6] Such functional explanations of language change remain controversial: compare Lass (1997) 352–65.

[7] For a more sceptical account of this topic, see Ritt (2003).

Chaucer appears to play on the 'northernness' of *their* in the character-ization of two northern students in *The Reeve's Tale*. The important early Hengwrt manuscript of the *Canterbury Tales* regularly uses *they* for the subject form but *hem* and *here* for the object and possessive forms. However, it has *thair* just once, in the speech of one of these northern students (although even they still have *hem*, not *them*): 'A wilde fyr on thair bodyes falle.'[8]

From this examination of the third-person plural pronoun forms we can identify several features that are typical of Scandinavian borrowing in English:

- The close formal and structural similarities between English and Scan-dinavian have important implications for the sort of borrowing that we find, including closed-class items such as *they*.
- A borrowed word often has rather complex relationships with a native form that is similar in both form and meaning, and that is usually directly cognate. Sometimes, it is impossible to tease the two words apart fully.
- Because the heaviest Scandinavian borrowing occurred in parts of Britain from which we have very limited contemporary textual docu-mentation, we often have to use linguistic clues to estimate when borrowing is likely to have occurred.
- There is often a 'delay' in influence showing up in many of our sources, as a result of internal spread between varieties of English.
- The considerable difference between varieties of English in this period makes it particularly difficult to generalize about the nature or extent of Scandinavian influence. Even today, regional varieties of English closest to the areas of most intensive contact with Scandinavian show much more Scandinavian-derived vocabulary than those from other areas.

There is some other evidence of Scandinavian influence on English pronoun forms. See section 10.2.2 on *ik* as a Middle English and Older Scots variant of *ich*, *I*. There is also a single occurrence of the Scandinavian form *hanum* in

---

[8] Chaucer *The Reeve's Tale* line 252, cited from Lloyd-Morgan (2003); corresponding to line 4172 of *The Canterbury Tales* in Benson et al. (1987). On the linguistic aspects of the use of northern forms in this tale, see Tolkien (1934), but also Horobin (2001) 99. The use of some northern forms by the two students in this tale and of some East Anglian forms by the reeve who narrates the tale has provoked much debate, since it is very unusual in Chaucer's works; for a sophisticated discussion of the possible motivation, see Machan (2003) 111–38.

place of Old English *him* for the third-person singular masculine in an eleventh-century inscription on a sundial from the church in Aldbrough in Yorkshire.[9]

The pronoun *she* is also very often listed in histories of English as also showing Scandinavian influence. This is much more problematic. As noted, in some varieties of early Middle English the pronoun forms for third-person singular masculine and third-person singular feminine could both be *hē*. This gender ambiguity was eventually resolved by the adoption of a new feminine pronoun type reflected by modern English *she*, first recorded as *scæ* in the mid twelfth century. In Middle English *she* is typically southern, varying with a related form *sho, scho* in the north. The origin of these forms is much debated. They probably had their origin in the Old English forms *hēo*, *hīo*, and (originally accusative) *hīe*, although other possibilities are difficult to eliminate entirely. The processes of change in word form involved in the development of *she* and *sho* are complex and disputed: probably there was stress shift in the diphthong, from a falling to a rising diphthong, and a sound change /hj/ > (ultimately) /ʃ/, as well as (in some accounts) cross-influence between different form types. Scandinavian influence has frequently been posited as explanation for both the stress shift and the sound change giving /ʃ/, but this is very debatable: see Britton (1991), Laing and Lass (2014) for satisfactory accounts of *she* that do not require Scandinavian influence.[10]

Such debatable cases abound in the field of Scandinavian borrowing, and the criteria on which judgements can be made will necessarily figure strongly in the remainder of this chapter.

9.4 Periodization

9.4.1 Scandinavian borrowings attested in Old English

Relatively few Scandinavian loanwords are found in texts of the Old English period and even fewer in sources that date from before the Norman Conquest. Kastovsky (1992 321) puts the number of borrowings attested up to *c.*1100 at approximately 150. Pons-Sanz (forthcoming) lists 185 items (including some phrases) that can reasonably confidently be regarded as

---

[9] See Howe (1996) 154–5.

[10] See also Howe (1996) 145–54 for a summary of the very extensive literature on the origin of this pronoun form.

borrowed from early Scandinavian in Old English and also lists large numbers of less likely cases.[11] Interestingly, quite a few of these items did not survive into Middle English, in spite of the generally much higher incidence of Scandinavian loanwords in the later period.

Many of the borrowings attested in Old English belong to semantic fields which correlate with areas of well-known Scandinavian technological or cultural innovation. For instance, loanwords in the area of ships, seafaring, and sea-borne raiding and warfare include: names of various different types of ships, including *barþ*, *barda* (also *barþa*), *cnear*, *flēge*, *scegð*;[12] also *hā* 'oar-thole', *hamele* 'rowlock', *wrang*, *wranga* (probably) 'hold (of a ship)', and (perhaps) *hæfen* 'haven, port'.[13] The second element of *bātswegen* 'boatman' (> modern English *boatswain*, *bosun*) certainly shows a Scandinavian loan (see section 10.2.4), although it is uncertain whether the compound is itself a borrowing (if so, of a compound not attested in the later Scandinavian languages) or whether it shows a hybrid formation, from an Old English first element and a borrowed second element. In the case of *būtsecarl* (or *butsecarl*) 'shipman, member of a naval levy' it seems very likely that the Old English word does show borrowing of a compound not attested in the later Scandinavian languages, since neither element occurs as a simplex in Old English (even as a borrowing). There are also probable loan-translations in this semantic area: *æscman* 'shipman, sailor, pirate' (compare Old Icelandic *askmaðr*), *hāsæta* 'oarsman, rower' (compare Old Icelandic *háseti*), *stēormann*, *stēoresmann* 'pilot, master of a ship' (compare Old Icelandic *stýrimaðr*; also *stjórnamaðr*), *wederfest* 'weatherbound' (compare Old Icelandic *veðrfastr*), although the nature of our documentation for both Old English and early Scandinavian leaves many doubts in this area.

[11] Some of the main scholarly contributions on Scandinavian borrowings in Old English are Hofmann (1955), Peters (1981a, 1981b), Wollmann (1996), Pons-Sanz (2007), and the comprehensive account in Pons-Sanz (forthcoming); there are also important evaluations in Kastovsky (1992), Gneuss (1993), and also (although focusing principally on Middle English) Björkman (1900–2).

[12] Identifying which sort of ship is denoted in each case is complicated, albeit very interesting; for some generally conservative appraisals, see the *DOE*; see also Thier (2009) for discussion and references to the (extensive) literature, and also for the reasons for rejecting the hypothesis of Scandinavian borrowing in the case of *snacc*, another name of a type of ship.

[13] On *hæfen* see the detailed account (sceptical of Scandinavian origin) in Pons-Sanz (forthcoming) Appendix 3.

It is often assumed that Old English *æsċ* 'warship' shows semantic borrowing, with analogy operating on the following lines:

> early Scandinavian **askr* 'ash (tree)' : 'small ship, barque' = Old English *æsċ* 'ash' : 'warship'

It is also sometimes suggested that *healdan* 'to hold' may have acquired the sense 'to proceed, steer' in a similar way. However, certainty is very often elusive in this area. If we return to the example of *æsċ* 'warship', Townend (2002 203) argues that this is in fact a loanword, in which a 'switching code' has operated, resulting in substitution of native sounds for their usual Scandinavian equivalents. Thier (2009) adduces evidence for a quite different explanation, arguing that Old English *æsċ* and early Scandinavian **askr* (Old Icelandic *askr*) are cognates that both denoted ships, with no borrowing involved.

Significant numbers of loanwords and other borrowings are also found in the Old English period in the semantic fields of war, law, social ranks, and coins and measures, these last three reflecting the introduction of Scandinavian, especially Danish, administration in many areas (and, of course, Scandinavian dominance at a national level at various times). Compare e.g. *marc* (modern *mark* = measure of weight or unit of currency), *hūsting* (modern *husting*) 'assembly for deliberative purposes', *hūscarl* 'retainer or member of the household troops', *bryniġe* 'coat of mail', and *grið* 'peace'. The important loanword *lagu* (modern *law*) first occurs specifically with reference to the legal customs of the Danes. Compare also *bōnda* 'householder' (compare Old Icelandic *bóndi*) and *hūsbōnda* 'householder' (modern *husband*; compare Old Icelandic *húsbóndi*); *hūsbōnda* may show a loanword, or may show an English formation from *hūs* and *bōnda* on the model of the Scandinavian compound.[14] *Fēolaga* (modern *fellow*) 'partner, associate, fellow, comrade' shows a loan blend, with Old English *feoh* substituted for its Scandinavian cognate (compare Old Icelandic *félagi*).

There are also borrowings attested in Old English texts that do not fit so neatly into these semantic categories, such as *loft* 'air' (modern *loft* 'attic'), *rōt* 'root' (modern *root*), or *scinn* (modern *skin*) 'skin, fur', although trade or general social interaction would explain most of these examples.[15]

---

[14] Compare Durkin (2009) 51–2.

[15] A very good analysis of the semantic categories shown by Scandinavian loanwords attested in Old English is provided by Peters (1981a), partnered by an examination of their relationships with other items in the same semantic fields in Peters (1981b).

One very notable item is *tacan* (modern *take*), which is attested in late Old English in two manuscripts of the *Anglo-Saxon Chronicle* (manuscript D and the First Continuation of the *Peterborough Chronicle*, manuscript E) and in one homily (and also in a compound, *oftacan* 'to catch up with'). This eventually ousted the usual native synonym *niman* entirely, earliest in the east midlands, the north-west midlands, and the north, only much more gradually coming to predominate in the south-west midlands and the south. The reflex of *niman* remains in common use in parts of England down to the fifteenth century, but is rare by the sixteenth century.[16] When *nim* is found in Early Modern English, it is very often in the meaning 'to steal, pilfer', showing narrowing in the word's range of meaning, as well as pejoration (compare also the name of Shakespeare's thieving Nim).

Sometimes the case for Scandinavian borrowing of an important word in late Old English is much shakier: compare Durkin (2009 261–4) and Pons-Sanz (forthcoming) Appendix 3 on *plough*, for which the tenuous early evidence in both Old English and Scandinavian makes earlier scholarly assumptions of a Scandinavian loan into late Old English seem less than secure.

9.4.2 Borrowing as reflected in Middle English and in later sources

The great majority of English loanwords from early Scandinavian are first attested in Middle English.

Significant evidence for Scandinavian borrowing can be found in some of the earliest Middle English texts. The long homiletic poem entitled the *Ormulum* is the work of an Augustinian canon called Orm (a name of Scandinavian origin) who probably lived in south Lincolnshire; the dating is controversial, but Orm may have started work on the text as early as the middle of the twelfth century and continued well into old age.[17] Even after allowances are made for its considerable length (around 20,000 lines survive), it contains a very significant number of words for which Scandinavian origin can reasonably be argued: over two hundred[18] (although if we

---

[16] On the history of these two words, see the very detailed study by Rynell (1948), who also makes extended comparisons with a number of other word pairs of native and Scandinavian origin. See also the more recent study by Wełna (2005).

[17] See especially Parkes (1983).

[18] A search on the *MED* for 'ON' (= Old Norse) as 'language of etymon' and 'Orm.' in quotation stencil, i.e. entries giving early Scandinavian as language of origin and

remove all doubtful cases then the core of absolutely certain Scandinavian borrowings will necessarily be much smaller than this). This total includes many words of certain or very likely Scandinavian origin that are of common occurrence in modern English, such as (in their modern English forms) *to anger, awe, to bait, bloom, boon, booth, to die, to egg* (*on*), *to flit, ill, law, low, meek, to raise, root, to scare, skill, skin, to take, though, to thrive, wand, to want, wing*; a number of the borrowings it shows are not found at all in Old English texts.[19] Perhaps most interestingly of all, as noted in section 9.3, it contains some of the earliest evidence for three of the most important Scandinavian borrowings, the pronoun *they*, and the related object form *them* and possessive *their*. The *Ormulum* is an entirely new composition and it is normally assumed that it is probably a reasonably faithful reflection of contemporary speech. (Johannesson (2005) even suggests that the use of these Scandinavian pronoun forms may represent a deliberate attempt on Orm's part to address a popular audience in language that they would find familiar. However, this remains a very speculative suggestion.)

An interesting comparison is presented by another text of very similar date and (probably) localization, the *Peterborough Chronicle*. This is the name given to manuscript E of the *Anglo-Saxon Chronicle*, a copy made at Peterborough in the early twelfth century and then continued with annals dealing with contemporary events. Its rather complex textual history is well summarized in the Index of Sources of the *Linguistic Atlas of Early Middle English* (Laing 2011):[20]

> A neat round hand... wrote the entries up to the annal for 1121 at one time. It continued adding entries at intervals up to the end of the entry for 1131 (The First Continuation), as is evident from the changes in the colour of the ink. A second scribe... wrote, all at one time, the annals for 1132–1154, in a more compressed and later type of script. It is assumed that the text was written in or shortly after 1154.

The annals for 1132–54 are known collectively as the Second or Final Continuation. Since they appear to have been written *c*.1154, they are

---

including a quotation from the *Ormulum*, gives 263 results. Brate (1884) finds approximately 170 separate borrowings and many more derivatives that could also have been borrowed, but his methodology would not be embraced by most modern scholars, although his survey remains useful for being based on the full text of the *Ormulum*.

[19] See further Rynell (1948) 59–69, Townend (2002) 208–10.

[20] On the history of this text, see also the detailed discussion in Irvine (2004). For discussion of an extract, see section 13.1.1.

sometimes taken as showing the first Middle English text, because they fall just after the (very arbitrary) period division of 1150; crucially, they deal with recent events and must be of recent composition. Here there are very few words of likely Scandinavian origin that are not recorded in Old English texts: *harns* 'brains', *both*, and perhaps also *till* 'to' (although this could show some continuity with rare Old English (Northumbrian) *til*: see section 10.8) and *brennen* 'to burn' (although this may be partly or entirely of native origin, as a metathesized variant of the ancestor of *burn*).[21] However, the text is very short and, as we will see below, a statistical comparison with the language of the *Ormulum* gives results that differ much less dramatically.

If we look first at how the density of Scandinavian borrowings differs in the different parts of the *Peterborough Chronicle*, Skaffari (2002) examines borrowings in the Copied Annals (up to 1121), the First Continuation (1122–31), and the Final Continuation (up to 1154), which together amount to about 21,000 words of text. He finds 45 Scandinavian borrowings in total, including semantic borrowings as well as loanwords. The semantic loan *eorl* 'earl' is the commonest, found in the Copied Annals, First Continuation, and Final Continuation. The loanword *oc* 'but' is the next commonest and is found in the First Continuation and Final Continuation; Skaffari notes the similarity in word form to the native equivalent *ac*. Next in frequency is *gærsume* 'treasure', although this last appears in the annal for 1128, thus not appearing in the Final Continuation (the French loanword *tresor*, that gives rise to modern English *treasure*, appears from 1137). The token frequencies are 16 per 1,000 words in the Copied Annals, 13 per 1,000 words in the First Continuation, and 23 per 1,000 words in the Final Continuation. Thus the frequency goes up markedly in the final part, written *c.*1154. The third-person pronoun forms remain the native ones, even in the Final Continuation.

If we turn now to a comparison of the Final Continuation of the *Peterborough Chronicle* with the *Ormulum*, Skaffari (2009) is a survey of Scandinavian and French loanwords in early Middle English, based on text samples taken from the *Helsinki Corpus of English Texts* and using the etymologies of the *OED* and *Middle English Dictionary* (*MED*). His survey includes an 8,850-word sample from the *Ormulum*, in which he finds 358 examples of 68 different loanwords (i.e. 358 tokens of 68 types), while in the

---

[21] On Scandinavian borrowing in the *Peterborough Chronicle,* see especially Clark (1952–3), Kniezsa (1994), Skaffari (2002), Skaffari (2009).

2,610 words of the Final Continuation of the *Peterborough Chronicle* he finds 38 examples of 16 different loanwords (i.e. 38 tokens of 16 types). Skaffari's normalized figures, allowing for the different sample sizes, put the type counts rather closer, at 7.7 for the *Ormulum* and 6.1 for the *Peterborough Chronicle* (which is, in turn, only just ahead of the figures found for a number of important texts from the south-west midlands). Thus, the much larger number of Scandinavian loanwords found in the *Ormulum* could just be a factor of its greater length. On the normalized frequency count the *Ormulum* remains way ahead, at 40.5 compared with 14.6 for the *Peterborough Chronicle*. However, this may owe a great deal to the frequency with which a few items of core vocabulary occur, especially the pronoun *they*.

The Final Continuations of the *Peterborough Chronicle* and the *Ormulum* may well be extremely close to one another both chronologically and geographically. The *Ormulum* has been very tentatively localized to Bourne in south Lincolnshire (see Parkes 1983) and the findings of dialect geography agree with a localization in south Lincolnshire (see Laing (2011) 161–3). If the localization in Bourne is accepted, this is only about fifteen miles north of Peterborough (with no obvious geographical obstructions intervening) and it is just possible that Orm may have begun his work as early as the time when the final annals were being added to the *Peterborough Chronicle*, thus the generational gap could have been very small.

If we take the evidence of all parts of the *Peterborough Chronicle* and the evidence of the *Ormulum* together we can thus (very tentatively) make some interesting observations. Although the material in the hand of the Copied Annals and First Continuation of the *Peterborough Chronicle*, written down roughly 1121–31, certainly contains Scandinavian loanwords (including some not found in the Final Continuation), the frequency with which Scandinavian loanwords occur is considerably higher in the Final Continuation. This is true even if we are comparing just the First Continuation, composed 1121–31, with the Final Continuation, *c.*1154. It is thus very possible that we are observing a significant generational difference. This impression is reinforced by the data of the *Ormulum*, apparently written nearby by someone very possibly of much the same generation as the author of the Final Continuation of the *Peterborough Chronicle*. However, the language of the *Ormulum* is also different from that of the Final Continuation in very significant ways, most notably its use of the Scandinavian-derived pronoun *they*. (As we see in section 12.1.3, there are also very significant differences in the incidence of French-derived words in each text, with the Final Continuation in this instance showing a much higher frequency than the *Ormulum*.)

In the survey in Skaffari (2009) based on *Helsinki Corpus* data for the period 1150–1250, the normalized counts for the *Ormulum* and the *Peterborough Chronicle* Final Continuation are respectively the highest and second-highest scores for both types and tokens of Scandinavian origin in all of the seventeen texts examined. This clearly bears some relationship to their provenance as eastern texts. However, the overall picture is by no means a simple one, and Skaffari finds that the most significant differences are between texts that are original compositions in Middle English and texts that are either copies of or modelled closely on Old English texts, rather than between texts of different regional provenances. It has long been known that Scandinavian-derived words are found in puzzlingly high numbers in early Middle English texts of south-west-midland origin (Dance (2003) is a masterly study of this topic) and, although much work remains to be done, it is clear that the early Middle English sources do not present an entirely uncomplicated picture of heavily Scandinavian-influenced lexis in the east and north, and lightly Scandinavian-influenced lexis in the west and east.

The transition from Old English to Middle English does constitute a clear watershed in the volume of Scandinavian-derived lexis that we find in written English sources. (We return in section 9.4.3 to the difficult question of when the borrowing actually occurred.) The majority of the Scandinavian loanwords in English are first attested in Middle English texts, but not by any means all in the earliest Middle English texts. However, a good deal of Scandinavian-derived lexis only appears rather later, either in very late Middle English texts or later still.[22] Compare e.g. the certain or probable Scandinavian loanwords: *whisk*, first found at the end of the fifteenth century, *billow*, *scuffle*, both with sixteenth-century first attestations, *ruckle* 'to make a rattling or gurgling sound', first securely attested in 1700, or *to nag*, first attested a1728. Some probable loanwords are found only in modern dialect evidence, e.g. *rim* 'rung of a ladder', *maun* 'to manage (to), to control'. The linguistic and historical evidence points to these words being borrowings resulting ultimately from the Scandinavian settlements, but, if so, either (a) they must have existed in earlier centuries only in varieties of English for which we have no early textual evidence (of which

---

[22] Compare Bator (2006) for an interesting comparison of Scandinavian loanwords first attested in the fifteenth century with those last attested in the same century.

there are many), or (b) perhaps a word belonged to the vocabulary of one or more writers who simply did not use it in their surviving writings. In some cases, the register of a borrowed word was probably an important factor in preventing its earlier appearance in written sources.

In a useful analysis, Hug (1987 7–9) looks at all words of Scandinavian origin in the *Oxford Dictionary of English Etymology* (*ODEE*), which presents a selective wordlist based on that of the *OED*, and which also draws data on the dating of words and (for the most part) on etymologies from the full *OED*. Hug finds 348 words in total (although this will include some modern borrowings from Scandinavian languages in later times) and divides them up by the century of their first attestation. The largest totals are for words with first dates in the thirteenth and fourteenth centuries (74 and 70 respectively, beside 40 for the twelfth century), but there are also significant totals for words with first dates in the fifteenth, sixteenth, and seventeenth centuries (35, 28, and 30 respectively). These numbers, derived from *ODEE*, are certainly too low, reflecting a very selective wordlist, but their chronological distribution is nonetheless very instructive. (A search on the electronic *MED* gives 1,436 entries that mention 'ON' (i.e. 'Old Norse') in the etymology, although not all of these are borrowings.)

9.4.3 The likely date of borrowing and its context

Since spoken Scandinavian varieties are not thought to have persisted anywhere in England beyond the eleventh century or at the very latest the early twelfth,[23] any early Scandinavian loanwords borrowed from Scandinavian settlers in England must have entered English before the time of early Middle English sources such as the *Ormulum*, and the many much later dates of first attestation clearly reflect gaps in our record. However, it is much harder to know whether the bulk of the borrowing dates from the early period of Scandinavian settlement, from the late ninth century onwards, when surely the largest numbers of Scandinavian settlers arrived in England and took possession of English villages, serfs, and (in many cases) wives; or whether it mostly dates from rather later, when individuals and communities began to shift from bilingualism in Scandinavian and English to English monolingualism. If the latter scenario is true, many

---

[23] Compare Parsons (2001), Townend (2002), Townend (2006).

of the Scandinavian-derived words may show what some scholars would regard as a different phenomenon from lexical borrowing, namely language-shift-induced imposition, as bilinguals imported some Scandinavian elements into their own English as they shifted from using Scandinavian to using English.[24] A related question is how far English and early Scandinavian may have been mutually intelligible: it seems certain that some very rudimentary communication would have been possible even between monolingual speakers of English and early Scandinavian, for instance in very basic trading situations; whether much more than this was possible remains the subject of debate.[25]

Some features of the Scandinavian element in English point clearly to a context of intimate contact between speakers of the two languages, such as the relatively high proportion of basic vocabulary borrowed and the high proportion of words connected with everyday life, which already had perfectly serviceable synonyms in English. Another common phenomenon is the replacement of an inherited Old English word by a Scandinavian-derived cognate that differed only slightly in word form. In some cases this process may better be regarded as the remodelling of the inherited Old English word after its Scandinavian cognate, or even just the pronunciation of an English word with a Scandinavian 'accent'; section 10.2 looks at some examples. Whichever of these three mechanisms applied in a given case, we must still assume subsequent spread (or internal borrowing) within English, from varieties showing heavy Scandinavian influence to other varieties.

It is also notable that the Scandinavian-derived words found in Old English, especially in sources other than the very latest ones, lean rather more towards cultural borrowing, reflecting aspects of Scandinavian cultural impact on Anglo-Saxon society, although there are certainly exceptions (compare the examples given in section 9.4.1). However, this impression could result from the nature of our surviving Old English documentation, reflecting varieties and registers in which Scandinavian penetration was relatively slight: it is quite possible that extensive transfer of vocabulary was going on at precisely the same time in spoken use in the

---

[24] See especially Townend (2002) and also, for an earlier discussion of related issues, Hansen (1984). For much of the theoretical framework involved, see Thomason and Kaufman (1988).

[25] A recent careful analysis of the evidence is presented by Townend (2002).

areas of heaviest Scandinavian influence, but simply fails to be recorded in our (largely West Saxon) surviving records. An additional complication is that some of the most important phonological indicators of either borrowing from Scandinavian or influence on existing English words, as explored in section 10.2, are reflected barely, if at all, in the orthography of Old English.

One thing that the late appearance of many borrowings does indicate is how we need to qualify assertions that a particular word was 'in English' at a particular date. A word may occur very early in one variety, but take much longer to spread to other varieties, or it may stay regionally restricted for all of its life in English. It may even ultimately become obsolete without ever achieving any general currency.[26]

---

[26] Bator (2010) is a very interesting investigation of loanwords of Scandinavian origin that have become obsolete and the likely causes for this.

10

Identifying Scandinavian borrowings and assessing their impact

10.1 Identifying Scandinavian borrowings

Chapter 9 outlined some of the key difficulties in identifying both the date and the social and cultural context of the majority of early Scandinavian borrowings in English. The first part of this chapter looks more closely at how linguistic evidence can be used to identify Scandinavian borrowing (or, alternatively, Scandinavian influence on English word forms). Much in this section will necessarily be hedged with qualifications. Although we can say with confidence that the vocabulary of English shows considerable Scandinavian influence, once we move to individual word histories we are typically dealing in probabilities rather than certainties: in some cases we cannot be entirely certain that any Scandinavian influence occurred; in some others, we can be reasonably certain that there was some kind of influence, but the exact mechanism is uncertain. There are some cases where certainty is possible, but assessing degrees of likelihood is the rule rather than the exception.[1]

---

[1] Much of my discussion here is founded on Björkman (1900–2), which remains the fullest and most authoritative account of those words that can be identified as Scandinavian borrowings on firm formal grounds. Very important recent studies of methodology, especially as applying to more difficult cases, and to the interplay of different types of evidence, can be found in Dance (2003), Dance (2011), Dance (2012).

10.2 Words distinct in sound from their native cognates

Some of the clearest evidence for early Scandinavian influence on English lexis comes from cases where the following reasoning applies:

- cognate words existed in Old English and in early Scandinavian
- a word form is found in later English that clearly developed from one of the two
- formal criteria show that borrowing from the early Scandinavian word could have given rise to the later word form in English, but development from the Old English form could not have
- in the strongest cases, the further etymology demonstrates that it is highly unlikely that Old English could have had any (unattested) variant form that could explain the later English form.

In such cases the native Old English, early Scandinavian, and Scandinavian-influenced forms can conveniently be placed side by side. The following are some of the principal example words that are discussed in this section; in each case, the native Old English form and later developments from it are given to the left of the symbol |, while developments from a Scandinavian form are given to the right of it.

> OE *sċyrta* (> *shirt*) | Scand. (OIce. *skyrta*) > *skirt*
> OE *sċ(e)aða, sċ(e)aðian* | Scand. (OIce. *skaði, skaða* 'it hurts') > *scathe*
> OE *sċiell, sċell* (> *shell*) | Scand. (OIce. *skel*) > (northern) *skell* 'shell'
> OE *ċietel, ċetel* (> ME *chetel*) | Scand. (OIce. *ketill*) > *kettle*
> OE *ċiriċe* (> *church*) | Scand. (OIce. *kirkja*) > (northern) *kirk*
> OE *ċist, ċest* (> *chest*) | Scand. (OIce. *kista*) > (northern) *kist*
> OE *ċeorl* (> *churl*) | Scand. (OIce. *karl*) > (northern) *carl*
> OE *hlenċe* | Scand. (OIce. *hlekkr*) > *link*
> OE *ġietan* | Scand. (OIce. *geta*) > *get*
> OE *ġiefan* | Scand. (OIce. *geva*, OSw. *giva*) > *give*
> OE *ġift* | Scand. (OIce. *gipt*, OSw. *gipt, gift*) > *gift*
> OE *ġeard* (> *yard*) | Scand. (OIce. *garðr*) > (northern) *garth*
> OE *ġearwe* | Scand. (OIce. *gervi*) > *gear*
> OE *bǣtan* | Scand. (OIce. *beita*) > *bait* 'to bait'
> OE *hāl* (> *whole*) | Scand. (OIce. *heill*) > *hail* 'healthy'
> OE *lāc* | Scand. (OIce. *leikr*) > (northern) *laik* 'game'
> OE *rǣran* (> *rear*) | Scand. (OIce. *reisa*) > *raise*
> OE *swān* | Scand. (OIce. *sveinn*) > *swain*
> OE *nā* (> *no*) | Scand. (OIce. *nei*) > *nay*
> OE *blāc* | Scand. (OIce. *bleikr*) > *bleak*
> OE *wāc* | Scand. (OIce. *veikr*) > *weak*
> OE *þēah* | Scand. (OIce. *þó*) > *though*

OE *lēas* | Scand. (OIce. *louss, lauss*) > *loose*
OE *æg* (> ME *ei*) | Scand. (OIce. *egg*) > *egg*
OE *sweoster, swuster* | Scand. (OIce. *systir*) > *sister*
OE *fram, from* (> *from*) | Scand. (OIce. *frá*) > *fro*

The phonological criteria on which this analysis is based are discussed in sub-sections 10.2.1–10.2.8. However, a general word of caution is necessary at the outset about what these examples actually show. It is easy to assume that all of the words listed on the right (*skirt, scathe*, etc.) are certain cases of Scandinavian loanwords. However, while they are pretty certain cases of some sort of Scandinavian influence, it is less certain that they all show straightforward loanwords: in some of these instances, it is perhaps more likely that what we have is substitution of the Scandinavian form for its similar-sounding native cognate within a particular bilingual speech community, with the Scandinavian form then gradually spreading at the expense of the native form.[2] In support of this hypothesis, compare section 10.7 on a small number of words that seem to show substitution of equivalent Scandinavian sounds in native Old English words even where there is no cognate Scandinavian word.

In some cases semantic considerations combine with formal ones to make it seem more certain that we definitely have a loanword. For example, *odd* shows borrowing of an early Scandinavian adjective with the same meaning (compare Norwegian *odde*, Old Swedish *odda*); it is ultimately cognate with Old English *ord* 'point'. The early Scandinavian adjective reflects a characteristic Scandinavian assimilation of the Germanic consonant sequence *rd > dd*.[3] The meaning of the early Scandinavian adjective suggests a secondary development from a derivative noun in the meaning 'triangle' (or pointed thing), hence 'three-cornered' or 'odd'.

In some cases there appears to be input from both a native and a Scandinavian word, but it is impossible to unpick precisely what the influence was from each source with total confidence. *Thursday* shows in Middle English (and later) some forms of the type *Thorisday,* which fairly certainly show Scandinavian influence. The typical Old English form is *Þunresdæg,* which probably explains the /u/ in the dominant later type *Thursday* (although this could also be explained by East Scandinavian input); the

---

[2] Compare Townend (2002) 207 and passim.
[3] On the various consonantal assimilations that are characteristic of early Scandinavian, see Townend (2002) 40.

loss of /n/ could be entirely a development within English, although Scandinavian influence has often been suggested.[4]

With these caveats in mind, we can look at the main phonological criteria shown by each of the example words listed above:

10.2.1 Absence of Old English /sk/ > /ʃ/

Many of the simplest examples stem from the Old English development of /sk/ to /ʃ/ (compare section 8.1.1). This occurred in initial position and medial position when followed by a front vowel (and in initial position sometimes even when followed by a back vowel or /r/), and in final position after a front vowel.[5] Paradoxically, the Old English spelling system did not reflect this change (except secondarily in the effect on the following vowel reflected by spellings such as *sċeaða*) and it is also not reflected by the spelling systems of many early Middle English texts.[6] In fact, the conclusion that the change occurred systematically in Old English is based in part on later evidence, once likely cases of Scandinavian borrowing or influence from other languages have been eliminated from the data. The reasoning is thus in some ways rather circular, but the 'fit' of the evidence with the hypothesis is such that most scholars have not been particularly troubled by it. For instance, we know that a native word like *sċip* regularly gives modern *ship* in all parts of Britain, not **skip*. Place names such as *Skippool* in Lancashire or *Skipsea* in Yorkshire are only apparent exceptions, since, although they may go back to Old English names in *sċip*, it is fairly certain that /sk/ results from later Scandinavian influence. (Compare though section 10.7 on *scatter*.)

One of the best-known examples is borrowed (or Scandinavian-influenced) *skirt* (compare Old Icelandic *skyrta*), beside *shirt*, which shows the reflex of the Old English cognate *sċyrta*; the semantic differentiation of garment worn on the lower body as opposed to garment worn on the upper body may have taken place in English, but if so it happened very early.

---

[4] Compare Björkman (1900–2) 180, Dance (2003) 439–40, Pons-Sanz (forthcoming) Appendix 3.

[5] Compare Hogg (1992a) 7.16 to 7.43, and especially 7.17(4).

[6] As noted in section 6.3, the dot distinguishing *sċ* from *sc* is a modern convention, based on the assumptions of philologists. On spellings like *sċeaða,* see section 8.1.1, Change G.

Similarly *scathe* (noun and verb) is assumed to show a borrowing from Scandinavian (compare Old Icelandic *skaði* 'harm, damage', *skaða* 'to harm'), rather than a continuation of Old English *sċ(e)aða* 'injurer, injury' and/or *sċ(e)aðian* 'to injure; to rob'. *Scale* (for weighing) may likewise reflect Scandinavian borrowing (compare Old Icelandic *skál*, beside Old English *sċealu*), although the stem vowel in English presents some complications.

In some cases the Scandinavian form appears only ever to have had relatively limited regional distribution, as in the case of Middle English (northern) *skelle* and English regional (northern) *skell* (compare Old Icelandic *skel*) beside the native form *shell*.

10.2.2 Absence of Old English /k/ > /tʃ/

Absence of palatalization and assibilation of /k/ before a front vowel (see section 8.1.1) is usually a good sign of Scandinavian borrowing or influence, although the possibility often cannot be ruled out that a word simply shows failure of this change in the (poorly documented) northern dialects of Old English. Thus, as noted in sections 4.3 and 7.5.1.1, the form *kettle* may show a borrowing from early Scandinavian of the same (ultimately Latin) word as Old English *ċietel* and *ċetel* (> Middle English *chetel*), or else remodelling of the native word after its Scandinavian cognate. Similarly, English regional (northern) and Scots *kirk* shows Scandinavian borrowing or influence beside native *church* (on the ultimate etymology, see section 8.2.1), as does northern *kist* (compare Old Icelandic *kista*) beside southern *chest* (the reflex of *ċist*, *ċest*—in both English and Scandinavian ultimately reflecting a Latin borrowing, compare section 6.3.1). Likewise northern *carl* (compare Old Icelandic *karl*) beside more distantly related southern *churl* (< Old English *ċeorl*—the vowel variation probably reflects variation at an early stage in Germanic). *Keel* may also belong here (compare Old Icelandic *kjǫlr* beside Old English *ċele*), although it may alternatively show a borrowing from a different language.

Similar considerations generally hold for the rather more complicated developments affecting *c* in medial and final positions. Thus (alongside *kirk* already mentioned) *link* probably reflects Scandinavian borrowing (compare Old Icelandic *hlekkr* beside Old English *hlenċe*) and perhaps similarly northern *benk* or *bink* beside southern *bench* (compare Old Icelandic *bekkr* beside Old English *benċ*; the forms *hlekkr*, *bekkr* with *kk* reflect a later assimilatory sound change in West Norse). *Mickle*, beside *much* (clipped < earlier *muchel, michel*), is probably chiefly due to Scandinavian influence, although there was also variation within the paradigm in Old English, since the environment for palatalization and assibilation did not occur in all inflected forms of this word. *Like* (as adjective, and hence as adverb and preposition) and *dike* (beside *ditch*) are similarly complex cases. *Ik* as Middle English and Older Scots variant of the first-person pronoun *I* (Old English *ić*) is probably the result of Scandinavian influence.

10.2.3 Absence of Old English /g/ > /j/ and /gg/ > /ddʒ/

Absence of palatalization of /g/ > /j/ before a front vowel indicates Scandinavian influence in the case of *get* (compare Old Icelandic *geta*) beside Old English *ġietan* and in the case of *give* (compare Old Icelandic *geva*, Old Swedish *giva*) beside Old English *ġiefan* (although the stem vowel of *give* has been variously explained: see Björkman (1900–2) 154–6), and likewise in the case of the related *gift* (compare Old Icelandic *gipt*, Old Swedish *gipt*, *gift*) beside Old English *ġift*. *Guild* probably also shows at least some influence from Scandinavian (compare Old Icelandic *gildi* with Old English *ġild*, *ġyld*). *Gear* shows Scandinavian influence (compare Old Icelandic *gervi*), the Old English cognates being *ġearwe* 'clothing, attire' and (slightly more distantly) the adjective *ġearu* 'ready, prepared' (> archaic or regional *yare*). Northern *garth* is of Scandinavian origin (compare Old Icelandic *garðr*), beside the native cognate *yard* (Old English *ġeard*). *Guest* is a more complex case, but probably belongs here, although it may show a blend of inherited and borrowed forms.

Developments within English in positions other than word-initial again pose many difficulties and uncertainties, and it is not certain (although it is likely) that alternations such as northern *rig* beside southern *ridge*, or northern *brig* beside southern *bridge*, are due to Scandinavian influence.[7] Likewise *to egg (on)* probably shows an early Scandinavian loan (compare Old Icelandic *eggja*, beside native *edge*, Old English *eċġ*, noun).

---

[7] Compare Hogg (1992a) §7.42 and further references given there. On the complex case of *bridge*, see Styles (2001) 292–6.

10.2.4 Absence of Old English development of Germanic *ai > ā

Germanic *ai developed to ā in Old English (and hence > ǣ when affected by i-mutation), but in Scandinavian it remains, being realized by ai or sometimes ei in Middle English borrowings.[8] Thus bait 'to bait' (and likewise also the noun bait) is clearly from Scandinavian (compare Old Icelandic beita 'to cause to bite, to hunt'), not from the Old English cognate bǣtan (< proto-Germanic *baitjan).[9] Likewise:

- hail 'healthy' is from Scandinavian (compare Old Icelandic heill), not from the Old English cognate hāl, which gives modern English whole. In Middle English the two words are sometimes found as a phrasal doublet, hail and hole.[10] (It is less certain whether the modern phrase hale and hearty reflects the Scandinavian loanword or the northern variant of its native cognate.) Scandinavian origin is also shown by the (ultimately related) interjection hail! and the corresponding verb to hail.
- English regional (northern) laik 'game' is from Scandinavian (compare Old Icelandic leikr) not from the cognate Old English lāc.
- Swain shows a Scandinavian borrowing (compare Old Icelandic sveinn), reflected already in Old English by the compound bātsweġen 'boatman' (> boatswain, bosun), the Old English cognate being swān 'herd, swine-herd'.
- Nay shows a Scandinavian borrowing (compare Old Icelandic nei), the Old English form nā giving modern (southern) no.
- Raise is from Scandinavian (compare Old Icelandic reisa), while its Old English cognate rǣran (< Germanic *raisian) gives modern English rear. Obviously, in this instance the consonant at the end of the root also differs, Old Icelandic reisa versus Old English rǣran. Here Old English retains r (by rhotacism) < *z (by Verner's Law) < proto-Germanic *s.[11]

---

[8] In fact there are a number of circumstances in which Middle English ei or ai spellings can ultimately reflect reflexes of Old English ā, particularly in the spelling systems of certain texts. Additionally, some Middle English borrowings reflect later East Scandinavian monopthongization of ei. There is a good discussion of difficult cases in Björkman (1900–2) 36–60.

[9] Compare Björkman (1900–2) 41.

[10] Compare Björkman (1900–2) 44.   [11] See Durkin (2009) 18–19, 181–2.

Bleak (Old English *blāc*, Old Icelandic *bleikr*) and *weak* (Old English *wāc*,
Old Icelandic *veikr*) probably belong in this group, the modern forms
resulting from a particular development of the Scandinavian diphthong
before /k/.[12] (The same development is seen also in the Scandinavian
borrowing *steak*, which does not have an Old English counterpart. The
distinct pronunciation of *steak* in modern English results from variation in
the early modern period:[13] in Middle English *bleak*, *weak*, and *steak* all had
the same vowel, open *ē* /ɛ:/.)

10.2.5 Germanic **au* > *ēa* in Old English (open *ē* in Middle English)

The Germanic diphthong **au* gives early Scandinavian *au* (realized by *au*,
ou, or close *ō* /o:/ in Middle English borrowings), but Old English *ēa*
(> Middle English /ɛ:/, normally termed open *ē*, in contrast to close *ē*, /e:/,
which is the reflex of Old English *ē*).

Window shows the reflex of a borrowing from Scandinavian (compare
Old Icelandic *vindauga*); the Scandinavian word shows a compound (literally 'wind eye') in which the second element is *auga* 'eye', cognate with Old
English *ēage* (> *eye*). *Though* reflects a borrowing of a Scandinavian form in
which *au* was monophthongized before *h*; the native form is Old English
þēah. *Loose* reflects Scandinavian borrowing (compare Old Icelandic *louss*,
lauss) rather than Old English *lēas*.

10.2.6 **jj* > *gg* in early Scandinavian

Egg is a distinctly Scandinavian form (compare Old Icelandic *egg*), the Old
English form being *ǣġ*. The Scandinavian form probably reflects a sound
change known as sharpening or alternatively Holtzmann's Law, by which
prehistoric **jj* > *gg*. (The proto-Germanic form of the root was probably
*ajj-.) In this instance the resulting variation in late Middle English is
reflected by a famous anecdote in Caxton's Prologue to *The Boke of
Eneydos*, in which a merchant who asks for eggs using the Scandinavian-
derived plural form *eggys* is not understood by a woman who only knows
the native form *eyren*: see section 13.1.5 for the passage in question.

---

[12] Compare Jordan (1934) §130.1.
[13] See Dobson (1968) II. §115; Durkin (2009) 189.

(The incomprehension may well have been genuine at this date: the *MED* records *egg* only from 1366 onwards, and predominantly in northern and north-east-midland use.)

10.2.7 **ui > y* in early Scandinavian

The modern form of *sister* points very strongly to borrowing from Scandinavian (compare Old Icelandic *systir*), while the forms *suster* and *soster,* which are also found in Middle English, are more plausibly explained as developments from the Old English cognate *sweoster, swuster.*

10.2.8 Loss of final nasals in early Scandinavian

Early Scandinavian loss of final nasals is probably reflected by *fro* 'from' (surviving in modern standard English chiefly in *to and fro*), which shows the reflex of northern Middle English *frā*, southern Middle English *frō* (with vowel rounding: compare Durkin (2009) 183), a probable Scandinavian borrowing (compare Old Icelandic *frá*). The Old English cognate *fram, from*, without loss of the final nasal, gives modern English *from.*

10.3 Borrowings with different derivational morphology from a cognate

We enter rather more difficult territory in some cases where we have a probable early Scandinavian borrowing and there is an Old English cognate, but this differs significantly in form because it shows a different stem-forming suffix. Thus it is normally assumed that *boon* and *loan* are Scandinavian borrowings because there are recorded Scandinavian forms that would explain the English words exactly (compare Old Icelandic *bón, lán*), but the attested cognate forms in Old English are respectively *bēn* and *lēn*, showing *i*-mutation as a result of having had a different Germanic stem-forming suffix with **-i-*. Similar considerations apply to *band*, later usually *bond* 'connection, fetter', beside native *bend.*

This is a different sort of case from those we have looked at so far, since it is possible that Old English could also have had (unattested) variants formed with the same Germanic suffix as the Scandinavian forms. The existence of such variants would not be very surprising, since stem class and gender do typically show a lot of variation in the early Germanic languages. Scandinavian borrowing is still likely in these cases, but it is not proven quite so categorically. (For some more problematic cases see Björkman (1900–2) 30 n. 1.)

A similar case is shown by *awe* (compare Old Icelandic *agi*), beside Old English *ege* with *i*-mutation. In the case of *axle-tree* (hence *axle*) the form with -*l* appears to have existed only in Scandinavian, replacing native *ax*. A much less certain example is shown by *fast* (= fasting, abstinence from food) beside the native (now obsolete) synonym *fasten* (Old English *fæsten*); Scandinavian borrowing provides an economical explanation, but so would a variant of the native form with loss of final /n/ followed by loss of the final vowel, since both of these processes are common in English in this period.

10.4 Words with no native cognate where formal grounds indicate borrowing

In some cases a Scandinavian word has no recorded Old English cognate but we can demonstrate that, had a cognate existed, it would have been distinct in form and therefore impossible as the direct antecedent of the later English word. Generally, in such cases we can be fairly certain that borrowing from Scandinavian has occurred, so long as there is no other viable competing etymology. Normally, the hypothesis is also dependent on assumptions about the further etymology of the Scandinavian word being correct.

Thus, if we work through the same formal criteria as outlined in sections 10.2.1–10.2.8:

10.4.1 Absence of Old English /sk/ > /ʃ/ , /k/ > /tʃ/, /g/ > /j/

Among words with /sk/ we find *scant* (compare Old Icelandic *skammr*: on the final -*t* in English, see section 10.5), *scare*, *score*, *skill*, *skin*, *skulk*, *skull* (although early examples of this word are chiefly in southern texts), *sky* (see further section 10.4.3), and (probably) *scowl*; also (in final position) *bask*. Similarly, with /k/ rather than /tʃ/ we find *kid* (compare Old Icelandic *kið*) and also *cast* (compare Old Icelandic *kasta*; a native cognate would have shown fronting of *a* and hence palatalization). Secure cases with

/g/ rather than /j/ all have Old English cognates, and are exemplified at section 10.2.3.

10.4.2 Absence of Old English development of Germanic *ai > ā

Middle English (and modern Scots and northern English) *lair* 'mud, clay' has no native cognate and the development of Germanic *ai* shows conclusively that it is from Scandinavian (compare Old Icelandic *leir*). Similar considerations apply for *steak:* see section 10.2.4 on the vowel development shown in this case.

10.4.3 Presence of early Scandinavian *i*-mutation (or *r*-mutation) of Germanic *eu

The form of *mire* points very strongly to borrowing from Scandinavian (compare Old Icelandic *mýrr*), rather than development from an unattested Old English cognate, which would have given **mēre* in forms developed from the Anglian dialects of Old English; the word is slightly more distantly related to Old English *mēos* 'moss' and more distantly still to Old English *mos*, modern English *moss*. Similarly, *sky* is a pretty certain borrowing (compare Old Icelandic *ský*), since the expected Middle English development from a cognate form in the Anglian dialects of Old English would be **shē*.

10.4.4 Presence of early Scandinavian development of *ǣ* as *ā*

The development of Germanic *ǣ* as *ā*, rather than as *ǣ* (in West Saxon) or *ē* (in Anglian and in Kentish: compare section 8.1.1), probably indicates Scandinavian origin in the case of *low* (compare Old Icelandic *lágr*, although this may have had a native cognate in Old English **lǣge* 'fallow, uncultivated'[14]). It is also reflected by a number of other words found only in Middle English, e.g. *brothe* 'fierce, grim' (compare Old Icelandic *bráðr*).

---

[14] Compare the *OED*'s entry for *lea | ley | lay* adj. (first attested in Middle English but perhaps implying an Old English precursor cognate with Old Icelandic *lágr*), and for place-name evidence compare also Smith (1956) at *lǣge*.

10.5 Borrowings that preserve aspects of Scandinavian morphology

A special case is shown by words that preserve aspects of their Scandinavian morphology in English. In a number of English loanwords from early Scandinavian final -*t* in the stem of the English word ultimately reflects the neuter adjective ending in Scandinavian; some examples among relatively common modern English words are *scant*, *thwart* 'athwart' (found in Middle English as adverb, preposition, and adjective), and *want* 'shortage, lack' (although, in this instance, association with the verb *to want* could provide an alternative explanation). In most cases specific explanations can be found for the adoption of forms showing Scandinavian morphology in English. For instance, English *thwart* may largely reflect the corresponding Scandinavian adverb, which itself shows use as adverb of the neuter of the corresponding adjective, and hence has -*t* (compare Old Icelandic *þvert*, adverb; *þverr*, adjective, neuter *þvert*). In the case of *want* 'shortage, lack' the adoption of the Scandinavian neuter adjective form as a noun may reflect reanalysis of particular contextual uses of the neuter adjective.[15]

Similarly, the final consonant cluster of *bask* reflects what is in fact a reflexive ending in early Scandinavian, rather than part of the verb stem (compare Old Icelandic *baþask*, later *baþast* 'to bathe (oneself)').[16]

Although *do* is certainly of native origin (not being found in Scandinavian), as is the preposition *at*, it is quite possible that the expression *at do* (> modern English *ado*) may reflect use of the corresponding preposition in early Scandinavian (compare Old Icelandic *at*) to introduce an infinitive (analogously to *to* in English).

10.6 Cases where borrowing is argued for on grounds other than word form

Some words are not attested in Old English (or only in contexts where Scandinavian borrowing at least seems possible), but do have plausible Scandinavian etymons, although the argument is not supported by clear formal criteria. That is to say, had a native cognate existed, it would not have differed in form in a way that would rule it out as antecedent of the later word.

---

[15] For further discussion of such cases, see Björkman (1900–2) 19–20.

[16] On the apparent loss of a reflexive ending in the cases of *thrive* and (a doubtful borrowing) *falter,* see the arguments to the contrary in Simpson (1981) 303.

This is a difficult area. There are plenty of words not recorded until after the Old English period for which an Old English antecedent is normally assumed on formal and etymological grounds, e.g. *minnow, mud, pimple, pound* (= enclosure), *to pry, rash, to waver*, and perhaps *moan*, so it is rather dangerous to assume that simply because a word is not found in Old English but does have a possible Scandinavian etymon it must necessarily be a Scandinavian borrowing. The evidence must be weighed carefully, for instance whether the word is found in any of the other West Germanic languages other than Old English, and what precisely its meanings are in each language, as well as whether it appears earliest in English in texts with a significant Scandinavian element (although this last consideration can be problematic and can lead easily to circularity). As Björkman points out in his classic study of the Scandinavian element in Middle English:

> Although the vocabularies of the two languages were to a very great extent identical, there must of course have been a considerable number of words peculiar originally to one or the other of the languages in question, but subsequently adopted by one language from the other. But we shall never be able to make out wholly in what points the vocabulary of one language differed from that of the other, and consequently the results drawn from presumed differences of vocabulary must be regarded as very uncertain.
>
> (Björkman (1900–2) 193.)

It is particularly difficult to assess the importance of early distribution in texts that show a lot of Scandinavian lexical evidence, coming from areas that are thought to have seen considerable Scandinavian settlement. Some words often thought to be of Scandinavian origin, such as the (apparently related) group *rug, rugged*, and *ruggy*, show an early distribution that shows little correlation with the main areas of Scandinavian settlement, but it is unclear how decisive a factor this should be in assessing the likelihood of them being Scandinavian borrowings.[17]

Lest all of this caution appears unnecessary, it is as well to consider the case of *trust*: none of the words in this family are found in Old English, and the noun, the verb, and a related obsolete adjective all have analogues in Scandinavian (compare Old Icelandic *traust*, noun; *treysta*, verb; *traustr*, adjective), but phonological considerations make it very difficult to explain

---

[17] See especially Dance (2003) on the interesting questions posed by the Scandinavian-derived lexis that is found in early Middle English texts from the south-west midlands, outside the Danelaw.

the English words as Scandinavian loanwords. Therefore, while scholarly opinions have differed, there is certainly strong support for the hypothesis that the English words reflect an unattested native cognate, which was then probably influenced in its subsequent development by association with the well-developed set of words attested in the Scandinavian languages.[18]

None of this means that we should dismiss the idea that any words for which we do not have decisive phonological evidence were borrowed from Scandinavian: clearly, very many words would have the same form regardless of whether they were borrowed or native, and the number of words that can be shown on formal grounds to be borrowings argues strongly that there are also borrowings among those words that show no clear formal criterion. The problem is that we can almost never be certain about individual cases; subtle differences in the approaches adopted by different researchers may have significant implications, and as Dance (2003 71) notes 'the most important tool remains . . . consistency in personal point of view and in its application'.[19]

Other fairly common modern English words for which similar considerations make Scandinavian borrowing extremely probable if not entirely provable include: *anger, bloom, booth, bound (for), calf* (of the leg), *to carp, to cow, to crawl, to die,*[20] *to droop, to flit, gap, to gape, to geld, to hap* (hence *happy, happen*), *to hit, ill,*[21] *leg, to lug* (hence *luggage*), *meek, raft* (originally in the sense 'beam'), *to ransack, reindeer,*[22] *rift, root, rotten* (on which see further later in this section), *same, seat, sly, stack, to take* (a strong verb), *to thrive* (another strong verb; also the related noun *thrift*), *to thrust, ugly, wand, to want, to whirl, wing.* In a few of these cases formal arguments could also be adduced, although not entirely conclusive ones.

[18] See especially the discussion in Dance (2000) 377.

[19] For a recent very careful consideration of the methodological issues involved, see Dance (2011) and also Dance (2012).

[20] For a very detailed summary of the evidence and various competing explanations for *die,* see Dance (2000).

[21] The likely Scandinavian etymon is of uncertain etymology; at least one of the suggested further etymologies would make it certain on formal grounds that English *ill* must be a borrowing, not a cognate; there is anyway little real doubt in this case: compare Björkman 171.

[22] There is an apparent Old English cognate of the first element, *hrān* 'reindeer', but this probably shows an earlier borrowing from early Scandinavian, with substitution of Old English *ā* for the Scandinavian diphthong (compare Old Icelandic *hreinn*), by analogy with the correspondences shown by other words.

Examples that are more doubtful (although in some cases only very marginally so) include *awkward*, *bank* (of earth), *bark* (of a tree), *birth*, *boulder*, *brink*, *bulk*, *cake*, *to call*,[23] *to clip* (= cut), *club* (= stick), *cog*, *crook* (= staff; hence *crooked*), *dank*, *to daze*, *dirt*, *down* (= feathers), *dregs*, *to dump*, *flat*, *flaw*, *to fling*, *to gasp*, *to gaze*, *gill* (of a fish), *to glitter*, *grime*, *to lift*, *muck*, *race* 'rush, running', *rag*, *raggy*,[24] *rump*, *scab*, *scalp*, *scrap*, *to scrape*, *to slant*, *slug*, *snare*, *wisp*, *wrong*, and (as noted above) *rug* and *rugged*, and (as derivatives of possibly borrowed words) *freckle*, *muggy*, *tattered*.

Very possibly all of these words are in fact Scandinavian borrowings, and in most cases this is at least the best guess available, but it is as well to bear in mind that the evidential basis is nowhere near as secure as it is for most of the words discussed earlier.[25]

Some words, like *main* (adjective), probably show some input from native Old English material and some from Scandinavian. There was probably some Scandinavian input (as well as from other languages) in the case of *creek*.

Some of these words are normally assumed without hesitation to be Scandinavian borrowings because they have fairly basic meanings and it is thought unlikely that they would not have been recorded in Old English had they existed; this argument is reinforced if we can identify an Old English word that usually realized the meaning in question, although here we are again hampered by our lack of detailed information about regional variation in Old English lexis because of the limited and skewed nature of our surviving texts. Words realizing basic meanings, if borrowed, are perhaps most likely to have been introduced by Scandinavian speakers shifting to English, rather than by English speakers in contact with Scandinavian speakers.

---

[23] Compare Dance (1999), but also Stanley (1969). The only Old English attestation of this word occurs in the poem *The Battle of Maldon*. For a recent appraisal of the many suggestions that have been made concerning Scandinavian-derived lexis in this poem and its significance, see Pons-Sanz (2008).

[24] On the difficult case of *raggy*, see the useful summary in Pons-Sanz (2011) 42–4.

[25] For more detail on most of these words see especially Björkman (1900–2) and the *OED*.

To take a few examples:

- As noted in section 9.4.1, *take* first appears in very late Old English, in contexts where borrowing from Scandinavian is plausible; this hypothesis is strengthened by the fact that this basic meaning is earlier realized by *niman*.
- Before its appearance in Middle English *anger* is found only in Scandinavian (compare Old Icelandic *angr*), the usual term in Old English in broadly this meaning being *wrǣþþu* (modern English *wrath*).[26]
- *Meek* has cognates in other West Germanic languages, but showing a different ablaut grade, hence reinforcing the idea that the English word is borrowed from Scandinavian.[27]

In some cases there is a native cognate, but it seems very unlikely to be the antecedent of the later word (on grounds other than form). Thus *seat* has an Old English cognate, but it is very rare and has the meaning 'ambush'. The adjective *wrong* is a more difficult case: it has cognates in other West Germanic languages (not in Old English), but these have the meanings 'sour, bitter; unpleasant, hostile', and this has led many scholars to the view that it is most likely that the English word (first attested in Old English in use as a noun) shows a Scandinavian borrowing (compare Old Icelandic *rangr* 'awry, not straight, wrong; unjust, unrighteous'; the initial consonant is preserved by Old Swedish *vranger*, Swedish *vrång*, Old and modern Danish *vrang*), although it is not impossible that the word was inherited in Old English and shows either semantic influence from early Scandinavian or a parallel development within English.[28]

Bloom 'flower' has no recorded Old English antecedent, but there is an Old Saxon cognate *blōmo*; the assumption of Scandinavian borrowing in English (compare Old Icelandic *blōm*, *blōmi*) is strengthened by the fact that early examples in Middle English are largely from northern and north-midland sources.

---

[26] It has been suggested that the adoption of *anger* may have been encouraged by association with Latin *angor* 'strangling, suffocation, anguish, torment, trouble'. On the possibility that *anger* in early use typically realized a new specific meaning, denoting anger without associated violence on the part of a person with little social power, see Diller (1994), Geeraerts et al. (2011).

[27] For the variety of words etymologically unrelated to *meek* found in this or similar meanings in Old English, see *TOE* categories 07.07, 07.07.01.

[28] For a recent discussion sceptical of the idea of Scandinavian influence, see Pons-Sanz (forthcoming) Appendix 3.

In other cases a mixture of inputs is likely: *miss* (verb) is found in Old English (not as a borrowing) but comparison of the Old English, Middle English, and Scandinavian evidence suggests that the native word was reinforced and perhaps also influenced semantically by the Scandinavian cognate (although no very clear pattern of Scandinavian-influenced meanings is evident); the noun *miss* could be entirely from Scandinavian. *Slaughter* is most likely from Scandinavian (compare Old Icelandic *slátr*), although related *slaught* is of native origin (and is related ultimately to *slay*), and the type of formation is paralleled by native *laughter*, thus there is nothing to rule out native origin completely.

A good example of the intertwined histories often shown by words of native and Scandinavian origin is shown by the verb *rot* and the (semantically and ultimately etymologically) related adjective *rotten*. The verb *rot* shows the reflex of an Old English weak verb *rotian*. It has cognates in other West Germanic languages, which are also weak, e.g. Old Frisian *rotia*, Middle Dutch *rotten*, Old Saxon *rotōn*, Old High German *rozzēn*. As a weak verb, it forms the past tense and past participle with *-ed*, and, as expected, we find adjectival use of the past participle *rotted* (first recorded in the thirteenth century in one of the manuscripts of the *Ancrene Wisse*: see further sections 12.1.3, 13.1.3 on this text). However, also first recorded in the thirteenth century (in a different manuscript of the *Ancrene Wisse*) is the adjective *rotten*, showing the *-en* ending that usually characterizes the past participles of strong verbs. Probably *rotten* does ultimately reflect the past participle of a strong verb (rather than an alteration of *rotted*), but the verb in question is a Scandinavian one rather than an English one. In a number of the Scandinavian languages similar forms are found (particularly important early examples being Old Icelandic *rotinn* and Old Swedish *rutin*) and it is normally assumed that these result from adjectival use of the past participle of a strong verb that is otherwise unattested. Old English *rotian*, Old Frisian *rotia*, etc. probably all reflect a weak verb derived ultimately from the same base as this strong verb (on formations of this type, see Durkin (2009) 114; there is also a related weak verb in North Germanic, but showing a different suffix). In English, what has probably happened is that *rotten* has been borrowed from Scandinavian (or alternatively speakers familiar with Scandinavian have substituted the strong type *rotten* for the weak type *rotted*); subsequently, *rotten* has simply been regarded as the adjective corresponding to *rot*. In later English, the adjective *rotted* is also still

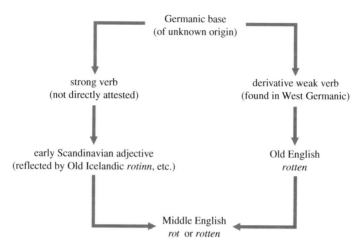

Fig. 10.1 Divergent developments from a shared base in early Scandinavian and in English, and convergence in Middle English as a result of borrowing.

found, although it is less common than *rotten*; conversely, *rotten* is occasionally found as the past participle of *rot*.[29] We can represent this divergence and subsequent confluence schematically, as in Fig. 10.1.

Bull has often been placed in the category of mixed input (especially as regards variants of the type *bole, bol, bolle*), or even regarded as a borrowing purely from Scandinavian, but it is not impossible that all forms of this word show native Old English origin (if so, reflecting an Old English word that is extremely poorly attested).[30]

Other words for which earlier hypotheses of Scandinavian borrowing are now often rejected include *ball* and *rid*. The assumption often made that *cut* is a Scandinavian borrowing is very doubtful. Some words for which Scandinavian borrowing cannot be ruled out but is probably less likely than native origin are *bag, cart, knife*, and perhaps also *shriek* (although regional forms with *skr-* probably do reflect Scandinavian influence) and *scold*.

---

[29] Some still more complex relationships with this word group, probably involving another borrowing from Scandinavian and also one from Dutch, are shown by the rather specialized word *ret* 'to macerate (especially flax or hemp) in order to soften the woody stem and separate the fibres from it', but this is best pursued in dictionaries.

[30] See especially Parsons and Styles (2000) 64–6, Dance (2003) 444.

10.7 Apparent substitution of Scandinavian sounds in native words and vice versa

Shatter and *scatter* pose interesting problems. In Middle English they overlap broadly in meaning and it is likely that they were originally variants of a single word. Since there is no obvious donor form in the Scandinavian languages and since there are words that may be cognates in other West Germanic languages (although these are rather doubtful), it is normally assumed that *shatter* and *scatter* both show developments from an unattested word of native origin, Old English **sc(e)aterian* and that the forms in /sk/ probably reflect substitution of typically Scandinavian /sk/ for native /ʃ/, by analogy with the correspondences found in pairs of cognate words. If so, this perhaps happened among Scandinavian speakers shifting to English. Alternatively, the Old English word could perhaps have been borrowed into Scandinavian varieties in Britain and then borrowed back into English.[31] Thorson (1936 2 n. 1) gives some examples of the same phenomenon apparently shown by other words in modern English dialects. Townend (2002 86–7) gives a number of examples of similar phenomena apparently occurring in place names, such as *Saltmarske*, in which the second element was originally Old English *mersċ* 'marsh', or *Riskenton*, in which the first element was originally Old English *risċen* or *rysċen* 'rushy'. These are different from cases in which the cognate early Scandinavian lexical item has apparently been substituted for its native equivalent, as discussed in section 10.2.

It is also likely that in some cases native sounds were substituted for their Scandinavian equivalents in Scandinavian borrowings, by analogy with the correspondences found in pairs of cognate words. One possible case is *sheer*, which could show substitution of /ʃ/ for /sk/ in Middle English *skēr(e* (modern English regional *skeer*; < Scandinavian: compare Old Icelandic *skǽrr*), although this case is complicated by the existence of the native cognate *shīr(e* (Old English *sċīr*), with different root vowel. See also n. 22 on Old English *hrān*, and also section 10.8 on *dream*.

---

[31] For some further possibilities as regards this word, see Björkman (1900–2) 123 and also the *OED*.

10.8 Words that probably show semantic influence from Scandinavian

Old English had *sēman* 'to settle (a dispute), reconcile (contending parties); to ratify, confirm (an agreement)', a derivative formation from *sōm* 'agreement'. The Middle English and modern verb *seem* meaning 'to appear to be, to be apparently' (and in earlier use also 'to be suitable to, befit, beseem') pretty certainly owes its meaning to Scandinavian influence: compare Old Swedish *söma* 'to befit, beseem' (< **sōmi-* 'fitting, seemly') and Old Icelandic *sóma* (past tense subjunctive *sæmðe*) 'to beseem, befit', both ultimately cognate with the Old English word. (On the subsequent sense development, see section 10.11.) What is less clear is whether the Middle English (and modern) word shows an entirely new borrowing from Scandinavian (as assumed by e.g. the *OED* and as would be plausible on formal grounds), or whether the existing word was influenced in meaning by one or more of the Scandinavian words (as assumed by Björkman (1900–2) 8 n. 1). It is pretty certain that *seemly* does show borrowing of a related word.

Dwell could show the reflex of Old English *dwellan*, but that word's core meaning is 'to lead astray'; the modern meaning 'abide, stay' is surely due to Scandinavian influence (compare Old Icelandic *dvelja* '(transitive) to delay', '(intransitive and reflexive) to tarry, stay'); but, again, it is difficult to say whether semantic influence or simply a fresh borrowing of the Scandinavian cognate has happened here.

Earl (Old English *eorl* 'nobleman, warrior') probably owes its use denoting a high-ranking noble to Scandinavian influence (compare Old Icelandic *jarl* 'earl, high-born nobleman or warrior');[32] in this case, word form argues against a separate borrowing from early Scandinavian.

In Old English the usual word in the meaning 'bread' is *hlāf* (modern English *loaf*, which is now only used in the countable meaning 'a loaf of bread'). Old English *brēad* (modern English *bread*) also occurs in this meaning, but rarely, and also occurs (just as rarely) in the meaning 'a bit, morsel (of bread)'. It has often been suggested that its later emergence as the usual word in the meaning 'bread' is due to either reinforcement or semantic influence (or both) from the Scandinavian cognate (compare Old Icelandic *brauð* 'bread').

---

[32] For summary of some concerns that have been raised about this (generally accepted) instance, see Pons-Sanz (2008) 426–7.

Modern English *dream* appears to be the formal reflex of Old English *drēam* 'joy, bliss, jubilation, celebration, mirth, frenzy, rejoicing, rapture, sound, music, noise', but the meaning 'dream' seems likely to reflect the influence of its possible Scandinavian cognate (compare Old Icelandic *draumr* 'dream'), particularly since it is first recorded in early Middle English texts from the east Midlands. However, it is difficult to be certain that the modern word does not show a loanword, with sound substitution by analogy with the sound correspondences between other pairs of native and Scandinavian cognates (compare section 10.7.) An argument in favour of the latter hypothesis is that the native and Scandinavian words appear to have had little semantic common ground, hence they may not have been readily associated with one another.

A much less certain example of Scandinavian influence is the verb *stint*. Old English *styntan* (rare) has the meaning 'to blunt, dull'; a derivative *āstyntan* also shows the meaning 'to check, stop'; the Scandinavian cognate has the meaning 'to shorten', and this was probably an important influence on the usual modern meanings of the English word, although the exact details are unclear. Another possible instance is the verb *clap*.

In most such cases we can really only deal in probabilities rather than absolute proof: we normally cannot entirely rule out the possibility that a meaning existed in Old English but happens not to be attested, and if we accept that there is Scandinavian influence, we normally cannot be certain that there was not simply a borrowing of the Scandinavian word, replacing the native word entirely (compare the examples discussed in section 10.2, and doublets discussed in section 10.11).

Such examples all (probably) show semantic loans (compare sections 1.2.2 and 8.3). The other major type of semantic borrowing, loan-translations, from Scandinavian are typically very difficult to spot, for two main reasons:

- the elements concerned are normally cognate, and it is difficult to rule out the possibility that Old English and Scandinavian simply shared a formation going back to common Germanic
- we often cannot rule out a loanword from Scandinavian, perhaps with (full or partial) remodelling after the cognate forms in Old English.

Compare *husband* and *boatswain* discussed in section 9.4.1. A possible example first recorded in late Middle English is the verb *mistake*; the second element of this formation certainly shows an earlier borrowing from early

Scandinavian, but it is possible that the formation may also partly be modelled on the early Scandinavian verb reflected by Old Icelandic *mistaka* 'to take by mistake, (reflexive) to miscarry'.

In a still more subtle process, it is possible that some words of rare occurrence in Old English may have been reinforced by their Scandinavian cognate, that is to say, they may have come to be used more often in English in Scandinavian-influenced areas because of familiarity with the cognate word in early Scandinavian: compare discussion of *miss* in section 10.6 and of *bread* above. Björkman (1900–2) comments also on *dale* and *till* 'to' in this regard. The case of *till* is particularly difficult. Its pattern of early Middle English appearances supports the hypothesis of Scandinavian borrowing (see especially Dance (2003)), but continuity with Old English (Northumbrian) *til* cannot be ruled out entirely, and it is unclear whether this Old English form was borrowed early from Scandinavian or shows a cognate form. Such phenomena are extremely difficult to detect with any confidence, given our lack of really secure knowledge about the actual currency of words in spoken Old English (as opposed to the frequency with which they occur in the surviving texts). Compare sections 7.5.1 and 11.4 on similar issues affecting different chronological layers of Latin and/or French loanwords.

10.9 Regional distribution of Scandinavian words

While it is clear that many words of early Scandinavian origin are found largely in sources of northern and north-midland provenance in their early history in Middle English, the field is a very difficult one and would benefit from a thorough review. Dance (2003), a survey of Scandinavian-derived vocabulary in early Middle English texts from the south-west midlands, both identifies the key problems as well as indicating some of the most promising lines for future research. As with all questions to do with Scandinavian-derived and Scandinavian-influenced words, much depends on the criteria by which such words are identified; additionally, the localization of Middle English texts, and of particular manuscript witnesses of Middle English texts, is an extremely difficult area, which has been revolutionized by the *Linguistic Atlas of Late Mediaeval English* (McIntosh et al. (1986)) and its more recent successor project the *Linguistic Atlas of Early Middle English* (Laing and Lass (2011)), and by the scholarship associated with these projects. All earlier scholarship on the distribution of Scandinavian-derived and Scandinavian-influenced lexis in Middle English needs to be reviewed carefully in the light of the findings of these projects.[33]

Useful insights can also be gained from looking at the distribution of Scandinavian-derived and Scandinavian-influenced lexis in modern English dialects, although the same provisos are necessary about how such lexis is identified. One of the most useful surveys is Thorson (1936), which draws on data from the *English Dialect Dictionary* (*EDD*), and for the most part classifies data according to the framework established by Björkman (1900–2). Thorson identifies (a) 275 'provable loans', (b) 322 'probable loans', (c) 48 'uncertain loans'. In his calculations, derivatives that seem to have been formed within English are not counted as independent words, but those that appear to be borrowed are. With many caveats about the unreliability of the data, he makes the following observations about the regional distribution of these words:

It [a table of his results] demonstrates the predominance of Scand. influence in the north, particularly the north-west, and secondly in the north midlands. It further shows a gradual lessening of Scand. elements as we pass southwards through Eastern England, and a continued decrease of these elements if we traverse the southern counties in a westerly direction. The borrowings are fewest in the London region where, because of the ascendancy of the literary language, not only dialect loan-words but dialect peculiarities as a whole have had the utmost difficulty in surviving.

(Thorson (1936) 6.)

Nouns predominate in his data, particularly reflecting the following semantic groups, in descending order of frequency (Thorson (1936) 7):

features of nature (mountains and hills, landmarks and plains, stones, bogs and
    watercourses etc.)
implements and tools
animals and parts of animals
persons and parts of the human body
woods, trees, plants, cereals, etc.
natural phenomena (fire, weather, etc.)

---

[33] For a summary of the earlier scholarship, see Dance (2003). Among the more important studies are Kaiser (1937) and McGee (1940). There are useful observations on the general picture in Burnley (1992). On the picture specifically in Older Scots texts, see the thorough survey of Kries (2003). Among studies that draw on later evidence are Thorson (1936: see main text above), Wall (1898), Kolb (1965). Bator (2007) draws on both medieval and later evidence for selected items.

things pertaining to agriculture
houses and building material, furniture
abstractions
social obligations (taxes, etc.)

Simple totals of loanwords in different dialects can be instructive, but leave out of consideration many very important factors. Thorson's classification into semantic groups is a very useful corollary. Another crucial issue is whether native synonyms are lost entirely, or whether we find a realignment of semantic relationships within a semantic field, and, if so, whether the more central meanings in the field are realized by the borrowed word. Section 10.11 looks at some test cases.

10.10 Impact of Scandinavian borrowing on English core vocabulary

Many Scandinavian borrowings belong to the everyday, familiar vocabulary of modern English. Among the words discussed in this chapter, we can identify fairly impressionistically the following items as belonging to contemporary everyday vocabulary, familiar to the average speaker of modern English:

- pronouns: *they, them, their*
- other function words: *both, though,* probably *till* (although see section 10.8); (archaic or regional) *fro,* (regional) *mun* (see section 10.11)
- verbs that realize very basic meanings: *die, get, give, hit, seem, take, want*
- other familiar items of everyday vocabulary (impressionistically assessed): *anger, awe, awkward, axle, bait, bank* (of earth), *bask, bleak, bloom, bond, boon, booth, boulder, bound (for), brink, bulk, cake, calf* (of the leg), *call, cast, clip* (= cut), *club* (= stick), *cog, crawl, dank, daze, dirt, down* (= feathers), *dregs, droop, dump, egg, to egg* (on), *fellow, flat, flaw, fling, flit, gap, gape, gasp, gaze, gear, gift, gill, glitter, grime, guest, guild, hail* (= greet), *husband, ill, kettle, kid, law, leg, lift, link, loan, loose, low, lug, meek, mire, muck, odd, race* (= rush, running), *raft, rag, raise, ransack, rift, root, rotten, rug, rump, same, scab, scalp, scant, scare, score, scowl, scrap, scrape, scuffle, seat, sister, skill, skin, skirt, skulk, skull, sky, slant, slug, sly, snare, stack, steak, thrive, thrust,* (perhaps) *Thursday, thwart, ugly, wand, weak, whisk, window, wing, wisp,* (perhaps) *wrong.*

Of course, it must be remembered that in many of these cases it is probable that a native cognate has been directly replaced by a very similar-sounding Scandinavian form and we may only wish to see this as lexical borrowing in a rather limited sense.

As elsewhere in this book, we can try to use (however problematically) the data compiled as part of the research in Haspelmath and Tadmor (2009) in order to obtain a slightly more objective estimate of the influence of Scandinavian borrowing on the basic vocabulary of contemporary standard English (compare section 2.3). In Anthony Grant's analysis[34] of the 1,460-meaning list used as a basis for the research in Haspelmath and Tadmor (2009), fifty-nine meanings are identified as usually being realized by a (certain, likely, or possible) Scandinavian borrowing in contemporary English (although in the framework adopted in this book some of these would better be identified as Scandinavian-influenced words):[35]

'anger', 'bait', 'bark', 'calf' (part of the leg), 'call' (included twice in different meanings), 'cast', 'club', 'crawl', 'crooked', 'die', 'dirty', 'egg', 'flat', 'get', 'gill', 'give', 'happy', 'hit' (see further section 16.3.1), 'husband', 'ill' (although the meaning is innovated in English: see section 10.11), 'law', 'leg', 'lift', 'low', 'raft', 'rag', 'raise', 'reindeer', 'rotten', 'same', 'scrape', 'seem' (in a meaning probably innovated in English: see sections 10.8, 10.11), 'sister', 'skin' (included both as noun and as verb), 'skirt', 'skull', 'sky', 'take', 'they', 'Thursday', 'ugly', 'want' (a meaning innovated in English: see section 10.11), 'window', 'wing', and (perhaps < the personal name *Gunnhildr*) 'gun'; (cases I would regard as more doubtful) 'bag', 'cart', 'scold', 'shriek', and (very doubtful) 'ball', 'cut', 'knife', 'sweep'; (compounds included on account of a borrowed element) 'whirlpool' (in which *whirl* is probably borrowed), 'low tide' (in which *low* is borrowed), 'netbag' (in which *bag* is perhaps borrowed), 'mistake' (in which *take* is fairly certainly borrowed; the formation may also partly be modelled on early Scandinavian: see section 10.8).

In some of these cases the word realizing the meaning is a derivative of a (potentially) borrowed word, rather than a borrowing itself: *dirty, crooked, happy, skin* (as verb). The meaning 'root' can probably be added to this list, although *root* is not identified as a borrowing by Grant.

In the Leipzig-Jakarta list of the hundred meanings that are least often borrowed cross-linguistically (as derived from this research), the following eight meanings (hence 8% of the total list) are normally realized by a Scandinavian borrowing or a Scandinavian-influenced word in modern English:

'egg', 'give', 'hit', 'leg', 'root', 'skin', 'take', 'wing'

---

[34] See <http://wold.livingsources.org/vocabulary/13> and compare Grant (2009).

[35] Grant, like other researchers on the WOLD project, ranks each item from 1 to 5 for the probability that the word is a borrowing, but I have not noted this here, referring instead to my own analysis in this chapter.

Chapter 16 looks again at these particular cases in the context of the overall impact of loanwords on the development of the basic vocabulary of modern standard English.

The 1,000 and 100 most frequent words in contemporary British English as reflected by the *BNC* are looked at in section 2.2. As noted there, 6% of the words in the most frequent 1,000 ultimately reflect Scandinavian borrowing and 7% in the most frequent 100, namely *they, their, get, take, give, like, want*.[36]

10.11 The relationships of Scandinavian-derived lexis with other English words

In many instances borrowing of Scandinavian loanwords has had interesting consequences for other items in a semantic field. In some cases there is simple replacement in the core meaning, as of native *warp* by borrowed *cast* (although this was itself later replaced in everyday, unmarked use by *throw*, an innovated meaning of an inherited word). *Sky* has replaced native *heaven* in the meaning 'sky' except in archaic or poetic use, but *heaven* has remained usual in religious meanings, showing semantic narrowing and specialization, and ultimately considerable dissociation from the meaning 'sky' (see further section 16.3.3). Similarly, borrowed *skin* is usual in the core meaning 'skin', native *hide* remaining in the narrower meaning 'the skin of an animal, especially when tanned or dressed' (and in archaic and poetic use more widely). Following the (probable) borrowing of *bark*, native *rind* became more restricted in meaning, no longer referring to the outer layer of a tree. In Old English the usual terms for 'wing' are either the plural of *feþer* 'feather' or the related (singular) *fiþere* 'wing'; both are eventually lost after borrowing of *wing*, with the result that the word *feather* ultimately shows semantic narrowing. Borrowed *die* has eventually ousted from the core meaning 'to die' numerous native synonyms such as *starve* (narrowed to 'to die of hunger') and *swelt* (lost completely from the standard language, although its other meaning 'to be overcome by heat' survives in the derivative *swelter*). Native *craft* and borrowed *skill* retain much more overlap (and

---

[36] The lemmatized *BNC* frequency list of Leech et al. (2001) treats *they* and *them* together, hence 'they' here reflects instances of *they* and *them* combined.

the range of meanings of both terms was affected by the relationship with the French and Latin borrowing *art*).

Similar patterns can often be observed in pairs of cognate words. Borrowed *root* and (ultimately cognate) native *wort* at first show fairly stable differentiation, *root* denoting the parts of a plant below ground and *wort* a plant (having denoted also roots in Old English). Later, *wort* was largely displaced by the Latin and French borrowing *plant*. Native *blossom* shows semantic specialization in the meaning 'flower of a tree', while the (probably ultimately related) borrowed *bloom* has eventually become a highly register-specific item beside the French borrowing *flower*. Scandinavian *hail* and native *whole* are clearly distinguished in meaning in modern English. Their Middle English antecedents show much more overlap, and their overlap in meaning and close formal similarity is exploited in the phrase *hail and hole*. Scandinavian *raise* and native *rear* have only very limited semantic overlap in modern English.

It is important to bear in mind that the foregoing comments all relate to meaning relations in standard modern English. In most cases the current distribution of meanings between two or more words has only developed very slowly and often the relationships within a semantic field are different in different varieties of English.

The diachronic dimension is well illustrated by some instances where a Scandinavian-derived word realizes a core meaning in modern English, but that meaning is one that the word has developed within English. The meaning 'to desire' of *want* developed within English from 'to lack', being securely attested only from the eighteenth century. Similarly, use of *seem* in the modern core meanings 'to appear to be, to be apparently' very probably shows an English development from the borrowed (or Scandinavian-influenced) meaning 'to befit, beseem' (compare section 10.8). In British English (although not in many other varieties) *ill* is the usual word for 'sick' in predicative use, but this is a meaning that was not borrowed from Scandinavian, but was innovated in English in the fifteenth century; *ill* was borrowed as a near-synonym of (etymologically unrelated) native *evil*, but is now only archaic in this meaning.

As with *ill* and *sick*, the words realizing particular meanings often differ between different regional varieties of English. The Scandinavian borrowing *stern* (also *starn*), related to native *star* (in Middle English typically *sterre*), is now restricted to Scots and northern English varieties. *Mun* 'must' is an important function word in many regional varieties of modern English; in Britain it is found from Scotland as far south as Oxford-shire and Berkshire. In many regional varieties the preposition *till* realizes many of the functions shown by *to* in standard English (e.g. *give it till him*), in addition to temporal meanings.

It is notable that a Scandinavian loanword sometimes provides a major term in a semantic field where most of the terms in modern English are of French and/or Latin origin. Scandinavian *earl* has come to form part of the basic hierarchy of the nobility, in which the other terms are all immediately of French origin: *baron, viscount, earl, marquis, duke.* Scandinavian *law* stands out among the legal vocabulary of modern English (perhaps eased by its coincidental formal resemblance to French *loi* and Latin *lēg-, lex* and their derivatives).[37]

Generally, Scandinavian loanwords and native words are almost impossible to distinguish in modern English in terms of register, unlike (in many but not all cases) Latin or French loanwords. Hug (1987) is an important attempt to look at relationships between Scandinavian and native words among nouns denoting various features of the natural world. She concludes that 'in most cases no definite reasons could be assigned to the survival of a word' (Hug (1987) 395), but also notes that:

> [One] determining factor is certainly the number of synonyms constituting a semantic field and their various meanings. We have seen that the smaller a semantic field is and the more general the meaning of its constituents, the greater is the chance of survival of a foreign word with a comparatively narrow meaning.
>
> (Hug (1987) 395.)

We return to this topic in chapter 16, with an investigation of the impacts of loanwords from Scandinavian, French, and Latin on several semantic fields, as reflected by the data of the *OED* and *HTOED*.

10.12 Borrowed word-forming elements and influence on other aspects of the grammatical system

The inflectional and derivational morphology of early Scandinavian bore many resemblances to that of Old English and early Middle English, and, where differences occurred, substitution of the native equivalent was very common. This is one of the factors that generally make it very difficult to tell

---

[37] Compare Fischer (1989) 113, Dance (2003) 314–15, Skaffari (2009) 171.

whether derived forms from early Scandinavian bases show formations within English or were borrowed along with their bases direct from early Scandinavian. It is probably also an important part of the explanation for why large-scale lexical borrowing from early Scandinavian had only a limited impact on the derivational morphology of English, especially in comparison with the huge (but slow) impact of French and Latin derivational morphology on English. (For this reason, a discussion of the mechanisms by which affixes are borrowed into another language is postponed until section 14.4.)

Similarity to native forms has probably played a role in some instances where Scandinavian affixes clearly form new English words. Middle English *-laik* occurs in a small number of formations on native bases (especially in the *Ormulum*); two examples are (in Orm's unique orthography) *clænleȝȝc* 'cleanness' and *grediȝleȝȝc* 'greediness'. It is possible that an altered form of this suffix is shown by the second element of *knowledge*, although other explanations are possible. It is likely that the use of this suffix in English was aided by its formal similarity to the native suffix *-lāc* (although the functions of the two were rather different: *-laik* is suffixed to adjectives in a similar way to *-ness*, while *-lāc*, later *-lock*, is suffixed to verbs and nouns).

Some words of early Scandinavian origin have become common as the first element of compounds within English, e.g. *ill-*, *low-*, and some scholars would regard these as prefixes.

The usual modern English form *-ly* of the adjective- and adverb-forming suffixes may be due to early Scandinavian influence (compare Old Icelandic *-lig*), the regular Middle English developments of the native form being *-lich* and *-like*.

The ending *-and* (as opposed to *-end*) forming the present participle in northern varieties of English may be partly or even wholly due to early Scandinavian influence.

The frequency with which new verbs ending in *-en* (chiefly with inchoative or factitive meaning) arise in Middle English and early modern English may partly reflect Scandinavian influence, since this ending is fairly frequent in words borrowed from or influenced by early Scandinavian, probable examples including Middle English *bliknen* 'to turn pale', *bolnen* 'to swell', *mourknen* 'to rot', *slokenen* 'to extinguish', *þarrnen* 'to lack, to lose, to be absent'.[38]

---

[38] See the short survey in Björkman (1900–2) 14–17, who suggests similar influence also on formations in *-le* (chiefly denoting rapid movement or sounds), although here

Borrowing of function words and closed-class grammatical items such as *they* and (in many varieties) *mun* has already been noted (see sections 10.10, 10.11). The increasing frequency of phrasal verb constructions in English has frequently been ascribed to Scandinavian influence (as also sometimes to Celtic or French), but the case remains unproven. It has also often been suggested that the close contact of two closely related and structurally and grammatically similar languages may have hastened the erosion of the Old English system of inflectional morphology and the transition from a more synthetic to a more analytic grammatical system (i.e. from a system that relies predominantly on grammatical endings to convey grammatical relations to one that relies more heavily on word order), but this remains very controversial.[39]

the evidence seems generally weaker (one interesting example is presented by *niggle*). On the rather complex histories of both endings and their development as productive suffixes, see also Marchand (1969) §4.28, §4.59. See also Miller (2004).

[39] See Miller (2012) for a recent overview of this topic.

Conclusions to part IV

A fair amount is known about the historical context for contact between English and early Scandinavian, but there is troubling uncertainty about a number of key points. Firstly, about the amount of Scandinavian settlement in mainland Britain, and its nature. Secondly, about the date, circumstances, and nature of the contact that led to the bulk of the lexical borrowing into English. The Old English literary records show that Old English certainly contained some loanwords from early Scandinavian from the earliest periods of contact onwards. Many, but not all, of these words belong to specific semantic areas, such as seafaring, warfare, or law, where differences between Anglo-Saxon and Scandinavian culture would readily have prompted lexical borrowing. What is much less certain is whether already in this period there were spoken varieties of Old English, particularly in areas of the most intense contact between Anglo-Saxons and Scandinavian incomers, which already contained most of the Scandinavian loanwords that are found in Middle English. Many of the words that are conventionally referred to as loanwords could alternatively show importations, introduced by speakers of Scandinavian as they switched to using Old English. Such words may subsequently have spread from one variety of English to another by a process of internal borrowing. If so, it is quite possible that many of the words may have entered English only very late in the period of use of early Scandinavian as a spoken language in England. The linguistic evidence is unfortunately rather equivocal on this point: most of the words were clearly in some variety of English early enough to participate in the major early Middle English sound changes, but this still leaves a large chronological window open, and many of the words could have entered English either in mid to late Old English or in very early Middle English.

The close genetic relationship between Old English and early Scandinavian presents particular difficulties. Where cognates existed in both languages, sound changes in Old English or in early Scandinavian can sometimes show that a later English word must have been borrowed from early Scandinavian into English, although in many cases it is impossible to rule out the possibility that the native Old English word has instead been influenced in form by the early Scandinavian cognate, or even by general Scandinavian speech habits in varieties of English heavily influenced by Scandinavian. One argument against the latter hypothesis is that there are relatively few cases of the type discussed in section 10.7, where assumption of the influence of Scandinavian speech provides a solution for a word history that would otherwise be difficult to explain. However, to have more certainty on this latter point one would need to make a thorough survey of all potential cases in English dialects and in Scots, and this has not been done to date.

In cases where there is no native cognate, word form (in combination with the ulterior etymology) can sometimes show early Scandinavian borrowing fairly conclusively. However, this leaves a large number of words for which the case for borrowing from early Scandinavian is circumstantial, and, whatever set of criteria we choose to apply in making assessments, there will always remain many words about which we must admit that there is honest doubt whether they are of native or Scandinavian origin (or a mixture of the two).

Whatever yardstick we adopt, it is clear that borrowing from early Scandinavian has ultimately had a very significant impact on the core vocabulary of modern English, including even the closed-class grammatical vocabulary. Generally, the Scandinavian origin of words is completely invisible to speakers who do not have a detailed knowledge of etymology and historical philology. However, in some areas, such as the derivational morphology of modern English, there is relatively little impact from Scandinavian, at least in comparison with the huge influence from French and Latin in Middle English and beyond. This is probably in large part a result of the close relationship between the languages, so that many words could be accommodated to the existing derivational morphology of English with very little modification. The same linguistic factors probably eased borrowing into areas of core vocabulary, although this would not have happened in the absence of the particular social and cultural circumstances of Scandinavian contact in Britain.

Part V

Borrowing from French and Latin in Middle English

Introduction to part V

The chapters in this part of the book deal with processes that were of crucial importance for the history of the lexis of English; indeed, they show the first part of a long historical arc that will continue through into chapter 14. Middle English borrowing from French and Latin was on a massive scale, and had implications and consequences that continued to be worked through in Early Modern English and even later. Had the Norman Conquest never occurred, it is likely that Latin borrowing would have continued on much the same pattern as described in part III. A good deal of borrowing from French would also have been likely: in the medieval and early modern periods (and beyond) most major European languages show considerable borrowing from French, particularly those near to France geographically, e.g. Dutch and German. But English borrowing from French and from Latin (frequently via French in the medieval period) is different and really rather unusual both in extent and in kind.

As seen in section 2.1, if we look at the composition of the vocabulary of modern English, Latin and French are by far the most prolific contributors of loanwords, whether we take as our yardstick the wordlist of a very comprehensive dictionary such as the *OED*, or a dictionary intended for learners of English. As seen in section 2.2, a similar picture emerges even if we narrow the focus to the 1,000 most frequent words in a corpus of contemporary English, and an analysis of the *OED*'s chronological data for these high-frequency words showed that the overwhelming majority were first borrowed in the Middle English period. It is only when we narrow the focus to the 100 most frequent items that loanwords from early Scandinavian are more numerous than those from French and/or Latin. When the focus was shifted to words realizing basic meanings in section 2.3, a broadly similar picture was seen, with loanwords from Latin and French considerably outstripping loanwords from any other source in the full list of 1,460 meanings on which the Leipzig-Jakarta survey was based, but loanwords from early Scandinavian being more frequent among the 100 meanings most resistant to borrowing.

The fact that loanwords from French or Latin are scarce among the basic, closed-class grammatical words of modern English (with no startling instances such as Scandinavian *they*) is what we would expect from a typical borrowing situation where there has not been language shift in the first language of a large proportion of a population. The thing that is most unusual about the lexical borrowing from French and Latin is its sheer volume, which in turn led to some huge changes in the nature and structure of the vocabulary of English:

- The derivational morphology of English was (eventually) completely transformed by the accommodation of whole word families of related words from French and Latin, and by the analogous expansion of other word families within English exploiting the same French and Latin derivational affixes (especially suffixes).
- Not only was a good deal of native vocabulary simply lost, but many other existing words showed meaning changes (especially narrowing) as semantic fields were reshaped following the adoption of new words from French and Latin.
- The massive borrowing of less basic vocabulary, especially in a whole range of technical areas, led to extensive and enduring layering or stratification in the lexis of English, and also to a high degree of dissociation in many semantic fields (e.g. the usual adjective corresponding in meaning to *hand* is the etymologically unrelated *manual*).

The Norman Conquest was a crucial first step in this process, but it was not the only important factor, and it is also important to realize that the shape of the vocabulary of English did not change overnight. For example, some of the word-forming elements that entered English from Latin and French did not become fully productive in English until the Early Modern period.

However, it is clear that by 1500 the pattern was set and most of the most significant borrowing from French had already occurred. Although the biggest influx of words from Latin was only just beginning at this point, the majority of the Latin loanwords that would eventually form part of the basic or high-frequency vocabularies of modern English had already been borrowed by 1500, and the later voluminous borrowing of Latin words built on the receptivity that English had by this point developed to words of French or Latin origin. Additionally, continuing frequent exposure to these languages, especially among the learned, led to reinforcement of earlier borrowings, as they acquired new senses from the donor language.

The three chapters in part V look primarily at events that occurred before 1500 and part VI primarily at events after 1500. However, there are many continuities across the two periods and the chronological division is not maintained very rigidly. The chapters in part V look most closely at borrowing of words from French and Latin in the multilingual society of later medieval England, and at the tests by which we can (or cannot) identify a word as borrowed from French, Latin, or from a (certain or probable) mixture of inputs from both languages. They also examine the extent to which borrowing from Anglo-French can be distinguished from borrowing from continental French. Consideration of the long-term effects of this borrowing on the nature and structure of the vocabulary of English is largely held over for part VI.

Chapter 11 looks at the nature of the contact situation, and at the methodology for identifying and classifying loans. Chapter 12 examines the extent of Middle English borrowing from these two languages and looks also at how far specifically Anglo-French loans can be distinguished from continental French ones. Chapter 13 begins with an examination of loanwords of all origins in a selection of passages from earlier and later Middle English. This provides some practical illustrations of the differing impact of loanwords from Latin and/or French in comparison with loanwords from early Scandinavian, a topic that is returned to in a longer historical perspective in chapter 16. Chapter 13 ends with a brief look at some of the difficult but important multilingual documents surviving from later medieval England, in which we can observe language contact up close.

11

Exploring the contact situation and identifying loans

11.1 Sources of data

In this period we have a good deal of dated information for Middle English, continental French and Anglo-French, and for classical and post-classical Latin. Dictionaries provide the main point of access for this data, although they do not all provide the same level of coverage, and almost all are better in their coverage of literary than non-literary texts.[1] In general, the language of records (especially everyday business records) is covered least well by the dictionaries; this is largely because such text types are rarely found in the

---

[1] The most useful dictionary sources are: for Middle English, the *MED* and *OED*; for Anglo-French: the *Anglo-Norman Dictionary* (*AND*; the new major revision is accessible only online); for continental French (in some cases also with some coverage of Anglo-French): *Altfranzösisches Wörterbuch* (*AFW*; complete), *Französisches etymologisches Wörterbuch* (*FEW*; complete and now in course of revision), *Dictionnaire étymologique de l'ancien français* (*DEAF*; so far published only for a very limited portion of the alphabet, but invaluable for this); *Dictionnaire de moyen français* (*DMF*); *Trésor de la langue française* (*TLF*; some revised etymologies are being incorporated in the online edition); for medieval Latin: *Dictionary of Medieval Latin from British Sources* (*DMLBS*; approaching completion), *Revised Medieval Latin Word-List* (*RMLW*; largely superseded by *DMLBS*, although still useful since it covers a slightly longer date-range), and also (not concentrating on British material) Niermeyer and Du Cange, and (for words recorded in classical Latin, which are excluded from most of the dictionaries of medieval Latin) the *Oxford Latin Dictionary* (*OLD*) and (for very comprehensive coverage) *Thesaurus Linguae Latinae* (*TLL*; not yet complete). See under Dictionaries in the References section for full details of each.

sorts of completely faithful editions on which lexicographical and other philological work ideally depends. This is particularly the case with the (extremely numerous) records that have Latin as the matrix language (i.e. the language that provides the core grammatical vocabulary)[2] but contain many embedded vernacular words. See section 13.2 for further discussion and examples of such texts.

There are also problems with the dating of our evidence. Because of the uncertainties of manuscript transmission, we may choose (as typically in the *MED* and *OED3*) to give primacy to the date of the earliest manuscript witness in which a word is recorded, or alternatively (as generally in the first edition of the *OED* and still in much French lexicography) to the known or presumed date of original composition of texts. There are no easy solutions here and detailed word studies need always to pay attention not just to dictionary dates of first attestation but to the complex layers of manuscript transmission that lie behind much of the evidence.[3]

It also needs to be borne in mind that, even if unlimited resources were expended on making each dictionary the most perfect possible reflection of the surviving evidence, supported by tagged and parsed corpora of every manuscript witness of every surviving text, we would still be confronted with a picture containing many gaps and apparent contradictions. For instance, many more English texts survive from roughly the fourth quarter of the fourteenth century onwards than from earlier Middle English. This is almost certainly a very fair reflection of the fact that much more was written down in English from this time onwards. However, English was in everyday spoken use by the vast majority of the population throughout this period and we have to accept that the first use of a word in a surviving written document will not necessarily be the same as the first date of spoken use. (Although, in the case of more technical language, it may sometimes be extremely probable that we do have a genuine first use.) This is of course true to some extent of every period, but when we are looking at the Middle

---

[2] On the concept of the matrix language of a mixed-language text see further Myers-Scotton (2002) 10–16.

[3] Much of the most important work in this area has been done in connection with the *Linguistic Atlas of Late Mediaeval English* (McIntosh et al. 1986) and the *Linguistic Atlas of Early Middle English* (Laing and Lass 2011); on the different modes of transmission of different witnesses of texts see especially Benskin and Laing (1981), Laing (2004), and the Introduction to Laing and Lass (2011).

English period it is particularly important not to be seduced by the apparent certainty of the dates that we find in dictionaries (or, reproduced from dictionaries, elsewhere). The dated evidence that we have for each language is extremely valuable and much use is made of it in the course of this chapter, but it always needs to be approached with a measure of caution.

11.2 Multilingualism in later medieval Britain

In the period between the Norman Conquest and the mid fifteenth century English showed a complex interaction with both Latin and Anglo-French in ways that changed considerably over time and that also showed considerable complexity within any given sub-period.

The scholarship of the past several decades has drawn attention to the importance of English/French/Latin trilingualism in England (and to a certain extent in other parts of Britain). This had a transformative effect on the development of the lexis of English. The post-Conquest population of mother-tongue speakers of Anglo-French was tiny (see more on this subject later in this section). As we will see later in this chapter, it is likely that relatively little lexical borrowing is attributable directly to the impact of this speaker group, although some important words were certainly borrowed at this time. Much more influential in the long term was the fact that for almost all of the Middle English period it would have been more or less impossible to pursue any mode of life that involved literacy without having considerable, probably native-like, competence in Anglo-French and Latin, as well as in English. Latin was the language of the Church, but appears to have been learnt primarily through the medium of French until well into the fourteenth century. Government and legal business was typically recorded in either Latin or Anglo-French, as was almost any commercial business. A good deal of business appears also to have been conducted in Anglo-French, as for instance in legal pleading or in parliament. This situation gradually changed in the late fourteenth and fifteenth centuries, as English began to be used in an ever-increasing range of professional functions. Both the extended period of trilingualism and the subsequent period of language shift in particular technical functions had important consequences for the vocabulary of English. In sociolinguistic terms, this was change from above. The crucial language users were not the peasantry, who were probably mostly monolingual throughout this period. However, it was change within the community of speakers who had English as their mother tongue: Latin and (Anglo-)French words, forms, and meanings were adopted in the English of these trilingual individuals, especially when they said or wrote things in English that they were accustomed to saying or writing in Latin and/or French. Some of these words, forms, and meanings spread from specialist to more general discourse, and from the usage of particular social groups to the usage of the general population, but many others did not. When they did spread, the process was often very gradual indeed.

In this book I refer to French as used in Britain as Anglo-French. The term 'Anglo-Norman' is also frequently used, especially in the title of the *Anglo-Norman Dictionary*, and, following this, in other sources, notably the *OED*. Many scholars today prefer the term 'Anglo-French', because there was considerable input from varieties of French other than the Norman one even in William the Conqueror's invading army and there was substantial contact with and input from different continental varieties over the subsequent centuries. However, the new edition of the *AND* currently in preparation retains 'Anglo-Norman' in its title for reasons of historical continuity, and it is very likely that both terms will continue in use for some time to come.[4] My use of the term 'Anglo-French' in this book has the additional advantage of allowing the useful shorthand '(Anglo-)French' for the very many cases where it cannot be ascertained whether input into English has occurred from insular or continental French, or from both.

For several hundred years after the Conquest, English became forced out of official functions almost entirely, at least in writing. In Anglo-Saxon England the vernacular had been quite widely used in official functions, but, by the twelfth century, writs (or written instructions) were normally in Latin, as were the records of the new types of bureaucratic activity of the state, such as the Pipe Rolls, which recorded the state's financial business conducted at the Court of the Exchequer. Latin of course remained the international language of the Church and, with the appointment of Frenchmen to nearly all of the leading positions in the Church, it is not surprising that the thriving native traditions of religious writing in English suffered a very severe setback. In many ways, this brought England more into line with the situation in most of western Europe, as noted by Clanchy:

---

[4] See further the discussion by William Rothwell in the preface to the new edition of the *AND* (Rothwell 2005); for some different perspectives, see also Wogan-Browne (2009a).

Latin made quick progress because it was the written language with which William's clerks (in both the ecclesiastical and modern sense), from Archbishop Lanfranc of Canterbury downwards, were most familiar. In the eyes of contemporaries on the European continent Latin was the only language of record; a person unfamiliar with it was illiterate . . . In increasing the use of Latin writing, the Norman Conquest brought England into the mainstream of medieval literate communication. At the same time, in the short term, the Conquest may have caused a reduction in literacy (in the modern sense of being able to read and write the language one speaks), because it divorced writing further from everyday speech.

(Clanchy (1993) 27.)

When we gradually find a vernacular coming to be used in secular technical functions, such as financial record-keeping, legal records, or records of parliamentary business, that vernacular is at first much more typically Anglo-French than English. Vernacular literature shows a similar pattern: Britain saw a significant flowering of vernacular literature in the twelfth century, but this was predominantly in Anglo-French, not in English.[5] Ironically, the well-established traditions of vernacular (i.e. English) writing in Anglo-Saxon England may have had some influence in fostering post-Conquest vernacular writing, since the early Anglo-French literary flowering is rather precocious in comparison with literary activity in French on the continent. But nonetheless, as a language of writing, English after the Conquest stood hugely in the shadow of both Latin and French, and it is not until the late fourteenth and (especially) the early fifteenth centuries that we can see English becoming the default choice as language of writing in various official functions.[6] The second half of the fourteenth century also saw significant landmarks in the history of the official use of spoken English, such as the Statute of Pleading of 1362 specifying (albeit with little impact) that pleading in the law courts should be in English rather than French, or the opening of parliament in English for the first time in the same year.[7] It is also only from the later fourteenth century onwards that we come once more to have a continuous, confident tradition of literary composition in English.

---

[5] For overviews of Anglo-French literature, see Short (1995), Short (2007) 31–5, and further references given there.

[6] Compare Ormrod (2003), Harriss (2005) 46.

[7] For much fuller listing of key events in both oral and written usage, compare Williams (1975) 68–81, Kibbee (1991), Baugh and Cable (2002) 127–57, Miller (2012) 6.16; also Short (2007) 28–9 for some critical comments on the uses sometimes made of such dates, and Machan (2002) on the dangers of a teleological bias in interpreting such data. See also Smith (1992) for an overview of the sociolinguistic situation.

If we look at the other side of the coin, John Gower's *Mirroir de l'Omme* is a substantial literary work in Anglo-French dating from the late fourteenth century (although the heyday of literary composition in Anglo-French was very much earlier), and record-keeping in Anglo-French extends well into the fifteenth century.[8] However, it is only in the special case of the language of the law that writing in French for practical purposes survived beyond 1500 in Britain.[9]

It is important to bear in mind that throughout these centuries English remained the principal language in everyday spoken use. After the Conquest, there were clearly speakers of Anglo-French in most of the key positions of power in the country. How long Anglo-French remained anyone's first, native language is a difficult question and perhaps a naive one given the bilingualism that must before long have existed in the higher orders of society. It is also fairly clear that patterns of language use showed significant shifts and changes among the higher social orders in the twelfth century; even among those who had Anglo-French as their first language, some degree of bilingualism was probably at least useful (perhaps helped by the prevalence of English wet nurses for noble infants). It is very unlikely that by the early thirteenth century anyone other than the royal family, some of the feudal aristocracy, and some of the highest clergy had Anglo-French as their mother tongue.[10]

However, recent work on Anglo-French suggests rather strongly that up until the last few decades of the fourteenth century considerable competence in Anglo-French was normal among the educated portion of the population, at a level of balanced bilingual competence that suggests learning of Anglo-French in very early childhood. In an important recent study, Ingham (2012) argues that there were two major shifts in the history of Anglo-French. In the first half of the thirteenth century, increasing

---

[8] For some interesting analysis of the changing relationships between French and English, especially from a literary perspective, see Butterfield (2010).

[9] For important discussions of the languages used in legal functions in post-Conquest England, see Brand (2000), Ormrod (2003), Ormrod (2009).

[10] Compare Berndt (1965), Kibbee (1991), Short (2007) 12. On the very complex issues surrounding language and anti-foreigner sentiment in thirteenth-century England, see Machan (2003) 21–69. There is a useful summary of some of the most valuable anecdotal evidence on spoken use of Latin, French, and English in the period up to the early thirteenth century in Bartlett (2000) 482–91. On the likely later linguistic situation among royalty, see Lusignan (2009).

separation between the baronial classes on either side of the English Channel led to a decrease in the numbers of people even in the great households of
England who had significant exposure from a very early age to French as
spoken by continental native speakers. Ingham detects the impact of this in
an increasing divergence between the phonologies of continental and insular
French, and specifically in changes in the phonology of Anglo-French that
reflect increasing influence from the sound system of English. However, he
maintains that key syntactic phenomena show very little influence from
English until the late fourteenth century. For instance, up until roughly
the 1370s, written Anglo-French shows native-like command of such features as gender agreement and oblique pronouns, once the effects of sound
changes involving the reduction of unstressed vowels are taken into account:
thus, people who were writing Anglo-French in England appear to have
been very competent bilinguals and (as shown by the sound changes dis-
played by the French they wrote) they were bilingual in English and Anglo-
French, not continental French.[11] If such findings are borne out by further
research, they make a radical difference to the traditional picture of Anglo-
French in the late thirteenth and fourteenth centuries as (to caricature only
slightly) a half-learned jargon employed only in writing. If we follow Ingham's view, the fairly rapid decline of Anglo-French as a language of record
in the late fourteenth and early fifteenth centuries follows shortly after the
loss of widespread native-like command of Anglo-French among the literate
in England. Elementary education would clearly have been of crucial
importance in establishing and maintaining balanced bilingualism of this
sort, and it is thus significant that Latin seems generally to have been taught
through the medium of French, not English, until well into the fourteenth
century.[12] Latin was the medium of all advanced education and its early
mastery was a primary aim of the earliest stages of a grammar school
education; hence, the medium in which Latin was taught has important
implications for the linguistic abilities of the educated portion of the population. Ingham (2012) suggests that Anglo-French was acquired in the 'song
schools' which it appears that many pupils attended from around age 5,

---

[11] Compare also Trotter (2003a), Trotter (2003b) on late Anglo-French as forming
part of a dialect continuum with continental French, rather than an isolated (moribund)
variety.

[12] Compare Ingham (2009); on languages in education, see also Kristol (1990), Hunt
(1991), Orme (2006).

before beginning grammar school at 7 (although details about elementary education in the period are scarce); Ingham suggests that acquisition of French as an everyday medium of school instruction and communication at this age would explain many of the characteristics of Anglo-French, and that very high mortality rates, particularly among urban populations, in the Black Death in the 1340s to 1360s may well explain the dramatic shift found in the late fourteenth century. The extracts in section 13.1.4 give the comments of two contemporary writers on the changing situation in the course of this century.

The ability to speak some sort of French to some sort of functional level is likely to have remained fairly widespread among most educated people until the early fifteenth century and probably beyond, although it is uncertain whether in the fifteenth century even educated people (except lawyers) may have been called upon actually to speak any French except when speaking to a Frenchman (or other foreigner). Nonetheless, major historical events such as the English occupation of much of northern France in the fifteenth-century phase of the Hundred Years War[13] led to significant continuing face-to-face contact between English speakers and speakers of (various varieties of) continental French, and the enclave around Calais remained in English hands until the middle of the sixteenth century. There were innumerable everyday contacts through trade. Additionally, encounters with French as the most prestigious written vernacular in western Europe continued apace.

The relationship between English and Latin was very different from that between English and Anglo-French. Latin was central to the medieval Church, both as its international language and at a national and local level, and knowledge of Latin was a defining characteristic of a cleric, even if the cleric with poor Latin became a stock satirical topos. In the fourteenth century (very minimal) ability to read Latin became established by statute as sufficient justification for pleading benefit of clergy and hence transfer of a case from the secular to the ecclesiastical courts, with generally more lenient penalties. Those employed in administrative positions in the national government were predominantly clerics until very late in the Middle Ages and high-ranking civil servants were often rewarded with a bishopric.[14] The 'laicization' of the various branches of the royal secretariat (chancery, privy seal office, and signet office) belongs to the late fourteenth

---

[13] Compare Curry et al. (2010).

[14] See the summary of some 'careers in royal administration' in Prestwich (2005) 62–6.

and early fifteenth centuries; the poet Geoffrey Chaucer, clerk of the royal works, is an important early example of the higher ranking lay administrative class; his slightly later contemporary Thomas Hoccleve was a clerk in the privy seal office and married only after giving up on his hopes of an ecclesiastical benefice.[15] Scholarship remained barely separable from the Church in this period and Latin was likewise the international language of scholarship.

Until at least the end of the fourteenth century the linguistic competence demanded of anyone involved with any level of government business was probably considerable. Prestwich comments thus on the situation in the thirteenth and early fourteenth centuries:[16]

> The main language of government was Latin. . . . Most charters and writs were in Latin; this was also the language of accountancy, not just in the rolls produced by the exchequer, but also in the myriad of manorial accounts kept by landlords, great and small. French was also used. Much of the more private royal correspondence was in French, and by the early fourteenth century this was the language used for the accounts of the royal chamber. In the royal law courts the records were kept in Latin, while pleading took place in French. It was only among the lower levels of the hierarchy of the courts that English may have been employed.
>
> (Prestwich (2005) 56.)

Away from the world of government, Rothwell (2010) points to the importance and popularity of Anglo-French texts on estate management among the landed classes in the second half of the thirteenth century, although it is notable that this is a semantic area where there was relatively little transfer of technical terminology to English, in comparison with the language of the various professions.

In some ways, the sociolinguistic distinctions of status and function between Latin, French, and English in late medieval England were similar to the distinctions found between different dialects of English in contemporary monolingual English-speaking countries: in some situations and functions Latin was the appropriate language to use, in others French, and in others English.[17] Linguists often describe such a situation as showing di- or triglossia, i.e. the use of two or three different varieties or different

---

[15] Compare Harriss (2005) 41–7; on Hoccleve, see also Burrow (2008).

[16] Compare also Clanchy (1993) for analysis of lives and careers that took in chancery, law courts, the Church, and mercantile and civic record-keeping.

[17] For an extended argument along similar lines, see Machan (2003).

languages in different social situations. The fact that different languages were involved (i.e. trilingualism), not different dialects of a single language, had important implications: English gradually took on more and more functions at the expense of French and Latin, but as it did so it had to acquire whole new areas of vocabulary, in order to perform new functions. Typically, this was done by borrowing from Latin and French.

The books owned by particular individuals can also give important insights into this trilingual society. As Clanchy notes:

An educated Englishman in the thirteenth century would have become familiar with a variety of writings over his lifetime—charters to safeguard his landed property, royal writs for litigation, homilies for devotion, romances for entertainment, and so on. Among the forty or so volumes which Guy de Beauchamp, earl of Warwick, gave by charter to Bordesley Abbey in 1306 are books of the Bible, meditations and saints' lives, romances and histories, a book of physic and one of surgery, a child's primer, an encyclopaedia, and 'a little red book in which are contained many diverse things'. All the books are described as 'romances', meaning that they are in French and not Latin. A step down the social scale, the Northamptonshire gentleman, Henry de Bray of Harlestone, copied out with his own hand in Latin at the age of fifty-two (in 1322) a compilation for the instruction of his heirs containing a general description of the world, a more detailed description of England (its counties, bishoprics, kings and Cinque Ports), extracts from the Domesday Book and other royal records, information about Northamptonshire feudal and local government, a list of own tenants, the dimensions of Harlestone common field and the village, a table of measures, records of his expenses, and numerous copies of documents concerning his property.

(Clanchy (1993) 81–2.)

Chapter 13 looks in detail at what selected passages from texts in English and in other languages of medieval England can tell us about this linguistic situation. Before that can be attempted, it is necessary to consider in detail the methodology by which loanwords of different origins can be identified.

11.3 Borrowing from French, Latin, and French and/or Latin

11.3.1 Background

In the Middle English period, many words can be shown to come directly from French, with French the main determiner of the word's form and meaning in English, and Latin at most a secondary influence. A smaller but still considerable number can be shown with some confidence to be solely from Latin, not French. In very many cases, we cannot say with complete confidence that a word is from French rather than Latin, or vice versa, and in most of these cases composite origin from both languages seems the likeliest scenario. (For estimates of the totals of each type and their chronological breakdown, see section 12.1.) This partly reflects facts about the history of English and the nature of the language contact with French and Latin. However, it also owes a great deal to some facts about the history of French and it is best to start by considering these.

French is historically developed from Latin and the bulk of its core vocabulary has developed 'naturally' from spoken Latin, showing a good many phonological and morphological (as well as semantic) developments during its history. However, since before the date of our earliest substantial literary texts in French and continuing up until the present day, French has also borrowed words from Latin. These borrowings have sometimes replaced and sometimes coexisted with earlier developments of the same Latin word (in the latter case, often with some semantic distinction). Sometimes a word has been borrowed once and begun to show formal developments within French, and then the same Latin word has been borrowed again, leading to further etymological doublets. Additionally, some French words have been altered in form on the model of their Latin antecedent (or sometimes, on the basis of incorrect identification of a supposed Latin antecedent), rather than being replaced by a completely new borrowing.

This has led to some rather complex layering in the vocabulary of French, which in turn has fed into some even more complex layering in the vocabulary of modern English.

For example, (Anglo-)French *pes*, *pais* (modern French *paix*) is the regular development of Latin *pāx* 'peace', or more accurately of the oblique stem shown by its accusative singular *pācem*. It is a word that almost certainly formed part of the vocabulary of the variety of Vulgar Latin from which French developed, and both the diphthong and the development of /k/ > /s/ show the expected developments in a word of this phonological shape. (The final *x* of the written form of the modern French word shows a classicizing respelling under the influence of the Latin word.) On the other hand, the verb *pacifier* 'to pacify' (Old French *pacefier*) is a borrowing of Latin *pācificāre*, rather than an inherited part of the lexis of French. Thus, the two words ultimately belong to the same etymological 'family', but they have entered French by very different routes.

To take another example, the noun *main* 'hand' is an inherited part of the vocabulary of modern French, regularly developed from Latin *manus*, while the adjective *manuel* 'manual' shows an Old French borrowing of Latin *manuālis*. It is important to note that this sort of borrowing goes back to a very early stage in the documented history of Old French, and has continued to happen ever since.

This situation in French is one cause of some of the very complex patterning that we find in the lexis of English. The English word *peace* (Middle English *pais*, *pees*, etc.) first appears in the Final Continuation of the *Peterborough Chronicle* in the middle of the twelfth century (thus in the earliest text conventionally taken to show Middle English rather than late Old English). Its form indicates clearly that it is from (Anglo-)French *pes*, *pais*, rather than from Latin *pāx*. (The monophthongization of /ai/ is an expected development in (Anglo-)French.) The early semantic history in English closely parallels that in both French and Latin. It is notable as an early borrowing in a core meaning. The principal existing English words it replaced were *friđ* and *griđ* (the latter being an Old English borrowing from Scandinavian: compare section 9.4.1). Of these, *frith* barely survives beyond the early Middle English period, in one or two very restricted specialized uses. *Grith* remains quite frequent in Middle English (and occurs in some very limited contexts even later than this), although in later Middle English it occurs largely in verse texts in which its use was probably stylistically marked. (Later uses of both *frith* and *grith* are often in formulae paired with a more recent synonym, e.g. *frith and grith* or *peace and grith*.) *Peace* thus shows a word clearly borrowed from French, not Latin, in the early Middle English period, which has come to occupy the central place in an important lexical field in modern English.

English *pacify* shows a rather different pattern. It is first attested in the late fifteenth century, and very probably owes something both to Latin *pācificāre* and to the French borrowing of this *pacefier*, *pacifier*; at least, there is nothing in its form to rule out either origin, and the range of senses is similar in each language (although figurative uses such as 'to appease' and 'to calm' appear to have closer parallels in French than in Latin).

This example illustrates a further important feature of the Middle English reception of French and Latin words: the patterns of morphological adaptation of the endings of Latin words in Middle English were largely determined by the shape that the same endings had in French. Thus Latin verbs in *-ficāre* typically end in *-fy* in Middle English, because they had the form *-fier* in French. Earlier examples that established the pattern include *signify* (first attested in the thirteenth century), and *crucify*, *justify*, *specify* (all first attested in the fourteenth century). Similar patterns include:

- Latin *-īa* > French *-ie* > English *-y*, in e.g. *glory, fury*
- Latin *-tāt-, -tās* > French *-té* (in Anglo-French also *-tet, -teth*) > English *-ty* (earlier *-teð, -te, -tee*), in e.g. *bounty, plenty, poverty, subtlety*[18]
- Latin *-bilis* > French *-ble* > English *-ble*, in e.g. *noble, stable, possible*
- Latin *-āntia* > French *-ance* > English *-ance*, in e.g. *circumstance, ignorance, abundance*
- Latin *-entia* >
    i. (in words that French inherited from Latin) French *-ance* > English *-ance*, in e.g. *countenance, resistance*
    ii. (in words that French borrowed from Latin) French *-ence* > English *-ence*, in e.g. *penitence, obedience, conscience, continence* (a doublet of *countenance*)

For many common endings, this early transmission through French set the pattern that has remained for the adaptation of subsequent Latin borrowings throughout the history of English. Compare e.g.:

- *maleficence* (1533) < Latin *maleficentia*
- *occurrence* (1539), either < post-classical Latin *occurrentia* or formed directly on English *occurrent*
- *resistible* (1629) < post-classical Latin *resistibilis*
- *perfectible* (1635) < post-classical Latin *perfectibilis*

In late Middle English and early modern English some new patterns come increasingly to distinguish Latin loanwords, e.g. we find that Latin *-entia* or *-āntia* more typically give English *-ency* or *-ancy,* rather than *-ence* or *-ance*. The formation of English verb stems in *-ate* < Latin past participial stem in *-āt-* becomes especially frequent. Section 14.2 looks at these processes more closely. Additionally, some later changes in continental French created further distinctions between English and French word forms in words ultimately of Latin origin; e.g. Latin *-ōrius* gives rise to Anglo-French and Old French *-orie* and hence English *-ory*, but in Middle French and modern French a further development to *-oire* is found. See further section 12.2.2, as likewise on *-aire* beside *-arie*. However, many endings remained unaffected by such developments: even in modern English, a word borrowed either from a Latin word ending in *-bilis* or a French word ending in *-ble* will still

---

[18] See further section 11.3.4 on words in *-ty*.

end in *-ble* in English. See section 14.4 on the process by which affixes were borrowed and came to form new words within English.[19]

Finally, the example of *manual* already touched on highlights another feature of the effects of borrowing from French and Latin on the vocabulary of English, namely a radical dissociation in many word groups (compare section 1.1 on this term). Thus *manual*, a borrowing from Latin, is the usual adjective corresponding in modern English to the noun *hand*, but the two words show entirely unrelated bases that speakers have no way of relating to one another formally. We can compare the situation in French, where such pairs as *main* and *manuel* do not show a transparent derivational relationship, but at least retain a phonetic resemblance to one another (as, rather more remotely, do even *paix* and *pacifier*, and English *peace* and *pacify*).

11.3.2 Borrowings solely from French

Many words are clearly identifiable as Middle English loanwords from French, not Latin. Most examples fall into one of two categories:

1. The word does not exist in Latin.
2. The word does exist in Latin, but the word form in English indicates borrowing from French, not Latin.

The first category, where the word does not exist in Latin, can usefully be subdivided into two groups:

(i) The English word is borrowed from a French word belonging to a word family that does not exist in (documented) Latin, i.e. it has been formed within the history of French, or has entered French (or the parent variety of Vulgar Latin) from another source, e.g. from a Germanic language, as in the case of *choice*, *range*, *rank*, *scorn*, or *wait*.

(ii) More commonly, the English word shows a derivative formation within French (or in some cases Vulgar Latin) on a stem of Latin origin, e.g. (among the high-frequency words discussed in section 2.2) *agreement*, *department*, *government*. In some cases the original

---

[19] For fuller listings of affixes found in French and/or Latin words in English, see Marchand (1969), Miller (2006), Miller (2012), although none of these works deal in any detail with questions of determining the immediate donor language.

derivative status of words of this type is entirely opaque in English, e.g. (again among the words discussed in section 2.2) *age*, *certain*, *company*, *degree*, *duty*, *force*, *size*, *stage*, *very*.

Even in cases like these, forms are frequently found in post-classical Latin that appear to have been borrowed from French and these sometimes cannot be eliminated entirely from consideration as etymons of the English word. For instance, in the case of *range* post-classical Latin has the forms *ranga*, *rangea*, *raingia* 'range, row'; if any of these retained pronunciation of *g* as [dʒ] it is just possible (although unlikely) that the word could have entered English partly via these Latin forms. (Such considerations apply to most of the words that have entered English < French < Vulgar Latin < Celtic, as described in section 5.3.)

In the second main category, an English word can be shown by its form to reflect borrowing from French rather than Latin, because the French word, although originally inherited or borrowed from Latin, has undergone significant change in word form in French that is also reflected by the English borrowing. This is typically change affecting the word stem, because most derivational suffixes in French are of Latin origin and the patterns of substitution described in section 11.3.1 mean that they are seldom secure proof of French rather than Latin origin.

The example of *peace*, < (Anglo-)French *pes*, *pais* rather than its etymon Latin *pāc-*, *pāx*, was discussed in section 11.3.1. There are many other clear examples, such as (drawing examples from the high-frequency words discussed in section 2.2 and in each case giving only the barest sketch of the etymology):

- *chance* < (Anglo-)French *chance* < Latin *cadentia*
- *change* < (Anglo-)French *changer* < post-classical Latin *cambiare* (ultimately of Celtic origin)
- *city* < (Anglo-)French *cité* < Latin *cīvitāt-*, *cīvitās*
- *clear* < (Anglo-)French *cler* (modern French *clair*) < Latin *clārus*
- *close* (verb) < (Anglo-)French *clos*, feminine *close*, past participle (or *close*, present subjunctive) of (Anglo-)French *clore* < Latin *claudere* (past participial stem *claus-*);[20] similarly *close* (adjective) < (Anglo-)French *clos* (as above)

---

[20] See section 6.3.1 for Old English *clūse*, ultimately reflecting borrowing of the same Latin etymon.

- *cost* (noun) < (Anglo-)French *cost* (modern French *coût*) < *coster* (> English *cost*, verb) < Latin *constāre*
- *couple* < (Anglo-)French *couple* < Latin *cōpula*
- *course* < (Anglo-)French *cours* < Latin *cursus*
- *cover* < (Anglo-)French *cuvrir, couvrir* < Latin *cooperīre*
- *enter* < (Anglo-)French *entrer* < Latin *intrāre*
- *fail* < (Anglo-)French *faillir* < a morphological variant of Latin *fallere*
- *foreign* < (Anglo-)French *forain* < post-classical Latin *foranus*
- *join* < (Anglo-)French *joign-* (infinitive *joindre*) < Latin *iungere*
- *large* < (Anglo-)French *large* < (feminine of) Latin *largus*
- *letter* < (Anglo-)French *lettre* < Latin *littera*
- *measure* (noun) < (Anglo-)French *mesure* < Latin *mensūra*
- *to pay* < (Anglo-)French *paier* < Latin *pācāre*
- *people* < (Anglo-)French *peuple* < Latin *populus*
- *point* < (Anglo-)French *point* < Latin *punctus*
- *poor* < (Anglo-)French *povre, poure* < Latin *pauper*
- *price* < Anglo-French *price, prise*, (Anglo-)French *pris* < Latin *pretium*
- *reason* < (Anglo-)French *raison* < Latin *ratiōn-, ratiō*[21]
- *rule* < (Anglo-)French *riule* < Latin *rēgula*
- *save* (in Middle English also *sauve*) < Anglo-French *saver*, (Anglo-)French *sauver* < Latin *salvāre*
- *term* < (Anglo-)French *terme* < Latin *terminus*
- *treat* (in Middle English also *trait*) < Anglo-French *treter*, (Anglo-)French *traiter* < Latin *tractāre*

In many cases verbs have (probably) been borrowed from a particular stem alternant in the paradigm of a French verb. Thus *appear* is probably < (Anglo-)French *aper-*, the stressed stem (found for instance in the present subjunctive *apere*) of *aparer* (< Latin *appārēre*), although in Anglo-French *aper-* does sometimes occur as stem throughout the paradigm, as a result of analogical levelling, and this may instead explain the English form *appear*. In either case, borrowing directly < Latin *appārēre* is not plausible. Similarly in the case of *claim* we find:

> *claim* < either Anglo-French *claimer* or (Anglo-)French *claim-*, stressed stem of *clamer* < Latin *clamāre*

---

[21] Compare later *ratio* and *ration*, showing borrowing of the Latin nominative and oblique stem respectively.

A very frequent pattern is shown by English verbs in *-ish*, which are generally from French verbs in *-ir* showing an extended stem (occurring in some parts of the paradigm) ending in *-iss-* (developed ultimately from Latin inchoative verbs in *-isc-*). The change from *-iss* to *-ish* is normally assumed to show a phonological development that occurred in Anglo-French,[22] although there is little to say that it could not have taken place in English instead. A typical example is:

> *punish* (in early use also *punisse*) < (Anglo-)French *puniss-*, extended stem of *punir* < Latin *pūnīre*

Others include: *abolish, accomplish, banish, blandish, blemish, brandish, burnish, cherish, demolish, embellish, establish, finish, flourish, furbish, furnish, garnish, impoverish, languish, nourish, perish, polish, ravish, relinquish, replenish, tarnish, vanish, varnish.* In most, but not all, of these cases the French verb has a Latin etymon, but in all such cases this can fairly confidently be ruled out as direct etymon of the English verb, because of the presence of the *-ish* ending in English. Because *-ish* shows an extension to a verb stem, it resembled a suffix and could very easily be applied by analogy to other verb stems in English. We thus sometimes find forms in *-ish* occurring as remodellings of English verbs not borrowed from French verbs in *-ir*, for example:

> *famish*, which originated as a variant of *fame* 'to starve (someone)' < (Anglo-)French *afamer*
> *admonish*, which originated as a variant of *admonest, amonest* < (Anglo-)French *amonester*, Middle French *admonester* (compare section 14.3)

Publish may show an alteration of (very rare) *publy*, or, as is probably more likely in view of its range of forms and meanings, may show a borrowing directly from (Anglo-)French *publier*, with *-ish* employed as though it were a derivational suffix for accommodating French verb stems into English. (Unless there was actually variation in verb class in (Anglo-)French that has not (yet) been identified in the lexicographical record and a form **publir* existed beside *publier*.)

This tendency to behave like a derivational suffix means that even *-ish* cannot be used as a completely safe formal test of French, not Latin, origin. For example, in the sixteenth century *distinguish* could show borrowing

---

[22] Compare Short (2007) 107.

directly from (Anglo-)French *distinguer* and/or its etymon Latin *distinguere*, or could show remodelling of late Middle English *distingue*. (Compare also *extinguish* discussed in 16.3.3.)

As the example of *-ish* shows, there are no really safe short cuts by which whole classes of words can be classified as of French not Latin origin. It is always essential to look into each word history individually, since exceptions to general rules can and do occur.

11.3.3 Borrowings solely from Latin

Borrowings solely from Latin tend to be much more difficult to identify than borrowings solely from French. In the case of words solely from French, there are typically strong arguments from word form: we can see that a word like *peace* is from French and not Latin because the English word form reflects changes that took place in French. By contrast, most Middle English words borrowed from Latin could easily have occurred as learned borrowings in French as well, in forms corresponding to those found in English. (See chapter 14 on how this situation changes somewhat in late Middle English and Early Modern English.) Therefore, in identifying borrowings solely from Latin, we are normally reliant on negative evidence, that a particular word form is not attested in French, or not at a particular date, or not in a particular meaning.

The 1,000 most frequent words in the *BNC* can once again be used as a test sample, in order to achieve some objectivity in the examples selected. It is notable that in this set of high-frequency words (see section 2.2) there are probably no words that can be identified entirely confidently as borrowings solely from Latin in the early Middle English period. Some such borrowings certainly did occur in this period, but they are rather rare (see section 12.1 for numerical analysis). The sample does provide some interesting examples from later Middle English, three of which are discussed in detail here:

Example 1: *produce* and *product*

Produce (verb) seems a safe example of a fifteenth-century borrowing solely from Latin *prōdūcere*. The equivalent word in French is *produire*, recorded from the early fourteenth century onwards (although apparently not in Anglo-French); a learned Middle French form *producer* is found in the early fifteenth century, but is very rare. Additionally, English shows in the late fourteenth century slightly earlier use of *product* as a past participle, < Latin *prōductus*, past participle of *prōdūcere*. The noun *product* (first attested in the mid fifteenth century) can likewise probably be attributed solely to borrowing from Latin (< *prōductum*), since the corresponding

French noun is the formally distinct *produit*, and is attested only from the mid sixteenth century. But for another noun in the same word family, *production* (also first attested in the mid fifteenth century), borrowing from either French or Latin seems equally possible.

Example 2: *provide*

Provide, first attested in the early fifteenth century, is probably a borrowing solely from Latin *prōvidēre*. The regular French development of Latin *prōvidēre* is (Anglo-)French *purveer*, French *pourvoir* (with numerous formal variants); English *purvey* (*c.*1300) clearly shows a borrowing of this. There is very limited evidence in Anglo-French for forms of the type *provider*, *providre*, earliest in the fourteenth century, in the technical meanings 'to appoint by papal provision' and (in reflexive use) 'to be beneficed by papal provision'. Since English *provide* is found in a much wider range of meanings, it seems reasonably safe to assume that it is a borrowing from Latin. In fact, in early use it shows very considerable semantic overlap with earlier *purvey* and it could be regarded as a substitution, reflecting the prestige of Latin, of the clearly Latinate form *provide* for the earlier French borrowing *purvey*.

Example 3: *idea* and *ideal*

Idea (first attested late fourteenth century) seems, on formal grounds, a clear borrowing from Latin *idea* (although the form *idee* attested from the mid sixteenth century may show French influence). However, the later semantic development of the word very probably owes something to semantic influence from Middle French *idee* or modern French *idée*, including the modern core meaning 'conception, notion', which is not part of the meaning of the word in classical or medieval Latin. The related adjective *ideal* is probably also primarily a borrowing from Latin (< post-classical Latin *idealis*), but in this instance the evidence comes from relative dates of first attestation: English *ideal* is first recorded in the mid fifteenth century, but Middle French *ideal* only in the mid sixteenth.

It will be noted that the examples in this section have involved a good deal of qualification and hedging. This is a true reflection of the difficulty of assessing the data. Most cases can be made to appear more categorical, but only at the cost of being rather cavalier with the data.

11.3.4 Borrowings from French and/or Latin

It is noted in several of the case studies in section 11.3.3 that semantic influence from French was likely, even if the corresponding French word could be ruled out as etymon on formal grounds. The same holds true for Latin semantic influence on many of the words discussed in section 11.3.2. The close semantic similarity of cognate words in medieval French and medieval Latin has important consequences when we come to consider the very large number of English words that could on formal grounds show borrowing from either Latin or French.

Example 1: *procession*

To take a first example that illustrates some of the main issues in miniature, *procession* occurs very sparingly in Old English as a borrowing of post-classical Latin *procession-*, *processio* (frequently with Latin case endings). In a late Old English interpolation among the copied annals in the *Peterborough Chronicle*[23] it occurs again as *procession*, perhaps showing continuity with the form found in earlier texts, or perhaps showing a new borrowing from Latin. In the early Middle English Final Continuation of the same source we find *processiun* (a form also found once in a different late Old English text). This form probably indicates a borrowing from Anglo-French, or at least the influence of contact with Anglo-French, since *-iun* (as well as *-ion*) is frequently found in Anglo-French in words showing the reflex of Latin *-iōn-*, and indeed in this case we find (from the *AND*) that Anglo-French has the form *processiun*, as well as *processione* and (like continental French) *procession*. In the rest of the Middle English period we continue to find forms ending in *-ion* and forms ending in *-ioun*, and the likeliest hypothesis would seem to be that this word shows multiple inputs, from French as well as from Latin (compare the discussion of *pacify* in section 11.3.1). However, it is also at least possible that the word was borrowed once only, from Latin, and that forms in *-iun* or *-ioun* merely show French influence, with the word *procession* being reshaped either directly after Anglo-French *processiun*, or on the general model of Anglo-French words in *-iun*, *-ioun*, reflecting the general level of influence of Anglo-French in the post-Conquest period. The word is semantically simple and there is nothing in the semantic history to help clarify the exact transmission of the word into English.

Words that could show input from either French or Latin or both are extremely common in the Middle English period. In order to prevent the selection of examples in this section being entirely capricious, all of the following examples are again drawn from the words discussed in section 2.2, which fall within the 1,000 most frequent words in the late twentieth-century *BNC* corpus.

---

[23] Compare section 9.4.2 on the complex textual history.

Example 2: *action* and *act*

Action presents similar formal issues to *procession*, although it is first attested in English only in the late fourteenth century. It shows early forms of the types *actioun* and *action*. The former type is attested earliest (by a very small margin) and hence borrowing from Anglo-French seems the likeliest initial input. The range of early meanings could be accounted for equally well by borrowing from French or Latin, or partly from each. It may seem on first consideration that the most parsimonious (or logically most economical) explanation is to assume that the word was borrowed entirely from French, since at least some of the forms point in this direction. However, the semantic history is against the assumption of once-and-for-all foreign-language input. It is clear that a number of the core meanings of the word are the result of foreign-language input, e.g. 'activity', 'act', 'deed', 'proposal', 'measure', 'policy', 'legal proceeding'. Given the situation of complex interaction of three languages in late medieval England, it would seem rash to assume that all of the influence came from (Anglo-)French and none from Latin. What is less clear is the precise mechanism: it is theoretically possible that the word became well established in English in a single meaning as a result of borrowing from one language only and that all of the other meanings result from secondary semantic borrowing; however, it is also possible that there were multiple separate instances of borrowing, perhaps from both Latin and French, and that these gradually coalesced to give a single polysemous English word.

In the case of the related noun *act* (late fourteenth century), the semantic richness of the English noun (which is attested in a wide variety of meanings in the late fourteenth and fifteenth centuries) seems best accounted for by borrowing chiefly from Latin *āctus* and (related) *āctum*, since (Anglo-)French *acte* appears to have been somewhat more limited in its range of meanings and uses, being found most characteristically in legal use in Anglo-French, and being found only very rarely in continental use before the fifteenth century. However, this does not necessarily mean that the (Anglo-)French word had no input at all.

In view of the balance of evidence available for each word in each language, it would be brutally reductive to assign English *action* entirely to borrowing from French (because of the early forms of the type *actioun*) and *act* (noun) entirely to borrowing from Latin (because some of its early meanings are attested in Latin but apparently not in French earlier than in English). Rather, it would seem likeliest that both words owe at least something to borrowing from each language, and it would also seem highly plausible that *action* and *act* have influenced one another semantically within English.

On the other hand, the verb *act* (first attested in the second half of the fifteenth century in technical legal uses, but only from the late sixteenth century in more general uses) does appear to be solely a Latin borrowing (from *āct-*, past participial stem of *agere*), since French has *agir* not **acter*; although, again, it is likely that in English *act* as noun exerted considerable influence on the development of *act* as verb. (Conversion from the noun *act* within English is less likely on semantic grounds than borrowing from Latin.)

Example 3: *person*

To take a yet more complex example, *person* is first recorded in English in the early thirteenth century in the *Ancrene Wisse*, a text for the guidance of a group of anchoresses.[24] In both form and meaning it could as easily come from either Latin *persōna* or (Anglo-)French *person, persone, personne*. Some of the Middle English forms, such as *persoun*, point strongly to borrowing of similar forms from Anglo-French. Forms such as *parson, parsoun* could also be from similar forms in (Anglo-)French, although they could equally show a parallel formal development within Middle English, since both languages frequently show lowering of *e* to *a* before *r*.[25]

The meaning history of English *person* suggests continuing influence from French and Latin over several hundred years. In the *Ancrene Wisse* the word occurs in two meanings, 'an individual human being' and 'a role or character'. The first of these meanings shows a fairly continuous history in English, but the second is not recorded again until the sixteenth century, when it probably shows a re-borrowing. Other meanings that were pretty certainly borrowed from (Anglo-)French and/or Latin include: 'each of the persons of the Trinity (in Christian theology)', first recorded in the early fourteenth century, and 'the living body or physical appearance of a human being', 'an individual considered with regard to his or her outward appearance', 'an individual corporate body recognized by the law as having certain rights and duties', 'grammatical category of person (i.e. first, second, or third person)', and 'important personage', which are all first recorded in the late fourteenth or early fifteenth century, as are the phrasal constructions *in one's own person* and *in one's proper person*. The relevant models for these senses and constructions are all found in French and Latin in the thirteenth century or earlier (some go right back to classical Latin) and therefore there are two possibilities: English could have borrowed *person* in all of this complexity in the thirteenth century, but we simply fail to have evidence of this until our much richer documentation of the late fourteenth century and onwards; or new senses could have continued being borrowed from the source language, considerably after the date of the original borrowing. As we see in section 14.6, many other word histories point very strongly to continued borrowing of senses over a long period of time

The specialization of the form *parson* in the meaning 'parson' (i.e. a rector or vicar) belongs to the history of the English word; in (Anglo-)French and medieval Latin this is simply one of the meanings of the word for 'person'.

Example 4: *colour*

Colour occurs from the Middle English period onwards in forms of the type *colour*, which strongly suggest at least influence from (Anglo-)French, and forms of the type *color*, which could be from either Latin or French. In both Latin and French a wide

---

[24] The same text is also sometimes called *Ancrene Riwle*: see further section 13.1.3.

[25] For discussion of the sound change involved, see Durkin (2009) 191–5.

variety of both literal and figurative meanings are found ('hue', 'complexion of the face', 'colouring matter', 'stylistic ornament', etc.), which are in turn also shown by the English word.

Further examples in brief

To pick out just a few further examples from the words from the (modern English) high-frequency list examined in section 2.2, *accept, application, capital, element, general*,[26] *history, natural*,[27] *nature, present* (verb and adjective),[28] *question, use* (noun), and *use* (verb) could all equally be from Latin or (Anglo-)French, and could well show some input from each. Once the pronunciation of medieval Latin and the patterns of naturalization discussed in section 11.3.1 are taken into account, there is no reason why transmission via French is necessitated to explain the English outputs of such forms as Latin *acceptāre* 'to receive, accept', *applicātiōn-, applicātiō* 'action of attaching or joining', (later) 'application, action of putting into practice', *capitālis* 'capital', *elementum* 'element', *generālis* 'general', *historia* 'history', *nātūra* 'nature', *nātūrālis* 'natural', *praesentāre* 'to present', *praesent-, praesēns* 'present', *quaestiōn-, quaestiō* 'question', *ūsus* 'use (noun)', or *ūs-*, past participial stem of *ūtī* 'use (verb)'.

In some instances questions of word form may make borrowing from one language rather than another seem more likely. For instance, it may seem likelier that *quality* (first attested in English *c.*1300), *opportunity* (*a.*1387), *security* (*a.*1425) are from (Anglo-)French *qualité, opportunité, securité*, rather than showing borrowing of Latin *quālitāt-, quālitās, opportūnitāt-, opportūnitās*, and *sēcūritāt-, sēcūritās* with remodelling of the ending on the French pattern. However, there are certainly counterexamples from at least the late fourteenth century where words ending in *-ty* seem with varying degrees of certainty to be borrowings primarily from Latin, such as:

- *actuality* (*a.*1398; French *actualité* is only found much later in corresponding meanings);
- *ponderosity* 'heaviness' (?*a.*1425; the word is only attested somewhat later in French in the corresponding meaning, and the earliest English attestation translates Latin directly);
- *mediety* 'a half' (?1440; the usual French word is *moitié* (> English *moiety* 1444), and the Latinate type is not found in French until the sixteenth century and then only in a very narrow meaning).

---

[26] The use of the noun in the specific meaning 'highest-ranking officer of an army' is a sixteenth-century development that ultimately reflects influence from either Spanish, French, or Italian.

[27] In this instance continuing semantic influence from French is likely in Early Modern English.

[28] Use of the verb in the meaning 'to stage or put on (a play)' from the sixteenth century onwards almost certainly shows later influence from French: see section 14.6.

11.3.5 Likely mechanisms of borrowing

It remains a difficult question whether most of the words discussed in section 11.3.4 are best regarded as borrowings from French *or* Latin or from French *and* Latin. As often as not no single form or meaning points incontrovertibly to input exclusively from one language or the other, and even when such forms or meanings occur we may choose to attribute them to later influence on an already borrowed word. As already noted in the discussion of *action*, this opens up a broader question of whether words of this type are borrowed once and for all (and then may show continuing influence from French and Latin), or whether they emerge from multiple separate instances of borrowing, perhaps from both Latin and French, which have gradually coalesced to give a single polysemous English word.

As already noted, semantic borrowings are also shown by many words that can be identified reasonably confidently as loanwords from just French or just Latin. As shown by the case of *idea* in section 11.3.3, this semantic borrowing can often be from the 'other' language (i.e. from Middle French *idee*). This sort of gradual borrowing of new senses from either Latin or French often extends beyond Middle English into the Early Modern period (see section 14.6).

If we take a broader perspective, and consider the social and cultural circumstances considered in section 11.2, the complexities of the language situation in medieval England place considerable strain on the notion of lexical borrowing as a once-and-for-all process: many of these word histories are highly suggestive of multiple inputs, in some cases from (Anglo-) French and in others from Latin, sometimes in literary contexts and sometimes in spoken ones, sometimes in the context of learned religious or secular discourse, sometimes in more practical contexts of record-keeping or conducting legal or other official business. Sometimes considerations of word form show that a particular meaning must be a semantic borrowing, if it is borrowed at all; e.g. Middle French *idee* can only have influenced English *idea* by semantic borrowing, rather than showing a loanword. More typically, we cannot tell whether a word has been borrowed from one language in one meaning and then shown subsequent semantic borrowing (and maybe also formal influence: compare discussion of *processiun* in section 11.3.4), or whether it has been borrowed separately in different contexts on different occasions, and gradually coalesced and merged to give the kind of richly polysemous English word that we find represented in historical dictionaries such as the *OED* or the *MED*. It is the combination of our knowledge of the multilingual language contact situation with our detailed knowledge of the histories of each word in Latin, French, and English that makes the case for multiple inputs compelling, even if the precise mechanisms normally remain uncertain in individual cases.[29]

Chapter 12 offers a chronological analysis of the totals of loanwords of each type found in each fifty-year period between 1150 and 1500. As is seen there, words from French and/or Latin show both their absolute peak and their peak as a proportion of all new words in the period 1350–1450, precisely when English was expanding its range of functions considerably in official and formal contexts, and this strongly supports the hypothesis of multiple inputs, as particular individuals switched from Latin or French to English in various aspects of their professional lives. However, it will be useful to consider one further topic beforehand: the reinforcement or re-borrowing of words that had been borrowed from Latin during the Old English period.

11.4 Reinforcement or re-borrowing of words borrowed in Old English

As was already touched on in section 7.5.1, many words that are found in Old English as loanwords from Latin could show either re-borrowing or reinforcement from French and/or Latin in Middle English. An interesting sample is again provided by those words that feature among the 1,000 most frequent items in the *BNC*, considered in section 2.2.

In some instances, formal criteria demonstrate that there is no direct line of continuity. In Old English, borrowing of Latin *oleum* is shown by *ele* 'oil', which survived until the fifteenth century in occasional attestations. However, from the early thirteenth century new form types are shown, broadly (with a good deal of variation) *oil* and *oili*. These new form types fairly clearly show a new borrowing, from Anglo-French *oylie*, (Anglo-)French *oile*. By the late fourteenth century the *oil* type is dominant in the surviving texts (generally spelt *oyle* or *oile*). However, at least some speakers evidently identified the new word with the old one, since *ele* shows a new form type *eli* in the thirteenth and fourteenth centuries, apparently arising from association with *oili*.

---

[29] Compare Schweickard (1986) on the difficult case of the multiple etymologies often identified in Romanian lexicography, where it is less clear that either the evidence or the nature of the contact situation have been considered in such detail.

We can also be reasonably confident that a re-borrowing has occurred in some cases where there are no clinching arguments from word form. In Old English (only in Northumbrian texts) we find *plæce*, *plæse*, *plætse* in the meaning 'open space in a town, public square, marketplace', showing a borrowing of Latin *platea* (compare section 6.3.1). We then find *place* again in early Middle English in the meaning 'room, available space', earliest in the *Ancrene Wisse*. This almost certainly shows a new borrowing, from (Anglo-)French *place*, and it is very unlikely that there is any continuity between the Old English and Middle English use.

Part occurs in Old English (in Ælfric's *Grammar*) in grammatical use, denoting a 'part of speech'. It is next attested in this meaning in English in a fifteenth-century manuscript copy of a fourteenth-century text. However, from early in the fourteenth century it is attested in the meanings 'portion' and 'piece or section', and slightly later in the meanings 'portion of a human or animal body' and 'aspect or constituent of something'. All of these uses can readily be explained as resulting from Middle English borrowing from French and/or Latin, and, although it is certainly not impossible, it seems unlikely that there was any continuity of use from Old English, in which the word gives every appearance of having been a technical word of very limited use. *Title* is a broadly similar case, albeit less clear cut.

Some words occur in Old English only in sources from after the Conquest and (Anglo-)French could have been part of the input right from the outset. *Accord* is found in very late Old English and early Middle English, chiefly in annals of various dates in the *Peterborough Chronicle*, in which it could show borrowing from either (Anglo-)French or post-classical Latin. It probably shows continuity with *accord* in subsequent use in English, although it is notable that neither the verb nor the noun nor any other word in this word family (e.g. *accordant*, *according*, etc.) is particularly frequent in thirteenth-century texts. *Market* perhaps shows a similar case, of (probably) post-Conquest borrowing from Latin or French, although it could alternatively be from a form in another Germanic language (ultimately borrowed from Latin).

Alongside these words, there are other words in the *BNC* high-frequency list that probably do show continuity between Latin borrowings in (pre-Conquest) Old English and the modern English word, albeit with a strong possibility of continuing input from French and Latin in the Middle English period: e.g. *master*, *plant*, or *table* (in this last case, the core modern meaning definitely reflects post-Conquest input).

The names of the months make a particularly interesting group.[30] *March* and *May* were probably only borrowed post-Conquest, from either Latin or French. Likewise *February*, although this only shows (Anglo-)French input in forms of the type *Feverer*. The other month names all occur in pre-Conquest texts as borrowings from Latin. (Although Old English also had non-borrowed names for all of the months of the year.) In the case of *January*, the Anglo-French form differs considerably from the Latin form and we can be reasonably confident that direct (Anglo-)French input is limited to Middle English forms of the type *Janever*. In the cases of *June*, *July*, and *April* we can be certain that Middle English variants of these month names of the types *Juyn, Juyl, Averil* show (Anglo-)French input; so could the normal modern forms of each of these month names, since (Anglo-)French also had forms of the types *jun, junie, julie, aprill, aprille*. *September, October, November, December* could all show input from either Latin or (Anglo-)French, likewise *August*, which in Anglo-French shows forms much closer to the Latin and English types than modern French *août*. What we cannot be certain of is what the precise mixture of inputs was: these month names could have shown continuity from the Old English period with little or no significant later influence, or they could show a convergence of (possibly learned) early borrowings with post-Conquest re-borrowing from French and/or Latin, or there could be complete discontinuity between the Old English and Middle English words.

Besides these, there are cases such as *school* where any input from (Anglo-)French could only be semantic, because of the formal dissimilarity of the French cognates; and some where sound changes in English also rule out later re-borrowing from Latin, e.g. *box, pound, street*. Some more difficult cases are noted in section 7.5.1.

We thus have at least two different clines. There are some cases where we can be pretty certain that there is continuity, others where we can be pretty certain that there is none, but there are very many uncertain cases at various points along the cline. Similarly, there are some cases where we can be pretty certain that there was at least some later input from (Anglo-)French, others where we can be pretty certain that there was not (except perhaps in the form of semantic influence), but again, there are very many uncertain examples somewhere in between.

---

[30] *March, April, May, June, July* all fall within the most frequent 1,000 items in the *BNC*, the others just outside.

12

Quantifying French and Latin contributions to Middle English

12.1 Chronological breakdown

12.1.1 Latin, French, and Latin and/or French borrowings in English lexicography and lexicology

Many traditional accounts of English etymology have focused primarily on questions of word form and have also shown a bias towards identifying the language of ultimate origin of words; thus, words that come ultimately from Latin, like *pacify* or *procession*, have often been treated as Latin borrowings, regardless of the possibility of transmission via French, and borrowing from French has tended to be acknowledged only where word form makes this very clear, as in the case of e.g. *peace*. Thus, all of the words discussed in sections 11.3.3 and 11.3.4 would be classified as Latin borrowings, and borrowing from French restricted to words of the type discussed in section 11.3.2. More recently, a number of scholars have been much more receptive to the implications of borrowing via French. In particular, fuller dictionaries of Old French, Middle French, and Anglo-French (see section 11.1) have made possible much more detailed and better informed comparison of the lexical histories of words in English and French, enabling us to form judgements about the likelihood of transmission via French on the basis of the relative dating of particular forms and meanings in each language, as well as our knowledge of the realities of the language contact situation. This has led to something of a (quiet) revolution in the study of French and Latin borrowing in Middle English, with significant implications for the overall picture of borrowing from each source language.[1]

12.1.2 Analysis of the data of the *MED* and *OED3*

The *Middle English Dictionary* (which provides very full coverage up to the early fifteenth century and some coverage up to the end of the fifteenth century)[2] gives the following picture:

> Total of words (including those inherited from Old English): 53,925
> Etymologies that refer only to French (including Anglo-French):[3] 8,624 (16%)
> Etymologies that refer only to Latin:[4] 6,445 (12%)
> Etymologies that refer to both: 5,709 (11%)

Thus 39% of all headword entries are from French or Latin. (It should be noted that the etymologies in the *MED* are very brief and do not reflect extensive research; in particular, relatively little account was taken of the range of meanings found in each language.)

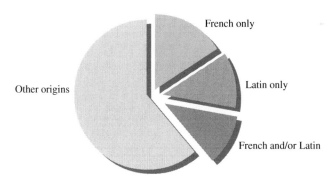

Fig. 12.1 Words from French, Latin, and French and/or Latin as a proportion of all headword entries in the *MED*.

---

[1] For a study based on the practice of the *MED*, see Coleman (1995); on the policy of *OED3* in this area, see further Durkin (2002b).

[2] On the policies of the *MED*, see Lewis (2007).

[3] Search on 'OF' (Old French) and 'AF' (Anglo-French) in etymologies.

[4] Search on 'L' (Latin) and 'ML' (medieval Latin) in etymologies.

A total of 10,023 etymologies in the *MED* mention Old English,[5] in most instances indicating that the word in question existed already in Old English. If we subtract this total from the 53,925 total number of headwords and recalculate the percentages, in order to focus on those words that entered English in the Middle English period, we get the following results:

Etymologies that refer only to French (including Anglo-French): 20%
Etymologies that refer only to Latin: 15%
Etymologies that refer to both: 13%

Thus 48% of all headword entries first recorded in the Middle English period are from French or Latin.

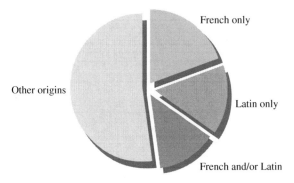

Fig. 12.2 Words from French, Latin, and French and/or Latin as a proportion of all headword entries first recorded in the Middle English period in the *MED*.

In *OED3* medieval borrowings from French and/or Latin are being assessed on essentially the basis described in section 11.3. Accordingly, some are etymologized solely from French, some solely from Latin, and some are etymologized as from French 'and its etymon' Latin or (in cases where it is less certain that both inputs are found) French 'or its etymon' Latin. Working on this basis has given the following statistical picture in the parts of *OED3* so far published (drawing again, as elsewhere in this book, on the alphabetical sequences A to ALZ and M to R):

Total of words first attested 1150–1499 (in this sample): 11,624
Etymologies from French (including Anglo-French) only: 2,482 (21%)
Etymologies from Latin only: 1,537 (13%)
Etymologies from both: 1,130 (10%)

---

[5] Search on 'OE'.

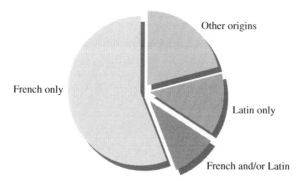

Fig. 12.3 Words from French, Latin, and French and/or Latin as a proportion of all headword entries first recorded in the Middle English period in *OED3*.

Thus 44% of all headword entries first recorded in the Middle English period are loanwords from French or Latin.

The figures from each dictionary are very similar. The differences in the proportions of words from French only, Latin only, and French and/or Latin mostly stem from the tendency in the *MED* to assess etymologies largely on grounds of word form, without detailed comparison of the range of meanings and relative dating in each language, at least not on the scale that is attempted in *OED3*. The *OED3* total for 'other origins' is probably higher than that in the *MED* because the *OED* gives a greater number of compounds the status of separate headwords, on account of their later importance in the history of English. Additionally, it should be borne in mind that the *OED3* sample is drawn from half of the letter A and all of the letters M, N, O, P, Q, R, and the relative frequencies of words of different origin are not identical through all letters of the alphabet. However, the overall level of similarity, in two different dictionaries with different editorial policies and procedures, is perhaps more striking than the level of divergence.

A breakdown of the *OED3* figures by half-century gives a much more detailed picture, represented graphically in Figs 12.4–12.8. Loanwords already attested in Old English are excluded from these figures, because they cannot easily be accommodated into the chronological framework of fifty-year periods. In fact, the number of such words is relatively very small: 238 in the parts of *OED3* so far completed, including cases where *OED3* has an Old English first date but there is probably discontinuity between the Old English word and the later use (e.g. cases such as *part* discussed in section 11.4

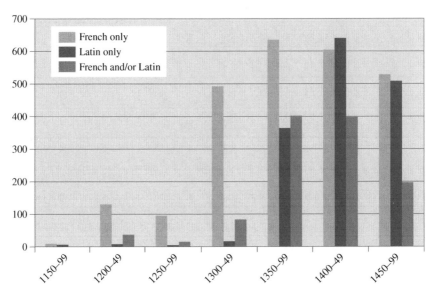

Fig. 12.4 Absolute numbers of new words from each source per half-century (in *OED3*, A–ALZ, M–R).

or *note* discussed in section 7.5.1).[6] Very few French loans are found in sources from before 1150, but this is probably in part a result of the nature of our sources. *Proud* (giving rise to *pride*: compare section 8.1.5) and *tower* appear to have been among the earliest; among those found in late annals of various manuscripts of the *Anglo-Saxon Chronicle* are *arblast* (a cross-bow), (probably) *chancellor* (as *cancelere*: compare section 12.2.1 on the phonology), *chaplain* (as *capelein*: compare section 12.2.1), (probably) *clerk*,[7] *duke*, *nativity* (in the distinctive early form *natiuiteð*), *prison*, *service*, *war*, and perhaps *castle* in the sense 'castle' (compare sections 5.3.3, 7.5.2, 12.2.1, and also 13.1.1), and perhaps also *market* (although this word may not be from French at all: compare section 11.4); compare also section 11.4 on cases like *accord* that may show input from both Latin and French.[8]

---

[6] The figures derived from the *MED* given here do in fact include a number of such items, since some words, such as *procession* (*MED prōcessiŏun*) are etymologized in the *MED* simply as mixed borrowings from French and Latin, with etymologies not explicitly noting their appearance in Old English texts.

[7] Early instances of the French loanword *clerc*, *clerk* cannot easily be told apart from Old English *clerc*, an occasional variant of the Latin loanword *cleric*.

[8] Skaffari (2002) provides a particularly useful analysis of those borrowings from both Latin and French that are found in both the Old English and the Middle English parts of manuscript E of the Chronicle, the *Peterborough Chronicle*.

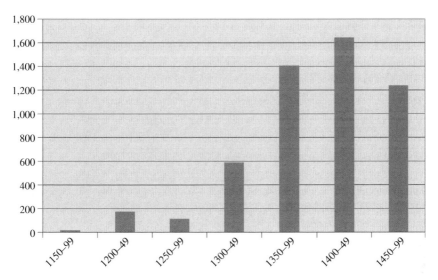

Fig. 12.5 Absolute numbers of French and Latin loanwords per half-century, combined totals (in *OED3*, A–ALZ, M–R).

Some trends can be picked up immediately from these graphs based on *OED3*. The combined totals of absolute numbers of loanwords from French, Latin, and French and/or Latin shown by Fig. 12.5 begin to increase considerably from the first half of the fourteenth century, go up again hugely in the late fourteenth century, and reach their peak in the early fifteenth century, before declining slightly in the later fifteenth century.

However, some immediate provisos are in order if we are looking at absolute numbers of loanwords. As shown by Fig. 12.6, the number of *OED3* headwords (of whatever origin) with first dates in the first half of the fourteenth century is much greater than for earlier fifty-year periods and the total for the second half of the fourteenth century is more than double again, remaining very high for both halves of the fifteenth century. This probably partly reflects actual lexical expansion: certainly, it is only fairly seldom that we have to assume that a word was current very much earlier than its date of first attestation in order to explain the relationships within a group of words.[9] However, the very big increase in the second half of the fourteenth century probably also reflects some peculiarities of our data: there is simply a much greater quantity of surviving Middle English material

---

[9] Although this is sometimes one of a range of possible explanations: see section 13.1.3 on *departunge* 'departing' in the *Ancrene Wisse*.

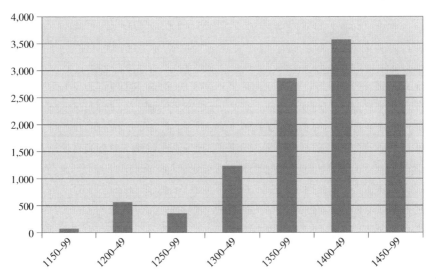

Fig. 12.6 Totals of all *OED3* headwords (of any origin) with first dates in each half-century.

available for lexicographical research from the mid fourteenth century onwards. This is especially the case if, as in the *MED* and *OED3*, the primary date assigned to most Middle English evidence is the date of the manuscript in which a text is preserved, rather than the (presumed or known) original date of composition of the text: this means that a number of texts that were probably composed in the early fourteenth century or earlier receive a primary date in the late fourteenth or fifteenth centuries, on account of the dates of the surviving manuscripts. In many cases the caution lying behind this approach is probably very well grounded, since the word in question may not have been present in the original form of the text. We can seldom be entirely certain that this is not the case; but it is doubtless also true that many words did exist rather earlier than the dictionary dates suggest.

It is thus rather important to look closely at the graphs in Figs 12.7 and 12.8, showing loanwords from each source as a proportion of all new words in each half-century. The combined totals in Fig. 12.8 show a much less dramatic picture than Fig. 12.5. Loanwords from French, Latin, and French and/or Latin collectively make up 29% of all *OED* first attestations even in the second half of the twelfth century and over 30% in both halves of the thirteenth century. There is still, though, a substantial increase in the fourteenth century, only now both halves of the fourteenth century show similarly high levels, with loanwords from these sources making up 47% of

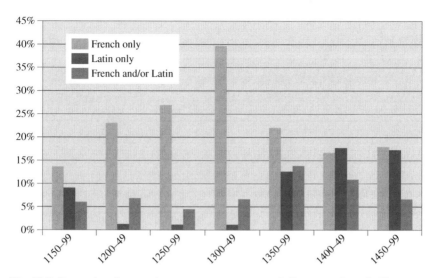

Fig. 12.7 Borrowings from each source as a percentage of all new words per half-century.

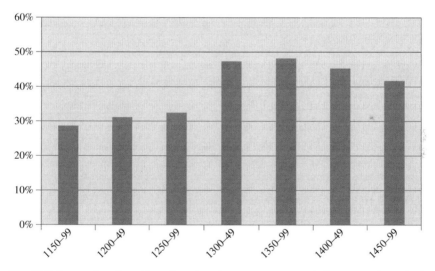

Fig. 12.8 Borrowings from French and Latin as a percentage of all new words per half-century, combined totals.

all new words in the first half of the fourteenth century and 48% in the second, before the level falls away a little in the fifteenth century.

These broad trends are in fact very similar to those found by earlier studies deriving absolute and relative figures from data taken from either the first edition of the *OED* or *MED*.[10] As shown by Fig. 2.6 in chapter 2,

[10] For some notable earlier studies see Mossé (1943), Zettersten (1969), Scheler (1977) 52, Dekeyser (1986), Dekeyser and Pauwels (1990).

the fourteenth century is the period in which the combined contribution from French and Latin makes up the highest proportion of the total of new words at any stage in the history of English.

If we turn to Figs 12.4 and 12.7, it is very obvious that there are clear differences between the patterns shown by words from French only, from Latin only, and from French and/or Latin. (Compare Figs 2.4 and 2.6 in chapter 2, which carry the same figures through to the present day.)

Words from French only show the earliest peak; this comes in the late fourteenth century if we look at absolute numbers (Fig. 12.4), and in the early fourteenth century if we look at the proportion of all new words (Fig. 12.7). Fig. 12.7 shows that they also make up a much higher proportion of the total of new words in the late twelfth, thirteenth, and early fourteenth centuries than the words from Latin only or from Latin and/or French; indeed, in the thirteenth century and the first half of the fourteenth, they are overwhelmingly the most numerous type. In the period 1350–99 they still constitute the most numerous category, although by a smaller margin. After 1400 words from Latin only become equally frequent. (This trend continues markedly after 1500, as shown by Figs 2.4 and 2.6 in chapter 2. Chapter 14 looks at this more closely.)

Words from French and/or Latin show a very distinctive pattern, being much more numerous in the 100-year period 1350–1450 than they are at any other time (Fig. 12.4), and making their largest contribution as a proportion of all new words in English in the period 1350–99, closely followed by 1400–49 (Fig. 12.7). This is interesting, because it correlates very clearly with the period when English was coming to be used as the default language in writing in many contexts where Latin and/or French had earlier been the norm. It seems very unlikely that this correlation is accidental: we are seeing the tail end of a period of trilingualism, in which an individual might be called on to express the same concepts in English, French, or Latin, either in speech or writing. It is therefore unsurprising that when English comes to be used as a written medium in functions where one or both of the other languages had previously been used, we find that this is very often done using precisely those words that were equivalent and familiar in both of the other languages of this trilingual society.

If we compare this data with the analysis in section 2.2 of the histories of the 1,000 most frequent words in contemporary English, as reflected by the *BNC*, it is very noteworthy that words from Latin only (of any date of borrowing) are far less numerous in this highest-frequency component of the

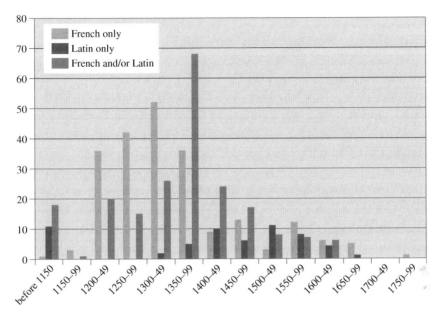

Fig. 12.9 Numbers of new words from each source per half-century as reflected in the 1,000 most frequent words in the *BNC*.

lexis of contemporary English than are words either from French only or from French and/or Latin. Fig. 12.9 takes a more fine-grained approach, dividing the material into fifty-year periods. The period 1300–1499 saw the highest totals of borrowings of words from French and/or Latin among these high-frequency words, while words from French only are most frequent in the period 1200–1399. Loanwords from Latin only are much more concentrated in the late Middle English period. This points once more to the importance of borrowing in both early Middle English and later Middle English to the shaping of the core lexis of modern English. Of course, words that are high-frequency words in modern English were not necessarily high-frequency words in Middle English; section 14.7 and chapter 16 look at this topic more closely. However, this approach does shed useful light on the date of borrowing of those words that have come to be most significant in modern English. The correlation with the general pattern in Figs 12.4–12.8 is notable.

In the analysis of the 'basic vocabulary' list forming the basis for the *WOLD* project in section 2.3, French borrowing was found to predominate even more strongly in Middle English, and this was again spread fairly evenly across the whole of the Middle English period.

12.1.2.1 Semantic borrowing Finally, although semantic borrowing does not form the main focus of this chapter, it is worth recording here the totals of cases found in the comparable part of *OED3*.

Looking first at semantic borrowing from French: if we leave aside words borrowed from French (and/or Latin) that show continuing semantic influence from French (compare discussion in section 11.3), there are approximately 300 *OED3* entries first dated before 1500 that do *not* have French as direct etymon but do show some (certain or possible) semantic influence from Anglo-Norman, Old French, or Middle French at some point in the dictionary entry (although it should be noted that Middle French extends up to 1600 and a number of the matches show semantic influence from Middle French after 1500). Thus the phrase *writ of right close* (recorded under the *OED* headword *right* n.) shows a loan translation of Anglo-French *bref de dreit clos*. In many cases, when the elements are themselves of French origin, it can be difficult to tell whether one has a loan translation or a direct loan, e.g. *receiver general* (earliest recorded as *receyvour generall*) is probably a loan translation of Anglo-French *receivur general* but could be a direct loan. Additionally, there are cases like *popular*, identifiable on formal grounds as a borrowing from Latin, but probably showing considerable semantic influence from French *populaire*; compare similarly *idea* in section 11.3.3.

If we turn now to semantic borrowing from Latin: there are just over 300 *OED3* entries first dated between 1150 and 1500 that do *not* have Latin as direct etymon but do show some (certain or possible) semantic influence from Latin (although in some cases long after the end of the Middle English period). For instance *black salt* was formed as a loan translation of Latin *sal niger*, while *knowingly* in its rare early meaning 'recognizably' shows a loan translation of Latin *cognoscibiliter*, but in its slightly later meaning 'consciously, intentionally' it shows a loan translation of a different Latin word, *scienter*. Sometimes the input may be from either French or Latin, or both: *freehold* may show a loan translation of either Anglo-French *franctenement* (or *franctenance*) or of Latin *tenementum liberum*, or of both; likewise *plainsong* is modelled on either Latin *cantus planus* or French *plain chant*, or both (as also is much later *plainchant*).

Although instances of semantic borrowing are often difficult for dictionaries to detect, the very small size of these numbers in comparison with the numbers of loanwords is indicative of how heavily the borrowing of loanwords predominates over other types of lexical borrowing in this period.

12.1.3 Studies based on particular texts or corpora

A useful counterbalance to the sort of data based on first dates of attestation looked at in section 12.1.2 is to look instead at the usage of particular Middle English texts in order to gain an impression of the frequency with which loanwords occur in actual use. Dekeyser (1986) reports on an exercise by students coding the etymologies of all of the words in thirteen selected passages of early Middle English and late Middle English of between 300 and 600 words in length; the early Middle English passages are mostly thirteenth century, although a rather later (unspecified) passage from Richard Rolle is also included; the late Middle English passages are all from the second half of the fourteenth century or the fifteenth century. He groups together all words of French, Latin, or French and/or Latin origin as 'Romance', but he does also give the percentage for Latin only (although his criteria for assessing etymologies were not identical to those underlying my figures in section 12.1.2). The sample is very small and somewhat skewed by the inclusion of Rolle in the early part, but the results are nonetheless interesting:

> eME:
> Type frequency: 91.5% 'English', 8.5% 'Romance'
> Token frequency: 94.4% 'English', 5.6% 'Romance' (1.4% of which are pure 'Latin')
>
> lME:
> Type frequency: 78.8% 'English', 21.2% 'Romance'
> Token frequency: 87.5% 'English', 12.5% 'Romance' (2.5% of which are pure 'Latin')

Thus there is a marked increase in the incidence of Romance words in the later Middle English texts, more than doubling, whether we look at the type frequency (i.e. the number of different words of Romance origin encountered) or the token frequency (i.e. the total number of occurrences, including multiple occurrences of the same word). However, the token frequency remains low even in late Middle English, at only 12.5%. This is partly because so much of the high-frequency core grammatical vocabulary remains of native (or occasionally Scandinavian) origin, but partly also because even the most important Romance borrowings tend only to gain in frequency rather slowly and do not become very high-frequency words until long after the date of their initial borrowing. Section 14.7 and chapter 16 look at some ways of exploring this further.

Studies based on the analysis of corpus data are still few and far between. Skaffari (2009) looks at both Scandinavian and French loanwords in the sub-period "ME I" (1150–1250) in the *Helsinki Corpus*; Latin loanwords are omitted, as are words of mixed or uncertain French/Latin origin. Some of his findings as regards Scandinavian loanwords are looked at in section 9.4.2. As noted by Skaffari (2009 136–7), there are some difficulties concerning the material included in this part of the *Helsinki Corpus*. It has some post-1150 copies of texts of Old English composition and, at the other end of the chronological span, Laȝamon's *Brut*, both manuscripts of which date from later than 1250, although the date of original composition is disputed. However, looking at this portion of the *Helsinki Corpus* does mean that samples from most of the major English sources surviving from this period are examined. Skaffari's etymological data are based on the *MED* and *OED*. His method is to include words for which the *MED* posits mixed French/Latin origin if and only if the corresponding etymology in *OED2* (which in nearly all cases goes back to the first edition of 1884–1928) gives French as sole primary etymon. (Very few entries of revised *OED3* had been published when this research was carried out.) The words looked at by Skaffari thus correspond roughly to 'French only' in my data in section 12.1.2; this is not so great a problem as it would be for an analysis of late Middle English text samples, since, as seen in section 12.1.2, loanwords solely from French constitute the largest category in early Middle English. Even applying this rather narrow definition of a French borrowing, Skaffari finds that in his sample as a whole the number of different words borrowed from French outnumbers those borrowed from Scandinavian: there are 294 different French loanwords, beside 206 Scandinavian ones (i.e. these are the totals of different types); among the 294 French loanwords, nouns predominate much more than they do among the Scandinavian loanwords (a further indication that borrowing from French has a more typical profile than borrowing from Scandinavian, from a cross-linguistic, typological perspective: compare section 2.3). The token frequencies, i.e. the frequency with which a French borrowing or a Scandinavian borrowing occurs, are very similar for each source: 8.3 occurrences per thousand words for French borrowings, 8.2 per thousand for Scandinavian borrowings. Both of these figures are extremely low, especially when one bears in mind that 8,850 (8%) of the total 113,020 words in the sample are taken from the *Ormulum*, with its high incidence of Scandinavian-derived high-frequency items such as the third-person plural personal pronoun.

Skaffari finds that the difference in the incidence of French loanwords is very great between different texts in this early period, much more so than for Scandinavian loanwords. Broadly the same story is found both for type frequencies, i.e. the totals of different words of French origin in each text sample, and for token frequencies, i.e. the frequency with which any French words occur. The figures for the *Ormulum* are tiny, far lower than those for most of the early Middle English compositions (as opposed to copies of earlier texts). Not very far ahead of it is Laȝamon's *Brut*, a later text, but deliberately archaizing in style and diction. The Final Continuation of the *Peterborough Chronicle*, on the other hand, although composed earlier, shows much higher type and token frequencies for French loanwords than the *Ormulum* does: the normalized type frequency is twelve times higher and the normalized token frequency is just under ten times higher.[11] (This is, of course, data that is intended to omit words of uncertain, or mixed, French or Latin origin.) The totals of French loanwords in the *Peterborough Chronicle* and *Ormulum* thus differ much more strikingly than the totals of Scandinavian loanwords examined in section 9.4.2. The figures for French loanwords in the *Peterborough Chronicle* are not dissimilar to those for most of the texts in the cluster of thirteenth-century south-west-midland texts known collectively as the Katherine Group (after one of the texts, a verse life of St Katherine).[12] However, more than double the type frequency or token frequency of the *Peterborough Chronicle* is shown by another text that is very close in date and language to the Katherine Group, the *Ancrene Wisse*. The very high rate of occurrence of French loanwords in the *Ancrene Wisse* has been noted by many other researchers.[13] It is striking that the incidence of French loanwords could vary so much from text to

[11] See table 9 in Skaffari (2009) 179.

[12] It is often observed (e.g. Burnley (1992) 438) that words of French origin are significantly more frequent in early sources from the west of England than in those from the east. Although the raw figures from the major surviving texts appears to bear this out, statistical analysis suggests a less clear picture (see Skaffari (2009) 185–8). The small number of surviving texts and the very large differences between individual texts of similar localization perhaps cast some doubt on how confidently we should extrapolate from this that words of French origin were actually used more often in the west than in the east in this period.

[13] Clark (1966) 117–24 found very similar results in a much earlier comparison of French loanwords in the *Ancrene Wisse* and the Katherine Group texts. The listing and analysis of French borrowings found in a portion of the text by Zettersten (1969) is also extremely valuable.

text, including near neighbours like the *Peterborough Chronicle* and the *Ormulum*, or the *Katherine Group*, *Ancrene Wisse*, and Laȝamon's *Brut* (another south-west-midland text). Subject matter probably has some part to play here, but so probably do the different lives and experiences of individual writers; section 13.1.3 looks at one of the pieces of data that has been used to support the hypothesis that the author of the *Ancrene Wisse* may be an early exhibitor of the sort of confident trilingualism that characterizes much of the literate portion of later medieval English society.

Statistical comparisons of the incidence of French- and Latin-derived words in earlier and later Middle English are still in short supply, but there is no doubt that their incidence increased dramatically by the end of the Middle English period. As already noted, the research by Dekeyser, based on (very small) text samples, gave an overall type frequency of 21.1% for later Middle English. The counts for some major authors are far higher than this. Mersand (1939) found approximately 52% of Chaucer's total vocabulary to be of French or Latin origin (4,189 words out of a total of 8,072), including compounds in which at least one element was of French or Latin origin, and including words formed with suffixes of French or Latin origin;[14] the data presented in Cannon (1998), working from a different set of data and with a different methodology, gives a revised figure of approximately 42% (3,820 words out of a total of 9,117).[15] The numbers presented in Kaplan (1932) give an identical figure of 42% for Chaucer's contemporary Gower (1,948 words out of a total of 4,648). These figures are far higher than the type frequencies found by analysis of (very small) text samples in the research by Dekeyser already cited, which gave an overall type frequency of 21.1% for later Middle English and in which the passage from Chaucer looked at gave a type frequency of only 15.5%. This is doubtless a reflection of the rarity of very many of the words of Latin and/or French origin, only a small proportion of which will appear in any given passage; therefore, the larger the sample looked at, the higher the type frequency will be. As several larger scale studies have confirmed, many of the loanwords in Chaucer (and likewise in Gower) are of very infrequent occurrence, many

---

[14] On the methodology employed, see Mersand (1939) 40–3.

[15] See Cannon (1998) 58 n. 42; compare also Cannon (1996). Cannon's total in fact also includes words of Italian origin, but the number of these is tiny. (See further section 15.2.4 on this topic.)

only being found once.[16] This is borne out also by the token frequencies found in Dekeyser's (very small) study, which gave 12.5% for the later Middle English passages taken collectively, 8.3% for the passage from Chaucer taken in isolation. Section 14.7 looks at how Helsinki Corpus data can help illuminate the very gradual increase in frequency shown by many loanwords of French and Latin origin over an even longer historical perspective through into Early Modern English.

12.2 Anglo-French and continental French

One issue has been left rather in the background in the discussion so far: can we tell how often it is possible, probable, or even certain that a loanword has entered English specifically from Anglo-French rather than from continental French, and vice versa? Clearly, by the Early Modern period the vast majority of loanwords are from continental French, because Anglo-French had only the most tenuous continuity as Law French. But if there was a shift to borrowing principally from continental French, can we tell when this happened?

This section looks at the main ways in which both distinctively Anglo-French loanwords and distinctively continental French loanwords can be identified. It looks at some of the problems of data and evidence, and this involves some fairly detailed comparison of data from various dictionaries. It also attempts to evaluate what proportion of loanwords can be assigned with reasonable confidence to either one source or the other, and will look at what this means for the overall picture of lexical borrowing in Middle English.

12.2.1 Methodology

In earlier scholarship, the phonological characteristics of the English loanwords were the main criterion for identifying loanwords from

---

[16] Cannon (1998) 129–34, in an interesting if idiosyncratic study, provides some figures on words that occur in only one text by Chaucer; he provides the statistic that the proportion of Chaucer's words (of all origins) that occur in only one of his works is 40% (counting each prologue and tale in the *Canterbury Tales* as a separate work). Scheps (1979) looks at words that occur only once in Chaucer's works, and finds that such words occur approximately once every twenty-seven lines in the *Canterbury Tales* (less frequently in most of his earlier works).

Anglo-French. This was largely because other data was in very short supply. Thus, in the older literature, borrowing specifically from Anglo-French is often illustrated by pairs of etymological doublets such as:

- *cattle* and *chattel* (< classical Latin *capitāle*)
- *catch* and *chase* (< post-classical Latin **captiare*, formed ultimately on classical Latin *capere*, *capt*-); in early use in English *catch* has meanings including 'to chase, to pursue' as well as 'to catch'
- *castle* and *chateau* (< classical Latin *castellum*).

In each of these pairs, the initial consonant of the second word shows a sound change /k/ > /tʃ/ (later /ʃ/) before /a/ that occurred in some varieties of French, including the varieties that served as the basis of modern standard French. In some other varieties, for instance in Picardy and in parts of Normandy, this change did not occur; it is frequently absent in Anglo-French. English forms such as *cattle*, *catch*, and *castle* (if this is not from Latin) reflect borrowings of forms without this change, presumably from Anglo-French. However, one thing that recent research has made clear is that Anglo-French was dialectally mixed, and extreme caution is needed before one starts inferring from these sorts of philological generalizations that certain words must be borrowings from Anglo-French and others conversely can only be from continental French. If we return to the three examples given above, *chateau* is first recorded in English in the eighteenth century and, unless there are huge gaps in the lexicographical record, we can be certain that this word shows a re-borrowing from continental French. *Chase* and *chattel* are both more complicated. As regards *chase*, the *AND* records a large number of spellings for the reflex of Latin **captiare*, including:

chacer, chacier, chacher, chachier, chascer, chaszer, chaiser, chiacer, cacher, cachier

It can be dangerous to assume a one-to-one correspondence between spellings and pronunciation in Anglo-French texts, but nonetheless this range of spellings makes it highly likely that Anglo-French had a range of forms from which both English *catch* and *chase* could have been borrowed. *Catch* is first recorded in English in the early thirteenth century, *chase* in the early fourteenth. The neat divide between an Anglo-French loanword *catch* and a continental French loanword *chase* thus appears at the least rather shaky on close inspection: both could have been borrowed into English from Anglo-French. In the case of *cattle* and *chattel*, the evidence of the *AND* suggests that forms with /tʃ/, not /k/, were by far the commonest in Anglo-French, and it is very likely that both *cattle* and *chattel* are borrowings into English from Anglo-French. (The semantic narrowing from 'property' to 'livestock, cattle' shown by *cattle* may well have occurred within English, although Anglo-French does have *chatel vif*, literally 'live property', in the sense 'livestock'.)

As already illustrated by this initial discussion, the *AND* gives us a powerful tool for investigating which English words are likely to be of Anglo-French origin: we can look at the *AND* for evidence of which words are actually attested in Anglo-French, and in which spellings and with which meanings. When this evidence is compared with what we find in dictionaries of continental French, we can start to draw some conclusions about the likely extent of the distinctively Anglo-French contribution to the vocabulary of English on a good evidential basis. Considerable caution is still required: the lexicographical coverage of medieval continental French has very many gaps where regional varieties are concerned, and the early parts of the *AND* are currently being transformed in a much needed second edition. Furthermore, there are areas for which our surviving data can never tell us as much as we might like: see section 12.2.4 on how Middle English data can sometimes provide evidence for words that are not attested in Anglo-French. Nonetheless, in the rest of this section the core methodology rests on comparison of the documentary record for English, Anglo-French, and continental French, largely as reflected by the available historical dictionaries.[17]

Many words can be identified as being almost certainly part of the Anglo-French contribution to English simply because they are not recorded in continental French sources. That is to say, there is positive evidence that the word existed in Anglo-French and no evidence that it existed in continental French. One example among the words in the 1,000 most frequent contemporary English words discussed in section 2.2 is *duty*. Other examples are *arrival* and *departure*, both of which have etymons attested in Anglo-French but not in continental French.[18] In other cases the word is attested in

---

[17] See section 11.1 for listing of the main dictionaries concerned.

[18] Compare Rothwell (1998). In the case of *departure* there is an interesting twist, in that the Middle English word is attested earlier than the Anglo-French one. In this case this is probably an accident of the historical record, but compare also section 13.1.3 on the complications presented by the earliest example of *departing* in English.

continental sources, but not in a meaning that is central to the use in English. Thus *moat* in the meaning 'castle hill, mound' could reflect borrowing from either continental French or Anglo-French, but the meaning 'defensive ditch' is specific to Anglo-French and Middle English (and also British Latin), and the chronology of the attestations in each language suggests that the sense was not innovated in Middle English. A similar situation is found in the case of *dungeon* in the meaning 'dungeon' rather than 'keep' and likewise in the case of *apparel* in the meaning 'clothing', *purchase* in the meaning 'to acquire' (as well as in a number of other specialised meanings), and *travel* in the meaning 'to travel' (rather than 'to work').[19] The next section looks at how considerations of form and date can also sometimes point strongly to specifically Anglo-French borrowing, before in section 12.2.3 we look at evidence pointing to borrowing specifically from continental French and in section 12.2.4 at cases where English words point to the existence of unrecorded donors in Anglo-French.

12.2.2 Distinctively Anglo-French loanwords as documented in *OED3*

Typically, etymologies in *OED3* give etymons from both Anglo-French and continental French if plausible donor forms are attested in both varieties. In the roughly one-third of *OED3* so far completed, there are approximately 345 words given a direct etymon from Anglo-French but not from continental French. These etymologies have been determined on the basis that a suitable etymon is recorded in Anglo-French and:

- there is no evidence for the relevant word in continental French
- or the word is found in continental French, but differs significantly in form
- or it is found in continental French but not in the relevant meaning(s)
- or it is found in continental French in the relevant form(s) or meaning(s), but at too late a date to be a plausible etymon for the English word.

However, in some of these cases borrowing from Anglo-French is not certain: in particular, in some cases a word could alternatively be from Latin and in others it could be a formation within English rather than a borrowing.

---

[19] For more on these examples, see Rothwell (1991), Rothwell (2005), Short (2007) 23, 136.

To take some illustrative examples from each of these categories (some of which overlap to some extent):

(i) There is no evidence for the relevant word in continental French:

hoggaster,[20] *lettuce, minstrelsy, mischievous, pageant, paramount, pedigree*,[21] *perambulation* (probably also partly < Latin), *rape, remainder, reredos*

(ii) The relevant word exists in continental French, but is very rare, or is only attested later than the English word:

effectual, margin, penthouse,[22] *profess* (probably also partly < Latin), *pumice*

(iii) The Anglo-French etymon differs significantly in form from its continental French equivalents:

palsy, in early use also *palasy, parlesy* (compare Anglo-French *palasie, parlesie* with continental French *paralisie*)
pantry (compare Anglo-French *pantrie* with continental French *paneterie*),
pautener 'rascal' (compare Anglo-French *pautener* with continental French *pautonier*)
pavior 'person who lays paving' (compare Anglo-French *paviour* with continental French *paveur*)
pocket (compare Anglo-French *pokete* with continental French *pochette*)
pronoun (compare Anglo-French *pronoun* with continental French *pronom*)
relent (compare Anglo-French *relenter* with continental French *ralentir*)
remedy (compare Anglo-French *remedie* with continental French *remede*).

(In each case here I have greatly simplified the evidence for ease and simplicity of presentation.)

In some cases the formal differences are rather systematic:

Changes in continental French meant that earlier *-orie* and *-arie* were replaced almost invariably by *-oire* and *-aire*, but this was not usual in Anglo-French; compare *refectory* (first attested *c.*1451) or *possessory* (1425), although either of these could alternatively be from Latin (and remodelling of a continental French word in *-oire* or *-aire* can seldom be ruled out entirely).

---

[20] A formation in a French suffix on an English base (*hog*), then borrowed into Middle English from Anglo-French.

[21] In Anglo-Norman this is a phrase, *pee de gru*, literally 'crane's foot'. It is an interesting question as to how long English speakers remained aware of this metaphor: compare Allan (forthcoming).

[22] The word occurs earliest in forms of the types *pentis, pendize*, reflecting Anglo-French *pentis*; the later form *penthouse* results from folk-etymological association with *house*.

The typical ending of agent nouns, Anglo-French -er beside continental French -eur, can be another important criterion in the case of later loanwords, although here the situation is rather more complex. Likewise for the adjective suffix -ous in Anglo-French beside -eux in continental French.

(iv) The Anglo-French etymon differs significantly in meaning from its continental French equivalents:

> *mortmain* (found in different legal meanings in insular and continental use), *quoit* (not found with reference to the game in continental French).

Many of the words are connected with the law. Indeed, some whole families of related legal terms, e.g. *amerce, amercement, amerciable, amerciament,* and *amerciate,* show input from Anglo-French and/or from medieval Latin words that were themselves either borrowed from or modelled on Anglo-French; this word family simply does not exist in continental sources, except in occasional echoes of Anglo-French use. No other semantic area is particularly predominant.

Such loanwords are found with English dates of first attestation right down to the end of the fifteenth century (and in some cases even later), although words connected with law greatly predominate among words with late dates of first attestation and most of the other words with late first dates could well have existed earlier in English, but either do not occur in the surviving sources, or have not yet been picked up by lexicographical research. The evidence of loans into English thus sadly provides no very clear indication of when Anglo-French ceased to influence English directly in fields other than law. (Loans from what is normally termed Law French continue well into the sixteenth century and beyond, albeit in relatively small numbers. For instance, *asset*[23] and *mandamus*[24] both have sixteenth-century first dates of attestation in English. They could show late borrowings from Law French, or they could have been borrowed earlier but have so far escaped notice in any earlier documents.)

As a proportion of the 2,385 loanwords from some variety of French that *OED3* records for the Middle English period, a total of 345 words

---

[23] *Asset*, originally found only in the plural *assets*, is from Anglo-Norman and Law French *assetz*, a specific use as noun of the adverb meaning 'enough, sufficiently' (Middle French, French *assez*).

[24] *Mandamus* is from Anglo-Norman and Law French *mandamus*, the name of a type of royal writ, in turn from classical Latin *mandāmus* 'we command', in the wording of the writ.

exclusively from Anglo-French is rather low, amounting to only 14.5%.[25] However, the evidential test has been set very high: these are the cases where the evidence is overwhelmingly in favour of borrowing from Anglo-French, not continental French. Many more words may have been borrowed solely from Anglo-French, but we are unable to establish this by the method of comparing the forms and meanings recorded for each variety of French with those recorded for the Middle English word.

12.2.3 A test case: words identified as loanwords from continental French in the parts of *OED3* that overlap with *AND2*

The preceding section looked at likely cases of distinctively Anglo-French loanwords in English. We can also learn a great deal from looking at the reverse situation: Middle English words that seem to be specifically from continental French, not Anglo-French.

What we can say about distinctively Anglo-French or distinctively continental French borrowing in Middle English depends a great deal on the quality and detail of our lexicographical resources. The first edition of the *OED* was prepared without the benefit of any dictionary of Anglo-French and it is well known that a great deal had to be left out even of the first edition of the *AND*. New editions of both the *OED* and *AND* are now in course of preparation and online publication, and it is particularly interesting to look at those parts of *OED3* (comprising A to ALZ plus some smaller sequences of entries in the letters A to L) that have been prepared with the benefit of material from the second edition of *AND*.[26] Comparison of these two resources gives a lexicographical 'state of the art' as it stands at present: *OED3* has drawn on the *MED* for antedatings and other valuable examples of English use, and has also compiled etymologies that draw extensively on the available resources for continental French (as well as for medieval and earlier Latin), while *AND2* gives greatly enhanced documentation on Anglo-French. If a word (or a spelling or a meaning of a word) is not found in *AND2*, then this is a good indication that it is not yet known to

---

[25] In fact, the total becomes very slightly lower if words with first attestations in English later than 1500 are removed.

[26] During 2012 revised *AND* entries were also published for M, but *OED3* entries have not yet been reviewed in light of this newly revised documentation.

historical lexicographers as existing in Anglo-French. Durkin (2012) makes this comparison in detail and it will be summarized below.

In the relatively small alphabetical subsections of A to L in *AND2* and *OED3* that can be compared directly, *OED3* has 270 words that have a first date between 1150 and 1500, and that have a form from some variety of French given as a primary etymon (in many cases alongside a Latin form as probable co-etymon). Among these 270 words:

- In 29 cases (just under 11%) the direct etymon is identified as distinctively Anglo-French, not continental French (although in some of these cases there is also a probable Latin co-etymon); some examples are among the words discussed in section 12.2.2.
- In 183 cases (just under 68%), there is a viable Anglo-French etymon, but borrowing from continental French would also be perfectly possible from the point of view of word form and meaning. In these cases it is perfectly possible for an Anglo-French origin to be presumed, but it cannot be demonstrated purely on the basis of the lexicographical record.
- In 59 cases (just under 22%), an etymon from continental French only, and not from Anglo-French, is given in *OED3*, because a suitable etymon is not documented even in *AND2*, nor has *OED*'s research uncovered any Anglo-French evidence elsewhere.

It is this last category that is looked at further here. In some cases, borrowing from Latin is also possible, and in some of these (including several plant names and a number of terms from medical discourse) there is no strong reason for supposing that the borrowing is not solely from Latin. The following are some representative examples:

(i) Words likely to be from French only (not Latin):

abolish (c.1475), *address* (as noun; a.1325), *addresseress* (a.1492), *ballad* (1458), *conservatrice* (a.1450), *conserve* (as noun; a.1393), *franc* (c.1405), *hogmanay* (1443, in a one-off early attestation, from Yorkshire rather than Scotland), *image* (as verb; c.1390), *imaginative* (a.1398), *labourage* (a.1460), *languager* (1484)

(ii) Words from French and/or Latin:

ablution (c.1405), *abound* (as adjective; c.1425), *absinth* (c.1429), *activity* (a.1425), *alterable* (?a.1425), *analogy* (?a.1425), *animosity* (?a.1475), *application* (a.1398), *arterial* (?c.1425), *cankerous* (c.1425), *civility* (c.1384), *climate* (a.1393), *communicable* (a.1398), *conservative* (a.1398; earliest as noun), *economic* (a.1393), *economy* (?1440), *facility* (?a.1425), *imaginable* (?c.1400), *intelligible* (a.1382), *liberality* (a.1387)

In some of these cases, from both group (i) and group (ii), closely related English words in the same word family do have likely Anglo-French (partial) etymons, e.g. *address* verb (beside *address* noun), *conserve* verb (beside *conserve* noun), *active* (beside *activity*), *alter* (beside *alterable*). Thus, the absence of evidence for the corresponding word in Anglo-French could simply be an accident of the historical record. Some of these words could alternatively be explained as being formations within English rather than loanwords, e.g. *conserve* noun could be < *conserve* verb, and *address* verb could be < *address* noun; *cankerous* could be an English derivative from *canker*.

Ballad (first attested 1458 in English) and *abolish* (*c.*1475) stand out most in this sample as words that can be fairly confidently assigned to borrowing from French and that belong to word families that appear not to be represented in Anglo-French at all. (*Ballad* could perhaps be explained by borrowing from Occitan rather than French, although there is certainly no strong indication of this.)

Section 12.2.5 looks at some of the implications of this data, but first it is advisable to look at some cases where the English data is best explained by hypothesizing the existence of an unattested Anglo-French word.

12.2.4 Evidence in English lexicography for unrecorded Anglo-French words, forms, or meanings

The approximately 33% of *OED3* so far published contains around 100 etymologies that suggest the possible and, in some cases, very probable existence of an Anglo-French word that is not recorded by the *AND*, and for which the *OED* editors are unaware of any evidence in documents written in Anglo-French. However, it should be noted that many of these cases come from words in the alphabetical range M to R, which has not yet been covered by *AND2*, and Anglo-French evidence may well come to light for *AND2*. The following paragraphs present some of the more striking examples and identify some characteristic types.[27] In most cases, the English words appear to reflect derivative or compound formations that are not securely attested in Anglo-French; in some cases, the English words appear to reflect characteristically Anglo-French form variants of other French words.

---

[27] For a fuller account, see Durkin (2012).

In many cases a vernacular word occurs in documents that have Latin as their matrix language earlier than the first appearance of the corresponding word in contextual English use. (See section 13.2 on texts of this type.) Typically, it is unclear whether we have evidence for earlier currency of the English word, or whether we have evidence for a corresponding word in Anglo-French that has not (yet) been entered in the lexicographical record. Some examples are noted in the *OED3* entries for:

> *galanga* 'galangal', *galantine* 'type of sauce', and *drug* (which are all recorded in continental French, but not in Anglo-French);
> *hotte* 'shed, hut',[28] *osmund* 'type of iron' (a word ultimately of Scandinavian origin), *parpen* 'dressed stone running through a wall from one side to the other', *parrel* 'item of rigging', *pliers*, *polancre* 'kind of pulley', *potteler* 'pot or tankard' (also found as a surname), *pouldron* 'piece of shoulder armour' (in form *paltron*), *pram* 'type of flat-bottomed boat',[29] *rocher* 'rock', *roller* 'cylinder on which something can be rolled', *rubble*.[30]

Section 13.2 looks in more detail at the questions posed by such texts. In the case of *purpitle* 'choir screen' all of the evidence is ambiguous in this way and thus it is possible that the word may have existed in Middle English only, or in Anglo-French only, or (probably more likely) in both.

In many cases, surnames (especially occupational ones) appear to imply the existence of a vernacular word, but it is unclear whether the word concerned is Anglo-French or Middle English (or both). Some examples where a surname occurs earlier than any (other) evidence for the English word and there is no (other) evidence for an Anglo-French equivalent are noted in the *OED3* entries for:

> *cellar* 'cellarer', *imager* 'producer of images', *marler* 'person who digs marl', *murenger* 'officer responsible for keeping city walls in good repair', *oiler*, *paliser* 'maker of fences', *psalterer* (probably) 'person who plays the psaltery', *quilter, quoiter, rager, roller* 'maker or seller of parchment rolls', *rounger* 'person who clips coins', as well as many others.

---

[28] In this instance the uncertain occurrence is in fact later than the examples in contextual English use. For detailed discussion of this example, see section 13.2.

[29] This is a borrowing (ultimately) from Dutch, not clearly attested in English until the sixteenth century, but found as a vernacular word in late fourteenth-century Latin documents from England.

[30] This word is of uncertain etymology. It may perhaps be related to *rubbish*, which does have parallels in Anglo-French (*robous, robouse, roboise, rubbouse*, etc.) and Latin (*rebbussa, robusium, robousa, robusum*), but it is entirely unclear in which language (English, French, Latin, or another language) the word originated.

In the case of *ointer* 'dealer in grease, lard, or tallow' all of the evidence is ambiguous in this way and thus, like *purpitle* already mentioned, it is possible that the word may have existed in Middle English only or in Anglo-French only, or it may have existed in both.

In a small but interesting group of cases, Middle English word forms can be explained by hypothesizing the existence of unattested Anglo-French forms showing characteristic formal developments in Anglo-French (although often alternative explanations are also possible), e.g. *mean* 'to mediate' (compare Middle French *moyenner*), or form variants of *message* of the type *massage*.

Two parallel cases are shown by *remainer* '(in legal use) remainder' and *reseiser* 'royal act of resuming possession upon discovery of an error that had led to property being delivered out of royal possession'. It is clear that both of these terms ultimately reflect the French pattern of forming a noun by conversion of a verbal infinitive, but what is less clear is whether we therefore have evidence for unattested Anglo-French nouns *remainer* and *reseiser*, or whether the nouns have been formed within English by analogy with other borrowed nouns, as seems likely in the case of some later English words on this pattern, such as *superviver* (1542) or *accruer* (1662).

Some Middle English etymologies suggest (with varying degrees of likelihood) the existence of unattested words or forms that may have existed in either Anglo-French or continental French, examples being *osprey* or *penalty*. In the case of *rabbit* the likely etymon *rabotte* is attested later in French regional use; the word is probably ultimately a French derivative formation on a base borrowed from Dutch, but there is no medieval French evidence from either England or the continent. In the case of *purlin* 'horizontal beam that runs along the length of a roof' the corresponding word *porloigne* is attested in continental French, but not in this meaning.

Sometimes an English word strongly suggests an unattested Anglo-French semantic model. *Freeboard* and especially its semantic equivalent post-classical Latin *francbordus* 'right to a strip of land outside a boundary marked by a hedge' seem to reflect an unattested Anglo-French **franc bord*, with English *freeboard* showing a loan translation of this, and Latin *francbordus* a borrowing.

12.2.5 Some conclusions

Careful use of dictionary data, in conjunction with traditional philological approaches in the identification of form types characteristic of different varieties of French, can be revealing about the distinctively Anglo-French contribution to the vocabulary of English.

The proportion of French loanwords that can be identified as specifically Anglo-French is small: 14.5% in the sample looked at in section 12.2.2, and even lower, 11%, in the smaller sample looked at in section 12.2.3. In the small sample of comparable *AND2* and *OED3* data looked at in section 12.2.3, the proportion of words apparently borrowed only from continental French was actually considerably higher, at 20%. However, in many of these cases the borrowing could be entirely from Latin rather than from French. Additionally, as shown in section 12.2.4, there are many cases where the most plausible etymological hypothesis is to assume the existence of an unattested word, form, or meaning in Anglo-French, and this could also be the explanation for at least some of the cases considered in section 12.2.3.

Finally, it is striking that all of the examples of the type illustrated in section 12.2.3, where a plausible etymon is attested in continental French but not in Anglo-French, date from the last quarter of the fourteenth century or later, i.e. none date from the period in which English stood substantially in the shadow of Anglo-French as a language of record. It will be very interesting to see whether this finding from a very small sample continues to be borne out when it becomes possible to make a greater number of direct comparisons between data in *OED3* and *AND2*. On present evidence, we can say that there is little to contradict the hypothesis that Middle English borrowing was largely from Anglo-French rather than continental French up until about 1375, even if the proportion of cases where we have positive evidence to support this hypothesis remains low.

13

Example passages from English and multilingual texts

This chapter illustrates some of the main topics discussed in part V and also some from part IV, through a series of passages from Middle English texts with commentaries on the loanwords from French, Latin, and early Scandinavian that they show. This is followed by a short examination of some representative multilingual texts and the evidence they provide about the linguistic practice of late medieval England.

13.1 Example passages from Middle English texts with commentary

In each passage, loanwords are marked with bold type and derivative formations with a loanword as their base are marked with bold type plus underlining.

13.1.1 Passage 1: from the Final Continuation of the *Peterborough Chronicle*

The closing sentences of the annal for 1140 from the Final Continuation, written *c.*1154 (see section 9.4.2):[1]

> Þa ferde he [i.e. Henry] mid micel færd into Engleland & wan **castles**, & te king ferde agenes him mid micele mare ferd. & **þoþ**wæthere fuhtten hi noht, **oc**

[1] Cited from Irvine (2004). I have silently included expansions and emendations which Irvine indicates in her text; none of these makes a material difference to the interpretation of any of the lexical borrowings noted in this particular passage. See section 9.4.2 on the textual history of this source.

ferden þe **ærcebiscop** & te wise men betwyx heom & makede ðat **sahte** ðat te king sculde ben lauerd & king wile he liuede & æfter his dæi ware Henri king, & he helde him for fader & he him for sune, & sib & **sæhte** sculde ben betwyx heom & on al Engleland. Þis & te othre foruuardes þet hi makeden suoren to halden þe king & te **eorl** & te **biscopes** & te **eorles** & rice men alle. Þa was þe **eorl** underfangen æt Wincestre & æt Lundene mid micel wurtscipe, & alle diden him manred & suoren þe **pais** to halden, & hit ward sone suythe god **pais** sua ðat neure was here. Þa was þe king strengere þanne he æuert her was, & te **eorl** ferde ouer sæ, & al folc him luuede for he dide god **iustise** & makede **pais**.

Then he [i.e. Henry, the future King Henry II] went into England with a great army and won castles, and the king [i.e. King Stephen] marched against him with a much bigger army. And nevertheless they did not fight, but the archbishop and the wise men went between them and made an agreement that the king should be lord and king while he lived, and after his day Henry should be king, and they should hold each other as father and son, and there should be peace and concord between them and in all England. The king and the earl and the bishops and the nobles and all the rich men swore to uphold this and the other agreements that they made. Then the earl was received with great honour at Winchester and at London, and all paid homage to him and swore to abide by the peace, and it soon became a very good peace, such as never was before. Then the king was stronger than he ever was before, and the earl went over the sea, and all the people loved him because he administered justice appropriately and made peace.

- *Castles*: in the meaning 'castle, fortress' *castle* occurs earliest in manuscripts of the Anglo-Saxon Chronicle from the late eleventh century and later, probably showing a new borrowing from (Anglo-)French *castel* (showing a form preserving /k/ before /a/: see section 12.2.1) and perhaps also post-classical Latin *castellum*. (See section 6.3.3 for the earlier borrowing *castel*, *cæstel* 'village, small town'.)
- *Þoþwæthere* 'nevertheless': the first element is the early Scandinavian loanword *though* (compare section 10.2.5); the formation may show a remodelling of Old English *þēah-hwæþere*, with substitution of Scandinavian *though* for the native equivalent (and cognate) *þēah*.
- *Hi* 'they', *heom* 'them': the native third-person plural pronoun forms are retained.
- *Oc* 'but': a conjunction borrowed from early Scandinavian. This is the most frequently occurring early Scandinavian loanword in this text: compare section 9.4.2.
- *Ærcebiscop* 'archbishop', *biscopes* 'bishops': the reflexes of Old English (or earlier) borrowings from Latin: see sections 6.3.1, 6.3.2. (*Rice* 'rich' probably ultimately reflects an even earlier borrowing from Celtic: see section 4.2.)

- *Sahte, sæhte* 'agreement, settlement, peace, concord': an important late Old English loanword from early Scandinavian. See further under the passage from the *Ancrene Wisse* below. Note the pairing of native and borrowed synonyms (or near synonyms) in *sib & sæhte*.
- *Eorl, eorles* 'earl, earls': an important (fairly certain) semantic loan from early Scandinavian: see section 10.8, and also sections 10.11, 9.4.2.
- *Pais* 'peace', *iustise* 'justice': this is the earliest text to record either of these major (Anglo-)French loanwords. Note how in this passage *pais* 'peace' occurs in near proximity to *sib* and *sahte* in partly overlapping meanings.

13.1.2 Passage 2: from the *Ormulum*

Second half of the twelfth century: see section 9.4.2. Lines 7392–7:[2]

> Forr ȝiff **þeȝȝ** herenn ohht off Godd,
>   & **skirrpenn** þær onnȝæness,
> Þa beþ hemm ȝarrkedd mare inoh
>   & werrse **pine** inn helle
> Þann iff **þeȝȝ** haffdenn herrd itt nohht,
>   Ne **skarnedd** tær onnȝænness.

Because if they hear anything about God, and behave contemptuously against it, then there is prepared for them a greater amount of and worse suffering in Hell, than if they had not heard it, and had not acted scornfully against it.

- *Þeȝȝ* 'they' (but *hemm* 'them'): see section 9.4.2 on the use of the Scandinavian-derived third-person plural personal pronoun forms in this text.
- *Skirrpenn* 'to behave contemptuously': another early Scandinavian loanword.
- *Pine* 'suffering, torment': probably a very early Latin borrowing in Old English (see sections 6.2.1, 6.3.1).
- *Skarnedd* 'acted scornfully': one of the very few French loanwords in this text, the first attestation of *to scorn* < (Anglo-)French *escarnir*, ultimately a borrowing into the Romance languages from a Germanic language. (*Escarnir* is a distinctively Anglo-French or northern

---

[2] Cited from White (1852).

continental French form, showing preservation of /sk/ before /a/, beside central and southern *escharnir*. The English variant with /o/ which became the dominant form in English has not been adequately explained.)

13.1.3 Passage 3: from the *Ancrene Wisse*

Early thirteenth century. A text offering spiritual guidance for a group of anchoresses (compare discussion of this text in section 12.1.3). From part 4, section 59:[3]

> Vre Lauerdes leaste wordes, þa he steah to heouene ant leafde his leoue freond in uncuðe þeode, weren of swote luue ant of **sahtnesse**: *Pacem relinquo uobis; pacem meam do uobis*, þet is, '**Sahtnesse** Ich do imong ow; **sahtnesse** Ich leaue wið ow.' Þis wes his **druerie** þet he leafde ant ʒef ham in his **departunge**. *In hoc cognoscentis quod dicipuli mei sitis, si dilectionem ad inuicem habueritis*. Lokið nu ʒeorne for his deorewurðe luue hwuch a mearke he leide upon his icorene þa he steah to heouene: *In hoc cognoscentis quod, et cetera*. 'Bi þet ʒe schulen icnawen', quoð he, 'þet ʒe beoð mine **deciples**, ʒef swete luue ant **sahtnesse** is eauer ow bitweonen.' Godd hit wite (ant he hit wat), me were leouere þet ʒe were alle o þe **spitel**-uuel þen ʒe were ontfule oðer feol iheortet.
>
> Our Lord's last words, when he ascended into heaven and left his dear friends in a strange land, were of sweet love and of peace: 'I leave peace with you; I give you my peace'; that is, 'I establish peace among you; I leave peace with you'. This was his love that he left and gave them in his departing. 'In this you shall know that you are my disciples, if you have love for one another.' Look now carefully, on account of his precious love, what sort of a sign he laid upon his chosen ones when he ascended into heaven: 'In this you shall know, etc.' 'By that you shall know', he said, 'that you are my disciples, if there is always sweet love and peace between you.' Let God know it (and he knows it), it would be preferable to me that you were all suffering with leprosy, than that you were spiteful or foul-hearted.

This passage, like very many others in the *Ancrene Wisse* and in many other Middle English religious texts, comments directly on verses from the Latin (Vulgate) Bible. Even when texts are not directly translated from Latin or French, there is often a dialogue with material in another language, whether explicitly, as here, or more implicitly.

---

[3] Taken from Millett (2005) 94–5. On the history of the alternative names *Ancrene Wisse* (which occurs in the text itself) and *Ancrene Riwle* (an invention of modern scholars), see Wada (2003a).

- *Deciples* 'disciples': Middle English (and hence modern English) *disciple* probably partly shows continuity with Old English *discipul* (< Latin) and partly shows a new borrowing from (Anglo-)French and Latin; the modern word form is entirely consistent with the hypothesis that the word was borrowed anew from (Anglo-)French in the post-Conquest period, but other narratives are certainly possible.

- *Sahtnesse* 'reconciliation, peace': *sahte* (on which see commentary on passage 1 above) and its derivative *sahtnesse* are used frequently in the language of the *Ancrene Wisse*; the (Anglo-)French loanword *peace* also occurs (as *pes, peis*), but more typically in the meaning 'rest, peace and quiet'.[4]

- *Druerie* 'love': this is the earliest text to record this loanword from (Anglo-)French (which is more commonly found denoting secular, especially courtly, love); the French word is probably ultimately of Gaulish origin (compare section 5.3).

- *Departunge* 'departing': this is the earliest attestation of *departing* in English. It is also earlier than the earliest attestations of *depart*, which is found from around 1300 (in one instance in a text probably composed in the mid thirteenth century but preserved in slightly later manuscripts). The early occurrence of this apparent derivative is also interesting. It may be evidence that the verb was also found in English at this date. Alternatively, it could have been formed within English directly on the French verb stem. Trotter (2003c) groups this with some similar examples in *Ancrene Wisse*, arguing that they may reflect the confident trilingualism of the author and the author's circle, who may have formed hybrid words on Romance bases with native affixes without there necessarily being prior borrowing of the base. A persuasive case is made for this, although in this particular instance there remains the strong possibility that the word *depart* did exist in English at this date and our surviving documents simply fail to show it: compare comments on the next word below.

- *Spitel-uuel* 'leprosy': this is a compound of *spitel* 'place of quarantine for lepers' and *evil*. *Spitel* is, like *hospital*, ultimately < Latin *hospitālis*. However, in this rather unusual instance, the word in the aphetic form *spitel* (i.e. with loss of the initial vowel) appears to have entered English

---

[4] See further Dance (2003) 191, 228, 372.

not through Anglo-French (in which this form type is very rare) nor directly from Latin, but probably via another Germanic language, most likely Middle Dutch or Middle Low German. This compound is the earliest evidence for *spitel* in English, but there is evidence for slightly earlier currency of the word in England in the late twelfth-century surname *Spitelman*.

13.1.4 Passage 4: from John Trevisa's translation of Ranulf Higden's *Polychronicon*

Higden's Latin work was written in the early fourteenth century.[5] In the passage below, the text from 'Þys manere was' onwards is an interpolation by Trevisa, which he himself dates 1385. I cite the text as it appears in London, British Library, manuscript Cotton Tiberius D. vii. of *c.*1400 (as given in Sisam (1921) 148–9); I do so because, aside from the importance of Trevisa's content (on which compare section 11.2), there are some additional points of interest in the scribal language of this particular manuscript. The manuscript is localized to Gloucestershire in *LALME* (McIntosh et al. 1986: vol. I. 107).

> Þis **apeyryng** of þe **burþ**tonge ys by**cause** of twey þinges. On ys for chyldern in scole, aȝenes þe **vsage** and **manere** of al oþer **nacions**, buþ **compelled** for to leue here oune **longage**, and for to **construe** here **lessons** and here þinges a Freynsch, and habbeþ suþthe þe Normans come furst into Engelond. Also **gentil** men children buþ ytauȝt for to speke Freynsch fram tyme þat a buþ yrokked in here cradel, and conneþ speke and playe wiþ a child hys **brouch**; and oplondysch men wol lykne hamsylf to **gentil** men, and fondeþ wiþ gret bysynes for to speke Freynsch, for to be more ytold of.
>
> Þys **manere** was moche **y-vsed** tofore þe furste **moreyn**, and ys seþthe somdel **ychaunged**. For Iohan Cornwal, a **mayster** of **gramere**, **chayngede** þe lore in **gramerscole** and **construccion** of Freynsch into Englysch; and Richard Pencrych lurnede þat **manere** techyng of hym, and oþer men of Pencrych, so þat now, þe ȝer of oure Lord a þousand þre hondred foure score and fyue, of þe **secunde** kyng Richard after þe **Conquest** nyne, in al þe **gramerscoles** of Engelond childern leueþ Frensch, and **construeþ** and lurneþ an Englysch, and habbeþ þerby **avauntage** in on syde, and **desavauntage** yn anoþer. Here **avauntage** ys þat a lurneþ here **gramer** yn lasse tyme þan childern wer ywoned to do. **Disavauntage** ys þat now childern of **gramerscole** conneþ no more Frensch þan can here left heele, and þat ys harm for ham and a scholle **passe** þe se and

---

[5] On the complexities of dating the Latin text, see the brief account in Taylor (2004).

trauayle in **strange** londes, and in meny **caas** also. Also **gentil** men habbeþ now moche yleft for to teche here childern Frensch.

This damaging of the mother tongue is for two reasons. One is that children in school, against the usage and manner of all other nations, are compelled to put aside their own language, and to write their lessons and compositions in French, and have done so since the Normans first came to England. Also the children of the gentry are taught to speak French from the time that they are rocked in their cradle and know how to speak and play with a child's bauble; and rustics want to make themselves more like the gentry, and seek to speak French with great industry, in order to be more highly thought of.

This manner of doing things was much used before the first plague, and has changed somewhat since. For John Cornwall, a teacher of grammar, changed the teaching in the grammar school to English rather than French, and [likewise] the [Latin] translation exercises; and Richard Pencrych learned that manner of teaching from him, and other men in turn from Pencrych, so that now, in the year of Our Lord 1385, the 9th year of the second King Richard after the Conquest, in all the grammar schools of England children put aside French, and write and learn in English, and thus they have an advantage on one side, but a disadvantage on another. Their advantage is that they learn their grammar in less time than children were accustomed to do. The disadvantage is that now grammar school children know no more French than their own left heel, and that is a problem for them if they should cross the sea and work in foreign countries, and in many other circumstances also. Also the gentry have now greatly ceased teaching their children French.

It is notable that (in the language of this particular manuscript) the third-person plural personal pronoun forms are reflexes of native forms, not the Scandinavian borrowings, even in the subject form *a* 'they'. The past participle normally has the prefix *y-* (the reflex of Old English *ġe-*), as in *ytauȝt, yrokked, ytold, ywoned*; in borrowed verbs this is slightly more sporadic, as here in *y-vsed, ychaunged*, but *compelled*. There are many words of (Anglo-)French or Latin origin, including a number that are attested for the first time in this text:

(Anglo-)French: *manere* 'manner' (*a.*1225), *ychaunged, chayngede* 'changed' (*c.*1225), *passe* 'pass' (*c.*1225), *brouch* 'trinket, bauble' (*c.*1230), *lessons* (*c.*1230), *caas* 'cases, circumstances' (*a.*1250), *trauayle* 'work' (*c.*1275), *avauntage* 'advantage' (*c.*1300),[6] *longage* 'language' (*c.*1300), *strange* 'foreign' (*c.*1300), *vsage* 'usage' (*c.*1325), *moreyn* 'plague' (*a.*1382; this text provides the *MED*'s earliest example in this sense), *desavauntage, disavauntage* (*a.*1387, earliest in this text), *gramere, gramer* 'grammar' (*a.*1387,

---

[6] The later spelling with *ad-* results from the influence of Latin words beginning with *ad-*: compare section 14.3.

earliest in this text); (derivatives and compounds) *bycause* 'because' (*c.*1375; < *cause*, *c.*1230), *apeyryng* 'damaging' (*a.*1387, earliest in this text), *gramerscole* (*a.*1387, earliest in this text).

(Anglo-)French and/or Latin: *gentil* 'noble, belonging to the gentry' (*a.*1250; 1222 in the compound *gentil man*), *y-vsed* 'used' (*a.*1250), *secunde* 'second' (?*a.*1325), *nacions* 'nations' (*c.*1330), *Conquest* (*c.*1350), *compelled* (*c.*1384; this text provides the *MED*'s earliest example in this sense), *construccion* 'construction', here specifically 'translation for the sake of interpretation' (*a.*1387, earliest in this text).

Latin: *mayster* 'master', *scole* 'school' (Old English), *construe, construeþ* 'construe, write' (*a.*1387, earliest in this text).

Notably, there are no certain Scandinavian loanwords in this passage, only the rather uncertain *burþ* 'birth'.

13.1.5 Passage 5: from Caxton's Prologue to *The Boke of Eneydos*

Date: 1490. Text cited from Gray (1985).

> That **comyn** Englysshe that is spoken in one shyre **varyeth** from another. Insomuche that in my dayes **happened** that **certayn marchauntes** were in a shippe in Tamyse, forto have sayled over the see into Zelande, and for lacke of wynde, **thei** taryed atte forlond, and wente to lande forto **refreshe them**. And one of **theym** named Sheffelde, a **mercer**, cam into an hows and axed for mete; and **specyally** he axyd after **eggys**. And the goode wyf answerde that she coude speke no Frenshe. And the **marchaunt** was **angry**, for he also coude speke no Frenshe, but wolde have hadde **egges**, and she understode hym not. And thenne at laste another sayd that he wolde have eyren. Then the good wyfe sayd that she understood hym wel. Loo, what sholde a man in thyse dayes now wryte – **egges** or eyren? **Certaynly** it is harde to **playse** every man, by**cause** of **dyversite** and **chaunge** of **langage**. For in these dayes every man that is in ony **reputacyon** in his **countre** wyll utter his **commynycacyon** and **maters** in suche **maners** and **termes** that fewe men shall understonde **theym**.

A translation is probably unnecessary for this text if the loanwords are glossed:

> Scandinavian: *thei* 'they', *theym, them* 'them', *egges, eggys* 'eggs'; (derivatives) *angry, happened*.

> (Anglo-)French: *maners* 'manners' (*a.*1225), *marchaunt* 'merchant' (*c.*1225), *chaunge* 'change' (or perhaps 'variation') (*c.*1230), *maters* 'matters' (*c.*1230), *mercer* (*c.*1230, showing borrowing of a specifically Anglo-French form), *termes* 'terms' (*c.*1230), *countre* 'country' (*a.*1300), *certayn* 'certain' (*c.*1300; hence *certaynly c.*1300), *langage* 'language' (*c.*1300), *refreshe* 'refresh, obtain refreshments' (*a.*1382), *playse* 'please' (*c.*1350).

(Anglo-)French and/or Latin: *comyn* 'common' (*c.*1300), *dyversite* 'diversity' (*a.*1382), *varyeth* 'varies' (*a.*1382), *reputacyon* 'reputation' (*c.*1390), *commynycacyon* 'communication' (1419); (derivatives and compounds) *bycause* 'because' (*c.*1375; < *cause*, *c.*1230), *specyally* 'specially, specifically' (*c.*1325; < *special*, *c.*1230).

(Note also *taryed* 'tarried': of unknown origin; attested only from the late fourteenth century, but frequent from this date.)

Caxton illustrates regional variation in English with the example of *egges* and *eyren*; in this case the variation results from survival of native *eyren* in some areas, beside the early Scandinavian loanword *egges* (compare section 10.2.6). Note that native *eyren* retains the *-en* plural, which is rare in Caxton's language and survives in the modern standard language only in a few isolated cases, such as *oxen*, whereas *egges* shows what is already in Caxton's language the regular plural ending *-s/-es/-ys*.

Words of French and Latin origin occur much more frequently in this passage and in the passage from Trevisa than in the early Middle English passages (even though they were also picked to illustrate interesting loanwords). Note that they occur more densely in the more technical discussion of language than in the narrative account of the merchants and their communicational difficulties. Note also the pairing of synonymous or nearly synonymous terms, *commynycacyon and maters, maners and termes*, and perhaps also *dyversite and change*, since 'change' here may mean (synchronic) variation rather than change over time. This use of paired terms is very characteristic of late Middle English and also of early modern English, and probably partly reflects rhetorical style,[7] and partly a real need for communicational clarity in an age of rapid lexical change.

The next few sentences of the same passage give further illustration of Caxton's linguistic attitudes and intended practice, and also of the frequency of loanwords in late Middle English prose, and are worth quoting in full:

> And som **honest** and grete **clerkes** have ben wyth me, and **desired** me to wryte the moste **curyous termes** that I coude fynde. And thus bytwene **playn, rude**, and **curyous**, I stande **abasshed**. But in my **judgemente**, the **comyn termes** that be dayli used ben lyghter to understonde than the olde and **auncyent** Englysshe. And forasmoche as this **present** booke is not for a **rude** uplondyssh man to **laboure** therin ne rede it, but only for a **clerke** and a noble **gentylman** that

---

[7] Compare Adamson (1999) 556–9 on the multiplication of synonyms as a rhetorical device in Early Modern English.

feleth and understondeth in **faytes** of **armes**, in love, and in **noble chyvalrye**, therfor in a **meane** bytwene both, I have **reduced** and **translated** this sayd booke into our Englysshe, not over-**rude** ne **curyous**, but in suche **termes** as shall be understanden by Goddys **grace**, **accordynge** to my **copye**.

13.2 Some examples from multilingual texts and texts not in English

Since this book has discussed in detail the impact of medieval multilingualism on the vocabulary of English, it is only sensible to look also at some passages that are not from monolingual English texts.

My first example comes from a text that is (arguably) a monolingual Anglo-French text. Jefferson (2000) examines the records of the Goldsmiths' Company (one of the livery companies of the City of London) from the fourteenth and fifteenth centuries. These are kept in Anglo-French, and entries relating to goldsmithry show a confident and comprehensive Anglo-French technical vocabulary, at least until the end of the fourteenth century. By contrast, Jefferson draws attention to an entry recording money expended on building work, where a great deal of vocabulary of English origin occurs (the italicization of words of Middle English origin is mine):

Item, al *tyler* xij s. Item pur iiij[MI] *tieles*, pris xxvj s. viij d. Item, pur *rooftiel*—ij s. vij d. Item, pur *tylpyns* vij d. ob. Item, pur *lathes* al celour—x s. x d. Item pur *lathenaylle* a tut l'overaygne – xx s. v d. ob.

What we have here is a record of payments to a tiler, and for tiles, roof tiles, tile pins, laths for the ceiling, and for lath nails for all of the work. The grammatical vocabulary is Anglo-French (except for Latin *item* conventionally beginning each entry), and so are *celour* 'ceiling' and *overaygne* 'work'. The remainder of the nouns are all Middle English in origin. However, *tieuler* 'tiler', *tieule* 'tile', and *lath* 'lath' are headwords in the *AND*, because these words occur frequently enough in Anglo-French texts (for the most part in similar texts to this one) to merit this status, even if they are of Middle English origin (and are indicated as such in the *AND*). The other Middle English words in this passage are (Middle English) compounds of these three words. Should these words therefore simply be regarded as Middle English loanwords occurring in an Anglo-French text? However, if we bear in mind that the scribe pretty certainly had English as his mother tongue, it is certainly also possible to construe what is happening here rather differently, as a switch to largely English terminology in written records when building work is discussed. It is not just for Middle English that the boundaries of the lexis are hard to define, but, to a certain extent, for all three of the major languages of later medieval England. (It is also worth noting that the general phenomenon of records being kept in languages other than that in normal daily spoken use by the majority of the local population is a widespread one in medieval Europe, although my discussion here focuses on later medieval England.[8])

When the matrix language of a text, i.e. the language that provides its core grammatical vocabulary, is Latin, it is at least possible to apply a formal criterion: words that are borrowed into Latin (in however fleeting a way) show accommodation to the rich Latin system of inflectional endings and any words that do not are code switches to a vernacular. The marks of suspension used to represent the endings in very many manuscripts can in fact make things rather more ambiguous than this. An example of this is shown by *pro officio plumbar'* standing for *pro officio plumbarii* 'for the office of the lead-worker' in the 1350 quotation from the Durham Abbey account rolls given later.

In some late medieval English accounts, we find a situation where typically the matrix language is Latin but very many of the nouns are in the vernacular. Determining which vernacular is extremely difficult, especially since recent research has suggested that the (etymologically French) definite article *le* (and the plural *les*) appear to be used in such texts to flag a switch to a vernacular, but that vernacular may be either Anglo-French or Middle English (or maybe even another vernacular).[9]

In section 12.2.4 an illustration was given of some of the lexicographical difficulties that are posed by such evidence, when we cannot tell whether a particular example shows a Middle English or an Anglo-French word. The list given in section 12.2.4 was of words that are not otherwise recorded in Anglo-French. One of the words mentioned there was the very rare Middle English word *hotte* 'hut', recorded in two fourteenth-century chronicles. This is of uncertain etymology: word form would suggest a connection with Middle English *hott, hotte, hote, hutte* 'basket' (which is a borrowing from Anglo-French), but the meaning is much closer to that of *hut* (which is found in English only from the sixteenth century onwards, borrowed from

---

[8] For an interesting discussion of French used as a language of record in predominantly Dutch-speaking areas, see Lusignan (2012).

[9] See Trotter (2010) 59–60, Wright (2010).

another Germanic language, at least partly via French). This word seems to make another appearance in the accounts of Durham Abbey (cited here in the style in which it appears as a quotation in *OED3*):[10]

> ?*c*.1450 in J. T. Fowler *Extracts Acct. Rolls Abbey of Durham* (1898) I. 239 Pro car. 7 fother meremii a le hote usque ad ortum abbathie.

The entry records payment for the carriage of seven cartloads of timber from the hut to the abbey garden. The Durham Abbey account rolls show Latin as the matrix language, with very extensive use of embedded lexical items from both English and French. Rothwell (1999 654) comments:

> The broad distinction made by the scribes is that English is usually found in lists of farm or household implements, the parts of a cart, building materials, local fish, etc.— in sum, anything produced in the locality or in neighbouring areas. French, on the other hand, is the language chosen as a rule for lists of imported products—fabrics, tableware, furnishings, furniture, a wide range of fruits and spices—and for what might be termed architectural features of important buildings, as distinct from humbler constructions such as cowsheds. This distinction, however, is not absolute.

Looking again at the quotation given above, we may note that *fother* 'cartload' is a word of Middle English origin and the subject matter is one of the types for which Rothwell notes that English is usually found. It is therefore tempting to regard this instance of *hote* as most probably English, especially since the word otherwise occurs only in English contexts, but this is far from definitive proof. The complications may become clearer if we turn now to a word that definitely was borrowed into English from (Anglo-) French. *Plane*, denoting the tool used by a carpenter or builder for planing or smoothing, is found in Middle English from the first half of the fifteenth century (interestingly, earliest in glosses on Latin words in Latin-English glossaries). The following example from the same Durham Abbey accounts probably shows the English word, because of the plural ending -*ys* (which is at least not typical of Anglo-French):

> 1404 in J. T. Fowler *Extracts Acct. Rolls Abbey of Durham* (1899) II. 397 In custodia Plumbarii, 2 planys.

---

[10] Typically in lexicographical work, because of practical constraints, material can only be taken from printed editions, as here, rather than directly from the source manuscript. Such editions often expand manuscript abbreviations silently, and great care must be taken when interpreting such evidence.

('In the keeping of the lead-worker, two planes.') The following earlier examples, one of them again from the Durham Abbey accounts, are much more ambiguous:

> 1350 in J. T. Fowler *Extracts Acct. Rolls Abbey of Durham* (1899) II. 550
> Uno Plane et aliis instrumentis pro officio plumbar', emptis, 2 s. 5 d.
>
> 1399 in J. Raine *Fabric Rolls York Minster* (1859) 18 Instrumenta carpentariorum...
> Item, j plane de ere.

('For one plane and other tools bought for the office of the lead-worker, 2 shillings and 5 pence.'; 'Tools of the carpenters... Item, one plane made of metal.') Since the word is definitely of (Anglo-)French origin, it may seem safest to assume that these examples show the Anglo-French word. However, as already seen from both the Goldsmiths' Company records and the Durham Abbey accounts, the vocabulary of building is an area where English words abound in records kept in Latin and even in records kept in Anglo-French. We may therefore perhaps wonder whether these examples might not show some slight support for the idea that the word may have been borrowed into Middle English by this date. (The *HTOED* records no earlier synonym, so we do not know what other name the builders using these tools may have called them by.) It is useful also to pause to consider the experience of writing or reading records such as these, particularly since just about anyone who was literate and had any connection with any sort of business would have had some contact with texts of this type. As we have seen, the matrix language of the Durham Abbey accounts is Latin, but the vernacular items embedded in it are not flagged as belonging either to French or to English. It is likely that the experience of using such documents would have led to some blurring of the distinction between the lexicons of the two vernacular languages: certainly, the only distinction evident in these texts is between Latin and 'vernacular', and it may be that, beyond the core vocabulary of each language, speakers made little practical distinction between the lexis of French and the lexis of English.[11]

A further interesting text type is the macaronic sermon, the subject of a detailed study by Wenzel (1994). The following brief extract is from a sermon preserved in an early fifteenth-century manuscript:

---

[11] See for instance Trotter (2010) for illustration and investigation of these issues. Compare also Schendl (forthcoming), Schendl and Wright (2011a).

> Dixi eciam quod venit et **doith** omni die **by grace of þe godhede**. Karissimi, debetis intelligere quod **it farith** per graciam Dei **as it doith** per solem.[12]

Wenzel suggests, controversially, that such sermons should be taken essentially at face value, as evidence for mixed-language preaching, in a variety in which code switching from Latin to the vernacular was commonplace, and perhaps in some cases exploited for rhetorical effect.[13]

To turn finally to another sort of multilingual document, the following is a short extract from a letter of 1403 from Richard Kingston to King Henry IV, cited by Schendl (forthcoming).[14] The letter begins in Anglo-French, switches to English, and then reverts to Anglo-French. This may therefore seem a very straightforward sort of mixed-language text, in which Anglo-French and English occur in neatly demarcated sections, and can be treated quite separately. However, the reality seems to be rather more complicated than this. The passage I quote here comprises the last sentence of the first part in French, followed by the section in English:

> Mon tressouveraigne et tresredoute Seignour. [...] please a vostre tresgracieuse Seignourie entendre que a jourduy, apres noo[ne] [...] q'ils furent venuz deinz nostre countie pluis de CCCC des les rebelz de Owyne, Glyn, Talgard, et pluseours autres rebelz [...] Qar, mon tresredoute Seigneur, vous trouverez pour certein que si vous ne venez en vostre propre persone pour attendre [apres] voz rebelx en Galys, vous ne trouverez un gentil que veot attendre deinz vostre dit Countee.
>
> War fore, for Goddesake, thinketh on ȝour beste Frende, God, and thanke Hym as He hath deserved to ȝowe; and leveth nought that ȝe ne come for no man that may counsaille ȝowe the contrarie; for, [...] the Walshmen supposen and trusten that ȝe schulle nought come there, ... And that hit plese ȝowe of ȝour hegh Lordeship for to have me excused of my comynge to ȝowe, [...] for to with stande the malice of the Rebelles this day.[15]

---

[12] Wenzel (1994) 125; the emboldening of vernacular words is Wenzel's. Wenzel translates: 'I have further said that he comes to people and does so every day through the grace of his godhead. Beloved, you must understand that it goes with the grace of God as it does with the sun.'

[13] On different views on this topic see Schendl and Wright (2011b) 25.

[14] Also cited in Schendl (2002) 254–6.

[15] Translated by Hingeston (1860) 155–9 as: 'My most sovereign and most dread Lord, may it please your most gracious Lordship to consider that to day, after noon [...] there were come into our county more than four hundred of the rebels of Owen, Glynn, Talgard, and many other rebels besides [...] For, my most dread Lord, you will find for certain that, if you do not come in your own person to await your rebels in Wales, you will not find a single gentleman that will stop in your said county. Wherefore, for God's

As Schendl notes, the use of *Rebelles* in the part of the letter written in English is particularly interesting. *rebel* is recorded earlier in English, but in the general meaning 'person who or thing which resists authority or control', and, as noted by *OED3*, 'esp[ecially] in early use with reference to a person who resists divine or spiritual authority'. The meaning shown here, 'person who refuses allegiance or obedience to, or who fights against, an established government or ruler', is first attested slightly later in English contexts, *c.* 1425. This presents a very interesting possibility. We appear to have a new first attestation for this particular meaning in English, but in the context of a multilingual letter in which Anglo-French *rebelle* has just been used three times in exactly the same way. As Schendl observes:

On the basis of the dictionary evidence, it might be justified to classify *rebelles* in the English context as a code-switch back into French, taking up the closely preceding multiple use of the term in the French text. This is, in my view, an impressive example of how a mixed-language text may reflect the dynamic process of lexical integration of French lexemes into English: first, as in the present letter, as a switch in a bilingual text (or in bilingual speech), later, however, as an increasingly established borrowing. This is further support for the increasingly held view that code-switching and borrowing are not distinct phenomena for multilingual speakers, but rather form a continuum.

The debate surrounding code switching is complex and somewhat fraught,[16] even without the added complicating factors concerning how we identify code switching in historical texts. However, it is clear that an examination of multilingual practice is key to understanding many developments in the lexical history of Middle English.

sake, think on your best friend, God, and thank Him, as He hath deserved of you; and leave nought that you do not come for no man that may counsel you the contrary: for, [...] the Welshmen suppose and trust that you shall not come there, ... And that it please you of your high Lordship to have me excused of my coming to you, [...] for to withstand the malice of the rebels this day.'

[16] Compare section 1.2.2 and references given there.

Conclusions to part V

Lexical borrowing in the Middle English period is of crucial importance both for the lexis of Middle English and for the later lexical history of English. In chapters 14 and 16 we will look at some of the long-lasting impact on the structure of semantic fields, and at the exploitation of lexical variation for stylistic effect and for the development of new stylistic and technical registers. We will also look at the often very slow process by which borrowed words gain in frequency and become more fully embedded in the borrowing language, developing or acquiring new meanings, giving rise to new compound or derivative formations, and spreading to different registers. In the present summary we will concentrate instead on what generalizations can be drawn about the chronology and the circumstances of the borrowing.

As sketched in section 11.2, the period from the Norman Conquest to 1500 saw many very significant shifts in patterns of language use in England (and in other parts of Britain). French monolingualism among the ruling elite was almost certainly at its most widespread in the post-Conquest late Old English period, in which we still find very few loanwords from French in our (very limited) English sources. Many more French loanwords are found in the early Middle English period and it is quite likely that some of these may be attributable to language shift from French to English by some members of the elite, although other explanations are also very plausible. However, by all measures the later Middle English period seems at least as significant for borrowing from French as earlier Middle English, even when the focus is narrowed to words realizing basic meanings, or to words that have become high-frequency items in later English. When, as in Fig. 12.7 in section 12.1.2, we adjust the figures to reflect the numbers of loanwords as a proportion of the numbers of all new words recorded per fifty-year period (as a corrective for the uneven chronological distribution of the surviving texts) it is the sub-period 1300–50 that stands out as by far the most prominent for the borrowing of loanwords solely from French. When loanwords that may be from French and/or Latin, and loanwords solely from Latin are also taken into account, the period after 1300 comes to appear much more significant than the period before 1300, and the late fourteenth century and the fifteenth century come more sharply into focus as a key period for borrowing of loanwords.

  If we try to map these observations to contemporary changes in language use in society, it is the changes in the range of uses of English, especially in technical functions and in the mundane record-keeping of the business world, that begin to appear of central importance, at least as much as the earlier shift in first language by the majority of the ruling elite. Until the late fourteenth century Anglo-French seems to have been acquired in early childhood and with a near-native proficiency by an important and influential component of society, as a language of business and professional life. The decline of Anglo-French in these uses appears to be closely linked to the increase in French loanwords in English. Similarly, the spread of English in official and professional functions is inextricably linked with the wider picture of borrowing from both French and Latin. The complex linguistic history of medieval England involves many intricate stories of interaction between languages, but certainly not the least important among them is the late medieval increase in the use of English as a language for government, the law, business, religious discourse, and many other aspects of cultural and intellectual life. This is a process in which our written records doubtless in many instances lag considerably behind spoken use, but nonetheless it is clear that any account that neglects to pay close attention to the last two Middle English centuries as well as the first two will miss many developments of key importance for the lexical history of English.

Part VI

Loanwords into English after 1500; How Borrowing has Affected the Lexicon

Introduction to part VI

The final three chapters deal with two distinct but closely interrelated topics. Firstly, they look at new loanwords after 1500, and at trends that can be traced in lexical borrowing in Early and Later Modern English. Secondly, they look at some ways in which the long-term effects of loanwords on the overall shape of the vocabulary of English can be traced.

The part on loanwords after 1500 is itself divided into two chapters, the first dealing with loanwords from Latin and French, and the second with loanwords from other sources, concentrating on a selection of cases. This division is partly because the volume of borrowings from Latin and French is greater than from other sources, especially in Early Modern English, but also because the patterns over time are very different.

In the late sixteenth and seventeenth centuries, borrowing from Latin reached its zenith in terms of absolute numbers of new words recorded in a very large dictionary such as the *OED*, but new borrowings had nothing like the long-term effect on the high-frequency or basic vocabularies of English that earlier ones had. Very many of the new loanwords are restricted in register, to more formal language or (increasingly in the eighteenth and nineteenth centuries) to scientific or technical vocabularies; indeed, the formal and technical registers of English that develop in this period are

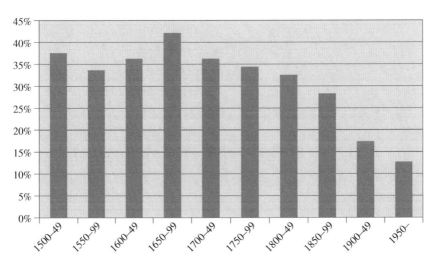

Fig. VI.1 Loanwords as a proportion of all new words.

largely characterized by their use of Latinate vocabulary. French continued to contribute considerable numbers of new loanwords, but these constituted nothing like the proportion of all new words that they did in Middle English. In the nineteenth and twentieth centuries, although new loanwords from French and (especially in the language of the sciences) Latin remain numerous, they do not make up anything like the same proportion of all new loanwords in English as in earlier centuries. (This picture would, however, be rather different if all scientific words formed from elements ultimately of Latin origin were taken into account. These have shown a remarkable expansion from the nineteenth century onwards, as have formations from elements ultimately of Greek origin. See sections 14.8 and 14.9 on the approach taken to such words in this book.)

Fig. VI.1 shows how the proportion of all new words in English that are loanwords has changed in each fifty-year period from 1500 to the present day, as reflected by *OED3* data (drawing on A–ALZ and M–RZ, and collapsing the period before 1150 together). The overall picture appears to be one of fairly steep decline in modern times, especially in the late nineteenth and twentieth centuries. However, the picture is rather different if, as in Fig. VI.2, we separate loanwords from Latin and French from loanwords from other sources. If we do this, it becomes clear that the decline in the proportion of all new words that are loanwords is largely due to a very steep

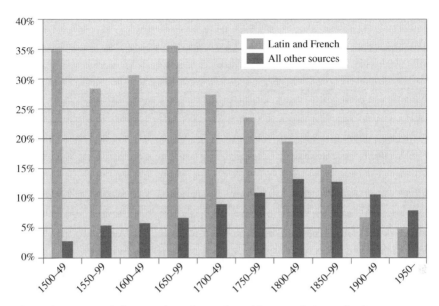

Fig. VI.2 Loanwords from Latin and French, and loanwords from all other sources, as a proportion of all new words.

decline in the numbers of loanwords from Latin and French, even though Latin and French remain the biggest single donor languages even in modern times. The proportion of all new words that are borrowed from other languages has in fact shown an upward trend over a long historical perspective, although it too appears to have declined somewhat from a nineteenth-century peak in the course of the twentieth century.

This long-term picture becomes even more striking if the Middle English period is taken into account as well: in Middle English, if we leave aside borrowings from early Scandinavian (which are difficult to date with precision, as explored in part IV) and from the Celtic languages (which are few in number, as explored in chapter 5), almost all loanwords from other languages appear to have been mediated through French or Latin: the one major exception not yet looked at in this book is Dutch and its close relation Low German, which we will look at in section 15.2.1.

In the Early Modern period, English gradually becomes receptive to loans from a wider range of other European languages (especially from Romance languages other than French, as we will investigate in section 15.2). Over subsequent centuries, with the advent of the colonial era and of direct trading links with a much broader range of nations and cultures, it begins to receive loanwords from a huge variety of languages from many different corners of the globe. However, as the range of donor languages has greatly broadened, the patterns of borrowing shown by English have become much less remarkable, from a typological perspective, than what is found in Middle English. Gradually, English has shifted to a pattern of borrowing that is more typical among the languages of the world: new words continue to be borrowed as new things or concepts are encountered, or as a result of the particular prestige of a certain foreign-language culture in a particular sphere; if a new thing or concept becomes central to daily life, a borrowed word may also become commonplace, for instance *potato*, *tomato* (both from South American languages via other European languages), or today even *sushi* (from Japanese) in many English-speaking communities. However, it is only rarely the case in modern English that a newly borrowed word replaces an existing word as the usual referent for a particular meaning. Also, since relatively few modern loanwords have entered the common core of the vocabulary, any assessment of the rate of borrowing of new loanwords in modern English, or of the relative numbers of words borrowed from different languages, will vary according to whose English we are examining: for instance, New Zealand English has many Maori loanwords not found elsewhere, while South African English has loanwords from many different donor languages that have not (yet) spread to other varieties of English; at the same time, the vocabulary of people belonging to various social or cultural groups will share many loanwords that cut across the boundaries between different world varieties of English (compare section 1.5 on the vocabulary of wine lovers, for instance).

The final chapter will seek to illustrate and investigate this gradual shift through an examination of change in some basic areas of the English lexicon over a very long historical perspective. It will look at how earlier borrowings have in many cases only very slowly established themselves as the usual referent in core meanings. It will also examine how more recent borrowings (many of them still either directly or indirectly from Latin) have typically led to enrichment of semantic fields, making it possible to draw more nuanced distinctions of meaning, or to signal differences of register or stylistic level through vocabulary selection, but have not typically led to replacement of existing lexical items.

In these last three chapters, even more than in preceding ones, it will only be possible to touch upon some of the most important aspects of lexical borrowing across a long period of more than five hundred years, in which

English has shown a remarkable expansion in its number of speakers and in their global geographical spread. This is all the more the case since new loanwords in this period have had relatively little impact on the common core vocabulary, certainly in comparison with the radical changes of the Middle English period. Since 1500 the most dramatic changes have involved the expansion of the lexical resources of English and the exploitation of these resources for realizing differences of meaning or of stylistic register, as well as in the borrowing of new words to denote things and concepts that had not previously been named in English. These are all developments characterized by large volumes of new words, and hence in a study of this scale they cannot be treated exhaustively, and can only be investigated through some test cases.

14

Borrowing from Latin and French after 1500

14.1 The development of written English after 1500

From the advent of the age of printing (introduced in Britain in the 1470s) and especially from the late sixteenth century onwards, the nature of our evidence for tracing the linguistic history of English changes dramatically. There is an enormous amount of data from printed books. Nearly all of this data reflects a particular variety of written English, based largely on the usage of London and surrounding areas, which formed the foundation of modern standard English.[1] The descendant of this variety is employed in formal writing with remarkably little variation around the world today.

The portrait of the development of the lexicon of English presented by the *OED* indicates a remarkable increase in the number of new words recorded in this period. This may in part be a reflection of the multiplication in sources of data, although, as we will see in section 14.1.3, there is no simple correlation between the numbers of new words recorded and the numbers of books published in any given year. Indeed, there are other reasons for thinking it very unlikely that a large proportion of the words first encountered in Early Modern English sources could have existed in Middle English without being detected: we do not find the sorts of large-scale disparities in dates of attestation within word groups that would be expected if there were major problems with our evidence base. In this period first dates of

---

[1] For a short overview of the key developments in the Early Modern period, see Nevalainen (2006).

attestation must still be treated with great caution, but the overall picture of very considerable lexical expansion in Early Modern English is not seriously in doubt.

As reflected by Fig. 2.5 in section 2.1, there is a dramatic bulge in the overall numbers of new words recorded in the *OED* from approximately 1550 to 1700. There is then a significant drop in the eighteenth century (which we will look at in more detail in section 14.1.3), followed by a new, even greater peak in the nineteenth and twentieth centuries. There are many complex factors lying behind these patterns, but probably the most important are the expanding functions of written English and stylistic factors affecting how English was written.

14.1.1 The expanding functions of English; changes in relationships between writing in English, Latin, and French

During the Early Modern period, English came to be used as a written language in an increasing range of functions, especially as a language of learning and of religious discourse. In many respects, this built on developments already found in the late Middle English period.

Very gradually, the vernacular came to replace Latin as a language of publication for the learned. This process was slow, because Latin retained the very significant advantages of being both prestigious and understood by scholars internationally. On the other side of the coin, the vernacular was readily accessible to a wider readership within the English-speaking community and was the native language of authors, rather than being a language acquired through education. See section 14.1.4 for some of the debate about lexis that these developments sparked.

For a long time, English (and other European vernaculars) also stood rather in the shade of French as the most prestigious among the vernacular languages. We can see this, for instance, in the frequency with which Early Modern English translations of the Greek and Latin classics used existing French translations as an aid (either by choice or through force of circumstances).[2] In the Early Modern period, French still also had an important role as a cultural mediator of influences from much of the rest of the world for Anglophone society. Although the number of loanwords directly from other European languages increases and some loans begin to be found

---

[2] Compare Braden (2010) 96–7, Carver (2010) 360–1.

directly from languages outside Europe as trade and colonialism opened up new and wider perspectives (as will be explored in chapter 15), still French acted as an important window on the wider world for England, as shown by the high number of loans from other Romance languages that are mediated through French. In the areas of high culture and technical knowledge, this was often a result of mediation of knowledge through French-language texts: compare section 15.2.4 on Italian words entering English via French in the sixteenth and seventeenth centuries, for example.

In Later Modern English, an important factor is the explosion of French publications in the natural sciences and other areas of technical knowledge in the eighteenth and nineteenth centuries, followed in the later nineteenth century by a similar explosion of scholarly and technical publications in German. The modern dominance of English as the first choice language for publication in most areas of scholarship is a much more recent phenomenon; in the nineteenth century English still, on the whole, came a rather clear third to French and German for the reporting of important results in international scholarship.

14.1.2 Stylistic developments in the written language

Intricately connected with the history of the functions of English is the history of style, as modes of expression in written English (both literary and technical) developed.

The stylistic bias towards Latinate diction already evident in what is termed the 'aureate' style of the fifteenth century laid the foundations for the dominant Renaissance styles of the sixteenth and first half of the seventeenth centuries.[3] The enormous prestige of Latinate forms is reflected by the extent to which earlier borrowings were replaced by new ones that were of more clearly Latinate form. This is shown most notably by the frequent replacement of earlier borrowings from a French or Latin present tense stem with new formations from the Latin past participial stem (typically in -*ate*), and also in the respelling of earlier borrowings to conform more closely to (sometimes mistaken) Latin etymons (see sections 14.2, 14.3).

---

[3] On the aureate style, see especially Burnley (1992), Blake (1992a), Adamson (1999); on lexical developments in Early Modern English in general, see Nevalainen (1999); on the development of the literary language from the late fifteenth century through to the present day, see the masterly two-part study of Adamson (1999, 1998).

However, there were also important forces at play in the rhetorical norms of the period. The most highly valued quality overall was 'copy' (Latin *cōpia* 'abundance, plenty, fullness in expression'), reflected in such stylistic features as pairing of near or full synonyms (which became so ubiquitous that sets of three or more equivalents were often resorted to for real emphasis), or playing on various etymologically related words within a passage. This dominant factor in the rhetorical style of the period, coupled with the enormous prestige of Latinate word forms, may help explain the very high density of Latin loanwords in this period. Many of the new loanwords were very rare words, often slight variants on existing loanwords, and hence eminently exploitable in the thirst for highly demonstrative 'copy' in the employment of language.

From approximately the mid seventeenth century there is a significant shift in the most favoured styles in writing: the strong prestige of Latinate lexis remains, but in a context where variation is less favoured than classicism and lucidity. As detailed by Adamson (1999), the earlier emphasis on *cōpia* or 'copy' was succeeded by a new emphasis on *perspicuitās* or 'perspicuity', where clarity of expression was prized more highly than piling up multiple synonyms or playing on the derivational or etymological relationships among a group of words. Very interestingly, though, a significant decline in the numbers of new words recorded is not found until somewhat later, in the eighteenth century. This is an intriguing phenomenon that would benefit from much more detailed study, beyond the scope of this book: very probably two major factors are the continuing growth of specialist technical vocabulary and of distinct stylistic registers (on which see the test cases in chapter 16), and the further growth of existing word families (compare section 14.5).

In the eighteenth century the continuing prestige of classicism was coupled with a strong impulse towards codification, reflected in grammars and dictionaries. As already noted, the eighteenth century shows a considerable dip in the numbers both of loanwords and of new words of all origins, as reflected by the *OED* (compare Fig. 2.5 in section 2.1, and Figs VI.1 and VI.2 in the introduction to part VI). (See section 14.1.3 for the reasons for thinking that this does reflect a genuine trend in the history of English lexis, at least as represented by the surviving evidence, rather than simply, as often suggested, reflecting factors to do with the compilation of the *OED*.)

Concurrent with these changing fashions in literary and rhetorical style went the development of increasingly differentiated registers in English lexis. Frequent use of Latinate lexis is often one of the key markers differentiating more formal and elevated styles of language from the informal and the everyday. Additionally, registers specific to particular topics of discourse, e.g. medical or scientific, have their own developing technical vocabularies, and typically draw directly or indirectly on the lexical resources of Latin in order to name specific phenomena or processes. They also have their own typical stylistic characteristics, where a bias towards Latinate lexis often predominates. Both phenomena at least in part reflect the switch from the use of Latin in writing about such topics.

In the nineteenth century there was an enormous expansion in technical vocabulary, corresponding to the rapid expansion of new fields of scientific and technical research. There is a focus on developing expanded and more precise terminologies and nomenclatures, especially in describing the natural world. The nineteenth-century peaks in borrowings from Latin and Greek are very largely attributable to the exploitation of words and word-forming elements from Latin and Greek in the development of new technical vocabulary. Borrowings from French and German in this period are also dominated by technical words, mostly formed from elements ultimately of Latin or Greek origin. How such words are classified makes a very considerable difference to the overall totals of borrowings from each source in this period: section 14.8 will discuss in detail the approach taken in *OED3* and in this book. In the twentieth century and beyond the coining of new technical vocabulary continues at a rapid pace, mostly using word-forming elements ultimately of Latin or Greek origin, but increasingly the words themselves are formed within English on the model of other existing words showing the same elements, and often in meanings rather different from those that the same elements have in Latin or Greek. In the framework adopted in *OED3* and in this book, such words are not regarded as showing loanwords, for reasons that will be examined in detail in section 14.9.

Alongside these developments in technical vocabulary, the nineteenth century is pivotal in a further shift in the patterns of lexical borrowing in English. In the Early Modern period new loanwords from Latin or French typically belong to more formal registers and are crucial to the development of distinct formal registers in the lexis. This association with formal registers remains the case for new Latin loanwords in Later Modern English, except that they now more often carry overt connotations of technicality or precision rather than of polite or literary formality. In the same time period, borrowing from French gradually becomes much more similar to borrowing from any other modern language and much more clearly distinct from borrowing from Latin. French loanwords continue to outnumber those from any other modern vernacular, but, once we put to one side those loanwords that reflect the use of French (like German and English) as one of the international languages of scholarship, a large proportion of the new loanwords belong to semantic areas where French culture has particular influence or prestige, or can be seen to be motivated by attempts to reference the general air of sophistication perceived to be associated with all things French. The period of radical reshaping of the lexis of English through new loanwords from French is clearly over by the nineteenth century and, accordingly, French loanwords of the last two hundred years will be considered alongside those from German, Italian, Spanish, etc. in chapter 15.

14.1.3 A re-examination of the data surveyed in chapter 2 in light of these factors

The factors so far considered in this chapter help explain the patterns shown by graphs that were looked at briefly in section 2.1. Here we look more closely at the data in two of these graphs for the period from 1300 to the present day.

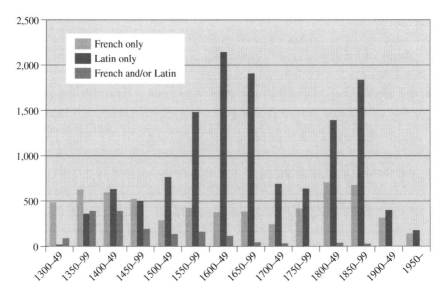

Fig. 14.1 Loanwords from French, Latin, and French and/or Latin in parts of *OED3* so far completed, arranged chronologically, 1300–present.

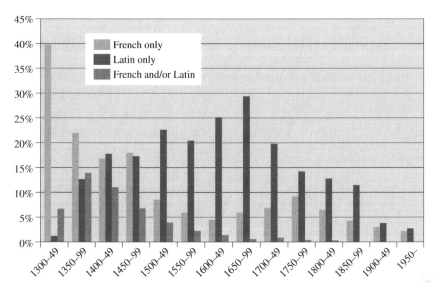

Fig. 14.2 Loanwords from French, Latin, and French and/or Latin as a proportion of all new words, as reflected by parts of *OED3* so far completed, 1300–present.

The data in Figs 14.1 and 14.2 tell very different stories for French and Latin. If we begin with French, the absolute totals in Fig. 14.1 show a complex picture of relatively small variations. If we include words from French and/or Latin, then the period 1350–1450 shows a clear peak in the absolute totals, but not very dramatically ahead of the totals found in the nineteenth century. However, when we look at borrowings from French (and from French and/or Latin) as a proportion of all new words, as shown in Fig. 14.2, there is a clear falling away after 1500. From the mid sixteenth century onwards the proportion fluctuates either side of 5%, reaching its highest point in the second half of the eighteenth century. From the mid nineteenth century onwards it begins to fall away rather dramatically. It is interesting that there does not appear to be any close correlation between the totals of new loanwords from French and the sporadic but large-scale immigration of Huguenots to England, especially to Kent and London, from the mid sixteenth century to a peak in the late seventeenth century, as well as to other predominantly English-speaking areas in the Americas and elsewhere; any numerical reflection of borrowing from this large community of French native speakers appears to be drowned out by the constant influence of French culture and French learning from across the Channel. Another factor is probably that there was intermittent but

cumulatively substantial immigration from various French-speaking communities, both in France and e.g. in parts of the Spanish Netherlands,
throughout the Early Modern period.[4]

The absolute totals of loanwords from Latin in Fig. 14.1 show rather
more dramatic fluctuations. By far the largest absolute totals are in the
periods 1550–1649 and 1800–99. The high nineteenth-century figures need
to be approached with caution for two reasons. Firstly, most of these Latin
loanwords belong to the language of science, and the vast majority have had
little or no impact outside very specific specialist vocabularies. As already
touched upon, the majority of these words show deliberate coinages by
modern scientists, drawing on the lexical resources of Latin (and Greek)
in order to supply suitable names for newly encountered or identified
phenomena. As we will explore further in section 14.8, their status as
loanwords is problematic and they must stand somewhat to one side from
the main narrative of this book. A large proportion of the nineteenth-
century (and eighteenth- and twentieth-century) loanwords from French
also belong to the language of science, reflecting the status of French as one
of the international languages of scientific publication in this key period of
expansion of scientific research. See further sections 14.8 and 15.2.8 on this.

The second reason for caution in approaching the figures for nineteenth-
century loanwords from Latin becomes clear if we look again at Fig. 14.2,
where the total of Latin loanwords as a proportion of all new words in fact
shows a decline from the eighteenth century, as part of a gradual decline
from a peak of 27% in the second half of the seventeenth century to merely
2% in the second half of the twentieth century.

It is also notable in both Figs 14.1 and 14.2 that, although words that may
be from French and/or Latin continue to be found beyond 1500, they
become much less significant numerically. As we will see in sections 14.3
and 14.4, this at least partly correlates with an increasing preference for
word forms of distinctly Latinate form in the Early Modern period.

This data is all derived from the *OED*, specifically from those parts of
OED3 so far completed (and more specifically the contiguous alphabetical
ranges A–ALZ and M–RZ). A question that has been long debated is
whether this sort of data could be telling us more about the circumstances
of the *OED*'s compilation and the decisions made by its editors than it does

---

[4] Compare Lambley (1920) for a detailed study of the impact of French speakers on
various different levels of English society during the sixteenth and seventeenth centuries.

about the historical growth and development of the vocabulary of English. In particular, Schäfer (1980 53) found striking similarities between the pattern of first dates in the first edition of the *OED* and the numbers of works from each year cited as sources in the *OED*'s bibliography. However, as Schäfer himself acknowledged, the bibliography in the first edition of the *OED* was not at all comprehensive. Before we return to this question of what the *OED* did or did not read, it will be useful to get an overview of the surviving sources of data for this period. We can get a comprehensive picture of this from the *English Short Title Catalogue* (*ESTC*), which seeks to record all books published in English before 1800, drawing on data from a number of major research projects. The graph in Fig. 14.3 shows the overall pattern.[5] With the interesting exception of some turbulent peaks and troughs in the mid to late seventeenth century, these figures show a fairly steady, and very dramatic, increase over time. A comparison with Fig. 2.5 in section 2.1 is very instructive. The very high levels of new words with first dates of 1550–1699 in comparison with the much lower totals for

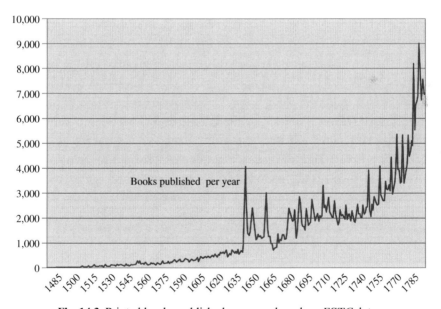

Fig. 14.3 Printed books published per year, based on *ESTC* data.

[5] Data taken from <http://estc.ucr.edu/stcdates.html>. See also <http://estc.ucr.edu/ESTCStatistics.html> for a series of very useful detailed charts based on this data.

1500–49 and 1700–99 does not correspond at all closely to the graph for publication of printed sources. In particular, even if we allow for the non-survival of a good deal of earlier material, it is clear that the eighteenth century did not see a dip in the production of new books, corresponding to the dip in first attestations of new words. The *ESTC* data only goes up to 1800, but after 1800 the volume of printed material continues to increase very dramatically.

Thus we can be fairly happy that the *OED*'s pattern of peaks and troughs in numbers of new words recorded for each year does not simply map the availability of sources for reading for the dictionary. However, it could still be the case, theoretically, that the patterns shown by the *OED* reflect over-emphasis on some periods or neglect of others in the reading underlying the *OED*'s compilation: in addition to Schäfer's comments on Early Modern English, similar suggestions have often been made with regard to documentation for the eighteenth century in the *OED*.[6] In this context, it is important to note that my figures are drawn from *OED3*, which has mostly been compiled in the era of vast text databases for English post-1500. *OED3* can now draw on *Early English Books Online* (*EEBO*) and *Eighteenth-Century Collections Online* (*ECCO*) in the search for first examples of words, and additionally its reading of Middle English sources is complemented by the independent reading of sources conducted for the *MED*. In particular, *ECCO* makes a huge proportion of the surviving eighteenth-century material available in searchable form and it has been drawn on in research for *OED3* since 2004;[7] Google Books now also offers access to very extensive collections of eighteenth-century material, if approached with due caution. Use of these resources is making it possible to antedate some existing *OED* words to the eighteenth century and to add some new words with eighteenth-century first dates, but it appears to remain the case that there are fewer new words recorded in eighteenth-century sources than in those from either the seventeenth century or the nineteenth. Fig. 14.4 shows data from one of the most recently completed sections of *OED3*, A–ALZ,

---

[6] For a summary and analysis, see Brewer (2007).

[7] In this context it should be noted in particular that all of the content of *ECCO* is electronically searchable, whereas only a portion of the content of *EEBO* is currently searchable in this way. Thus reliance solely on these tools would if anything lead to an over-representation of eighteenth-century material, although this is in practice largely offset by the *OED*'s other sources of data.

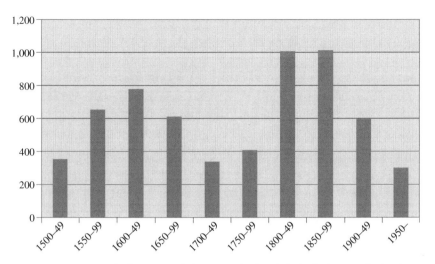

Fig. 14.4 Totals of all new words in *OED3* in the alphabetical range A–ALZ.

which has been worked on making careful use of *ECCO*, Google Books, and other resources; a clear dip in the eighteenth century is still found.

Thus, it seems likely that we can approach *OED3*'s data on the numbers of new words found in each period as a reasonably faithful reflection of what is shown by the surviving sources of data for each period, certainly post-1500. Our surviving data is less extensive for the Middle English period and we do not have text databases like *EEBO* to enable us to search the same proportion of the surviving material, but, as already noted in section 14.1, there are good reasons for supposing that the picture of increased growth in the lexis of English post-1500 is not an entirely false one. (Compare also the discussion of the dating of Middle English words in 12.1.2.)

Of course, the data looked at so far in this section takes no account of the penetration of loanwords into the high-frequency vocabulary of modern English, or into its basic vocabulary. It is when we take these perspectives into account that the differences between borrowing pre- and post-1500 become really dramatic, as already seen in sections 2.2 and 2.3.

In the high-frequency data from the *BNC* examined in section 2.2, seventy-three of the words borrowed from French, Latin, or French and/or Latin are first attested later than 1500. This is only 15% of the total. Even this figure is in need of some qualification: many of the first dates are from *OED2* and may well be antedated considerably in *OED3*; additionally, approximately 40% of these words belong to word families that already had some presence in Middle English. Thus *national* is first attested in 1581, but the base word in its family, *nation*, is first attested in *c.*1330; a similar situation holds for e.g. *central* (earlier *centre*), *association* (earlier *associate* verb), *procedure* (earlier *proceed*), and *success* (earlier *succeed*). On such growth of word families through continuing borrowing and through derivational processes within English, see further section 14.5. In a different pattern, *describe* is preceded by *descrive* (and also *description*), *basis* by *base*, and *fact* (found earliest in the sense 'deed') by *feat*. In cases like these, the later Latinate borrowing acts to some extent as a substitute for an earlier cognate and broadly synonymous French loanword. However, it is likely that many of the earlier borrowings have only very gradually come to be high-frequency words in English (see section 14.7).

The data based on analysis of the *WOLD* basic meaning list in Fig. 2.10 in section 2.3 shows an even more dramatic dropping off after 1500, with only 4% of the loanwords being first attested later than this. However, it is only in the period after 1500 that many of the earlier borrowings have come to be the usual realization of a particular basic meaning in English (see further chapter 16). It is possible that the same future could ultimately await more of the words borrowed after 1500, although it is clear that most of the major realignments in existing semantic fields as a result of borrowing from Latin and French belong to the Early Modern period or earlier.

14.1.4 Attitudes towards loanwords in English

From the Early Modern period onwards there is much more information available on attitudes towards loanwords in English, in the form of comments from contemporaries. Such comment surviving from the sixteenth and seventeenth centuries is particularly important for the light that it sheds on a period of very rapid growth and change in the vocabulary of English, and also for the possibility that such attitudes may have had an impact on borrowing patterns.

In the sixteenth century there are comments from neologizers justifying their adoption of new words, usually on the basis that English requires them in order to address new subject matter; some of the earliest and best known are from the humanist scholar and diplomat Sir Thomas Elyot in the early 1530s. Such comment forms part of a larger debate about the appropriate functions of

English as a written language.[8] Slightly later, there are also some purists, who sought to use loanwords sparingly; perhaps most famously, the staunch Protestant, royal tutor, and first regius professor of Greek at the University of Cambridge, Sir John Cheke, made use of many derivatives or adaptations of either native or long-established words in place of ultimately Latin or Greek loanwords in his translation of the New Testament in the early 1550s, using for example *wisards* (i.e. *wizards*) rather than *magi*, *crossed* rather than *crucified*, *tollers* rather than *publicans* (i.e. tax-gatherers), or *hunderder* (i.e. *hundreder*) rather than *centurion*, although many relatively recent loanwords do also occur in his translation.[9]

   A particular focus of debate in the second half of the sixteenth and early seventeenth centuries is around what were termed inkhorn terms, essentially newfangled words, with the focus very clearly on loanwords. One important document is Thomas Wilson's *Art of Rhetorique* (1560), in which he comments:

> Among all other lessons this should first be learned, that wee neuer affect any straunge ynkehorne termes, but to speake as is commonly receiued.

Wilson singles out French and Italian loanwords for particular comment:

> He that commeth lately out of Fraunce, will talke French English and neuer blush at the matter. An other chops in with English Italienated, and applieth the Italian phrase to our English speaking.

Of course, at this date it is impossible for Wilson to avoid the use of many earlier borrowings, such as *affect, strange, common, receive* in the first sentence quoted here, and there is not the slightest indication that this is what he or his contemporaries actually had in mind; in fact, he makes the point himself that words such as *communion* or *prerogative* have enriched the language. As an example of the style he disapproves of, Wilson offers a letter that is probably his own invention, but is described as 'a letter deuised by a Lincolneshire man, for a voyde benefice, to a gentleman that then waited vpon the Lorde Chauncellour'. The first sentence is:

---

   [8] An excellent account is provided by Barber (1997) 42–102. Very useful analysis and reproductions of extracts from many of the key texts are provided by Görlach (1991).

   [9] For a careful account, placing Cheke and other purists in their national and international intellectual contexts, see Gray (1988).

> Pondering, expending, and reuoluting with my selfe, your ingent affabilitie, and ingenious capacity for mundaine affaires: I cannot but celebrate, & extol your magnifical dexteritie aboue all other.

Unfortunately, it is impossible to be certain which Wilson intends to be the most egregious inkhorn terms in this letter. A thorough and very useful analysis is provided by Barber (1997 57–60), based chiefly on a comparison with the *OED*'s data for each word. Nearly all of the words are found in other texts, but some are recorded earliest in this letter. Barber noted that twenty-five of the words in this letter had *OED* first dates later than 1500, and these are probably the likeliest targets of Wilson's criticism: *accersited* adj., *adepted* adj., *adjuvate* v., *antique* adj., *celebrate* v., *clemency* n., *collaud* v., *condisciple* n., *contemplate* v., *dexterity* n., *dominical* adj., *extol* v., *fatigate* v., *frivolous* adj., *illustrate* adj., *impetrate* v., *invigilate* v., *magnifical* adj., *obtestate* v., *panion* n., *revolute* v., *scholastical* adj.,[10] *sublimity* n., *superiority* n., *verbosity* n. (Two of these words, *sublimity* and *superiority*, have now been antedated to before 1500 for *OED3*.) What is most striking is that a number of these words (e.g. *antique, celebrate, contemplate, dexterity*) have become commonplace in modern English; the same is true of many of the words and phrases that are explicitly singled out for criticism by later contributors to the inkhorn debate.[11] On the other hand, some of these words (e.g. *accersited, adjuvate*) appear never to have attained any degree of frequency in English, and are now obsolete. The loanwords in Wilson's letter are nearly all markedly Latinate in form and, notably, there is not one Italian loanword among them, in spite of Wilson's specific mention of Italian. This is also common to several of the other documents from this debate.

It is very hard to tell whether comment of this sort had any major impact on the borrowing of new loanwords into English or on the integration of existing ones. Certainly, purism never attained the importance in Early Modern English that it did in some other Germanic languages in the same period, most notably in German.[12] In seventeenth-century German we often find that a loan formation from native elements largely replaces an earlier loanword: for instance *Mundart* 'dialect' in place of earlier *Dialect*, or *Wörterbuch* 'dictionary' in place of *Lexicon* or *Nomenclator*. Such

---

[10] This is in fact attested once in Middle English as part of a work title.

[11] For examples, see Barber (1997) 60.

[12] For a long perspective, see Geers (2005).

replacement is relatively rare in English. Very probably a major cause of this is the extent to which English had already borrowed from French and Latin during the Middle English period, with the result that many French and Latin derivational endings had not only become very familiar in English but had begun to be employed in forming new words. There was no clear dividing line between new loanwords from French and Latin, and those words that had already become fully established as part of the core vocabulary of English; instead there was a fuzzy border area of moderately frequent words showing derivational suffixes that were already familiar from dozens or even hundreds of other words. However, it is clear from other evidence that the steep increase in new words in this period was keenly felt by language users: for instance, it is notable that the earliest monolingual English dictionaries from the first half of the seventeenth century are all essentially dictionaries of 'hard words', chiefly Latinate loanwords.[13]

Some different, complimentary perspectives can be gained directly from writings of the period. For instance, very often in Shakespeare's plays comic effects derive from characters' failure to use the right word when they attempt to use high-prestige borrowed vocabulary. Typically, the speakers concerned are members of the lower or social orders who are attempting to sound 'grand' or to 'speak up' to social superiors. Often, these Shakespearean instances engage in richer patterns of textual irony, but this does not detract from their significance as indicators of the social and cultural context of loanwords. Compare in *The Merry Wives of Windsor* Mistress Quickly's *alligant* for *elegant* (2.2.65), *speciously* for *specially* (3.4.105, 4.5.104), *erection* for *direction* (3.5.38), or in *Much Ado About Nothing* Dogberry's *desertless* for *deserving* (3.3.9), *senseless* for *sensible* (3.3.22), *comprehend* for *apprehend* (3.3.25), *decern* for *concern* (3.5.3), *odorous* for *odious* (3.5.15), *dissembly* for *assembly* (4.2.1), or *opinioned* for *pinioned* (4.2.66).

The inkhorn debate lost steam in the course of the seventeenth century, but after the Restoration of the Monarchy in 1660 there was new criticism of overuse of French loanwords.[14] Of course, the new king and his closest associates had spent a long period of exile in France and their use of French

---

[13] Compare Béjoint (forthcoming).
[14] See Nevalainen (1999) 359–60, Barber (1997) 62.

is well documented;[15] it is therefore unsurprising that recent Gallicisms provided a focus for social comment. It is interesting that the numbers of new French loanwords recorded in this period show no particular fluctuation; in fact *OED3* records slightly more new French loanwords for the 1650s, under the Commonwealth, than for the 1660s, and the pattern is the same in unrevised parts of the *OED* as well. Probably this is because the Gallicisms that attracted negative comment were emblematic ones representative of the usage of a small social group, against a background of continued borrowing in a wide range of social and cultural contexts. Adverse comment on French loanwords continued in the eighteenth century, with words and phrases such as *opiniatre, sortie, volupty, dernier resort, beaux arts* attracting criticism on the grounds of redundant synonymy;[16] it is notable that these items show widely differing levels of frequency in later English, *sortie* having become common in military use and beyond, while *opiniatre* is now entirely obsolete (although in the eighteenth century it is recorded as adjective, noun, and verb). The figures in Fig. 14.1 show only a very slight fall in the number of new French loanwords in the eighteenth century, compared with a much steeper fall in the number of Latin loanwords. Such criticism continued in the nineteenth century,[17] when the overall figures for loanwords from French are rather higher, although this apparent rise is mostly due to the large number of scientific and technical words that entered English immediately from French, whereas the ire of purists was directed much more at the use of French words in fashionable social discourse.

14.2 Morphological differentiation between Latin and French borrowings

In late Middle English and Early Modern English some new morphological patterns come increasingly to distinguish Latin loanwords from French loanwords. By far the most frequent type are verbs borrowed from the Latin past participial stem, ending in either *-t-* or *-s-*, rather than from the

---

[15] See especially the extensive account from the viewpoint of French linguistic history in Brunot (1917) vol. V, 147–94. However, see also Lambley (1920) on the extent of the knowledge and use of French in court and gentry circles throughout the sixteenth and seventeenth centuries.

[16] See further Nevalainen (1999) 360, Görlach (2001) 162–5.

[17] For discussion and examples, see Görlach (1998), Görlach (1999) 107–11.

present stem, as is typical for earlier borrowings. This pattern developed from the borrowing of Latin past participle forms as participles or adjectives in English, sometimes via French; thus *perfect* verb (*a.*1398, formerly stressed on the first syllable) was preceded by *perfect* adjective (*c.*1300; earliest in the forms *perfit, parfit* < (Anglo-)French); the ultimate etymon is classical Latin *perficere*, with past participial stem *perfect-*.[18] The largest number of these English verbs from Latin past participial stems (about 78% of the total in *OED3*) end in *-ate*, reflecting the most numerous class of verbs in Latin, which end in *-āre*, with past participial stem ending in *-āt-*. Thus *communicate* (1529) is < classical Latin *commūnicāt-*, past participial stem of *commūnicāre*. For formations from other Latin past participial stem types, compare e.g. *infect* (*a.*1387) < classical Latin *infect-*, past participial stem of *inficere*,[19] or *supervise* (1541) < post-classical Latin *supervis-*, past participial stem of *supervidere*. Fig. 14.5 gives the totals for each fifty-year period, as reflected by the parts of *OED3* so far completed (approximately a third of the whole dictionary).

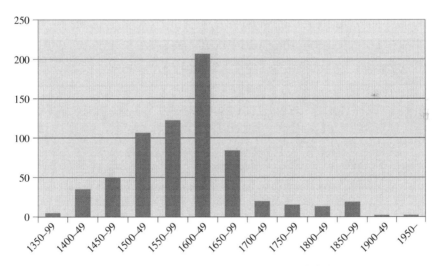

Fig. 14.5 Verbs formed from Latin past participial stems.

[18] Opinions differ on the precise mechanism of this development: see *OED*'s account at *-ate* suffix[3] and also Reuter (1934).

[19] In this instance *infecter* also exists in Middle French, but from roughly the same date as the English verb, and with the various meanings attested in a slightly different chronological sequence, hence it seems very unlikely as primary etymon of the English word.

The total rises fairly steadily from a very low beginning in the second half of the fourteenth century to a peak in the first half of the seventeenth century, before falling again very dramatically. If the totals are compared with the totals for all Latin borrowings in *OED3* given in Fig. 2.4 in section 2.1, it will be seen that the curve is fairly similar for the Early Modern period, i.e. borrowings of this type make up a fairly steady proportion of Early Modern borrowings from Latin. It is in the period 1500–49 that borrowed verbs of this type make up the highest proportion of all loanwords from Latin, constituting approximately 13% of all words from Latin, including those from Latin and/or French, in comparison with 10% in the period 1600–49.

An interesting characteristic of such borrowed verbs is that there are often parallel borrowings ultimately from the present stem of the same Latin verb, often via a distinctive form in French. Typically there is overlap in meaning in early use, after which one form becomes either obsolete or very rare; the survey by Reuter (1936) suggests that overall the survival rate for the past participle types and the present stem types is fairly even, although among the present stem types the survival rate is highest among those attested relatively early, before the past participle type became well established.[20] To take a few examples of doublets, one of which is now either rare or obsolete:

- *subverse* (1590) is a rare later synonym of *subvert* (*a.*1382); likewise *retardate* (1613) beside earlier *retard* (1490), *adaptate* (1638) beside *adapt* (1531), *educt* (1568) beside *educe* (?*a.*1475), or *molestate* (1543) beside *molest* (*a.*1425)
- *abominate* (1597) has a rare earlier synonym *abomine* (*c.*1500); likewise *preponderate* (1611) is preceded by *preponder* (1599 in a corresponding meaning).

When both types survive, the two verbs normally become distinguished in meaning to at least some extent. For example:

- *resonate* (1648) shows considerable semantic overlap in its early history with the doublet *resound* (*c.*1405; < French); likewise *adjudicate* (1655) beside *adjudge* (1399; < French), or *pulsate* (1674) beside *pulse* (?*a.*1425; < Latin).

[20]   See Reuter (1936) 17–18.

Sometimes there is likely to have been no historical overlap:

- *supervise* (1541) was preceded by rare *supervide* (*c.* 1475; probably obsolete before *supervise* was borrowed).
- *pulverate* (1615) was preceded by rare *pulver* (*c.* 1425 in a single attestation), as well as by the now usual *pulverize* (also *c.* 1425, < postclassical Latin *pulverizare*).

In the examples from Wilson's inkhorn letter discussed in 8.2.5, compare *fatigate* and *revolute*: the latter is a rare synonym of *revolve*, a Middle English borrowing, while the former considerably antedates *fatigue* as a verb in English.

In about 20% of the cases reflected by Fig. 4 there is at least one parallel borrowed from the present stem that is earlier than the borrowing from the past participial stem, as reflected by *OED3*'s data. The chronological breakdown of these is given in Fig. 14.6 and is very similar to the overall pattern in Fig. 14.5.

Thus it appears that the early seventeenth century also shows the high-water mark for the formation of verbs from a Latin past participial stem that either replace or compete with an earlier borrowing from the present stem of the same verb.

The next most numerous class of loanwords that show a distinctively Latin form comprises agent-nouns in *-or*, shown by Fig. 14.7. These show a

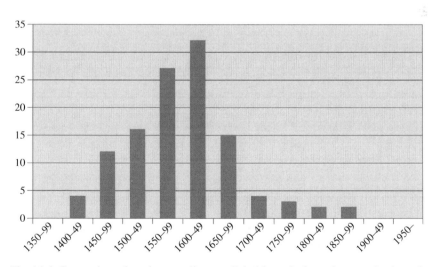

Fig. 14.6 Cases where there is an earlier parallel ultimately from the same Latin verb.

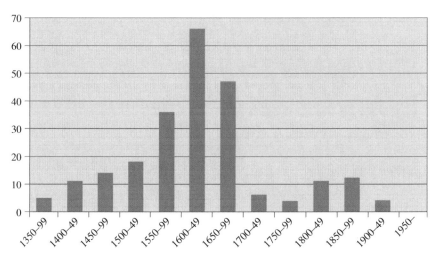

Fig. 14.7 Words ending in *-or* probably borrowed from a Latin word ending in *-or*.

very similar pattern to Fig. 14.5. In approximately 10% of cases there is a related earlier English formation in *-er*, thus *promotor* (1517) is preceded by *promoter* (1384), *reconciliator* (*a*.1567) by *reconciler* (*c*.1531). Since *-or* is a productive suffix in English in this period, often varying with *-er* in parallel formations that could equally be regarded as spelling variants, it is possible that some of the apparently borrowed words in *-or* could in fact be coincidental formations within English, formed on the previously borrowed verb.

After these, the two next most numerous classes are nouns and adjectives borrowed from Latin ending in *-ory* or *-ary* (as opposed to English formations in these elements), which again show a broadly similar chronological pattern (Fig. 14.8), although without a peak in the period 1600–49. Some examples include:

- *minatory* (1532), *promontory* (1548), *reconciliatory* (1581), *adulatory* (1587), *placatory* (*a*.1640);
- *subsidiary* (1543), *processionary* (1597), *supernumerary* (1605), *pulmonary* (1668), *obituary* (1701).

In all of these cases plausible Latin etymons exist and borrowing from Latin is assumed in *OED3*, although in some cases formation within English from earlier borrowings in the same word family cannot be ruled out entirely. Corresponding words in (continental) Middle French and modern

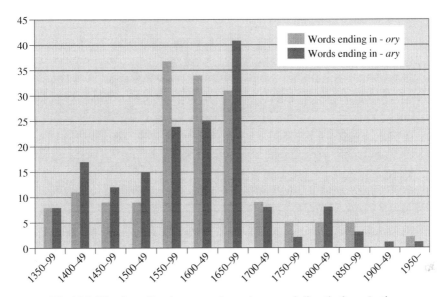

Fig.14.8 Words ending in -*ory* and -*ary* borrowed directly from Latin.

French regularly end in -*oire* or -*aire* (compare sections 11.3.1, 12.2.2), e.g. *minatoire, promontoire, reconciliatoire, adulatoire, subsidiaire, processionaire, supernumeraire, pulmonaire*.

All of these morphological types distinguish Latin loanwords from French ones and they are important in contributing to the increasingly Latinate as opposed to Romance flavour of a good deal of English lexis from the end of the Middle Ages onwards. However, their importance should not be exaggerated, since in no fifty-year period do all of the types examined here combined amount to more than 18% of all words borrowed from Latin.

14.3 Latinate spelling forms and the respelling or remodelling of earlier borrowings

Related to the phenomena discussed in section 14.2, the Early Modern period also sees very frequent remodelling of earlier borrowings after their (ultimate) Latin etymons. This phenomenon is not restricted to this period, nor is it restricted to English: compare the discussion in section 11.3.1 of the many waves of renewed influence from classical Latin on the lexis of French. However, in Early Modern English two factors came together rather powerfully: firstly, the predominating fashion for Latinate word forms, and secondly, the gradual process of narrowing of the repertory of spelling variation found in printed sources. When selections were made for particular form types out of a pool of existing variants, these were typically Latinate ones. For instance, spellings such as *perfeccione* or *perfeccioun* for *perfection*, an early Middle English loanword from (Anglo-)French and Latin, barely survive into the sixteenth century. In this instance a parallel process in French means that *perfection* is also the usual form in Middle French. More radical remodelling is shown by another word in the same family, modern English *perfect*. From the fourteenth century forms such as *perfit*, *parfit* are found (among many others), indicating that the initial borrowing was from (Anglo-)French *perfit*, *parfit*. The Latinate type *perfect* is found only from the middle of the fifteenth century, but predominates by the end of the sixteenth. In this instance modern French has retained an earlier form type, *parfait*.

A similar case is shown by *admonish*. This was borrowed in the fourteenth century as *amonest* < (Anglo-)French *amonester*. The ending was remodelled in the fifteenth century as a result of association with verbs in *-ish* (compare section 11.3.2), which is when we also first find spellings with *ad-*, after the ultimate etymon classical Latin *admonēre* (perhaps also after equivalent forms in Middle French); by the end of the sixteenth century *admonish* and *admonishe* are the only spellings remaining in use in print in England.

Cases of respelling or remodelling cannot always be distinguished with certainty from cases of wholesale replacement. In a case such as *absolve* replacing earlier *assoil* we can be fairly certain that we have a late Middle English borrowing of classical Latin *absolvere* that comes in the course of the Early Modern period to replace entirely both the corresponding (Anglo-)French loanword *assoil* and the semi-Latinized form *absoil*. It is less certain whether we have replacement or remodelling in cases like *describe* coming to be used where *descrive* was previously used (compare section 14.1.3).

It is clear that in many cases change in spelling did not necessarily entail immediate change in pronunciation, especially when the addition of letters or sounds was involved. Modern English *corpse* shows an etymologically motivated respelling of earlier *cors*, *corse*, a Middle English borrowing < (Anglo-)French *cors* (also respelt *corps*) < classical Latin *corpus*. In this case there is abundant evidence in the Early Modern period for pronunciations without /p/ long after *corps* or *corpse* had become the usual spellings;[21] in modern English, *corpse* is distinct in both spelling and pronunciation from the later re-borrowing *corps*, as also in morphology (plural *corpses* beside plural *corps*), but these distinctions did not become well established until the late eighteenth century.

Respelling or remodelling on the basis of false etymological assumptions is not at all uncommon. There are stand-alone cases such as *scissors*, in which the interpolation of *c* in the written form results from etymologically unfounded association with classical Latin *scissor* 'cutter' or its etymon *scindere* 'to cut', whereas the word is in fact a Middle English borrowing (first attested as *cisours*, *sisours*) from a French word ultimately < classical Latin *cīsōrium* (a derivative of *caedere*). Compare similarly the examples of *scent* in section 16.3.2 and of *island* in section 16.3.3.

In other cases etymologically motivated remodelling of a group of words spilled over into analogous remodelling of other words. For instance, Latin words with the prefix *ad-* regularly showed *a-* in Old French, but *ad-* was frequently restored under classicizing influence in both French and English, as for instance in *adventure* (earlier *aventure*); in the case of *advance*, the same remodelling was applied to a word that ultimately reflected an etymon with Latin *ab-*, not *ad-*.[22]

14.4 Affixes of Latin and French origin in English word formation

One of the most profound and far-reaching effects of lexical borrowing from Latin and French is that large numbers of derivational affixes originally of Latin or French origin (or in many cases Latin and French origin) have become naturalized in the derivational system of English, for instance (among very, very many similar examples) *ante-*, *pre-*, *pro-*,[23] *sub-*, *super-*, *-al*, *-ate*, *-ation*, *-ic*, *-ity*, *-ment*; some are ultimately of Greek origin, such as *anti-*, *-ize*, *macro-*, *micro-*, *proto-*. We can say as shorthand that such affixes have been borrowed from Latin, French, or Latin and/or French, but the process is rather different from the borrowing of a loanword. These affixes

---

[21] Compare Dobson (1968) II. §442.

[22] For most of the examples discussed in this section and others like them, see Scragg (1974), although much of the discussion there is rather superficial. Compare also Salmon (1999), Upward and Davidson (2011).

[23] In the meaning 'before' *pro-* reflects a distinct prefix ultimately of Greek origin.

have entered English as a result of a two-part process: firstly, words have been borrowed into English containing the affix; secondly, new words have been formed within English containing the affix, on the model of the borrowed words. (See section 14.9 on the special case presented by formations from neoclassical combining forms in modern English.)

A good example is provided by the suffix *-age*. In (Anglo-)French, *-age* is a noun-forming suffix with a variety of (partly overlapping) functions, forming:

- collective nouns, e.g. *bagage, plumage, potage*;
- nouns denoting the office, function, or condition of the person or class of persons denoted by the base noun, e.g. *baronnage, vassalage, vilainage*;
- nouns of action (from verbs), e.g. *equipage, mariage, portage*;
- nouns denoting charges, taxes, or duties of various kinds, e.g. *murage, pontage*.

Some words show meanings from more than one of these categories, e.g. *baronnage* can also denote barons collectively; *passage* can denote (among many other meanings) 'action of passing' and 'ferry toll'. The French affix is the reflex of Latin *-aticum*, originally the neuter of the adjective-forming suffix *-āticus* (> French *-atique*, English *-atic*), although in the case of many word pairs, such as French *passage* and medieval Latin *passaticum* or French *message* and medieval Latin *messaticum*, it is uncertain whether the Latin word gave rise to the French word or vice versa (i.e. the Latin word could be a medieval formation on the model of the French one). Certainly, the French suffix lies behind the suffix *-agium* that we find frequently in medieval Latin, including in variants such as *passagium* beside *passaticum*.

In English, loanwords ending in *-age* are found from early Middle English, e.g. *heritage, pottage*. In course of time, all of the categories listed here are represented in English by numerous borrowings, including borrowings of all of the French words given as examples here (English *baggage, plumage*, etc.). In very many cases, it is uncertain whether the borrowings into English are from (Anglo-)French words in *-age* or from Latin words in *-agium*, and it is likely that many words had multiple inputs.

Examples of new words in *-age* formed within English are probably found from at least the fifteenth century, e.g. *peerage* and *mockage*. In both of these instances the bases (*peer, mock*) are themselves loanwords from

(Anglo-)French; the reason for assuming that *peerage* and *mockage* were formed in English is that we have no evidence for parallel forms in (Anglo-) French or Latin. It is possible that such examples could come to light and then the assumption that these show English formations would have to be reconsidered. In the multilingual situation of later medieval England certainty can be elusive even in the case of words formed on bases that are etymologically of English origin. For example, *hidage* 'tax assessed at a certain quota for each hide of land' certainly shows as its first element English *hide* 'measure of land' (Old English *hīd*); Latin *hidagium* is found from the twelfth century, and Anglo-French *hidage* from the fourteenth. However, there is no clear evidence for English *hidage* before the fifteenth century. It is hard to believe that it did not exist earlier: there would have been a clear need to refer to the tax in English, and the lack of earlier examples must surely reflect the dominance of Latin and French as languages of record-keeping in medieval England. However, there is no good reason for thinking that the word was formed in English rather than in Latin or French, simply because it has an English word as its base: it was very likely coined in Latin or French in the early post-Conquest period and thence passed into English. A safer example of an English formation may be shown by *barnage*, probably in the meaning 'childhood', found in a single Middle English attestation in the late fourteenth-century alliterative poem *Cleanness*, probably formed on the native word *barn* 'child' and not paralleled in French or Latin.[24]

In the sixteenth and seventeenth centuries new words in *-age* become common and there can be no reasonable doubt that suffixation in *-age* was the origin of many new English words; some typical examples are *ballastage*, *boatage*, *housage*, *manufacturage*, *motherage*, *neighbourage*, *postage*, *raftage*, *suppage*. Even if new evidence comes to light that makes it appear more likely that some individual examples are instead borrowed from or modelled on French or Latin words, the general picture is clear that in this period *-age* frequently formed new English words. Further new examples are also found in later centuries, although gradually the formation of new words in *-age* has become less frequent.

---

[24] There is a useful list of other possible cases in Lloyd (2011) 273, although the inclusion of *outrage* as a possible example of a formation on a native base seems to show a misconception.

This example illustrates some of the key difficulties in the study of borrowing of Latin and French affixes in English, including affixes that are now extremely frequent in English, such as *-ment* or *-ation*. In the discussion of *-age* I have thus far avoided the difficult term 'productive'. Different scholars take very different views of what constitutes morphological productivity, even in contemporary English where there is no shortage of lexical data and in situations where borrowing can be eliminated as a major complicating factor.[25] In a diachronic and multilingual perspective, it becomes yet more difficult to determine what sort of evidence shows that an element had become 'productive' in English. The existence of a number of formations on bases of native origin is normally a sure sign (although compare the case of *hidage* already mentioned); it is also a very conservative one, since it would be expected that bases clearly not of French or Latin origin would be among those most resistant to showing new analogous formations of this type. If we set the bar as high as this, then only a very few French or Latin affixes can be said with confidence to have been productive before the end of the Middle English period. If we accept as evidence of productivity formations on French or Latin bases that are not paralleled in French or Latin, then we have rather more evidence, but of a less fail-safe sort, since it is always possible that there are simply gaps in our records for French and Latin. Even less certain evidence is provided by cases where the English word is attested earlier than parallels in French or Latin, or in a distinctive meaning; we may feel that we would need to have very many such instances before we felt confident that we were not simply seeing the consequences of deficiencies in the dictionaries of French and Latin. Additionally, some scholars suggest that a few scattered instances of formations on Germanic bases do not necessarily demonstrate productivity, but may simply show sporadic instances of analogous word formation. This qualification seems very reasonable, but, if it is accepted, quite where to draw the line becomes very problematic. For some different approaches, see Dalton-Puffer (1996), Miller (1997, 2006, 2012), Lloyd (2011).

Detailed exploration of this vast contribution to the lexical resources of modern English is outside the scope of a book on loanwords and, fortunately, there are good surveys of the full range of borrowed affixes in English. From a diachronic perspective, Nevalainen (1999) is excellent on

---

[25] See especially the discussions in Bauer (2001), Plag (2006).

those found in Early Modern English, while Marchand (1969) offers comprehensive coverage of the full historical range. There is also excellent documentation in Miller (2006) and Miller (2012); Cowie (2012) presents some further recent perspectives on Early Modern English.

The importation of whole families of related affixes has had some far-reaching consequences for the word-formation patterns of English. One notable phenomenon is that various new patterns of allomorphy have become established. Thus many borrowed adjectives end in -ic /ɪk/ and this suffix has become highly productive in English (by any definition of productivity). Many abstract nouns corresponding semantically to such adjectives end in -icity /ɪsɪti/. The same alternation of /k/ and /s/ has been carried over into English formations on the same pattern. Thus, when the loanword *electric* (a. 1626) gives rise to an English derivative in -ity, *electricity* (1646), this shows the same pattern as borrowed word pairs such as *rustic* (?1440) and *rusticity* (1531). Similarly, abstract nouns in -ity formed on adjectives in -able or -ible regularly end in -bility (not *-blity), on the model of borrowed word pairs.[26] Another very important ultimate consequence of the borrowing of so much vocabulary from French and Latin, particularly morphologically complex words, and of the establishment of word-formation patterns involving affixes of French and Latin origin, is that the stress system of English has changed radically, from a characteristic Germanic system focused on the beginning (or left-hand edge) of the word, to a complex mixed system, in which the end (or right-hand edge) of the word has become more important.[27]

One major consequence of the borrowing of French and Latin affixes that is very important for the narrower topic of this book is that we often cannot tell whether a particular word that is ultimately a derivative formation shows (i) a formation within English or (ii) a loanword from Latin or French. Compare the discussion of the ambiguity of many words ending in -or, -ory, or -ary discussed in section 14.2, and for further illustration see *adapter* and *adaptor* and similar cases discussed in section 14.5.

---

[26] For a detailed introductory account of these phenomena, see Stockwell and Minkova (2009).

[27] For an overview from a historical perspective and further references, see Minkova (2012) and compare also Lass (1999a) for an introductory account.

14.5 Test cases: selected word families in English

Much of the expansion of the lexis of English in the Early Modern period and later results from the growth of word families surrounding French and/ or Latin loanwords. This occurs both by borrowing of further related words and by derivation within English, sometimes using native affixes, sometimes borrowed ones, often on the model of words in French and/or Latin. Frequently such word families contain many competing synonyms; typically, over a very long timescale, certain synonyms become dominant in the most central uses, while the others may become rare or obsolete, or may become more specialized in meaning or register.

The pair of verbs *adapt* (1531) and *adaptate* (1638) were touched on already in section 14.2. The wider word family to which they belong provides a typical illustration of some of these processes.

In Middle English we find only a single example of *adapted*, in the early fifteenth-century English translation of Guy de Chauliac's *Grande Chirurgie*. This may imply earlier currency of the verb *adapt* in English, or may be formed directly on the verb stem of either Middle French *adapter* or classical Latin *adaptāre*. A formation on the Latin past participial stem would be more usual, but this is *adaptāt-*, not **adapt-*, and hence the more expected word form would have been **adaptated*. (See further below for a cluster of later analogous cases in the same word family.)

If we do not assume that earlier borrowing is implied by *adapted*, the verb *adapt* is securely attested from 1531. The recorded spellings and meanings and the early contexts of use make it likely that the transmission was partly direct from (the present stem of) Latin *adaptāre* and partly via French *adapter*, as in many other cases in this period, on the same pattern as the Middle English cases discussed in section 11.3.4. The same is probably true of *adaptation* (1597).

In the seventeenth century we find increasing semantic overlap and redundancy in new formations. For instance, the nouns *adapting* (1610) and *adaption* (1615) occur in similar uses to existing *adaptation*, while *adaptness* (1657) is followed soon after by *adaptedness* (1673). Likewise, as already noted, the verb *adaptate* (1638, formed on the Latin past participial stem) is found beside existing *adapt*. We also find *adapt* as adjective (1658) beside earlier *adapted*: this form probably results from analogy with cases where the Latin past participial stem is identical to the English present stem, such as *content*, *distract*, or *erect*, although it could alternatively show a borrowing from the rare post-classical Latin adjective *adaptus* (found beside the normal participial adjective *adaptatus*); compare similarly *adaption*, *adaptly*, *adaptness*, all formed on a stem *adapt-*.

This profligacy continues in the eighteenth century with *adaptment* (1739) being added to the existing repertoire of abstract nouns and the agent noun *adapter* (1753) being followed swiftly by *adaptor* (1764). In the nineteenth century, *adaptive* (1734) is joined by *adaptative* (1815), *adaptational* (1849), and *adaptorial* (1838), leading to further profligacy in the cluster of derived nouns *adaptiveness* (1815), *adaptativeness* (1841), and *adaptableness* (1833). Additionally, *adaptivity* (1840) is found alongside earlier *adaptability* (1661), which itself antedates *adaptable* (1692). In the early twentieth century *adaptationalism* (1922) arises beside earlier *adaptationism* (1889, originally modelled on German *Adaptationismus*).

Very few of these words show direct borrowing from Latin or French (probably just *adapt* verb, *adaptate*, *adaptation*, and maybe *adapt* adjective), but a number of others are best explained as hybrid or analogous formations on Latin stems. The group as a whole illustrates the impact of the borrowing of a handful of key words in giving rise to an extended word family over time, including many full or partial synonyms. In some cases synonyms may have arisen accidentally, as speakers were simply ignorant of the existence of earlier formations; some others could result from misrecollection of earlier words. In the nineteenth century, some terms become more associated with particular subject fields, derivative formations on *adaptation* being common in biology, for instance. However, such profligacy and redundancy is typical of such word families in English well into the Later Modern period, well beyond the period in which 'copy' was particularly in vogue in literary style.

For the most part the chronology of these formations shows the sequence that we would expect, although *adaptability* precedes *adaptable* by several decades, perhaps showing a failure in the chronological record, or perhaps showing a genuinely earlier formation (in *-ability*) directly on the verb stem. So far as relationships with other word groups are concerned, there is considerable semantic overlap with the verbs *adjust*, *alter*, *modify*, and their satellites, and more limited overlap with *frame*, *fashion*, *accommodate*, *dispose*, *suit*, *fit*, and with the adjectives *apt* and *appropriate*, as well as with many other words.

If we look more briefly at some of the other word families touched on in section 14.2, we can find some similar patterns:

In the same word family as *retard* (1490) and *retardate* (1613) we find, all in broadly overlapping ranges of meanings:

> abstract nouns: *retardation* (*c*.1437; < French and Latin), *retardance* (1550), *retarding* (1585), *retardment* (1640; < French), *retardure* (1751), *retardency* (1939), *retardancy* (1947)
>
> adjectives, broadly meaning 'causing retardation': *retardant* (1642; probably < Latin), *retarding* (1654), *retardative* (1705; formed on the Latin stem), *retardive* (1787), *retardatory* (1843), *retardent* (1881)
>
> agent nouns: *retarder* (1644), *retardant* (1824), *retardent* (1858).

In the same word family as *resonate* (1648) we find:

> abstract nouns: *resonance* (*a*.1460; < French), *resonancy* (1611; perhaps < Latin), *resonation* (1824).

In the same word family as *pulsate* (1674) and *pulse* (?*a*. 1425) we find:

> abstract nouns: *pulsation* (?*a*. 1425; < French and Latin), *pulsing* (*a*.1525), *pulsating* (1829)
>
> adjectives: *pulsative* (*a*.1398; < French and Latin), *pulsatile* (?*a*. 1425; < French), *pulsing* (1559), *pulsive* (1600; formed on the Latin stem), *pulsatory* (1613; formed on the Latin stem), *pulsant* (1642; < Latin), *pulsating* (1742).

Cases like these illustrate vividly the considerable confusion and profligacy caused by the influx of Latin and Romance suffixes into the word-forming arsenal of English, in conjunction with varying morphological types in the base words borrowed from French and Latin. Additionally, they show how etymologies can be rather uncertain in such clusters of words: for instance, *pulsatory* can be explained, as above and as in *OED3*, as a formation in *-ory* on the Latin past participial stem *pulsāt-*, but it could alternatively be explained as an alteration of *pulsative* with suffix substitution, or, again without recourse to Latin, as a formation arising by analogy from *pulsation*, after such pairs as *accusatory* and *accusation*.[28]

In most of the word families looked at in this section, new loanwords are outnumbered by formations within English, but nonetheless such 'filling out' of the word families surrounding earlier borrowings accounts for a considerable proportion of the new loanwords from Latin and French

---

[28] On pairs of adjectives in *-ive* and *-ory* and patterns of competition and differentiation between them, see Kaunisto (2008) and see also Kaunisto (2007) for an extended survey of adjectives in *-ic* and *-ical*.

found in Early Modern English and later: compare section 14.1.3 on such words even among the 1,000 most frequent words in the *BNC*.

14.6 Continued semantic borrowing shown by earlier loanwords

In section 11.3 some examples were treated in detail where a word identified on formal grounds as a loanword from Latin nonetheless shows considerable semantic influence from French (e.g. *idea*), and also cases where a loanword that may on formal grounds be from either Latin or French appears to show semantic input from both languages (e.g. *action, person*). In the case of *person*, it was noted that the continuous history of the meaning 'a role or character' in English dates only from the sixteenth century, probably resulting from continuing influence from Latin in this period. It is quite a common phenomenon that words borrowed from French and/or Latin in Middle English (or in some cases even in Old English) show new senses from either source language during the Early Modern period, in just the same way as *person*. For example the verb *present* shows a semantically complex Middle English borrowing from French and/or Latin (earliest recorded in English *c.*1300), but the meaning 'to stage or put on (a play)' (earliest in English in 1573) appears to result from semantic influence from Middle French (in which this meaning is first recorded in 1561). Similarly, in the same word family, *presence* is a Middle English borrowing from French and Latin (earliest recorded in English *c.*1330), but its use with reference to the impressive or handsome bearing of a person (first attested 1570) appears to show semantic influence from a meaning of Middle French *presence* that is itself not recorded before the sixteenth century. In a sense this is no more than the tail end of the process of multiple semantic inputs seen in Middle English and explored in section 11.3. Where there are no distinguishing formal criteria (typically resulting from sound change in English, French, or Latin), it is normally impossible to determine whether such continuing semantic influence shows re-borrowing of the source word from the source language (i.e. giving a separate English word that has converged with the earlier borrowing) or a semantic borrowing affecting the previously borrowed word.

   This phenomenon is of particular interest here because it may be one of the factors that help explain the phenomenon looked at in section 14.7, namely the gradual increase in frequency shown over a long time period by many of the Middle English borrowings from Latin and French.

14.7 Increasing word frequency over time

A key theme of this book has been that a borrowed word's first attestation in English is not the only significant fact in its history. In sections 14.3 and 14.6 we have seen some of the processes of subsequent influence from the donor word that can affect borrowed words long after the date of their first appearance. It can be more difficult to detect what is probably a very typical, even usual process, namely that a borrowed word gradually increases in frequency of occurrence. This may simply be a result of internal spread in the borrowing language, as a word comes to be used by an increasing number of speakers and perhaps also in an increasing number of contexts. We have seen some good examples of this when looking at the history of Scandinavian borrowings in English. In some situations it may also partly result from continuing influence of the donor language, as speakers of the borrowing language continue to encounter the donor word in just the sorts of situations that led to the initial borrowing. This is very likely to have been an important factor during the long contact between English, French, and Latin in the Middle English and Early Modern periods.

If these processes do indeed apply, then we should expect to find that many individual French or Latin borrowings in the Middle English and Early Modern periods gradually increase in frequency in our surviving records, and also that we find an increasing proportion of French or Latin words among the most frequent words in English over time. We look in this section, somewhat experimentally, at whether the tools available today make it possible to test this hypothesis.

In section 2.2 we looked at the origins and dates of first attestation of the loanwords found in the 1,000 most frequent words in contemporary English, as reflected by the *BNC*. The *Helsinki Corpus of English Texts*, which was compiled in the 1980s, is small in comparison with many of its successors, but offers a good opportunity for comparing a balanced selection of Middle English texts with a similar selection of Early Modern English texts. Its smaller sub-periods (e.g. 1420–1500, 1500–70) make a finer diachronic focus possible. However, there are severe limitations to the sorts of comparisons that we can make, arising from the degree of spelling variation found in Middle English and in Early Modern English.

There are now numerous word frequency lists for modern English, based on tagged and parsed versions of contemporary English corpora. As discussed in section 2.2, these normally do not distinguish between distinct homonyms, such as *rest* in *to take a rest* (a word of native, Germanic origin) and *rest* in *the rest of* (a French loanword). Such homonymy is fairly limited in modern English, at least among the highest-frequency words. The picture is rather different if we look at Middle English or Early Middle English, where the high degree of spelling variation that is found means both that there are many more homonyms (or at least homographs), and also that individual lexemes show considerable spelling variation, as e.g. *maner*, *manere* for 'manner' or *tyme*, *time* for 'time'. A syntactically parsed corpus (such as the parsed Penn-Helsinki corpora) can distinguish between *rest* as verb and as noun, and also between e.g. *art* 'art' and *art* second-person singular of 'be', but it cannot distinguish between the two *rest* noun homonyms, nor can it group together the various spelling variants of *manner* or *time*. The implications of this become clear when we consider that even the thousand most frequent spelling forms in the Early Modern component of the Helsinki Corpus (1500–1710) include for instance both *act* and *acte*, *maner* and *manner*, *part* and *parte*, *time* and *tyme*, and further spelling variants will be found for each of these items in lower frequency numbers. Recently some steps have been made in trying to develop tools that can identify some major patterns of spelling variation in Early Modern English texts,[29] but we are a long way from having tools that could do this for Middle English.

If we look just at what the most frequent spelling forms are in various diachronic portions of the Helsinki Corpus, and compare these with one another and with contemporary English data from the *BNC*, we certainly seem to see a dramatic increase in the incidence of words of French and/or Latin origin over time. In the Middle English component of the Helsinki corpus, covering the period 1150–1500, around 1,000 spelling forms show a frequency of 0.01% or higher. In the Early Modern component, covering the period 1500–1710, a little over 900 spelling forms show a similar frequency. This is after matches for proper names have been removed from the results. Among those 1,000 spelling forms from the period 1150–1500, approximately 70 (7%) are for words borrowed from French or Latin, or both. Among the 900 spelling forms from the period 1500–1710, this total has shot up to *c.*170 (19%). We thus seem to have a dramatic increase in words of

---

[29] For information on a tool that promises to do this for English post-1600, see <http://ucrel.lancs.ac.uk/VariantSpelling/> and further references given there.

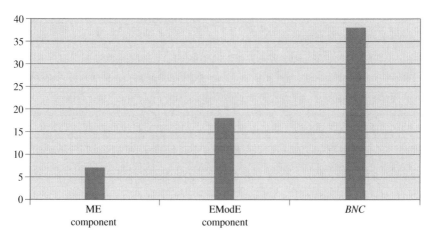

Fig. 14.9 The proportion of words of French and/or Latin origin among high-frequency spellings in Helsinki Corpus data for Middle English and Early Modern English, alongside a comparable sample from the *BNC*.

French or Latin origin among the most frequent strings in Early Modern English. If we make a similar analysis of the 900 most frequent spelling forms in contemporary English in the *BNC*, we again find a dramatic increase in the incidence of words of French or Latin origin, as shown by Fig. 14.9. A similar picture is shown if we look more narrowly at high-frequency spelling forms in the Helsinki Corpus's sub-periods 1420–1500 and 1500–70, as shown by Fig. 14.10. These figures need to be treated with extreme caution, because they are almost certainly considerably skewed by the gradual decrease in the degree of spelling variation shown by the highest-frequency words, which are largely of native origin. However, the sharp increase either side of 1500 remains particularly striking.

Even more interesting, and probably rather more robust, is what we find if we look at the *OED* dates of first attestation for each of the words that figure among the high-frequency strings in the Helsinki Corpus data for 1500–1710:

7	were originally Old English borrowings from Latin (mostly reinforced by later Romance borrowing)
4	show first dates from the twelfth century
*c.*77	show first dates from the thirteenth century
*c.*73	show first dates from the fourteenth century
*c.*9	show first dates from the fifteenth century

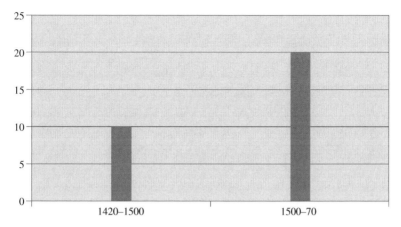

Fig. 14.10 The proportion of words of French and/or Latin origin among high-frequency spellings in Helsinki Corpus data for 1420–1500 and 1500–70.

The languages of origin are as follows:

*c.*115   from French only
*c.*46   from French and/or Latin
*c.*9   from Latin

Thus, the words that figure in the high-frequency list for 1500–1710 were all borrowed before 1500, they were mostly borrowed before 1400, and borrowings from French greatly predominate.

These figures make an interesting comparison with the Present-Day English data derived from the *BNC* that was looked at in section 2.2 and (in sharper chronological focus) in section 12.1.2. Although the *BNC* data shows that borrowings first attested in the thirteenth and fourteenth centuries still predominate among high-frequency words, the data from the Helsinki Corpus for 1500–1710 is markedly different: words first attested in the thirteenth century make up a bigger share and words first attested later than 1400 make up a far smaller share. The difference is even more striking when we look at languages of origin, with words borrowed solely from French predominating much more strongly in the Early Modern material.

One further point of interest is that a large proportion of the words that occur among the most frequent spelling forms in the Helsinki Corpus material still figure among the 1,000 most frequent words in Present-Day English as reflected by the *BNC*. The exceptions are interesting, apparently for the most part reflecting changes in the most frequent topics of discourse (as well as differences in the balance of text types between the Helsinki Corpus and the *BNC*), rather than radical changes in the meaning or usage of particular words. Among the loanwords that are most frequent in the Helsinki Corpus data for 1500–1710 but do not appear among the 1,000 most frequent in the *BNC* are *honour*, *justice*, *manner*, *noble*, *parliament*, *pray*, *prince*, *realm*, *religion*, *supper*, *treason*, *usury*, *virtue*.

If extensive corpora of Middle English and Early Modern English become available that distinguish between the many homographic spelling forms found in texts of these periods, it should become possible to make far more precise observations about the increasing penetration of loanwords into the high-frequency vocabulary of English over time. The methods that I have employed here, looking at spelling forms rather than a lemmatized word list, must leave a very large margin for error, especially because the incidence of spelling variation and of homographic forms has decreased over time, making diachronic samples not strictly comparable. However, even with these caveats in mind, the data examined here suggests striking differences between the high-frequency vocabularies of late Middle English, Early Modern English, and Present-Day English, and suggests strongly that, on average, words borrowed from French and Latin have taken a period of centuries rather than decades to become fully established in the high-frequency vocabulary of English. In particular, the sixteenth century appears to have been a crucial period in the establishment of many earlier borrowings in frequent, everyday use (at least in written English). In chapter 16 we will take a complementary approach, to look further at what it is possible to deduce about the processes by which a loanword can come to be the usual word employed in a particular core meaning.

14.8 Modern scientific formations from elements ultimately of Latin and Greek origin

As already noted, the high absolute totals of borrowings from Latin in the nineteenth century reflected by *OED3*-derived data in Fig. 14.1 in section 14.1.3 owe a great deal to *OED*'s detailed coverage of the expanding vocabulary of scientific discourse. Even though this period actually shows a decline in the proportion of all new words that are loanwords from Latin (see Fig. 14.2 in section 14.1.3), such high absolute totals are still worthy of investigation. Most of these words fall into one of two groups:

1. They are words formed by modern scientists from one or more Latin (or Greek) elements, either with endings that are identical to those found in classical Latin (or sometimes ancient Greek), or using the naturalized forms of those same endings that are found in the modern vernacular languages. See section 14.8.1.

2. They are loanwords from the Latin employed by modern scientists in the systematic terminology of various disciplines, especially taxonomy and medicine: see section 14.8.2 below on this scientific Latin, which has a rather special (and difficult) status, since it is mostly used in discourse that is otherwise entirely framed in modern vernacular languages.

14.8.1 Formations in modern vernacular languages from Latin or Greek elements

Some typical examples are:

- *abietene* a type of liquid hydrocarbon mixture (1872) < classical Latin *abiet-*, *abiēs* fir tree + the (borrowed) suffix *-ene*
- *oleiferous* yielding or bearing oil (1804) < classical Latin *oleum* oil + the (borrowed) combining form *-iferous* (see section 14.9 on combining forms)
- *acarpous* not producing fruit (1871) < ancient Greek ἄκαρπος (*ákarpos*) without fruit + the (borrowed) suffix *-ous*.

In the example of *acarpous*, the suffix *-ous* is simply an adjective-forming suffix, signalling the word class to which the borrowed word belongs. In the examples of *abietene* and *oleiferous*, the second element brings part of the meaning content and we have a newly created complex word, incorporating a newly borrowed foreign-language word stem. The preliminary discussion in section 1.2.2 noted the challenges presented by such words for traditional typologies of lexical borrowings. Words of this type make up the vast majority of the 2,747 borrowings from Greek listed in section 2.1, as well as a very high proportion of modern borrowings from Latin.

Many such words originated in discourse in other modern vernacular languages, especially French and German. We could regard the English equivalents as formations from the same elements within English on the model of the foreign-language words, or alternatively as loanwords with remodelling either after the equivalent word-forming elements in English or after the ultimate Latin or Greek etymons. For example:

- *papaverine* a type of crystalline alkaloid (1848) < classical Latin *papā-ver* poppy + the (borrowed) suffix *-ine*, after German *Papaverin* (1848, in the work that the first English example translates); or alternatively, < German *Papaverin* with remodelling of the ending after the usual English equivalent *-ine*
- *pileorhiza* layer of parenchymatous tissue in a plant (1849) < classical Latin *pīleus* cap + *-o-* (borrowed) connective element + ancient Greek ῥίζα (*rhiza*) root, after French *piléorhize* (1846); or alternatively, < French *piléorhize* with remodelling after the Latin and Greek words
- *plagihedral* having crystalline faces of a particular type (1816) < ancient Greek πλάγιος (*plágios*) oblique, slanting + the (borrowed) combining form *-hedral*, after French *plagièdre* (1797); or alternatively, < French *plagièdre* with remodelling after *-hedral*.

The former analysis is normally adopted in *OED3* in cases where the composition of the word is likely to have been relatively transparent to other experts in the field; were it not, the numbers of loanwords from German and French in section 2.1 would be rather higher, and those from Latin and Greek would be appreciably lower. Even excluding words of uncertain analysis such as these, scientific vocabulary makes up a considerable proportion of the loanwords from French in this period, for example:

- *pectase* a plant enzyme (1852) < French *pectase* (1848) < *pect-* (clipped from *pectine* or *pectose*) + the suffix *-ase*
- *raffinose* a type of trisaccharide sugar (1876) < French *raffinose* (also 1876) < *raffiner* to refine + the suffix *-ose*.

A very large proportion of the loanwords from German recorded in *OED3* are scientific or technical words broadly of this type. As noted in section 2.1, there are 1,310 words given as loanwords from German in the parts of *OED3* so far completed. A total of 854 of these are first recorded in the nineteenth century, and well over half of these are scientific or technical words containing elements drawn ultimately from Latin or Greek. (This is excluding examples such as *papaverine* above, where the German word is taken simply to be the model for the English word.) For example:

- *ontogenesis* development of an individual organism from the earliest embryonic stage to maturity (1875) < German *Ontogenesis* (1866) < the combining form *onto-* + *Genesis* genesis

- *paraffin* (1835) < German *Paraffin* (1830) < classical Latin *parum* too little, barely + classical Latin *affīnis* closely related, akin.

As already noted, such words are open to subtly different etymological interpretations, and this can have a big impact on how many loanwords from each source are recorded by a particular dictionary (as also does the extent to which a particular dictionary chooses to cover scientific and technical vocabulary of this type).[30] To a certain extent they are internationalisms that can be taken up by specialists using any of the modern European vernaculars either unchanged (except by various regular phonological substitutions in the spoken form) or with only minimal morphological adaptation. As noted in section 1.5, in most German scholarship a general distinction is made between 'borrowed words' (Lehnwörter) and 'foreign words' (Fremdwörter), the former category being taken to include only the most thoroughly naturalized borrowings (especially early ones), and the latter containing just about everything else. In this tradition, words such as *Ontogenesis* and *Paraffin* are normally entered in dictionaries of Fremdwörter; however, their status as such is rather difficult, since they are words that have been coined within German by German scientists and, in this respect, they are more a part of the lexis of German than they are of the lexis of Latin or Greek of any era.

Section 14.9 will look at those combining elements of Latin and Greek origin that have become established as part of the word-forming repertoire of modern (largely scientific or technical) English, albeit with their own distinctive word-forming patterns. It will be argued here that when such formations follow an established pattern they should not be regarded as loanwords. However, we should look first at a particular category of borrowing complete Latin words, albeit from Latin that is typically used embedded in discourse that is otherwise entirely framed in a modern vernacular language.

---

[30] For instance, in the first and second editions of the *OED*, much of the material covered in this section and in sections 14.8.2 and 14.9 is subsumed under the heading 'modL' (i.e. modern Latin), while in *Webster's Third New International Dictionary* (1961) most of the material in this section and in section 14.9 is dealt with using the formulation ISV 'International Scientific Vocabulary' (see Gove 1966, Gove 1968).

14.8.2 Scientific Latin

If we turn now to the other category identified at the beginning of section 14.8, very many of the later Latin loanwords recorded in the *OED* (just under 50% of those from the nineteenth century, for example) are from what *OED3* terms scientific Latin. This term is used to denote the systematic use in various specialist fields of vocabulary that:

- is Latin in form (i.e. it shows Latin case endings)
- frequently occurs collocated with one or two other Latin words in short noun phrases
- but is typically embedded in texts written in a vernacular language.

The two most important fields are medicine and, above all, taxonomy, i.e. the systematic naming of living organisms. In modern taxonomy, plants and animals are named using binomial expressions that identify both the genus to which an organism belongs and the species within that genus. Thus a lion is identified as *Panthera leo*, the species *leo* in the genus *Panthera*, while a tiger is *Panthera tigris*, the species *tigris* in the genus *Panthera*. Single names are then used for each of the larger-scale units in the taxonomy: the genus *Panthera* in turn belongs to the family *Felidae*, and so on. Similarly, the English oak (or pedunculate oak) is called *Quercus robur*, while some other species in the same genus are the sessile oak, *Quercus petraea*, and the cork oak, *Quercus suber*. In plant names the second word, the specific epithet, is an adjective agreeing in gender with the genus name. In animal names the second word, the specific name, is a noun, and therefore the binomial is simply a collocation of two nouns. This use of terminology was systematized in broadly its current form by the Swedish scientist Linnaeus in a series of (Latin) works from the 1730s and 1750s, although the use of binomials in more or less systematic ways extends back much earlier (indeed, it has its roots in Aristotle). It has been carried over into the usage of modern zoologists and botanists, who will use this Latin terminology in the same way irrespective of which vernacular language they are writing. The status of scientific Latin in modern times is theoretically rather problematic: when a newly identified organism is named officially, this terminology is employed in a (very brief) formal description written entirely in Latin (or at least, this was the invariable practice until very recently), but otherwise it is employed embedded in vernacular sentences, including on the occasion of its first coinage. In the sentence 'the lion, *Panthera leo*, like other members of the genus Panthera, belongs to the family Felidae', *Felidae* and *Panthera* are unnaturalized loanwords just like any others discussed in this book and, although it is conventionally italicized, *Panthera leo* is an unnaturalized borrowed phrase, consisting of two collocated nouns. The main reason for according these items a different status as 'scientific Latin' is that they are so perceived by their users, who consider them to belong to the international Latin terminology of taxonomists, and who use them in formally consistent ways (e.g. specific epithet must agree with the genus name in a plant name, family names are feminine and plural, etc.), regardless of which language they are using them embedded within.

A very few examples drawn from *OED3* entries are:

- The phylum name *Arthropoda* first appears in English in 1854 (and the anglicized form *arthropod* in 1861). It was coined by C. T. E. von Siebold in a book written in German in 1846 and is formed from elements of Greek origin.

- The genus of shrubby poppies *Romneya* was coined in English in 1845 by W. H. Harvey from the name of the Irish astronomer Thomas Romney Robinson.

- *Bulimus* is the name of what was formerly thought to be a genus of land and freshwater snails; the thinking of zoologists has moved on, and this is no longer thought to be a distinct genus. Accordingly, the name was suppressed by the International Commission on Zoological Nomenclature in 1957, having been first attested in an English sentence in 1801. It first appears in a work written in Latin in 1777, I. A. Scopoli *Introductio ad historiam naturalem*. However, Scopoli's form *Bulimus* is probably an error for earlier *Bulinus*, coined by the French naturalist A. Adanson, in a French work, in 1757, alongside its French equivalent *bulin*; the origin of both the scientific Latin and the French words is French *bulle* bubble (plus the diminutive suffix -*in*).[31]

Similarly, in medicine, Latin terminology is used as an international point of reference in anatomy and in the names of some diseases. For instance, the terminologies of anatomy, histology, and embryology approved by the International Federation of Associations of Anatomists use Latin as their reference language, with glosses in English;[32] thus the left ventricle of the

---

[31] See further *OED3* for more detail on this rather complex case.
[32] See <http://www.unifr.ch/ifaa/>

heart is identified as the *ventriculus sinister*, its anterior cusp as the *cuspis anterior*, and so on. Such phrasal units are hence found in English, e.g. *globus pallidus* denoting part of the lenticular nucleus of the brain (1872; coined originally in a German context).

14.9 Neoclassical compounding in English and other modern vernaculars

Closely related to words of the type discussed in section 14.8.1 is a particular type of word formation that is found in modern English, and in various other modern European vernaculars, on the model of compounding patterns in Latin and Greek. Words formed in this way are not loanwords, but they show an important aspect of the impact of Latin and Greek on modern technical vocabulary. It is probably easiest to begin with some illustrative examples. The following words are all first recorded in the last quarter of the nineteenth century and are (on the strength of present knowledge) neither loanwords nor adaptations of words found earlier in another language:

> *aerobiosis, biomorphism, cryogen, nematocide, ophthalmopathy, plasmocyte, proctoscope, rheophyte, technocracy*

The majority of such words belong to scientific registers, but many do not. What they all have in common is that they are composed of two bound forms, i.e. elements that are not independent words (in English). In all of the examples listed the first element ends with the connecting vowel *-o-*, ultimately following patterns of word formation in Latin and Greek. Combining with other affixes is not normally a property of affixes in English, and hence elements such as *aero-*, *-biosis*, *bio-*, *-morphism* are normally identified as a separate word class, neoclassical combining forms. Many of these elements can also occur compounded with independent words, e.g. *aeroallergen*, *biohazard*, but what distinguishes them from other affixes is that they are frequently found compounded with other bound forms.[33]

There are scattered examples of such formations from the late sixteenth and early seventeenth centuries that appear not to be formed after a foreign-language model, e.g.:

- *polycracy* government by the many (1581), from two elements ultimately of Greek origin

---

[33] Compare Bauer (1983) 213–16, Durkin (2009) 108–11.

- *pantometer* an instrument for measuring angles and heights (1597), from two elements ultimately of Greek origin
- *multinomial* consisting of or involving more than two terms connected by the signs + or – (1608), from two elements ultimately of Latin origin.

All early examples are somewhat problematic, since until the pattern has become well established they are best regarded as analogous formations. By the middle of the seventeenth century some elements (e.g. *auto-*, *poly-*, *-latry*, *-logy*, *-vorous*) begin to show multiple formations that do not have clear foreign-language models, but it is only from the early nineteenth century that such formations begin to be extremely frequent. Typically, elements ultimately of Greek origin combine with other elements ultimately of Greek origin, and elements of Latin origin with other elements of Latin origin, but there are many exceptions that show hybrid formations.

Like the words discussed in section 14.8.1, these formations typically belong to the international language of science and move freely, often with little or no morphological adaptation, between English, French, German, and other languages of scientific discourse. They are often treated in very different ways in different traditions of lexicography and lexicology; however, those terms that are coined in modern vernacular languages are certainly not loanwords from Latin or Greek, even though they may be formed from elements that originated in such loanwords.

14.10 Summary and conclusions

The history of loanwords from French and from Latin after 1500 presents a complex set of interrelated narratives. From the Early Modern period onwards, borrowing from French and Latin develops along increasingly divergent pathways. Throughout the Early Modern period, both languages contribute greatly to the development of distinct registers in the vocabulary of English, in the emerging technical vocabularies of the sciences and many other fields of study, or in the vocabulary differences that help distinguish formal language from informal, or the literary from the non-literary.

In Early Modern English, word form increasingly distinguishes Latin loanwords from French loanwords, although there remain many word histories where formal input from both languages is likely, as well as many where word form points to borrowing solely from Latin but word meaning indicates at least some semantic input from French.

The total of loanwords from French remains reasonably steady in absolute numbers, but, as a proportion of all new words found in English, it falls away dramatically after 1500, never to return to anything close to the levels found in late Middle English. Words borrowed from French after 1500 make a very much smaller contribution than those borrowed before 1500 to the high-frequency vocabulary of modern English, or to its basic vocabulary (as reflected by basic meaning lists).

The total of loanwords from Latin after 1500 increases greatly in terms of absolute numbers; even as a proportion of all new words, the figures found in Early Modern English are similar to those found in late Middle English (higher, if words from Latin and/or French are omitted). However, as with French loanwords, the contribution of Latin loanwords first recorded after 1500 to the high-frequency and basic vocabularies of modern English is much smaller than that made by loanwords from before 1500. Latin loanwords in Early Modern English increasingly show restriction to particular technical or stylistic registers of English, rather than contributing to the general vocabulary. Additionally, many new loanwords (and many more new derivative formations within English) expand the word families surrounding earlier borrowings.

The Early Modern period was also important for the increase in frequency of use shown by earlier, medieval loanwords from Latin and French, and for the process by which earlier loanwords eventually came to oust native synonyms as the usual word employed in a particular meaning (a process examined more closely in chapter 16).

From the eighteenth century onwards, the differences in the patterns of borrowing from French and Latin become yet more marked. French loanwords continue to be numerous (more numerous than those from any other modern language), but they become easier to classify into distinct groups: those that reflect the role of French as an international language of scholarship (as examined in this chapter), and those that reflect areas of French cultural influence or prestige (as will be surveyed briefly in chapter 15, in comparison with borrowing from other European languages).

Borrowing from Latin in the same period follows a much more distinctive pathway. The lexical resources of Latin (and increasingly also of ancient Greek) are exploited in the rapidly expanding vocabulary of the modern sciences. Words that already existed in classical or medieval Latin are employed in new technical meanings in the scientific Latin of modern scientists, and are used increasingly often embedded in vernacular sentences.

Even more often, Latin words or word-forming elements are used to form new compound words, either in scientific Latin, hence preserving their Latin morphology, or in new formations within the modern vernaculars. Hence Latin words and word elements have become ubiquitous in modern technical discourse, but frequently in new compound or derivative formations or with new meanings that have seldom if ever been employed in contextual use in actual Latin sentences.

15

Loanwords from other languages: test cases

15.1 Introduction

So far this book has largely concentrated on loanwords from French, Latin, the Scandinavian languages, the Celtic languages, and (in sections 14.8 and 14.9) Greek. This is for reasons outlined in chapter 2: French and Latin are by a considerable margin the most frequent donors of loanwords to the vocabulary of modern English, whether we look at the wordlist of a very large dictionary such as the *OED* (see section 2.1), or at the 1,000 most frequent words in the *BNC* (see section 2.2); if the focus is narrowed to the 100 most frequent words in a corpus, the distinctive contribution of early Scandinavian comes much more into focus. A similar pattern is found if one looks instead at the words that usually realize basic meanings in modern English (see section 2.3). Greek has been discussed alongside the contribution of Latin to the modern vocabulary of science, since (as outlined in sections 14.8 and 14.9) the contribution of the two languages is to a large degree inseparable. Loanwords from the Celtic languages were discussed in detail in chapter 5 for the rather different reason that they are so few, in spite of what is likely to have been a long-lasting close contact between speakers of English and of Celtic languages.

This chapter casts its net a little wider. In particular, it looks at loanwords from those languages (or groups of languages) other than Latin, French, the Scandinavian languages, and the Celtic languages that figure among the twenty-five most prolific sources of loanwords, as reflected by *OED3* and listed in section 2.1.

The chapter looks at these languages in two groups. Firstly, languages of Europe. Those that figure among the twenty-five most prolific sources in section 2.1 are (in descending order) German, Italian, Spanish, Dutch, Portuguese, Russian, Afrikaans, Yiddish, and Middle Low German. (The modern Scandinavian languages fall just outside the twenty-five most prolific inputs: see section 2.1.) Greek is also treated in overview here, drawing together strands already discussed in chapter 14. This section ends with a brief re-examination of recent loans from French, as it will be argued that over time borrowing from French has come closer and closer to the pattern of borrowing seen from other European languages, although the numbers of loans remain rather greater.

Secondly, the chapter looks at loanwords from languages from outside Europe. The formulation 'languages from outside Europe' is here intended to refer to languages that are either not spoken as a native language in Europe, or have only come to be spoken in Europe by immigrant communities in recent centuries. This section looks briefly at each of the languages that figure among the twenty-five most prolific sources listed in section 2.1: Japanese, Arabic, Sanskrit, Maori, Hindi, Hebrew, Persian, Malay, Urdu, and Chinese. (The distinction between 'languages of Europe' and 'languages from outside Europe' is not intended as an absolute one. In particular, a strong case could be made for placing Hebrew in either grouping, in the context of its history of direct and indirect contacts with English.)

Some characteristics are common to almost all of the cases examined in this chapter. With the significant exception of Dutch and Low German, there are few if any direct loans before 1500 from any of these languages. In some cases, like Maori, the chronological time depth is significantly shallower.

This chapter makes use of quantitative data from those parts of *OED3* so far completed, as a way of measuring each language's changing contribution over time to a very large wordlist such as the *OED*'s. This should not be equated simplistically with each language's contribution to the vocabulary of 'English'. The *OED*'s reading and sampling encompasses as wide as possible a variety of text types from as wide as possible a range of different varieties of English from all around the world. Loanwords are included according to their frequency of use within particular varieties as well as across different varieties; many are labelled as being restricted to use entirely or primarily within one particular variety. Historical dictionaries that are restricted in coverage to a particular variety of English typically contain higher totals of loanwords belonging solely to that variety than the *OED* does, just as they typically contain higher totals of words of all origins that belong solely to that variety (compare for example the discussion of the *Dictionary of New Zealand*

English (*DNZE*) in section 15.3.6). No dictionary could ever hope to list all items of foreign-language origin (or indeed of any other origin) that ever occur in a particular language or variety: compare the discussion of the basic methodological and theoretical difficulties in chapter 1. What a dictionary like the *OED* can do is present a good reflection of those words that have been recorded with some frequency in written use in a range of text types over a period of years, including both items that are restricted to a particular variety (labelled as such) and those that have wider currency.

Throughout this book, most attention has been given to those words that have entered the everyday vocabulary of English, particularly that core of vocabulary that is (with certain significant differences) common to all of the major varieties of English around the world. In this perspective, what is most striking about the full *OED* list of loanwords from each of the languages looked at in this chapter is how few words there are that have (yet) entered the everyday vocabulary of international English. Relatively few can be expected to be known by the average native speaker of English, regardless of local origin or knowledge of other languages. Although there are exceptions, those loanwords that have entered this layer of generally familiar vocabulary are often not direct loanwords, but have instead entered English via other languages. Very many of the most familiar words borrowed ultimately from other European vernaculars have entered English via French; this is especially true of those that entered English earliest. Very many of the most familiar words borrowed ultimately from languages from outside Europe, especially the chronologically earlier borrowings, have been borrowed wholly or partly via other European languages.

Each section of this chapter therefore presents a selection of the most notable direct borrowings from each language, with the *OED* date of first attestation. These are not to be taken as representative of what is typical of borrowing from each language, but rather as an indication of the high-water mark of lexical influence on English in general use internationally.

At the end of this chapter I draw together some general observations on what is typical of the semantic categories shown by the loanwords surveyed throughout the chapter. Before the language-by-language survey begins, some further initial contextualization is needed concerning the changing social, cultural, and geographical contexts of contact between English and other languages over the period surveyed here.

In the first part of this chapter, looking at loanwords from other languages of Europe, a frequent theme is how other European languages have frequently acted as the conduit for borrowing of words ultimately from geographically more distant languages. This can be seen, for instance, in the borrowing of words directly from Spanish or Portuguese that ultimately reflect contact with indigenous languages of the Americas. Additionally, with the geographical expansion of English, contact with other European languages has often occurred in locations outside Europe. This can be seen, for instance, in contact with Spanish in the United States, or with Dutch (and its descendant Afrikaans) in South Africa, as well as with both of these languages in many other locations.

As will be shown by the second part of this chapter, English has also increasingly come into direct contact with languages from outside Europe. This results from a number of historical, social, and cultural developments, especially:

- Widening trading contacts and colonial expansion from Britain from the late sixteenth century onwards, leading to the establishment of majority English-speaking communities in areas where previously other languages had been spoken, and where contact with other languages persisted (e.g. in North America, Australia, or New Zealand), and leading also to the use of English as the language of colonial administration in areas where it remained the first language of only a very small minority (e.g. in South Asia, many parts of Africa, and many parts of South-East Asia).
- Increasing immigration from a broadening range of countries into majority English-speaking communities in Britain (especially from post-colonial times onwards), and (in various different historical circumstances) in North America, Australia, etc.
- Increasing use of English as a language of communication, at a national and international level, in business, in administration, in higher education and research, both in post-colonial environments and, increasingly, in places where English was never a language of colonial administration, as a result of processes of globalization.

The increasing globalization of English has added significant new complexity to the picture of lexical borrowing in English. As new varieties of English have developed in an increasing range of speaker communities worldwide, it becomes more and more important to ask questions about whose English a word has been borrowed into. Additionally, contact between an expanded range of 'Englishes' has added a new dimension to the phenomenon of internal borrowing of lexis between varieties of English.

15.2 Loanwords from other European languages

15.2.1 Dutch (and Afrikaans) and Low German

Use of the terms 'Low German' and 'High German' may require some initial explanation. From the perspective of the early history of the Germanic languages, Dutch, Low German (the earliest stage of which is normally termed Old Saxon), and High German are three separate West Germanic languages, even though they have very complex dialectal relationships. See the diagram in section 4.1. Subsequently, High German, reflecting varieties originally spoken only in the south (in the more upland or 'High' areas), has spread as a standard variety to northern Germany as well. As a consequence of this, modern spoken varieties that show the reflexes of Middle Low German (to the extent that they survive at all) now exist in a context of diglossia with High German in northern Germany, i.e. Low German varieties are used in some social contexts, chiefly informal and intimate ones, while High German is used in others. (With the changing sociolinguistic relationship between Low German and High German, compare the discussion of Scots and southern standard English in section 1.5.)

Loanwords into English from Dutch (including Flemish) and Low German are normally considered together, because it is so difficult to tell them apart. This is partly because word forms in both languages were, and to some extent still are, so similar, and partly because the social and cultural circumstances of borrowing into English are also often hard to tell apart. 'Low Dutch' is sometimes used as a collective cover term for borrowings from either or both languages into English, although it is important to note that Low Dutch is not itself a language name, but simply a terminological shorthand for referring to a complex situation.

As already noted in section 2.1, the number of Dutch loanwords in *OED3* in the revised ranges A–ALZ and M–RZ (a little under a third of the full dictionary) is comparatively low (under 400), and the proportion does not appear to be significantly higher in those parts of the *OED* not yet revised. The number that can be distinguished confidently as being only from Low German is tiny (barely over twenty in *OED3*; the total rises to fifty-five if all words that may show some Low German input are taken into account). Absolute numbers of loanwords are not the only factor to which we should pay attention: although quite small, the total of Dutch loanwords is after all higher than that from the important donor of basic vocabulary items, early

Scandinavian. However, borrowing from Dutch and Low German has had almost no impact on the high-frequency vocabulary of modern English (see section 2.2), although it has had some impact on certain areas of the basic vocabulary (see 2.3, and examples in chapter 16).

If we take a diachronic perspective, Dutch and Low German, taken together, have a very long history of contributing loanwords to English. They are the most frequent source of loanwords in Middle English after French, Latin, and early Scandinavian, considerably exceeding the Celtic languages.[1] The overall pattern, of both absolute totals and loanwords as a proportion of all new words recorded in each fifty-year period, is given in Fig. 15.1.

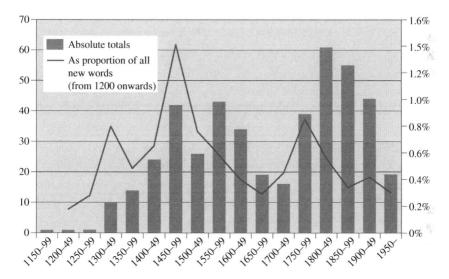

Fig. 15.1 Loanwords from Dutch, Low German, and Afrikaans, as reflected by *OED3* (A–ALZ and M–RZZ).

---

[1] In those parts of *OED3* so far completed, loanwords with first dates between 1150 and 1500 borrowed (perhaps, probably, or certainly) directly from Dutch or Low German exceed those from all of the Celtic languages in the same period by a margin of more than six to one. The results of a search on the field 'language of etymon' in the *MED* are more difficult to interpret, because occurrences as etymon are not distinguished from other occurrences in an etymology (for instance, one match for 'Celtic' is the etymology of *gloi* 'straw, thatching' which in fact reads 'MDu. *gloy* & OF *glui*; ?ult. Celtic'); however, it is clear that mentions of Dutch, Flemish, or Low German in *MED* etymologies far exceed those of Celtic or of any of the individual Celtic languages.

As this figure shows, it is in the Middle English period that Dutch and Low German are most significant as a proportion of all new words in English, and especially in late Middle English (discounting a blip caused by very small numbers overall in the twelfth century), although the absolute totals are higher in later centuries. There was probably also considerable borrowing from continental West Germanic varieties in the Old English period, but the very close similarity of the languages, as well as the lack of detailed information on many aspects of social and cultural interaction, make this very difficult to detect.[2] Many of the words borrowed into Middle English reflect close trading connections or seafaring contacts, and probably also close interaction of populations, resulting from successive waves of immigration to England, especially by Flemings; compare *deck* (originally in sense 'roof, covering'), *to dote*, *groat*, *groove*, *hop* (plant), *luck*, *malmsey*, *measles*, *mesh*, *nap* (of cloth), *to nip*, *peg*, *pickle*, *pip* (= disease of poultry), *to prate*, *rack* 'barred frame', *roe* (= spawn of fish), *rover* 'pirate', *school* (= shoal), *skipper*, *wainscot*; also (from Middle Low German) *trade*. A key term in the important wool trade is *pack*, although it is impossible entirely to rule out the possibility that this word (of unknown further etymology) was a borrowing from English into Dutch rather than vice versa. The word *clock* was probably introduced by experts in the relevant technology (as reflected by the fact that uses in the meaning 'bell' have always been rare in English outside the context of automated bell-ringing devices). In some of the other cases already mentioned it is impossible to be absolutely certain that the word shows a borrowing rather than the reflex of an otherwise unattested Old English cognate. Normally such certainty is only available in cases where the absence of an English sound change or the presence of a Dutch or Low German one demonstrates borrowing: the situation is similar to that explored with reference to early Scandinavian borrowings in part IV, with the added complication that there are fewer sound changes distinguishing English from Dutch and Low German. The same problem even affects some words first attested much later than the Middle English period, especially those found in regional varieties for which earlier evidence is in very short supply.

The fullest study of words of Dutch or Low German origin in English remains that of Bense (1939), who drew his data chiefly from the first edition

---

[2] Compare Gneuss (1993) 131–4.

of the the *OED*.[3] Bense's study groups loanwords from Dutch and Low German together under the collective heading 'Low Dutch', although at the level of individual word histories he frequently distinguishes between input from each language. His companion work, Bense (1925), provides a summary of the main historical contexts of contact.[4] Bense discusses over 5,000 words, for most of which he considers Low Dutch origin at least plausible; this is thus much higher than the *OED*'s etymologies suggest. His total includes some words ultimately of Dutch origin that have definitely entered English via other languages, e.g. *plaque* (from a French word that ultimately has a Dutch origin), and also many semantic loans; *OED3* has over 150 of these in parts so far revised, e.g. *household* (*a.*1399) or *field-cornet* (1800, after South African Dutch *veldkornet*). Nonetheless, Bense does make a case for direct borrowing from Dutch for many words for which the *OED* does not posit a Dutch etymon; even if one agrees with the *OED*'s (generally more conservative) approach in all cases, Bense's suggestions are by no means absurd, and his work highlights very well the difficulty of being certain about the extent of the Dutch contribution to the lexis of English.

Words from Dutch or (less commonly) Low German first attested after 1500 show similar general patterns to those before 1500. There is a somewhat greater overall emphasis on words particularly associated with aspects of life in the Low Countries or with items of Dutch trade or manufacture, although there are numerous words that have come to be used in modern English with little or no conscious association with Dutch; compare e.g. *spit* 'spade-depth' (1508), *uproar* (1526), *to snap* (1530), *pad* 'path, road' (1567; now preserved only in the compound *footpad*), *reef* (1579), *to beleaguer* (1590), *wiseacre* (1595), *to split* (1597), *to plunder* (1632; this word could alternatively have been borrowed from High German), *easel* (1634), *slim* (1657), *maelstrom* (1659), *smuggler* (1661), *kink* (1678), *snuff* (1678), *genever* (1689; now somewhat rare, but formerly much more common), *walrus* (1728), or *advocaat* (1895),[5] alongside words that retain more obvious

---

[3] There is also useful material in Llewellyn (1926), Toll (1926), Smithers (1941, a review of Bense), Sijs (2010).

[4] Among more recent accounts from historians, compare Barron and Saul (1995), and, on immigrant communities in early modern England in general, Luu (2005), Goose and Luu (2005).

[5] Loss of the association with Dutch is suggested in particular by pronunciations with absence of final /t/.

Dutch associations such as *younker* (1505), *palsgrave* (1539), *polder* (1602), or *mevrouw* (1734), and very many rarer words.[6] Many words show a limited regional distribution, in most cases probably reflecting localized contact: compare e.g. *haar* 'wet mist' (1662), found in eastern English regional varieties and in widespread use in modern Scottish English.[7]

From the late sixteenth century onwards, loanwords are found that reflect Dutch trading or colonial activities outside Europe, e.g. *mangosteen* (1598; ultimately < Malay, partly via Dutch), *mace* 'traditional unit of weight in Malaysia and Indonesia' (1598; < Dutch < Malay), *moree* 'kind of fine Indian cotton cloth' (1625; < Dutch < Malay), *soya* (1679; Dutch < Malay < Japanese), *muntjac* (1771; < Dutch < Sundanese, a language spoken in Java).

Many loanwords reflect contact between Dutch and English speakers outside Britain. Borrowings in North America reflect both the language of the early Dutch colonists and the Dutch spoken by subsequent waves of immigrants.[8] Some examples include:

- *coleslaw* (1794; subsequently borrowed to other varieties of English)
- *cookie* (from the late eighteenth century in North America, apparently directly from Dutch; found slightly earlier in Scottish English, denoting a plain bun)[9]
- *bowery* (1809; earlier as a proper name).

---

[6] For a listing and some analysis of Dutch loanwords and semantic loans found in *OED2*, see Otter (1990). Some of the words listed here will of course be antedated in the course of work on *OED3*. Others may well have been borrowed earlier than their dates of first attestation in English contexts; see Wright (1996) for numerous examples of Dutch or Low German words in mixed-language documents from London, suggesting currency in at least one of the languages of medieval England earlier than the dictionary record suggests, and compare also discussion of this topic in Hendriks (2012).

[7] On Dutch borrowings in Scots, see Macafee (1997), Tulloch (1997), and also Murison (1971). An interesting attempt to look at the regional distribution of words of possible Dutch or Low German origin in later English dialects has been begun by Chamson (2010), Chamson (2014); this could have significant implications for exploring the likelihood of borrowing in particular instances.

[8] For a detailed survey of this topic prepared for a popular audience, see Sijs (2009).

[9] It is unclear whether the word is also found (before modern US influence) in Scottish English denoting a biscuit as opposed to a bun: compare the positive assertion in the *Scottish National Dictionary* that it is not with the apparently contradictory evidence in the *English Dialect Dictionary*.

Compare also *waffle* (1744), *spook* (1801), *boss* (1806), and probably also *dope* (first half of the nineteenth century). An instance of a borrowing from Low German-speaking colonists in North America that has subsequently spread to other varieties of English is probably shown by *cranberry* (1672).

In South Africa the contact with speakers of South African Dutch and its later reflex Afrikaans has been long-lasting and is reflected by large numbers of loans. The earliest of them even antedate British seizure of the Cape Colony in 1795. The *Dictionary of South African English* lists a little under two thousand items borrowed from South African Dutch or Afrikaans (including semantic loans); several hundred of these are listed also in the *OED*, although most are labelled as belonging only to South African English. Some notable examples include:[10] *rhebok* 'type of antelope' (1775), *springbok* (1775), *aardvark* (1785), *klipspringer* 'type of antelope' (1785), *muishond* 'mongoose' (1796), *snoek* 'snake mackerel' (1797),[11] *mealie* 'maize' (1801), *meerkat* (1801), *commandeer* (1810), *biltong* 'dried meat' (1815), *aasvoel* 'vulture' (1821), *padloper* 'type of tortoise' (1821), *spoor* (1823), *agterryer* 'mounted groom, lackey' (1824), *oubaas* 'elderly white man' (1824), *wildebeest* (1821), *laager* (1834), *allemagtig* 'good Lord!' (1837), *trek* (1846), *mos* 'new wine, must' (1864), *Voortrekker* (1872), *rooibos* (1893), *baasskap* 'domination' (1935), *apartheid* (1944). It is notable that, while English has freely borrowed Dutch and Afrikaans names of African animals and plants, many of these borrowed words do not themselves show borrowings from indigenous languages, but instead show new descriptive compounds, e.g. *aardvark*, *aasvoel*, *klipspringer*, *muishond*, *rooibos*, *springbok*, *wildebeest*; or transferred uses of existing words from European Dutch, e.g. *reebok* 'roebuck', *snoek* 'pike', *padloper* 'tramp', or *meerkat* 'type of monkey'.[12] However, there are also many loanwords from South African Dutch or Afrikaans that are themselves relatively recent loanwords from other languages, reflecting some of the varied inputs in South African history, e.g. *kraal* (1731; < Portuguese), *quagga* (1731; probably < Khoekhoe), *commando* (1790; < Portuguese), *mebos* 'confection

---

[10] I have followed the dates given in the *Dictionary of South African English* for words not yet revised for *OED3*.

[11] Familiarity with this word in British English largely results from importation of canned snoek in the hungry years following the Second World War.

[12] The same word was borrowed much earlier into Middle English from Middle Dutch as *mercat*.

made from dried apricots' (1793; < Japanese), *pondok* 'makeshift shack' (1815; < Malay < Arabic), *bobotie* 'type of curry dish' (1870; probably < Malay).

As already noted, South African English itself also shows many loanwords that (either certainly or probably) come directly from other languages of South Africa, e.g. *gnu* (1786; < Khoekhoe and San), *sambal* 'highly seasoned condiment' (1815; < Malay), *imbongi* 'praise poet or public orator' (1836; < Xhosa and Zulu; hence also *mbongo* 'yes-man'), *tsetse* (1849; < Tswana), *ngaka* 'traditional healer' (1871; < Southern Sotho, Northern Sotho, and Tswana), *nyala* 'type of large antelope' (1899; < Tsonga and Venda), *roti* 'Indian flat-bread' (1903; < Hindi and Urdu; found earlier in other varieties of English, e.g. in India), *giya* 'type of traditional dance' (1905), *domba* 'period of initiation of young Venda girls into womanhood' (1931; < Venda). As reflected by the data of the *Dictionary of South African English* such loanwords are, however, greatly outnumbered by borrowings from Dutch and Afrikaans.

15.2.2 High German and Yiddish

The picture is rather different as regards loanwords from modern German, the descendant of the High German dialects of central and southern Germany, now used as the standard language throughout all of Germany. As noted in section 2.1, loanwords from German have the fourth highest total overall if we look just at the raw figures in those parts of *OED3* so far completed. Pfeffer and Cannon (1994), a survey based on the data of the *OED* and other major dictionaries plus a selection of specialist dictionaries, lists 5,380 loans, plus an appendix of 621 items not yet entered into major English dictionaries. However, their listing includes both loanwords and various types of semantic borrowing; loan translations (such as *beer cellar* after *Bierkeller*, *swan song* after *Schwanengesang*) and loan blends (such as *liverwurst* < German *Leberwurst*) make up about 15% of the total; they also include some semantic loans such as *weak* and *strong* in designating verb classes (after the philological use of *schwach* and *stark* by Jacob Grimm). Their list is also increased in size by the inclusion of a number of proper names that are recorded in attributive or allusive uses in dictionaries (e.g. *Lohengrin*, *Siegfried*). Examination of a list like the one provided by Pfeffer and Cannon confirms an observation already made in section 14.8.1: a large proportion of the German loanwords in English are words formed from elements ultimately of Latin or Greek origin (e.g. *paraffin*, *ontogenesis*, or *ozone*) and such words belong largely to technical, especially scientific, discourse (with exceptions such as *paraffin* or *ozone* that have spread to more general use as the things they denote have come to be known more widely).

Pfeffer and Cannon provide a broad analysis of their data into subject areas; those with the highest numbers of items are (in descending order) mineralogy, chemistry, biology, geology, botany; only after these do we find two areas not belonging to the natural sciences: politics and music. The remaining areas that have more than a hundred items each (including semantic borrowings) are medicine, biochemistry, philosophy, psychology, the military, zoology, food, physics, and linguistics. Nearly all of these semantic areas reflect the importance of German as a language of culture and knowledge, especially in the latter part of the nineteenth century and early twentieth century.

Mineralogy, the most numerous category in Pfeffer and Cannon's survey, does show a number of German loanwords not ultimately formed from Latin or Greek elements, with e.g. *bismuth* (1668), *quartz* (1676), *cobalt* (1728), *meerschaum* (1784), reflecting the long German tradition in this field (and still longer traditions in mining and metallurgy); however, more typical of the very large number of borrowings in this subject area are words such as *polybasite* (1830), *alloclase* (1866), or *sphaerite* (1886), showing formations from elements ultimately of Latin or Greek origin, and arguably in many cases better analysed as English formations on a German model rather than direct loanwords from German (compare discussion in section 14.8.1). Examples of Latinate German loanwords belonging to the general sphere of education are *semester* (1826) and *seminar* (1889).

Loanwords that are more distinctively German in form, reflecting German words composed of elements that are either of native origin or have long been assimilated in the general vocabulary of German, typically denote things or concepts of German invention or manufacture, e.g. (following the *OED*'s judgements on the English spelling and capitalization for each word): *pumpernickel* (1738), *Liebfraumilch* (1833), *poltergeist* (1848), *Zeitgeist* (1848), *doppelganger* (1851), *kindergarten* (1852), *Lied* (1852), *rucksack* (1853), *Realpolitik* (1872), *kapellmeister* (1873), *leitmotiv* (1880), *Wunderkind* (1891), *Schadenfreude* (1895), *Festschrift* (1898), *Bildungsroman* (1910), *lederhosen* (1937), *Gesamtkunstwerk* (1939); most are nouns, but for exceptions compare e.g. *ersatz* (1875), *abseil* (1908).

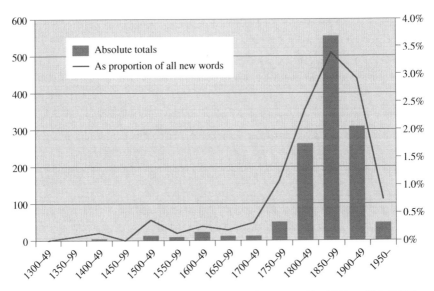

Fig. 15.2 Loanwords from German, as reflected by *OED3* (A–ALZ and M–RZZ).

A number of loanwords reflect the experience of the two World Wars and the politics of the interwar years, e.g. *lebensraum* (1905; but very rare in English before the Nazi period), *Machtpolitik* (1916), *putsch* (1919), *diktat* (1922), *Nazi* (1930), *Führer* (1934), *Gestapo* (1934), *panzer* (1938), *Blitzkrieg* (1939), *Sieg Heil* (1940), *Stalag* (1940).[13] Most borrowings of this type will be apprehended by most English speakers as Germanisms, one indicator of this being that many nouns still retain the German capitalization of the initial letter when used in English. *Rucksack* and *abseil* are perhaps the words among those listed here that are least likely to be perceived as Germanisms, in the case of *rucksack* because of the identification of the second element with its English cognate *sack* (with consequent substitution of /s/ for /z/), and in the case of *abseil* probably because of folk-etymological association of the second element with *sail*, leading to a remodelled pronunciation as /ˈabseɪl/, obscuring the German origin of the word. A word that few English speakers will identify as being of German origin is *noodle* (1779), probably because the food it denotes is not particularly associated with Germany for most contemporary speakers. In many cases a German

[13] For a stimulating brief discussion putting lexical innovation during the two World Wars in the broader context of the first half of the twentieth century, see Beal (2004) 29–34.

loanword coexists alongside a loan-translation of the same German term, which is typically of more frequent occurrence in English, e.g. *Weltanschauung* (1868) beside *world-view* (1848), *Machtpolitik* (1916) beside *power politics* (1901). The overall pattern as shown by *OED3* is given in Fig. 15.2. Both the absolute total and the percentage of all new words that are loanwords from German show their highest totals in the second half of the nineteenth century, in which the total of German loanwords is not far behind that from French. There are no German loanwords among the high-frequency or basic vocabulary items surveyed in sections 2.2 and 2.3.

Loanwords from varieties of German spoken in North America are mostly limited to regional varieties of US or Canadian English, or are found in occasional use more widely with specific reference to the practices of particular communities that have traditionally spoken German. For example, loanwords from Pennsylvania German (often called Pennsylvania Dutch) include *ponhaus* 'scraps of pork, etc. stewed with meal and pressed into large cakes' (1869) or *rumspringa* 'period of adolescence in which boys and girls are given greater personal freedom' (1963). The interjection *ouch* (1838) may be a North American borrowing from German *autsch* that has subsequently spread to other varieties of English, but it is not certain that it does show a German loanword. A more certain case is shown by *pretzel* (1831; < German *Bretzel*), earliest recorded in US English, and which probably spread from there to other varieties of English (especially in view of the word's distinctive form, which probably reflects the unaspirated quality of the initial consonant in southern German varieties).

A few loanwords could be from either German or Yiddish, and could show input from both, e.g. *schmaltz* (1935). Yiddish loanwords are found in many varieties of English where there have been Yiddish-speaking Jewish immigrant communities; some are much more widely known, largely as a result of linguistic spread within English, e.g. *mazeltov* (1675 in an isolated early borrowing from Hebrew that is explained contextually, subsequently from the nineteenth century), *nosh* (1892), *schmooze* (1897), *pastrami* (1899), *oy vey* (1914), *bagel* (1919), *schlep* (1922), *putz* (1928), *klezmer* (1929), *maven* (1950), *mensch* (1930), *kvetch* (1964).[14] Among these examples, *mazeltov*, *schmooze*, *klezmer*, and *maven* are all ultimately from Hebrew; see section 15.3.2 for further examples where transmission of Hebrew words via

---

[14] For a classic account intended for a popular audience, see Rosten (2001), and compare also Steinmetz (2001).

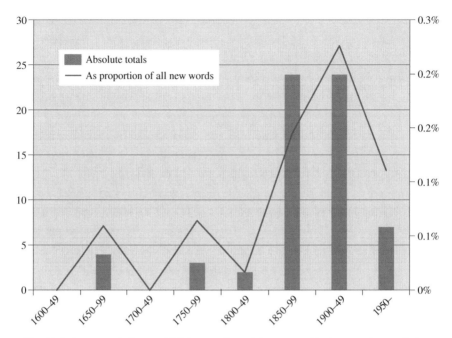

Fig. 15.3 Loanwords from Yiddish, as reflected by *OED3* (A–ALZ and M–RZZ).

Yiddish is very probable. Yiddish loanwords may often be perceived as Americanisms by speakers of other English varieties, because of the considerable international social and cultural impact of Jewish communities in the United States (especially in New York), although there may be long histories of use within Jewish communities elsewhere (e.g. in London). This perception is probably true to the extent that it is primarily the use of these words in some varieties of US English that has led to their familiarity to non-Jewish English speakers elsewhere. Fig. 15.3 gives the overall pattern shown by *OED3*, in which the (very small) totals of loanwords are concentrated mostly in the second half of the nineteenth century and the first half of the twentieth.

15.2.3 Spanish and Portuguese

There are very few loanwords directly from Spanish attested in Middle English; *cork* is one likely example and *fustic* another. A single very late Middle English borrowing directly from Portuguese may be shown by *marmalade* (1480), since the English word is recorded earlier than the corresponding word in other European languages (e.g. Middle French *marmeline* (1541), *mermelade* (1573), Spanish *mermelada* (1570), Italian *marmellata* (1579)); it may reflect trading links between Portugal and England. However, the fact that Portuguese *marmelada* is itself first recorded only in 1521, hence later than the English word, shows that arguments based solely on the first dates of attestation in each language must be approached with some caution. (See further section 15.2.5 on this example.) A rare early borrowing from Catalan may be shown by *pinionade* 'kind of comfit or conserve made with pine nuts' (1329), although it may alternatively be from Old Occitan (the Romance variety spoken in southern France).

Between 1500 and 1550 the number of words borrowed directly from Ibero-Romance languages (i.e. Spanish, Portuguese, or Catalan) increases somewhat; borrowing is mostly from Spanish, as in the case of *armada* (1533), *maize* (*a.*1544), and (probably) *gaberdine* 'type of loose upper garment of coarse material' (1520; hence the later cloth name *gabardine*).[15] Among these, *maize* is particularly interesting as a very early example of what was later to become an important phenomenon: a borrowing ultimately of a word from the New World (in this case Taino *mahiz* or *mahís*) via Spanish (or Portuguese in many later cases).

Loanwords from Spanish become much more frequent after 1550 through to the mid seventeenth century. These reflect the later stages of the Golden Age of European Spanish culture, and also the wider European impact of Spanish discoveries and conquests in the New World. The absolute totals in both *OED2* and in the parts of *OED3* so far revised present a very similar picture from this point onwards: see Fig. 15.4 for tabulation of the *OED3* data. There is a decline in the absolute number of Spanish loanwords in the later seventeenth century and a further decline in the eighteenth century, followed by a sharp rise in the early nineteenth. This rise probably reflects the intense contacts between English and Spanish speakers in the context of the westward expansion of English-speaking settlers in North America (compare the example loanwords below). From the mid nineteenth century the absolute totals again fall away steadily. The totals as a proportion of all new words in each period show much less dramatic variation and a slightly different pattern overall: relative to the number of new words of any origin recorded in *OED3*, the late sixteenth-century peak appears more significant and the eighteenth-century dip rather less dramatic. From the nineteenth

---

[15] For a detailed survey of the material up to the mid sixteenth century, see Dietz (2007).

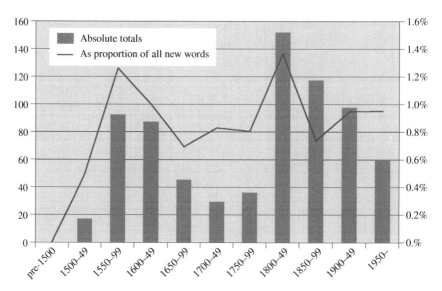

Fig. 15.4 Loanwords from Spanish, as reflected by *OED3* (A–ALZ and M–RZZ).

century onwards the question of whose English we are examining also becomes particularly important, since some varieties of English (particularly US English) show many more loanwords from Spanish than other varieties (and where other varieties do show loanwords they are in some cases probably via US English rather than directly from Spanish).[16]

Algeo (1996) is a survey based on *OED2* and the evidence of other dictionaries,[17] with an analysis into semantic groupings of the loanwords first recorded in each century up to 1900. Plants, animals, food, and drink make up a significant proportion of the loanwords in all centuries from the sixteenth to the nineteenth; many reflect Spanish discoveries and conquests in the New World, and many of these are ultimately from indigenous languages. Otherwise, the loanwords reflect a wide range of categories, mostly connected with culture and society. The category Algeo identifies as 'human beings by occupations and qualities' has a significant presence in the data for all centuries, as does 'meteorology and topography'; 'entertainment' also has a significant presence, especially among the later loanwords;

---

[16] For some interesting investigations of this question from a wide range of perspectives, see the contributions to Rodríguez González (1996).

[17] As with most of the other surveys drawn on in this section, not all of Algeo's etymologies agree with the *OED*'s, and I would differ from him on a number of cases.

loanwords connected with 'cowboys, cattle, and horsemanship' come to prominence in the nineteenth century. A broadly similar semantic pattern is shown by the twentieth-century loanwords surveyed by Cannon (1996a) and also in the *OED*'s data.

Among Spanish loanwords that are likely to be used by most speakers of contemporary English without particular consciousness of their Spanish origin, and certainly not with reference only to Spanish-speaking cultures, are: *machete* (1575), *mosquito* (1572), *tobacco* (1577), *anchovy* (1582), *plantain* 'type of banana' (1582; 1555 as *platano*), *alligator* (1591; earlier *lagarto*; the later form reflects misapprehension of the Spanish definite article as part of the word stem), (probably) *cockroach* (1624), *guitar* (*a*.1637, perhaps via French), *castanet* (1647; perhaps via French), *cargo* (1657), *plaza* (1673), *jerk* 'to cure (meat)' (1707), *flotilla* (1711), *demarcation* (1728; perhaps via French), *aficionado* (1802), *dengue* (1828; the ulterior etymology is uncertain), *canyon* (1837), *bonanza* (1844), *tuna* (1881), *oregano* (1889). Words particularly associated with the American West include *rodeo* (1811), *stampede* (1828), *vamoose* (1834, from the first-person plural imperative, 'let us go'), *lariat* (1835). A more general association with the Spanish-speaking world is probably retained by e.g. *sombrero* (1599), *quadroon* (1707), *poncho* (1717), *fandango* (1776), *cigarillo* (1832), *amigo* (1837), *gazpacho* (1845), *salsa* (1846; 1975 denoting the dance, showing a re-borrowing), *oloroso* (1876), *enchilada* (1887), although the strength of the association will differ for different speakers.

Words that originate in languages from outside Europe and have entered English via Spanish include *cocoa* (1555, as *cacao*; < Nahuatl), *iguana* (1555; < Arawak), *potato* (1565; probably < Taino),[18] *papaya* (1598; probably < Taino or Arawak), *chocolate* (1604; < Nahuatl), *tomato* (1604; < Nahuatl),[19] *chilli* (1662; < Nahuatl), *avocado* (1697; a folk-etymological alteration of a Nahuatl word), *barbecue* (1697; from a language of the Caribbean), *puma* (1771; < Quechua), *coyote* (1824; < Nahuatl), *abalone*

---

[18] On the complex patterns of transmission and semantic histories shown by the words for the potato and the sweet potato in various European languages, see Durkin (2009) 146–8; see this also on the (unexplained) final vowel in the modern English form (< Spanish *patata*, a form also found in early use in English).

[19] Earliest in English as *tomate*. The modern form *tomato*, attested from the eighteenth century onwards, probably results from association with *potato*: see further Durkin (2009) 145–6.

(1850; < Rumsen, a Costanoan language of northern California), *marijuana* (1874; perhaps < Nahuatl).

It begins to become harder to identify many loanwords after 1900 that most English speakers will understand without glosses, and many of those that are most widely known belong to the fields of food and drink (although the repertoire of particular individuals will of course vary widely); compare e.g. food and drink terms such as *huevos rancheros* 'Mexican egg dish' (1901), *guacamole* (1920; < Nahuatl), *pina colada* (1920), *burrito* (1934), *mojito* 'type of cocktail' (1934), *tostada* 'deep-fried cornmeal pancake' (1945), *chipotle* 'dried and smoked jalapeño pepper' (1950; < Nahuatl), *seviche* 'raw fish dish' (1951), *sangria* (1961), *fajita* (1971), or words from other semantic fields such as *paso doble* (1927), *mano a mano* 'confrontation', (as adjective and adverb) 'head to head' (1950), *manoletina* 'decorative pass in bullfighting' (1952), or *apartotel* (1965).

Loanwords from Portuguese remain much less frequent than those from Spanish. They are at their most frequent between the late sixteenth century and the early eighteenth. Very many reflect Portuguese colonialism and trade in the New World and in the East. Some notable examples are: *betel* (1553; < Malayalam), *pintado* 'type of fine cotton cloth imported from India' (*a.*1575), *albacore* 'type of tuna' (1579), *mango* (1582; probably < Malayalam), *pagoda* (1582), *monsoon* (1584; < Arabic; the word may have entered English partly via Dutch), *palanquin* (1588; ultimately < Sanskrit), *mandarin* (1589; < Malay), *banyan* 'Indian trader' (also in *banyan tree*) (1597; probably < Arabic, ultimately < Sanskrit), *sargasso* 'gulf weed' (1598), *brinjal* (1611; < Arabic, ultimately < Sanskrit), *moray* (eel) (1624), *pickaninny* (1653; probably via a Portuguese-based pidgin), *mongoose* (1673; < Marathi), *teak* (1698; < Malayalam), *palaver* (1707; probably via early West African Pidgin), *piranha* (1710; < Tupi), *cuspidor* (1779). Fig. 15.5 presents the overall pattern from *OED3* data.

Very many words could show borrowing from either Spanish or Portuguese, and many of these may show some input from both sources; compare e.g. *caste* (1555), *hurricane* (1555; < Taino), *Negro* (1555), *banana* (1577; probably < a Bantu language), *molasses* (1582), *flamingo* (1589), *grandee* (1599), *yam* (1657; probably < a Bantu language), *pimento* (*c.*1660), *naseberry* (1679),[20] and likewise the terms of racial classification *mulatto* (1591)

---

[20] This word shows folk-etymological alteration in English: see Durkin (2009) 58, 203, 254–5.

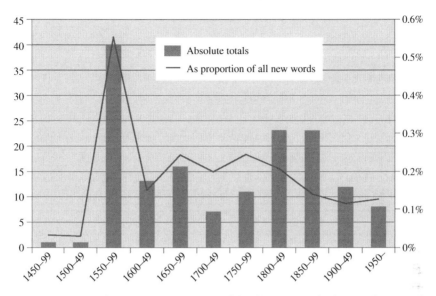

Fig. 15.5 Loanwords from Portuguese, as reflected by *OED3* (A–ALZ and M–RZZ).

and *mestizo* (1598). Such etymologies, from Spanish and/or Portuguese, make up 23% of the *OED3* data reflected in Fig. 15.5. For the period 1550–1699 they average 32% of the total. See further the discussion in section 15.2.5 on the more general formal issues that can make it very difficult to distinguish loanwords from various different Romance languages in Early Modern English.

15.2.4 Italian

There are few secure instances of loanwords directly from Italian in Middle English. Dietz (2005) looks at some of the most frequently suggested cases and whittles the list down to very few indeed. Of the words he considers, *vecke* 'old woman' (1390) and the coin name *sold* (?1448) are probable direct Italian loanwords. It is also possible that *bank*, denoting a financial institution (?c.1475), shows some direct input from Italian. Dietz also lists *orchil* 'type of red dye' and *marchpane* 'marzipan', but in the former case borrowing from French cannot be ruled out, and in the latter case the earliest evidence for English use cannot be securely dated earlier than 1516. A rather larger number of words of Italian origin probably entered Middle English via other languages, e.g. (via French) *alarm* (c.1400), *brigand* (?*a.*1400), *florin* (1303), *million* (*c.*1390), or (probably via Latin) *ducat* (*c.*1384). In some cases, such as the nautical term *mizzen* (1416), the mode of transmission is entirely unclear, and there is little to rule out transmission directly from Italian, although also nothing to rule out transmission via any of several other languages.

In the early to mid sixteenth century the number of direct Italian loanwords does not increase greatly, although there are notable examples such as *archipelago* (*c.*1503), *arsenal* (1511), *nuncio* (1512), *artichoke* (1531), *ballot* (1549; as both noun and verb, although both may be partly via French), *cupola* (1549), and (probably) *dispatch* (verb, 1517).[21] In the later sixteenth century the volume of loanwords increases greatly, including some words noted in section 2.2 as occurring in the 1,000 most frequent items in the *BNC*: *manage* (1561), *per cent* (1568; although probably strictly a loan translation), *post* 'position, office, job' (1562; although partly via French). Pinnavaia (2001) presents a detailed analysis of the Italian borrowings recorded in the *OED* (second edition); she includes semantic loans and loan blends as well as loanwords, although loanwords predominate in her data. She finds that the period 1550–1600 has the highest (absolute) total of Italian borrowings, followed by a gently descending curve to the end of the eighteenth century, and then a fresh rise (at least in absolute numbers) in the nineteenth century (although never reaching quite the level of the late sixteenth), followed by another decline in the twentieth. The parts of *OED3* so far published present a similar picture for the absolute totals of loanwords, although with not nearly so sharp a decline in the twentieth century: see Fig. 15.6. However, if one looks at Italian loanwords as a proportion of all new words, the eighteenth century appears as something of a peak rather than a dip, given the higher ratio of Italian loanwords among the relatively few words first attested in this period, reflecting continuing strong cultural influence from Italy. If we assume that the *OED*'s data reflects limited lexical innovation as shown by surviving textual sources, as seems reasonable (compare section 14.1.3), it is very interesting to note that Italian loanwords appear somewhat to buck this general trend.

Pinnavaia makes a detailed analysis of the borrowings into semantic categories. Some interesting trends are observable: words in semantic fields such as plants, social groups, behaviour, warfare, architecture, and money/

---

[21] Although often suggested, it is far from certain that *bankrupt* shows any direct Italian input: see discussion in Dietz (2005) 605–6.

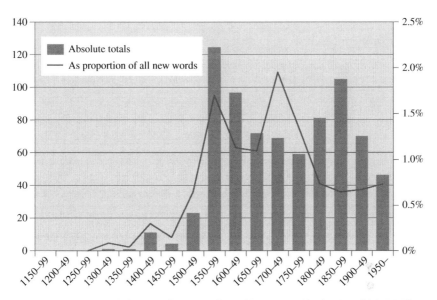

Fig. 15.6 Loanwords from Italian, as reflected by *OED3* (A–ALZ and M–RZZ).

finance/commerce have peaks in the Early Modern period, and make up a considerable proportion of all Italian borrowings in this period. Music and opera (followed less closely by pictorial art) are very prominent in the eighteenth and nineteenth centuries. Food and drink show a considerable increase from the early nineteenth century and predominate among the twentieth-century borrowings, a picture amply borne out by *OED3*'s data on more recent loanwords; compare for example *pistachio* (1598),[22] *macaroni* (1616), *broccoli* (1699), *semolina* (1784), *pesto* (*a.*1848), *salami* (1852), *minestrone* (1871), *pepperoni* (1888), *grappa* (1893), *linguine* (1920), *risotto* (1821), *pizza* (1825), *pasta* (1827), *spaghetti* (1845), *scampi* (1928), *al dente* (1935), *espresso* (1945), *cappuccino* (1948), *sambuca* (1971). Loanwords belonging (originally) to the sphere of music include *violin* (1579), *madrigal* (1584), *opera* (1648), *adagio* (1680), *allegro* (1683), *sonata* (1694), *oratorio* (1727),[23] *soprano* (1730), *duet* (1735), *sotto voce* (1737), *libretto* (1741), *aria* (1742), *coda* (1753), *prima donna* (1782), *finale* (1783). Terms belonging (originally) to other areas of the arts, the applied arts, or architecture include *cameo* (1561), *portico* (1579), *miniature* (*a.*1586), *gesso* (1596), *capriccio* (*a.*1616), *grotto* (1617), *balcony* (1618), *pergola* (*a.*1641), *novella*

---

[22] Earlier *pistace* is from French.
[23] Earlier in isolated use denoting a pulpit.

(1677), *terracotta* (1722), *ballerina* (1789), *studio* (1819), *replica* (1824; earlier in the meanings 'reply, response' and in the musical sense 'repeat'), *graffiti* (1851). Names for buildings with a particular function or for parts of an urban space include *seraglio* (1581), *piazza* (1583), *bazaar* (1588),[24] *ghetto* (1611), *casino* (1789). A selection of more notable words from other semantic areas are *tarantula* (1561), *scope* (1562, earliest denoting a target in shooting), *pedant* (*a.*1586, although this is probably partly via French), *stiletto* (1611), *umbrella* (1611), *regatta* (1612), *volcano* (1613), *sirocco* (1617), *manifesto* (1620), *generalissimo* (1621), *fuse* (1647), *vista* (1657, earliest as *visto*, on which see discussion in section 15.2.5), *al fresco* (1717), *influenza* (1743), *imbroglio* (1753), *bravo* (1761 as interjection), *tufa* (1777), *bravura* (1787), *confetti* (1815), *contessa* (1819), *vendetta* (1855), *fascism* (1921), *ciao* (1929), *paparazzo* (1961). Some words have shown considerable semantic extension in English, e.g. *miniature, cameo, studio.*

In Early Modern English many Italian words continued to enter English via French. Significant words of Italian origin that entered English (certainly or probably) via French after 1500 include *artisan* (*a.*1538), *partisan* (1542), *race* 'group connected by common descent or origin' (*a.*1547), *lottery* (1567), *populace* (1572), *musket* (1574), *panache* (1584), *concert* (1590), *to attack* (1600), *gazette* (1607), *pedal* (1611), *parasol* (1616), *risk* (1621), *burlesque* (1656), *attitude* (1668), *caprice* (1673; earlier borrowed directly as *capriccio*), *riposte* (1707), *fracas* (1727). See further the following section on some of the methodological difficulties in determining the precise mode of transmission in many cases.

15.2.5 Distinguishing Romance inputs in Early Modern English

As already noted, until well into the Early Modern period (and in some cases even later) it is often very difficult to distinguish precisely which Romance language a word has entered English from; this results from formal similarities between cognate forms in different Romance languages and also from the fact that morphological patterns that were established in borrowing French words into English were in many cases continued when borrowing words with cognate suffixes from other Romance languages. Additionally, there is a certain amount of instability and straightforward

---

[24] As with many other words in Early Modern English, Italian here acted as the means of transmission of a word from outside Europe, in this case ultimately from Persian.

unpredictability in the forms that early loanwords from Romance languages other than French show in English.

To begin with some relatively simple examples:

- *Adjutant* (1622), in early use also *ayudant*, could plausibly show a loanword from either Spanish *ayudante* or Portuguese *ajudante*, and very likely shows some input from both; in either case, the form *adjutant* reflects remodelling after the further etymon of both words, classical Latin *adiūtant-*, *adiūtāns*, present participle of *adiūtāre* 'to assist'; French *adjutant* shows similar remodelling, but is first attested considerably later than the English form and hence in this instance can be eliminated from consideration as etymon of the English word.
- *Mustachio* (1551), which is attested in a wide variety of spellings in early use, including *mostacho*, *mustacho*, probably reflects borrowing of both Italian *mustacchio* and Spanish *mostacho*; compare likewise *nave* (1501), *peccadillo* (1591), *punctilio* (1596).
- *Capitana* 'ship of an admiral or commander, flagship' (1596) probably shows borrowing from both Spanish *capitana* and Italian *capitana*; it occurs directly translating both words, and in contexts that refer clearly to either a Spanish or an Italian ship, as well as to ships with a similar function in other fleets (e.g. a Turkish one).
- *Padre* 'Christian clergyman, Roman Catholic priest' (1584) probably shows borrowing from Italian *padre*, Spanish *padre*, and Portuguese *padre*: it occurs in localized reference to priests in countries where each of these languages are spoken, as well as in more generalized use.

The variability and unpredictability in form shown by many early loanwords from Romance languages other than French can be illustrated through a brief investigation of words showing the suffixes *-ade* and *-ado*.

The suffix *-ade* first entered English in loanwords from French, e.g. *ballade* (a.1393). It ultimately reflects Latin *-āta*, but only indirectly: the regular reflex of Latin *-āta* in French is *-ée*, whereas in other Romance languages a dental consonant is preserved, e.g. Spanish *-ada* or Italian *-ata*. French *-ade* reflects borrowing into French of words with the reflex of Latin *-āta* in other Romance languages, e.g. Old French *balade* < Old Occitan *balada*. New formations occurred in French on the model of borrowed words, e.g. *oeillade* 'glance' or *arquebusade* 'shot from a harquebus', both of which were subsequently borrowed into English. On the model of borrowed words like these, occasional new formations are found in English from the late seventeenth century, most notably *blockade*. Additionally, in English the French pattern of substitution of *-ade* is also sometimes found when words are borrowed from other Romance languages, e.g. (as noted in section 15.2.3) *pinionade*, probably from either Catalan *pinyonada* or Old Occitan *pinhonat*. Compare also *brocade* (earlier also *brocardo*, *brocado*, *brocard*) < Spanish *brocado*, or *renegade* (earlier *renegado*) < Spanish *renegado*. *Masquerade* (1587) probably shows borrowing from both French *mascarade*, *Masquerade* and from Italian *mascherata*.

The history of *-ado* is rather more complicated. In English words such as *renegado* 'renegade' (1573; < Spanish) or *crusado* 'Portuguese coin bearing the figure of a cross' (1544; < Portuguese), *-ado* straightforwardly reflects borrowing of Spanish or Portuguese words in *-ado* (showing the reflex of Latin *-ātus*). However, it often occurs also in English borrowings of Spanish or Portuguese words ending in the equivalent feminine suffix *-ada*, e.g. English *carbonado* (1575, occasionally also *carbonada*) from Spanish *carbonada*; compare also *tornado* (1589), apparently from Spanish *tronada* 'thunderstorm'.[25] In English, *-ado* can also occur as the ending of words that more commonly (and regularly) show *-ade*, as e.g. *masquerado*, *mascarado*, variants of *masquerade* (on the etymology of which see above). The converse occurs in cases like *renegade* (1611), a remodelling of *renegado* (although perhaps also influenced by earlier *renegate* 'apostate'), or *brocade*, earlier *brocado* (1588; < Spanish *brocado* and/or Portuguese *brocado*). A less common pattern is illustrated by *poignado* 'small dagger' (?a.1549), a remodelling of *poniard* (1533; < French *poignard*).

The reasons for this interchangeability of suffixes is uncertain: Dietz (2005 608–12) presents a persuasive case that restrictions on the range of vowels found in final position in the sound system of Early Modern English played a major part. Among the example words listed above, compare *visto*, a common variant of *vista* down to the early nineteenth century, apparently arising simply from uncertainty about the quality of final vowels in Italian loans.

The resulting situation is one where the exact route of transmission of particular words and word forms is often very uncertain. For instance, to return to the example of *marmalade*, *OED3* records the following spellings

---

[25] The form of the English word *tornado* may perhaps result from association with Spanish *tornado*, the past participle of *tornar* 'to turn, return', although metathesis would also satisfactorily explain the change in the stem of *tronada*.

as all being found in the Early Modern period (arranged here according to their endings):

> marmalade, marmelade, marmilade, marmulade, marmylade, mermalade, merme-
>   lade, mormelade
> marmalad, marmelad, marmilad, marmylad
> marmaled
> marmalado, mermelado
> marmalate, marmelate, marmulate, marmylate
> marmalat, marmalatt, marmilat
> marmalet, marmfaalett, marmelett, marmlet, marm'let, marmolet, marmulet
> marmalit
> marmeleta

It would be tempting to try to assign some of these forms to multiple inputs from other languages (compare e.g. Italian *marmellata*, French *marmelat*, post-classical Latin *marmelatum*), but, in addition to the chronological difficulties already noted, the variety of form shown by other words in -*ade* in the same period suggests that the variation could have arisen entirely within English.

15.2.6 Greek

Loanwords from Greek constitute the third highest total overall in Fig. 2.1 in section 2.1. The vast majority of these are from ancient Greek; or more precisely, they are either from Greek in the period up to 300 BC that is technically denoted ancient Greek, or they are from Greek of the subsequent Hellenistic Greek period from 300 BC to AD 300. Very few indeed come from modern Greek.

Words ultimately from Greek have already been discussed at many points in this book. Up to 1500, nearly all cases probably entered English via Latin, hence the history of words ultimately from Greek in English is part of the history of words directly from Latin. Compare the discussion of words ultimately of Greek origin in Old English in section 8.2.1.

In the Early Modern period, some direct knowledge of Greek became more widespread among the highly educated, especially among scholars (including biblical scholars), and we begin to find cases where transmission solely from Greek seems possible. Fig. 15.7 tabulates those cases where *OED3* posits at least some input directly from Greek. However, it should be noted that, in all cases from before 1500, direct input from Latin is also

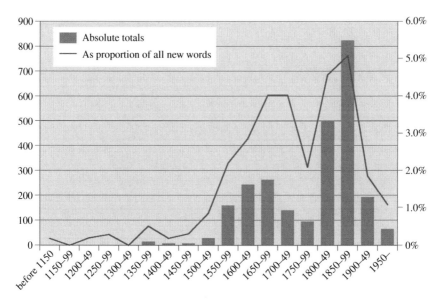

Fig. 15.7 Loanwords from Greek, as reflected by *OED3* (A–ALZ and M–RZZ).

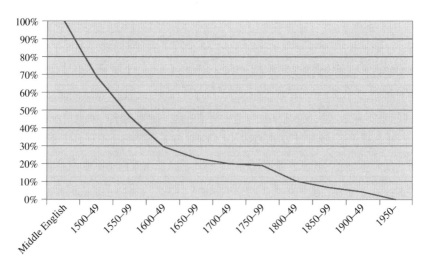

Fig. 15.8 The proportion of Greek loanwords that have entered English partly via Latin, as reflected by *OED3* (A–ALZ and M–RZZ).

posited and it is very likely that in all of these cases the initial transmission was via Latin, with direct input from Greek occurring only later in a word history. Fig. 15.8 gives the proportion of Greek loanwords in *OED3* that are indicated as partly from Latin. (In the data from more recent centuries in

Fig. 15.8, some cases show hybrid words, from a Latin element in combination with a Greek one, rather than transmission via Latin.)

The history of Greek loanwords in Later Modern English is complicated by a different set of factors, already examined in chapter 14. The peak of Greek loanwords in the late nineteenth century, and the generally high levels in the early nineteenth and twentieth centuries, are largely attributable to new coinages formed from Greek elements in the expanding vocabulary of the sciences. As examined in section 14.8.1, the majority of such words show the compounding of two or more words or word elements of Greek origin to create an entirely new word within English, and their status as loanwords is somewhat difficult. Additionally, the productivity of affixes ultimately of Greek origin has been examined in section 14.4 and the role of neoclassical combining forms of Greek origin in section 14.9.

The phenomenon of borrowing a single word from ancient Greek as a single loanword in English, not mediated through Latin, is largely a phenomenon of the Early Modern English period. The total of these runs to hundreds of loanwords. Some examples of commoner words where *OED3* does not posit transmission via Latin include *acme* (*a.*1568), *meiosis* (1550), *mimesis* (1550), *onomastic* (1576), *pathos* (1579), *pederasty* (1603), *oligarch* (*a.*1610, but rare before the nineteenth century), *polymath* (1624), *orthodoxy* (1630), *palindrome* (*a.*1637), *polyglot* (1650), *miasma* (1665), *nous* (1678), and derivative formations on Greek words, such as *polemical* (1615), *misogynist* (1620), *prismatic* (1668). Even in a carefully selected list such as this, there are few words that have penetrated completely into everyday language and that do not convey some connotation of learning. Most direct Greek loanwords in English belong firmly to the learned vocabulary of particular specialist fields. Additionally, there are few words where the possibility of transmission via Latin (or in some cases French) can be eliminated entirely: among the words listed above, several are found commonly in Latin contexts from the Middle Ages and later, and this may have been the route of transmission into English. The decisions made concerning the etymologies of such words in *OED3* typically indicate that there is no particular reason to suspect that the transmission was not directly from Greek, since it occurred in a period when Greek was being studied in English-speaking communities and there is no clear sign of transmission via another language, but we can rarely be entirely certain that the transmission was not mediated through Latin or a vernacular.

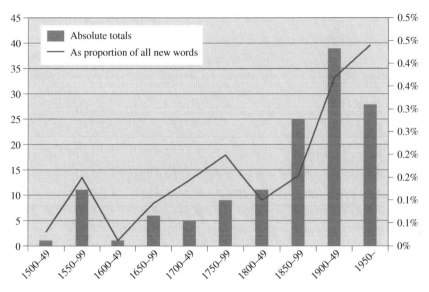

Fig. 15.9 Loanwords from Russian, as reflected by *OED3* (A–ALZ and M–RZZ).

15.2.7 Russian

Russian is the one European language among the top twenty-five sources listed in section 2.1 that has yet to be considered at all in this book. Fig. 15.9 gives the overall pattern, as shown by *OED3*. The numbers of loanwords are very low overall and probably very little weight should be given to the fluctuations shown from the mid sixteenth century to the mid nineteenth (although the late sixteenth-century spike is shown also by the totals in the full *OED* wordlist). Down to the mid nineteenth century, the loanwords largely denote aspects of Russian culture or society, e.g. *boyar*, *tsar*, *verst* (all 1555), *rouble* (1557), *muzhik* 'peasant' (1587), *protopope* 'senior priest' (1591), *pope* 'parish priest' (1662), *copeck* (1698), *tsarevich* (1710), *knout* (1716), *yurt* (1780), *rayon* 'area surrounding a city, fortress' (1830; later in specific Soviet use denoting an administrative area), *samovar* (1830), *babushka* (1834), *oblast* (*a.*1837), or products of the natural world, e.g. *beluga* (1591, but much later denoting the caviar as opposed to the fish). *Mammoth* (1706) is a rare example that has come to be used without any specifically Russian associations; *steppe* (*a.*1670) has currency as a general geographical term, as well as denoting the Central Asian 'Great Steppe'. *Parka* is first attested in 1625, but until the late nineteenth century is restricted to use denoting the traditional garment worn by peoples of the Arctic. Although *vodka* (1802–3) is very widely drunk and is produced in many other countries, its marketing and branding in the English-speaking world typically plays on its Russian origin, reinforcing consciousness of the Russian origin of the word.

Many loanwords from the second half of the nineteenth century and later likewise have reference to aspects of Russian culture and society in general or to Russian products, as e.g. *borsch* (1884), *borzoi* (1887), *dacha* (1896), *matryoshka* (1946), but a distinct strand is shown by words relating to politics and in particular to communism and its antecedents, as well as to political violence, as *duma* (1870), *kulak* (1877), *intelligentsia* (1883), *pogrom* (1891), *Bolshevik* (1907), *Presidium* (1907), *Soviet* (1917), *Menshevism* (1920), *Politburo* (1923), *agitprop* (1925), *troika* (1945; 1842 denoting a type of vehicle drawn by three horses), *Gulag* (1946), *nomenklatura* (1958), *samizdat* (1967), *glasnost* and *perestroika* (both 1986). Compare also *sputnik* (1957), reflecting Soviet technological success, and the name of the art movement *Suprematism* (1920).

15.2.8 Recent loanwords from French revisited

These brief surveys of loanwords from some of the other major European donor languages help put Later Modern English borrowing from French in perspective. During the eighteenth and nineteenth centuries there is a very gradual shift from the patterns found in the sixteenth and seventeenth centuries. If we take the same method as applied in sections 15.2.1 to 15.2.7 to loans from other European donor languages and pick out some of the most notable French loanwords, in the sixteenth and seventeenth centuries the volume of loanwords is so great that sampling of words recorded just in a single year is sufficient to give an impression of the variety of words being borrowed. Among loanwords first recorded in 1550 we find (including words from French and/or Latin) *barbarian, baton, buffoon, cassock, decadence, demolition, embark, encouragement, germ, gratify, heredity, humid, imbecile, incivil, monologue, pistolet, rampart, sack* 'plundering', *superb, timid, torture.*[26] In 1600: *attack* (as verb), *avenue, carnage, couscous, defrock, dessert, dose, drollery, gazelle.* In 1650: *carousel, despotic,*

---

[26] This list includes sources with the approximate dating *c.*1550 and is hence a much longer list than for most individual years.

patrol; also (from French and/or Latin) *decapitation, periodic*. In the words from the three sample years there are some words restricted to particular areas of discourse (e.g. *cassock, defrock, pistolet*) or to more formal registers (e.g. *gratify, incivil, drollery*), but many others that belong to the vocabulary of everyday life, familiar to almost all speakers of modern English, and used as the normal everyday name for a particular thing or concept.

If we proceed with ten-year samples taken from the beginning of each fifty-year period from 1700 onwards, there are some gradual shifts in the types of loanwords that we find. In these samples I have excluded words showing probable multiple inputs, which in any case become significantly rarer in this later period, and also words that could alternatively be explained as derivatives from earlier borrowings. I have included only items likely to be familiar to a fairly wide cross-section of speakers of modern English; most are included in large desktop dictionaries such as *The Oxford Dictionary of English*.[27]

Among the words first attested 1700–09, there are a handful of words in common culinary use (*cutlet, terrine, meringue, mirabelle, rissole*), a type of fabric (*velours*), an item of furniture (*escritoire*), a casino term (*croupier*), one from fencing (*riposte*), and some terms from architecture, fortification, or construction (*caisson, ramp*, and also *console*, found earliest with reference to architecture, and *envelope*, earliest attested with reference to fortification, but found also in several other borrowed senses, including 'cover for a letter', in the early decades of the century; compare also *debris*, although this is recorded earliest in English in figurative use). There is only one word belonging to the general abstract vocabulary of English: *crucial*.

Among the words first attested 1750–9, there is a less clear division into semantic fields that are particularly associated with French cultural influence, but it is more obvious that the words are spread along a cline from words that have entered the general vocabulary of English without any strong association with France or French culture to others that remain clear Gallicisms. At the one end of this cline are *decompose, dentist, evaluation, mentor, optimism* (all of which are likely to be apprehended as Latin rather than French loans), *manoeuvre*, probably also *banal, duvet, fete*, and *morale*, and perhaps *gauche*. Towards the other end of the cline are

---

[27] For much more extensive listing of French loanwords, grouped chronologically and with some semantic analysis, based largely on the documentation of the first edition of the *OED*, see Mackenzie (1939).

dénouement, embonpoint, ennui, friseur, née, papier mâché, persiflage, sang-froid, vignette, vis-à-vis.

Among the words first attested 1800–9, words belonging to (or originating in) scientific or technical vocabulary become more prominent: *chrome, centigram, centilitre, centimetre, galvanize, lignite, mastodont, tannin, urea, vaccine.* Besides these, there are names of pieces of furniture (*chaise-longue, chiffonier*), terms from literature or the arts (*bibliomane, littérateur, écossaise*), names of drinks (*absinthe, vermouth*), a military term (*fusillade*), and a term used with historical reference to feudalism (*suzerain*). In addition to some of the scientific or technical words already mentioned (e.g. *chrome, vaccine*), some other words have become unmarked members of the everyday vocabulary of modern English, most notably *abattoir, analogue, escarpment, restaurant, surveillance, utilize*; some items that remain more marked stylistically are *exigeant, debacle, retroussé, tirade*, and the borrowed phrase *tour de force.*

In 1850–9 there are further scientific and technical terms: *bolide, carnivore, gyroscope, herbivore, vacuole*, or (from the worlds of architecture and antiquities) *crenellate, dolmen.* There is a clutch of words in more or less unmarked use in contemporary English: *altruism, barrage, beige, chic, communiqué, delimit, derail, extradition, fiancée, juxtapose, opt, ponce, provocateur*, probably also *milieu*; at the more marked end of the cline are *flâneur* and phrasal constructions such as *à deux, c'est la vie, crème de cassis, n'est-ce pas, nom de plume, petit bourgeois, prix fixe.*

In the two twentieth-century samples 1900–9 and 1950–9, there are transport terms, *metro* (1904) and *garage* (1902; a high-frequency word, although still varying between more and less naturalized pronunciations), as well as *marque* (1906, originally used specifically of motor vehicles), and *motocross* (1951) from motor sports. From elsewhere in the world of sport come *touché* (1904) and *pétanque* (1955). There are terms from the arts, *pointillism* (1901), *art nouveau* (1908), *musique concrète* (1952), *nouvelle vague* (1959), as well as *discotheque* (1954) from the world of popular music, and *rapportage* (1903) denoting a style of writing. Terms for food and drink are the largest single category: *pêche Melba* (1902), *Pernod* (1908), *reblochon* (1908), *Viognier* (1908), *oeuf en cocotte* (1909), *pistou* (1951), *rouille* (1951), *amuse-bouche* (1959). The world of fashion is represented by *prêt-à-porter* (1957), and politics and economics by *Gaullism* (1950) and *dirigisme* (1951). A field of study is denoted by *codicology* (1953) and a new technology by *microfiche* (1950). A period in French social and cultural history is denoted by *belle époque* (1952). There is a further borrowed noun phrase, *amour fou* (1902), and an idiomatic phrase, *plus ça change* (1955).

As these examples illustrate, there are progressively fewer words that belong simply to the register of everyday polite or semi-formal discourse (as will be examined further in chapter 16). In the nineteenth century, when the absolute numbers of new French loanwords are very high (compare section 14.1.3), a high proportion of the loanwords reflect the prominence of French as a language of scholarship and research. It is notable that, as discussed in section 15.2.2, the second half of the nineteenth century is the period in which the total of loanwords from German comes closest to that from French, again largely reflecting lexical innovation in scholarly writing in German.

Outside this learned or technical level of the vocabulary, French loanwords in Later Modern English are more and more restricted to certain fields of social or cultural activity in which France is particularly renowned or prestigious (e.g. food and drink, music, fashion). In the twentieth century, as the number of new borrowings declines, so this trend becomes even more marked, as does the tendency for non-technical borrowings to remain marked Gallicisms (although some may of course show further naturalization over time).[28] It is often the words that are more Latinate and less transparently French in form that have become most thoroughly embedded in the English lexicon, as well as some items denoting institutions or practices that have become commonplace in the contemporary world. As comparison with loanwords from Italian, Spanish, German, or Dutch shows, gradually borrowing from French has become more similar to that from other major European languages. Loanwords from French remain more numerous than those from any of these other languages (although only ahead of German by a whisker in the later nineteenth century),[29] but borrowing from French is much less different in kind than it was in earlier centuries.

---

[28] Compare Schultz (2012a) and the summary account in Schultz (2012b) for a useful analysis of twentieth-century borrowings from French, divided into subject fields; her data draws on both revised and unrevised parts of the *OED*, and includes semantic loans as well as loanwords.

[29] For numerical analysis of very recent borrowings, see Durkin (2006).

15.3 Loanwords from languages from outside Europe

The changing circumstances of borrowing from languages from outside Europe have already been sketched in section 15.1. (See introduction to this chapter on what is meant by the formulation 'languages from outside Europe' as used here.) This section looks at each of the languages that figure among the twenty-five most prolific sources listed in section 2.1 (Japanese, Arabic, Sanskrit, Maori, Hindi, Hebrew, Persian, Malay, Urdu, Chinese). It is only possible to look very briefly at each of these languages here, but the section ends with two slightly longer discussions of loanwords from Maori and from Japanese as contrasting test cases. Throughout this section I will for the most part avoid the discussion of words that derive from proper names, such as names of fabrics derived from the names of towns, except where there is clear evidence of mediation via a distinct form or meaning in the local language.

15.3.1 Arabic

The number of direct loanwords from Arabic reflected by the *OED* is relatively small, but there is an unusually large number of indirect loans via other languages.[30] It is uncertain whether there are any loanwords directly from Arabic before 1500; apparent cases, such as the star name *Aldebaran* (*a.*1393), probably just reflect a gap in the historical record for the language of transmission (in this case, like most others, probably Latin or French). However, many words ultimately of Arabic origin entered English in the Middle English and Early Modern periods. Many of these reflect the indebtedness of Western Europe to Arabic thinkers and writers, both for their own original contributions to knowledge and for their transmission of learning from Antiquity; compare e.g. *alchemy* (*c.*1390), *almanac* (*c.*1392), *nadir* (*c.*1392; originally in astronomical use), *cipher* (1399; later *zero* ultimately shows the same origin), *alkali* (?*a.*1400), or *algebra* (*a.*1400 with reference to treating fractured bones, 1551 with reference to mathematics). Others are more general cultural loans or names of traded goods, such as *saffron* (*c.*1200), *mattress* (*c.*1300), *galangal* (?*a.*1325), *syrup* (1398), *crimson*

---

[30] For a general survey of Arabic words in English, based largely on documentation from the second edition of the *OED* and from selected other dictionaries, see Cannon (1994).

(1416), or *ream* (1482), while others again have reference specifically to aspects of the Arabic world, e.g. *caliph* (1393) or *mosque* (?*a.*1425). Many of these words entered English only after a long route of transmission via numerous other languages and often in forms that bore little resemblance to the Arabic word forms; *syrup* is ultimately from Arabic *sharāb* (*sherbet* and *sorbet* are both ultimately related), *ream* from Arabic *rizma* (formerly also †*razma*), and *mosque* from Arabic *masjid* (in some colloquial pronunciations *masgid*). In all of these cases, it is highly unlikely that the Arabic word has had any direct impact on any stage of the word's history in English.

Small numbers of (probable) direct borrowings are found in Early Modern English and the numbers subsequently climb modestly, peaking round about 1800: see Fig. 15.10 for the picture presented by *OED3*. In many cases, especially earlier in this period, it is difficult to be certain that a loan has come directly from Arabic rather than via another language; typically, the most that can be said is that there is no clear evidence of transmission via another language arising from considerations of word form, word meaning, or the earliest contexts of use, and there is at least some contemporary evidence for direct contact between English speakers and Arabic speakers. Most of these loans relate specifically to aspects of

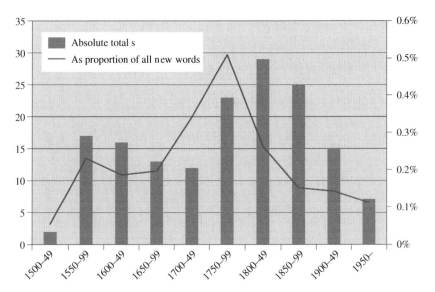

Fig. 15.10 Loanwords from Arabic, as reflected by *OED3* (A–ALZ and M–RZZ), 1500–present.

Arabic culture (or to Islam), e.g. *hashish* (1598), *madrasa* (1616), *hammam* (1625), *kohl* (1799), *hadj* (1847), *hijab* (1885), *mujahidin* (1887). Greater currency is shown by some of the large number of later loanwords ultimately of Arabic origin that have entered English wholly or partly via French (in many cases at the end of a longer chain of transmission), e.g. *carat* (1552), *magazine* (1583), *giraffe* (1594), *couscous* (1600), *assassin* (1603), *sequin* (1613), *alcove* (1655), or via other European languages, e.g. *artichoke* (1531; < Italian), *coffee* (1598; < a form in another Germanic language), *alfalfa* (1767; < Spanish).

15.3.2 Hebrew

Hebrew ranks somewhat lower among the twenty-five most prolific donor sources than Arabic, but, like Arabic, it also shows an unusually large number of indirect loans, especially in earlier centuries. For instance, *alleluia*, *amen*, *pharoah*, and *rabbi* are among words that occur (mostly in very restricted contexts) already in Old English texts (although their Middle English and later currency may reflect re-borrowing). However, it is unlikely that there any direct loans from Hebrew before the Early Modern period, earlier instances having almost certainly been mediated through Latin and French (sometimes < French < Latin < Greek < Hebrew). In the sixteenth century we begin to find some words that may have entered English directly from Hebrew, for instance *homer* 'type of dry or liquid measure' or *log* 'type of liquid measure', both in Tyndale's Bible translation. Fig. 15.11 gives the pattern after 1500, as shown by *OED3*. Most loanwords reflect biblical use or Jewish religious or cultural traditions, e.g. *shekel* (1560; now also used with reference to the modern Israeli unit of currency), *sanhedrim* (1588), *Midrash* (1613), *mitzvah* (1723). Many nineteenth-century loans are either probably or certainly via Yiddish, e.g. *goy* (1841), *kosher* (1851), *chutzpah* (1891), *golem* (1897); see also section 15.2.2 for further entirely certain cases. Some loans reflecting the revival of Hebrew as a language of everyday discourse in modern Israel include *kibbutz* (1931), *kippah* 'skullcap' (1964), or *Shoah* (1967).[31]

---

[31] For an account, intended for a popular audience, of some of the Hebrew words and phrases that are most familiar among English speakers, see Glinert (1992).

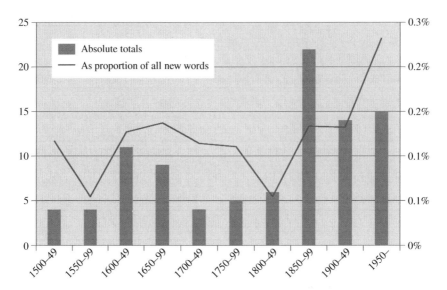

Fig. 15.11 Loanwords from Hebrew, as reflected by *OED3* (A–ALZ and M–RZZ), 1500–present.

15.3.3 Languages of South Asia

Fig. 15.12 groups together *OED3* data on borrowing from Sanskrit, Hindi, Persian, and Urdu together with other languages of South Asia, among which the next highest totals of loanwords are from (in descending order) Tamil, Bengali, Marathi, Sinhala, Panjabi, Malayalam, Pashto, Tibetan, Telugu, Gujarati, Rajasthani, Assamese, and Nepali.[32] I have here interpreted South Asia very broadly, including Persian, Pashto, and Tibetan, because the majority of direct loanwords from these languages in the *OED* reflect contact as a result of British colonialism in South Asia (although Persian words have certainly entered English through many other channels, directly and especially indirectly). I have aggregated the figures in this way because distinguishing between loanwords from several of the major languages of South Asia is particularly problematic. Some of the hardest

---

[32] On loanwords in the context of British colonialism in South Asia in general the classic work remains one from the nineteenth century, revised at the beginning of the twentieth, Yule and Burnell (1903); a work that is in many ways a successor to this is Lewis (1991); see also Rao (1954), Hawkins (1984), Muthiah (1991), Hankin (1992). For a general survey of Persian words in English, based largely on documentation from the second edition of the *OED* and from selected other dictionaries, see Cannon and Kaye (2001).

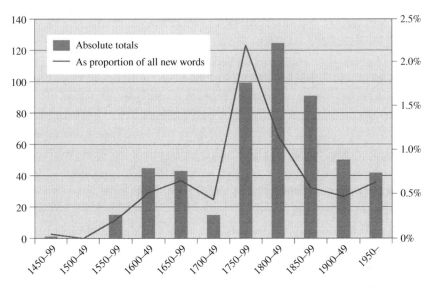

Fig. 15.12 Loanwords from languages of South Asia, as reflected by *OED3* (A–ALZ and M–RZZ).

problems are posed by loanwords from Indic languages, and especially Hindi and Urdu. In contemporary use, Hindi denotes a language spoken in northern India, used as the official language of the federal government of India, and containing a good deal of formal and technical lexis borrowed from (closely related) Sanskrit; Urdu denotes a language used in Pakistan and parts of northern India, which has the status of national language in Pakistan, and which contains a good deal of formal and technical lexis borrowed from (less closely related) Persian or (unrelated) Arabic. In pre-partition India, the situation was rather more complicated, and assigning English words as borrowings from one language or the other presents many problems. *OED3* takes an approach that to some extent reflects the further etymology of the borrowed words. Broadly, words that are ultimately from Sanskrit (or a closely related Indic variety) and that have a distinct form or meaning in English reflecting a Hindi form or meaning are given as loanwords from Hindi; words that could be explained plausibly as borrowings directly from Sanskrit are presented as Sanskrit loans; words that originate in Persian or Arabic and show mediation through an Indic language are presented as loanwords from Urdu.

The pattern shown by Fig. 15.12 is interesting: the peak in absolute numbers of loanwords from 1750 to 1899 correlates closely with British

colonial involvement with South Asia, although the drop in the first half of
the twentieth century is perhaps somewhat surprising, as is the rather earlier
peak in the second half of the eighteenth century in the proportion of all new
words in the *OED* that is made up by loanwords from South Asia. It would
appear that the lexical influence was strongest early in the period of British
colonial expansion in the region, probably as new aspects of material and
social culture were encountered. Some early cases may show borrowing via
other European languages, for instance Portuguese (compare examples in
section 15.2.3). As the examples below show, most of the loanwords that
have had the biggest impact on general English usage are also first attested
in the early nineteenth century or earlier; in fact, many are concentrated in
the seventeenth century, early in the period of direct involvement of British
merchants with South Asia, and considerably before the major military
expansion of the British East India Company. A notable exception to this
general trend is the vocabulary of South Asian food and drink, which is
currently becoming better known outside expatriate communities in majority English-speaking communities (especially in Britain) as a result of the
spread and popularity of restaurants reflecting various South Asian cuisines.
Food and drink terms make up a sizable proportion of the twentieth-century
loanwords, and many of the terms with considerably earlier dates of first
attestation have only recently come to be widely known.

Words that have entered general English usage (at least in Britain) include

> (< Sanskrit) *pundit* (1661), *mantra* (1795), *nirvana* (1801); (< Hindi) *puttee* (1882;
> now in less common use); (< Hindi and Panjabi) *pukka* (1619); (< Urdu and Persian)
> *pyjamas* (1801), *pashmina* (1850); (probably ultimately < Gujarati) *coolie* (1622);
> (< Tamil and Malayalam) *pariah* (1613); (< Tibetan) *polo* (1872)

Outside the *OED3* revised sequences, some of the most notable words of
South Asian origin that are now typically used with little or no consciousness of their origin are

> *chintz* (1614), *cot* 'small bed' (1634), *juggernaut* (1638), *shawl* (1662), *bungalow*
> (1676), *dungaree* (1696), *catamaran* (1697), *shampoo* (1762, originally as verb), *jungle*
> (1776), *cheetah* (1781), *chit* (1785; clipped < *chitty* (1698)), *bangle* (1787), *dinghy*
> (1810), *thug* (1810), *yoga* (1818), *loot* (1839), *gymkhana* (1861), *khaki* (1863), *cushy*
> (1915); see also below on food and drink terms

Additionally, for most speakers probably no more than vaguely 'Eastern'
associations attach to items such as *hookah* (1763) or *ganja* (1800), while
cultural items such as *guru* (1613) or *karma* (1827), or clothing terms such as

sari (1785) or *burka* (1836) are clearly identified with a particular culture, but known to all speakers. A rare example of an item with greater currency in North America than in Britain is the cloth name *nainsook* (1790). For some examples of borrowings from South Asian languages into South African English see section 15.2.1. A number of South Asian loans are now rather dated slang, such as *choky* 'prison' (1608), *deck* or *dekko* 'a look (at something)' (1853), or *blighty* 'home, Britain' (1915).

Food and drink terms include:

> (< Hindi) *mung* (bean) (1611), *raita* (1832), *saag* (1852), *aloo* (1916), *pakora* (1932), *chaat* (1954), *aloo gobi* (1974); (< Persian and Urdu) *paneer* (1954), *kulfi* (1966); (< Urdu) *masala* (1780), *naan* (1780), *rogan josh* (1934), *mughlai* (1936), *pasanda* (1961), *murgh* (1976); (< Persian and Hindi) *pilau* (1609); (< Tamil) *poppadom* (1820); (< Bengali) *jalfrezi* (1979); (< Marathi) *patia* (1954); also, outside the *OED3* revised material, many further familiar items such as *ghee* (1665), *dal* (1698), *chupatti* (1810).

However, relatively few culinary terms of South Asian origin are frequent outside of discussion explicitly of South Asian food; exceptions to the general rule are *curry* (1598), *punch* (as name of the drink) (1600), *kedgeree* (1662), *chutney* (1813), *mulligatawny* (1784), which are probably all used by at least some speakers with little consciousness of their South Asian origin.

Terms that continue to have more obvious association with South Asia include

> (< Sanskrit) *raja* (1555), *maharaja* (1676); (< Hindi) *rupee* (1612), *punkah* (*a.*1625), *mahout* (1662), *babu* (1763), *nautch* (1777), *raj* (1781), *bindi* (1872); (< Persian and Urdu) *maidan* (?1551), *purdah* (1621), *nazir* (1648); (< Urdu) *nabob* (1612).

Terms with reference to the religions of South Asia include

> (< Sanskrit) *Rigveda* (1767), *Mahabharata* (1768), *Maharishi* (1785), *om* (1785), *mandala* (1859); (< Persian and Urdu, in some cases also partly < Arabic) *masjid* (1594), *mullah* (1613).

15.3.4 Malay

Borrowing from Malay, as reflected by Fig. 15.13, shows a broadly similar pattern to borrowing from languages of South Asia, although the numbers concerned are very small.[33] The peak in the absolute number of loanwords

---

[33] On the difficulties posed by identification of the immediate donor language in the case of many loans occurring in South-East Asia, and also on the problems of labelling caused by changes in the modern use of language names such as Malay and Indonesian, see Fraser Gupta (2008).

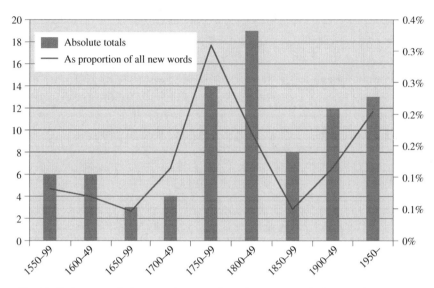

Fig. 15.13 Loanwords from Malay, as reflected by *OED3* (A–ALZ and M–RZZ).

again falls in the first half of the nineteenth century and the highest peak in the percentage of all loanwords is in the late eighteenth century. The comparatively high figures in the second half of the twentieth century are interesting, but it should be noted that the numbers of words involved are very small; the *OED* as a whole (rather than just *OED3*) shows a larger peak in absolute totals in the first half of the nineteenth century, but then twentieth-century totals slightly lower than those in the second half of the nineteenth century. Some notable loanwords include *sago* (1555), *durian* (1588), *gong* (*c.*1600), *cassowary* (1611), *paddy* (1623, earliest in the meaning 'rough or unhusked rice', later in the meaning 'paddy field'), (probably) *compound* 'enclosure' (1679), *orangutan* (1699), *kapok* (1735), *agar-agar* (1769), *gecko* (1774), *pangolin* (1774), *caddy* (for tea) (1792), *sarong* (1834), *rupiah* (1914), *nasi goreng* (1924), *satay* (1934); perhaps also *bamboo* (1598; probably via Dutch), *launch* 'small vessel' (1697; via Spanish); for some further examples of indirect loans via Dutch or Portuguese see sections 15.2.1 and 15.2.3. Those words that have become most thoroughly established in English use date disproportionately from the earlier part of the chronological range. As in the case of South Asian languages, some loanwords result from contact with emigrant communities in various different geographical localities where English is spoken: compare the examples of loanwords in South African English in section 15.2.1.

15.3.5 Chinese

Fig. 15.14 shows the pattern for loanwords from Chinese as reflected by *OED3*; the pattern shown by the whole of the *OED* is similar, although the earliest loanwords date from rather earlier, in the second half of the sixteenth century. (Here I will group together Cantonese, Mandarin, and other varieties under the single language name Chinese.) Notable examples include *ginseng* (1654), *yin* and *yang* (both 1671), *chop*-stick (1699), *tao* (1704), *feng-shui* (1797), *kow-tow* (1804), *qi* (1850), *yuan* (1921 denoting the currency), *mah-jong* (1922), *gung ho* (1942), *kung-fu* (1966); the food terms *lychee* (1588), *kumquat* (1699), *ketchup* (1711), *loquat* (1820), *bok choy* (1847), *chop-suey* (1888), *fu yung* (1917), *dim sum* (1948), *hoisin* (1957); and the tea terms *cha* (1616), *pekoe* (1713), *souchong* (1761), *oolong* (1845), and indirectly also *tea* itself (1655). Some words in the *OED* reflect borrowing from extraterritorial varieties of Chinese, such as *kiasu* 'person governed by self-interest' (1978), a borrowing used in English in South-East Asia (especially Singapore), from Chinese as used in South-East Asia. Some are confined largely or wholly to English as used in specific localities where Chinese is either the majority language or the first language of a large part of the population, as e.g. in Hong Kong English or Singapore English. The *OED* as yet contains very few loans directly reflecting China's recent

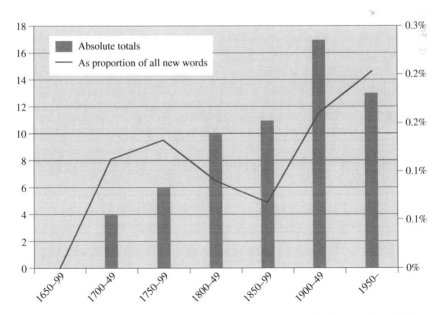

Fig. 15.14 Loanwords from Chinese, as reflected by *OED3* (A–ALZ and M–RZZ).

economic and technological advances; *taikonaut* (1998) apparently shows a blend of Chinese *tai kong* 'outer space' and English *astronaut*.[34]

15.3.6 Maori

Maori ranks quite highly among the crude totals of loanwords reflected by the parts of *OED3* so far completed, as seen in the data presented in section 2.1. These words have all been borrowed over a comparatively short time span. Specialist New Zealand English sources record many more loanwords. However, there are pressing questions of whose English (if anyone's) many of these words belong to, which we will return to shortly.

Maori words in English offer an attractive case for slightly more extensive consideration for various reasons: the place of contact can be identified clearly; there is a clear chronological terminus a quo, Captain Cook's first voyage to New Zealand in 1769,[35] followed by trading contacts in the remaining decades of the eighteenth century and by missionary activity and European settlement from early in the nineteenth century; and the lexicon of New Zealand English and the contribution of Maori words to it have been well studied.

The *DNZE*, a historical dictionary ultimately on the model of the *OED*, records 746 words of Maori origin, amounting to over 10% of its full headword list. Nearly 69% of these are names of flora and fauna, 18% are words connected with social culture, and 13% are words connected with material culture.[36] However, many of these words are very rarely used even in New Zealand English, especially many of the names of flora and fauna,

[34] The topic of Chinese words in English is relatively little studied. For a selective survey of words of direct and indirect Chinese origin based largely on Hong Kong English, see Chan and Kwok (1985). For a somewhat eclectic survey of direct and indirect borrowings from Chinese (many via Japanese), as well as compounds and phrases formed from them, and semantic loans, as reflected by English dictionaries, see Cannon (1988). For a stimulating if critical account of the treatment of words and uses relating to China in *OED2*, see Benson (2001). For a historical account of Chinese English varieties, especially Hong Kong English, see Bolton (2003), and see also Cummings and Wolf (2011).

[35] On the immediate linguistic impact of Cook's voyages, including loanwords into English from Australian aboriginal languages (e.g. *kangaroo*) and from Polynesian languages other than Maori (e.g. *tattoo* and, specifically from Tongan, *taboo*) see Gray (1983).

[36] See Macalister (2006), drawing on Kennedy and Yamazaki (1999), although their terminology differs.

although there are exceptions among these, most notably *kiwi*. This is a borrowed bird name,[37] used as an emblem of New Zealand, and hence in a variety of extended uses, especially as a nickname for any of various national representatives (in sports, etc.) and (chiefly outside New Zealand) as a nickname for any New Zealander. Later (from the 1960s) it also came to be used as a name for the Chinese gooseberry, after it began to be grown in and exported from New Zealand.

Corpus-based studies that include both proper nouns and common nouns suggest that the frequency of items of Maori origin in New Zealand English written sources has climbed very gradually, reaching about six words per 1,000 by the year 2000, although the majority are proper nouns (see Macalister 2006).

Some characteristic loanwords include *marae* 'courtyard of a Maori meeting house, central open space in a Polynesian village, Polynesian sacrificial altar or sacred enclosure' (1769, in Cook's journal, although this was not published until later), *patu* or *patu patu* 'clublike instrument, used especially as a weapon or as a pestle' (*c*.1771 and 1769 respectively, in sources not published until later), *whare* 'hut' (1807; also found in rural use in New Zealand in compounds such as *whare boy*, *whare boss*, *back whare*, *bark whare*, indicating a considerable degree of integration into New Zealand English[38]), *Pakeha* 'New Zealander of European descent' (1817), *pa* 'fortified Maori village' (1823), *tui* 'the parson bird, Prosthemadera novaeseelandiae' (1823), *rimu* 'the red pine, Dacrydium cupressinum' (1835; 1820 as *demo*), *kaumatua* 'an elder' (1835), *aroha* 'sympathy, understanding, love' (1863), *kia ora*, used as a greeting or a farewell (1896 in a source not published until later; according to the *DNZE*, infrequent in non-Maori use between *c*.1940 and the 1980s). Some of these items are sometimes found in English from outside New Zealand, but almost always with explicit reference to New Zealand or its culture.

Most commentators agree that, in very broad outline, several distinct phases are observable in the borrowing of Maori words in New Zealand English.[39] An initial period of considerable receptiveness to loanwords was followed, from approximately the 1860s, by a long period in which Maori loanwords were less favoured, reflecting greater demarcation

---

[37] On the complexities of the original bird name, see *DNZE* at *kiwi*.

[38] Compare Bardsley (2001) on these uses.

[39] Compare discussion in Macalister (2006), Bartlett (2002), Deverson (1991).

and hostility (and in the 1860s even warfare) between largely urban English-speaking communities and largely rural Maori-speaking communities. The frequency of borrowing began to decline, as did the frequency with which some borrowed words were used; alternative names were often preferred to Maori loanwords, such as *parson bird* rather than *tui*, or *red pine* rather than *rimu*. The third suggested phase is much more recent and not yet reflected in detail by the coverage of the *OED* or *DNZE* (but see data from a recent corpus study in Macalister 2006). It is argued that since around 1970 the number of Maori loanwords in general use in New Zealand English has seen a considerable increase, especially as regards words connected with social culture; this is regarded as constituting a second major phase of borrowing, following the initial period of contact and colonization in the eighteenth and early nineteenth centuries. Following Macalister (2006), we can identify several connected factors motivating this recent change: a Maori-speaking population that is growing both in absolute terms and as a proportion of the population as a whole, and that is becoming less rural-based; positive support for Maori through language planning; greater prominence of Maori in political discussion in New Zealand; and more positive attitudes towards Maori language and culture among the general population. Considerations such as these are a reminder of the complex factors that lie behind actual language use. As well as new borrowings, these developments have probably led to revivals of earlier loanwords that had fallen into disuse or never secured widespread use, as well as to the increased use of some borrowings in a wider range of contexts (compare comments on *kia ora* above).[40] Notably, *OED3*'s coverage of recent words with high frequency in New Zealand English or with impact in other varieties has yet to pick up any recent entirely new loanwords from Maori post-1970 in the ranges A–ALZ and M–RZZ: see Fig. 15.15. The *DNZE* has examples such as *koha* 'gift, donation' (1982) or *kawa* 'protocol or etiquette accepted on a marae' (1983).

Another important factor in contemporary New Zealand society is phonology: the pronunciation of words of Maori origin (including proper names) is often regarded as an important indicator of the degree of sympathy with

---

[40] Deverson (1991) lists a number of loans 'coming into prominence and wider currency in the last few years'; of these, two have first dates in the 1980s in the *DNZE*, but others have first dates as far back as the nineteenth century.

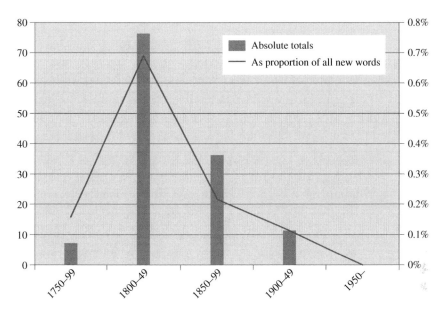

Fig. 15.15 Loanwords from Maori, as reflected by *OED3* (A–ALZ and M–RZZ).

Maori culture that speakers wish to convey;[41] modification of the pronunciation of existing loanwords is facilitated by continuing close contact between speaker groups.

15.3.7 Japanese

Like Maori, Japanese ranks highly among donor languages in modern English, as reflected by *OED3* data in section 2.1. Most of the borrowing has also occurred during a relatively short time span. It is an interesting contrasting case, since the borrowing does not reflect a colonial situation. Some important contact has involved English speakers living in or in close proximity to majority Japanese-speaking communities, e.g. traders at some points in Japan's difficult history of contact with the outside world, or the personnel of American military bases in the post-War period, or more recently ex-pat teachers or business people living in Japan. In other cases it has involved Japanese emigrant or ex-pat communities in majority English-speaking communities. In many instances, the most important factor has

---

[41] Compare Macalister (2005) xix, Deverson (1991).

been Western interest in various aspects of Japanese culture, such as food and drink, decorative and applied arts, or martial arts.[42]

Apart from proper names, a very few items in the sixteenth century could reflect direct contact with Japanese, most notably *bonze* 'Buddhist priest' (1588).[43] From the early seventeenth century there are rather more, e.g. *tatami* 'straw mat used as flooring' (1614), *furo* 'bath' (1615), *bento* 'lunch package' (1616), *maki-e* 'type of lacquerware' (1616), *mochi* 'rice cake' (1616), *mikan* 'type of small citrus' (1618). These words are a selection from among those first recorded in English in the letters and papers of named individuals involved in early Western trading links with Japan;[44] however, it seems very unlikely that any of them were known to anything more than a very small circle of English speakers in the early seventeenth century, nor that they have shown a continuous history in English from this period onwards. The *OED* records *furo* and *mikan* again in isolated examples from the early eighteenth century, in J. G. Scheuchzer's English translation, printed in 1727, of the German manuscript account by Engelbert Kaempfer of his 1690–92 journey to Japan.[45] Apart from these examples in a translation of an account by a German traveller, none of these words are recorded in English again before the mid to late nineteenth century. This is not surprising, because Western (and all external) contact with Japan was tightly controlled as a matter of state policy from the early seventeenth century until the forcible opening up of Japan to foreign trade following the US intervention under Commodore Matthew C. Perry in 1853.

From this period onwards, many loanwords from Japanese show a gradual transition from occurring solely in works describing Japanese culture, to rather more widespread use, in referring to aspects of Japanese culture that have been embraced more widely in Western countries and elsewhere. Some items, like *judo* (1888) or *sushi* (1893), may even be beginning to loosen their tight association specifically with Japan for some

---

[42] For a detailed survey based largely on the *OED* (second edition) and other dictionaries, see Cannon (1996b); see also Evans (1997) for a near-contemporary survey, based on reading of US written sources from between 1964 and 1995.

[43] The dates I give throughout this section are taken from *OED Online*. Cannon (1996b) suggests earlier first dates for many of these words, many of which will eventually be incorporated in *OED3*.

[44] See especially Farrington (1991), Farrington (2008), Thompson (1883).

[45] Scheuchzer (1727).

speakers; *rickshaw* (1879) has long had generic associations with the Far East rather than specifically with Japan. This is distinct from the situation shown by words such as *tofu* (1880), where a word of Japanese form has long also been used as the usual English word rendering the related Chinese *doufu* from which the Japanese word was itself originally borrowed. A special case is shown by *tsunami* (1897), which, since it denotes a wide-spread natural phenomenon, can be used freely in English without any implicit associations with Japanese (or even generalized Eastern) culture, and is now preferred by most speakers to the misleading term *tidal wave*. A few words, like *futon* (1876), are acquiring uses and meanings distinct from their usual meanings in Japanese (in this instance, denoting a low-lying bed with a thin mattress, rather than simply a Japanese bed quilt).

Some other notable Japanese loanwords, in rough semantic groupings, are terms relating to food and drink: *sake* (1687), *soy* (1696), *mirin* 'sweet alcoholic liquid resembling sake (used in cooking)' (1874), *shiitake* (1877), *sashimi* (1880), *nori* '(type of) edible seaweed' (1892), *soba* (1896), *wasabi* (1903), *tempura* (1920), *udon* (1920), *teriyaki* (1961), *dashi* 'fish stock' (1961), *ramen* (1962), *umami* (1963), *shabu-shabu* (1970), *teppan-yaki* (1970); terms denoting aspects of Japanese material culture: *yukata* 'light kimono' (1822), *netsuke* (1876); terms relating to Japanese culture and society: *katakana* 'one of the syllabic scripts used in writing Japanese' (1727), *hiragana* 'the usual syllabic script used in writing Japanese' (1822), *noh* (1871), *kimono* (1886), *geisha* (1887), *haiku* (1899), *kabuki* (1899), *ikebana* 'Japanese flower arrangement' (1901), *kanji* 'character (of Chinese origin) used in the ideo-graphic writing system of Japan' (1920), *bonsai* (1950), *shiatsu* (1967); terms connected with warfare, martial arts, combat, or violence: *samurai* (1727), *hara-kiri* (1856), *seppuku* 'hara-kiri' (1871), *ju-jitsu* (1875), *sumo* (1880), *banzai* 'shout or cheer used in greeting the emperor or in battle' (1893), *kendo* (1921), *basho* 'sumo contest' (1940), *kamikaze* (1945 with reference to suicide aircraft attacks; earlier with reference to the 'divine wind' of Japanese tradition), *aikido* 'martial art form' (1955), *karate* (1955), *ninja* (1964); names of (ornamental) fish: *koi* (*carp*) (1727), *shubunkin* (1917); and an interjection bidding farewell, *sayonara* (1875). The overall pattern, as reflected by *OED3*, is shown in Fig. 15.16, although it should be noted that many of the first dates of attestation from before the mid-nineteenth century are likely to show isolated first uses, with a long gap following before the period of fairly continuous use in English.

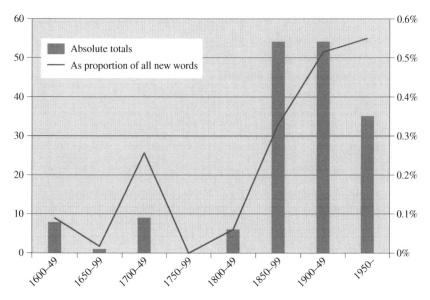

Fig. 15.16 Loanwords from Japanese, as reflected by *OED3* (A–ALZ and M–RZZ).

15.4 Some common themes

This brief survey of lexical influence from the remainder of the twenty-five most prolific sources of loanwords has drawn out some common themes, as well as some differences between the patterns of borrowing from particular languages.

For nearly all of these languages, certain semantic categories tend to predominate: terms for food and drink, names of flora and fauna, names of imported goods of various sorts, and words relating to aspects of local material and social culture. The majority of the loanwords can be connected directly with newly encountered objects or concepts (or newly encountered varieties of already known objects or concepts) that English speakers have come into contact with chiefly in the linguistic context of the language from which the loanword has been borrowed, e.g. *polder* or *coleslaw* from Dutch, *kindergarten* or *pumpernickel* from German, *plaza* or *gazpacho* from Spanish, *ballerina* or *risotto* from Italian, *paddy* or *satay* from Malay, or *kow-tow* or *lychee* from Chinese. Nouns greatly predominate, although occasional loanwords in other word classes are found. In other words, the pattern is very much in line with the sort of borrowing we would expect a language to show from its near neighbours. The range of donor languages is on a near-global scale, because of the wide geographical spread of English in modern times, and its role as a language of trade and of colonialism, and latterly as an international language of communication and scholarship. There are some distinctive trends shown by particular languages: for instance, Italian stands out for the number of words relating to high culture of various kinds, especially music, fine arts, and architecture; this clearly correlates with the particular status of Italy in these fields in a certain historical period.

The discussion of loanwords from Romance languages other than French, as well as of borrowing from many languages from outside Europe, has brought renewed focus on the importance of distinguishing between direct and indirect borrowing, as well as casting light on the practical difficulties that can be encountered in making this distinction in certain cases, particularly in any period when both direct and indirect borrowing are known to be taking place.

German and Greek stand out in the discussion because of the huge numbers of words belonging to scientific and technical vocabularies, pene-trating in volume into a distinctive area of lexis (compare the patterns shown by Figs 15.2 and 15.7 with others in this chapter); in this respect, the late nineteenth-century input from German is very similar to that from French, and the contribution from Greek in Later Modern English is extremely similar to that from Latin. If the contributions to scientific and technical terminology are factored out, then the pattern of borrowing from French in Later Modern English becomes similar in nature (if still larger in scale) to that from other European languages, while the level of borrowing from Latin outside these areas is very low in Later Modern English.

In comparison with the borrowing from French, Latin, and (especially) early Scandinavian in earlier centuries, there is relatively little impact on the high-frequency or basic vocabularies of English from borrowings first attested after 1500, and almost none in Later Modern English. However, the brief discussion in section 15.2.8 has brought into focus a topic also discussed in chapter 14, namely the huge impact of French and Latin in Early Modern English on the expansion of the higher-register vocabulary of English. The contribution of both French and Latin in this area has fallen considerably in Later Modern English, outside the special area of scientific and technical terminology. Chapter 16 will revisit this topic from a slightly different perspective, in order to round out the picture of the changing impact of loanwords on the development of the lexis of English over time.

16

Long-term effects of loanwords on the shape of the English Lexicon

This final chapter takes stock of how the shape of the vocabulary of English has changed and developed over a long timeframe as a result of the integration of loanwords. Its starting point is meanings rather than words; how the words that realize particular meanings have changed over time. It looks at how the availability of full or near synonyms has often been exploited in order to realize finer distinctions in meaning, or to establish different stylistic registers. It considers some examples where the set of meaning relations found in a semantic field appear to have been transformed in more radical ways as a result of borrowing of loanwords. The emphasis throughout is on using empirical data to explore this topic.

Four major (partly overlapping) inputs already considered in detail in this book figure very largely in the narrative that emerges from the examples discussed here: early loanwords from Latin, loanwords from early Scandinavian, Middle English loanwords from French and Latin, and Early Modern English loanwords from French and Latin.

16.1 Some key questions

As noted in chapter 1, there are various ways in which the degree of integration of a loanword in the lexis of English can be assessed. We can look at formal issues, such as naturalization in pronunciation or morphology, or we can consider whether the word gives rise to new compound or derivative formations in English, or whether it shows new meanings developed within English. Often less tangible but no less important are questions concerning currency and use:

- Which people is a word used by? Is it used by the general population, or only by speakers of a particular regional variety, or only by people belonging to a particular profession or with an interest in a particular field?
- In which sorts of contexts is it found? Is it in general, everyday, unmarked use, or is it found only in formal or technical registers, or only in literary use, or only in informal registers?

An important way of gauging this is to investigate what the relationships are that the loanword shows with other words of similar or related meaning, within a particular semantic field:

- Is the loanword the usual word in contemporary English realizing a particular meaning? If it is not, can we identify what the restrictions are on its use?
- From a diachronic perspective, can we trace how relationships within the semantic field have shifted and developed over time?
- In particular, if a loanword is the usual word in contemporary English realizing a particular meaning, can we trace how this situation has come about over time?
- Was the loanword the first word to denote a particular concept in English? If so, perhaps it denotes a technical innovation, or perhaps it denotes a particular activity or experience that had not previously been distinguished lexically? If not, what process of competition has it shown with native synonyms? Can we trace when the loanword began to be the usual word realizing a particular meaning?

16.2 The available research tools

Nearly all of the questions sketched in section 16.1 are much easier to ask than to answer. When we are looking at the history of a well-documented language like English, there is a great deal of relevant data in historical dictionaries like the *OED* (and the *DOE*, *MED*, *A Dictionary of the Older Scottish Tongue* (*DOST*), *The Scottish National Dictionary* (*SND*), and so on). There are two main challenges in using this data for the purposes sketched above.

Firstly, historical data on relative frequencies can be very hard to come by. As seen in section 7.5.2, the *DOE* offers frequency numbers for Old English, based on its near comprehensive electronic corpus of surviving texts, the challenge for researchers being to judge how to interpret this data, given the biases and gaps in our surviving documentation. The *OED*, *MED*, *DOST*, and *SND* do not offer such data, nor do most of the historical dictionaries of other regional varieties. The *OED* normally only comments on frequency when a word is very rare in a particular meaning in a particular period. Its paragraphs of quotations illustrating each meaning of a word normally only contain one or two quotations per century for the period up to 1800, and three or four per century for the period after 1800. This quota is easily met for all but the rarest items (especially for modern English), hence the density of quotation evidence in the *OED* generally yields little information about the relative frequency of words; indeed, in cases where additional quotations are given, these will tend to have been supplied in order to reflect additional nuances of meaning or variation in word form, rather than to reflect currency. For Middle English there is often less evidence available, and the *MED*'s quotation paragraphs are normally more generously filled, often containing a large proportion of the available examples for less common words, but they must also be used with caution when estimating word frequency.

Searchable text collections for the period before 1500 are still limited in extent and have not been compiled in order to give a representative sampling of regional varieties or text types, hence they are of limited usefulness for lexicological purposes. As seen in section 14.7, carefully profiled representative historical corpora of medieval (and later) English are at present very small, and can tell us little about word frequency beyond the core grammatical vocabulary and the most frequent tier of general vocabulary items. For the period after 1500, searchable collections of electronic texts begin to be much more useful for estimating word frequency, if approached with due caution. *EEBO* presents in searchable electronic form such a large proportion of the surviving material printed in English up to 1700 that we can be reasonably confident that it can tell us useful things about the composition of the vocabulary of the emergent standard written language. However, care must be taken to frame searches in such a way as to collect together all of the likely spelling variants of a word and to eliminate coincidental homographic spellings of other words. This latter task will normally have to be done by hand: compare section 14.7 on the general difficulties in this area. For the eighteenth century, *ECCO*, although laborious to use, can with perseverance yield a very full picture of eighteenth-century usage, at least as reflected by the surviving printed sources. For the nineteenth century and later, large corpora such as Mark Davies's *Corpus of Historical American English* (*COHA*) are transforming corpus-based research, particularly when used in conjunction with vast (but indiscriminate) text collections such as *Google Books*. All of these resources are much easier to use if we are interested in comparing the frequencies of words than if we are interested in particular meanings of words; the same is true of tools such as Google's Ngram Viewer.[1] If meanings are our object of study, as they are in this chapter, then reliable results will generally only be obtained by coding each example by hand, which can rapidly turn a very large database into a hindrance rather than a help. Even if each example is coded by the researcher, disambiguation of word meanings is notoriously difficult, and it cannot be expected that every example will fit neatly into the broad semantic tendencies that are identified as separate word meanings in dictionaries.[2] Searching for particular collocates, as will be examined briefly for some examples in this chapter, can sometimes provide a useful shortcut where the semantic distinctions are very clear cut, but the results must be approached with caution.

The second big challenge in investigating questions of this sort is that, traditionally, historical dictionaries have been relatively easy to use if we want to explore a set of related word forms, but there have been very significant obstacles in the way of exploring a group of related meanings. Not least, it has been extremely difficult to identify what all of the members of a semantic field are, especially from a diachronic perspective. The advent of the *Historical Thesaurus of the OED* (*HTOED*) makes this much simpler. In essence, *HTOED* is a semantic classification of (nearly) all of the individual senses of each word in the *OED*, with additional information on words and senses obsolete before the end of the Old English period (which are mostly omitted from the *OED*). The printed *HTOED* volumes of 2009 draw on data from *OED1* and its Supplements, but not from revised and updated *OED3*. However, as part of *OED Online,* it is possible to use a version of the *HTOED* data that is being updated in step with *OED3*.

---

[1] On Ngrams, see Michel et al. (2011).
[2] For a brief discussion of this topic and further references, see Durkin (2009) 225–7.

The structure of the *HTOED* has three overarching divisions into 'the external world', 'the mental world', and 'the social world', which lead down to individual semantic categories and subcategories, via a branching structure at up to twelve levels. These categories and subcategories consist of synonyms or near synonyms, although the terms within a category often differ in precise meaning, and usually differ in frequency, register, stylistic level, or regional distribution. It should be borne in mind that the *HTOED* reflects the level of abstraction from actual historical data that is shown by the sense divisions of the *OED*. Sometimes an *OED* sense has been broken down into more than one node in the *HTOED*, but nonetheless many individual semantic nuances are necessarily smoothed out of the resulting structure. Typically, *HTOED* categories group together near synonyms or items with closely related meanings, rather than full synonyms. A relatively simple example of this is shown by *root* in the meaning that *OED3* defines as:

> The part of a plant or tree, normally underground, which attaches it to the ground (or other supporting medium) and conveys water and nutrients from the ground to the body of the plant or tree.

This sits in the *HTOED* structure under 'the external world > the living world > plant > part of plant > root', where it is listed alongside the synonyms and near synonyms:

> *more* (early Middle English; in Old English 'edible root, root vegetable'), *master-root* (*c*1330), *rooting* (*a*1400), *tap-root* (1601), *top-root* (1651), *tuberous root* (1668), *pivot* (1725), *spill* (1766), *tap* (1796), *tutty-more* (1873), *stem root* (1901)

Most of these words in fact denote particular kinds of roots and are not true synonyms of *root*; some are in general use, others have been restricted in register or regional distribution for some or all of their history. This is typical of very many *HTOED* categories and shows why the data must always be used in close conjunction with the *OED*'s definitions and illustrative quotations.[3]

---

[3] The dates that are given in the printed version of the *HTOED* reflect those found in *OED2*, not *OED3*. In this section I instead give dates from *OED Online*, thus reflecting *OED3* entries where they exist; for Middle English material, I give the *MED*'s dates rather than the *OED*'s in those instances where an *OED3* entry has yet to be published.

16.3 Some test cases

One characteristic that the *HTOED* has in common with the *OED* is its massive scale: the printed version contains approximately 797,600 meanings each assigned a place within a structure of 236,400 categories and subcategories. In order to extract a manageable sample of data relating to some of the most basic areas of meaning, I will again make use of the basic meaning categories employed by the WOLD project. As outlined in section 2.3, this project looked at the origins of the words realizing a long list of 1,460 basic meanings, as identified by prior works in linguistics and anthropology, in a wide variety of languages worldwide. It then derived from this a much shorter 100-meaning 'Leipzig-Jakarta List of Basic Vocabulary' identified as being generally least resistant to borrowing. I will look first at what the data of the *HTOED*, *OED*, and other sources can reveal about loanwords realizing meanings in this 100-meaning Leipzig-Jakarta list. Then, to broaden the survey a little, I will look at two (contrasting) semantic areas in the much larger 1,460-meaning list on which the WOLD research was based: forty-nine meanings grouped under 'the senses' and seventy-eight grouped under 'the physical world'.

It should be borne in mind that the semantic categorization of the WOLD meaning lists is intended so far as possible to reflect what is typical in languages across the world, while the structure of the *HTOED* reflects the semantic history of English. Thus one of the WOLD basic meanings is assigned the name 'mountain or hill' but, as this name suggests, modern English (like many other languages) in fact uses different words depending on the size (and to some extent the shape and other physical characteristics) of the geographical feature being referred to. *Hill* is not a loanword, but *mountain* is, and this example is typical of how even the system of meaning relations in modern English is closely intertwined with the history of accommodation and integration of loanwords.

16.3.1 Test case 1: loanwords among the 100-meaning 'Leipzig-Jakarta List of Basic Vocabulary'

Section 2.3 looked briefly at the 100-meaning Leipzig-Jakarta list. The following meanings were identified as being normally realized by a borrowed word in modern British English:

Scandinavian (or Scandinavian-influenced): root, wing, hit, leg, egg, give, skin, take
French: carry, soil, cry, (probably) crush

As will by now be clear from discussion in the preceding chapters, this sort of synchronic statement reflects a rather complex set of historical developments. In each case, a borrowed word has come, over time, to be the usual word realizing a particular meaning in English. That meaning may be one that the word already had when it was borrowed from the donor language, or it may be a meaning that it has developed within English. In every instance there has been competition with native synonyms: there have been ways of expressing each of these core concepts throughout the recorded history of English, and the fact that a loanword is now the usual word realizing each of these meanings reflects historical change in the lexis of English. When we begin to look at these word histories one by one, we find a wide variety of different scenarios and outcomes.

To begin with the Scandinavian items, fairly straightforward replacement of an etymologically unrelated synonym is typified by the case of *take* replacing *nim*, the slow progress of which through different local varieties of English was traced in detail by Rynell (1948); see further the summary of this word history given in section 9.4.1. A slightly different situation is shown by *hit*. The basic meaning 'to hit, strike', was probably borrowed rather than innovated in English (it occurs as a meaning of Old Icelandic and modern Icelandic *hitta*, although the meaning 'to meet, encounter, come upon' is more common). The evidence of the *HTOED* shows that this lexical field has been well populated in English from the Old English period onwards. *Hit* occurs in late Old English in the meaning 'to meet, encounter', then in early Middle English in the meaning 'to hit, strike', and is found in very widespread use in this meaning later in the Middle English period.[4] Rather than showing competition with a particular prominent synonym, it appears slowly to have emerged as a fairly neutral way of expressing this particular meaning. Even today it continues to have very many informal, expressive synonyms, while in very formal use *strike* may be preferred (unlike *smite*, which is now largely a literary archaism).

In other cases, the semantic effects on existing words are rather more complex. Very often, an existing term shows semantic narrowing or specialization

---

[4] See Dance (2003) and also Pons-Sanz (forthcoming) for very interesting comments on the word's restricted distribution in late Old English and early Middle English.

rather than complete loss, as for instance native *hide* following the borrowing of *skin* (compare section 10.11 and further examples discussed there, and also examples in the remainder of this chapter).

Sometimes the borrowed word takes over only a component of the core meaning of an existing word, as in the cases of *wing* beside (simplifying slightly) native *feather*, or, at first, borrowed *root* beside native *wort*, until the semantic field was affected further by borrowing of *plant* from Latin and French (compare section 10.11). The effects of such a process on the structure of a semantic field are shown particularly clearly in the case of *leg* (first attested *c.*1300, although earlier currency could be implied by surnames). The Old English words that appear in the meaning 'leg', *sċeanca* (modern English *shank*) and *lim* (modern English *limb*), are also found in respectively narrower and broader meanings, in the case of *sċeanca* 'shank, lower leg' and in the case of *lim* 'limb (i.e. arm or leg)'. Therefore, although it was clearly possible to refer to a *leg* in Old English and be understood in context, it was only with the borrowing of *leg* that English acquired a word that, in its core meaning, meant 'leg' and only 'leg'. (As is often the case, the early Scandinavian donor form appears to have been rather more complex semantically: in Old Icelandic, *leggr* has the meanings 'leg' and 'hollow bone (of arms and legs)', and this latter meaning is reflected by compounds such as *armleggr* 'arm' and *fótleggr* 'leg'.)

The remaining items, *give* and *egg*, belong to a different category, where a native word is replaced by a Scandinavian cognate that differs only slightly in form; *give* replacing the native cognate *yive* (Old English *ġiefan*: compare section 10.2.3) and (although the formal difference is more considerable) *egg* replacing the native cognate *ei* (Old English *ǣġ*: compare section 10.2.6). As discussed in section 10.2, it is not entirely certain that all such cases should be regarded as showing borrowing at all, rather than Scandinavianization of an existing word. Certainly, the situation is different from one of competition between unrelated words that have no formal resemblance to one another.

The four French loanwords in this core 100-meaning list are also worth looking at in a little detail. *Carry* is recorded by the *MED* from *c.*1375. The usual native synonym was *bear*. When *carry* became more common than *bear* in the meaning 'to bear by bodily effort' is a very difficult question and one that cannot easily be answered using the currently available lexicographical tools; to the best of my knowledge, there has been no detailed study of the relationship between these words, along the lines of Rynell

(1948) on native *nim* and Scandinavian *take*. If we search on *EEBO* in texts from 1500–99 for *bear it* and *carry it*, applying *EEBO*'s filters to search for variant spellings and inflected forms, *bear it* is about twice as frequent as *carry it*, but then *bear* shows greater polysemy in this period (in such meanings as 'to tolerate', 'to give birth to', or (in *bear witness*) 'to testify'), and a detailed study would be required in order to tease the various meanings apart. Looking for some likely direct objects (e.g. *bag, baggage, load, pack, sack, wood*) suggests that *carry* may already be the more common verb in this meaning in the sixteenth century. In *EEBO* texts from 1600–99, a similar search finds *carry it* considerably more common than *bear it*, even before we attempt to distinguish different meanings of *bear*. Thus it appears very likely that *carry* was the basic word in this meaning by the seventeenth century (at least in the ancestor of modern standard English), but it may already have been much earlier. Productivity in forming new derivatives, compounds, or phrasal constructions within English can also be a useful indication of the degree of integration of a loanword (although the listing of these in dictionaries, which will be relied on for data here, is by no means exhaustive). For *carry*, the *MED* records the derivative *carrier* from the late fourteenth century, but this may well show a borrowing from (Anglo-)French; it also records idiomatic uses in *to carry one's course* 'to pursue one's course' and *to carry warnestore* 'to collect provisions'; better evidence of productivity is shown for Early Modern English by (among items recorded in the *OED*) the phrasal constructions *to carry out* (1526; 1605 in the meaning 'to put into execution'), *to carry through* (1608), *to carry on* (1609), or the noun compound *carry tale* (1577).

The other three cases are all rather more complex, albeit in differing ways. *Cry* is certainly the usual verb in modern English in the meaning 'to weep, shed tears', having long replaced *weep* as the usual choice in this meaning. However, the meaning 'to weep, shed tears' for *cry* is an innovation within English (attested from *c.*1532) and is not part of the meaning of the borrowed French verb, which is first recorded in English in the early thirteenth century in the meaning 'to beg (someone for something)'. Consciousness of the polysemy of *cry*, and in particular its use to describe both vocal and silent manifestations of emotion, may even have led some speakers to avoid using it in the meaning 'weep'. The *OED* (1926) commented on the native synonym *weep*:

In mod.English somewhat rare in non-literary use, being superseded by *cry*; recently a sense of the inappropriateness of that verb as applied to silent manifestations seems to have in some degree revived the colloquial currency of *weep* in the sense 'to shed tears'.

In the case of *soil* (recorded in this meaning from *c.*1400) it is not clear that the situation is entirely settled even in contemporary English; there are complex relationships with *earth*, *ground*, and *dirt*, differing regionally as well as by register. As regards productivity within English, there is some evidence for conversion to a verb even in Middle English (although *soil* 'to dirty' shows a different borrowing), but there are relatively few early derivatives or compounds; those that are found include *soiled* 'having a particular or specified kind of soil' (*c.*1645), *soil bound* (1688), *soily* 'of the nature of soil' (1747). Compare also the idiom *to change one's soil* (1555).

Crush (first recorded *c.*1350 in this meaning, and competing with *bruise* and *break* in early use) is etymologically difficult and may not be a borrowing from French at all. Additionally, the semantic category 'to crush/grind', identified as a basic meaning in the WOLD list, maps rather awkwardly to English words, as is shown by the use of both 'crush' and 'grind' in identifying the category. The *HTOED* places these meanings in different categories and arguably they are semantically distinct categories in English.

Thus a preliminary examination of these eight Scandinavian and four French loanwords has illustrated a number of different outcomes in the English lexicon, even though, in each case, the loanword has come to be the more or less default realization of a core meaning in at least some varieties of English. Existing words with the same meaning may eventually be replaced outright and either become entirely obsolete, or become obsolete in the relevant meaning, but remain current in other meanings. Alternatively, existing words may show semantic narrowing, retaining a portion of the relevant meaning; or they may remain in the same meaning, but become restricted to different registers of usage. In cases like *leg*, a loanword may fill a gap in the system, by providing for the first time a clear one-to-one mapping between a particular word form and a particular core meaning. In cases like *cry*, the core meaning may be one that a loanword has innovated during its history within English. Some cases, like *soil*, are clearly less definitive than others, and what is the usual word meaning 'soil' will differ both according to whose English we are talking about and, to a certain extent, according to level of formality.

In the case of some of the other meanings in the WOLD 100-meaning list, a borrowed word has become usual for an important subset of the category. Like 'to crush/grind' (and 'mountain or hill' discussed in section 16.3.3), the meaning 'the stone/rock' is identified by two different English words in the

WOLD meaning list, reflecting the fact that modern English typically employs different words for large and small pieces of stone; the *OED*'s evidence suggests that *stone* is rare in countable meanings except denoting 'a piece of rock of small or moderate size' after 1500, the French and post-classical Latin borrowing *rock* being the usual modern English word for 'a large stone, a boulder' (first attested in this meaning *a.*1413, although attested much earlier denoting a cliff or crag[5]), as well as in some varieties, such as US English, being used of much smaller objects. This mismatch between the WOLD categories and the lexical structures of English reflects the fact that no two languages are identical in the set of meanings that are realized by distinct word forms. In modern English, complex or anomalous semantic distinctions often (although by no means always) show the traces of earlier processes of accommodation of loanwords.

For other meanings in the list, what we identify as the 'usual' word will depend to a large extent on register and context. For instance, in the meaning 'far' both the Latin loanword *remote* and the French and Latin loanword *distant* are common in adjectival use, especially when occurring attributively, and especially in higher registers. For the meaning 'big' the French loanword *large* is arguably more usual than *big* in formal and even in fairly neutral registers.

If one works through all of the *HTOED* categories corresponding to the meanings in the Leipzig-Jakarta 100-meaning list, there are only twenty-two (i.e. just over a fifth of the total) for which the *HTOED* records no borrowed synonyms:

> ash, to blow, bone, to do/make, to hear, horn, in, to laugh, louse, not, to suck, thigh, this, tongue, water, what?, who?, wood, yesterday, 1SG, 2SG, 3SG pronouns [i.e. the first-, second-, and third-person singular personal pronoun forms]

More typically there are at least some minor, register-specific synonyms recorded, and sometimes there are very many, most often from French and/or Latin. Their dates of first attestation typically cluster in the fifteenth century and (especially) in Early Modern English, correlating with the large-scale lexical expansion and the growth of new stylistic registers in this period. For instance, for the meaning 'sweet' the *HTOED* gives the following (in all instances, the dates given are for use in the relevant

---

[5] See section 6.3.3 for currency in Old English, although the word was probably re-borrowed in early Middle English.

meaning, and reflect the dates currently given in the *OED* or *MED*, following the procedure explained in footnote 3):

> *douce a.*1399; *dulcet* 1440; *luscious c.*1475; *mellite* ?1440; *dulce* 1568; *marmalade* 1617; *ambrosian* 1632; *dulcid* 1657; *dulcorous* 1676; *dulceous* 1688; *saccharaceous* 1689; *saccharic* 1945;

Additionally, showing derivatives of borrowed words, there are:

> *sugarish c.*1450; *nectared c.*1595-; *marmalady* 1602; *sugar-candyish* 1874

The following two sections look beyond the 100-meaning list of items most resistant to borrowing, to two semantic areas in the much larger 1,460-meaning list on which the WOLD research was based: 'the senses' and 'the physical world'.

16.3.2 Test case 2: the senses

Basic vocabulary relating to the senses is learned early and is often considered rather resistant to borrowing. As Sylvia Adamson comments on the vocabulary of Early Modern English:

> Saxon words are associated with private and intimate discourse and their semantic range is characteristically experiential: they encode perceptions, emotions, evaluations.
>
> (Adamson (1999) 573.)

If one looks just at the 49 meanings in this semantic area included in the 1,460-meaning list used for the WOLD research, and investigates each of these meanings in the *HTOED*, it is striking how much impact there is from loanwords, especially those from French and/or Latin. A very few meanings appear never (or at most only extremely rarely) to be realized by loanwords:

> to hear, light (= not dark), salty

For the majority of meanings, loanwords are found only as relatively (or in some cases extremely) minor, largely register-restricted, synonyms of the usual (non-borrowed) word:

> bitter, black, blunt,[6] bright, clean, cold, dark, dry, to feel, green, hard, heavy, hot, light (as opposed to heavy), to listen, to look, loud, red, rough (as opposed to smooth), to see, sharp, to shine, to show, to smell (intransitive), to smell (transitive), smooth, to sniff, soft, sour, stinking, sweet (on which see section 16.3.1), warm, wet, white, wrinkled, yellow

---

[6] The word *blunt* itself is first found in early Middle English (earliest in figurative use) and is of uncertain origin; the case for borrowing from early Scandinavian has yet to be made convincingly, although the suggestion has sometimes been made.

In contrast, a loanword borrowed from French, Latin, or both has come to be the usual word realizing a meaning in the following cases (again, the dates given are for use in the relevant meaning):

- **'To pinch':** *pinch* (*c.*1230) becomes well established in this meaning during the Middle English period, although native synonyms such as *twinge* or *twitch* survive into Early Modern English. Early derivatives and compounds of *pinch* include *pinching* (*c.*1230), *pincher* (1368), *pinch-penny* (?*c.*1425), *pinch* (noun; *c.*1450), *pinchpence* (1540), *pinch fist* (*c.*1580), *pinchcrust* (1582), *pinchfart* (1592), *penny-pinching* (1600). (There are also numerous later borrowed synonyms, including *nip*, which is probably from Dutch.)

- **'Colour':** *colour* (*c.*1300 in the meaning 'a colour', *a.*1398 in the abstract meaning 'colour') rapidly supplants *hue*. In sixteenth-century texts searchable on *EEBO*, *colour* is roughly twenty times more common than *hue* (including spelling variants, and even without separating out homographic forms of other words); the *OED* (1899) comments that *hue* 'appears to have become archaic in prose use about 1600'. *The OED* and *MED* both record a huge number of derivatives and compounds, especially of the similative type shown by e.g. *rose colour* (*a.*1382) or *orange colour* (1512) (i.e. 'the colour of a (usually pink or light crimson) rose', 'the colour of a (ripe) orange').

- **'To taste':** *taste* (*c.*1300) rapidly replaces native *smatch* (not found after 1500 in transitive use), although competition continues longer with other loanwords such as *savour*. Apparent derivatives in Middle English are probably all borrowed from French (except for the very predictable *tasting c.*1384), but in Early Modern English we find e.g. *tastesome* (1598), *tastelessness* (1600), *tasteless* (1603), *tasteful* (1611). The *MED* records idiomatic uses such as *to taste death* 'to die', *to taste under tooth* 'to test by biting'.

- **'Sound':** the *HTOED* offers no earlier synonym of *sound* (*c.*1300) in the general meaning 'thing heard' in early Middle English, although it does record words with this meaning in Old English, and there are certainly many more specific terms for particular types of sound recorded in Middle English. As regards productivity, the *MED* records the compounds *thunder sound* and *name sound* 'the sound of someone's name' and a number of idiomatic phrases; derivatives and compounds include *soundly* 'full of sound' (1435), *soundful* (*a.*1500), *sound-board* (1504), *soundish* (1530), *sound-hole* (1611), *soundless* (*a.*1616). (The borrowed

verb *sound* is also first attested *c.*1300, whence *sounding a.*1382 and
sounder 'person or thing that makes sound' *a.*1425.)

- **'To touch':** *touch* (*c.*1300) became the usual word in this meaning
  during the Middle English period, replacing native *reach* and the earlier
  Scandinavian loanword *take*; there is also a rather complex overlap
  with native *feel*. Early derivatives and compounds include *touching*
  (noun; *c.*1300), *touching* preposition 'concerning' (*c.*1390), *touchable*
  (*a.*1400), *toucher* (1423), *touchstone* (1481), *touch-powder* (1497), *touch-
  hole* (1501).

- **'Blue':** *blue* (*c.*1330) shows a surprisingly late borrowing of such a basic
  colour term. The French word is itself ultimately of Germanic origin,
  but the Old English cognates *blǣ* and *blǣwen* are poorly attested
  and appear usually to have the meaning 'dark blue', especially with
  reference to textiles, *hǣwen* having been the more usual word in the
  meaning 'blue'.[7] The early Scandinavian cognate is also borrowed
  into Middle English as *blō*, (northern) *blā*, but usually in the meanings
  'blackish blue' or 'bluish grey'. By the end of the Middle English
  period *blue* is firmly established as the usual word in the meaning
  'blue', with *haw* (the reflex of *hǣwen*) surviving after this date only in
  Scots, and the borrowed partial synonyms *azure*, *inde*, and *glawke* all
  being rare.

- **'Fragrant':** *fragrant* is recorded from *c.*1450,[8] although arguably *sweet-
  smelling* remains the more likely word in some less formal registers.
  Fragrant is one of a very large number of words with this meaning that
  are either borrowed from French and/or Latin, or derived from French
  and/or Latin loanwords: see the end of this section for the full list, and
  compare especially *aromatic* (fifteenth century), *perfumed* (1538). Early
  derivatives are *fragrantly* (?1521), *fragrantness* (1616).

- **'Quiet':** *quiet* is recorded in English from the late fourteenth century,
  but the specific, narrowed meanings 'making little noise' and 'free from
  noise' (as opposed to 'peaceful, tranquil') only become fully established
  during the Early Modern period; in earlier use partial synonyms such
  as *still* or *soft* are more frequently found with reference to sound.

---

[7] For a detailed study, see Biggam (1997), and also Biggam (2006) specifically on the
replacement of *hǣwen* by *blue*.

[8] See the *MED* for fifteenth-century examples, not yet included in the *OED*.

A word derived from a probable early Scandinavian loanword is the usual modern realization of a meaning in the case of 'dirty' (see sections 10.6, 10.10 on *dirt*; *unclean* and *filthy* are native synonyms of *dirty*). In the meaning 'brackish' (i.e. somewhat salty), *brackish* (*a.*1552) is a derivative of *brack* (*a.*1522), a likely Dutch loanword (while *brinish* is a native synonym).

For some of these meanings there is also a large set of borrowed minor synonyms or near-synonyms. For 'fragrant' the *HTOED* records the following items that are either loanwords or formed on loanwords, again showing a heavy concentration of words first attested in the fifteenth century or in Early Modern English:

> *aromatic* (?*a.*1425); *redoling* (*c.*1429); *balmy* (?*a.*1439); *redolent* (?*a.*1439); *odorate* (?1440); *fragrant* (*c.*1450); *well-savouring* (*c.*1450); *flagrant* (*a.*1475); *aromatical* (?*a.*1475); *aromatous* (1483); *embalmed* (*a.*1529); *perfumed* (1538); *savoury* (1560); *balm-like* (1569); *aromatizate* (1576); *Sabaean* (*a.*1586); *sweet-scented* (1591); *reperfumed* (1593); *balm-breathing* (1595); *nectared* (*c.*1595); *spiced* (1600); *fuming* (1601); *fumed* (1612); *scentful* (1612); *balsam* (1624); *perfumy* (1625); *ambrosian* (1632); *spicy* (1650); *aroma-olent* (1657); *suaveolent* (1657); *aromatized* (1661); *scented* (1666); *ambrosial* (1667); *essenced* (1675); *balsamy* (1687); *flavorous* (1697); *balsamic* (1714); *well-scented* (1726); *flavouriferous* (1773); *aromal* (1848); *euodic* (1868, in specific use in Chemistry)[9]

Some of these compound and derivative formations are formed from words that had already existed in English for centuries, and whose origins may no longer have been perceived by speakers. For example, *well-scented* is formed on *scent*, found as both noun and verb from the early fifteenth century, and borrowed from the (Anglo-)French verb *sentir*. In this instance, the etymologically inappropriate respelling of earlier *sent* as *scent* (probably by association with *science* and related words) is a particularly clear indicator that the true etymology was no longer perceived, although such a respelling also suggests that the word was nonetheless perceived to be part of the Latinate vocabulary. *Flavorous* is a formation on a noun that had been borrowed in the fifteenth century, with a suffix that had long become fully naturalized and was, by this date, used freely to form adjectives on the bases of any origin (a base being a word or other element to which a suffix is added). However, even formations such as these illustrate the gradual expansion of the English lexicon with compound and derivative formations on borrowed

---

[9] The *HTOED* category includes also *well-aired* and *scenty* but neither fits the semantic category as well as most of the other items do.

bases. The number of formations on non-borrowed bases in this semantic category from Middle English onwards is much smaller:

sweet-smelling (*a.* 1382); *well-smelling* (*c.* 1385); *merry* (*a.* 1398); *soft* (*a.* 1500); *nosy* (1892)

16.3.3 Test case 3: the physical world

If we turn finally to some data from a rather different area of human experience, 'the physical world', the WOLD 1,460-meaning list has 79 relevant meanings from this area.[10] No borrowing or negligible borrowing is shown by the following meanings, as reflected by data in the *HTOED* and *OED*:

ash, charcoal, coal, embers, to freeze, light (noun), loam, low tide, snow, tide, water, weather, wood (the material)

Only minor borrowing (and in the case of French and Latin words, mostly register-restricted) is shown for the following meanings (although see the footnotes below for some significant differences in particular varieties of English):

beach, to blaze,[11] bolt of lightning, to burn (transitive), to burn (intransitive),[12] cliff or precipice,[13] cloud, darkness, dew, earthquake, fire, firewood, foam, fog, high tide, ice, lake, land, lightning, mainland, to melt, moon, mud, powder, rain,[14] rainbow,

---

[10] A further five meanings, 'the arctic lights', 'the jade or jadeite', 'the lagoon', 'the savanna', and 'the short dry season', will not be considered here, since they do not refer to aspects of the physical world in the British Isles (although the northern lights are sometimes seen in northerly parts). Another meaning from the WOLD list, 'the match', will be omitted here because the history of technological development complicates the history of *match* and its relationships with other words, and the meaning also sits rather oddly with others in the 'physical world' category.

[11] In this meaning, native *blaze* varies rather freely with French *flame* (*c.* 1390 as verb; see below on the related noun); early Scandinavian *low* has significant regional currency.

[12] A notable late date of first attestation is shown by the early Scandinavian loan *swither*, first recorded in the nineteenth century in English regional use, although related *swithe* is found from early Middle English in transitive use.

[13] The possible Celtic loanword *crag* can have this meaning in Scots. Additionally, a steep (although normally not sheer) hill side, especially rising from water, is often denoted by the probable early Scandinavian loanword *brae* in Scots, although in this instance the use denoting a landscape feature probably reflects a metaphorical development in English, from 'eyebrow' to 'brow of a hill'.

[14] In fact, the *HTOED* lists no borrowed synonyms for *rain*, since it puts borrowed *precipitation* in a different category, 'precipitation', although this is a debatable decision.

river mouth,[15] rough (of sea), sand, sea, shade or shadow, shore, smoke, spring or well, star, steam, storm, sun, thunder, waterfall, wave, whirlpool,[16] wind, world

A loanword from French and/or Latin has become the usual word realizing a meaning in modern English in quite a number of cases:

- **'Cave':** *cave* (*a.*1300) is more common than *den* by Early Modern English, if not earlier, although the evidence of the *MED* and the *MED Corpus* collection of online texts suggests that *den* still has strong currency in late Middle English. Early compounds recorded by the *MED* include *hell cave*, *fosse cave* (in uncertain precise meaning), and the verbal noun *cave-keeping*.

- **'Plain':** the evidence of *EEBO* suggests that *plain* (*c.*1325) is the dominant term in this meaning by the sixteenth century, if not earlier. Early compounds include *plain-country* (*c.*1487) and *plain-land* (1489); the *MED* also records some phrasal uses, e.g. *hilles and plaines*, *valleies and plaines*.

- **'Valley':** *valley* (*c.*1300) is more common than native *dale* by the sixteenth century in the emerging standard language. The evidence of the *MED* and the *MED Corpus* suggests that the fifteenth century is the key period of competition in southern texts.[17] The related loanword *vale* appears to have rivalled *valley* in frequency for much longer, before becoming a stylistically marked, high-register variant in modern use. So far as the degree of integration of *valley* is concerned, the *MED* records numerous uses in metaphorical expressions, deeply influenced by Latin religious discourse, and also records the derivatives *valleyed* and (probably) *to valley*. Early compounds in the *OED* include *valley-gate* (1535), *valley-side* (1575), *valley-lily* (1597).

- **'Ocean':** *ocean* (*c.*1300) seems to have supplanted *the deep* in frequency by the beginning of the Early Modern English period, but the relationship with *sea* remains a complex one down to the present day, with usage differing considerably according to variety, register, and level of

---

[15] The early Scandinavian loanword *firth* has an important place in distinctively Scots lexis.

[16] The first element of *whirlpool* is probably a Scandinavian loanword (compare section 10.6), but the compound appears to be entirely an English formation.

[17] This is an area of vocabulary where particular varieties of English often show significant differences, reflecting different contact situations; for instance, the loanword from Scots Gaelic *glen* has an important place in distinctively Scots lexis.

formality (in general, *ocean* is rather more common in North American than British English in non-technical use). Early compounds recorded by the *OED* include: *ocean water* (*a.*1500), *ocean flood* (1557), *ocean-deep* (1590), *ocean main* (1590), *ocean wave* (1590); the *MED* records earlier phrasal uses, as well collocations including *sea ocean, ocean sea,* and *great ocean* in use as proper names.

- '**Air**': the evidence of dictionaries and electronic text databases suggests that *air* (*c.*1300) competes with native *lift* in the general meaning 'the air' to the end of the Middle English period, but *lift* became regionally restricted in its distribution very soon after this. Both words can also mean 'the sky' in earlier use, in which meaning Scandinavian *sky* eventually became the dominant term. When referring specifically to the effects of air on human health, *air* appears to dominate even in early use. The *MED* records the compounds *atempre air, strong air, sweet air, infect air, evil air, thick air,* and some phrasal uses; among early derivatives and compounds in the *OED* are: *airy* (*a.*1398), *open air* (? *a.*1425; as noun), *airish* (*c.*1450), *aired* (1505), *well-aired* (1505), *airlike* (1567), *airsome* (1584), *air hole* (1601).

- '**Flame**': *flame* (*c.*1375) competes with native *leye* in later Middle English, but *leye* barely survived into Early Modern English except in regional use. The *MED* has *flame funeral* 'funeral pyre' and phrasal uses (e.g. *flame of fire*) as well as the derivatives *flamy* and *flamely* (both *c.*1450); among other early compounds and derivatives in the *OED* are *open flame* (1583), *flame-coloured* (1598), *flameful* (1605), *flameless* (1606).

- '**Bay or gulf**': before the borrowing of *bay* (*c.*1400) and *gulf* (?*a.*1425 in this meaning) the concepts seem only poorly distinguished from 'harbour' or 'inlet'. Compounds and derivatives for both words appear first to be attested rather late: *bay-man* (1641),[18] *gulfy* (1594), *gulf-breasted* (1598), *gulf-eating* (?1611), *gulf-stomached* (?1611).

- '**Soil**': see section 16.3.1 on *soil*.

- '**Cape**': *cape* (*a.*1395) shows a complex interaction with a number of native and borrowed terms, among them (native) *ness, head, foreland, headland, peak, bill, reach,* (of unknown origin) *nook, snook,* (Celtic) *mull,* (French) *point,* (Latin) *promontory,* with significant local

---

[18] Earlier *bay-salt* (*a.*1464) probably reflects the proper name of the *Baie de Bourgneuf*: see Twemlow (1921).

differences in the currency or use of terms, and also differences between technical and lay usage. There are further terms with very limited geographical distributions, such as (Scandinavian) *noup* or *scaw* in Shetland or Orkney. There is also a complex interaction with such words found in place names, many of which originated in a language other than English (e.g. a Celtic or Scandinavian language) but which retain some degree of transparency as descriptive names for some English speakers. No early compounds or derivatives of *cape* are recorded by the dictionaries.

- **'Calm (of sea)':** *calm* is found from *a.*1393, earliest in this meaning. An *EEBO* search indicates that *calm sea* is much commoner than equivalent constructions with prominent synonyms such as *still sea*, *plain sea*, or *smooth sea* even in the sixteenth century; likewise for the construction *the sea was/is calm*.

- **'Constellation':** *constellation* is found from *a.*1398 in this meaning; its relationships with earlier (borrowed) *sign*, *image*, etc. are difficult to trace in detail because of the complexity of astronomical and astrological concepts in early modern Europe.

From early Scandinavian we find:

- **'Sky':** *sky* is first attested in the thirteenth century. As discussed in section 10.11, the usual native synonym is *heaven*, which ultimately showed semantic narrowing and specialization. See also previous list on overlap with *air* and *lift* in this meaning in earlier use.

A Dutch loanword is shown by:

- **'Reef':** *reef* (1579) is the earliest item recorded in this meaning in the *HTOED* except for the Scots item *skelly* (1513, of uncertain origin). However, numerous earlier synonyms are recorded for more specific subsidiary categories in the thesaurus structure, such as 'sandbank' and 'mudbank'.

In the meaning 'the swamp', it is possible (but by no means certain) that *swamp* (1624, earliest in North America) is from Low German; *bog* in the same meaning (mid sixteenth century) is from Scottish Gaelic; earlier *marsh* and *fen* are among the native synonyms.

Additionally, in Early Modern English the French loanword *isle* comes close in frequency to *island*, which is itself a native word, but remodelled in spelling as a result of association with borrowed *isle*. In modern standard English, *isle* is largely restricted to archaic or literary registers.

A loanword has become the usual realization for a subset of a category in the following cases:

- **'Mountain or hill':** *mountain* (first attested in late Middle English, < French) and (in earlier use) *mount* have long been the usual terms for a mountain (in the case of *mount*, the word perhaps already had this status even in Old English: see section 7.5.3). As noted in section 5.1, Old English *dūn* 'hill' may show a significant early borrowing from Celtic in this same semantic field. *Fell* and *bank* are loanwords from early Scandinavian that remain important terms in some varieties of English.
- **'River or stream':** *river* (*c.*1300, < French) very quickly became the dominant term for a large natural watercourse.
- **'Woods or forest':** *forest* (*c.*1330, < French) very quickly became the dominant term for a large area of woodland.
- **'Rock or stone':** on *rock* (*a.*1413) see discussion in section 16.3.1.

In a number of cases in the 'physical world' group the interaction of technical and general vocabularies is also very clear. For example:

- **'To light (a fire)':** *light* (an inherited word) and *kindle* (perhaps an English formation, or perhaps borrowed from early Scandinavian) belong to similar neutral or informal registers (although *kindle* may now have a rather archaic or literary air for many speakers), while the Latin loanword *ignite* (1823) belongs to technical registers.
- **'To extinguish':** *extinguish* (from Latin) is recorded in this meaning from the mid-sixteenth century, but native *put out* remains more usual in informal and unmarked registers even in contemporary English.

16.4 Conclusions

In these three test cases, the WOLD meaning lists have been used as a way of imposing some limits on what could otherwise be a wayward and serendipitous investigation of the riches of the *HTOED*, in order to concentrate as far as possible on words realizing the meanings that are most central in modern English.

The investigation of the core 100-meaning list in section 16.3.1 showed rather more considerable impact from early Scandinavian than from French or Latin on the list of words that are the usual, default realization of a basic meaning in modern English. It also revealed difficulties in identifying what is the usual word in various meanings, in ways that are revealing about the structure of the English lexicon. Even at this basic level of the vocabulary, there are significant differences between different varieties of English, and there is also significant variation between registers, formal and informal, technical and non-technical. In this last area, the contribution from French and Latin loanwords begins to look much more significant, particularly in the fifteenth century and in Early Modern English. In some cases, a semantic category does not map neatly to a single word in English, and this frequently (if by no means always) reflects the way that loanwords have been accommodated into the lexical system of English.

The next two test cases of the senses and the physical world are far apart semantically, but in both sets of meanings the input of French and/or Latin borrowings is considerable, and much more considerable than that from early Scandinavian or from any other source, at least if our focus is on the standard language, as typically encountered in formal, written English.

In the case of the semantic field of 'the senses', all of the words that have come to be the usual realizations of basic meanings in modern English were first attested in Middle English, nearly all before 1400. The latest of these borrowings, *fragrant*, is also the one that seems least unequivocally to be the default realization of the meaning in question in everyday, unmarked modern English usage. Borrowings that occurred after 1500 are numerous among the minor, register-restricted synonyms for many of these meanings, as exemplified by 'fragrant'.

The test case of the physical world shows even more clearly the divergence of vocabulary in different registers of modern English. Some Middle English borrowings such as (French) *air, cave, flame* (noun), *plain, valley*, or (Scandinavian) *sky* incontrovertibly have the status of the usual realization of a meaning in everyday, standard modern English. In a number of cases, loanwords have been exploited in order to realize distinctions in meaning between larger and smaller instantiations of a particular feature of the physical world that appear natural to speakers of modern English but are not necessarily shared cross-linguistically, such as between *mountain* and *hill, river* and *stream, rock* and *stone*, or (perhaps rather less robustly) *forest* and *wood*. In the case of some other borrowings, such as *ocean, cape, ignite*, or *extinguish*, much more depends on register and stylistic level: for instance, the distinction between *ocean* and *sea* may be part of the linguistic competence of the average school leaver, but nonetheless *sea* has a much greater claim to be the default word for any of the bodies of salt water on the earth in everyday, unmarked use; *ignite* and *extinguish* are both commonplace in technical discourse, but the everyday words are clearly *light* and *put out*.

Taken together, these test cases show how difficult it is to quantify the impact of loanwords on the core vocabulary of English. However, in spite of these difficulties, they shed a useful light on some key developments in the history of English lexis. In Middle English and earlier, many instances of lexical borrowing (from early Scandinavian, or from French or Latin) led to the eventual replacement of native terms as the usual realization of a basic meaning in unmarked, everyday modern English. Large numbers of other Middle English and later borrowings from French or Latin have not become the usual, unmarked term in this way, but have added greatly to the available pool of lexical variation. Typically, they have been exploited in the development of distinct registers in modern English, either by contributing to a large set of near synonyms that can be drawn upon in literary language, or by contributing terms that can be used to mark distinctions between technical and informal language. The fact that 'Latinate' can be used as an approximate cover term for the lexis of more formal or elevated language in modern English testifies to the far-reaching effects of these processes.

Various of the examples discussed here have touched on the impact of loanwords on the set of meaning relations within a semantic field. Another way of approaching this topic is to look at the impact of lexical borrowing on the whole of a group of closely related terms. A classic example is provided by the set of kinship terms in English. The terms for the immediate relatives *father*, *mother*, *brother*, *sister*, *son*, and *daughter* are all inherited, except *sister*, which shows an early Scandinavian loan replacing a native cognate (compare section 10.2.7); but, at one remove in lineality, *uncle*, *aunt*, *nephew*, and *niece* are all French loanwords; and, at one remove in generation, the prefixation of *grand-* in *grandfather*, *grandmother*, *grandson*, and *granddaughter* shows a French loan element. However, things are rather less neat in some other parts of this semantic field. The adjectives corresponding to *brother* are either *brotherly* or (borrowed) *fraternal*. Likewise to *father* correspond *fatherly* or *paternal*, and to *mother* either *motherly* or *maternal*. In each of these cases the fact that English has retained different, unrelated word-forms in identical or very similar meaning is exploited for distinctions of register or level of formality. The situation is rather different in the case of *sister*, for which *sisterly* is overwhelmingly the default adjective, *sororial* and *sororal* being much rarer than *fraternal*, *paternal*, or *maternal*. The reason for this is not at all clear; euphony is perhaps a factor, the forms *sororial* and *sororal* being perceived as clumsy or inelegant in sound. If we turn our attention to the non-gender-specific terms for a parent, these show loanwords as the usual forms for both the noun and the adjective: *parent* and *parental*. Likewise *filial* is the gender-neutral adjective corresponding to both *son* and *daughter*. *Avuncular* corresponds reasonably frequently to *uncle*, although it is somewhat marked stylistically; *uncle-ish* barely occurs. *Aunt* has no usual corresponding adjective, *materteral*, *materterine*, and *auntly* all being very rare (except, in the case of the first two words, in various kinds of specialist technical discourse involving family or kinship relationships, where the desire for an adjectival form outweighs the unfamiliarity of the technical words). Corresponding to *grandfather* and *grandmother* the usual, stylistically unmarked adjectives are *grandfatherly* and *grandmotherly* rather than *grandpaternal* and *grandmaternal*, while *grandparental* corresponds to *grandparent*, but is relatively rarely used.

The set of kinship terms in English thus shows rather patchy integration of loanwords in various parts of the system. However, in addition to these changes in the words realizing particular meanings, it is also clear that the integration of French loanwords coincided with significant changes in the structure of the semantic field of kinship terms in English, as explored by Fischer (2002). Old English has distinct words for 'father's brother' (*fædera*) and 'mother's brother' (*ēam*), and for 'father's sister' (*faðu*) and 'mother's sister' (*mōdrige*). It has this in common with other medieval Germanic and Celtic languages, and also with earlier stages in the history of Latin. This was a natural state of affairs in societies where a wife would normally go to live with her husband's extended family; hence, a child's relationships with paternal uncles and aunts would be significantly different from those with maternal uncles and aunts. In particular, a special connection was felt to exist between a male child and his mother's brother (Old English *ēam*), presumably as a protector figure from the maternal household external to the extended paternal household in which the child was living. In late Antiquity the distinction between paternal and maternal siblings was lost in Latin, probably reflecting social and cultural change in Roman society, and this was the situation inherited by the Romance languages, including French. In Middle English the French loanword *uncle* replaced both *fædera* and *ēam*, and similarly the French loanword *aunt* replaced both *faðu* and *mōdrige*. Of course, the concepts 'father's brother' and so on can still be distinguished in English using phrasal constructions, but the simplification in the system of core terms points to an important shift in what were perceived as the most significant family relationships, resulting in a system, as well as a set of terms, similar to that found in French and Latin. Thus in this instance both the set of terms and the set of meaning relations between them can be seen to show particularly clearly the impact of lexical borrowing. The study of historical change and development in semantic fields in English is still in its infancy, but it is clear that the integration of loanwords has been the catalyst for many very significant changes.[19]

---

[19] An example that I have deliberately avoided here is the set of terms for 'an animal' and 'meat of this animal' *pig* (or *sow*) and *pork*, *cow* (or *ox*) and *beef*, *calf* and *veal*, *sheep* and *mutton*. Some popular works on the history of English relate the history of the relationships between the terms in a way that differs little from the early nineteenth-century novelist Sir Walter Scott's assumptions in his historical novel *Ivanhoe*, which he explained thus in reaction to a query from his printer: 'Surely the strongest possible badge of the Norman conquest exists in the very curious fact that while an animal remaind alive under the charge of the Saxon slaves it retaind the Saxon name *Sow Ox* or *calf* – when it was killd & became flesh which was only eaten by the Normans the Sow became Porc the ox *boeuf* or beef the calf *veau* or veal.' (See editorial notes in Scott [1820] (1998) 511–12.) See Kornexl and Lenker (2011) for an overview of the problems with this account. There is much here that remains to be explored in detail, but we can note in brief: (i) Modern English happily uses e.g. *lamb*, *rabbit*, *chicken*, *turkey*, *duck* for the name of both the animal and the meat, just as French does. (ii) Old English in fact had lexicalized means of distinguishing between the meanings 'animal' and 'meat of this animal', but they were phrasal and transparent, as they are for instance in modern German. (iii) In Middle English *beef*, *pork*, *mutton*, *veal*, *venison*, and even *bacon* can all occur denoting an animal as well as its flesh, and the shift to the modern pattern occurred much later than the period in which Scott's account places it.

17

General conclusions and pointers for further investigation

This book set out to examine the impact of loanwords on the lexicon of English, taking as its main datasets the wordlist of the largest dictionary of English, the *OED*, as well as the 1,000 most frequent words in a contemporary English corpus, and an extensive list of basic meanings developed for work on a wide variety of languages worldwide.

The *OED*'s wordlist is huge, including a good many rarer words, some restricted to particular geographical varieties of English, others restricted to particular areas of technical or specialist discourse, and some others that are simply rare. However, even the *OED* is very far from containing every word that has ever occurred in discourse in English: because of the nature of the English lexicon (or indeed the lexicon of any language) it would be impossible for any dictionary ever to do this. Loanwords are one of the areas where the lexicon is very readily extendible. As demonstrated in chapter 15, a survey of loanwords from a wide range of languages that have all contributed significant numbers of words to at least some varieties of English shows how an examination of the *OED*'s wordlist can bring to light those (relatively few) words that have achieved broad general currency in English worldwide, as well as a large number of words that have achieved some significant level of currency, whether in a particular geographical variety of English, or e.g. among botanists or historians, or among enthusiasts for a particular type of cuisine.

Looking at high-frequency words and at words in basic meanings provides a useful counterbalance to looking at the *OED*'s full wordlist. In particular, these approaches bring to light how borrowing from early Scandinavian shows an unusual pattern: there is a significant impact on the most basic levels of the vocabulary, as shown by the 100 highest-frequency words or by the 100 most basic meanings (and as illustrated most strikingly by the personal pronoun *they*), but numbers of loanwords in the overall *OED* wordlist are much lower than those from a number of other languages. Even in the 1,000 highest-frequency words or the full WOLD basic meaning list, the contribution from early Scandinavian drops to a level much lower than that from French or Latin. Also, as seen in part IV and also in chapter 16, the distribution of Scandinavian loanwords differs considerably among geographical varieties in Britain. As examined in detail in part IV, the unusual patterns of lexical influence from early Scandinavian are a clear reflection of the nature of the contact between speech communities and also owe a great deal to the close family relationship between English and early Scandinavian. This latter factor also leads to some of the most challenging but interesting etymological problems in identifying loanwords.

The examination of borrowing from Celtic languages in chapter 5 brought to light some important negative observations. Close geographical proximity of speech communities, even on the same landmass, will not always lead to large-scale reciprocal lexical borrowing. Whatever conclusions we draw from the difficult issue of the tiny number of loanwords from Celtic languages in our surviving Old English records, we also cannot avoid the fact that the general vocabulary of modern English shows very little borrowing at any date from any of the Celtic languages, particularly not if we compare the impact from other neighbouring languages such as French or Dutch. Sadly, we cannot escape the sobering conclusion that this is largely a result of the relatively low esteem in which speakers of Celtic languages have generally been held by speakers of English over many centuries. Even where language switch from a Celtic language to English has taken place, there appears to have been relatively little carrying over of words to the new language and, subsequently, very little spread of such words to the general vocabulary of English, doubtless reflecting the low prestige of these speaker communities.

Borrowing of loanwords from Latin runs as a backbone through the chronological narrative of this book. Some loanwords can be traced to common Germanic (as can some from Celtic), and a cluster of fairly common words appear to reflect borrowing into West Germanic along the Rhine. Old English shows more loanwords from Latin than from any other source, by a considerable margin, chiefly reflecting the impact of Christianity and of Latin as the language of learning. Many date from earlier than our earliest surviving literary records, but identifying precisely when they entered English and in what context poses many difficult problems. Later Old English borrowings are less often the focus of study for modern scholars, but they pose many interesting questions, not least what their degree of currency in English ever was and, in a longer historical perspective, whether they show any degree of continuity with words found in Middle English that could theoretically show the reflexes of these Old English borrowings or could alternatively show re-borrowings from Latin and/or French after the Norman Conquest. Although such words are too few to make any significant difference to the overall numbers of words entering Middle English, they raise interesting questions about what degree of receptivity there may already have been to new borrowings.

In Middle English the impact from both French and Latin is huge, by any measure. Part V showed how an apparently rather dry etymological question, whether words show direct borrowing from French or from Latin or from both sources, opens up very interesting perspectives on the patterns of borrowing in Middle English, both as reflected by the general wordlist of the *OED* and by high-frequency and basic vocabulary. The peak in the impact of words borrowed solely from French comes comparatively early; borrowing solely from Latin is much more characteristic of later Middle English and especially of the transitional period leading into Early Modern English; borrowing from French and/or Latin shows perhaps the most interesting pattern of all, exhibiting a very marked peak in the period approximately 1350–1450, which correlates significantly with the period when English was coming to take over many formal and written functions from both Latin and French.

In Early Modern English, direct borrowing begins to be found from a wider range of languages, but loanwords from French and Latin continue to outnumber those from any other source. However, new borrowings from neither language have anything like the impact on the high-frequency or basic vocabularies of English that is shown by words first attested in Middle English, although there is some evidence that some earlier borrowings only became really established as high-frequency words and as the usual, default realization of a particular basic meaning during this period. Distinctive morphological patterns come to distinguish Latin loanwords from French ones more often. The absolute totals of Latin loanwords increase greatly, although the increase appears somewhat less significant if viewed as a proportion of all new words recorded in English. Loanwords from Latin and from French, and new derivative formations from them, come to be exploited much more widely in the development of new stylistic registers in the vocabulary of English.

In Later Modern English, it becomes much more important to distinguish between technical, especially scientific, vocabulary and the general lexicon. The *OED* wordlist shows large numbers of loanwords from Latin and French as well as from Greek and German, but a very high proportion of these words belongs to the rapidly expanding terminology of technical fields and especially the sciences. This terminology is largely formed from elements ultimately of Latin or Greek origin, and is broadly international. The main languages of international scholarly publication have been French, German, and (only latterly) English, and this correlates closely with the patterns of borrowing of technical and scientific vocabulary that we find between different European languages in this period. Some new borrowings from Latin and French are still found that are motivated by the desire to provide a more 'elegant' or formal term in general non-technical discourse, but they form only a tiny proportion of the total. Generally, borrowing from French has fallen into a pattern much more similar to that from other European vernaculars, once the large volume of technical and scientific terms is set to one side.

In the changing contexts of English use internationally, especially in a post-colonial environment where English has a dominant position as an international language of communication in a globalized business environment, patterns of borrowing from languages from outside Europe are also gradually showing more convergence with the patterns of borrowing from European languages. This is, however, in a context where the impact of new loanwords on the general international vocabulary of English appears to be at its lowest level since at least the Norman Conquest. There are certainly very many new loanwords entering English discourse, but more than ever before we must ask questions about whose English they are found in. A very promising avenue for future research is in developing better ways of tracking the spread of new words, including loanwords, between different varieties of English worldwide.

Loanwords are often perceived as an easy or somewhat peripheral topic. I hope to have shown in this book that neither of these things is true, certainly so far as the lexical history of English is concerned. Loanwords pose many etymological challenges, especially if we make a serious effort to maintain the important distinction between direct and indirect borrowing. Estimating the impact of loanwords on the lexis of English over time opens up even bigger and harder questions. English is a particularly well-documented language for most of its history, although some of the most important episodes of borrowing fell in precisely those periods for which we have least documentation. However, even when we have abundant documentation, as we have for published written English in the Early Modern period for example, developing the right methodologies to explore the changing lexicon and the place of loanwords within it remains hugely challenging, and is a field that is really still in its infancy.

The present research environment offers some interesting ways forward, as do wider developments in such areas as the digitization of earlier texts and their exploitation for historical, literary, and linguistic research. Loanwords have a key role in the development of the lexicon, whether they offer ways of expressing new concepts, or new ways of expressing existing concepts. They may lead to the loss of an existing word, or to semantic narrowing or specialization, or to a split between different registers. Investigating their history opens up new perspectives on the historical development of a culture and a society. Indeed, finer-grained analysis offers the potential to gain insight into a plurality of cultures and societies that share a common core of vocabulary but within which there are significant differences in the lexicons of particular groups or individuals. Ultimately, language is a vehicle of thought and expression, and the reception of loanwords into the system of a language is one of the ways in which a language changes and develops, and with it the resources of that language for formulating thoughts and communicating them to others.

This book has been closely involved with the analysis of empirical data. Close engagement with such data is the best way to carry forward any investigation of loanwords. In the hope that at least some readers will want to conduct their own investigations, a companion website offers some pointers for using various resources to explore and research loanwords in English further. Since much of the data in this book has come from a dictionary in progress, *OED3*, the website will also provide updates as and when the *OED*'s ongoing revision makes a significant difference to any of the datasets discussed in this book.

References

General works cited by author

Adams, James N. 2003. *Bilingualism and the Latin Language*. Cambridge: CUP.

Adams, James N. 2007. *The Regional Diversification of Latin, 200 BC–AD 600*. Cambridge: CUP.

Adamson, Sylvia 1998. 'Literary language', in Suzanne Romaine (ed.) *The Cambridge History of the English Language. Vol. iv: 1776–1997*. Cambridge: CUP. 589–692.

Adamson, Sylvia 1999. 'Literary language', in Lass (1999b) 539–653.

Ahlquist, Anders 1988. 'Of unknown (?) origin', in *Studia Anglica Posnaniensia* 21 69–73.

Algeo, John 1996. 'Spanish loanwords in English by 1900', in Rodríguez González (1996) 13–40.

Allan, Kathryn (forthcoming 2013). 'An inquest into metaphor death: exploring the loss of literal senses of conceptual metaphors', in R. Fusaroli and S. Morgagni (eds.) *Conceptual Metaphor Theory: Thirty Years After*, special issue of *Journal of Cognitive Semiotics* 8.

Ball, Martin J. and Müller, Nicole (eds.) 2009. *The Celtic Languages*. 2nd edn. London: Routledge.

Barber, Charles 1997. *Early Modern English*. 2nd edn. (1st edn. 1976). Edinburgh: EUP.

Bardsley, Dianne 2001. 'On first looking into Kiwi ruralspeak', in *NZWords* 5 1–3.

Barney, Stephen A. 1985. *Word-Hoard: An Introduction to Old English Vocabulary*. 2nd edn. New Haven: Yale University Press.

Barron, Caroline and Saul, Nigel (eds.) 1995. *England and the Low Countries in the Late Middle Ages*. New York: St. Martin's Press.

Barry, Michael V. 1969. 'Traditional enumeration in the North Country', in *Folk Life* 7 75–91.

Bartlett, Maria 2002. 'Utu: A bit of give and take?', in *NZWords* 6 6–7.

Bartlett, Robert 2000. *England Under the Norman and Angevin Kings 1075–1225*. Oxford: OUP.

Bassett, Steven 2000. 'How the West was Won: The Anglo-Saxon Takeover of the West Midlands', in *Anglo-Saxon Studies in Archaeology and History* 11 107–18.

Bator, Magdalena 2006. 'Scandinavian loanwords in English in the 15th century', in *Studia Anglica Posnaniensia* 42 285–99.

Bator, Magdalena 2007. 'The Scandinavian element beyond the Danelaw', in *Studia Anglica Posnaniensia* 43 167–80.

Bator, Magdalena 2010. *Obsolete Scandinavian Loanwords in English*. Studies in English Medieval Language and Literature 26. Frankfurt am Main: Peter Lang.

Bauer, Laurie 1983. *English Word-Formation*. Cambridge: CUP.

Bauer, Laurie 2001. *Morphological Productivity*. Cambridge: CUP.

Bauer, Renate and Krischke, Ulrike (eds.) 2011. *More Than Words: English Lexicography and Lexicology Past and Present: Essays Presented to Hans Sauer on the Occasion of his 65th Birthday – Part I*. Frankfurt am Main: Peter Lang.

Baugh, Albert C. and Cable, Thomas 2002. *A History of the English Language*. 5th edn. New Jersey: Pearson.

Beal, Joan C. 2004. *English in Modern Times 1700–1945*. London: Arnold.

Béjoint, Henri (forthcoming). 'Dictionaries for general users: history and development; current issues', in Philip Durkin (ed.) *The Oxford Handbook of Lexicography*. Oxford: OUP.

Bense, J. F. 1925. *Anglo-Dutch Relations from the Earliest Times to the Death of William the Third*. Den Haag: Martinus Nijhoff.

Bense, J. F. 1939. *A Dictionary of the Low Dutch Element in the English Vocabulary*. First published in five parts, from 1926. Den Haag: Martinus Nijhoff.

Benskin, Michael 2011. 'Present indicative plural concord in Brittonic and early English', in *Transactions of the Philological Society* 109 158–85.

Benskin, Michael and Laing, Margaret 1981. 'Translations and *Mischsprachen* in Middle English manuscripts', in Michael Benskin and Michael L. Samuels (eds.) *So meny people longages and tonges: philological essays in Scots and mediaeval English presented to Angus McIntosh*. Edinburgh: The Editors. 55–106. Substantially reprinted in McIntosh et al. (1986) Vol. 1, §3.

Benson, Larry D., Pratt, Robert, and Robinson, F. N. (eds.) 1987. *The Riverside Chaucer*. 3rd edn. Oxford: OUP.

Benson, Phil 2001. *Ethnocentrism and the English Dictionary*. London: Routledge.

Bergs, Alexander and Brinton, Laurel (eds.) 2012. *English Historical Linguistics*. 2 vols. Handbücher zur Sprach- und Kommunikationswissenschaft / Handbooks of Linguistics and Communication Science 34.1–2. Berlin: De Gruyter.

Berndt, Rolf 1965. 'The linguistic situation in England from the Norman Conquest to the loss of Normandy (1066–1204)', in *Pragensia Philologica* 8 145–63; reprinted in Lass (1969) 369–91.

Berndt, Rolf 1989. *A History of the English Language*. 3rd edn. Leipzig: VEB Verlag Enzyklopädie.

Bierbaumer, Peter 1975–9. *Der botanische Wortschatz des Altenglischen*. Vols. 1–3. Frankfurt am Main: Peter Lang.

Biggam, Carole P. 1997. *Blue in Old English: An Interdisciplinary Semantic Study*. Amsterdam: Rodopi.

Biggam, Carole P. 2006. 'Political upheaval and a disturbance in the colour vocabulary of early English', in Carole P. Biggam and Christian J. Kay (eds.) *Progress in*

Colour Studies. Volume I: Language and Culture. Amsterdam: Benjamins. 159–79.

Birkhan, Helmut 1970. *Germanen und Kelten bis zum Ausgang der Römerzeit : der Aussagewert von Wörtern und Sachen für die frühesten keltisch-germanischen Kulturbeziehungen*. Österreichische Akademie der Wissenschaften: Philosophisch-Historische Klasse, 272. Vienna: Hermann Böhlaus.

Björkman, Erik 1900–2. *Scandinavian Loan-Words in Middle English*. 2 vols. Halle (Saale): Niemeyer.

Blake, Norman 1992a. 'The literary language', in Blake (1992b) 500–41.

Blake, Norman (ed.) 1992b. *The Cambridge History of the English Language. Vol. II: 1066–1476*. Cambridge: CUP.

Bliss, A. J. 1952–3. 'Vowel-quantity in Middle English borrowings from Anglo-Norman', in *Archivum Linguisticum* 4 121–47, 5 22–47; reprinted in Lass (1969) 164–207.

Bolton, Kingsley 2003. *Chinese Englishes: A Sociolinguistic History*. Cambridge: CUP.

Braden, Gordon 2010. 'Translating procedures in theory and practice', in Braden et al. (2010) 89–100.

Braden, Gordon, Cummings, Robert, and Gillespie, Stuart (eds.) 2010. *The Oxford History of Literary Translation in English: Volume 2: 1550–1660*. Oxford: OUP.

Brand, Paul 2000. 'The languages of the law in later medieval England', in Trotter (2000) 63–76.

Brate, Erik 1884. *Nordische Lehnwörter im Orrmulum*. Halle (Saale): E. Karras.

Breeze, Andrew 1993. 'Celtic etymologies for Old English *cursung* "curse", *gafeluc* "javelin", *staer* "history", *syrce* "coat of mail", and Middle English *clog(ge)* "block, wooden shoe", *cokkunge* "striving", *tirven* "to flay", *warroke* "hunchback"' in *Notes and Queries* 238 287–97.

Breeze, Andrew 2002. 'Seven types of Celtic loanword' in Filppula et al. (2002) 175–81.

Bremmer, Rolf H. 2009. *An Introduction to Old Frisian: History, Grammar, Reader, Glossary*. Amsterdam: Benjamins.

Brewer, Charlotte 2007. 'Reporting Eighteenth-Century Vocabulary in the Oxford English Dictionary', in John Considine and Giovanni Iammartino (eds.) *Words and Dictionaries from the British Isles in Historical Perspective*. Newcastle upon Tyne: Cambridge Scholars Publishing. 109–35.

Britton, Derek 1991. 'On Middle English *she*, *sho*: a Scots solution to an English problem', in *North-Western European Language Evolution* 17 3–51.

Brook, G. L. 1947. *English Sound-Changes*. Manchester: MUP.

Brüch, Josef 1951. 'Die Herkunft des Wortes *kaufen*', in *Zeitschrift für deutsches Altertum und deutsche Literatur* 83 92–103.

Brunot, Ferdinand 1917. *Histoire de la langue française, des origines à 1900. Vol. V: Le français en France et hors de France au XVIIe siècle*. Paris: Armand Colin.

Burnley, David 1992. 'Lexis and semantics', in Blake (1992b) 409–99.

Burrow, J. A. 2008. 'Hoccleve, Thomas (*c.*1367–1426)', in *Oxford Dictionary of National Biography*, OUP, 2004; online edn., January 2008 [<http://ezproxy.ouls. ox.ac.uk:2117/view/article/13415> accessed 20 December 2011].

Butterfield, Ardis 2010. *The Familiar Enemy: Chaucer, Language, and Nation in the Hundred Years War.* Oxford: OUP.

Cameron, Kenneth 1996. *English Place Names.* New edn. London: Batsford.

Campbell, Alistair 1959. *Old English Grammar.* 2nd corrected reprint 1968. Oxford: OUP.

Campbell, James 1982a. 'The end of Roman Britain', in Campbell (1982b) 8–19.

Campbell, James (ed.) 1982b. *The Anglo-Saxons.* London: Phaidon.

Cannon, Christopher 1996. 'The Myth of Origin and the Making of Chaucer's English', in *Speculum* 71 646–75.

Cannon, Christopher 1998. *The Making of Chaucer's English: A Study of Words.* Cambridge: CUP.

Cannon, Garland 1988. 'Chinese borrowings in English', in *American Speech* 63 3–33.

Cannon, Garland 1994. *The Arabic Contributions to the English Language: An Historical Dictionary.* With the collaboration of Alan S. Kaye. Wiesbaden: Harrassowitz.

Cannon, Garland 1996a. 'Recent borrowings from Spanish into English', in Rodríguez González (1996) 41–60.

Cannon, Garland 1996b. *The Japanese Contributions to the English Language: An Historical Dictionary.* Associate editor Nicholas Warren. Wiesbaden: Harrassowitz.

Cannon, Garland and Kaye, Alan S. 2001. *The Persian Contributions to the English Language: An Historical Dictionary.* Wiesbaden: Harrassowitz.

Capelli, C.; Redhead, N.; Abernethy, J. K.; Gratrix, F.; Wilson, J.; Moen, T.; Hervig, T.; Richards, M.; Stumpf, M.; Underhill, P. A.; Bradshaw, P.; Shaha, A.; Thomas, M. G.; Bradman, N.; and Goldstein, D. B. 2003. 'A Y Chromosome Census of the British Isles', in *Current Biology* 13 979–84.

Carver, Robert H. F. 2010. 'Prose Satire', in Braden et al. (2010) 333–46.

Chamson, Emil 2010. *The Continental West Germanic Heritage in Late Modern English Dialects: An Etymological Investigation of the English Dialect Dictionary.* Unpublished Ph.D. thesis, University of Innsbruck.

Chamson, Emil 2014. 'Revisiting a millennium of migrations: contextualizing Dutch/Low-German influence on English dialect lexis', in Simone E. Pfenninger, Olga Timofeeva, Anne-Christine Gardner, Alpo Honkapohja, Marianne Hundt, and Daniel Schreier (eds.), *Contact, Variation, and Change in the History of English.* Amsterdam: Benjamins. 281–304.

Chan, Mimi and Kwok, Helen 1985. *A Study of Lexical Borrowing from Chinese into English with Special Reference to Hong Kong.* Hong Kong: Centre of Asian Studies, University of Hong Kong.

Clanchy, Michael 1993. *From Memory to Written Record: England 1066–1307.* 2nd edn. Oxford: Blackwell.

Clark, Cecily 1952–3. 'Studies in the vocabulary of the *Peterborough Chronicle*, 1070–1154', in *English and Germanic Studies* 5 67–89.

Clark, Cecily 1966. '*Ancrene Wisse* and *Katharine Group*: a lexical divergence', in *Neophilologus* 50 117–24.

Clark, Cecily 1992. 'Onomastics', in Hogg (1992c) 452–89.

Clark Hall, J. R. 1960. *A Concise Anglo-Saxon Dictionary*. 4th edn. (1st edn. 1894). Toronto: University of Toronto Press.

Coates, Richard 1982. 'Phonology and the lexicon: a case study of Early English forms in -gg-', in *Indogermanische Forschungen* 87 195–222.

Coates, Richard 2000. 'Evidence for the persistence of Brittonic in Wiltshire', in Coates and Breeze (2000) 112–16.

Coates, Richard 2002. 'The significance of Celtic place-names in England', in Filppula et al. (2002) 47–85.

Coates, Richard 2006. 'Behind the dictionary-forms of Scandinavian elements in England', in *Journal of the English Place-Name Society* 38 43–61.

Coates, Richard 2007. 'Invisible Britons, the view from linguistics', in Higham (2007) 172–91.

Coates, Richard and Breeze, Andrew, with a contribution by Horowitz, David 2000. *Celtic Voices, English Places: Studies on the Celtic Impact on Place-Names in England*. Stamford: Shaun Tyas.

Coleman, Julie 1995. 'The chronology of French and Latin loan words in English', in *Transactions of the Philological Society* 93 95–124.

Cowie, Claire 2012. 'Early Modern English: Morphology', in Bergs and Brinton (2012) Vol. I 604–20.

Cummings, Patrick J. and Hans-Georg Wolf 2011. *A Dictionary of Hong Kong English: Words from the Fragrant Harbor*. Hong Kong: Hong Kong University Press.

Curry, Anne; Bell, Adrian; Chapman, Adam; King, Andy; and Simpkin, David 2010. 'Languages in the Military Profession in Later Medieval England', in Ingham (2010b) 74–93.

Dalton-Puffer, Christiane 1996. *The French Influence on Middle English Morphology: A Corpus-based Study of Derivation*. Berlin: Mouton de Gruyter.

Dance, Richard 1999. '*The Battle of Maldon*, l.91, and the origins of *call*: a reconsideration', in *Neuphilologische Mitteilungen* 100 143–54.

Dance, Richard 2000. 'Is the verb die derived from Old Norse? A review of the evidence', in *English Studies* 81 368–83.

Dance, Richard 2003. *Words Derived from Old Norse in Early Middle English: Studies in the Vocabulary of the South-West Midland Texts*. Tempe, Ariz.: Arizona Center for Medieval and Renaissance Studies.

Dance, Richard 2011. '"Tomar□an hit is awane": Words derived from Old Norse in four Lambeth Homilies', in Jacek Fisiak and Magdalena Bator (eds.) *Foreign Influences on Medieval English*. Frankfurt am Main: Peter Lang. 77–127.

Dance, Richard 2012. 'English in contact: Norse', in Bergs and Brinton (2012) Vol. II 1724–37.

Davies, Mark and Gardner, Dee 2010. *A Frequency Dictionary of Contemporary American English*. New York and London: Routledge.

Dekeyser, Xavier 1986. 'Romance Loans in Middle English: A Re-Assessment', in Dieter Kastovsky and Aleksander Szwedek (eds.) *Linguistics across Historical and Geographical Boundaries: In Honour of Jacek Fisiak on the Occasion of His Fiftieth Birthday*. Vol. 1. Berlin: Mouton de Gruyter. 253–65.

Dekeyser, Xavier and Pauwels, Luc 1990. 'The demise of the Old English heritage and lexical innovation in Middle English: two intertwined developments', in *Leuvense Bijdragen* 79 1–23.

Delamarre, Xavier 2001. *Dictionnaire de la langue gauloise*. Paris: Errance.

Denison, David 1985. 'The origins of periphrastic DO: Ellegård and Visser reconsidered', in R. Eaton; O. Fischer; W. Koopman; and F. van der Leek (eds.) *Papers from the 4th International Conference on English Historical Linguistics*. Amsterdam: Benjamins. 45–60.

Denison, David 1993. *English Historical Syntax: Verbal Constructions*. London: Longman.

Deverson, Tony 1991. 'New Zealand English lexis: the Maori dimension', in *English Today* 7(2) 18–25.

De Vriend, Hubert Jan 1984. *The Old English Herbarium and Medicina de Quadrupedibus*. Early English Text Society: Original Series, 286. Oxford: OUP.

Diensberg, Bernhard 1997. 'Three etymological cruxes', in Raymond Hickey and Stanisław Puppel (eds.) *Language History and Linguistic Modelling: A Festschrift for Jacek Fisiak on his 60th Birthday*. Vol. 1. Berlin: Mouton de Gruyter. 457–65.

Dietz, Klaus 1992. Review of Wollmann (1990), in *Kratylos* 37 142–51.

Dietz, Klaus 2005. 'Die frühen italienischen Lehnwörter des Englischen', in *Anglia* 123 573–631.

Dietz, Klaus 2007. 'Das frühe iberoromanische Lehngut des Englischen', in *Anglia* 124 549–80.

Dietz, Klaus 2011. 'Sprachkontakt im Lichte der altenglischen Toponymie: Das frühe lateinische Lehngut', in Wolfgang Haubrichs and Heinrich Tiefenbach (eds.) *Interferenz-Onomastik: Namen in Grenz- und Begegnungsräumen in Geschichte und Gegenwart*. Saarbrücken: Kommission für Saarländische Landesgeschichte und Volksforschung e. V.

Diller, Hans-Jürgen 1994. 'Emotions in the English lexicon: A historical study of a lexical field', in Francisco Moreno Fernández, Miguel Fuster, and Juan Jose Calvo (eds.) *English Historical Linguistics 1992*. Amsterdam: John Benjamins. 219–34.

Dobson, Eric J. 1968. *English Pronunciation 1500–1700*, 2nd edn. 2 vols. Oxford: OUP.

Durkin, Philip 2002a. 'Changing documentation in the third edition of the *Oxford English Dictionary*: sixteenth-century vocabulary as a test case', in Teresa Fanego, B. Méndez-Naya, and E. Seoane (eds.) *Sounds, Words, Texts and Change: Selected Papers from 11 ICEHL, Santiago de Compostela, 7–11 September 2000*. Amsterdam: Benjamins. 65–81.

Durkin, Philip 2002b. '"Mixed" etymologies of Middle English items in *OED3*: Some questions of methodology and policy', in *Dictionaries* 23 142–55.

Durkin, Philip 2006. 'Lexical Borrowing in Present-Day English', in *Oxford University Working Papers in Linguistics, Philology, and Phonetics* 11 26–42.

Durkin, Philip 2009. *The Oxford Guide to Etymology*. Oxford: OUP.

Durkin, Philip 2011. 'An Influential Voice in the Germanic Etymologies in the First Edition of the *OED*: Correspondence Between Early Editors and Eduard Sievers', in Bauer and Krischke (2011) 23–38.

Durkin, Philip 2012. 'Etymological research on English words as a source of information about Anglo-French', in David Trotter (ed.) *Present and Future Research in Anglo-Norman: Proceedings of the Aberystwyth Colloquium, 21–22 July 2011.* Anglo-Norman Online Hub: Aberystwyth. 101–7.

Eisenberg, Peter 2011. *Das Fremdwort im Deutschen*. Berlin: de Gruyter.

Evans, D. Ellis 1983. 'Language Contact in pre-Roman and Roman Britain', in H. Temporini and W. Haase (eds.) *Aufstieg und Niedergang der römischen Welt* 29:2. Berlin and New York: W. De Gruyter. 949–87.

Evans, Jeremy 1990. 'From the End of Roman Britain to the "Celtic West"', in *Oxford Journal of Archaeology* 9 91–103.

Evans, Toshie M. 1997. *A Dictionary of Japanese Loanwords*. Westport, Connecticut: Greenwood Press.

Farrington, Anthony 1991. *The English factory in Japan, 1613–1623*. 2 vols. London: The British Library.

Farrington, Anthony 2008. 'Cocks, Richard (bap. 1565, d. 1624)', in *Oxford Dictionary of National Biography*, OUP, 2004; online edn., January 2008 [<http://www.oxforddnb.com/view/article/47038> accessed 18 August 2012].

Felixberger, Joseph 2002. 'Das gallische Substrat im etymologischen Wörterbuch des Französischen', in Sabine Heinemann, Gerald Bernhard, and Dieter Kattenbusch (eds.) *Roma et Romania. Festschrift für Gerhard Ernst zum 65. Geburtstag.* Tübingen. 79–94.

Felixberger, Joseph 2003. 'Sub-, Ad- und Superstrate und ihre Wirkung auf die romanischen Sprachen: Galloromania', in Gerhard Ernst, Martin-Dietrich Gleßgen, Christian Schmitt, and Wolfgang Schweickard (eds.) *Romanische Sprachgeschichte: ein internationales Handbuch zur Geschichte der romanischen Sprachen.* Vol. 1. Berlin: Walter de Gruyter. 594–607.

Feulner, Anna Helene 2000. *Die griechischen Lehnwörter im Altenglischen*, Texte und Untersuchungen zur englischen Philologie 21. Frankfurt am Main: Peter Lang.

Filppula, Markku 2009. 'The rise of *it*-clefting in English: areal-typological and contact-linguistic considerations', in *English Language and Linguistics* 13 267–93.

Filppula, Markku 2010. 'Contact and the early history of English', in Hickey (2010) 432–53.

Filppula, Markku, Klemola, Juhani, and Paulasto, Heli (eds.) 2008. *English and Celtic in Contact* (Routledge Studies in Germanic Linguistics 13). New York and London: Routledge.

Filppula, Markku, Klemola, Juhani, and Pitkänen, Heli (eds.) 2002. *The Celtic Roots of English* (Studies in Languages 37). Joensuu: University of Joensuu.

Finkenstaedt, Thomas and Wolff, Dieter with contributions by H. Joachim Neuhaus and Winfried Herget 1973. *Ordered Profusion: Studies in Dictionaries and the English Lexicon*. Heidelberg: Winter.

Fischer, Andreas 1989. 'Lexical change in Late Old English: From æ to *lagu*', in Andreas Fischer (ed.) *The History and the Dialects of English: Festschrift for Eduard Kolb*. Heidelberg: Winter. 103–14.

Fischer, Andreas 2002. 'Notes on kinship terminology in the history of English', in Katja Lenz and Ruth Möhlig (eds.) *Of dyuersitie & chaunge of langage: Essays Presented to Manfred Görlach on the Occasion of his 65th Birthday*. Anglistische Forschungen 308. Heidelberg: Winter. 115–28.

Fischer, Andreas 2003. 'Lexical borrowing and the history of English: A typology of typologies', in Kastovsky and Mettinger (2003) 97–115.

Förster, Max 1921. *Keltisches Wortgut im Englischen: Eine Sprachliche Untersuchung*. Halle (Saale): Niemeyer.

Forsyth, K. 1997. *Language in Pictland: the case against 'Non-Indo-European Pictish'*. Studia Hameliana 2. Utrecht: de Keltische Draak.

Fraser Gupta, Anthea 2008. 'English words from the Malay world', in *Notes and Queries* 55 357–60.

Frere, Sheppard 1999. *Britannia: a History of Roman Britain*. 3rd edn. further revised. London: Folio Society.

Frings, Theodor 1957. *Grundlegung einer Geschichte der deutschen Sprache*. Dritte erweiterte Auflage. Halle (Saale): Niemeyer.

Frings, Theodor 1966. *Germania Romana: Vol. I*. Zweite Auflage besorgt von Gertraud Müller. Mitteldeutsche Studien. Halle (Saale): Niemeyer.

Frings, Theodor and Müller, Gertraud 1968. *Germania Romana: Vol. II. Dreißig Jahre Forschung Romanische Wörter*. Mitteldeutsche Studien. Halle (Saale): Niemeyer.

Funke, O. 1914. *Die gelehrten lateinischen Lehn- und Fremdwörter in der altenglischen Literatur von der Mitte des X. Jahrhunderts bis um das Jahr 1066*. Halle (Saale): Niemeyer.

Gardner-Chloros, Penelope 2010. 'Contact and Code-Switching', in Hickey (2010) 188–207.

Garrett, Andrew 1998. 'On the origin of auxiliary *do*' in *English Language and Linguistics* 2 283–330.

Geeraerts, Dirk, Gevaert, Caroline, and Speelman, Dirk 2011. 'How *anger* rose: Hypothesis testing in diachronic semantics', in Kathryn Allan and Justyna Robinson (eds.) *Current Methods in Historical Semantics*. Berlin: Mouton de Gruyter. 109–32.

Geers, Maria 2005. 'A contrastive study of linguistic purism in the history of England and Germany', in Nils Langer and Winifred W. Davies (eds.) *Linguistic Purism in the Germanic Languages*. Berlin: Walter de Gruyter. 97–108.

Gelling, Margaret 1977. 'Latin loan-words in Old English place-names', in *Anglo-Saxon England* 6 1–13.

Gelling, Margaret 1984. *Place-Names in the Landscape*. London: Dent.

Gelling, Margaret 1992. *The West Midlands in the Early Middle Ages*. Leicester: Leicester University Press.

Gelling, Margaret and Cole, Ann 2000. *The Landscape of Place-Names*. Stamford: Shaun Tyas.

Glinert, Lewis 1992. *The Joys of Hebrew*. New York and Oxford: OUP.

Gneuss, Helmut 1955. *Lehnbildungen und Lehnbedeutungen im Altenglischen*. Berlin: Erich Schmidt.

Gneuss, Helmut 1993. '*Anglicae Linguae Interpretatio*: Language Contact, Lexical Borrowing and Glossing in Anglo-Saxon England', in *Proceedings of the British Academy* 82 107–48; reprinted with addenda in Gneuss (1996b).

Gneuss, Helmut 1996a. 'Latin loans in Old English: A Note on their Inflexional Morphology' in Gneuss (1996b) section VI 1–12.

Gneuss, Helmut 1996b. *Language and History in Early England*. Variorum Collected Studies Series. Aldershot: Ashgate.

Goose, Nigel and Luu, Lien (eds.) 2005. *Immigrants in Tudor and Early Stuart England*. Brighton: Sussex Academic Press.

Görlach, Manfred 1991. *Introduction to Early Modern English*. Cambridge: CUP. (Original German edn. 1978 *Einführung ins Frühneuenglische*. Heidelberg: Quelle und Meyer.)

Görlach, Manfred 1998. 'French in 19th-century Britain', in Manfred Görlach *Aspects of the History of English*. Heidelberg: Winter. 179–99.

Görlach, Manfred 1999. *English in Nineteenth-Century England: An Introduction*. Cambridge: CUP.

Görlach, Manfred 2001. *Eighteenth-Century English*. Heidelberg: Winter.

Gove, Philip B. 1966. 'Etymology in Webster's Third New International Dictionary', in *Word: Journal of the Linguistic Circle of New York* 22 7–82.

Gove, Philip B. 1968. 'The International Scientific Vocabulary in Webster's Third', in *Journal of English Linguistics* 2 1–10.

Graham-Campbell, James; Hall, Richard; Jesch, Judith; and Parsons, David N. (eds.) 2001. *Vikings and the Danelaw: Select Papers from the Proceedings of the Thirteenth Viking Congress, Nottingham and York, 21–30 August 1997*. Oxford: Oxbow.

Grant, Anthony 2009. 'Loanwords in British English', in Haspelmath and Tadmor (2009) 360–83.

Gray, Douglas 1983. 'Captain Cook and the English Vocabulary', in Stanley and Gray (1983) 49–62.

Gray, Douglas (ed.) 1985. *The Oxford Book of Late Medieval Verse and Prose*. Oxford: OUP.

Gray, Douglas 1988. 'A note on sixteenth-century purism', in Eric G. Stanley and Terry F. Hoad (eds.) *Words: For Robert Burchfield's Sixty-Fifth Birthday*. Cambridge: D. S. Brewer. 103–19.

Green, D. H. 1998. *Language and History in the Early Germanic World*. Cambridge: CUP.

Grzega, Joachim 2003. 'Altenglisch bisc(e)op und seine germanischen Verwandten' in *Anglia* 120 372–83.

Hamer, R. F. S. 1967. *Old English Sound Changes For Beginners*. Oxford: Blackwell.

Hankin, Nigel B. 1992. *Hanklyn-Janklin, or A Stranger's Rumble-Tumble Guide to Some Words, Customs and Quiddities Indian and Indo-British*. Delhi: Banyan Books.

Hansen, Bente H. 1984. 'The historical implications of the Scandinavian linguistic element in English: a theoretical evaluation', in *North-Western European Language Evolution* 4 53–95.

Harriss, Gerald 2005. *Shaping the Nation: England 1360–1461*. Oxford: OUP.

Haspelmath, Martin 2009. 'Lexical borrowing: concepts and issues', in Haspelmath and Tadmor (2009) 35–54.

Haspelmath, Martin and Tadmor, Uri (eds.) 2009. *Loanwords in the World's Languages: A Comparative Handbook*. Berlin: De Gruyter Mouton.

Haugen, Einar 1950. 'The analysis of linguistic borrowing', in *Language* 26 210–31.

Hawkins, R. E. 1984. *Common Indian Words in English*. Delhi: OUP.

Hendriks, Jennifer 2012. 'Contact: German and Dutch', in Bergs and Brinton (2012) Vol. II 1659–70.

Hickey, Raymond (ed.) 2010. *The Handbook of Language Contact*. Oxford: Wiley-Blackwell.

Higham, Nicholas J. 2002. 'The Anglo-Saxon/British interface: history and ideology', in Filppula et al. (2002) 29–46.

Higham, Nicholas J. (ed.) 2007. *Britons in Anglo-Saxon England* (Publications of the Manchester Centre for Anglo-Saxon Studies 7). Woodbridge: Boydell Press.

Hills, Catherine M. 1979. 'The archaeology of Anglo-Saxon England in the pagan period: a review', in *Anglo-Saxon England* 8 297–329.

Hines, John 1990. 'Philology, archaeology and the adventus Saxonum vel Anglorum', in Alfred Bammesberger and Alfred Wollmann (eds.) *Britain 400–600: Language and History*. Heidelberg: Winter. 17–36.

Hingeston, F. C. 1860. *Royal and Historical Letters During the Reign of Henry the Fourth. Vol. I: A.D. 1399–1404*. London: Longman, Green, Longman, and Roberts.

Höfler, Manfred 1981. 'Für eine Ausgliederung der Kategorie <Lehnschöpfung> aus dem Bereich sprachlicher Entlehnung', in Wolfgang Pöckl (ed.) *Europäische Mehrsprachigkeit: Festschrift zum 70. Geburtstag von Mario Wandruszka*. Tübingen: Niemeyer. 149–53.

Hofmann, Dietrich 1955. *Nordisch-Englische Lehnbeziehungen der Wikingerzeit*. Copenhagen: Einar Munksgaard.

Hogg, Richard M. 1982. 'Two geminate consonants in Old English?', in John Anderson (ed.) *Language Form and Linguistic Variation: Papers Dedicated to Angus McIntosh*. Amsterdam: Benjamins. 187–202.

Hogg, Richard M. 1992a. *A Grammar of Old English: Vol. 1: Phonology*. Oxford: Blackwell.

Hogg, Richard M. 1992b. 'Phonology and Morphology', in Hogg (1992c) 67–167.

Hogg, Richard M. (ed.) 1992c. *The Cambridge History of the English Language. Vol. I: The Beginnings to 1066*. Cambridge: CUP.

Holman, Katherine 2001. 'Defining the Danelaw', in Graham-Campbell et al. (2001) 1–11.

Horobin, Simon C. P. 2001. 'J.R.R. Tolkien as a Philologist: A Reconsideration of the Northernisms in Chaucer's Reeve's Tale', in *English Studies* 82 97–105.

Howe, Stephen 1996. *The Personal Pronouns in the Germanic Languages: A Study of Personal Pronoun Morphology and Change in the Germanic Languages from the First Records to the Present Day* (Studia Linguistica Germanica 43). Berlin: Walter de Gruyter.

Hug, Sibylle 1987. *Scandinavian Loanwords and their equivalents in Middle English.* Bern: Peter Lang.

Hunt, Tony 1991. *Teaching and Learning Latin in Thirteenth-Century England*, 3 vols. Cambridge: D. S. Brewer.

Ingham, Richard 2009. 'Mixing languages on the manor', in *Medium Aevum* 78 80–97.

Ingham, Richard 2010a. 'The transmission of later Anglo-Norman: some syntactic evidence', in Ingham (2010b) 264–82.

Ingham, Richard 2010b. *The Anglo-Norman Language and its Contexts.* York: York Medieval Press.

Ingham, Richard 2012. *The Transmission of Anglo-Norman: Language History and Language Acquisition.* Amsterdam: Benjamins.

Irvine, Susan 2004. *The Anglo-Saxon Chronicle: A Collaborative Edition.* Vol. 7: MS E. Cambridge: D. S. Brewer.

Jackson, Kenneth H. 1953. *Language and History in Early Britain: A Chronological Survey of the Brittonic languages, First to Twelfth Century A.D.* Edinburgh: EUP.

Jackson, Kenneth H. 1955. 'The Britons in southern Scotland', in *Antiquity* 29 77–88.

Jefferson, Lisa 2000. 'The language and vocabulary of the fourteenth- and early fifteenth-century records of the Goldsmiths' Company', in Trotter (2000) 175–211.

Johannesson, Nils-Lennart 2005. 'Old English versus Old Norse vocabulary in the Ormulum: the choice of third person plural personal pronouns' <http://www2.english.su.se/nlj/ormproj/info/heore97_rev.pdf>—earlier version published in Gunnel Melchers and Beatrice Warren (eds.) *Studies in Anglistics* (1995) Stockholm: Almqvist & Wiksell International. 171–80.

John, Eric 1982. 'The end of Anglo-Saxon England', in Campbell (1982b) 214–39.

Jones, Charles (ed.) 1997. *The Edinburgh History of the Scots Language.* Edinburgh: EUP.

Jordan, Richard 1934. *Handbuch der Mittelenglischen Grammatik.* 2nd edn., rev. H. C. Matthes. Heidelberg: Winter.

Kaiser, Rolf 1937. *Zur Geographie des mittelenglischen Wortschatzes.* (Palaestra 205). Leipzig: Mayer & Müller.

Kaplan, Theodore H. 1932. 'Gower's Vocabulary', in *Journal of English and Germanic Philology* 31 395–402.

Kastovsky, Dieter 1992. 'Semantics and vocabulary', in Hogg (1992c) 290–408.

Kastovsky, Dieter 2010. 'Translation Techniques in the Terminology of Ælfric's Grammar: Semantic Loans, Loan Translations and Word-Formation', in Merja Kytö, John Scahill, and Harumi Tanabe (eds.) *Language Change and Variation from Old English to Late Modern English: A Festschrift for Minoji Akimoto*. Bern: Peter Lang. 163–74.

Kastovsky, Dieter and Mettinger, Arthur 2003. *Language Contact in the History of English*. 2nd revised edn. (1st edn. 2001). Frankfurt am Main: Peter Lang.

Kaunisto, Mark 2007. *Variation and Change in the Lexicon: A Corpus-based Analysis of Adjectives in English Ending in -ic and -ical*. Amsterdam and New York: Rodopi.

Kaunisto, Mark 2008. 'The Rivalry between English Adjectives Ending in -*ive* and -*ory*', in Roderick W. McConchie, Alpo Honkapohja, and Jukka Tyrkkö (eds.) *Selected Proceedings of the 2008 Symposium on New Approaches in English Historical Lexis (HEL-LEX 2)*. Somerville, MA: Cascadilla Proceedings Project. 74–87.

Kennedy, Graeme and Yamazaki, Shunji 1999. 'The influence of Maori on the New Zealand lexicon', in John Kirk (ed.) *Corpora Galore: Analyses and Techniques in Describing English*. Amsterdam: Rodopi. 33–44.

Kibbee, Douglas A. 1991. *For to Speke French Trewely: The French Language in England, 1000–1600: Its Status, Description and Instruction*. Amsterdam: Benjamins.

Klemola, Juhanni 2002. 'Periphrastic DO: Dialectal distribution and origins', in Filppula et al. (2002) 199–210.

Kluge, Friedrich 1909. 'Gotische Lehnworte im Althochdeutschen' in *Beiträge zur Geschichte der deutschen Sprache und Literatur* 35 124–60.

Kluge, Friedrich 2002. *Etymologisches Wörterbuch der deutschen Sprache* edn. 24 [1st edn. 1883], Elmar Seebold (ed.). Berlin: de Gruyter.

Kniezsa, Veronika 1994. 'The Scandinavian elements in the vocabulary of the Peterborough Chronicle', in Francisco Fernández, Miguel Fuster, and Juan José Calvo (eds.) *English Historical Linguistics 1992: Papers from the Seventh International Conference on English Historical Linguistics, Valencia, 22–26 September 1992*. Amsterdam: Benjamins. 235–45.

Koivulehto, Jorma 2002. 'Contact with non-Germanic languages II: relations to the East', in Oskar Bandle et al. (eds.) *The Nordic Languages: An International Handbook of the History of the North Germanic Languages*. 2 vols. Berlin: Walter de Gruyter. 583–94.

Kolb, Eduard 1965. 'Skandinavisches in den nordenglischen Dialekten', in *Anglia* 83 127–53.

Kornexl, Lucia 2003. '"Unnatural words"?—Loan-formations in Old English glosses', in Kastovsky and Mettinger (2003) 195–216.

Kornexl, Lucia and Lenker, Ursula 2011. 'Culinary and other pairs: lexical borrowing and conceptual differentiation in early English food terminology', in Bauer and Krischke (2011) 179–206.

Kries, Susanne 2003. *Skandinavisch-schottische Sprachbeziehungen im Mittelalter: der altnordische Lehneinfluss*. Odense: University Press of Southern Denmark.

Kristol, A. 1990. 'L'enseignement du français en Angleterre (XIIIème–XVème siècles): les sources manuscrites', in *Romania* 111 289–330.

Laing, Margaret 2004. 'Multidimensionality: time and space and stratigraphy in historical dialectology', in Marina Dossena and Roger Lass (eds.) *Methods and Data in English Historical Dialectology*. Bern: Peter Lang. 49–96.

Laing, Margaret 2011. *A Linguistic Atlas of Early Middle English: Index of Sources*, in Laing and Lass (2011).

Laing, Margaret and Lass, Roger 2011. *A Linguistic Atlas of Early Middle English, 1150–1325*, version 2.1 [<http://www.lel.ed.ac.uk/ihd/laeme1/laeme1.html>]. Edinburgh: The University of Edinburgh.

Laing, Margaret and Lass, Roger 2014. 'On Middle English she, sho: A refurbished narrative', in *Folia Linguistica Historica* 35 201–240.

Laker, Stephen 2009. 'An explanation for the early phonemicisation of a voice contrast in English fricatives', in *English Language and Linguistics* 13 213–26.

Lambert, Pierre-Yves 1995. *La langue gauloise: description linguistique, commentaire d'inscriptions choisies*. Paris: Errance.

Lambley, Kathleen 1920. *The Teaching and Cultivation of the French Language in England in Tudor and Stuart Times*. Manchester: MUP.

Lapidge, Michael, Blair, John, Keynes, Simon, and Scragg, Donald (eds.) 1999. *The Blackwell Encyclopaedia of Anglo-Saxon England*. Oxford: Blackwell.

Lass, Roger (ed.) 1969. *Approaches to English Historical Linguistics: An Anthology*. New York: Holt, Rinehart, and Winston.

Lass, Roger 1994. *Old English: A Historical Linguistic Companion.* Cambridge: CUP.

Lass, Roger 1997. *Historical Linguistics and Language Change*. Cambridge: CUP.

Lass, Roger 1999a. 'Phonology and morphology', in Lass (1999b) 56–186.

Lass, Roger (ed.) 1999b. *The Cambridge History of the English Language. Vol. iii: 1476–1776*. Cambridge: CUP.

Leech, Geoffrey, Rayson, Paul, and Wilson, Andrew 2001. *Word Frequencies in Written and Spoken English: based on the British National Corpus*. London: Longman.

Lehmann, Winfred P. 1986. *A Gothic Etymological Dictionary: Based on the Third Edition of Vergleichendes Wörterbuch der Gotischen Sprache by Sigmund Feist*. Leiden: E. J. Brill.

Leisi, Ernst 1955. *Das heutige Englisch: Wesenszüge und Probleme*. Heidelberg: Winter.

Leisi, Ernst and Mair, Christian 1999. *Das heutige Englisch: Wesenszüge und Probleme*. 8th edn. Heidelberg: Winter.

Lewis, Ivor 1991. *Sahibs, Nabobs and Boxwallahs: A Dictionary of the Words of Anglo-India*. Bombay: OUP.

Lewis, Robert E. 2007. *Middle English Dictionary: Plan and Bibliography: Second Edition*. Ann Arbor: University of Michigan Press.

Llewellyn, E. C. 1926. *The Influence of Low Dutch on the English Vocabulary*. Publications of the Philological Society. Oxford: OUP.

Lloyd, Cynthia 2011. *Semantics and Word Formation: The Semantic Development of Five French Suffixes in Middle English*. Frankfurt am Main: Peter Lang.

Lloyd-Morgan, Ceridwen 2003. *The Hengwrt Chaucer: Standard Edition on CD-ROM*. CD-ROM published by Scholarly Digital Editions, Leicester.

Lockwood, William B. 1993. *The Oxford Dictionary of British Bird Names* (revised edn. of *The Oxford Book of British Bird Names*, 1984). Oxford: OUP.

Loporcaro, Michele 2011. 'Syllable, segment and prosody', in Martin Maiden, John Charles Smith, and Adam Ledgeway (eds.) *The Cambridge History of the Romance Languages: Vol. i: Structures*. Cambridge: CUP. 51–108.

Lucas, Peter J. and Lucas, Angela M. (eds.) 2002. *Middle English from Tongue to Text. Selected Papers from the Third International Conference on Middle English: Language and Text, held at Dublin, Ireland, 1–4 July 1999*. Frankfurt am Main: Peter Lang.

Luick, Karl 1914–21. *Historische Grammatik der englischen Sprache: Vol. I*. Stuttgart: Tauchnitz.

Lusignan, Serge 2009. 'French language in contact with English: social context and linguistic change (mid-13th–14th centuries)', in Wogan-Browne (2009b) 19–30.

Lusignan, Serge 2012. *Essai d'histoire sociolinguistique: le français picard au Moyen Âge*. Paris: Garnier.

Lutz, Angelika 2009. 'Celtic influence on Old English and West Germanic' in *English Language and Linguistics* 13 227–49.

Luu, Lien Bich 2005. *Immigrants and the Industries of London, 1500–1700*. Hampshire, England: Ashgate.

Macafee, Caroline 1997. 'Older Scots lexis', in Jones (1997) 182–212.

Macafee, Caroline 2002. 'A history of Scots to 1700', in *A Dictionary of the Older Scottish Tongue*. Vol. XII: xix–clvii (see also <http://www.dsl.ac.uk/dsl/>).

Macafee, Caroline and Anderson, Alan 1997. 'A random sample of Older Scots lexis', in *Transactions of the Philological Society* 95 247–78.

Macalister, John 2005. *A Dictionary of Maori Words in New Zealand English*. Oxford: OUP.

Macalister, John 2006. 'The Maori presence in the New Zealand English lexicon, 1850–2000: evidence from a corpus-based study', in *English World-Wide* 27 1–24.

McClure, Peter (forthcoming). 'Personal and surname dictionaries', in Philip Durkin (ed.) *The Oxford Handbook of Lexicography*. Oxford: OUP.

McGee, Alan Van Keuren 1940. *The Geographical Distribution of Scandinavian Loan-Words in Middle English, with Special Reference to the Alliterative Poetry*. Ph.D. thesis, Yale University.

MacGillivray, H. S. 1902. *The Influence of Christianity on the Vocabulary of Old English*. Halle (Saale): Niemeyer.

Machan, Tim W. 2002. 'Politics and the Middle English language', in *Studies in the Age of Chaucer* 24 317–24.

Machan, Tim W. 2003. *English in the Middle Ages*. Oxford: OUP.

McIntosh, Angus, Samuels, Michael L., and Benskin, Michael (eds.) 1986. *A Linguistic Atlas of Late Mediaeval English* (with the assistance of Margaret Laing and Keith Williamson) 4 vols. Aberdeen: Aberdeen University Press.

Mackenzie, Fraser 1939. *Les relations de l'Angleterre et de la France d'après le vocabulaire. Vol. II. Les infiltrations de la langue et de l'esprit français en Angleterre: gallicismes anglais.* Paris: Droz.

Marchand, Hans 1969. *The Categories and Types of Present-Day English Word-Formation: A Synchronic-Diachronic Approach.* 2nd edn. Munich: Beck.

Matasović, Ranko 2009. *Etymological Dictionary of Proto-Celtic.* Leiden Indo-European Etymological Dictionary Series. Vol. 9. Leiden: Brill.

Mersand, Joseph 1939. *Chaucer's Romance Vocabulary.* 2nd edn. (1st edn. 1937). New York: Comet Press.

Michel, Jean-Baptiste; Shen, Yuan Kui; Aviva Presser, Aiden; Veres, Adrian; Gray, Matthew K.; The Google Books Team; Pickett, Joseph P.; Hoiberg, Dale; Clancy, Dan; Norvig, Peter; Orwant, Jon; Pinker, Steven; Nowak, Martin A.; and Erez Lieberman, Aiden 2011. 'Quantitative analysis of culture using millions of digitized books', in *Science* 331 176–82.

Milfull, Inge 2009. 'PULEGE and PSYLLIUM: Old English plant names in p- in the *Oxford English Dictionary*', in Peter Bierbaumer and Helmut Klug (eds.) *Old Names—New Growth: Proceedings of the 2nd ASPNS Conference, University of Graz, Austria, 6–10 June 2007, and Related Essays.* Frankfurt am Main: Peter Lang. 121–143.

Miller, D. Gary 1997. 'The morphological legacy of French: borrowed suffixes on native bases in Middle English', in *Diachronica* 14 233–64.

Miller, D. Gary 2004. 'The Morphosyntactic Legacy of Scand-English Contact', in Marcin Krygier and Liliana Sikorska (eds.) *For the Loue of Inglis Lede.* Frankfurt am Main: Peter Lang. 9–39.

Miller, D. Gary 2006. *Latin Suffixal Derivatives in English and their Indo-European Ancestry.* Oxford: OUP.

Miller, D. Gary 2012. *External Influences on English: From its Beginnings to the Renaissance.* Oxford: OUP.

Millett, Bella (ed.) 2005. *Ancrene Wisse: A Corrected Edition of the Text in Cambridge, Corpus Christi College, MS 402 with Variants from Other Manuscripts.* Drawing on the uncompleted edition by E. J. Dobson, with a glossary and additional notes by Richard Dance. Vol. 1. (Early English Text Society No. 325.) Oxford: Early English Text Society.

Minkova, Donka 2012. 'Linguistic levels: prosody', in Bergs and Brinton (2012) Vol. I 113–28.

Mossé, Fernand 1943. 'On the chronology of French loan-words in English', in *English Studies* 25 33–40.

Murison, David 1971. 'The Dutch element in the vocabulary of Scots', in A. J. Aitken, Angus McIntosh, and Hermann Pálsson (eds.) *Edinburgh Studies in English and Scots.* London: Longman.

Murray, James A. H. 1888. 'General Explanations', in James A. H. Murray (ed.) *A New English Dictionary on Historical Principles*. Vol. I: A and B. Oxford: OUP. xvii–xxiv.

Muthiah, S. 1991. *Words in Indian English*. Delhi: Indus.

Myers-Scotton, Carol 2002. *Contact Linguistics: Bilingual Encounters and Grammatical Outcomes*. Oxford: OUP.

Nevalainen, Terttu 1999. 'Lexis and Semantics', in Lass (1999b) 322–458.

Nevalainen, Terttu 2006. *An Introduction to Early Modern English*. Edinburgh: Edinburgh University Press.

Orme, Nicholas 2006. *Medieval Schools: from Roman Britain to Renaissance England*. New Haven: Yale University Press.

Ormrod, W. Mark 2003. 'The use of English: language, law, and political culture in fourteenth-century England', in *Speculum* 78 750–87.

Ormrod, W. Mark 2009. 'The language of complaint: multilingualism and petitioning in later medieval England', in Wogan-Browne (2009) 31–43.

Otter, Alice G. den 1990. 'Lekker scrabbling: Discovery and exploration of once-Dutch words in the online Oxford English Dictionary', in *English Studies* 71 261–71.

Parkes, Malcolm B. 1983. 'On the Presumed Date and Possible Origin of the "Ormulum": Oxford, Bodleian Library, MS Junius 1', in Stanley and Gray (1983) 115–27.

Parsons, David N. 2001. 'How long did the Scandinavian language survive in England? Again', in Graham-Campbell et al. (2001) 299–312.

Parsons, David 2011. 'Sabrina in the thorns: place-names as evidence for British and Latin in Roman Britain', in *Transactions of the Philological Society* 109 113–37.

Parsons, David N. and Styles, Tania 2000. *The Vocabulary of English Place-Names*. Vol. 2: *brace – cæster*. Nottingham: Centre for English Name-Studies.

Pattison, John E. 2008. 'Is it necessary to assume an apartheid-like social structure in Early Anglo-Saxon England?', in *Proceedings of the Royal Society B: Biological Sciences* 275 2423–9.

Pattison, John E. 2011. 'Integration Versus Apartheid in Post-Roman Britain: A Response to Thomas et al. (2008)', in *Human Biology* 83 715–33.

Pelteret, David A. E. 1980. 'Slave raiding and slave trading in early England', in *Anglo-Saxon England* 9 99–114.

Pelteret, David A. E. 1995. *Slavery in early medieval England from the reign of Alfred until the twelfth century*. Woodbridge: Boydell Press.

Peters, Hans 1981a. 'Zum skandinavischen Lehngut im Altenglischen', in *Sprachwissenschaft* 6 85–124.

Peters, Hans 1981b. 'Onomasiologische Untersuchungen zum skandinavischen Lehngut im Altenglischen', in *Sprachwissenschaft* 6 169–85.

Pfeffer, Alan J. and Cannon, Garland 1994. *German Loanwords in English: An Historical Dictionary*. Cambridge: CUP.

Pfeifer, Wolfgang 2000. *Etymologisches Wörterbuch des Deutschen*. 5th edn. Munich: Deutsche Taschenbuch Verlag.

Philippa, Marlies 2003–9. *Etymologisch woordenboek van het Nederlands*. 4 vols. Amsterdam: Amsterdam University Press.

Pinnavaia, Laura 2001. *The Italian Borrowings in the* Oxford English Dictionary*: A Lexicographical, Linguistic and Cultural Analysis*. Rome: Bulzoni.

Plag, Ingo 2006. 'Productivity', in Bas Aarts and April McMahon (eds.) *The Handbook of English Linguistics*. Oxford: Blackwell. 537–56.

Pogatscher, Alois 1888. *Zur Lautlehre der griechischen, lateinischen und romanischen Lehnwörter in Altenglischen*. Strassburg: Trübner.

Polenz, Peter von 1967. 'Fremdwort und Lehnwort sprachwissenschaftlich betrachtet', in *Muttersprache* 77 65–80.

Polomé, Edgar C. 1983. 'The linguistic situation in the western provinces of the Roman Empire', in H. Temporini and W. Haase (eds.) *Aufstieg und Niedergang der römischen Welt* 29:2. Berlin and New York: W. De Gruyter. 509–53.

Pons-Sanz, Sara 2007. *Norse-Derived Vocabulary in Late Old English Texts: Wulfstan's Works, a Case Study* (*North-Western European Language Evolution* supplement 22). Odense: University Press of Southern Denmark.

Pons-Sanz, Sara 2008. 'Norse-derived terms and structures in *The Battle of Maldon*', in *The Journal of English and Germanic Philology* 107 421–44.

Pons-Sanz, Sara 2011. 'The etymology of the word-field of Old English *hōre* and the lexico-cultural climate of eleventh-century England', in *Nottingham Medieval Studies* 55 32–48.

Pons-Sanz, Sara (forthcoming). *The Lexical Effects of Anglo-Scandinavian Linguistic Contact on Old English*. Turnhout: Brepols.

Poplack, Shana 2004. 'Code-switching' in U. Ammon, N. Dittmar, K. J. Mattheier, and P. Trudgill (eds.) *Sociolinguistics: An International Handbook of the Science of Language and Society*. 2nd edn. Berlin: Walter de Gruyter. 589–96.

Poplack, Shana and Dion, Nathalie 2012. 'Myths and facts about loanword development', in *Language Variation and Change* 24 279–315.

Poplack, Shana and Meechan, Marjory 1998. 'How languages fit together in code-mixing', in *International Journal of Bilingualism* 2 127–38.

Poplack, Shana, Sankoff, David, and Miller, Chris 1988. 'The social correlates and linguistic processes of lexical borrowing and assimilation', in *Linguistics* 26 47–104.

Poppe, Erich 2009. 'Standard Average European and the Celticity of English intensifiers and reflexives: some considerations and implications', in *English Language and Linguistics* 13 251–66.

Prestwich, Michael 2005. *Plantagenet England 1225–1360*. Oxford: OUP.

Rao, G. Subba 1954. *Indian Words in English: a Study in Indo-British Cultural and Linguistic Relations*. Oxford: OUP.

Reuter, Ole 1934. *On the Development of English Verbs from Latin and French Past Participles*. Societas Scientiarum Fennica: Commentationes Humanarum Litterarum VI.6. Helsinki: Akademische Buchhandlung.

Reuter, Ole 1936. *Verb Doublets of Latin Origin in English.* Societas Scientiarum Fennica: Commentationes Humanarum Litterarum VIII.4. Helsinki: Akademische Buchhandlung.

Ringe, Donald R. 1984. 'Germanic "ē2" and *r', in *Die Sprache* 30 138–55.

Ringe, Donald R. 2006. *From Proto-Indo-European to Proto-Germanic.* Oxford: OUP.

Ritt, Nikolaus 2003. 'The spread of Scandinavian third person plural pronouns in English: Optimisation, adaptation and evolutionary stability', in Kastovsky and Mettinger (2003) 279–304.

Roberge, Paul 2010. 'Contact and the History of Germanic Languages', in Hickey (2010) 406–31.

Rodríguez González, Félix 1996. *Spanish Loanwords in the English Language: A Tendency towards Hegemony Reversal.* Berlin: Mouton de Gruyter.

Rosten, Leo 2001. *The New Joys of Yiddish.* Revised by Lawrence Bush. (1st edn. 1968.) New York: Random House.

Rothwell, William 1991. 'The missing link in English etymology: Anglo-French', in *Medium Ævum* 60 173–96.

Rothwell, William 1998. 'Arrivals and departures: the adoption of French terminology into Middle English', in *English Studies* 79 144–65.

Rothwell, William 1999. 'Sugar and spice and all things nice: from Oriental bazar to English cloister in Anglo-French', in *Modern Language Review* 94 647–59.

Rothwell, William 2005. 'Preface: Anglo-French and the *AND*', in *Anglo-Norman Dictionary*, 2nd edn., Vol. i: A–C. London: Modern Humanities Research Association. v–xx.

Rothwell, William 2010. '*Husbonderie* and *manaungerie* in later medieval England: a tale of two Walters', in Ingham (2010b) 44–51.

Rotsaert, Marie-Louise 1977. 'Vieux-haut-allem. *biscof* / gallo-roman **(e)bẹcobo*, **(e)bẹscobǝ* / lat. *episcopus*', in *Sprachwissenschaft* 2 181–216.

Rynell, Alarik 1948. *The Rivalry of Scandinavian and Native Synonyms in Middle English, Especially* Taken *and* Nimen *(with an excursus on* Nema *and* Taka *in Old Scandinavian).* (Lund Studies in English 13.) Lund: Håkon Ohlssons Boktryckeri.

Salmon, Vivian 1999. 'Orthography and Punctuation', in Lass (1999b) 13–54.

Salway, Peter 2001. *A History of Roman Britain.* Revised edn. Oxford: OUP.

Samuels, Michael 1985. 'The Great Scandinavian Belt', in Roger Eaton et al. (eds.) *Papers from the 4th International Conference on English Historical Linguistics.* Amsterdam: Benjamins 269–81; reprinted in Margaret Laing (ed.) 1989. *Middle English Dialectology: Essays on some Principles and Problems.* Aberdeen: Aberdeen University Press. 106–15.

Sanchez, Christina 2008. *Consociation and Dissociation: An Empirical Study of Word-Family Integration in English and German.* Tübingen: Narr.

Sanchez-Stockhammer, Christina 2009. 'What makes a word dissociated? A contrastive study of the English and German vocabulary', in Lars Eckstein and Christoph Reinfandt (eds.) *Anglistentag 2008 Tübingen.* Proceedings of the Conference of the German Association of University Teachers of English, Vol. 30. Trier: WVT. 459–69.

Sauer, Hans 2003. 'The morphology of the Old English plant-names', in Carole P. Biggam (ed.) *From Earth to Art: The Many Aspects of the Plant-World in Anglo-Saxon England*. Amsterdam: Rodopi.

Schäfer, Jürgen 1980. *Documentation in the O.E.D.: Shakespeare and Nashe as Test Cases*. Oxford: OUP.

Scheler, Manfred 1977. *Der englische Wortschatz*. (Grundlagen der Anglistik und Amerikanistik 9.) Berlin: Erich Schmidt.

Schendl, Herbert 2002. 'Code-choice and code-switching in some early 15th century letters', in Lucas and Lucas (2002) 247–62.

Schendl, Herbert (forthcoming). 'Multilingualism and code-switching as mechanisms of contact-induced lexical change in late Middle English', in Daniel Schreier and Marianne Hundt (eds.) *English as a Contact Language*. Cambridge: CUP.

Schendl, Herbert and Wright, Laura (eds.) 2011a. *Code-switching in Early English*. Berlin: Mouton de Gruyter.

Schendl, Herbert and Wright, Laura 2011b. 'Code-switching in Early English: Historical background and methodological and theoretical issues', in Schendl and Wright (2011a) 15–46.

Scheps, Walter 1979. 'Chaucer's use of nonce words, primarily in the *Canterbury Tales*', in *Neuphilologische Mitteilungen* 80 69–77.

Scheuchzer, J. G. 1727. tr. Engelbert Kaempfer *The History of Japan*. London. (Reprinted 1906 (in 3 vols). Glasgow: James MacLehose and Sons.)

Schrijver, Peter C. H. 1999. 'The Celtic Contribution to the Development of the North Sea Germanic Vowel System, with Special Reference to Coastal Dutch', *North-Western European Language Evolution* 35 3–47.

Schrijver, Peter C. H. 2002. 'The rise and fall of British Latin: evidence from English and Brittonic', in Filppula et al. (2002) 87–110.

Schrijver, Peter C. H. 2007. 'What Britons spoke around 400 AD', in Higham (2007) 165–71.

Schrijver, Peter C. H. 2009. 'Celtic influence on Old English: phonological and phonetic evidence' in *English Language and Linguistics* 13 193–211.

Schultz, Julia 2012a. *Twentieth Century Borrowings from French to English: Their Reception and Development*. Newcastle upon Tyne: Cambridge Scholars Publishing.

Schultz, Julia 2012b. 'Twentieth-century borrowings from French into English—an overview', in *English Today* 110 3–9.

Schweickard, Wolfgang 1986. 'Etimologie distinctivă. Methodische Überlegungen zur Herkunftsbestimmung neuerer Entlehnungen des Rumänischen am Beispiel des sportsprachlichen Vokabulars', in Günter Holtus and Edgar Radtke (eds.) *Rumänistik in der Diskussion*. Tübingen: Narr. 129–63.

Scott, Sir Walter [1820] 1998. *Ivanhoe*. Graham Tulloch (ed.). Edinburgh: Edinburgh University Press.

Scragg, Donald 1974. *A History of English Spelling*. Manchester: MUP.

Seebold, Elmar 1970. *Vergleichendes und etymologisches Wörterbuch der germanischen starken Verben.* The Hague: Mouton.

Serjeantson, Mary S. 1935. *A History of Foreign Words in English.* London: K. Paul.

Short, Ian 1995. 'Anglo-Norman Literature', in Peter France (ed.) *The New Oxford Companion to Literature in French.* Oxford: OUP. 28–32.

Short, Ian 2007. *Manual of Anglo-Norman.* Anglo-Norman Text Society, Occasional Publications Series, No. 7. London: Anglo-Norman Text Society.

Sijs, Nicoline van der 2009. *Cookies, Coleslaw, and Stoops: The Influence of Dutch on the North-American Languages.* Amsterdam: AUP.

Sijs, Nicoline van der 2010. *Nederlandse woorden wereldwijd.* Den Haag: Sdu.

Simpson, John 1981. 'Notes on Some Norse Loans, Real or Supposed, in S*ir Gawain and the Green Knight*', in *Medium Aevum* 50 301–4.

Sisam, Kenneth (ed.) 1921. *Fourteenth Century Verse and Prose.* Oxford: OUP.

Skaffari, Janne 2002. 'The non-native vocabulary of the Peterborough Chronicle', in Lucas and Lucas (2002) 235–46.

Skaffari, Janne 2009. *Studies in Early Middle English Loanwords: Norse and French Influences.* Anglicana Turkuensia 26. Turku, Finland: University of Turku.

Smith, A. H. 1956. *English Place-Name Elements.* 2 vols. Cambridge: CUP.

Smith, Jeremy J. 1992. 'The use of English: language contact, dialect variation and written standardisation in the Middle English period', in Tim. W. Machan and C. T. Scott (eds.) *English in its Social Contexts.* New York: OUP. 47–68.

Smith, Jeremy J. 2007. *Sound Change and the History of English.* Oxford: OUP.

Smithers, G. V. 1941. Review of Bense (1939), in *The Review of English Studies* 17 494–9.

Stanley, Eric G. 1969. 'Old English "-calla", "ceallian"', in Derek Pearsall and R. A. Waldron (eds.) *Medieval Literature and Civilization: Studies in Memory of G. N. Garmonsway.* London: Athlone Press. 94–9.

Stanley, Eric G. 2003. 'Old English *The Fortunes of Men*, lines 80–84' in *Notes and Queries* 50 265–8.

Stanley, Eric G. and Gray, Douglas (eds.) 1983. *Five Hundred Years of Words and Sounds: A Festschrift for Eric Dobson.* Cambridge: D. S. Brewer.

Stefenelli, Arnulf 1996. 'Thesen zur Entstehung und Ausgliederung der romanischen Sprachen' in Günter Holtus, Michael Metzeltin, and Christian Schmitt (eds.) *Lexikon der Romanistischen Linguistik* 2/1. Tübingen: Niemeyer. 73–90.

Steinmetz, Sol 2001. *Yiddish and English: the story of Yiddish in America.* 2nd edn. (1st edn. 1986). Tuscaloosa, AL and London: University of Alabama Press.

Stockwell, Robert and Minkova, Donka 2009. *English Words: History and Structure.* 2nd edn. (1st edn. 2001). Cambridge: CUP.

Styles, Tania 2001. 'Scandinavian elements in English place-names: some semantic problems', in Graham-Campbell et al. (2001) 288–98.

Sykes, Bryan 2006. *Blood of the Isles: Exploring the Genetic Roots of Our Tribal History.* London: Bantam.

Szemerényi, Oswald J. L. 1996. *Introduction to Indo-European Linguistics*. Oxford: OUP. (Translation of Szemerényi, Oswald J. L. 1990. *Einführung in die vergleichende Sprachwissenschaft*. 4th edn. Darmstadt: Wissenschaftliche Buchgesellschaft).

Tadmor, Uri 2009. 'Loanwords in the world's languages: findings and results', in Haspelmath and Tadmor (2009) 55–75.

Tadmor, Uri, Haspelmath, Martin, and Taylor, Bradley 2010. 'Borrowability and the notion of basic vocabulary', in *Diachronica* 27 226–46.

Taylor, John 2004. 'Higden, Ranulf (*d.* 1364)', in *Oxford Dictionary of National Biography*. OUP [<http://ezproxy.ouls.ox.ac.uk:2117/view/article/13225> accessed 13 December 2011].

Thier, Katrin 2009. 'Ships and their Terminology between England and the North', in Matti Kilpiö; Leena Kahlas-Tarkka; Jane Roberts; and Olga Timofeeva (eds.) *Anglo-Saxons and the North, Essays Reflecting the Theme of the 10th Meeting of the International Society of Anglo-saxonists in Helsinki, August 2001*. Tempe, Arizona: Arizona Center for Medieval and Renaissance Studies. 151–64.

Thomas, Mark G., Stumpf, Michael P. H., and Härke, Heinrich 2006. 'Evidence for an apartheid-like social structure in early Anglo-Saxon England', in *Proceedings of the Royal Society B: Biological Sciences* 273 2651–7.

Thomas, Mark G., Stumpf, Michael P. H., and Härke, Heinrich 2008. 'Integration versus apartheid in post-Roman Britain: a response to Pattison', in *Proceedings of the Royal Society B: Biological Sciences* 275 2419–21.

Thomason, Sarah G. 2001. *Language Contact: An Introduction*. Edinburgh: EUP.

Thomason, Sarah G. 2003. 'Contact as a source of language change', in Brian D. Joseph and Richard D. Janda (eds.) *The Handbook of Historical Linguistics*. Oxford: Blackwell. 687–712.

Thomason, Sarah G. and Kaufman, Terrence 1988. *Language Contact, Creolization, and Genetic Linguistics*. Berkeley: University of California Press.

Thompson, Edward Maunde 1883. *Diary of Richard Cocks Cape-Merchant in the English Factory in Japan 1615–1622 with Correspondence*. 2 vols. London: Hakluyt Society.

Thorson, Per 1936. *Anglo-Norse Studies: An Inquiry into the Scandinavian Elements in the Modern English Dialects*. Amsterdam: N. V. Swets en Zeitlinger.

Timofeeva, Olga 2010. 'Anglo-Latin Bilingualism Before 1066: Prospects and Limitations', in Alaric Hall, Olga Timofeeva, Ágnes Kiricsi, and Bethany Fox (eds.) *Interfaces between Language and Culture in Medieval England: A Festschrift for Matti Kilpiö*. Leiden: Brill. 1–36.

Tolkien, J. R. R. 1934. 'Chaucer as a Philologist: The Reeve's Tale', in *Transactions of the Philological Society* 1–70.

Tolkien, J. R. R. 1963. 'English and Welsh', in Henry Lewis (ed.) *Angles and Britons: O'Donnell lectures*. Cardiff: University of Wales Press. 1–41.

Toll, J-M. 1926. *Niederländisches Lehngut im Mittelenglischen*. Halle (Saale): Niemeyer.

Townend, Matthew 2002. *Language and History in Viking Age England: Linguistic Relations Between Speakers of Old Norse and Old English*. Studies in the Early Middle Ages 6. Turnhout: Brepols.

Townend, Matthew 2006. 'Contacts and conflicts: Latin, Norse, and French', in Lynda Mugglestone (ed.) *The Oxford History of English*. Oxford: OUP. 61–85.

Trotter, David (ed.) 2000. *Multilingualism in Later Medieval Britain*. Cambridge: D. S. Brewer.

Trotter, David 2003a. 'Not as eccentric as it looks: Anglo-French and French French', in *Forum for Modern Language Studies* 39 427–38.

Trotter, David 2003b. 'L'Anglo-Normand: Variété insulaire ou variété isolée?', in *Médiévales* 45 43–54.

Trotter, David 2003c. 'The Anglo-French lexis of *Ancrene Wisse*: a re-evaluation', in Wada (2003b) 83–101.

Trotter, David 2010. 'Bridging the Gap: The (Socio-)linguistic Evidence of Some Medieval English Bridge Accounts', in Ingham (2010) 52–62.

Tulloch, Graham 1997. 'Lexis', in Jones (1997) 378–432.

Twemlow, J. A. 1921. 'The etymology of "Bay-salt"', in *English Historical Review* 36 214–18.

Upward, Christopher and Davidson, George 2011. *The History of English Spelling*. Oxford: Wiley Blackwell.

van der Auwera, Johan and Genee, Inge 2002. 'English *do*: on the convergence of languages and linguists' in *English Language and Linguistics* 6 283–307.

Vennemann, Theo 2010. 'Contact and prehistory: The Indo-European Northwest', in Hickey (2010) 380–405.

Wada, Yoko 2003a. 'What is *Ancrene Wisse*?', in Wada (2003b) 1–28.

Wada, Yoko (ed.). 2003b. *A Companion to Ancrene Wisse*. Cambridge: D. S. Brewer.

Wall, A. 1898. 'A contribution towards the study of the Scandinavian element in the English dialects', in *Anglia* 20 45–135.

Ward-Perkins, Bryan 2000. 'Why did the Anglo-Saxons not become more British', in *English Historical Review* 115 513–33.

Wartburg, Walther von 1969. *Évolution et structure de la langue française*. Neuvième édition. Berne: Francke.

Watts, Victor 2004. *The Cambridge Dictionary of English Place-Names*. Cambridge: CUP.

Weale, Michael E.; Weiss, Deborah A.; Jager, Rolf F.; Bradman, Neil; and Thomas, Mark G. 2002. 'Y chromosome evidence for Anglo-Saxon mass migration' in *Molecular Biology and Evolution* 19 1008–21.

Weinreich, Uriel 1953. *Languages in Contact: Findings and Problems*. New York: Linguistic Circle of New York. (Reprinted 1964 The Hague: Mouton.)

Wełna, Jerzy 2005. '*Nim* or *take*? A competition between two high frequency verbs in Middle English', in *Studia Anglica Posnaniensia* 41 53–69.

Wenzel, Siegfried 1994. *Macaronic Sermons: Bilingualism and Preaching in Late-Medieval England*. Ann Arbor: University of Michigan Press.

Wermser, Richard 1976. *Statistische Studien zur Entwicklung des englischen Wortschatzes*. Bern: Francke.

White, Robert M. 1852. *The Ormulum: Now First Edited from the Original Manuscript in the Bodleian*. Oxford: OUP.

Williams, Joseph M. 1975. *Origins of the English Language: A Social and Linguistic History*. New York: The Free Press.

Winford, Donald 2010. 'Contact and Borrowing', in Hickey (2010) 170–87.

Wogan-Browne, Jocelyn (ed.) 2009a. 'General introduction: What's in a name: The "French" of "England"', in Wogan-Browne (2009b) 1–13.

Wogan-Browne, Jocelyn (ed.) 2009b. *Language and Culture in Medieval Britain: The French of England c.1100–c.1500*. York: York Medieval Press.

Wohlgemuth, Jan 2009. *A Typology of Verbal Borrowings*. Berlin: Mouton de Gruyter.

Wollmann, Alfred 1990a. *Untersuchungen zu den frühen Lehnwörtern im Altenglischen: Phonologie und Datierung*. Texte und Untersuchungen zur englischen Philologie 15. Munich: Fink.

Wollmann, Alfred 1990b. 'Lateinisch-Altenglische Lehnbeziehungen im 5. und 6. Jahrhundert' in Alfred Bammesberger and Alfred Wollmann (eds.) *Britain 400–600: Language and History*. 373–96.

Wollmann, Alfred 1993. 'Early Latin loan-words in Old English' in *Anglo-Saxon England* 22 1–26.

Wollmann, Alfred 1996. 'Scandinavian Loanwords in Old English', in Hans Frede Nielsen and Lene Schøsler (eds.) *The Origins and Development of Emigrant Languages: Proceedings of the Second Rasmus Rask Colloquium, Odense University, November 1994*. North-Western European Language Evolution Supplement 17. Odense: Odense University Press. 215–42.

Wright, Laura 1996. *Sources of London English: Medieval Thames Vocabulary*. Oxford: OUP.

Wright, Laura 2010. 'A Pilot Study on the Singular Definite Articles *le* and *la* in Fifteenth-Century London Mixed-Language Business Writing', in Ingham (2010) 130–42.

Wright, Roger 1982. *Late Latin and Early Romance, in Spain and Carolingian France*. Liverpool: Francis Cairns.

Wright, Roger (ed.) 1996. *Latin and the Romance Languages in the Early Middle Ages*. Pennsylvania: Penn State Press.

Wright, Roger 2002. *A Sociophilological Study of Late Latin*. Utrecht Studies of Medieval Literacy, Vol. 10. Turnhout: Brepols.

Yule, Henry and Burnell, A. C. 1903. *Hobson-Jobson: A Glossary of Colloquial Anglo-Indian Words and Phrases, and of Kindred Terms, Etymological, Historical, Geographical and Discursive*. (New edn., William Crooke (ed.).) London: Murray.

Zettersten, Arne 1969. 'French loan-words in the Ancrene Riwle and their frequency', in *Mélanges de philologie offerts à Alf Lombard a l'occasion de son
soixante-cinquième anniversaire par ses collègues et ses amis.* Lund: Gleerup
227–50.

Dictionaries, reference works, and databases cited by title

AFW: *Altfranzösisches Wörterbuch*, 1925–2002. Adolf Tobler, Erhard Lommatzsch,
and Hans H. Christmann (eds.). Wiesbaden: Franz Steiner.

ALD: *The Advanced Learner's Dictionary of Current English*, 1963. A. S. Hornby
(ed.). 2nd edn. (1st edn. 1948; earlier edn. published as *Idiomatic and syntactic
English dictionary* Tokyo Institute for Research in English Teaching, 1942).
London: OUP. (See also *OALD*.)

AND: *The Anglo-Norman Dictionary*, 1977–1992. Louise W. Stone, T. B. W. Reid,
and William Rothwell (eds.). London: The Modern Humanities Research Association. *Anglo-Norman Dictionary: revised edition, A–C; D–E*, 2005. William
Rothwell, Stewart Gregory, and David Trotter (eds.), 2 vols. London: MHRA.
(online publication) *Anglo-Norman Dictionary: revised edition, F–M*. Funded by
AHRC, employing two research assistants, 2003–12. (At time of access published
A–L.) <www.anglo-norman.net>

DEAF: *Dictionnaire étymologique de l'ancien français*, 1971–. Kurt Baldinger,
Frankwalt Möhren, and Thomas Städtler (eds.). Tübingen: Niemeyer. <www.
deaf-page.de>

DMF: *Dictionnaire de moyen français*, version 2010. ATILF – CNRS & Nancy
Université. <http://www.atilf.fr/dmf>

DMLBS: *Dictionary of Medieval Latin from British Sources*, 1975–. R. E. Latham,
David Howlett, and Richard Ashdowne (eds.). Published to fascicle XIV, Reg-
Sal. Oxford: OUP (for the British Academy).

DNZE: *The Dictionary of New Zealand English*, 1997. H. Orsman (ed.). Oxford:
OUP.

DOE: *The Dictionary of Old English*, 1986–. Angus Cameron, Ashley Crandell
Amos, and Antonette diPaolo Healey (eds.). Published to G. University of
Toronto. <http://www.doe.utoronto.ca>

DOST: *A Dictionary of the Older Scottish Tongue*, 1931–2002. Sir William
A. Craigie, A. J. Aitken, James A. C. Stevenson, and Marace Dareau (eds.).
Oxford: OUP. Available online as part of Dictionary of the Scots Language:
<http://www.dsl.ac.uk/dsl/>

DSAE: *A Dictionary of South African English on Historical Principles*, 1996. Penny
Silva (ed.). Oxford: OUP.

Du Cange: Glossarium Mediae et Infimae Latinitatis, 1883–87. Charles du Fresne,
sieur du Cange (ed.); new edn. Léopold Favre. (1st edn. 1688.) Reprinted 1954 in 5
vols. Graz: Akademische Druck- und Verlagsanstalt.

ECCO: *Eighteenth-Century Collections Online*, see <http://gale.cengage.co.uk>

EDD: *The English Dialect Dictionary*, 1898–1905. Joseph A. Wright (ed.). London: Henry Frowde (at the expense of Joseph Wright); subsequently Oxford: OUP. Electronic version in preparation at University of Innsbruck: <http://www.uibk.ac.at/anglistik/projects/speed/>

EEBO: *Early English Books Online*, see <http://eebo.chadwyck.com/home>

FEW: *Französisches etymologisches Wörterbuch: Eine Darstellung des galloromanischen Sprachschatzes*, 25 vols., 1922–78; 2nd edn. in course of publication. Founding editor Walther von Wartburg. Basel: Zbinden.

GSL: *A General Service List of English Words*, 1953. Michael P. West. London: Longman.

HTOED: *Historical Thesaurus of the Oxford English Dictionary*, 2009. Christian Kay, Jane Roberts, Michael Samuels, and Irené Wotherspoon (eds.). Oxford: OUP.

MED: *Middle English Dictionary*, 1952–2001. Hans Kurath, Sherman Kuhn, and Robert E. Lewis (eds.). Ann Arbor: University of Michigan Press. Available online at: <http://quod.lib.umich.edu/m/med/>

Niermeyer: *Mediae Latinitatis Lexicon Minus*, 1976. J. F. Niermeyer (ed.). Leiden: Brill.

OALD: *The Oxford Advanced Learner's Dictionary*, 2010. Joanna Turnbull (ed.). 8th edn. (1st edn. 1948: see under *ALD*). Oxford: OUP. Searchable online at <http://oald8.oxfordlearnersdictionaries.com/>

ODEE: *The Oxford Dictionary of English Etymology*, 1966. Charles T. Onions (ed.), with the assistance of G. W. S. Friedrichsen and Robert W. Burchfield. Oxford: OUP.

OED: *The Oxford English Dictionary*. Sir James A. H. Murray, Henry Bradley, Sir William A. Craigie, and Charles T. Onions (eds.) 1884–1928; *Supplement and Bibliography* 1933. *Supplement*, 1972–1986; Robert W. Burchfield (ed.). 2nd edn. 1989; John A. Simpson and Edmund S. C. Weiner, (eds.). *Additions Series*, 1993–1997; John A. Simpson, Edmund S. C. Weiner, and Michael Proffitt (eds.). Oxford: OUP. 3rd edn. (in progress) *OED Online*, March 2000–, John A. Simpson (ed.), <www.oed.com>.

OLD: *Oxford Latin Dictionary*, 1968–82. P. G. W. Glare (ed.). Oxford: OUP.

RMLW: *Revised Medieval Latin Word-List*, 1965. R. E. Latham (ed.). Reprinted 1980 with new Supplement. London: OUP, for the British Academy.

SND: *The Scottish National Dictionary: designed partly on regional lines and partly on historical principles, and containing all the Scottish words known to be in use or to have been in use since c. 1700*, 1931–1976. William Grant and David D. Murison (eds.). *Supplement* 2005. Edinburgh: Scottish National Dictionary Association. Available online as part of Dictionary of the Scots Language: <http://www.dsl.ac.uk/dsl/>

SOED: *Shorter Oxford English Dictionary*, 2007. Angus Stevenson (ed.) 6th edn. (1st edn. 1933 as *The Shorter Oxford English Dictionary on Historical Principles*, Charles T. Onions (ed.)). Oxford: OUP.

TLF: *Trésor de la langue française: Dictionnaire de la langue du XIXe et XXe siècle (1789–1960)*, 16 vols., 1971–1994. Paul Imbs and Bernard Quemada (eds.). Paris: Gallimard. Searchable online (incorporating some revised etymologies) at: <http://atilf.atilf.fr/tlf.htm>

TLL: *Thesaurus Linguae Latinae*, 1900–. Published to Vol. X.2, Fascicle XVII, pulso – pyxodes. (Until 1999) Leipzig: Teubner; (2000–2006) Munich: KG Saur (from 2007) Berlin: Walter de Gruyter.

TOE: *Thesaurus of Old English*, 1995. Jane Roberts and Christian Kay (eds.), with Lynne Grundy. King's College London Medieval Studies XI. Amsterdam: Rodopi.

Webster's Third New International Dictionary, 1961. Philip B. Gove (ed.). Springfield, MA: G & C Merriam Co.

General Index

Word Index

(This index is selective. In particular, It excludes most example words discussed under particular donor languages in chapter 15.)

cited personal names and place names

Old English

Printed and bound by CPI Group (UK) Ltd, Croydon, CR0 4YY